Beware the Evil Eye

BEWARE
THE EVIL EYE

The Evil Eye in the Bible and the Ancient World

—Volume 3—

The Bible and Related Sources

JOHN H. ELLIOTT

CASCADE *Books* · Eugene, Oregon

BEWARE THE EVIL EYE
The Evil Eye in the Bible and the Ancient World
Volume 3: The Bible and Related Sources

Cascade Books
An Imprint of Wipf and Stock Publishers
199 W. 8th Ave., Suite 3
Eugene, OR 97401

www.wipfandstock.com

PAPERBACK ISBN 13: 978-1-4982-0500-9
HARDCOVER ISBN 13: 978-1-4982-8578-0
EBOOK ISBN: 978-1-5326-0103-3

Cataloguing-in-Publication data:

Name: Elliott, John Hall.

Title: Beware the evil eye : the evil eye in the Bible and the ancient world / John H. Elliott.

Volume 3: The Bible and Related Sources

Description: Eugene, OR: Pickwick Publications, 2016 | Includes bibliographical references and index.

Identifiers: ISBN: 978-1-4982-0500-9 (paperback) | ISBN: 978-1-4982-8578-0 (hardcover) | ISBN 978-1-5326-0103-3 (ebook)

Subjects: LCSH: Evil eye—Biblical teaching. | Evil eye—Mediterranean region. | Envy. | Title.

Classification: GN475.6 E45 2016 v. 3 (print) | GN475.6 (ebook)

Manufactured in the U.S.A.   07/21/16

For

Norman K. Gottwald,

socialist pioneer and activist exegete extraordinaire,

fellow BASTARD
(Bay Area Seminar on Theology and Related Disciplines),

co-founder and fellow-officer of the Center and Library
for the Bible and Social Justice,

faithful friend

"Remember that an Evil Eye is a wicked thing.
What has been created more evil than an Evil Eye?"

(SIRACH 31:13)

"Is your Evil Eye envious because I am generous"?

(MATTHEW 20:15)

CONTENTS

ILLUSTRATIONS

PREFACE

THIS FOUR VOLUME STUDY traces evidence of Evil Eye belief and practice in the ancient world from Mesopotamia (c. 3000 BCE) to Late Roman Antiquity (c. 600 CE), with particular attention to the Bible and post-biblical traditions of Israel and early Christianity.

Belief in the Evil Eye is a long-standing and widespread folk concept that some persons are enabled by nature to injure others, cause illness and loss, and destroy any person, animal or thing through a powerful noxious glance emanating from the eye. Also known as "fascination" (Greek: *baskania*; Latin: *fascinatio*), this belief holds that the eye is an active organ that emits destructive emanations charged by negative dispositions (especially malevolence, envy, miserliness, and withheld generosity). These emanations arise in the heart or soul and are projected outward against both animate and inanimate objects. The full constellation of notions comprising the Evil Eye complex includes the expectation that various prophylactic words, gestures, images, and amulets have the power to counter and avert the damaging power of the Evil Eye.

From its likely origin in ancient Sumer (3000 BCE) and its early spread to Egypt and the Circum-Mediterranean region, to its later movement eastward to India and westward and northward to Europe, the belief eventually made its way from "old worlds" to "new." It now constitutes a cultural phenomenon with personal, social, and moral implications that has spanned the centuries and encircled the globe.

Beware the Evil Eye concentrates on the Evil Eye phenomenon in the ancient world, with new and extensive attention to mention of it in the Bible and the biblical communities of Israel and early Christianity. Volume 1 opens with an introductory overview of references to, and research on, the Evil Eye from the ancient past to the modern present (chap. 1). Chapter 2 of Vol. 1 examines Evil Eye belief and practice in ancient Mesopotamia and Egypt. Volume 2 is devoted to the extensive evidence on the subject in ancient Greece and Rome. Within the geographical and cultural matrix detailed in these first two volumes, the evidence of Evil Eye belief and practice in the Bible is now examined in the present volume (Vol. 3). A final volume (4) considers post-biblical evidence of Evil Eye belief and practice in Rabbinic Israel (chapter 1) and early Christianity (chap. 2) through Late Antiquity (c. 600 CE). Concluding reflections on the import and implications of our study (chap. 3) close this final volume.

This study is the first full-scale monograph on the Evil Eye in the Bible and the biblical communities (Vols. 3 and 4). Its analysis of Evil Eye belief and practice in Mesopotamia, Egypt, Greece, and Rome (Vols. 1 and 2) summarizes a century of research since the milestone two-volume study of Siegfried Seligmann, *Der böse Blick und Verwandtes* (1910) and describes the ecological, historical, social, and cultural contexts within which the biblical texts are best understood. Throughout this four-volume work we are treating the Evil Eye in antiquity, not as an instance of vulgar superstition or deluded magic, but as a physiological, psychological, and moral phenomenon whose operation was deemed explicable on rational grounds; for discussion see Vol. 1, pp. 26–27.

ACKNOWLEDGMENTS

MY THANKS TO PROFESSORS Gary Stansell and Dennis C. Duling for their critical reading of and feedback on the material for this volume, chaps. 1 and 2 respectively, and to Professor Richard L. Rohrbaugh for reviewing the entire manuscript. Conversations with Professor Mark Nanos on this subject of common interest were also most fruitful. Thanks, further, to all the many friends, students, and colleagues in the USA and abroad for their generous contributions of Evil Eye anecdotes, Evil Eye bibliography, and Evil Eye amulets for this Evil Eye project. My gratitude abounds again to K. C. Hanson, peerless editor, and to Ian Creeger, patient and expert typesetter, for midwifing this third baby to its final delivery, unscathed by the Evil Eye.

ABBREVIATIONS

ANCIENT PRIMARY SOURCES

OLD TESTAMENT (HEBREW, GREEK, LATIN)

Aquila	Greek translation of Aquila
HT	Hebrew text of Old Testament (alias MT= Massoretic Text)
LXX	Greek text of Old Testament
Symmachus	Greek translation of Symmachus
Vulg	Latin text of the Bible (Vulgate = Jerome's *Vulgata*)

Gen	Genesis
Exod	Exodus
Lev	Leviticus
Num	Numbers
Deut	Deuteronomy
Josh	Joshua
Judg	Judges
1–2 Sam	1–2 Samuel
1–2 Kgdms	1–2 Kingdoms LXX
1–2 Kgs	1–2 Kings
1–2 Chr	1–2 Chronicles
Ezra	Ezra
Esther	Esther
Job	Job

Ps/Pss	Psalms
Prov	Proverbs
Qoh/Eccl	Qoheleth/Ecclesiastes
Song	Song of Songs (Song of Solomon)
Isa	Isaiah
Jer	Jeremiah
Lam	Lamentations
Ezek	Ezekiel
Dan	Daniel
Mic	Micah
Nah	Nahum
Zech	Zechariah
Mal	Malachi

APOCRYPHA

Ep Jer	Epistle of Jeremiah
1 Macc	1 Maccabees
2 Macc	2 Maccabees
3 Macc	3 Maccabees
4 Macc	4 Maccabees
Sir	Sirach (Jesus ben Sira) (Vulgate: Ecclesiasticus)
Sus	Susanna
Tob	Tobit
Wis	Wisdom of Solomon

PSEUDEPIGRAPHA

APOT	*The Apocrypha and Pseudepigrapha of the Old Testament in English.* 2 vols. Edited by R. H. Charles. Oxford: Clarendon, 1913
Ascen. Isa.	*Ascension of Isaiah*
2 Bar.	*2 Baruch*
3 Bar.	*3 Baruch*
Jos. Asen.	*Joseph and Asenath*

Jub.	*Jubilees*
L.A.B.	*Liber antiquitatum biblicarum* (Pseudo-Philo)
OTP	*The Old Testament Pseudepigrapha.* 2 vols. Edited by James H. Charlesworth. Garden City, NY: Doubleday, 1983
Ps-Phoc.	*Pseudo-Phocylides*
T. 12 Patr.	*Testaments of the Twelve Patriarchs*
T. Ash.	*Testament of Asher*
T. Benj.	*Testament of Benjamin*
T. Dan	*Testament of Dan*
T. Gad	*Testament of Gad*
T. Iss.	*Testament of Issachar*
T. Jos.	*Testament of Joseph*
T. Jud.	*Testament of Judah*
T. Levi	*Testament of Levi*
T. Naph.	*Testament of Naphtali*
T. Reub.	*Testament of Reuben*
T. Sim.	*Testament of Simeon*
T. Zeb.	*Testament of Zebulun*
T. Job	*Testament of Job*
T. Mos.	*Testament of Moses*
T. Sol.	*Testament of Solomon*

NEW TESTAMENT

Matt	Matthew
Rom	Romans
1 Cor	1 Corinthians
2 Cor	2 Corinthians
Gal	Galatians
Eph	Ephesians
Phil	Philippians
Col	Colossians
1 Thess	1 Thessalonians
2 Thess	2 Thessalonians
1 Tim	1 Timothy

2 Tim	2 Timothy
Tit	Titus
Jas	James
1 Pet	1 Peter
Rev	Revelation

PHILO OF ALEXANDRIA

Abraham	*On the Life of Abraham*
Agriculture	*On Agriculture*
Cherubim	*On the Cherubim*
Dreams	*On Dreams*
Drunkenness	*On Drunkenness*
Flaccus	*Against Flaccus*
Joseph	*On the Life of Joseph*
Migration	*On the Migration of Abraham*
Moses	*On the Life of Moses*
Names	*On the Change of Names*
Posterity	*On the Posterity of Cain*
Prelim. St.	*On the Preliminary Studies* (a.k.a. *De congressu*)
QG	*Questions and Answers on Genesis 1, 2, 3, 4*
Rewards	*On Rewards and Punishments*
Sacrifices	*On the Sacrifices of Cain and Abel*
Spec. Laws	*On the Special Laws*
Virtues	*On the Virtues*

JOSEPHUS, FLAVIUS

Ag. Ap.	*Against Apion*
Ant.	*Antiquities of the Jews*
Life	*The Life*
War	*Jewish War*

DEAD SEA SCROLLS

1QM	War Scroll
1QS	Rule of the Community
4Q200	4QTobit
4Q424	4QWisdom
4Q477	4QDecrees
4Q510	4QSongs of the Sage
4Q525	4QBeatitudes

RABBINIC WRITINGS

Arak.	*Arakin*
Avot	*Pirke Avoth*
b.	*Babylonian Talmud (Bavli)*
B.B.	*Bava Batra*
Ber.	*Berakhot*
B.M.	*Bava Metzi'a*
Gen. Rab.	*Genesis Rabbah*
m.	*Mishnah*
Ned.	*Nedarim*
Num. Rab.	*Numbers Rabbah*
Sanh.	*Sanhedrin*
Shabb.	*Shabbat*
Sifre Num.	*Sifre Numbers*
Ta'an.	*Ta'anit*
y.	*Jerusalem/Palestinian Talmud (Yerushalmi)*

GREEK AND ROMAN WRITINGS

Aelian

Var. hist.	*Varia historia*

Aeschines

Tim.	*In Timarchum*

Aeschylus

Prom.	*Prometheus vinctus*

Alexander of Aphrodisias

Prob. phys.	*Problemata physica*

Anth. Pal.	*Anthologia Palatina/Palatine Anthology.* Published as *Anthologia Graeca.* 13 vols. Edited by F. Jacobs. 1794–1803; revised 1813–1817

Aristophanes

Equit.	*Equites*
Frag.	Fragment

Aristotle

De sensu	*De sensu et sensibilibus*
Eth. eud.	*Ethica eudemia*
Frag.	Fragment
PA	*de Partibus Animalium*
Phgn.	*Physiognomonica*
Rhet.	*Rhetorica*

Aristotle (Pseudo-)

Prob. phys.	*Problemata physica*

Athenaeus

Deipn.	*Deipnosophistae*

Cicero

Cael.	*Pro Caelio*
De or.	*De oratore*
Orat. pro dom.	*Oratio pro domo sua*
Verr.	*In Verrem*

Democritus

Frag.   Fragment

Dio Cassius

Hist.   *Historia Romana/Roman History*

Dio Chrysostom

Orat.   *Orationes*

Empedocles

Frag.   Fragment

Epictetus

Disc.   *Discourses*

Euripides

Suppl.   *Suppliant Women*

Heliodorus

Aeth.   *Aethiopica*

Herodotus

Hist.   *Histories*

Hesiod

Frag.   Fragment

Horace

Serm.   *Sermones*

Juvenal

Sat.   *Satires*

Ovid

Met.   *Metamorphoses*

Persius

Sat.   *Satires*

Petronius

Sat.   *Satyricon*

Plato

Hipp. Min.   *Hippias Minor*
Prot.   *Protagoras*

Pliny the Elder

NH   *Natural History*

Plutarch

Cons. ux   *Consolatio ad uxorum*
De cap.   *De capienda ex inimicis utilitate*
De frat.   *De fraterno amore*
De recta   *De recta ratione audiendi*
De tranq.   *De tranquillitate animi*
Dion   *Life of Dion*
Is. et Os.   *De Iside et Osiride*
Mor.   *Moralia*
Prim. frig. *De primo fridgido.*
Quaest. Conv.   *Quaestiones Convivales (Convivial Questions/Table Talk)*

Quintillian

Inst. Orat. *Institutio Oratorica*

Suetonius

Vesp.   *Life of Vespasian*

Stobaeus, Johannes

Anth./Ecl.   *Anthologium/Eclogues*

Tacitus

Hist.   *Histories*

Theophrastus

Char.   *Characteres*
De sensu   *De sensu et sensilibus*

Virgil

Ecl.   *Eclogues*

Xenophon

Eq.   *De equitande ratione*
Mem.   *Memorabilia*

PAPYRI, INSCRIPTIONS, EPIGRAPHA

BGU   *Ägyptische Urkunden aus den Staatlichen Museen zu Berlin: Griechische Urkunden.* Berlin: Weidmann, 1895–. Vols. 1–4. Berlin: Weidmann, 1895–1912

CIG   Corpus inscriptionum graecarum. Edited by A. Boeckh. 4 Vols. Berlin, 1825–1877

Diels-Kranz, FVS   *Die Fragmente der Vorsokratiker.* Edited by Hermann Diels and Walter Kranz. 3 vols. 6th ed. Berlin: Weidmann, 1951–1952 (originally, 1903). Vol. 2. *Testimonia* 1–170 (siglum A); *Fragmenta* 1–298a (siglum B)

GMPT   *The Greek Magical Papyri in Translation, Including the Demotic Texts.* Edited by H. D. Betz et al. Chicago: University of Chicago Press, 1986

Kaibel, *Epigr. Gr.*   *Epigrammata Graeca ex lapidibus conlecta.* Edited G. Kaibel. Berlin: Reimer, 1878; Reprinted 1965

PGM   *Papyri Graece Magicae. Die griechischen Zauberpapyri.* 2 vols. Edited by K. Preisendanz. Berlin: Teubner, 1928 (vol. 1), 1931 (vol. 2). Vol. 3 with index, edited by K. Preisendanz, with E.

Diehl and S. Eitrem (1941/1942). 2nd revised edtion by A. Heinrichs. Stuttgart: Teubner, 1973–1974

P.Oxy.   *The Oxyrhynchus Papyri*. Edited by B. P. Grenfell and A. S. Hunt etc. 72 vols. London: Egypt Exploration Society, 1898–

P.Petr.   *The Flinders Petrie Papyri*. 3 vols. Edited by J. Mahaffy and J. Smyly. Dublin, 1891–1905

EARLY CHRISTIAN WRITINGS

Ambrosiaster (Pseudo-Ambrosius)

Comm. Gal.   Commentaria in Epistolam ad Galatas

Apost. Trad.   Apostolic Tradition

Barn.   Barnabas, Epistle of

1 Clem.   1 Clement

Clem. Alex. Strom.   Clement of Alexandria, Stromata

Did.   Didache

Gos. Thom.   Gospel of Thomas

Hermas   Shepherd of Hermas
Mand.   Mandates
Sim   Similitudes

Jerome

Comm. Gal.   Commentarius in epistulam ad Galatas

John Chrysostom

Catech. illum.   Catecheses ad illuminandos
Delic.   De futurae vitae deliciis
Hom. 1 Cor.   Homiliae in primum epistulam ad Corinthios
Hom. Eph.   Homiliae in epistulam ad Ephesios

Hom Gal.	*Homiliae in epistulam ad Galatas*
Hom. Gen.	*Homiliae in Genesim*
Hom. Matt.	*Homiliae in Matthaeum*
Paralyt.	*In paralyticum demissum per tectum*

Justin Martyr

| *1. Apol.* | *First Apology* |

Lactantius

| *Div. Inst.* | *Divine Institutes* |

| *Mart. Polyc.* | *Martyrdom of Polycarp* |

| *NTA* | *New Testament Apocrypha.* 2 vols. Edited by Edgar Hennecke and Wilhelm Schneemelcher. Translated by R. McL. Wilson. Philadelphia: Westminster Press, 1965 |

Polycarp

| Polyc. *Phil.* | *Polycarp to the Philippians* |

Tertullian

| *Virg.* | *De virginibus velandis* |

BIBLE TRANSLATIONS/VERSIONS

ASV	American Standard Version
BJ	Bible de Jerusalem
CEB	Common English Bible
Douay-Rheims	Douay-Rheims Version (translating the Latin Vulgate)
ESV	English Standard Version
Goodspeed	Edgar J. Goodspeed and J. M. Powis Smith, eds., *The Bible: An American Translation.* New edition with the Apocrypha. Chicago: University of Chicago Press, 1939
GNB	Good News Bible

JB	Jerusalem Bible
JPS	Jewish Publication Society. *Tanak: The Holy Scriptures according to the Masoretic Text* (1985)
KJV	King James Version
Luth	Luther Bibel
LXX	Septuagint (Greek OT)
NAB	New American Bible
NASB	New American Standard Bible
NEB	New English Bible
NIV	New International Version
NJB	New Jerusalem Bible
NJPS	Jewish Publication Society. *Tanak: The Holy Scriptures according to the Masoretic Text* (1999)
NKJV	New King James Version
NRSV	New Revised Standard Version
Phillips	J. B. Phillips, *The New Testament in Modern English*
REB	Revised English Bible
RSV	Revised Standard Version
RV	Revised Version
TEV	Today's English Version
Scholars Bible	The Scholars Bible
Vulg	Vulgata
Zink	Jörg Zink, *Das Neue Testament*
Zürcher Bibel	*Zürcher Bibel.* Zürich: Theologischer Verlag, 2007

ENCYCLOPEDIAS, LEXICA, SERIES, PERIODICALS

AB	Anchor Bible (see also AYB)
ABD	*The Anchor Bible Dictionary.* 6 vols. Edited by David Noel Freedman. New York: Doubleday, 1992
ANF	*Ante-Nicene Fathers*
ANRW	*Aufstieg und Niedergang der römischen Welt.* Edited by Hildegard Temporini and Wolfgang Haase. Berlin: de Gruyter, 1972–
APOT	*Apocrypha and Pseudepigrapha of the Old Testament.* 2 vols. Edited by R. H. Charles. Oxford: Clarendon, 1913

ArOr	*Archiv Orientálni*
AYB	Anchor Yale Bible
BAR	*Biblical Archaeological Review*
BDAG	*A Greek-English Lexicon of the New Testament and Other Early Christian Literature.* 3rd ed., revised and edited by Frederick W. Danker. Chicago: University of Chicago Press, 2000
BNTC	Black's New Testament Commentaries
BTB	*Biblical Theology Bulletin*
BThZ	*Berliner Theologische Zeitschrift*
BWA(N)T	Beiträge zur Wissenschaft vom Alten (und Neuen) Testament
CBQ	*Catholic Biblical Quarterly*
CCSL	Corpus Christianorum Series Latina 1954–
CSEL	Corpus Scriptorum Ecclesiasticorum Latinorum
Daremberg and Saglio	*Dictionnaire des antiquités grecques et romaines.* 10 vols. (5 double vols.). Edited by Charles Daremberg and Edmund Saglio. Paris: Hachette, 1877–1919
EDNT	*Exegetical Dictionary of the New Testament.* Edited by Horst Balz and Gerhard Schneider. 3 vols. Translated by James W. Thompson and John W. Medendorp. Grand Rapids: Eerdmans, 1990–93
FRLANT	Forschungen zur Religion und Literatur des Alten und Neuen Testaments
HERE	*Encyclopaedia of Religion and Ethics.* 13 vols. Edited by James Hastings et al. Edinburgh: T. & T. Clark, 1908–1926; 4th ed. (reprint), 1958
HNT	Handbuch zum Neuen Testament
HTKAT	Herders Theologischer Kommentar zum Neuen Testament
HTR	*Harvard Theological Review*
IDB	*The Interpreter's Dictionary of the Bible.* 4 vols. Edited by George Arthur Buttrick. Nashville: Abingdon, 1962
IDBSup	*The Interpreter's Dictionary of the Bible.* DB Supplement Volume. Edited by Keith Crim. Nashville: Abingdon, 1976
ISBE	*The International Standard Bible Encyclopaedia.* 4 vols. Edited by James Orr, et al. Revised ed. by Melvin G. Kyle. Chicago: Howard-Severance, 1929; revised and reedited by Geoffrey W. Bromiley. Grand Rapids: Eerdmans, 1979–88
JAC	*Jahrbuch für Antike und Christentum*

JAOS	*Journal of the American Oriental Society*
JBL	*Journal of Biblical Literature*
JE	*The Jewish Encyclopedia*. 12 vols. Edited by Isidor Singer. 3rd ed. New York: Funk & Wagnalls, 1927
JJS	*Journal of Jewish Studies*
JQR	*Jewish Quarterly Review*
JPOS	*Journal of the Palestine Oriental Society*
JSJ	*Journal for the Study of Judaism*
JSNT	*Journal for the Study of the New Testament*
JSOT	*Journal for the Study of the Old Testament*
JSP	*Journal for the Study of the Pseudepigrapha*
JTS	*Journal of Theological Studies*
KEK	Kritisch-exegetischer Kommentar über das Neue Testament
LCL	Loeb Classical Library
Louw and Nida, *GEL*	*Greek-English Lexicon of the New Testament Based on Semantic Domains*. 2 vols. Edited by Johanes P. Louw, Eugene A. Nida et al. New York: United Bible Societies, 1988
LSJ	*A Greek-English Lexicon*. 9th ed. Edited by H. G. Liddell, R. Scott, H. S. Jones, and R. McKenzie, with revised supplement. Oxford: Clarendon, 1996
Moulton–Milligan	James Hope Moulton and George Milligan. *The Vocabulary of the Greek Testament Illustrated from the Papyri and Other Non-Literary Sources*. London: Hodder & Stoughton, 1930
NIGTC	New International Greek Testament Commentary
NTD	Neues Testament Deutsch
NTG	*Novum Testamentum Graece*
NTS	*New Testament Studies*
OTE	Old Testament Essays
PGM	*Papyri Graece Magicae: Die griechischen Zauberpapyri*. 2 vols. Edited by K. Preisendanz. Berlin: Teubner, 1928 (vol. 1), 1931 (vol. 2). Vol. 3 with index, edited by K. Preisendanz, with E. Diehl and S. Eitrem (1941/1942). 2nd rev. ed. by A. Heinrichs. Stuttgart: Teubner, 1973–1974. ET: *Greek Magical Papyri*. Edited by Hans Dieter Betz, 1986
PsVTG	Pseudepigrapha Veteris Testamenti graece

PW   *Paulys Real-encyclopädie der classischen Altertumswissen-schaft.* Edited by A. F. Pauly. Vols. 1–6 (1839–1852). New Edition begun by G. Wissowa et al. 70+ vols. Stuttgart: Metzler, 1892–1980

RAC   *Reallexikon für Antike und Christentum.* 17+ vols. Edited by Theodore Klauser et al. Stuttgart: A. Hiersemann, 1950–

RGG³   *Die Religion in Geschichte und Gegenwart.* 6 vols. and index, Edited by Kurt Galling et al. 3rd edition. Tübingen: Mohr/Siebeck, 1957–65

RSPT   *Revue des sciences philosophiques et théologiques*

SBLRBS   Society of Biblical Literature Resources for Biblical Study

SNTSMS   Society for New Testament Studies Monograph Series

StTh   *Studia Theologica*

TBNT   *Theologischer Begriffslexikon zum Neuen Testament.* 3 vols. Edited by L. Coenen et al. 3ed. ed. Wuppertal: Brockhaus, 1967–72; 6th ed., 1983

TDNT   *Theological Dictionary of the New Testament.* 10 vols. Edited by Gerhard Kittel and Gerhard Friedrich. Translated and edited by Geoffrey W. Bromiley. Grand Rapids: Eerdmans, 1964–76

TDOT   *Theological Dictionary of the Old Testament.* 15 vols. Edited by G. Johannes Botterweck and Helmer Ringren. Translated by David Green. Grand Rapids: Eerdmans, 1974–2006

THAT   *Theologisches Handwörterbuch zum Alten Testament.* 2 vols. Edited by Ernst Jenni and Claus Westermann. Zurich: Theologischer Verlag, 1971–76

ThStK   *Theologische Studien und Kritiken*

TLOT   *Theological Lexicon of the Old Testament.* 3 vols. Edited by Ernst Jenni and Claus Westermann. Translated by Mark E. Biddle. Peabody, MA: Hendrickson, 1997

TRE   *Theologische Realenzyklopädie.* 36 vols. Edited by Gerhard Müller, Horst Balz, Gerhard Krause et al. Berlin: de Gruyter, 1976–2004

TUGAL   Texte und Untersuchungen zur Geschichte der altchristlichen Literatur

TWAT   *Theologisches Wörterbuch zum Alten Testament.* 2 vols. Edited by G. Johannes Botterweck and Helmer Ringren. 2nd ed. Munich: Kaiser, 1975–1976

TWNT	*Theologisches Wörterbuch zum Neuen Testament.* 10 vols. Edited by Gerhard Kittel and Gerhard Friedrich. Stuttgart: Kohlhammer, 1933–73
VT	*Vetus Testamentum*
ZAW	*Zeitschrift für die alttestamentliche Wissenschaft*
ZNW	*Zeitschrift für die neutestamentliche Wissenschaft*
ZWTh	*Zeitschrift für wissenschaftliche Theologie*

OTHER ABBREVIATIONS AND SIGLA

BCE, CE	Before the Common Era; Common Era (replacing BC/AD)
c.	*circa* ("about")
cent.	century
cf.	confer, see
chap.	chapter
col.	column
cp.	compare, contrast
ET	English translation
fl.	*floruit* ("flourished," was active at a certain time)
fig.	figure
frag.	fragment/s
FS	Festschrift
Grk	Greek
HT	Hebrew Text, a.k.a. MT (Hebrew Massoretic Text)
Illus.	Illustration
JHE	John H. Elliott (as translator)
lit.	literally
Lat	Latin
LXX	Septuagint (Greek text of Old Testament)
MT	Hebrew Massoretic Text a.k.a HT (Hebrew Text)
n.f.	neue Folge ("new series")
no(s)	number(s)
NT	New Testament
OT	Old Testament
P.	Papyrus

Pl.	Plate
pl.	plural
p(p).	page(s)
Prol.	*Prologus* ("Prologue")
Q	Qumran
Q	Q Sayings Source
SBL	Society of Biblical Literature
Vulg.	Vulgata (Jerome's Latin translation)
s.v.	*sub voce* ("under the [listed] word")
trans.	translation / translator
v.l.	*varia lectio* ("variant reading")
[ ]	Square brackets identify textual material supplied by the translator of the original source or by the present author (JHE)

I

THE OLD TESTAMENT, PARABIBLICAL LITERATURE, AND RELATED MATERIAL EVIDENCE CONCERNING THE EVIL EYE

INTRODUCTION

The Evil Eye was known, feared, and denounced in Israel and was mentioned often in its scriptures and parabiblical writings. Features of the belief and its accompanying practices in Israel and the Jesus movement are strikingly similar to those of other cultures of the Circum-Mediterranean world. Preceding volumes of *Beware the Evil Eye* have presented in detail evidence of Evil Eye belief and practice in Mesopotamia and Egypt (Vol. 1) and Greece and Rome (Vol. 2). This material describes the Mediterranean and Near Eastern matrix within which the biblical evidence of Evil Eye belief is properly understood—the focus of the present volume.[1] Israel and the Jesus movement, as will be shown, shared many aspects

---

1. Since an understanding of Israel's cultural matrix is presumed in what follows, readers of this present volume are encouraged to consult Vols. 1 and 2 for the evidence and broader context of Evil Eye belief and practice in the ancient Circum-Mediterranean world.

of Evil Eye belief and practice of their neighbors, albeit with distinctive emphases and differences to be discussed in due course.

The Evil Eye is mentioned repeatedly throughout the Old Testament, Israel's parabiblical writings, and New Testament, with a variety of terms and expressions. The Old Testament (Greek Septuagint) contains no less than *fourteen text segments* involving some *twenty explicit references to the Evil Eye* (Deut 15:9; 28:54, 56; Prov 23:6; 28:22; Tob 4:7, 16; Sir 14:3, 6, 8, 9, 10; 18:18; 31:13; 37:11; Wis 4:12; 4 Macc 1:26; 2:15; Ep Jer 69/70). This last text, the Epistle of Jeremiah 69/70, is the sole explicit biblical mention of an amulet specifically aimed at countering the Evil Eye (*prosbaskanion*, an anti-Evil Eye safeguard positioned in a cucumber patch). At least three further texts are also likely implied references to an Evil Eye (1 Sam 2:29, 32; and 18:9), with some other texts as more distant possibilities.[2] The Evil Eye is mentioned also in the Old Testament Pseudepigrapha, the Dead Sea Scrolls, and the writings of Philo and Josephus—all of which are discussed below.[3] The numerous references to the Evil Eye in Israel's rabbinic writings

2. The studies of the present author are the first to list *all* the likely biblical references to the Evil Eye; see Elliott 1988, 1990, 1991, 1992, 1993:67–69; 1994, 2004; 2005a, 2005b:159–64; 2007a, 2011, 2014, 2015. Earlier works offered only partial lists and in some cases included improbable texts. Elworthy (1958/1895:6, n. 7a), for example, lists Deut 28:54, 56; Job 7:8; Ps 35:21, 54:7, 59:10, 92:11; Prov 6:13, 23:6, 28:22; Isa 13:18; Lam 2:4; Ezek 9:5; Matt 6:22–23; 20:15; Luke 11:34; Mark 7:22 "with many others." His net, however, is too large and indiscriminating. Some texts he includes speak only of eyes and seeing, but not of an Evil Eye in particular (Job 7:8; Ps 35:21; Ps 54:7; 59:10; 92:11; Isa 13:18; Lam 2:4; Ezek 9:5). A winking eye (Prov 6:13) is not identified in antiquity as an Evil Eye. Seligmann (1910 1:12–14) lists three texts mentioning *[Me] aunenim* which he identifies, unconvincingly, as referring to an Evil Eye (Lev 19:26; Deut 18:10; 2 Kgs. 21:6), as well as Wis 4:12; Sir 14:8, 9, 10; Mark 7:22. He does not mention Matt 6:22–23 and specifically excludes Matt 20:15 and Gal 3:1 where he finds only "general conventional turns of phrase." He does, however, note Acts 13:6–12 and Paul's intense staring at and cursing of Elymas resulting in the latter's blindness (1910 2:436). Contenau (1947:261) mentions Deut 28:54, 56; Isa 13:18 and Luke 11:34 as biblical examples.

3. On the Evil Eye in Israelite and Jewish tradition and lore see Grünbaum 1877:258–66; Garnett 1891; Hirsch 1892; Elworthy 1895/1958; Blau 1898:152–56, 1907b; Grunwald 1901; Reizenstein 1904:291–303; Blau and Kohler 1907 5:280–81; Grunwald 1900:40–41, 47–48; M. Gaster 1910; Kennedy 1910; Montgomery 1910–1911; Seligmann 1910, 1922, 1927; Lilienthal 1924; Löwinger 1926; Peterson 1926:96–109, 1982; Roback 1938; Friedenwald 1939; Merlin 1940; Levi 1941; Meisen 1950:145; Goodenough 1953 2:238–41; Kötting 1954:474–76; S. Thompson 1956:121 (D 993), 364 366. (D 2071); Shrut 1960; Ginsberg 1961 index; Mowinkel 1962 2:3; Nador 1965; Trachtenberg 1970/1939:45, 48, 54–56, 97, 111, 133, 136, 139–40, 158, 161–62, 198, 219, 283; Noy 1971; Kirschenblatt-Gimblett and Lenowitz 1973; Anonymous, *Encyclopedic Dictionary of Judaica* 1974:181; Birnbaum 1975:462–63; Nador 1975; Moss and Cappannari 1976; Budge 1978/1930:212–38; Shachar 1981:20–21; Opperwall 1982b; Schrire 1982; Yamauchi 1983:187–92; Aschkenazi. 1984; Naveh 1985; Rosenbaum

(second–sixth centuries CE) and the material evidence from this period are examined in Vol. 4, chap. 1. Evil Eye belief and practice in the Jesus movement is examined in chapter 2 of this present volume; evidence of the belief in post-biblical Christianity through Late Antiquity is treated in Vol. 4, chap. 2.

THE MATRIX OF BIBLICAL EVIL EYE
BELIEF AND BEHAVIOR

To understand the biblical Evil Eye texts, it is essential to be aware of the physical, economic, social, and cultural environment in which Evil Eye belief and practice has been found to emerge and flourish. Beliefs and practices are products of, and responses to, the circumstances and conditions in which they emerge. The biblical communities of ancient Israel and early Christianity were among those cultures where Evil Eye belief originated and flourished, according to historical anthropologists. This includes Mesopotamia, Egypt, the ancient Near East, Greece and Rome, and the lands bordering on the coast of the Mediterranean Sea. The ecological conditions, economic and social circumstances, and cultural world of the Israelites, in general terms, were similar to those of their neighbors in many respects and were equally conducive to Evil Eye belief and practice.

The cultures of these areas, as characterized by anthropologists Vivian Garrison and C. M. Arensberg,[4] involve not only systems of writing and literary production, but also "complex stratified societies possessed of both milk animals (or nomadic herding populations) and grain fields (or stable peasant agricultural communities)."[5] The "symbiosis of part-cultures (landlord, bureaucrat, agriculturalist, herder, artisan) . . . the destructive effect

---

1985; Elliott 1988, 1990, 1991, 1992, 1993:67–69, 1994, 2005a, 2005b:159–64; 2007a, 2007b, 2008, 2011:118–22, 2014, 2015, 2016; Frankel and Teutsh 1991; Patai 1983:86–95; Lévy and Lévy Zumwalt 1987, 2002; T. H. Gaster 1989; Ross 1991; Ulmer 1991, 1992–93, 1994, 1998, 2003; Brav 1992/1908; Dundes 1992a:41–43, 1992b; Kotansky 1994:145, 298; Michaelides 1994:403–12; Schreiner 1996; Zumwalt 1996; Pilch and Malina 1998:59–63; Seawright 1988; Malina 2001b; Schroer and Staubli 2001:118–21; Lévy and Lévy 2002; Malul 2002:208–9, 267–68; 2009; Malina and Rohrbaugh 2003:50, 101–2, 176, 357–59; Kotzé 2006, 2007, 2008; Malina and Pilch 2006:359–62; Wazana 2007; Bohak 2008:152–53, 187, 249, 302, 322, 354, 373, 392; Nigosian 2008:45; Sinai 2008; Eshel 2010; Vukosavovic 2010; Avrahami 2011:152–53; Schmid 2012:81–89; Soderlund and Soderlund 2013; Tilford 2015a, 2015b. For Evil Eye belief and practice in nineteenth-century Palestine, see W. M. Thomson 1886 and Eiszler 1889.

4. Garrison and Arensberg 1976:286–328, esp. 294–97, summarizing the wealth of cross-cultural ethnographic data on Evil Eye cultures analyzed by J. M. Roberts 1976.

5. Garrison and Arensberg 1976:290.

of the nomadic herders upon settled village and state societies," and "the periodic redistribution of peasant fields typical of these societies created an environment of constant tension and conflict, suspicion and uncertainty."[6] The concept of an Evil Eye was a symptom of these conditions, tensions, and uncertainties: a fragile and unpredictible ecological environment; a precarious peasant-urban economy of mixed herding and agriculture made uncertain by conditions of topography, climate and limited technology, and rife with internal social tensions between agriculturalists and herders; technological specialization including metalworking, grain agriculture, domesticated large animals, milking or dairying; a subsistence base of bread, milk, and meat; economic and social disparities separating city populations and food-producing countrysides; peasant villages with fixed fields and a perception of limited resources; a redistributive economy in which periodic scarcity in produce called for forced sales at fixed prices in a centrally controlled market; highly economically and socially stratified societies involving few "haves" (2–3% of the population) in a world of mostly "have-nots" (97–98%) on the bare edge of subsistence; a symbiosis of part-cultures (landlord, bureaucrat, agriculturalist, herder, artisan), intense rivalries among villages, cities, tribes, and conceptual equals for resources perceived as scarce and limited so that one family's gain entailed another's loss (the notion of "limited good");[7] everyday life involving daily face-to-face contacts among members of families, occupational groups, village and urban neighborhood populations; high mortality and morbidity rates with infants and birthing mothers as prominent victims; weak or ineffective centralized means for resolving conflicts, enforcing law, or ensuring equitable distribution of resources, thereby resulting in recourse to patron-client arrangements and informal mechanisms of social control (such as Evil Eye accusations).

The poor state of sanitation and hygiene contributed to high infant mortality rates and frequent deaths of birthing mothers. In the absence of any scientific understanding of this connection, or of a consensus concerning the causes of illness in general, sickness was regularly attributed to the attack of hostile spirits and demons and an Evil Eye.[8] Babies and birthing mothers, infants, and children who had not reached their majority were deemed especially vulnerable to the Evil Eye and therefore in need of constant protection. These conditions contributed to a perception of life in

6. Ibid.:295.

7. On the concept of limited good see G. Foster 1965; 1972; Garrison and Arensberg 1976:295–97; Malina 1979, 2001:81–107; Pilch and Malina 1998:122–27.

8. Murdock 1980:38–40, 58, 62.

general as a continuous struggle for survival endangered by hostile, malevolent forces, both human and demonic. Culturally, the world was thought populated and controlled by high gods and a multiplicity of lesser divinities, demons, spirits, angels (benevolent and malevolent), "principalities and powers" (human and divine), patrons (human and divine), ghosts and phantasms, witches and sorcerers, diviners, soothsayers, spell casters, augurs, necromancers, conjurers, exorcists, dream interpreters, seers, alongside prophets, holy men, and sages. Decisions were made by casting lots and reading animal entrails. The causes of illness, misfortune, and disasters were thought to include angry or capricious deities, demons, unclean spirits, and hostile humans with their Evil Eyes. Protection against harm was sought by incantations and spells, lead tablets, amulets and apotropaics of various kinds. Hope for healing was placed on exorcisms and rituals, powerful words, names, gestures, and potent sounds. Trust was placed in the efficacy of blessings and curses and the power of extraordinary persons to feed and heal, receive divine revelation, ascend to the heavenly realms, and in general influence and harness the forces of nature. It was a world of male machismo, veiled and sequestered women, ocular aggression, and tension and envy between the poor and the privileged, natives and strangers, agriculturalists and herders, rival tribes and feuding neighbors. In this xenophobic world where only the privileged few had occasion and means to travel and where most of the population never set foot outside the village, strangers were regarded as likely enemies and thus feared of having a hostile Evil Eye. Everything of value, and especially the children, flocks, herds and means of livelihood, was thought vulnerable to the Evil-Eyed gaze of envy and therefore in need of concealment and protection. Amulets and other means of defense were enlisted for repelling the forces of evil, both human and transcendent.[9]

It was in such an environment and conceptual world that Evil Eye belief and practice flourished and expanded among the Mesopotamians,

9. See J. M. Roberts 1976:223–78 and Garrison and Arensberg 1976:294–302; also Boecher 1970; Derrett 1973 (describing life in Israel as the time of Jesus: "the social scene" [31–71], "economic and political scene" [73–100], and "the mental and intellectual scene" [101–159], the latter of which includes Evil Eye belief and practice [123]); Malina 2001; van der Jagt 2002; Klutz, ed. 2003; Nigosian 2008, among others. For basic features of the "common human pattern" of conceptualizing the world and experience (nature, life, thought, time, authority, work) prior to the Western enlightenment see Roheim 1958. On rivalry and conflict see Gouldner 1969. On demons and hostile forces, see Conybeare 1895–96; Tamborino 1909; Jirku 1912; Billerbeck 1926 4/1:501–35; Canaan 1929; Langton 1949; Eitrem 1950; Gordon 1957; T. W. Gaster 1962; Foerster 1964; Böcher 1970, 1981; Colpe et al. 1976; J. Z. Smith 1978; Ferguson 1984; Brenk 1986; Levack 1992, vols. 9 and 12; Page 1995; Cotter 1999:75–127; Vukosavovic 2010. On ocular aggression and the Evil Eye, see Gilmore 1982, esp. 197–200.

Egyptians, Greeks and Romans, Israelites and Christians. As we turn to the biblical communities and their writings, we will be looking at texts produced in this general environment and involving similar cultural mentalities.

The Pentateuch legislated, and the prophets inveighed, against the occult arts practiced by Israel's neighbors (e.g. Deut 18:9–14; Exod 22:17; Isa 3:16–4:1).[10] Egypt in particular was a target of condemnation. "Idols, sorcerers, mediums, and wizards" were claimed to populate the landscape and culture of Egypt (Isa 19:3). "Magic" and "sorcery" were more terminological weapons, however, than precisely defined practices. Attribution of magical practices and character flaws to the non-Israelite populations, projecting them back into hoary antiquity, and condemning them under Moses' name as foreign abominations, served to marginalize competing ideologies and reinforce Israel's distinctive self-identity. In what this magic and sorcery precisely consisted remains murky and unclarified. "Unlike the magic of artifact and inscription," Brian Schmidt argues, "magic in the Hebrew Bible has far less to say about the phenomenology of magic in ancient Israelite society and far more to tell about its function as a category of controlling matters of purity and pollution" (2002:259).

Israel's sacred writings make no connection between such proscribed magical practices and the Evil Eye. As indicated in Vol. 1, current disagreement and uncertainty concerning the very concept of "magic," and the absence of any direct explicit linking of the phenomenon of the Evil Eye with magic, has led us to avoid treatment of the Evil Eye in antiquity as an instance of sorcery or magical thought and practice."[11] This applies to the biblical evidence as well. The biblical communities did not equate the Evil Eye with sorcery or treat it as an instance of magic. They regarded it, as we shall see, as a phenomenon of nature, albeit noxious, and as a personal fault linked with conduct inconsistent with the will of God. It never is mentioned in biblical texts proscribing or denouncing customs or rituals associated with magic and conduct regularly linked with the practices of outsider Gentiles.[12] Conversely, where the Evil Eye is mentioned in the Bible, it is never labeled as an instance of magic, sorcery or the occult arts.

---

10. On Mesopotamian traditions and practice reflected in the proscriptions of "magical" actors and actions in Deuteronomy 18 see Schmidt 2002:242–59.

11. On this issue See Vol. 1, chap. 1, pp. 26–27, 61–66.

12. For example, Exod 7:11, 22; 8:18–19; 9:11; 22:18; Lev 19:21, 26, 31; 20:6, 27; Num 23:23; Deut 18:9–14; 1 Sam 28; 2 Kgs 9:22; 17:17; 21:5–6; 23:24; 2 Chron 33:6; Ps 58:5; Isa 3:3; 8:19; 47:9, 12; 57:3; Jer 27:9; Ezek 13:18–19; Dan 2:2; Mic 5:12; Nah 3:4; Mal 3:5; Wis 12:4, 17:7, 18:13; also *Ascen. Isa.* 2:5; *1 Enoch* 7:1, 64–65; *Jub.* 48:9–10; *L.A.B.* 34, 64; *T. Jud.* 23; Acts 8:9–24; 13:6–12; Gal 5:20; Rev 9:21; 18:23; 21:8, 22:15; *Barn.* 20:1; *Did.* 5:1 etc.

It is never condemned as a belief alien to Israel. Thus it appears that Evil Eye belief and practice was not included by the biblical communities under their rubric of magic and sorcery. The Evil Eye was dangerous, but not demonic. It worked mysteriously, but not magically. We respect this emic point of view of the biblical authors and treat Evil Eye belief and practice in the Bible as something distinct from what was named and condemned as "magic" or "sorcery." We examine it as it was envisioned by the ancients: as a phenomenon of nature, conferred by nature on certain humans identified as fascinators by particular physical and ethnic features; it could strike anyone anywhere, but neonates, infants, and birthing mothers were considered especially vulnerable; resort was deemed possible to a wide array of protective means and measures.

Having considered in the foregoing Vols. 1 (chap. 2) and 2 belief and practice concerning the Evil Eye (and its associations) in the larger world of the Bible—Mesopotamia, Egypt, Greece, and Rome—we are now in a position to examine traces of this belief and practice in the Bible itself and the biblical communities.

Belief in, and protective measures taken against, the Evil Eye were as widespread in the biblical communities as in the surrounding cultures, occasional voices to the contrary notwithstanding.[13] The more recent study of

---

13. Brav (1908/1992:46), for example, finds no mention of the Evil Eye in the biblical writings, taking *rah ayin* [*sic*] to mean rather "jealous/envious eye." "The sacred literature," he would have us believe, "is free from the stigma of this superstition" (1992:46), though it was "very prevalent" in Talmudic times" (1992:46). A similar position is taken by Nola Opperwall in her *ISBE* entry on the Evil Eye (1982b:210) in respect to all biblical references to the Evil Eye except Gal 3:1. Siegfried Seligmann's brief reference to the Evil Eye in the Bible (1910 1:12–13) is deficient and incorrect. Claiming that the Hebrews adopted Evil Eye belief from the Chaldeans, he gives Lev 19:26; Deut 18:10; and 2 Kgs 21:6 as OT texts mentioning persons, "Meaunenim /Aunenim," who, according to one opinion, bewitch through an envious eye; on this term *meônen* interpreted as "soothsayer," see more recently Jeffers 1996:78–81. In Seligmann's opinion, Wis 4:12 refers to fascination/Evil Eye; but Sir 14:8, 9, 10 and Prov 23:6 speak not of the Evil Eye but only of envy. In the New Testament, he allows that in Mark 7:22 Jesus mentions the Evil Eye, but that in Matt 20:15 and Gal 3:1 although the standard terminology for Evil Eye is employed, Jesus and Paul use it only for rhetorical effect and not because they actually believed in the "magical effect" of the Evil Eye (Seligmann 1910 1:13–14). On the other hand, the Jewish Mishnah, Talmud, and Kabbala, he observess, are replete with references to the Evil Eye (Seligmann 1910 1:14–16). Budge (1978/1930:359) states somewhat ambiguously that "The Hebrews were well acquainted with the Evil Eye and its dire effects, but it is not mentioned in the Old Testament, although it is clearly referred to in such passages as Deut xv.9 and Ps 141:4." He also adds Ps 23:6; Wis 4:12; and Sir 14:8, and states that "our Lord seems to refer to the Evil Eye" in Mark 7:22 and Matt 20:15 and that Paul "most certainly does" in Gal 3:1 (1978/1930:359). Later he adds David (1 Sam 18:9) and Balaam (Num 24:5) as biblical persons believed to possess the Evil Eye (1978/1930:364).

Rivka Kern Ulmer, *The Evil Eye in the Bible and Rabbinic Judaism*, devotes only four pages to the Evil Eye in the Bible (1994:1–4). She mentions Deut 15:9; 28:54, 56; 1 Sam 18:8–9 (the denominative verb "to eye" occurring only here in the Hebrew Bible); Prov 22:9 (a good eye signaling "a compassionate sharing of one's provisions with the poor"); Prov 23:6, 28:22; and Sir 14:10 and 31:13 (concerning an Evil Eye), and Isa 13:18 (regarding a destructive "eye of the Medes"). Unfortunately, she insists on distinguishing the sense of these *biblical* texts from *rabbinic* references to the Evil Eye. She asserts unconvincingly:

> Rabbinic interpreters later used these passages as the basis of the concept of an evil eye, but they [these biblical passages] can hardly be construed to refer to an evil or harmful power emanating from the human eye. The evil eye here [in the Bible] merely expresses malevolence, and it is the malevolent act, and not the eye itself, that afflicts other people. The only possible exception is found in the passage about the "eye of the Medes" which destroys everything: *Their eye shall not spare* children (Is 13:18). (Ulmer 1994:3)

This erroneous notion concerning the biblical Evil Eye texts is due in great part to her failure to examine biblical and rabbinic concepts of the Evil Eye in relation to Mesopotamian, Egyptian, Greco-Roman, and Christian Evil Eye traditions. This de-contextualized approach focuses primarily on rabbinic written sources and fails to consider the extensive amuletic evidence of Evil Eye belief and practice in biblical and post-biblical Israel. Her statement about the "eye of the Medes" suggests that she also wishes, perhaps like Aaron Brav (1908/1992), to purge the biblical communities of conventional notions and practice concerning the Evil Eye and allow them only to outsiders.

By contrast, the *rabbinic literature*, she indicates, shows a different view of the Evil Eye, from that of the Bible, involving "a power radiating from the eyes" and a view of the Evil Eye as an expression of "ill-will, envy, and selfishness," "niggardliness," and as both an "internal disposition" and an "externalized power" (Ulmer 1994:4–5). This view of the Evil Eye that she attributes to the rabbis is, of course, consistent with Evil Eye notions across the ancient Circum-Mediterranean, prior to, contemporaneous with, and subsequent to the Hebrew Bible references. Ulmer and others who deny repeated reference to this malignant power of the Evil Eye in the biblical writings assume, but fail to provide any evidence of, an isolation and divergence of the biblical communities and authors from the Evil Eye tradition and practice of their neighbors. Ulmer's 1994 study, while a useful assemblage and classification of references to the Evil Eye in the rabbinic literature, provides little attention to cultural context or cross-cultural influence and limited theoretical analysis. No light is shed here on the biblical texts.

Karl Meisen, in his rich 1950 article on the Evil Eye in antiquity and early Christianity, states that the Israelites knew the Evil Eye, but that "passages like Deut 28:54, 56; Prov 23:6; 28:22; Isa 13:8 etc. are insufficient" evidence of this belief in the Bible. No amulet against the Evil Eye is mentioned in the Hebrew Bible, he insists, and only the apocryphal and rabbinic literature of later time contain certain evidence thereof. Nevertheless, he concludes that the frequency and clarity of this later evidence point with "virtual certainty" (*ziemlicher Sicherheit*) to its existence in earlier times.[14] Such varied opinions may have influenced translators since the early twentieth century to translate actual references to the Evil Eye in the Bible not literally but according to assumed sense. The linguistic evidence of repeated references to the Evil Eye and malicious looking in the Bible, however, is indisputable; and the specific features of Evil Eye belief and practice recorded in the Bible, while distinctive, as we will note, also have much in common with those of the surrounding cultures. Particularly noteworthy in the biblical references to the Evil Eye is the focus on the Evil Eye of *humans,* with no reference to an Evil Eye demon, and the treatment of both Evil Eye and good eye as *moral* phenomena.

HEBREW AND GREEK OLD TESTAMENTS

In examining the Hebrew Bible and Greek Old Testament or Septuagint (LXX), we first will consider the terms and expressions employed for reference to the Evil Eye. Then we will examine in detail each of the relevant Evil Eye texts in the Old Testament and parabiblical writings. Finally, we will summarize our findings and note both the similarities and differences uniting and distinguishing Evil Eye belief and practice of the biblical communities from that of their neighbors. A following chapter will treat the New Testament Evil Eye references in similar fashion.

Hebrew and Greek Evil Eye Terminology

In the Old Testament (Hebrew and Greek), the chief formulations for the Evil Eye are *r" 'ayin* (verb), *ra' 'ayin,* (noun) *'ayin harah* in Hebrew, and in

---

14. Meisen 1950:145.

Greek, *ophthalmos ponêros, ophthalmos phthoneros* ("envious Eye") and various terms of the *bask-* family (*baskainô, baskania, baskanos, prosbaskanion*).

Expressions for Evil Eye (and Evil-Eyeing) in the Hebrew Bible

- *r'' 'ayin* (verb "be evil" [*r''*] + noun "eye" [*'ayin*] lit., "eye is evil;" also "do evil with the eye," "look maliciously with an Evil Eye," "to Evil Eye [someone]" Deut 15:9; 28:54, 56).[15]
- *ra' 'ayin* (adjective "evil" + noun "eye," lit., [someone] "evil of eye"), with "eye" as synecdoche for the entire person: "Evil-Eyed person," (Prov 23:6); see Prov 28:22 (*ish ra' 'ayin*, "person/man who is evil of eye;" "person/man with an Evil Eye."[16] The Aramaic for Evil Eye, *'ayna' bisha',* does not appear in the OT. "Evil Eye" can stand for the entire person with an Evil Eye (Prov 23:6); see also Sirach 14:10 (*'ayin ra'* / *ophthalmos ponêros phthoneros*).

Two other expressions are also likely references to an envious Evil Eye:
- *'ôyén* (participle of verb *'ayin,* lit., "eyeing [enviously]"), "staring at maliciously" (1 Sam 18:9)
- *me 'ôyén* (full participial form of the verb *'ayin,* lit., "eyeing [enviously]" "staring at maliciously") (1 Sam 2:29, 32)

Expressions for Evil Eye in the Greek Old Testament (LXX)

The Greek Old Testament (LXX) contains various explicit formulations for "Evil Eye." This includes expressions with *ophthalmos* ("eye"): *ophthalmos ponêros* (Sir 14:10), *ophthalmos ponêreuein* (Deut 15:9), *ophthalmos phthoneisthai* (Tob 4:7, 16; cf. Sir 14:10); *ophthalmos ponêros phthoneros* (Sir 14:10, the sole LXX occurrence of *phthoneros*; cf. *pleonektou ophthalmos* (Sir 14:9). This also includes expressions involving terms of the *bask-* family (13x): *baskanos* (*anêr baskanos,* Prov 23:6; 28:22; *anthrôpos baskanos,* Sir 14:3; *ponêros ho baskainôn ophthalmôi,* Sir 14:8; *baskanos,* absolute, 18:18; 37:11); *baskainein* (*baskainein tôi ophthalmôi,* Deut 28:54, 56; *baskainontos*

15. Beside meaning "be evil, do evil," the verb *r''* can mean "break, smash," which also fits the concept of the Evil Eye striking, breaking, and destroying—as in some Mesopotamian incantations. However, in Deuteronomy it denotes the action of a *human* with an Evil Eye and not an Evil-Eyed demon.

16. Wazana (2007:687) notes the absence of the phrase *'ayin harah* in the Hebrew Bible and its appearance only later in the rabbinic literature.

heauton, Sir 14:6, 8); *baskania* (Wis 4:12; 4 Macc 1:26; 2:15), and *probaskan-ion* (Ep. Jer. 69/70). Other formulations that are likely references to looking with an Evil Eye are *epiblepein . . . ophthalmôi* (1 Sam 2:29; cf. Deut 28:54, 56; Sir 14:8) and *hypoblepesthai* (1 Sam 18:9; cf. Sir 37:10).

The LXX rendering of the Hebrew *r" 'ayin* in Deut 15:9 is *ponêreusêtai ho ophthalmos sou*, "your eye is evil toward," a combination of noun (*ho ophthalmos sou*, "your eye") and verb (*ponêreusêtai*, "is evil toward"). The Greek, like the Hebrew, uses the verb "be evil" with "eye." Both also presume the connection of eye and heart.[17] The later passages of Tob 4:7 and 4:16 bear a close semblance in their formulation of noun (*ho ophthalmos sou*, "your eye") and verb ([*mê*] *phthonêsatô*, "not be envious"). The LXX render-ing of the Hebrew *r" 'ayin* in Deut 28:54 and 56 is *baskanei tôi ophthalmôi*, literally, "Evil-Eye with an eye," a combination of the verb *baskanei* and the noun *ophthalmos* also appearing in Sir 14:8. The verb *baskainein* also occurs in Sir 14:6. The related noun *baskania* appears in Wis 4:12, 4 Macc 1:26; and 2:15. The adjective/substantive *baskanos* occurs in Prov 23:6; 28:22; Sir 4:3; 18:18; 37:11, and the noun *probaskanion*, in Ep Jer 69/70.

The Greek *andri baskanôi* ("with an Evil-Eyed man/person," noun [*an-dri*]+ adjective [*baskanôi*]) renders Hebrew *ra' 'ayin* (Prov 23:6), with the LXX adding the noun *anêr* ("person").[18]

The Greek phrase *ophthalmos ponêros phthoneros* ("[A person with] an Evil Eye is envious of/begrudging of") renders Hebrew *'ayin ra' 'ayin* at Sir 14:10. As in Prov 23:6, "Evil Eye" stands here for the entire person.[19] *Ophthalmos ponêros* occurs in Sir 14:10 and Sirach 31:13, and in the New Testament in Matt 6:22–23/Luke 11:34–35; and Mark 7:22.

The LXX rendition of the Hebrew participle *'ôyén* ("enviously [Evil-] Eyeing") in 1 Sam 18:9 is *hypoblepomenos* ("looking askance"), a composite of *blepô* ("look") and *hypo* ("from under"), literally, "looking up from under the eyebrows." This Greek verb also occurs in in Sir 37:10–11, where "look-ing askance"(*hypoblepomenou*, v. 10a) also implies looking enviously with an Evil Eye (*zêlountôn*, v. 10b) and where an "envious rival wife" and an Evil-Eyed person (*baskanou*, 11) also are mentioned. In 1 Sam 2:29 LXX,

---

17. Deut 15:10 HT, paralleling 15:9 and reading "your heart is evil (when you give)," LXX renders, "you shall not grieve (*lypêthêsê*) in your heart (when you give)."

18. This addition in Greek clarifies the synecdoche of the Hebrew in which "Evil Eye" stands in for the entire person; cf. also Sir 14:10 and the Ugaritic incantation KTU[2] 1.96 [= RS 22.225 = CAT 1.96] discussed previously in Vol. 1, chap. 2.

19. The consistent Greek equivalent for the Hebrew adjective *ra'* ("evil") is *ponêros*, meaning "evil," "essentially bad." *Ponêros* is used of evil spirits (1 Sam 16:14, 23; Matt 12:45; Luke 7:21; 8:2, 11:26; Acts 19:12-16), evil demons (Tob 3:8), evil angels (Ps 78:49), evil beasts (Lev 26:6), and evil humans (Num 14:35; 1 Chr 2:3).

Hebrew m^e 'ôyén ("looking with an Evil Eye") is rendered "looking with a shameless eye," *epeblepsas. . . anaidei ophthalmôi*, involving another composite of *blepô*.

Thus the Septuagint employs two main conventional Greek expressions for the Evil Eye: (a) formulations with *ophthalmos* ("eye"): *ophthalmos ponêreuesthai* (Deut 15:9), *ophthalmos ponêros* (Sir 14:10, 31:13), *ophthalmos ponêros phthoneros* (Sir 14:10), *ophthalmos phthonein* (Tob 4:7, 16) and (b) formulations with terms of the *baskanos* word group: *baskainein tôi ophthalmôi* (Deut 28:54, 56; Sir 14:6, 8), *baskanos* (Prov 23:6, 28:22; Sir 14:3, 18:18; 37:11), *baskania* (Wis 4:12); *probaskanion* (Ep Jer 69/70). In addition, some synonyms for "looking askance," "looking with hostility or enviously or shamelessly with an Evil Eye" also appear (1 Sam 18:9; 1 Sam 2:29; Sir 37:10).

The article on the *bask-* wordfield by Gerhard Delling (1964) in the important and influential reference work, the *Theological Dictionary of the New Testament*, requires a comment, given its misleading content on this subject. Delling links *baskanos* (a denominative construction meaning "defamatory," "bewitching") with *baskô* and *bazô* (1964:594), and gives as the "original meaning" of *baskanos* "to do hurt to someone through unfavorable words" (ibid.:594). The verb, he claims, had three senses: (a) "to bewitch," (b) "to revile," and (c) "to envy." Added to the original meaning of (a), he continues, was "that of harm through hostile looks, so that (a) denotes 'specifically the simple but all the more sinister' witchcraft 'exercised through hostile looks or words' even though it might be unintentional."[20] He claims that "*baskanos* is attested from the 5th cent. B.C, *baskania* since Plato, *baskainô* since Aristotle" (ibid.:594). At present, however, the canon of ancient Greek literature covered by the *Thesaurus Linguae Graecae* gives a different and more up-to-date picture, as reflected above in the discussion of these terms in Vol. 2. In regard to the *bask-* word family. Delling claims that "it is not merely a question of magic through the evil eye but of any bewitching or hurting through men or non-human forces. Hence it is clear that, unless *baskainein* is given this narrower sense by the context, it does not have to denote the evil eye, but may equally well refer to other means of harming by magic" (ibid.:594–95). This is particularly misleading. Beside the problematic and unsubstantiated association of the Evil Eye with magic, this expanded sense of *baskania* etc. is by no means certain. So for the sake of linguistic consistency, in this study I have always rendered terms of the *bask-* word family with "Evil Eye." As to a connection with magic, Delling does correctly note that "*baskainein* is never used of other

20. Delling 1964:594, quoting Kuhnert 1909:2009.

magic which employs certain external means that acquire magical power by conjuration" (ibid.:595). But it is his categorization of the Evil Eye as magic that still remains problematic. Equally problematic is his taking none of the occurrences of *bask-* in the LXX or NT as referring to the Evil Eye. "In the LXX," he claims, "it means only 'to be unfavorably disposed to'" and in New Testament *baskainein* (Gal 3:1) supposedly has the sense of "to bewitch (by words)" (ibid.:595). This latter notion is clearly in error given the act of *looking* regularly implied by *bask-* terms, and given the repeated reference to eyes in both Gal 3:1 and 4:14 and the several other traces here of Evil Eye belief and practice, as our discussion of Galatians will indicate. It is hard to avoid the conclusion that Delling too seems intent on purging the Bible of any reference to the active and malevolent Evil Eye, rather than understanding what it entailed and implied. As a result, the article fails to illuminate the biblical passages containing these terms or other linguistic equivalents. Thomas Rakoczy levels a similar critique against Delling's entry.[21] Bauer-Danker-Arndt-Gingrich, *Greek-English Lexicon* (BDAG 2000), is a better lexical guide to the meanings of *baskania* etc. and the relevant literature.

The Latin Terminology of Jerome's Vulgate

Jerome's Latin Vulgate employs the standard Latin terminology for the Evil Eye (or envy as associated or equated with Evil Eye); namely, *oculus nequam* (Sir 14:10, 31:13; cf. Matt 6:23/Luke 11:34, Matt 20:15); *oculus malus* (Mark 7:22); *invidere* (Deut 28:54, 56; Prov 28:22; Sir 14:6) or *fascinatio* (Wis 4:12). The use of *invidere* to translate the Hebrew and Greek *Evil Eye*, e.g. Prov 28:22, also shows Jerome's sense of the virtual synonymity of *invidere/invidia* and *baskainein/baskania*.[22]

Original Languages and Translations

Examination of terminology in the original languages is essential for our analysis since all translations of the original Hebrew and Greek (and of Jerome's Latin Vulgate) are not simply translations but interpretations. These interpretations are conditioned and limited by the translators's knowledge of the cultural matrix of the terms employed and of the Evil Eye phenomenon itself, and by the assumptions of the translators's culture. The Latin Vulgate, the Syriac Peshitta, and the King James Version (KJV) generally

21. Rakoczy 1996:124 n. 383.

22. On the Latin terms *fascinare* etc. and *invidere* etc. see Vol. 2.

render the original texts with "Evil Eye." Other or later modern versions offer alternatives such as *Missgunst* ("begrudging," Luther), *neidischer Blick* ("envious glance, Zürcher Bibel), *squardo invidioso* ("envious glance," *Il Nuovo Testamento*); "jealousy" (TEV); and "envy" (RSV, NRSV, NEB, NAB, BJ). Translations that do not render the original Hebrew and Greek terms for "Evil Eye" or "looking, harming with an Evil Eye" as the same in the receptor language but that offer only an *assumed sense* of the original terms obscure for readers of the Bible that fact that the original texts explicitly mention the Evil Eye. In several Evil Eye texts, envy, for example, is explicitly mentioned or implied. The Evil Eye and envy, however, are allied but are not identical. Envy, we recall, is the emotion, and an Evil Eye is the physical organ—the malignant ocular glance—by which envy is conveyed. Rendering "Evil Eye" by "envy" in several instances confuses the matter. Translations often tell us more about the mindsets and culture of the translators than about the meaning of original terms in their original cultural settings. In this volume I will indicate the original Hebrew and Greek (and Latin) terms and will consistently translate Hebrew and Greek (and Latin) terms for Evil Eye with "Evil Eye," "to Evil Eye," "Evil-Eyed," "harm with an Evil Eye" etc. as the original terms require.

The Old Testament Evil Eye Texts

Our examination of Old Testament and related texts commences with those passages of the Hebrew and Greek Old Testaments that *explicitly* mention the Evil Eye. *Implicit* references will be treated next. Finally, passages will be discussed where reference to the Evil Eye has been claimed but where the evidence remains inconclusive.

In the Greek Bible (containing, beyond the Hebrew writings, the apocryphal writings), we find, as indicated above,[23] fourteen text segments involving twenty explicit references to the Evil Eye, an eye that is evil, malicious, hostile, envious, stingy, or greedy: Deut 15:9; 28:54, 56; Prov 23:6; 28:22; Sir 14:3, 6, 8, 9, 10; 18:18; 31:13; 37:10, 11; Wis 4:12; Tob 4:7, 16; 4 Macc 1:26; 2:15; Ep Jer 69/70. Many references appear in the so-called Wisdom Literature of the Old Testament. This is to be expected, given the interest of these writings in the practical concerns of everyday living. This body of literature concerning conventional wisdom has extensive affinities with the folk wisdom and folklore of Mesopotamian, Egyptian, Greek, and Roman traditions. Additional traces of the belief in the Intertestamental period

23. See above, p. 2.

appear in the Old Testament Pseudepigrapha,[24] the Dead Sea Scrolls,[25] Philo,[26] and Josephus.[27] The New Testament attests the persistence of Evil Eye belief within the communities of Jesus of Nazareth and the apostle Paul. Four explicit references to the Evil Eye (*ophthalmos ponêros*) are attributed to Jesus (Matt 6:22–23//Luke 11:33–34; Matt 20:15; Mark 7:22). In Paul's letter to the Galatians, the explicit question, "O uncomprehending Galatians, who has injured you with the Evil Eye (*tis hymas ebaskanen*)?" (3:1) is one explicit reference to the phenomenon, among several allusions (especially in 4:12–20). In the post-biblical centuries, as we shall see, Jewish and Christian concern over the Evil Eye and its prevention continued unabated through and beyond Late Antiquity. This is evident from the extensive literary, epigraphic, iconographic and archaeological evidence.

A wide range of evidence thus indicates that ancient Israelites and Christians shared with their pagan neighbors the ubiquitous fear of the Evil Eye and a constant concern for avoiding or warding off its destructive power. Varying nuances of Evil Eye belief in the biblical literature will become apparent in our examination of representative texts. Modern translations, with the exception of the KJV, generally tend to render the assumed *sense*, rather than the actual terms, of the Hebrew and Greek expressions for "Evil Eye." For our purposes, therefore, attention to, and comparison of, the *original languages* must be our point of departure. Comparison with the Latin translation of Jerome's *Vulgata* will provide a checkpoint for the Latin equivalents.

The Evil Eye Belief Complex in the Bible

To prepare for an examination of the Old Testament texts mentioning an Evil Eye, it will be useful to review how the eye in general was viewed in the biblical communities, along with consideration of other components of the Evil Eye belief complex that appear in the biblical texts. Most of these components we have already encountered in Mesopotamian, Egyptian, Greek, or Roman sources.

---

24. *T. Iss.* 3:2–3; 4:1–6 (*baskanos, ophthalmous ponêrous*); *T. Benj.* 4:2–4 (*skoteinon ophthalmon . . . phthonei . . . zeloi*); cf. *T. Dan* 2:5; *T. Sol.* 18:39; and possibly *Jos. Asen.* 4:11; and *2 Enoch* 52:7–8.

25. 4Q424, Frag. 1, lines 10–12; 4Q477 [4QDecrees], Frag. 1, col. 2.3–7; 1QS 7:13.

26. Philo, *Cherubim* 33; *Names* 95, 112; *Dreams* 1.107; *Moses* 1. 246; *Virtues* 170; *Flaccus* 29.

27. *War* 1.208; *Ant.* 1.188, 200, 260; 3.268; 6.59; 10.212, 250, 257; 11.265; *Life* 425; *Ag. Ap.* 1.72; 2.285.

The frequent references to the eyes of humans and of God in the Old Testament indicate how prominent the eyes were as means of apprehension of information and of perception of reality and truth, as indicators of internal states and affect, as instruments of communication and aggression, as means of moral evaluation, and as symbols of cognition and understanding. Yael Avrahami aptly speaks of the "centrality" and "supremacy" of sight in Israel's sensorium.[28]

The basic Hebrew term for "eye" ('ayin) appears in the Hebrew Bible with varying senses, designating (a) "spring": [of water, e. g., Gen 16:7) some twenty-three times or, more often, (b) "eye" (866+ times) referring to (b.1.) some human feature: physical eye (Exod 21:26); "eye of the land" or "face of the land" (Exod 10:15); the mental faculty of cognition (Gen 3:7, eyes opened); disposition, emotion ("your eye shall not pity them," Deut 7:16; "set their eyes to cast me to the ground," Ps 17:11); or the eye(s) of God (Deut 11:12; Judg 6:17; Prov 15:3 etc.).[29] The eyes conveyed a wide range of emotions including humility, arrogance, pity, defiance, dissimulation, generosity, miserliness, envy, malice, and hostility. As a verb, the action of "eyeing" involved looking with envy and malice (1 Sam 18:9). The semantic field also includes *chazah* and *ra'ah,* both actions of seeing.[30] In the Greek Old Testament (LXX, Septuagint), *ophthalmos* occurs almost 700 times and *omma,* ten times. Xavier Jacques's *List of Septuagint Words Sharing Common Elements* lists forty-seven words connected with the Greek root *op-* whose terms (including *ophthalmos, optesthai, opsis,* etc.) designate various aspects of seeing, vision, and the organ of the eye.[31] The semantic field of eye, seeing, looking, and experiencing in the OT is extensive and illustrates the great importance attributed to this human faculty.[32]

(1) Expressions in the Old Testament imply that the Israelites thought of the eye as having its own light. "The light of my eyes—it also has gone from me" (Ps 37 (38):10). "The light of the eyes rejoices the heart" (Prov

28. Avrahami 2011:263–73.

29. In the Aramaic sections of the Old Testament 'ayna' appears five times (Dan 4:31; 7:8 [twice], 20; Ezra 5:5). The Aramaic for "Evil Eye," 'ayna' bisha' does not occur.

30. The eye and other organs of body are usually feminine in Hebrew; but on occasion also masculine (Song 4:9b, 6:5; Job 21:20; Zech 4:10).

31. Jacques 1972 s.v. The Greek semantic field also includes *horaô, blepô, theaomai, theoreô* and their compounds.

32. On "eye" in the OT, see Cheyne 1899; Jenni and Vetter 1976:259–68; Stendebach 1989:31–48; Rosenzweig 1892 (OT and Talmud); Seligmann 1922:501–7; Wilpert and Zenker 1950; Deonna 1965 (symbolism of eye); Michaelis 1967; Opperwall 1982a; Avrahami 2011:263–73. For the rabbinic material, see Levy 1924 3:639–41; Jastrow 1950 2:1071–72.

15:30). "The Lord gives light to the eyes" (Prov 29:13). Loss of that light constitutes a progressive dimming of the eyes and eventually blindness.

(2) Like the surrounding cultures, the biblical communities viewed the eye as an *active* organ, projecting its light similar to the sun projecting its rays or a lamp casting light. Dan 10:2–9 records the vision of a male figure, whose "body was like beryl, his face like the appearance of lightning, his eyes like flaming torches . . ." (Dan 10:6). *1 Enoch* describes righteous Noah as having been born with eyes "like the rays of the sun" (106:5, 10). Like the sun or a lamp, they project lights: "when he opened his eyes the whole house lighted up" (106:2, 10). Philo, the Alexandrian Israelite historian, speaks of eyes "reaching out" and "acting upon subjects: "the light within us "goes forth towards the things seen" (*Abraham* 150–156).[33] Revelation 1:14 describes a figure with "eyes as flames of fire" (see also Rev 2:18, 19:12; cf. *1 Enoch* 106:5, 10).[34] Accordingly, one could speak of "casting the eye" (Gen 39:7; 44:21; 2 Sam 22:28; Job 16:9; Ps 34:15; 101:6; 145:15).[35] Seven lamps mentioned in a vision recorded by Zechariah are identified by an angel as "the [seven] eyes of the Lord, which range through the whole earth" (Zech 4:10). The equation of eye and lamp is explicitly made in the *Testament of Job*: "My eyes, acting as lamps, looked about" (*T. Job* 18:4). This same equation of eye and lamp recurs in the well-known saying of Jesus in Matt 6:22–23/Luke 11:33–36. Also, like lamps, the eyes can also become "dim" or "darkened," generally by age.[36] Sirach 18:18 states that an Evil Eye causes the dimming of the eyes (either one's own or, more likely, those of others). Jesus speaks of an Evil Eye constituting or causing total darkness in the body (Matt 6:23/Luke 11:34).

These passages illustrate the fact that the biblical communities shared with their neighbors what is called an extramission theory of vision. This theory of vision, which prevailed throughout antiquity. posited that the eye was an active organ that projected energy outward, similar to the rays of the sun or the glow of a lamp.[37] No writing of the Bible explains in detail how the eye was thought to function. From the texts illustrating the understanding

33. See Allison 1987:61.

34. *Pace* Aquaro 2004:32, who erroneously claims that the Hebrews differed from the Greek notion of emanations/rays exiting from the eye.

35. The notion of "casting" an Evil Eye is expressed in Italian with *jettatura,* which derives from the verb *jettare,* "to cast, throw."

36. See Gen 27:1; 48:10; Deut 34:7; 1 Sam 3:2; Job 17:7; Ps 69:23; Lam 5:17; Zech 11:17.

37. On the extramission theory of vision and its contrast to the intromission theory of vision that is now espoused by modern science, see Vol. 1, chap. 1, pp. 20–21, and Vol. 2, pp. 25–26, 71–72, 94–11.

of the eye as an active organ, however, it is clear that some version of the extramission theory of vision was en vogue among the biblical communities as it was throughout the ancient world. The process of vision and the action of an Evil Eye no doubt were understood in terms similar to those laid out by Plutarch and Heliodorus.[38]

(3) The eye was assumed to be connected to the heart, the seat of disposition and feeling, the cognitive and affective center of personal identity.[39] As Plutarch linked the eye and envy with the mind (*psychê*),[40] so biblical authors associated the eye with the *heart*, the seat of all dispositions, intentions, and emotions including envy, jealousy, miserliness, anger, hatred, malice, greed etc. Eye(s) and heart are regularly mentioned in tandem.[41] The psalmist sings of "integrity of heart . . . perverseness of heart, an arrogant heart" (Ps 101:2, 4, 5). "The light of the eyes rejoices the heart" (Prov 15:30). The heart rejoices from the enlightened eye (Ps 19:8). Correspondingly, the eye reveals and expresses the disposition and intentionality of the heart: "Walk in the ways of your heart and the sight of your eyes" (Eccl 11:9). One should not have "eyes and heart for dishonest gain and other evil" (Jer 22:17). The expression "the eyes of the heart" (Eph 1:17; *1 Clem.* 36:2) unites the two and appears to have been proverbial.

The eye or eyes express a variety of dispositions stirring in the heart: hostility (Job 16:9); hatred (Job 16:9; Ps 35:19; Prov 6:13); arrogance (Prov 6:17, 21:4; 30:13; Ps 101:5), humble trust (Ps 123:2), innocence (Ps 101:2); perverseness (Ps 101:4), mockery (Prov 30:17), sorrow (Job 3:10); sadness (Ps 6:7[8]; 31:9[10]; 88:9[10]; Jer 9:1, 18; Lam 1:16, 2:11); shamelessness (Sir 26:11); pity (Deut 7:16; 13:8; 19:13, 21; 25:12); insatiability (Eccl 1:8; 4:8; Prov 27:20; 30:17); desire, lust (Ps 73:7; Prov 17:24; Ezek 6:9; Sir 26:9), and, as we shall see, envy, miserliness, and greed as manifested in an Evil Eye. A winking eye reveals a conniving heart: "Whoever winks his eye plans evil deeds (Sir 27:22; cf. Ps 35:19; Prov 6:13; 10:10). *Ophthalmodoulia*, literally, "eye-service," denotes the vice of flattery and obsequiousness (Eph 6:6; Col 3:22). Blindness, the non-functioning of the eyes and result of their

38. On the Evil Eye texts of Plutarch and Heliodorus see Vol. 2. pp. 48–56 and 64–69, respectively.

39. See the fuller discussion below, chapter 2, in relation to Mark 7:22. On the linguistic nuances of the term "heart" (*léb*) and its idiomatic usage see Stolz 1971; Leeb 2008.

40. Plutarch, *Quaest. Conv.* 5.7.3; *Mor.* 681D–F, 682C

41. See Num 15:39; Deut 4:9; 15:9–10; 28:65, 67; 1 Sam 2:33; 1 Kgs 9:3; 14:8; 2 Kgs 10:30; 2 Chr 7:16; 16:9; 25:2; Job 15:12; Pss 19:8; 36:1; 101:3–5; Prov 15:30; 21:2, 4; 23:26; Eccl 2:10; 11:9; Lam 5:17; Ezek 6:9; 21:6; Mark 7:22. See also below, chap. 2 on Mark 7:18–23, where heart and Evil Eye are also associated; for "evil heart" see also 1 Sam 1:8.

"dimming," represents darkness and gloom (Isa 29:18) and can be regarded as caused by God or the gods as punishment for arrogance or *hybris* or for casting an Evil Eye.[42] The eye thus was the organ of seeing and witnessing, but also indicator of one's state of physical health, emotions, intentions, and moral character.

(4) In the case of an Evil Eye, chief among these emotions, as in Greek and Roman thought, was envy.[43] The eye and the process of seeing are linked regularly with the disposition of envy. Envy arises in the heart ("Do not let your heart envy sinners," Prov 23:17) and is conveyed outward through the eye, that is, an Evil Eye. "Saul (enviously Evil-) Eyed David" (1 Sam 18:9). Other formulations show the explicit association of Evil Eye and envy: "An Evil Eye is envious of (or 'begrudges') bread" (*Ophthalmos ponêros phthoneros ep' artôi*, Sir 14:10); "do not begrudge with your Evil Eye the alms when you give them," *mê phthonesatô sou ho ophthalmos . . .* (Tob 4:7, 16; lit., "do not envy with your eye . . ."; cf. also Sir 37:10, 11. As we shall discuss in greater detail below, envy is aroused by seeing the good fortune of others, comparing it with one's own condition, and concluding that another's gain has come at the cost of one's own loss. Distress from feeling inferior and short-changed prompts the wish that the good fortune of the other be destroyed. Seeing is a precondition of envying.

The Greek for "envy" in the LXX, translating the Hebrew *qanah*, is the *zêlos* family of terms (*zêlos, antizêlos, zêloô, zêlos, zêlotypeô zêlotypia, zêlôsis, zêlôtês, zêlôtos, homozêlia, parazêloô, parazêlôsis*); only the Greek biblical apocryphal writings contain terms of the *phthon-* family.[44] The Latin *invidia*, from which the English "envy" derives, and the verb *invidere*, from which *invidia* derives, make the association of Evil Eye and envy explicit, conceptually and linguistically. In the Vulgate, *invidere* (*invidus*) is the Latin equivalent of the Greek *baskainein* (*baskanos*, which renders the Hebrew of Deut 28:54, 56; and Prov 23:6; 28:22). *Invidere* (*in* + *videre*, lit.,

---

42. See Sophocles, *Oedipus at Colonus* 149–156; and Bernidaki-Aldous 1988. The apostle Paul was struck blind by God for seeking to harm God's people (Acts 9:1–8) and thereafter had his sight restored (Acts 9:17–19). Boughouts (1978:2), citing Schott 1931, refers to an Egyptian curse text mentioning Horus blinding the eyes of those casting an Evil Eye.

43. On envy in Israelite literature see Stumpf 1964; Sauer 1976; McKim 1982; de la Mora 1987; Schulz 1987; Dickie 1992; Pilch and Malina 1998:59–63, 209–12; Elliott 1992, 2007b, 2008; Kim 2001; Malina 2001b; Wazana 2007; Böttrich 2008; see also von Nordheim-Diehl 2012 (envy of God, the Devil, and humans in Second Temple Israel). On envy in antiquity (and its distinction from jealousy), see also Vol. 2, *Excursus on Envy* 83–113.

44. *Phthonein* (Tob 4:7, 16); *phthoneros* (Sir 14:10); *phthonos* (Wis 2:24; 6:23; 1 Macc 8:16; 3 Macc 6:7). See also *aphthonos* (3 Macc 5:2; 4 Macc 3:10); *aphthonôs* (Wis 7:13).

"to over-look") means "to look askance at, to look maliciously or spitefully at, to cast an Evil Eye upon."[45] *Invidia*, in turn, is the envy implicit in this evil glance. Thus, as the Greeks regularly associated envy (*phthonos*) with the Evil Eye and spoke of an *ophthalmos phthoneros* ("envious Eye"),[46] so the Romans reflected this association in their language through terms uniting the concepts of malevolent stare, envy, and Evil Eye. These associations have endured in Evil Eye cultures down through modern times.[47] It is essential to keep in mind that in antiquity envy was related to, but distinguished from, jealousy. The jealous person feared the loss of his possessions to a rival who sought to acquire them. The envious person grieved the good fortune and possessions enjoyed by others and wished them destroyed. Jealousy fears loss to self; envy wishes loss upon others. The husband's concern about his possibly adulterous wife in Numbers 5 and the ritual involved is a classic case of jealousy rather than envy. Saul, on the other hand, is not *jealous* of David but rather *envies* him (1 Sam 18:9).[48]

The accusation of enviousness, of course, could serve as a stereotype for putting down the "other," the stranger or the alien. Philo of Alexandria insisted that envy (*phthonos*) was a typical feature of the Egyptian nature (*Flaccus* 29). The accusation also has been leveled at one's own people. Centuries after Philo, Miguel de Unamuno directed the same charge against his own people, the Spaniards. On more than one occasion, the renowned author and former rector of the University of Salamanca declared envy to be a "deadly cancer" of the human spirit, but a vice characteristic of Spain in particular. "The national Spanish leprosy," he called it; "the ferment of Spanish social life."[49]

(5) Another disposition regularly associated in the Bible with an Evil Eye is miserliness, stinginess with one's resources, tight-fistedness, reluctance to be generous, giving only begrudgingly. "Be careful lest there be an evil thought in your heart . . . and your eye be evil against your needy neighbor and you give nothing" (Deut 15:9).[50] J. D. M. Derrett underscored the association in ancient Israelite society of the Evil Eye with "niggardliness,

---

45. Lewis and Short, *Latin Dictionary, s.v.*

46. Walcot 1978, esp. pp. 77–90 on the Evil Eye and envy.

47. Schoeck 1987 on envy and the Evil Eye; de la Mora 1987; Maloney 1976; Dundes, ed. 1992. Aquaro (2004:20–49), commenting on envy and the Evil Eye in the OT, unconvincingly sees "a much 'higher' and less superstitious understanding of envy in the Old Testament" than in its "Chaldean roots" (2004:49).

48. On this text see below, pp. 53, 65-66, 69, 70, 107, 183.

49. Cited by de la Mora 1987:55.

50. See also Deut 28:53–57; Tob 4:7–11, 16; Sir 14:3, 5, 8; Matt 6:22–23/Luke 11:34.

or meanness, in contexts where society expects, and rewards, generosity."[51] This Evil Eye of stinginess "is not a permanent characteristic, and can be remedied by a change in fortune or a change in attitude." Warning against this aspect of the Evil Eye is a distinctive feature of biblical commentary on the malevolent eye.

(6) Persons with an Evil Eye were thought capable of causing illness and great harm to others and even to themselves. Sigmund Mowinkel notes that "illness was thought to be brought about not only by God and supernatural beings, demons or evil spirits," but also by "the 'might' and supernatural 'power'—evil or good—of particular individuals. Beside prophets and priests, women and other humans deemed "different" were thought capable of "'the evil word,' 'the evil eye' and other 'damaging acts.' . . ." used by any person against another; the popular mind looked upon the evil word and the evil eye as in themselves potent agents of disaster."[52] These and further features of an Evil Eye will be discussed in greater detail below and in the following chapter.

(7) The Evil Eye, it was believed, could be averted by a variety of means and measures. Frequent mention is made, for example, of an array of amulets employed to protect against all forms of evil forces, including the Evil Eye. These included ear rings (Gen 35:4, associated with "household gods," cf. 31:19), Judah's signet ring (Gen 38:18, 25), nose rings, and moon/crescent amulets (Judg 8:21, 24, 26). Israelite women, Isaiah complains, wore "crescent moon amulets," other "amulets," "signet rings," "nose rings," and "veils" (Isa 3:18–23)—all for protection. At this time, we recall, "every ornament was an amulet" worn just as much for protection against evil forces as for ornamentation.[53] Animals, too, were protected with amulets; e.g. camels (crescents, Judg 8:21, 26) and horses (bells, Zech 14:20). Israelite soldiers under Judas Maccabeus, contrary to law, concealed amulets (*hierômata*, "sacred tokens of the idols of Jamnia") in their clothing (2 Macc 12:40), probably images of their protective deities similar to the images or "idols" of 2 Sam 5:21/1 Chr 14:12.

Illus. 1
Sketch of a crescent amulet for wearing, depicting a horned bull's head and a phallus (from Seligmann 1910 1:341, fig. 61).

Three features of specifically Israelite piety provided prophylaxis and served to ward off evil

---

51. Derrett 1995:68.

52. Mowinkel 1962 2:2–3.

53. So Kennedy 1910:439, among others.

forces in general and the Evil Eye in particular: (1) the donning of phylacteries (*phylaktêria*) at prayer (Exod 13:9, 16; Deut 6:8; 11:18; Matt 23:5); (2) the blue fringes or tassels (*tzitzit, kraspeda*) on the four corners of the prayer shawl (Num 15:37–41; Deut 22:12),[54] and (3) the *mezuzahs* affixed to the doorposts of domestic residences (Deut 6:9; 11:20).[55] On these three practices see below, pp. 100, 272–73, 282. Such protective practices of everyday

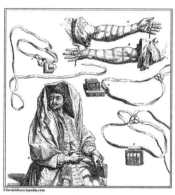

Illus. 2

Jewish phylacteries (from *Jewish Encyclopedia* 1906 10:24, reproducing an engraved drawing from Bernard Picart, 1725)

Illus. 3

Blue apotropaic tassels (*tzitzit*) on the four corners of the prayer shawl (*tallit*) worn by observant Jewish males during weekday morning services

54. Tassels and fringed objects, Egyptologist Budge reports (1978/1930:81), were thought by Egyptians to be "disliked by evil Spirits." "In ancient Pentateuch rolls, some of the letters have fringes attached to them," presumably for the same reason. For reference to these *tzitzit*/fringes in the New Testament, see Matt 9:20; 14:36; 23:5; Mark 6:56; Luke 8:44.

55. So Kennedy 1910:440; Nigosian 2008:45. On Hebrew and Jewish amulets (and charms) see also Peringer 1695;Rodkinson 1893; Blau 1898:86–93, 1907:546–50; 19142 M. Gaster 1900, 1910:451–55; Kennedy 1910; Montgomery 1910–11; Petrie 1914; Casanowicz 1917; Billerbeck 1928, vol. 4.1:529–33; Heller 1928; Kaufman 1939; Bonner 1950:302–3 and Plates XIV–XV, esp. Pl. XV, nos. 208–21; Goodenough 1953–68, vol. 2:153–295; vol. 3, nos. 379–81, 999–1209; Koetting 1954:474–476; Ben-Dor 1962:122; G. H. Davies 1962a, 1962b; Delatte and Derchain 1964, no. 371;Trachtenberg 1970/1939:132–52; Yitshaqi 1976; Budge 1978/1930:212–38 (Hebrew amulets), 283–90, 446–47 (Hebrew/Aramaic magic bowls, "devil traps"); T. W. Davies 1979; Harrison 1979; Peterson 1982; Schrire 1982; Yamauchi 1983:195–99; T. H. Gaster 1987; Naveh and Shaked 1987 (amulets and magic bowls); Kotansky 1991; Yardeni 1991; Barkay 1992, 2009 (oldest Israelite amulet, seventh–sixth cent. BCE); Schiffman and Swartz 1992; Ulmer 1994; Michaelides 1994; Keel 1996; Veltri 1996; Barkay et al. 2004; Schmitt 2004, 2012; Lincicum 2008; Vukosavovic 2010; Kosior 2014. On Egyptian amulets found in Palestine, see Rowe 1938; Hermann 1994, 2002.

life were shared by Israel with its neighbors and were prompted by a constant dread of the Evil Eye and other inimical forces. The specific *form* such apotropaics took in Israel's practice, however, illustrate Israel's distinctive mode of adaptation.

(8) Persons possessing a "good eye" are considered individuals of honor and integrity who are generous with their resources. Thus the sage observes, "He who has a good eye (*tov 'ayin*) will be blessed, for he shares his bread with the poor" (Prov 22:9, HT). The LXX renders this somewhat differently, with no mention of "good eye," but similarly praising generosity: "He who has mercy on the poor shall himself be maintained; for he has given of his own bread to the poor" (Prov 22:8a, b). An added statement equates "showing mercy" and "giving liberally:" "he that gives liberally secures victory and honor" (Prov 22:9c). Sirach 35:8–11 likewise shows that acting with a "good eye" (*agathos ophthalmos*) denotes enthusiastic, generous behavior:

Illus. 4
Mezuzah at the entrance to the Yochanan ben Zakai Synagogue, Old Jerusalem

> Glorify the Lord with a good eye (*en agathôi ophthalmôi*) (RSV: *generously*)
>   and do not stint the first fruits of your hands.
> With every gift show a cheerful face,
>   and dedicate your tithe with gladness.
> Give to the Most High as He has given and with a good eye
>   (*en agathôi ophthalmôi*) (RSV: *generously*) as your hand has received.
> For the Lord is one who repays,
>   and He will repay you sevenfold.[56]

The first biblical text explicitly contrasting a good and an Evil Eye is the saying of Jesus in Matt 6:22–23/Luke 11:34, involving an implied contrast of generosity ("integral eye") and miserliness ("Evil Eye").[57]

(8) The term "eye" could stand, *pars pro toto*, for the entire person. This is a case of synecdoche in which a part is employed to represent the whole.

---

56. On the good eye, see Seligmann 1910 1:244–51; Seligmann 1922:45off.; Deonna 1965:148–52. In the Greco-Roman world, a "good eye," was mentioned less frequently than "Evil Eye," and was attributed primarily to deities and transcendent figures (e.g., Zeus, sun, moon, justice); cf. Rakoczy 1996:227–45.

57. For this saying of Jesus see below, chap. 2; for this contrast in the Mishnah, see *m. Avot* 2:9; 5:13, 19; and Vol. 4, chap. 1.

"The eye that mocks a father and scorns to obey a mother will be picked out by the ravens of the valley and eaten by the vultures" (Prov 30:17). "No eye pitied you" (Ezek 16:5). "Do not eat the bread of an Evil Eye . . ." (i.e. of someone with an Evil Eye, Prov 23:6 HT; [LXX adds *anêr*, "someone"]). "An Evil Eye (i.e. someone with an Evil Eye) is envious (or begrudging) of bread, and it is absent from his table" (Sir 14:10). An "apple of someone's eye" denotes a favorite (Ps 17:8). The "apple of God's eye" was Israel (Deut 32:10; Zech 2:8.), a concept also illustrating how the Deity likewise was attributed eyes (Ezek 4:10) or an eye (Job 41:18) as a figurative expression of omniscience (Job 28:10; Ps 139:16; Prov 15:3), care (Judg 18:6; Ezra 5:5; 1 Pet 3:12), or judgment (Deut 7:16; 13:8; Ezek 5:11).[58]

Among these characteristics of the eye in the biblical writings are several features relevant more particularly to the Evil Eye. Additional salient features of Evil Eye belief and practice as found in Greek and Roman cultures (the notion of limited good connected with envy, features of typical Evil Eye possessors, types of typical victims, and protective strategies and devices) appear in the Bible as well and will be noted in due course. The rendition of the Hebrew and Greek for "Evil Eye" in various biblical versions (such as "envy," "jealousy," *Missgunst*, *squardo invidioso*, etc.) will be indicated and examined in the treatment of the Evil Eye texts that follows.

Explicit Evil Eye Texts

DEUTERONOMY 15:9 (15:7–11)

The first explicit reference to the Evil Eye, Deut 15:9, occurs in a legal prescription appearing in Deut 15 and describing appropriate behavior in the Year of Release.[59] The situation involves behavior when confronting a fellow Israelite in need and how one should respond. Deut 15:7–11 is part of a larger unit of material (15:1–23) dealing with the "year of release" and the canceling of debts (vv. 1–6); treatment of the poor, especially in relation to the year of release (vv. 7–11); the release of fellow Israelite slaves after six years of indentured service (vv. 12–18); and the consecration of unblemished firstling males of herd and flock for sacrifice (vv. 19–23).[60] The connection of vv. 7–11 to vv. 1–6 is part of a consistent compositional pattern

---

58. As also typical of other cultures; see Deonna 1965:99 and n. 2, 96–108.

59. Elliott 1991:156–58 is an earlier version of this material.

60. Regarding these so-called Sabbatical or Seven Year laws see also Exod 21:2–6; 23:10–11; Lev 25:18–22; Wright 1984. On these laws as a component of Israelite legal and other responses to poverty see Domeris 2007:156–68.

found in vv. 1–11, 12–18, and 19–23.[61] Each section opens with an older legal maxim which is then commented on and applied to the later and altered economic, political, and social situation presumed in the Deuteronomic Code (c. the reign of Manasseh, 687–642 BCE). Changes from an earlier situation included a settled urban society with a centralized sanctuary and political structure, a developing latifundialization, increased state taxes, and a resulting economic threat to the rural peasantry. The latter, often obliged in times of reduced harvests to float loans, had to bear the burden of the old sacral ordinance requiring a fallow land each seventh year. In vv. 1–11, this earlier ordinance (Exod 23:10–11; Lev 25:1–7), cited in v. 1, is then subjected in v. 2 to a legal interpretation taking into consideration the altered circumstances.[62] Here in Deuteronomy, the "release" is extended to a release of *debts* affecting creditors and creditees alike. Verses 3–11 shift from apodictic command and legal considerations to moral exhortation regarding the just treatment of the needy and potential borrowers.[63]

Within this literary and social context, vv. 7–11 exhibit a concern for the Evil Eye in conjunction with the treatment of needy fellow Israelites seeking loans when the year of release is imminent. The literary inclusion formed by the repetition of v. 7 in v. 11 frame and demarcate this unit of thought and indicate its main point, namely, generosity to any Israelite neighbor ("brother" used metaphorically) who is poor and in need.

Deuteronomy 15:7–11 reads as follows:

> 7. If there is among you in need, a member of your community in any of your towns within the land that the Lord your God is giving you, do not harden your heart or shut your hand against your needy neighbor 8. You should rather open your hand, willingly lending enough to meet the need, whatever it may be.

61. Von Rad 1966:104–8.

62. "In Deut 15:1–18," Sharon Ringe observes (1985:16–32, esp. p. 20), "there is no specific mention of the agricultural fallow year, but the terminology of 'release' and the reference to a seven-year period link the collection of laws to Exod. 21:2–6 and 23:10–11." For a later reinterpretation see Lev 25:1–7.

63. Similarly, vv. 12–18 begin with an older legal ordinance concerning slavery (Exod 21:1–11) which is reinterpreted for new circumstances. No longer is the "Hebrew" slave to be set free as a non-free foreigner, but as a "brother" Israelite who once was free and had sold himself in slavery to a fellow Israelite. Thus, by the time of the codification of laws reflected in Deuteronomy, the term "Hebrew" had come to identify the ethnic community of Israel rather than an alien economic class (Ringe 1985:20). Along with other modifications (von Rad 1966:107; Ringe 1985:21), vv. 12–18 focus, as do vv 1–11, on the generosity (vv. 13–14), emotions (vv. 16, 18), and experiential empathy (v. 15) of the agents. The same pattern recurs in vv. 19–23. An earlier legal maxim (v. 19a; cf. Exod 22:29b–30) is followed by "partly legal, partly homiletic accretion" (von Rad 1966:108).

9. Be careful lest there be an evil thought in your heart and you say: "The seventh year, the year of remission [of debts], is near," and *you look with an Evil Eye upon* your needy neighbor (lit., "and *your eye be evil* against your needy neighbor"), you give nothing, and your neighbor cry to the Lord against you, and you be guilty of sinning. 10. Give liberally and do not grieve in your heart when you do so; for because of this the LORD your God will bless you in all your work and in all that you undertake. 11. Since there will never cease to be some in need in the land, I therefore command you, "Open your hand wide to the poor and needy neighbor in your land." (JHE translation)

Reference to the Evil Eye occurs in verse nine. The Hebrew expression is, literally, *your eye be evil (rā'â 'êynkā)* (against your impoverished neighbor).[64] The Greek LXX gives an exact equivalent: "your eye be evil" (*ponêreusetai ho ophthalmos sou*). The Vulgate, "you avert your eyes" (*et avertas oculos tuos*), substitutes plural "eyes" for the singular (evil) eye and speaks of *turning one's eyes away* rather than looking malevolently at.[65] As usual, heart and eye are connected. Having an Evil Eye (v. 9) is connected with grieving in one's heart (v. 10), in this case regretting and resenting the need to be generous.[66] Malicious disposition (in the heart) is conveyed by malevolent agency (via the eye). The context makes clear that in this instance *an eye being evil*, or the *looking with an Evil Eye* or a *hostile glance*, involves a malicious disposition issuing in behaving hard-heartedly and tight-fistedly toward the needy, withholding aid, or giving only begrudgingly, or being miserly and stingy with one's resources. In this case, Evil-Eyeing someone with hostility is the opposite of feeling compassion, opening one's hand to the poor, and giving liberally and generously to the needy (15:8, 10, 11; cf. also 15:13–14). Compare the open hand of the good wife of Prov 31: "She opens her hand to the poor and reaches out her hands to the needy" (31:20).

64. The combination of this verb and noun occurs also in Deut 28:54, 56. For the verb *r''* as "be evil," see also Josh 24:5; as "do evil," Prov 24:19.

65. In his generally excellent study of the Evil Eye in Mesopotamian and related texts, J. N. Ford (1998:230) translates Deut 15:9 "and your eye be mean towards your needy brother." Imagining that a distinction between "magical" and "non-magical" is possible without any demonstration of this supposition, he asserts that this is "in a clearly non-magical context." In his Additions and Corrections (2000), Ford apparently takes issue with Elliott 1991 who, he says, "understands Deut 15:9 and similar passages to refer to the (magical) evil eye." In actuality I do refer to Deut 15:9, but not as an instance of a "magical evil eye." I rather consider such an etic distinction as futile and misleading. The words are a clear reference to looking with an Evil Eye.

66. For instances of eye and heart mentioned in tandem, see above, pp. 11, 16, 18–19, 25.

Whether or not a seventh year remission of debt (Deut 15:1) was actually practiced, the warning against begrudging generosity, stinginess, and withholding aid is the key point, a theme that appears repeatedly in the Hebrew Evil Eye tradition. Tobit's encouragement of his son to be generous in the giving of alms and not begrudging the gift with an Evil Eye (4:7, 16) is a clear echo of Deut 15:7–11, as we note below,[67] and illustrates the continuity of this theme in biblical references to the Evil Eye.[68] Derrett aptly emphasizes the association in ancient Israelite society of the "Evil Eye" with "niggardliness, or meanness, in contexts where society expects, and rewards, generosity." This Evil Eye of stinginess "is not a permanent characteristic and can be remedied by a change in fortune or a change in attitude."[69]

Verse 9 indicates that the situation of "the seventh year, the year of release" (cf. vv. 1–6), is still in view. With the year of release of debts imminent, a situation of tight credit is envisioned in which creditors would be reluctant to make loans which would soon be cancelled. Nevertheless, the hearers are urged to freely lend to the poor kinsman whatever he needs and to give generously (vv. 8, 11b). On the whole, this economic and social situation fits closely the circumstances where Evil Eye belief and practices tend to flourish, as outlined by anthropologists J. M. Roberts, V. Garrison, and C. M. Arensberg.[70] This includes the situation of peasant villages with fixed fields and limited production subject to the vagaries of nature and human-wrought disaster, grain agriculture competing with nomadic herders, peer rivalries and stratified society, peasant-urban redistributive economy, unstable government, and protection via patronage.

Mention of the Evil Eye in v. 9 thus comes as no surprise. Moreover, additional aspects of the Evil Eye phenomenon are also present. For one thing, the text reflects the assumed link of heart (vv. 7, 9, 10), including a "hardened" heart (v. 7) or resentful heart (v. 10), and an eye that acts evilly (v. 9).[71] Furthermore, as is typical in Evil Eye cultures, the Evil Eye is invoked here in an ambiguous situation where legal regulation is lacking and "matters of the heart," attitudes and moral dispositions, are of concern.

The issue at stake is the proper attitude and behavior of creditors toward borrowers, "haves" toward "have-nots," at a critical but legally unclarified

67. For Tob 4:7, 16 see below, pp. 57–60.

68. See also Deut 28:53–57; Prov 23:6; 28:22; Sir 14:8, 10; 18:18; Tob 4:7–11, 16; Matt 6:22–23; 20:15.

69. Derrett 1995:68. For opening of the hand to the poor as a gesture of generosity see also Prov 31:20; Ps 104:28; Sir 40:14.

70. J. M. Roberts 1976:234–78; Garrison and Arensberg 1976:286–328, esp. 294–97.

71. See also Prov 23:6–8; Sir 37:11–12; Matt 6:19–23; Mark 7:18–23; for envy and the heart, see Prov 23:17.

juncture just prior to the commencement of the year of debt release. Where execution of the law is unclear or uncertain, appeal to traditional values and beliefs take over, along with regard for the action, judgment and blessing of the Lord (vv. 7–10). As the Lord God has given (v. 7a), so his people should give (vv. 7b–8). Whereas an Evil Eye toward the needy brother is "sin" (v.9), the gift of a non-grudging eye and heart invites the Lord's blessing (v. 10). Giving liberally and generously (v.10) with an open hand (vv. 8, 11) is the antithesis to looking at someone with an Evil Eye and begrudging aid. This urging of generosity and reminder of divine recompense is a typical refrain of proverbial wisdom: see, for example, Prov 14:31; 19:17; 22:9; and 28:27:

> He who oppresses a poor man insults his [the poor man's]
>   Maker,
>   but he who is kind to the needy honors him. (14:31 RSV)

> He who is kind to the poor lends to the LORD,
>   and his good deed He will repay to him. (19:17)

> He who has a good eye will be blessed,
>   for he shares his bread with the poor. (22:9 RSV)

> He who gives to the poor will not lack,
>   but he who hides his eyes will get many a curse. (28:27)

The notion of the Evil Eye is invoked in Deuteronomy 15 as elsewhere when the focus is on wealth and the selfish accumulation of goods (cf. Prov 28:22), on the miserly refusal to share of one's substance (Deut 28:53–57), and on the neglect of the virtue of generosity and the begrudging of gifts and alms (Prov 23:6–8; Sir 14:3–4, 8, 10; 18:18; 37:11; Tob 4:1–21). Here too an Evil Eye is linked with a heart that is hardened to another's need and a hand that is shut to a poor brother in want.

Socially, this warning against an Evil Eye reflects the concern for mutual support and covenantal solidarity in a society plagued by economic disparity, conflict, suspicion of wealth, a perception of limited good, and occasions of severe deprivation. The Evil Eye behavior mentioned in Deut 28:54 and 56 envisions a desperate situation of famine in which husbands and wives begrudge with an Evil Eye food to even spouses, brother, and their own children (Deut 28:53–57).

Morally, exercise of the Evil Eye is identified as "sinning" (Deut 15:9), a violation of covenantal obligation and behavior incompatible with the experience of a generous God (vv. 7, 10–11). Generosity, on the other hand, is blessed by God (Deut 15:10). The principle at stake here is captured by the later words of Sirach and Tobit in the Greek Old Testament: "The bread of the needy is the life of the poor; whoever deprives them of it is a man of blood" (Sir 34:21). A passage in Tobit (4:1–21) encourages generosity to the poor and warns against ignoring their plight. Echoing the warning of Deut 15:9, but applying it not to a year of release but to the more recurrent and conventional action of almsgiving, a dying Tobit urges his son, "Do not begrudge with an Evil Eye the alms when you give them"(4:7a, 16; lit., "do not let your eye begrudge," *mê phthonesatô sou ho ophthalmos*). "Do not turn your face from any poor man, and the face of God will not be turned from you" (Tob 4:7b). Tobit 4:7, 16, like Deut 15:9 LXX, involve the formulation of "your eye" with verbs that are similar if not synonymous.[72] Further Evil Eye texts, Sir 14:10 and 18:15–18, criticize the Evil-Eyed begrudging of food and gifts, and likewise urge unconditional generosity.[73]

In his classic sociological study, *Ancient Judaism* (1952/1921), pioneering historical sociologist Max Weber had noted how pre-exilic Israel's economic ethic and its call for charity was likely "influenced by Egypt directly or by way of Phoenicia," an influence that was "strongest in Deuteronomic times."[74] Israel's ethic and focus on charity, nevertheless distinguished itself from that of Babylonia and Egypt.

> Nothing is transmitted from both these cultural areas [Babylonia, Egypt] which would equal or merely resemble a systematic ethical religious exhortation of the kind of Deuteronomy. Unlike pre-exilic Israel, Babylonia and Egypt knew no unified, religiously substructured ethic . . . In Israel this ethic was the product of the ethical Torah of the Levites continued for many generations, and of prophecy.[75]

The stress on charity was "one characteristic element of the old Israelite ethic."[76] "The formal law of debt bondage was . . . supplemented in the moral exhortation by far-reaching stipulations concerning payment of wages, debt remission, limitation on pledges, and general charity."[77] Weber expressly cites Deut 15:11 as one of "the most general formulations of these duties."[78]

Weber says nothing about the act of looking with a hostile Evil Eye that is proscribed in Deut 15:7–11. However, his singling out of this Deuteronomic passage as prime illustration of Israel's stress on charity toward the

---

72. On Tobit, see below, pp 57–61.

73. On these texts, see below, pp. 46–47.

74. Weber 1952/1921:258.

75. Ibid., 254–55.

76. Ibid., 255.

77. Ibid.

78. Ibid.

needy is significant. It helps us appreciate how a key expression of Israelite concern for the poor and a hallmark of Israel's ethic in general were opposed to the exercise of an Evil Eye. The Evil Eye is the antithesis to a spirit of generosity. Paired with a closed hand, it is an expression of miserliness and an eye that is blind toward, or little moved by, the plight of the poor and needy.

The translations upon which most Bible readers are dependent tend to obscure the fact that here at Deuteronomy 15, and in numerous other relevant instances, mention originally was made of an Evil Eye. While the King James Version (KJV) preserves in its rendition the reference to an Evil Eye, most modern versions offer what the translation teams of each assume to be the *sense* of the words, rather than a literal translation:

> KJV and JPS: *thine eye be evil (against thy poor brother)*
>
> RSV: *your eye be hostile*
>
> NRSV: *(you) view with hostility*
>
> NEB: *look askance at*
>
> NAB: *grudge help to*
>
> JB: *look coldly on*
>
> Goodspeed: *behave meanly to*
>
> TEV: *Do not refuse to lend him something*

These and similar translations capture one or more aspects of an Evil Eye, such as the mode of looking (with hostility or coldness or looking askance) or a mode of behavior (begrudging help, behaving meanly, refusing to lend). But they do not indicate to the readers that Deut 15:9 speaks explicitly of *behavior entailing a malignant ocular glance.* Among themselves, the versions show little consistency in their translations or in the aspects of Evil Eye behavior they choose to express. This is the case throughout the many biblical instances where "Evil Eye" appears in the original Hebrew or Greek. As a consequence, readers reliant on translations gain no impression of the abundance of biblical references to the Evil Eye and see no common threads among the Evil Eye texts. Nor do the translations always illuminate the social dynamics involved. These problems concerning the Bible versions—namely terminological multiplicity, translational inconsistency, and semantic unclarity—plague most of the renditions of biblical Evil Eye texts. The translations often result in inconsistent wordings from text to text, uncertainty of the connection of one text to another, and lack of clarity concerning the social dynamics involved. In its terminology, the KJV is a notable exception, usually reading "Evil Eye" where this is stated in the original Hebrew and Greek.

To document the existence and extent of Evil Eye belief and practice in the Bible and antiquity, and to address these problems, I have considered it advisable when translating the ancient texts to use a consistent set of terms and expressions such as "Evil Eye," an "eye being evil," "casting an Evil Eye" or "injuring with an Evil Eye." All my English translations of "Evil Eye" in the original languages include "eye" and "evil" for the sake of linguistic and semantic consistency. It has been suggested by some scholars that in the primary sources the term *envy* (Heb: *qanah*; Grk: *phthonos, zêlos*; Lat: *invidia* and their respective word families) can on occasion be a substitute for the expression "Evil Eye," an expression deemed to be too dangerous to utter. I, however, have used the translation "Evil Eye" only when the primary source has "Evil Eye" or some paronym thereof, while allowing for an implied reference to an Evil Eye whenever the closely linked emotion of envy is mentioned. Let us recall once more that in Evil Eye cultures, envy and Evil Eye are related but not identical. They related to each other as disposition (envy) and mechanism of conveyance (eye). Envy is a malice that is conveyed from one living entity at another by means of an Evil Eye, a malevolent glance, an eye looking askance, an eye overlooking. Moreover, an "eye being evil," or "Evil Eye," or "casting an Evil Eye," or "injuring with an Evil Eye" are not merely ancient and antiquated expressions, but rather references to what was taken to be a natural phenomenon of an eye operating in a malicious and harmful way toward a specific target.

DEUTERONOMY 28:54, 56 (28:53–57)

A double mention of the Evil Eye occurs in Deut 28:53–57. Looking with a hostile Evil Eye at others in need and selfishly withholding sustenance from them relate this passage to that of Deuteronomy 15. This passage falls within the concluding section of the book of Deuteronomy, chs. 28–34; and as a conclusion to Moses's second address (chs. 5–28). More specifically it occurs within the section 28:47–57 elaborating on the divine curses to befall Israel because of its nonobservance of the commandments and its failure to serve the Lord with joyfulness and gladness of heart (28:47). The details of the divine punishment and foreign attack reflect the gruesome experiences of Judah during the Neo-Babylonian invasion of 587 BCE in the reign of King Zedekiah (2 Kings 25). Judah, according to Moses's forecast, will be attacked and besieged by a merciless enemy, stripped of its cattle and food, and its population reduced to want and starvation (Deut 28:48–52). The besieged will finally resort to eating their own children: "and you shall eat the offspring of your own body, the flesh of your sons and daughters, whom the LORD your God has given you, in the siege and in the distress with which your enemies shall distress you" (28:53). In this situation of extreme deprivation and desperation, family members will be subject to the depraved Evil Eye of their very own relatives. Deuteronomy 28:54–57 reads:

> 54 The man, who is tender among you and delicately bred, will look with an Evil Eye (lit., *"his eye shall be evil," [téraʿ ʿēnó]*) against his fellow Israelite (lit. "brother"), against his beloved wife, and against the last of his children who remain to him, 55 begrudging them (for food) the flesh of his children that he is eating because he has nothing else left to him in the siege and in the distress with which your enemy shall distress you in all your towns. 56 The woman, who is tender among you and delicately bred, who would not venture to set the sole of her foot upon the ground for delicateness and tenderness, will look with an Evil Eye (lit., *her eye shall be evil [téraʿ ʿēnah]*) against her beloved husband, against her son, and against her daughter, 57 begrudging them (for food) the afterbirth that oozes from her genitals[79] and the baby that she bears; for she shall eat them herself secretly for lack of anything else (to eat), in the siege and in the distress with which your enemy shall distress you in your towns.

Here in the horrific situation of food shortage created by a siege and the throes of starvation, the extremes of human dispositions and behavior are depicted. Normally tender and refined fathers and mothers will act with an Evil Eye against each other and other family members, not only by cannibalizing their own children, but also in refusing a share, even of the placenta, to their starving households. The text constitutes the most extreme illustration of Evil Eye behavior in all of Scripture. In this most desperate of human situations, the most extreme manifestation of evil (as another text will describe the Evil Eye) will be unleashed.

As in Deut 15:9, the Hebrew speaks literally of "an eye being evil" (against someone), involving the combination of the noun "eye" and the verb "be evil." The Greek LXX translation shows that the translators took the Hebrew as referring to the Evil Eye. The husband's looking with an Evil Eye/ casting an Evil Eye (vv. 54–55) is paralleled by that of his wife (vv. 56–57). The context indicates that the Evil-Eyeing consists of behavior similar to that condemned in Deut 15:9; namely, withholding something that is desperately needed to survive—in this case something edible. That the only

79. Literally, "from between her *feet*," a euphemism for genitals; or, "from between her legs."

thing remaining to eat is the flesh of one's own children—and that even this is withheld from starving relatives by Evil-Eyeing husband and wife paints a macabre picture of extreme desperation and depravity. The selfish act of begrudgingly *holding back* something that is needed links this passage to that of Deut 15:9; Sir 14:8; and Tob 4:7, 16. The *withholding* of something to *eat* links this text with other biblical Evil Eye texts warning against an Evil Eye at occasions of *dining* (such as Prov 23:6; Sir 14:10; 31:12).

The LXX version of *téra' 'énó* and *téra' 'énah* in vv. 54 and 56 reads somewhat redundantly: *baskanei tôi ophthalmôi*, literally, *Evil-Eye with the [his] eye* (v. 54); *baskanei tôi ophthalmôi autês*, literally, *Evil-Eye with her eye* (v. 54). This Greek translation (third century BCE) shows that Israelites speaking and writing Greek were familiar with the standard Greek *bask-* family of terms that designated the "Evil Eye" and "Evil-Eyeing." It also shows that the Hebrew expressions *téra' 'énó* and *téra' 'énah* were understood by the LXX translators as references to the Evil Eye. Terms of this *bask-* word group appear elsewhere in the Bible designating an Evil Eye and its action.[80] The LXX juxtaposition of *ho haplos* and *hê haplê* (lit., "the *simple* man/woman") with *baskainein* ("to Evil Eye") is echoed in the juxtaposition of *ophthalmos haplous* (lit., "single eye") and *ophthalmos ponêros* ("Evil Eye") in Matt 6:22–23 (cf. Luke 11:34).

The Vulgate Latin verb *invidebit* (vv. 54, 57) indicates that Jerome regarded *invidere* ("to envy") as an apt rendition of the Hebrew "eye be evil against." The context and the sense of the passage rules out *invidebit* having the sense of "envy" here. It is therefore likely that *invidebit* is equivalent in sense to the LXX *baskanei*: "look with a hostile Evil Eye," "cast an Evil Eye upon." This is then an instance where *invidere* substitutes for, or is regarded as synonymous with, *fascinare*, as *phthonos* occasionally substitutes for *baskainen*; see Vol. 2 concerning the occasional substitution of "envy" for "Evil Eye" in Greek and Latin texts and inscriptions. Other instances of this equivalence of *invidus, invidere*, and *baskanos* occur in Prov 23:6 (LXX: *andri baskanô*; Vulg.: *homine invido*) and Prov 28:22, where for the Hebrew *'iš ra' 'ayin* the LXX has *anêr baskanos* and the Vulgate, *vir qui . . . invidet*.

Among conventional English language biblical translations of this passage, only the KJV and the Jewish Publication Society translation of the Masoretic Text (JPS) preserve the explicit reference to the Evil Eye contained in the original Hebrew: "his/her eye shall be evil." Other translations attempt to convey the assumed sense or implication of the Evil Eye reference: RSV, NAB: "will (be)grudge (food);" NEB, TEV: "will not share"; JB: "will glower

---

80. Prov 23:6; 28:22; Sir 14:3, 6, 8; 18:18; 37:11; Wis 4:12; 4 Macc 1:26; 2:15; Ep Jer 69/70; Gal 3:1.

at"; Goodspeed: "will act (so) meanly toward." This translational procedure is typical for most of the biblical Evil Eye references. As a consequence, the modern reader is left unaware of the biblical appearances of the Evil Eye phenomenon. The commentaries likewise rarely accord it any attention.

The Vulgate, RSV, and NRSV, on the other hand, translate according to the assumed *sense* of the action, but omit explicit mention of Evil-Eyeing. The Vulgate translates *invidebit* ("will overlook/look with envy at"). RSV reads: "will grudge food to" (v. 54), "will grudge to" (v. 56). NRSV reads "will begrudge food to" (v. 54); "will begrudge food to" (v. 56), "begrudging even the afterbirth" (v. 57). The action of grudging/begrudging is an aspect of Evil-Eyeing that fits several Evil Eye contexts. As a translation option here, however, it is insufficient without explicit reference to looking with an Evil Eye. To grudge or begrudge something is to give something or concede reluctantly, to resent giving something while preferring to retain it, such as offering food at a meal but really wanting to keep it for yourself (Sir 14:10; cf. Prov 23:6–8), or offering praise but really wanting to withhold it. To "be-grudge" can also imply *looking* resentfully at and *envying* someone's enjoyment of something.[81] Thus "grudge/begrudge" can be an aspect of looking with an Evil Eye in two possible ways: an Evil Eye *begrudgingly holding back* something, or an Evil Eye *begrudgingly envying* something enjoyed by another. In the present case, looking with an Evil Eye involves begrudgingly withholding something edible desperately needed by a relative for survival. The translation *grudge/begrudge*, however, without explicit mention of "looking with an Evil Eye" (as in the case of the RSV, NIV, etc.), obscures the fact that both the Hebrew and Greek speak expressly of *Evil-Eyeing*. Thus this translation, like other translations only according to sense,[82] fails to indicate that this is another Evil Eye text and that Deut 28:53–57 relates to Deut 15:7–11 and other biblical Evil Eye references.[83]

81. "Begrudge 1: to give or concede reluctantly. 2a: to look upon with reluctance or disapproval. 2b: to take little pleasure in: be annoyed by; 3: to envy the pleasure or enjoyment of" (*Webster's New Collegiate Dictionary*, 1977, *sub* grudge). "Grudge" derives from Middle English *grucchen, grudgen*, "to grumble, complain," fr[om] OF *groucier*. It is of Germanic origin, akin to Middle High German *grogezen*, "to howl": "to be unwilling to give or admit: give or allow with reluctance or resentment: begrudge <*grudged* the money to pay taxes>."

82. For example, NAB: "will (be)grudge (food)"; NEB, TEV: "will not share"; JB: "will glower at"; Goodspeed: "will act (so) meanly toward."

83. The claim has been made that Deut 28:53–57 prompted Paul's mention of *bas-kainein* in Gal 3:1 (S. Eastman 2001, mistranslating *ebaskanen* in Gal 3:1 as "put you under a curse" rather than "Evil-Eyed you." The conjecture is unconvincing and will be discussed in connection with our analysis of Paul and Gal 3:1; see below, chap. 2). Eastman's study illustrates how unfamiliarity with the phenomenon of the Evil Eye and its frequent mention in the Bible can lead to misleading translation and unconvincing

Israel's *Wisdom Literature*, where skill in everyday living, good sense, and sound judgment is the general theme, makes frequent reference to the Evil Eye and many of its diverse connotations. Its close relation and remarkable similarities to the wisdom traditions of Mesopotamia, Phoenicia, and Egypt include common thinking and practice concerning the Evil Eye, though with a more prominent accent on the human moral aspects of the Evil Eye.

Occasions of dining are one situation where the malice of an Evil Eye was anticipated. Proverbs 23:6–8 is a good illustration. Sirach 14:10 and 31:12–13 are also relevant and are discussed below. Deuteronomy 28:53–57, as we have seen, envisions a dire situation where the eating involved is cannibalism.

PROVERBS 23:6 (23:6–8)

Proverbs 23:6–8 is part of a sage's instruction to a student about conduct at meals (Prov 23:1–8, 20–21, 29–35). Verses 6–8 warn:

> 6 Do not eat the bread of *(someone with)* an Evil Eye;
>> do not desire that person's delicacies;
> 7 for that person is like one who reckons inwardly.
>> "Eat and drink!" s/he says to you;
>> but her/his heart is not with you.
> 8 You will vomit up the little you have eaten
>> and waste your pleasant words"

The Hebrew of v. 6 reads, literally, "do not eat the bread of an Evil Eye," with "Evil Eye" (*raʿ ʿayin*) standing *pars pro toto* for the entire malevolent person.[84] My English translation supplies "someone with" according to sense, following the LXX, which does the same by adding *anêr* ("man/person/someone"). The LXX omits "the bread of," adds "someone," and reads: "Do not eat with someone with an Evil Eye" (*Mê sundeipnei andri baskanô*). The Hebrew of Prov 28:22 has the fuller formulation: *'iš raʿ ʿayin*, "someone with an Evil Eye." The Vulgate renders the Hebrew with *homine invido*, also supplying "someone." The Latin adjective *invidus*, which can have the sense of "envious," in this instance is equivalent in sense to *baskanos* in the LXX

---

exegesis.

84. The eye, when referring to the organ of a human, can stand in for the entire person. This is a case of synecdoche in which a part is employed to represent the whole. For Evil Eye texts involving synecdoche see also Sir 14:9, 10; 31:13.

Greek version, and in rendering the Hebrew *ra' 'ayin* means not "envious" but "someone with an Evil Eye."[85]

KJV and JPS translate "him that hath an Evil Eye." RSV renders according to presumed sense: "a man who is stingy." Stinginess could entail resentful giving, although in this context of offering a banquet to guests, having and looking with an Evil Eye seems less a matter of stinginess than of *begrudging* the gift of food while serving it. Stinginess would keep the person from being hospitable in the first place. *Begrudging* the gift of food when serving it involves an internal disposition arising in the heart[86] and manifested through an Evil Eye—an emotion and action inconsistent with an act of apparent generosity. As in Deut 15:9, a connection of eye (v. 6) and heart (v. 7) is assumed, with the former giving expression to a disposition of the latter. The point is that the hospitality of Evil-Eyed persons is a sham in which courteous words of welcome mask evil intentions and a begrudging serving of food. Eating their food results not in a full stomach and a pleasant repast but in vomiting and wasted words. This theme of giving grudgingly, like refused generosity, we shall see, is a recurrent one among Old Testament Evil Eye texts; see Deut 15:7–9, 28:54–57; Prov 23:6–8; Sir 14:8, 10; 18:18; 37:11; and Tob 4:7, 16.

This passage is one of the instances in the Old Testament where the Evil Eye is expressly said to cause physical distress or illness; see also Sir 18:18 (the Evil Eye causes the eyes to melt, a "dimming of the eyes" = blindness or senescence); Sir 14:9 ("withers the soul"); and Sir 31:13 (causes "tears to fall from every face").[87] In the case of Deut 28:53–57, the deadly consequence of a begrudging Evil Eye, namely starvation and death, is implied rather than directly stated.

The predicament of eating with others and then vomiting because struck by an Evil Eye is the same as that discussed by Pseudo-Aristotle in *Problemata physica* (20.34 926 b20–31) cited in Vol. 2. Pseudo-Aristotle, we recall, indicates that dining with others aroused fear of being struck by an Evil Eye of a fellow diner. The vomiting caused by Evil Eye, it was believed, could be cured or forestalled by taking the herb rue prior to eating, an effect for which Pseudo-Aristotle provides a rational explanation. Both Prov 23:6–8 and Pseudo-Aristotle, *Prob. phys.* 20.34 record the belief that an Evil

85. For *invidus* or *invidere* with the sense of "Evil Eye" or "cast an Evil Eye" rather than "envy," see also Vulg Deut 28:54, 56; and Prov 28:22 (*vir qui invidet*, cf. LXX *anêr baskanos*).

86. "Her/his heart is not with you" = she/he is not disposed favorably toward you, which disposition is conveyed outward through an Evil Eye's glance causing vomiting.

87. Boughouts (1978:2) makes reference to an Egyptian curse text mentioning Horus blinding the eyes of those casting an Evil Eye, citing Schott 1931:106–10.

Eye could strike persons dining with others and could cause vomiting by those struck. Both indicate the same negative consequence of being stuck by an Evil Eye while eating, namely vomiting up the food. Pseudo-Aristotle explains how rue counteracts or cures the Evil Eye and its noxious effect. Proverbs 28:6–8 advises avoiding eating altogether with anyone possessing an Evil Eye. Proverbs 23:6–8 envisions a host, rather than any of the guests, that casts an Evil Eye; Pseudo-Aristotle in *Prob. phys.* 20.34 leaves the identity of the Evil-Eyed person unstated.[88]

Pseudo-Aristotle in *Prob. phys.* 20.34 does, however, mention that *eating greedily* was thought to arouse an Evil Eye, a notion expressed in another piece of biblical wisdom, namely Sir 31:12–13, one of two texts of the Wisdom of Jesus ben Sirach that also mention the Evil Eye in conjunction with dining and behavior at the table:

> A person with an Evil Eye begrudges bread;
> and it is lacking from her/his table. (Sir 14:10)

A second states:

> If you sit at a bountiful table,
> do not be gluttonous at it,
> and do not say "there is lots of food on it."
> Remember that an Evil Eye is a wicked thing.
> What has been created more evil than an (Evil) Eye?
> For this reason tears fall from every face. (Sir 31:12–13)

Both texts are discussed below (see pp. 40, 43–46 and pp. 48–52, respectively.). The sharing or non-sharing of food is just one instance of the various social exchanges where an Evil Eye was feared. Another important area of social interaction involved the acquisition of wealth and the refusal to share one's possessions with the needy.

Within a collection of wise sayings attributed to Solomon censuring the unrighteous and praising the righteous for conduct relating to wealth (Prov 25:1–29:27) is a statement concerning the behavior of one with an Evil Eye, Prov 28:22. It follows criticism of the quest for wealth (28:20), and is followed by censure of robbing one's parents (28:24), of greed, which stirs up strife (28:25), and of hiding one's eyes from the poor (28:27b).

---

88. The Egyptian *Instruction of Ptah-hotep* (c. 2414–2375 BCE) advised eating what is set before one and focusing on this rather than casting glances at the host and molesting him since this would offend the *ka*; see Lichtheim 1985 1:65, no. 7 (= 6, 11–12). This ancient Egyptian advice could have had the noxious glance of an Evil Eye in mind. If this is the case, it would involve an Evil-Eyeing of the host by the guest.

PROVERBS 28:22

Proverbs 28:22 states:

> A person with an Evil Eye hurries after wealth,
>> and does not know that want is sure to follow.

The Hebrew underlying "a person with an Evil Eye" is *'ish ra' 'ayin*, literally, "a man with an Evil Eye." The LXX *anêr baskanos* is an exact rendition of the Hebrew, although the full Greek text reads slightly differently:

> A man with an Evil Eye strives to be wealthy,
>> and is unaware that someone showing mercy will have
>>> power over him.[89]

The Vulgate reads:

> The man who hurries to become wealthy and *envies/Evil-Eyes*
>> others,
> is unaware that poverty shall come upon him.[90]

This Latin version shifts from a noun indicating a person with an Evil Eye to a verb, *invidere*, meaning "to envy," but here rendering the action of one with an Evil Eye. This formulation illustrates the frequent proximity and occasional synonymity of "envy" and "Evil Eye."[91]

KJV and JPS render literally: "he that hath an Evil Eye." RSV ("a miserly man") and NRSV ("the miser") again translate according to sense and make no mention of "Evil Eye." Compare also NEB: "the miser" (variant translation: "the man with the evil eye"); JB: "the man of greedy eye;" NAB, Goodspeed: "the avaricious man;" TEV: "selfish people." In this context the point has more to do with *greed* (yearning for what is not possessed, cf. vv. 24, 25) than miserliness (withholding what is possessed). The proverb forecasts a bitter twist of fate: the very state that an Evil-Eyed person seeks to avoid (i. e. poverty and want) is what will befall him because of his acquisitiveness/avarice/greed. This association of Evil Eye with greed and the quest for wealth appears also in Sir 14:3–8. Sirach 14:9 and 31:12–13 associate the Evil Eye with gluttony, which is greed at the dining table. The "insatiable eye" of the person mentioned in Eccl 4:4–8 may be a further mention of an Evil Eye filled with greed (on this text see below, pp. 74–75). The association of the Evil Eye, on the other hand, also with *reluctant giving*,

---

89. *Speudei ploutein anêr baskanos, kai ouk oiden hoti eleêmôn kratêsei autou.*

90. *Vir qui festinat ditari et aliis invidet, ignorat quod egestas superveniet ei.*

91. *Invidere* thus is used as a synonym and substitute for *fascinare*, "to Evil-Eye."

giving grudgingly, as found in Deuteronomy 15 and Deuteronomy 28, recurs elsewhere in the Greek Old Testament as well.

The Greek Old Testament (LXX) contains still further references to the Evil Eye. Several of these texts echo, or expand upon, motifs and themes already identified.

The *Wisdom of Jesus ben Sira,* another writing of Israel's Wisdom tradition, stands firmly in the tradition of Proverbs. In the Latin church and its Latin Vulgate the book was known as *Ecclesiasticus.* Originally written in Hebrew about 180 BCE, it was then translated into Greek (= LXX) by Ben Sira's grandson (c. 132 BCE).[92] Sirach makes multiple references to the Evil Eye: Sir 14:3–10; 18:18; 31:12–13; 37:10–11. Three of its instructions regarding the Evil Eye concern *dining and behavior at the table:* Sir 14:9, 10 and 31:12–13. Other instructions concern the Evil Eye and *wealth, greed, and envy* (Sir 14:3–8; 18:18; 37:10–11).

SIRACH 14:3–10

This passage constitutes the most extensive statement on the Evil Eye in the entire Bible of both Old and New Testaments. It contains multiple instances of standard Evil Eye terminology and mentions several features of the Evil Eye belief complex.[93] Sirach 14:3–10 reads:

> 3 Wealth is not fitting for a person of little account
>> and of what use is property to an Evil-Eyed person?
>
> 4 Whoever accumulates by depriving himself accumulates for others;
>> and others will live in luxury on his goods.
> 5 If a man is evil to himself,
>> to whom will he be good?
>> he will not enjoy his own riches.
> 6 No one is more evil than he who Evil-Eyes himself
>> and this is the retribution for his wickedness:
>
> 7 even if he does something good,
>> he does it unintentionally and betrays his wickedness in the end.

---

92. The value of the extant Hebrew fragmentary manuscripts from the Middle Ages is disputed. The edition by Israel Levy (1969) is used in this study, with the Greek LXX text, however, generally given precedence.

93. The technical terminology for "Evil Eye" includes *baskanos* (v. 3); *baskainein* (vv. 6, 8); and *ophthalmos ponêros* (v. 10); see also *ophthalmos* ("eye," vv. 8, 9); and *ponêros* ("evil," vv. 5, 6, 9, 10).

8 Evil is one who looks with an Evil Eye,
   turning away his face and disregarding people.

9 The (evil) eye of a greedy person is unsatisfied with a (single) portion;
   and an Evil Eye withers life.

10 A person with an Evil Eye is begrudging concerning bread;
   and it is lacking from his table.

The passage opens (v. 3) with the statement that an Evil-Eyed person is an unfitting possessor and manager of wealth (*ho ploutos, chrêmata*). The synonymous parallelism of v. 3a and 3b associates an *Evil-Eyed person* (*ish ra' 'ayin; anthrôpos baskanos*)[94] with a man (*anêr*) who is *mikrologos*, literally, "of little account." The topic of wealth (v. 3a, 3b and throughout vv. 3–10) suggests that "being of little account" and having an Evil Eye can entail either greediness to get more (v. 9) or miserliness or stinginess in reluctant giving (vv. 8, 10). The Vulgate of 14:3 translates *andri mikrologôi* with *viro cupido*, thereby opting for *greedy*. It renders *anthrôpôi baskanôi* with *homini livido* ("envious person"), thereby omitting explicit mention of "Evil Eye." It renders "Evil-Eyed person" (Hebrew, Greek) with "envious person" and makes envy a pendent to greed. RSV and NRSV make no mention of Evil Eye, but translate according to sense. RSV translates "stingy man" (v. 3a) and "envious man" (v. 3b); NRSV renders "small-minded person" and "miser," respectively. Verses 4–10 unfold the implications of v. 3.

Verses 4–7 form a unit in which a positive statement concerning a man aiding and being generous to others with his substance (v. 4) stands in contrast to a negative statement concerning an evil person with an Evil Eye who Evil-Eyes himself (vv. 5–7). Opposed to a man who deprives himself by generously putting his acquired goods at the service of others (v. 4) is one who is evil (*ponêros*) to himself[95] and consequently is not good (*agathos*) to anyone else. He does not enjoy his own property (*chrêmata*, like the *chrêmata* of the Evil-Eyed person, v. 3) (v. 5) in contrast to those who enjoy the largess of the generous person (v. 4). Being evil to himself (v. 5), he Evil-Eyes himself (*baskainontos heauton*) and no one is more evil (*ponêroteros*) than this! (v. 6a; cf. Sir 31:13).[96] RSV and NRSV translate *baskainontos* not

94. For the formulation *ish ra' 'ayin* see also Prov 28:22; for *anthrôpôi baskanôi* see the synonymous *andri baskanôi* (Prov 23:6).

95. The Vulgate renders *ponêros* (v. 5) with *nequam* ("evil"); RSV and NRSV render it with "mean."

96. *Baskainein*, the standard verb for "look with an Evil Eye," "cast, injure with, an Evil Eye," also occurs in Deut 28:54, 56; Sir 14:8; and in the NT, Gal 3:1. The Vulgate of v. 6 translates *qui sibi invidet*, with the verb *invidet*, usually meaning "envy," rendering *baskainontos*. *Invidere* here has the meaning not of "envying" oneself but of *Evil-Eyeing* oneself—one of multiple instances in the Vulgate where terms of the *invidia* family

literally but according to sense: "the man who is *grudging* to himself."[97] The retribution for his wickedness (*kakias*, v. 6b) and being evil (vv. 5, 6) is that he derives no satisfaction from his possessions (v. 5), thus harming himself as well with his own Evil Eye (v. 6). Even if he ever happens to do something right, he does it unintentionally, ultimately exposing his prevailing state of wickedness (*kakian*, v. 7).

In this unit of vv. 4–7, important recurrent aspects of the Evil Eye appear: generosity or stinginess in the handling of one's possessions (v. 4); the contrast of evil (*ponêros*, v. 5; *ponēroteros*, v. 6; cf. *kakia*, vv. 6, 7) and good (*agathos*, v. 5; also *agathois*, v. 4b);[98] the actuality of self-fascination, Evil-Eyeing oneself (v. 6, which is equivalent to being evil to oneself, v. 5);[99] the verdict that the Evil Eye is the *worst of evils* (v. 6a; so also Sir 31:13) and a result of being wicked (v. 6b); and the notions that any doing of good by the Evil-Eyed is unintentional and that his wickedness will be exposed in the end (v. 7). The likely "good" in view here is generosity with one's possessions, with a concern for the welfare of others. In this group-oriented culture typical of the biblical communities, the well-being of the community takes precedence over the advancement of self. The "evil," expressed in an Evil Eye, is illiberality, being miserly with one's goods, and refusing to share them with others (as in Deut 15:7–11; 28:54–57; Tob 4:7, 16). This ignoring and dishonoring of the needs of the group and its members brings harm to oneself as well as others. The neglect of the Evil-Eye possessor for the welfare of the group and his ungenerosity continues in the following verse.

Verse 8 condemns as evil (*ponêros*) one who looks with an Evil Eye (*ho baskainôn ophthalmôi*).[100] The participle *baskainôn* of v. 8 echoes the participle *baskainontos* of v. 6 and serves as a linkword joining v. 8 to vv. 4–7. The injuring with an Evil Eye (*baskainôn ophthalmôi*) of v. 8a (cf. Deut 28:54, 56 and *baskainontos*, v. 6) is paralleled in v. 8b by the verb "*looking away*" (*hyperorôn*),[101] which clarifies its sense here: an Evil-Eyed person averts his/ her face and disdainfully looks away from people (in need). The Vulgate

---

substitute for terms of the *baskanos* family.

97. Compare NEB: "who is grudging to himself"; NAB, TEV: "stingy with himself"; JB: "mean to himself."

98. The contrast appears also in Matt 6:22–23/Luke 11:34; and Matt 20:15.

99. This motif of self-fascination, we recall, is also mentioned by Theocritus (*Idylls* 6.39), Plutarch (*Quaest. Conv.* 5.7, *Mor.* 682B, 682EF), and the *Anth. Pal.* 11.192; see Vol. 2 for the texts.

100. *Ponêros* occurs in connection with both *baskanos* terms and *ophthalmos*, as in *ophthalmos ponêros*, v. 10.

101. Literally, "overlook" (*hyper* ["over"] + *horaô* ["look"]), then "look down upon," "look away from," "despise, disdain."

renders the Greek verbal clause *ho baskainôn ophthalmôi* with the nominal phrase *oculus lividi* (lit., "the eye of a livid/envious person"). While *lividus* generally means "envious," here again a Latin expression involving envy renders an explicit Greek reference to "Evil Eye." The Latin phrase is best understood as synonymous with *oculus malus* ("Evil Eye") and denoting a person with an envious Evil Eye.[102] RSV and NRSV render according to assumed sense, omitting explicit reference to Evil Eye; RSV: "Evil is the man with a *grudging eye*"; NRSV: "The *miser* is an evil person."[103] Being miserly and giving grudgingly are indeed both aspects of Evil-Eyed persons. Averting or turning away of one's face or eye can express either an unwillingness to give, as here, or a craving to get.[104] The verse is another instance where the Evil Eye involves refusing generosity toward others or giving only begrudgingly, as in Deut 15:7–9; 28:54–57; Sir 18:18; and Tob 4:7, 16.

Verse 9 continues the focus on the Evil Eye with "eye" (*ophthalmos*, v. 9a), and presumably "Evil Eye" (*ophthalmos ponêros*, v. 9b), connecting v. 9 to the Evil Eye injuring (*baskainôn*) of v. 8. The aspect shifts from miserliness to greed as another vice characteristic of an Evil Eyed person, and from reluctant giving to insatiable getting. Here the "eye of a greedy person" (*pleonektou ophthalmos*; Heb: "eye of covetousness," "covetous eye")[105] is a physical part of the body representing the entire person, as does "Evil Eye" (*ophthalmos ponêros*) in v. 10. The greediness of the Evil-Eyed person consists in her/his dissatisfaction with receiving only a portion of something rather than the whole. The adjacent reference to bread and table (v. 10) suggests that the "portion" is a portion of food. The LXX of v. 9b states the lethal effect of an Evil Eye on its possessor in rather curious terms: "and evil injustice withers life away" (*kai adikia ponêra anaxêrainei psychên*).[106] How injustice has this effect is far from clear, thereby raising the possibility of some textual error. A conjecture by I. Levi, editor of the Hebrew text of Sirach, plausibly proposes that the Hebrew original was *'ayin ra'* ("*an Evil*

---

102. The Vulgate depicts this Evil-Eyed person despising not others but *himself* (*despiciens animam suam*), a modification perhaps influenced by the same *animam suam* concluding v. 9.

103. Compare NEB, JB: "man with (or "who has") a grudging eye;" TEV: "a selfish man."

104. For proscription of the former see Sir 4:4–5: "Do not reject an afflicted suppliant, nor turn your face away from the poor. Do not avert your eye from the needy, nor give a man occasion to curse you." For censure of the latter see Sir 27:1: 'Whoever seeks to get rich will avert his eye."

105. RSV: "a greedy man's eye:" NRSV: "the eye of a greedy person."

106. RSV: "mean injustice;" NEB: "greedy injustice."

Eye") and that the LXX mistakenly read *'awón ra'* ("evil injustice").[107] This proposal makes sense from both a text-critical and cultural point of view and my translation of v. 9b therefore follows it. The textual misreading of the LXX involves only the confusion of the letter *waw* for the letter *yod*. Withering or drying up of the body, conventionally is traced not to injustice as the cause, but to the burning ocular rays of an Evil Eye.[108] Here, as in vv. 5–6, the Evil-Eye possessor himself is said to bring about his own injury and suffering—a withered soul.

From the Evil-Eyed person manifesting insatiable greed or avarice (v. 9), the focus returns in verse 10 to the association of the Evil Eye (*ophthalmos ponêros*) with envy/begrudging (*phthoneros*) and the trait of miserliness and stinginess. The subject of the sentence, "an Evil Eye" (*'ayin ra' 'ayin, ophthalmos ponêros*)," is a synecdoche (a part standing for the whole) and implies "a person with an Evil Eye":

> A person with an Evil Eye begrudges bread,
>> and it is lacking from her/his table. (Sir 14:10)

The Hebrew reads, literally, "The eye of an Evil Eye" (*'ayin ra' 'ayin*) . . .[109] The LXX adds the adjective *phthoneros* and reads, literally:

> An Evil Eye (*ophthalmos ponêros*) is envious/begrudging (*phthoneros*)
>> concerning bread (or *begrudges* bread),
>> and it is lacking from its [the Evil Eye's] table.[110]

The Vulgate varies somewhat in sense from the Greek, reading:
> An Evil Eye (*oculus malus*) focuses on evil things
>> and will not be satisfied by bread,
>> but will be needy and sorrowful at its own table.[111]

The Hebrew, Greek, and Vulgate all use "Evil Eye" to represent the entire person, as is the case in Prov 23:6. I have added "a person with (an Evil Eye)" according to sense. The Latin *oculus malus* is the exact linguistic equivalent of the Greek *ophthalmos ponêros*, which is the exact equivalent of the Hebrew *ra' 'ayin*. The Vulgate, however, presents the action not as a begrudging *giving* of bread but rather as an unsatisfied *getting* of bread.

107. Levi 1969:21, note on Sir 14:9b. In Sir 7:2 LXX, *adikou* ("injustice") renders Heb *'awón* as indicated by Skehan and DiLella 1987:258, note on v. 9b.

108. See Vol. 2 on the Evil Eye causing withering and dessication; also Dundes 1992b:257–312.

109. Hebrew text in Levy 1951:21.

110. *Ophthalmos ponêros phthoneros ep' artô, kai ellipês epi tês trapezês autou.*

111. *Oculus malus ad mala et non satiabitur pane, sed indigens et in tristitia erit super mensam suam.*

The adjective *phthoneros* modifying "Evil Eye" in the LXX illustrates the regular association of these terms in Greek. Although most frequently meaning "envious," the adjective, in certain contexts. as we have seen, can also denote a "begrudging" disposition and action, resentment conditioning one's giving. The sense of *phthoneros ep' artôi* is ambiguous. It could mean "is *envious* of the bread of *others*" (wishing it to be destroyed) or "is *begrudging* concerning the giving of *one's own* bread." With the first sense, the verse would speak of being *envious* of the bread of others (v. 10a) and (or, perhaps, because of) lacking bread at one's own table (v. 10b). With the second sense, the verse would speak of offering bread at one's own table but only begrudgingly. (One would not envy one's own bread with the wish to destroy it, but only the bread of another. One's own bread, however, one might give only grudgingly.) A begrudging of food would relate this verse to Deut 28:53–57, and a begrudging of aid, to Deut 15:7–11. The Vulgate offers no equivalent of the LXX *phthoneros* and is itself ambiguous, speaking of receiving bread but also of behavior at one's own table. Envy of others' food and the wish for its destruction would not necessarily prompt one to eliminate it from one's own table. Reluctance at sharing one's own food, however, could lead one to remove it from one's own table. The more likely sense of *phthoneros* here is the *begrudging* aspect of an Evil Eye manifested in the unwillingness of the Evil-Eyed person to part with his food altogether. As with other Evil Eye texts, the translators make choices determined not only by the terminology but also by the presumed social dynamics and intentions involved.

RSV and NRSV render according to assumed sense in context, omitting explicit mention of the Evil Eye: "A stingy man's eye (RSV, NRSV: "a miser") begrudges bread . . . and it is lacking at his table." *Stingy man* and *miser* are virtually identical in meaning, with both denoting being tight-fisted and unwilling to part with one's possessions, in this case one's food. The sense is thus similar to the disposition of the Evil Eye in Deut 15:9; 28:54, 56; Prov 23:6–8; and more immediately, Sir 14:4–7, 8. Being stingy or miserly and giving grudgingly are only one step removed from withholding aid and hospitality altogether.[112]

The gist of the entire statement of Sir 14:10 is ambiguous, with the most likely sense of *phthoneros* being not "envious (of the bread of others)" but "begrudging (of one's own bread)," as the RSV proposes. This reluctance

112. Absent from the Greek version of Sir 14:10 are words occurring in the Hebrew and Syriac: "A good eye causes bread to increase" and "a dry spring sends forth water upon his table" (perhaps representing a proverb). It is more likely that these are additions to Hebrew and Syriac texts and were designed to provide a positive statement to balance the negative, than that the LXX translators intentionally omitted these words.

to provide basic hospitality for dining and a stinginess with food as an aspect of the Evil Eye fit the immediate context, which speaks repeatedly of Evil-Eyed persons being miserly with their possessions and disregarding others (vv. 4–7 and 8). The link of Evil Eye and envy recurs at Sir 37:10–11. In the Bible, the phrase for Evil Eye, *ophthalmos ponêros*, appears again in Sir 31:13; Mark 7:22; and Matt 6:23, cf. Luke 11:34.

The alternate expression "good eye" (*tov 'ayin*) occurs only once in the Hebrew Bible, namely Prov 22:9, also as a synecdoche: "(A person with) *a good eye* will be blessed, for he shares his bread with the poor." The LXX reads differently: "He who shows mercy (*ho eleôn*) to the poor will be nourished; for he has given of his own bread to the poor." To this are added the words: "and he who gives liberally secures victory and honor," underscoring how honorable such generosity is. The RSV renders "good eye" as "He who has a *bountiful eye*"; the NRSV, "Those who are generous." The parallelism of Prov 22:9a and 9b indicates that having a "good eye" implies sharing one's possessions and hence being generous. Proverbs 22:9 is similar in sense to the additions to Sir 14:10 LXX and may have prompted the expansions. Sirach 14:10 LXX speaks of an Evil Eye causing bread to be absent from the table, with no mention of a good eye, and Prov 22:9 speaks of a good eye that shares bread with the poor, with no mention of an Evil Eye.[113]

Most translations do not make clear that Sir 14:3–10 has the Evil Eye in view from outset to close. The differing renditions of the RSV illustrate how this consistent focus is obscured when translations according to sense are preferred over literal translations: RSV "envious man" (14:3); "who is grudging toward himself" (14:6); "man with a grudging eye" (14:8); "a greedy man's eye" (14:9); "a stingy man's eye begrudges" (14:10). This is similarly true of the translation, for example, of *The Wisdom of Ben Sira* by P. W. Skehan and A. A. DiLella in their Anchor Bible commentary (1987). Their Comment speaks of "the evil of eye" and "the man evil of eye," but does not explain the Evil Eye phenomenon itself. The translation renders only according to perceived sense: "miser" (vv. 3, 8, 10); "stingy" (vv. 5, 6); "greedy" (v. 9a), "stinginess" (v. 9b), with no indication of the Evil Eye as the subject.

The consistent focus of Sir 14: 3–10, however, is the Evil Eye in its multiple aspects—an Evil Eye possessor's ungenerosity, miserliness and reluctant giving in general (vv. 3–8, 10) as well as Evil Eyed greed and gluttony (v. 9); the Evil Eye signaling being evil rather than good (v. 5), which in this context involves ungenerosity rather than generosity; the possibility of Evil-Eyeing oneself (vv. 5–7); the harmful effects of the Evil Eye, including the non-enjoyment of one's possessions (v. 5b) and the withering away of

---

113. On "good eye" see also below, pp. 77–78.

life (v. 9) by the eye's burning glance; the Evil Eye at dining expressing both gluttony (v. 9) and offering food grudgingly (v. 10). Both the personal and social ramifications of Evil Eye behavior are in view, involving both negative personal traits and self-injury, on the one hand, and impaired social relations and refusal of aid, food, and proper hospitality, on the other. The Evil Eye and Evil-Eyeing oneself are, in short, the worst of evils (14:6; also Sir 31:13). To have an Evil Eye and be miserly with one's goods was to lose their enjoyment and the honor such sharing would have earned. Evil Eye belief, in tandem with the ever-present quest for honor, reinforced the important code of hospitality and generosity in a world of limited good.

SIRACH 18:18

Sirach 18:18 occurs within the unit 18:15–18; the motif of "gift (vv. 15/18) forms an inclusion framing and setting off vv. 15–18. The passage entails advice concerning appropriate behavior when giving gifts or alms and echoes earlier Evil Eye statements about reluctant giving. Sirach 18:15–18 reads:

> 15 My son, do not mix reproach with your good deeds,
>   nor cause grief by your words when you present a gift.[114]
> 16 Does not the dew assuage the scorching heat?
>   So a word is better than a gift.
> 17 Indeed, does not a word surpass a good gift?
>   Both are to be found in a gracious man.
> 18 A fool is ungracious and abusive,
>   and the gift of *an Evil-Eyed person* (*baskanou*) makes the
>   eyes dim (*ektêkei ophthalmous*).
> (RSV with modifications by JHE)

The LXX has the conventional term *baskanos*, meaning "Evil-Eyed person."[115] In this contrast between a gracious person (vv. 15–17) and a fool (*môros*, v. 18a), the Evil-Eyed person is linked with a fool who is ungracious and abusive (v. 18b).[116] As in Deut 15: 7–11; Sir 14:8; and Tob 4:7–11, 16, an Evil-Eyed person is one who gives only grudgingly if at all. He also adulterates his gift with insulting comments (cf. v. 15), and this causes grievous

---

114. For the thought see also Sir 41:22b in a list of shameful actions.

115. For *baskanos* see also Sir 14:3; 18:18; 37:11; cf. *baskainein*, Deut 28:54, 56; Gal 3:1

116. Association with a *fool*, a profoundly denigrated individual, is thoroughly negative, especially in conventional proverbs extolling knowledge and wisdom.

harm. His reluctant parting with his gift "makes his eyes dim" (*ektêkei oph-thalmous*) or "melts his eyes," or "causes the eyes to waste away."[117]

The Vulgate reads, "A fool will reproach bitterly, and a gift of *one poorly taught* makes the eyes melt" (*Stultus acriter improperabit, et datus indisciplinati tabescere facit oculos*), replacing "Evil-Eyed person" with *one poorly taught*. The Vulgate's *facit tabescere* has same sense as LXX *ektêkei*; namely, "cause to melt gradually, cause to waste away."[118] An Evil Eye conventionally was compared to the sun and its scorching rays, as noted in Vol. 1, chap. 2, and was thought to cause a wasting or withering or drying up of the bodies of those its heat strikes. Dimming and darkening of the eyes could imply progressive blindness, usually a result of senescence,[119] or of grief (Job 17:7). Here the implication is that when an Evil-Eyed person gives a gift, her/his Evil Eye emits burning rays that melt and dissolve the eyes of the recipient and remove light from the eyes. Jesus also speaks of a body being made full of darkness by an Evil Eye (Matt 6:23/Luke 11:34). This idea of heat and melting is consonant with v. 16, which mentions dew assuaging the "scorching heat." Skehan and DiLella take the expression metaphorically: "the ungracious and 'grudging' manner in which he gives his gift ruins the excitement and expectation of the recipient."[120] A further implication of the statement is that accepting gifts from Evil-Eyed persons is highly dangerous and should be avoided.[121]

RSV and NRSV take the words to imply *grudging giving*. These versions omit explicit reference to "Evil-Eyed person" and translate according to sense: "the gift of a *grudging* man makes the eyes dim;" so also NEB: "a grudging giver;" JB: "a grudging man's gift;" NAB: "a grudging gift;" TEV: "a gift that you resent giving." For harm caused by an Evil Eye see also Prov 23:6–8 (causes vomiting at the table); Sir 14:5 (causes non-enjoyment of possessions), 6 (causes damage to self), 9 (withers life away); Sir 31:13 (tears fall from every face) and Wis 4:12 (obscures the good).

---

117. *Ektêkein* = "to melt out, pine or waste away, cause to waste away" (LSJ); cf. *têkein*: "melt."

118. *Tabescere* means "melt gradually, be dissolved, consumed." *Tabescat* also can mean "be consumed with envy" (Horace, *Serm.* 1.1.111). The noun *tabes* means "a wasting away"; for wasting away of the eyes see Tacitus, *Hist.* 4.81; Ovid, *Met.* 2.807.

119. See Gen 27:1 "when Isaac was old and his eyes were dim;" Gen 48:10; 1 Sam 3:2

120. Skehan and DiLella 1987:290.

121. For the noxious effect of an Evil Eye see also Prov 28:22; Sir 18:18.

Sirach 31:12–13 (15)

At the table, Sirach notes, the Evil Eye can also convey the dispositions of greed and gluttony. In the midst of advice on dining decorum (Sir 31:12—32:13), including eating in moderation (31:12–30), Sir 31:12–13 LXX instructs:

> 12 If you sit at a bountiful table[122] do not be gluttonous at it[123]
>   and do not say, "there is lots of food on it."
> 13 Remember that an Evil Eye (*ophthalmos ponêros*) is a wicked
>   thing (*kakon*).[124]
> What has been created more evil (*ponêroteron*) than an
>   (Evil) Eye *(ophthalmou)?*
> For this reason tears fall from every face.[125]

It is more likely here, however, that the point is that the Evil Eye, the most wicked of evils, causes universal weeping and sadness whenever and wherever it strikes: because of its profound wickedness, it brings tears to fall from every face. The translation of Skehan and DiLella of the more extensive Hebrew text is felicitous. However, rather than rendering "Evil Eye" (*ra'ah 'ayin*) explicitly, it opts for accentuating the gluttony and greed associated with an Evil Eye:

> Are you seated at a banquet table?
>   Bring to it no greedy gullet!
>   Say not, 'What a spread this is!'
> Remember, gluttony is a bad thing (Heb: *ra'ah 'ayin ra'ah*, lit.
>   "the Evil Eye is an evil thing")
>   God hates the eye's greed;
>   was ever any creature greedier?
> That is why it shifts from everything it sees,
>   and sends tears streaming down the face.[126]

---

122. Heb: "at the table of a great man."

123. *mê anoixês ep' autês pharugga sou*; literally, "do not open your throat at it."

124. Heb: *ra'ah 'ayin ra'ah.*

125. Or, "Therefore it causes tears to fall from every face." It has been suggested that the tears may be a wet antidote to the Evil Eye's scorching glance (Wazana 2007:689). Sirach 18:18 states that the Evil Eye melts the eyes or causes them to waste away.

126. Skehan and DiLella 1987:384. Oesterley, "Book of Sirach" (*APOT* 1:419–20) presents a translation of the additional lines contained in the Hebrew of v. 13 and comments on their redundancy: "The (man of) Evil Eye God hates, and He has created nothing more evil than him. For this—by reason of everything—the eye quivers, and from the face it makes tears." The similar Syriac reads: "the evil of the eye God hates, and He has created nothing more evil than it. Therefore the eye quivers by reason of everything."

The LXX of v. 13 has one of the conventional expressions for Evil Eye, namely *ophthalmos ponêros*, as does the Hebrew (*ra'ah 'ayin*). The Vulgate (Ecclus [Sir] 31: 12–15) reads:

> 12 Are you seated at a great table?
>   Do not be the first to open your mouth at it.[127]
> 13 Do not say. "There are many things that are upon it."
> 14 Remember that an Evil Eye (*oculus nequam*) is wicked (*malus*).[128]
> 15 What is created more evil (*nequius*) than an (Evil) Eye?[129]
>   Therefore when it looks, tears will be shed from every
>   face.[130]

In all three cases, the technical terms for "Evil Eye" in the respective languages are employed: *'ayin ra'ah*, *ophthalmos ponêros*, and *oculus nequam*.

The parallelism of vv. 12–13 (HT and LXX; Vulg: vv. 12–13 and 14–15) and the general context indicate that "Evil Eye" here is associated with the disposition of gluttony, being greedy for food at the table, and its harmful consequences.[131] Thus the translations of the RSV and NRSV ("do not be greedy . . . a greedy eye . . . what is more greedy than the eye?"), which render according to sense, are appropriate, even though, like Skehan and DiLella, they fail to indicate the explicit mention of "Evil Eye" in the original texts.[132]

An Evil Eye in dining situations, therefore, can involve either the begrudging offer of food by stingy hosts or the greedy grubbing of food on the part of gluttonous guests. Being gluttonous at meals is the opposite of eating in moderation and being considerate of fellow diners. Eating with a gluttonous Evil Eye will bring on vomiting, illness, heavy breathing in bed, sleeplessness, nausea and colic, all of which eating in moderation will avoid (Sir 31:19–21). In this context we find another reference to *vomiting* at the table: "If you are overstuffed with food, get up to *vomit* (*emeson porrô*), and you will have relief" (Sir 31:21; cf. Pseudo-Aristotle, *Prob. phys.* 20.34). In Sir 31:13 (as in 31:21) an Evil Eye causes physical discomfort or worse.

127. Cf. similarly Vulg Sir 31:21 [= Heb and LXX 31:18].

128. *Nequam* is an indeclinable adjective meaning *worthless, wretched, vile, evil*; *oculus nequam* is equivalent in meaning to *oculus malus*, both standard expressions for "Evil Eye." For *oculus nequam* see also the Evil Eye texts of Matt 6:23; 20:15; and Luke 11:34.

129. *Oculos,* standing for the *oculus nequam*, "Evil Eye," of v. 14.

130. *Ideo ab omni facie sua lacrimabitur, cum viderit.* The Vulgate adds "when it looks" (*cum viderit*), perhaps to clarify that the Evil Eye does not weep itself, but with its injurious glance causes its *victims* to weep.

131. Sir 18:33 also condemns gluttony.

132. The footnote of RSV v. 13, however, gives "evil eye" as a variant translation.

In the RSV and NRSV translations, the words *liberal, excellence, niggardly, niggardliness* (RSV) or *liberal, generosity, stingy, stinginess* (NRSV) convey the sense of the terms in this context and are more specific than the original Greek and Hebrew terms. They do not, however, mention the Evil Eye explicitly, although the RSV in a footnote allows the variant translation "evil eye." Other Bible Versions likewise render according to sense, many focusing on greed.[133] NAB opts for both gluttony and greed: "Remember that gluttony is evil. No creature is greedier than the eye: therefore it weeps for any cause."

This rendition illustrates a further point of divergence in the translations; namely the sense and rendition of the concluding words of v. 14 (15). Compare, for example,

Skehan-DiLella (Heb.): *That is why it shifts from everything it sees, and sends tears streaming down the face.*

LXX: *Therefore it sheds tears from every face.*

Vulg: *Therefore when it looks, tears will be shed from every face.*

CEB: *For this reason, every face sheds tears.*

Douay-Rheims: *Therefore shall it weep over all the face when it shall see.*

BJ/JB: *That is why it waters on every occasion.*

KJV Apocrypha: *Therefore it weepeth upon every occasion.*

NAB: *Therefore it weeps for any cause.*

NEB: *That is why it must shed tears at every turn.*

RSV: *Therefore it sheds tears from every face.*

NRSV: *Therefore it sheds tears for any reason.*

TEV: *That is why it sheds tears so often.*

These final words of the verse, introduced by "therefore" or equivalent expressions ("that is why," "for this reason," etc.), are taken by the translators to provide an *explanation* for the existence of some phenomenon associated with an Evil Eye (why all humans shed tears; why tears are shed on all occasions or for any cause). Or they are regarded as a *consequence* of an Evil Eye's action—the fascinator is brought to tears or the object of the Evil-Eyed glance is caused to weep. In any case, it is clear that the "eye" referred to here is not the ocular organ as such but an *Evil Eye*. The "eye" of v. 13b is the "Evil Eye" of v. 13a. It is not the ocular organ as such that is declared the most evil of things—such a notion would be singular in a body of writing that extols

133. For "greedy" see also BJ, JB, CEB, *La Biblia*, NAB, NEB, NRSV, and TEV.

the excellence and preeminence of the eye among the five sense organs. It is rather an *Evil Eye* that this wisdom saying censures, a malevolent eye, the exercise of which has palpable and dire consequences for possessor or victim or both.

If the earlier comment of v. 12, "there is lots of food on it," entails a compliment, this too would have Evil Eye implications. Evil Eye cultures, as we have noted, avoid admiring and praising because the admirer is suspected of envying the object admired and ruining it. Compliments normally are eschewed altogether,[134] so this case would represent an exception.

Finally, it is important to note how grievous the possession and casting of an Evil Eye was thought to be—"the very worst of all evils," as also stated in Sirach 14:6.[135]

The following verse, LXX Sir 31:14, may contain a further allusion to the Evil Eye. It reads:

> Do not reach out your hand for everything *you overlook,*
> and do not crowd your neighbor at the dish.[136]

The Vulgate (Sir 31:16 in the Vulgate versification) has a variant version:

> Do not reach out your hand first,
> lest, being defiled by envy (*invidia contaminatus*), you feel ashamed.[137]

Although the LXX and Vulgate vary, they both, each in its own way, suggest further implications of the Evil Eye. The LXX speaks of "overlooking" (*epibleptein*) which is an action of the Evil Eye (= Latin *in-videre,* "look over," "envy;" cf. *invidia* = "envy"). *Epibleptein* here likely indicates the "looking (*bleptein*) over (*epi-*)" of an Evil Eye. The Vulgate speaks of being defiled by envy (*invidia*), which is the chief emotion associated with the Evil Eye, but here could connote gluttony. It is thus likely that LXX Sir 31:14 continues the thread of vv. 12–13 and likewise refers to Evil Eye activity at the table; namely, scoping out the food in a gluttonous fashion.

This call for eating in moderation is followed by further dispositions associated with the Evil Eye: generosity or stinginess in the providing of food. Sirach 31:23–24 comments:

134. See Maloney 1976:102–48 on "Don't Say 'Pretty Baby'"; McCartney 1992:9–38 on praise and dispraise.

135. According to Sir 14:6 the worst of the Evil-Eye possessors is the one who Evil-Eyes himself/herself.

136. Literally, "do not reach out your hand wherever it looks (*epiblepsei*) . . ."

137. *Ne extendas manum tuum prior, et invida contaminatus erubescas.*

> People praise someone who is liberal (*lampron*) with food,
>   and their testimony to his generosity (*tês kallonês*, lit.,
>   "beauty") is trustworthy.
> The city complains about someone who is stingy (*ponêrôi*, lit.
>   "evil") with food,
>   and its testimony to his stinginess (*tês ponêrias*, lit., "evil"
>   is accurate.

Lampros means, literally, "luminous, glorious, sumptuous." In this dining context, a "luminous" person is one who is generous with his food, in contrast to an evil person, whose evil consists in his stinginess with food. The "evil" (*ponêros, ponêria*, v. 24) is typical of one with an Evil Eye (*ophthalmos ponêros*) refusing to share his food and resources (as in Deut 15:7–9; 28:54–57; Sir 14:8, 10; 18:18; Tob 4:7, 16). Accordingly, we may have here in Sir 31:23–24 another implied reference to the Evil Eye in a context already explicitly mentioning an Evil Eye (Sir 31:12–13). Greed and gluttony at table, like dissimulation of genuine hospitality, both manifestations of an Evil Eye, are thought to have deleterious consequences, both physical and social, as the Aristotelian tradition had noted.[138] Concern over an injurious Evil Eye at the table helps restrain gluttony and immoderation.

These meal scenarios illustrate a widespread fear of an Evil Eye active in dining situations in Israelite as well as Greco-Roman settings. This fear is still felt today and explains some defensive dining customs still employed. These include eating with one's back turned to the public or eating only in private or secluded booths so that potential Evil-Eyed persons cannot see and in envy cast their Evil Eye on those who dine. Another custom involving the Evil Eye in dining situations is the practice of giving the server of the meal a tip or *Trinkgeld*, as it is called in German, "money for a drink." Anthropologist George Foster explains in his illuminating article on envy,[139] that the tip is a "sop" given to the server to keep the waiter from becoming envious of the food served, casting an Evil Eye, and fouling the food. The German *Trinkgeld* is the money given to the waiter to purchase something for her/himself to drink (*trinken*). The English term "tip" most likely comes from "tippling" (drinking), and so, like the German *Trinkgeld*, is associated with drinking and dining and identifies a token amount of money given to the waiter to obtain for her/himself something to drink. The tip allows also the waiter to enjoy some food or drink, and motivates him to withhold any Evil Eye that could ruin the diner's food or cause vomiting.

---

138. See Pseudo-Aristotle, *Prob. phys.* 20.34, and the discussion in Vol. 2; also Elliott 1991:335 n. 38.

139. Forster 1972.

SIRACH 37:10–11

Another passage of Sirach warns against seeking counsel from, or giving counsel to, envious Evil-Eyed persons. Within a passage concerning counseling and counselors (Sir 37:7–15), both the self-interested (vv. 8–11) and the godly (vv. 12–15), Sir 37:10–11 advises:

> 10a Do not consult with one looking askance at you (with an Evil
>   Eye),
> 10b and conceal your counsel from those who envy
>   (*zêlountonôn*) you.
> 11 Do not consult with a wife about her envious rival co-wife,
>   or with a coward about war,
> with a merchant about barter,
>   or with a buyer about selling,
> with an Evil-Eyed person (*baskanou*) about generosity
>   or with a merciless person about kindness,
> with an idler about any work,
>   or with a seasonal laborer about finishing the job,
> with a lazy household slave about a large task.
> Pay no attention to these in any matter of counsel.

Instead, one is to associate with godly persons whom one "knows to be a keeper of the commandments, whose soul is in accord with your soul, and who will grieve with you if you fail" (Sir 37:12).

Verses 10 and 11 both refer to Evil-Eyed persons. The parallelism of vv. 10–11 indicates that that the person *looking askance (with an Evil Eye, hypoblepomenou*, v. 10a)[140] is equated with the *Evil-Eyed person ('ish ra'; baskanou)* of v. 11. The "one looking askance at you with an Evil Eye" (v. 10a), moreover, parallels "those who envy you" (*tôn zelountôn*) of v. 10b. This juxtaposition of *looking askance with an Evil Eye* and *envying* (see also "envious rival co-wife," v. 11) is consistent with the conventional association of Evil Eye and envy. The verb *hypoblepesthai* appears also in 1 Sam 18:9 where Saul "eyes" (Hebrew), or "looks askance" (LXX: *hypoblepomenou*) in envy at, David.[141] Looking askance remains a telltale feature of an Evil-Eyed person down to the present; cf. German *scheelen*, *Scheelauge* (Luther's translation of *ophthalmos ponêros* in Matt 20:15); *squardo maligno*, Mark 7:22 in *La Sacra Bibbia*). In this context, *zêlountes* (LXX; Vulgate: *zelantibus*) has the sense of *envy* not *jealousy* (against RSV and NRSV: "those who are *jealous* of

140. The participle *hypoblepomenou* of v. 10a (lit. *"who looks up from under* [*the eyebrows*]) denotes "looking askance with an envious Evil Eye" as in 1 Sam 18:9.

141. On the "oblique eye" and looking askance in Greek and Latin texts, see Vol. 2, pp. 8, 39, 45, 76, 102–103, 132–133, 272.

you.").[142] Envy, we recall, wishes harm and loss to others, while jealousy entails concern over losing what one himself possesses. The point of vv. 10–11 is that Evil-Eyed persons cannot give impartial advice and are not open to sound advice. This includes co-wives regarding their rivals and the topic of generosity, about which the tight-fisted Evil-Eyed know nothing.

Verse eleven specifies nine persons who "give counsel in their own interest" (v.7) and whose advice cannot be trusted. Among them is the Evil-Eyed person (*baskanos*)[143] who is described in v. 10 as one who looks askance with Evil-Eyed envy (*hypoblepomenou*). The trait of envy is captured in the Vulgate rendition: *viro livido*, an "envious man." Except for the last person mentioned (the domestic slave) in this list, the eight prior persons are matched with their domain of activity where their advice is distorted by self-interest: the wife (*gynaikos*) anxious about her co-wife (*antizêlou*) competing for the affection and time of their husband, the coward unreliable about putting life on the line in battle, the lazy interested only in shirking work etc. The reference is not to "women" in general (against RSV, NRSV), but to *co-wives* in particular who, in this polygamous culture, are rivals for the affection and favor of their husband and are vulnerable to the envy of the rival. The Greek term *antizêlos* (translating Heb. *zarar*, Lev 18:18) denotes a *rival co-wife* (see Sir 26:6) who is *envious* (*zêl-*) against (*anti-*) her other wifely competitors. *Antizêlos* echoes *zêlountôn* of the preceding v. 10b and likewise concerns envy, not jealousy (against RSV, NRSV: "jealous").[144] An envious rival wife wishes failure and harm to her rival and is no reliable source of sound counsel.[145]

The Evil-Eyed person (*baskanos*), in turn, should not be consulted about generosity. The Hebrew and Syriac read "generosity," reflecting the conventional notion of the Evil Eye as the opposite of generosity and liberality.[146] The LXX reads "gratitude" (*eucharistias*), as does the Vulgate (*gratiis agendas*). The implication here is that an Evil-Eyed person, like the others named, will give biased and unreliable advice about that to which he/she stands in contrast. The Evil-Eyed are miserly and deplore generosity.

---

142. Terms of the *zel-* word family have a wide range of meaning, including "feel intensely"; "have positive (or negative) feelings toward"; "(feel) enthusiasm for;" (feel) jealousy"; (feel) envy, envious"; "emulate, emulation"—all determined by context; see Vol. 2, "Excursus on Envy"; and Bell 1994, chap. 1.

143. For *baskanos* see also Prov 23:6; Sir 14:3; 18:18.

144. *Antizêlos*, with the meaning "envious one," is joined again with *baskanos* (and *ponêros*) in the *Martyrdom of Polycarp* 17:1, referring to the devil; on this text see Vol 4, Chapter 2.

145. For such rivalries see Gen 30:1 and 1 Sam 1:2–7.

146. See Deut 15:7–11; 28:53–57; Sir 14:3–8; Matt 20:15; possibly also Matt 6:22–23.

They also, however, are envious and incapable of gratitude, as illustrated later in Jesus's parable of the workers in the vineyard (Matt 20:1–15). The accompanying contrast of "merciless" and "kindness" is a parallel contrast and echoes "Evil-Eyed person" and "generosity." The RSV reads: "a grudging man about gratitude; NRSV: "a miser about generosity." Both capture aspects of the Evil Eye here but make no explicit mention of the Evil Eye itself, as is also the case with Skehan and DiLella's translation (1987:425). The point in general, which our Evil-Eye statement illustrates, is that counsel should not be sought from any whose self-interest or defects of character cloud their vision, including the envious and those with an Evil Eye.

WISDOM OF SOLOMON 4:12

The Wisdom of Solomon, another writing of Israel's broad wisdom tradition, was composed in Greek in the first century BCE, probably in Alexandria, Egypt. It makes one explicit reference to the Evil Eye and how it obscures everything good (4:12). Its Hellenistic Israelite author assumes the identity of Solomon, the all-wise ruler. The wisdom it shares is a conflation of Israelite and Greek thinking on universal reason, wisdom, and righteousness. Solomon, likewise the assumed author of Proverbs and Wisdom poetry in the Hebrew Bible, was viewed in later tradition as the wise man par excellence, adept also in occult wisdom as well.[147] This is indicated in the *Testament of Solomon* (which also refers to the Evil Eye) and by his inclusion on numerous anti-Evil Eye amulets bearing the "seal of Solomon" (*sphragis Solomonis*).[148]

The passage occurs among contrasts involving (a) the righteous in the hand of God (3:1–9) and the divine punishment of the ungodly (3:10–4:6) and (b) the blessedness of the righteous despite a premature death (4:7–15) in contrast to the shameful end of the ungodly (4:16–19). As an example of a righteous person who "died early" (4: 7), the figure of righteous Enoch is alluded to (vv. 10–15; cf. Gen 5:21–24; Sir 44:16). Loved by God (v. 10a), Enoch was "perfected in a short time" (v. 13). From the midst of sinners and wickedness (vv. 10b, 14b) he was quickly taken up to heaven by God (vv. 10b, 14b). The legend is recounted more extensively in the book of *1 Enoch*. In explanation of the statement that Enoch "was caught up lest evil (*kakia*) change his understanding or guile (*dolos*) deceive his soul" (v. 11), reference is made to the Evil Eye and its obscuring of what is good.

147. On the figure of Solomon see McCown 1922a; Preisendanz 1956; Duling 1975, 1984, 1985, 1993; Feldman 1976; Winston 1979; Verheyden 2012.

148. See below, respectively, pp. 71-72, 86-89 and also Vol. 4, chap. 1.

10 There was one who pleased God [Enoch] and was loved by him,
>   and while living among sinners he was taken up.
11 He was caught up lest evil change his understanding
>   or guile deceive his soul.
12 For *the Evil Eye of wickedness* obscures what is good,
>   and roving desire perverts the innocent mind.
13 Being perfected in a short time,
>   he fulfilled long years;
14 for his soul was pleasing to the Lord,
>   therefore the Lord took him quickly from the midst of wickedness.
15 Yet the peoples saw and did not understand,
>   nor take such a thing to heart, namely
> that God's grace and mercy are with his elect,
>   and he watches over his holy ones."

The LXX of Wis 4:12 reads: *baskania gar phaulotêtos amauroi ta kala, kai rhembasmos epithymias metalleuei noun akakon.* The Vulgate is a close translation of the Greek: *fascinatio enim nugacitatis obscurat bona/ et inconstantia concupiscentiae transverti sensum sine militia,* with Latin *fascinatio* rendering Greek *baskania.* This is the sole appearance of *fascinatio* in the Vulgate. Its related verb, *fascinare,* however, occurs in Gal 3:1 (*fascinavit*) translating the Greek verb *ebaskanen.* The occurrences of the *fascin-* terms are related; both are conventional refererences to the operation of the Evil Eye, as are their underlying Greek terms, *baskania* and *baskainen.*

In this passage, verse 12 states the reality underlying 4:11, which explains why Enoch was taken prematurely into heaven. God removed righteous Enoch from an exposure to the malicious Evil Eye of his neighbors because a fascinating Evil Eye obscures everything good. God thereby spared Enoch's innocent mind and moral character from being perverted by their roaming desire. The synonymous parallelism of v. 12a and v. 12b matches "a wicked Evil Eye" with "roving desire" (*rhembasmos epithymias*).[149] Does this association suggest that *epithymia* elsewhere in the Greek Bible could imply the working of an Evil Eye, as in the *coveting* of one's neighbor's house, or wife or domestic staff (Exod 20:17)? Joseph Lewis, *The Ten Commandments* (1946), made this claim, but without probative support.[150]

---

149. The *kakia* of v. 11 has its antithetical parallel in the *akakon* of v. 12.

150. *Epithymia* (*intense desire, craving, longing,* BDAG s.v.) connotes a strong desire to *acquire for oneself* rather than a wish for *someone else to lose* what she/he has. Like jealousy, the focus of *epithymia* is advantage to the self, rather than the dispossessing of another. It appears only rarely with "Evil Eye" (Philo, *Cher.* 33) but is not paired with Evil Eye and never serves as a synonym for *bask-* terms.

RSV and NRSV render *baskania* with "fascination," perhaps under the influence of the Vulgate. They do not explain, however, that *fascination* here has the ancient sense of *looking with an Evil Eye*. David Winston's Anchor Bible translation, "the witchery of evil," (Winston 1979:136) obscures the clear reference of the Greek (and later the Latin Vulgate) to the Evil Eye; he provides no comment on the term *baskania*.

The statement presumes that the Evil Eye was already present and operating in the period before the Flood and is the antithesis of everything good. It is a malicious manifestation of wickedness that obscures the good and perverts innocence, similar to craving covetous on the move.[151] Since the Evil Eye is so closely linked with envy, it is interesting to note that envy, specifically the Devil's envy, is said earlier in Wis 2:24 to have introduced death into the world, alluding to Gen 3–4.[152] The Evil Eye, however, is not directly linked with the Devil until post-biblical times, beginning with *Martyrdom of Polycarp* 17:1 (c. 156–157 CE).[153]

The moral implications of an Evil Eye are further evident in the books of Tobit and 4 Maccabees.

TOBIT 4:1–21 (VV. 7, 16)

The book of Tobit, a romantic tale composed in the second to first century BCE, from somewhere in the Eastern Mediterranean, tells of the tribulations of Tobit, a devoted Israelite of the Assyrian diaspora and his son Tobias, and the divine deliverance of the righteous. A further representative of Israel's wisdom tradition, the tale underscores, among other values, the importance of generosity to the needy and almsgiving (4:7–11, 16–17; 12:8–9; 14:2; 11), with Tobit himself and his "many acts of almsgiving" (1:3, 16–18; 2:1–8) as prime example.

At an important juncture of the story, Tobit, believing that he is dying, shares with his son Tobias his philosophy of life and how to live uprightly (4:1–21).[154] Twice in this discourse Tobit warns his son against acting toward others with a begrudging Evil Eye, in terms reminiscent especially of Deut 15:7–11. Tobit 4:5–11 and 16 read:

---

151. Its equation with "*roaming* desire" recalls the reference to the "roaming Evil Eye" found in Mesopotamian incantations; see Vol. 1, chap. 2.

152. On the tradition of the devil's envy, see 2 *Enoch* 31:3–6; *Life of Adam* 12–17; Theophilus, *Ad Autolycum* 2.29; Winston 1979:121–23; von Nordheim-Diehl 2012.

153. On this issue see Vol. 4, chap. 2.

154. This section is composed of a collection of conventional precepts and aphorisms put into the mouth of Tobit. It sums up the moral teaching of the book as a whole.

5 Remember the Lord our God all your days, my son,
    and refuse to sin or transgress God's commandments.
  Live uprightly all the days of your life,
    and do not walk in the ways of wrongdoing.
6 For if you do what is true,
    your ways will prosper through your deeds.
7 Give alms (*poiei eleêmosynên*) from your possessions to all
        who live uprightly,
    and *do not begrudge with an Evil Eye* the alms when you
        give them.
  Do not turn your face away from any poor man,
    and the face of God will not be turned away from you.
8 If you have many possessions,
    give alms from them in proportion [to what you have];
  if you have few possessions,
    do not worry about giving according to the little you have.
9 In this way you will be laying up a good treasure (*thêsaurizeis*)
    for yourself against the day of necessity.
10 For the generous giving of alms delivers from death
    and keeps you from entering the darkness (*skotos*);
11 and for all who practice it,
    giving alms is an excellent gift in the presence of the Most
        High . . .
16 Give of your bread to the hungry,
    and of your clothing to the naked.
  Give all your surplus as alms,
    and *do not begrudge with an Evil Eye* the alms when you
        give them.

Tobit 4:7, 16 LXX read: *mê phthonesatô sou ho ophthalmos en to poiein se eleemosynen*.[155] The formulation is, technically speaking, an implicit rather than explicit reference to the Evil Eye. "Eye" (*ophthalmos*) is not modified by "evil;" however, it is spoken of as an instrument for acting in an immoral,

155. The LXX text is that of Codices Vaticanus and Alexandrinus. The verses are absent from Codex Sinaiticus, which lacks vv. 7b–18. The textual tradition here and throughout Tobit is unclear and unsettled. Most of the biblical versions presume the longer recension, as does C. A. Moore, *Tobit* (1996), among others. Simpson 1913:211, on the other hand, claims on the basis of mss support that the words in v. 7 "seem to be an interpolation in R [recension in Cod. Vaticanus] from *v*. 16." A Hebrew fragment of Tob 4:4–7 found at Qumran (4Q200 frags, 2–3), is translated by García Martínez (1996:298): "[. . .] According to the size of your hands, my son, be [generous in doing] just deeds (alms), and do not wi[thdraw] [your face from any poor] person, so that from you [the face of God does] not [withdraw]" (vv. 6–7). It contains no explicit reference to the Evil Eye, but does support the likely originality of the readings of Codices Vaticanus and Alexandrinus.

envious manner (*mê phthonesatô*). The association, moreover, of *phthonein* and *ophthalmos* is conventional in Greek and Roman Evil Eye thought.[156] C. A. Moore's translation, "let not your eye be evil,"[157] makes reference to an Evil Eye explicit, as does my translation. Eye as instrument and linked with *phthonein* points unmistakably to an Evil Eye, as does its proximity in sense and sentiment to Deut 15:9. For this reason I have included the passage among the explicit Evil Eye texts. *Phthonein* generally means "to envy," and in this passage could be translated "do not let your (Evil) Eye be envious" or "do not look with an envious Evil Eye." However, the sense of the action here, similar to that of other Evil Eye texts (Deut 15:9, 28:54, 56; Prov 23:6; Sir 14:5–8, 10; 18:18; 37:11), is better communicated by translating *phthonesatô* with the verb *begrudge* (= "give reluctantly"), which is the rendering of the RSV and NRSV ("do not let your eye begrudge"). Envy of the possessions of another is not in view here; "begrudge" better specifies the disposition involved than does the more general "look with an Evil Eye" (where *phthonein* would be viewed as a substitute for *baskainein*).

The Vulgate of Tob 4:7 speaks explicitly neither of envy nor of the Evil Eye or begrudging, but only of "not averting your face from any poor person" (= LXX 4:7d).[158] Sirach 14:8, however, shows that "turning one's face and disregarding people" is equivalent to begrudging with an Evil Eye.

The translations vary in the manuscripts they render. Except for TEV, which puts the thought of v. 16 positively ("do it gladly"), they agree, however, on the sense of Evil Eye here as a "begrudging" Eye: "do not let your eye begrudge" (RSV, NRSV); "never give with a grudging eye "(NEB). Other versions, omitting v. 7b, also translate v. 16 "do not begrudge" (NAB); "do not do it grudgingly" (JB).

The passage recalls Deut 15:7–11 with its call for generosity toward the needy as opposed to Evil-Eyeing the poor and withholding assistance. Both texts also stress the response of God (Tob 4:7; Deut 15:10). Our passage also captures the spirit of Prov 28:27 ("He who gives to the poor will not want, but he who hides his eyes will get many a curse") and the call for generosity reflected in Sir 7:32–33: "Stretch out your hand to the poor, so that your blessing may be complete. Give graciously to all the living and do

156. Tob 4:7 and 16 are the only occurrences of the verb *phthonein* in the Greek OT.

157. Moore 1996:161, 162, 166.

158. Vulg. Tob 4:7: *Ex substantia tua fac elemosynam, et noli avertere faciem tuam ab ullo paupere; ita enim fiet ut nec a te avertatur facies Domini.* [Give alms from your possessions, and turn not your face from any poor person; and thus it shall be that the face of the Lord shall not be turned from you]. The Vulgate of 4:16 has no equivalent for the Greek LXX 4:16, and appears based on a different (inferior and shorter) text, perhaps an Aramaic text (so Moore 1996:xxiv).

not withhold kindness even from the dead." Such liberality is the opposite of giving reluctantly with an Evil Eye. Censure of the selfish withholding or begrudging of aid as a feature of Evil Eye conduct also appears, beside Deut 15:7–11, in Deut 28:54, 56; Sir 14:8, 10; 18:18; 37:11; Matt 6:22–23; and *m. Avot* 5:13. Rather than ever acting with a begrudging Evil Eye, Tobias is urged to always be generous and liberal with his charity.[159] As part of Tobit's parting instruction of his son about daily behavior in a righteous and generous fashion, this admonition against acting with an Evil Eye takes on special weight.

An evil demon by the name of Asmodeus plays a threatening role in the narrative.[160] It causes the death of seven bridegrooms of Sarah (Tob 3:8; 6:14), who eventually with trepidation marries Tobit's son Tobias. This demon, however, is not connected by the author with the Evil Eye, which is a human power here that Tobias is urged not to wield (4:7, 16). Blindness, conventionally thought to be a punishment for having and casting an Evil Eye, is a fate undergone by Tobit. This, however, is traced not to Tobit's having an Evil Eye, but to his being the victim of bird droppings falling on his eyes as he slept in an open air courtyard (3:9–10). Features like these convey the popular, folkloric caste of the Tobit narrative.

Religious as well as moral sentiments frame this instruction involving the Evil Eye and its counterpart, generosity, and relate these words of Tobit to other Evil Eye texts. The giving of alms and liberality toward poor coreligionists involves behavior consonant with the divine commandments and redounds in divine blessings (vv. 5–6, 11, 19). An Evil Eye manifested in a begrudging offer of alms, or the withholding of alms entirely, is contrary to the will of God (cf. Deut 15:7–11; Prov 23:6; Sir 14:5–8). To avert one's eye from a poor man's plight, like the begrudging of a gift, is the behavior of an Evil-Eyed person and results in God's averting His gracious face (v. 7). Human lack of generosity hinders the experience of God's generosity. Acting generously, on the other hand, amounts to "laying up a good treasure for yourself against a day of necessity" (v. 9), a notion echoed in Jesus' remark concerning the contrast of a good and an Evil Eye and laying up treasure in heaven (Matt 6:19–21). The encouragement to seek sound counsel, "Seek advice from every wise person and do not despise any useful counsel" (v. 18), recalls the Evil Eye text of Sir 37:7–12.

The story of Tobit underlines the moral implications of biblical Evil Eye belief and its bearing on social relationships and religious obligations.

---

159. For generosity and giving of alms see also Tob 1:17; 12:8–10; 14:11. "Alms" (*eleêmosunê*) occurs more often in Tobit (22x) than in any other book of the OT.

160. For Asmodeus see 3:8; 6:14–17; 8:1–3.

In a society marked by great disparity between the wealthy and the indigent and by the constant struggle over scarce resources, generosity is a lubricant that facilitates the smooth functioning of social interactions, while also a glue that binds together the haves and have-nots of the community.

The composition of Fourth Maccabees illustrates a further moral feature of the Evil Eye; namely its association with other dishonorable and malicious forms of conduct and its inclusion in lists of grievous vices.

4 MACCABEES 1:26; 2:15–16

The book of Fourth Maccabees, a philosophical discourse on the supremacy of reason and its mastery over all the passions of body and soul, was written by a Hellenistic Israelite of the Diaspora during the first century of the Common Era. As the fourth of the books associated with the revolutionary Judas Maccabaeus and his successors, this work is included in some but not all editions of the Septuagint. It is otherwise included among the Old Testament Pseudepigrapha. The book makes two references to the Evil Eye (1:26; 2:15), both in lists of vices.

The first reference to the Evil Eye (1:26) appears in a discussion of the four forms of wisdom (prudence, justice, courage/manliness, and temperance), prudence's rule over the passions of pleasure and pain, and the affections connected with pleasure and pain (1:18–23). The author then states (vv. 25–27):

> And there exists in pleasure (*têi hêdonêi*) a malicious disposition (*hê kakoêthês*) that is the most multiformed of all the affections (*tôn pathôn*). In the soul (*psychês*), it is arrogance, love of money, love of honor, contentiousness, and an *Evil Eye* (*baskania*). In the body (*to soma*), it is greediness at table, gormandizing, and solitary gluttony.

Here an Evil Eye is listed among five vices of internal disposition, which are distinguished from but related to three accompanying vices of external deportment at the table. These emotions, it is argued, can and must be brought under the control of reason, which is "the master of the passions" (1:30; cf. 2:9, 15). The Evil Eye is linked here, as elsewhere (Prov 23:6–8; Sir 14:9; 31:12–13), with gluttonous and greedy behavior at the dining table.

Building further on the previous point, the author states in 2:15–16 that

> Reasoning (*ho logismos*) appears to be master of the more violent affections—love of power, vain glory, arrogance, loud boasting,

and an Evil Eye (*baskanias*); for temperate understanding repels all these malignant affections, as it does wrath (*ton thymon*); for it conquers even this.

In this second passage, the Evil Eye (*baskania*) is again a final vice concluding another list of five vices, these denoted as violent affections. The Evil Eye, like all these violent and malignant emotions, is averted or overcome by reasoning and temperate understanding.

The Evil Eye, these pair of passages show, was believed to involve an internal human disposition—a thought consistent with the notion that the Evil Eye conveys a disposition arising in the human heart. It communicatess an immoderate and violent emotion that could nevertheless be brought under control through the exercise of reason and temperate understanding. Translations of *baskania* as "malice" (RSV) or "backbiting" (Townsend in Charles, *APOT* 1913 2:668, 669) fail to indicate the presence here of the standard Greek term for Evil Eye. The Evil Eye appears again in a biblical list of vices in Mark 7:21–22, where its internal origin (the heart, 7:21) also is stressed. The inclusion of the Evil Eye in these vice lists recalls the verdict of Sir 14:6 and 31:13 that the Evil Eye ranks first among all forms of wickedness.

Epistle of Jeremiah 69/70

This searing Israelite indictment of pagan idolatry and the mute lifelessness of idols contains the only explicit biblical reference to an apotropaic designed to ward off the Evil Eye (*prosbaskanion*, v. 69 LXX; v. 70 RSV). Purporting to be the copy of a letter written by the prophet Jeremiah to Judahites exiled in Babylon (597 BCE), it was likely composed around 317 BCE or later as a warning against Israelite attraction to foreign cults. Toward the conclusion of the address (vv. 69–72/70–73) a comparison is made between impotent heathen idols and an ineffective anti-Evil Eye apotropaic in a cucumber bed, a thorn bush on which every bird sits, and a corpse that is cast out into the darkness. Verse 69/70 reads:

> Like an *anti-Evil Eye apotropaic* (*probaskanion*) in a cucumber
>   bed that provides no protection,
>   so are their [non-Israelites] gods of wood, overlaid with
>   gold and silver.[161]

---

161. Ep Jer 69/70: *Hôsper gar en sikuêratôi probaskanion ouden phylasson ouden, houtôs hoi theoi autôn eisin xulinoi kai perichrusoi kai periarguroi.*

The critique of idols echoes that of Jer 10:1–16. Jeremiah 10 LXX, however, lacks an equivalent of the specific words of Ep Jer 69/70.[162]

The Greek term *prosbaskanion* denotes an anti-Evil Eye amulet. The noun belongs to the *bask-* (Evil Eye) family of terms, which occurs frequently in the LXX and the Greco-Roman world. Like the simplex form *baskánion,* meaning "anti-Evil Eye amulet" (Aristophanes, *Frag.* 592; Strabo, *Geog.* 16.4.17), the composite form *to probaskánion* also denotes an amulet or apotropaic designed to ward off an envious Evil Eye.[163] The grammarian Phrynichus Arabius of Bithynia (second century CE) notes the equivalency of terms and the identical functions they depict:

> *Baskánion,* or as the uneducated say, "*probaskánion*," is a human-like object, but varying a bit from human form, that artisans hang in their workshop so that their products are not damaged by the Evil Eye (*baskainesthai*). (*Praeparatio sophistica* 53.6)[164]

The reference in our text is not to an amulet worn on a person but to an apotropaic conventionally erected by owners in their gardens and fields to protect the crops from damage by the envious Evil Eyes of passers-by. Crops in the field were believed as vulnerable to the Evil Eye as children, horses, and cattle.[165] Roman domestic gardens, Pliny recounts, because of their quasi-sacred nature, were carefully protected by apotropaics (*satyrica signa*) against the "Evil-Eying of the envious" (Pliny, *NH* 19.19.50). These *satyrica signa* were grotesque figures resembling lustful Satyrs that displayed an exposed phallus serving like a *fascinum* (Latin for *baskanon*). They frightened away the Evil Eye, it was thought, like scarecrows scattered the birds in the field. At Pompeii, the garden of a Roman villa also was protected by apotropaic images of a Gorgo and the blue "eyes" of a peacock's tail.[166] Centuries

162. The Hebrew of Jer 10:5 reads: "They [i.e. the idols of the nations] are like scarecrows (*tomer*) in a cucumber field, and they cannot speak; they have to be carried, for they cannot walk. Do not be afraid of them, for they cannot do evil, neither is it in them to do good." The Greek of Jer 10 LXX varies from the Hebrew. Verses 6–8 MT are absent in the Greek and v. 9 MT is interposed between v. 5a and v. 5b. V. 5 LXX reads "They will set them up and they will not be moved (v. 5a); v. 5b reads: They must be carried [by others], for they cannot ride themselves. Do not be afraid of them, for they cannot do evil; and there is no good in them."

163. See Plutarch, *Quaest. Conv.* 5.7.3, *Mor.* 681F; BGU 3.954.9 (6th century CE). On *baskanon, baskanion, probaskanion* see Vol. 2, pp. 13-23, 23-38. On the Evil Eye in the rabbinic tradition see Vol. 4, chap. 1; and Ulmer 1994:33–61.

164. Julius Pollux (*Onom.* 7.108) uses the Latin equivalent to *baskania/probaskania,* namely *fascina* (plural of *fascinum*), in describing the anti-Evil Eye apotropaics protecting metalworkers' forges and products.

165. See Aulus Gellius, *Attic Nights* 9.4.

166. See Vol. 2.

later, Augustine observed and criticized the continued Roman practice of erecting *fascina* in fields to protect against fascination/the Evil Eye (*City of God* 7.21).[167] The point of the comparison in *Epistle of Jeremiah* is that human-made images of deities are no more effective in affording protection to humans than is an anti-Evil Eye apotropaic that cannot defend the crops of the field. The translation "scarecrow" (RSV)[168] fails to indicate that the apotropaic was employed to protect against the Evil Eye, but suggests to modern readers a straw-stuffed figure used to drive away birds.

The Vulgate incorporates the *Epistle of Jeremiah* in the book of Baruch as its sixth chapter. Baruch was the secretary of Jeremiah (Jer 32:12; 36:4). Verse 69 reads:

> For as a frightful thing (*formido*) in a garden of cucumbers
>   guards nothing,
>   so are their gods of wood, and of silver, and laid over with
>   gold.[169]

The noun *formido*, translating the LXX term *probaskanion*, is not a term for "Evil Eye." It can mean "fear, terror, dread" and in an extended sense, "frightful thing," "that which produces fear" (Virgil, *Georgica* 4.468) and then in this sense a frightening artifact made of different colored feathers.[170] It thus expresses the frightening aspect of the apotropaic device. Certain anti-Evil Eye apotropaics, Plutarch noted, did have such a strange aspect. "Their strange look attracts the attention of the [Evil] Eye (*tês opseôs*), so that it exerts less pressure upon its victims" (*Quaest. Conv.* 5.7.3, *Mor.* 681F). This might suggest that the amulet in the cucumber field was thought to work not by deflecting glances from envious Evil Eyes but by attracting those glances to itself and away from the succulent cucumbers.

Implicit References to the Evil Eye in the Old Testament?

Thus far we have considered *explicit* references in the Old Testament to the Evil Eye that employ standard Evil Eye terminology. There are, however, further texts that may include implicit references to the Evil Eye. Instances where mention is made of *looking* with envy, hostile intent, or greed may constitute implicit references to the Evil Eye, such as 1 Sam 18:9; 1 Sam 2:29;

167. On such apotropaics see Vol. 2, 217–64.

168. See also Ball in *APOT* 1:610.

169. *Nam, sicut cucumerario formido nihil custodit, ita sunt dii illorum lignei et argentei et inaurati.*

170. Seneca, *De ira* 2.12; Virgil, *Aeneid* 12.750; Horace, *Serm.* 1.8.4.

and 1 Sam 2:32.[171] This is likely in the case of 1 Sam 18:9, but less certain in the case of 1 Sam 2:29 and 2:32.

1 SAMUEL/1 KINGDOMS 18:8–9

Following David's heroic slaying of the Philistine warrior giant Goliath and Israel's slaughter of the Philistines (1 Sam 17:1–54), King Saul appointed diminutive David chief over the men of war (18:5). Saul and David returned from the battle and were met with great jubilation by women from all the Israelite cities (1 Sam/1 Kgdm 18:6). The throng sang out, "Saul has slain his thousands, and David his ten thousands" (18:7) Saul was alarmed and greatly displeased at this public acclaim of the "nobody" David and looked enviously at David, his young rival, for receiving greater praise than he, the king, had enjoyed:

> And Saul was very angry, and this saying ["Saul has slain his thousands, and David, his ten thousands"] displeased him (Heb lit., "it was evil in his eye").[172] He said, "They have ascribed to David ten thousands, but to me they have ascribed only thousands; all he now lacks is the kingdom!" And Saul enviously (Evil)-Eyed (*ŏyén*) David from that day on. (18:8–9)

The Hebrew participle *ŏyén*, a paronym of the noun *'ayin* ("eye"), means, literally, "looking at," "eyeing" (someone), with the participle indicating an ongoing action.[173] Occurring only here in the Hebrew Bible, the context makes it clear that the verb implies "looking with envious hostility at," "envious Evil-Eyeing."[174] Saul's action here is a classic case of envy conveyed by looking with an Evil Eye. Regarding the subordinate youth David as a rival for popular acclaim, Saul resents that the upstart has received greater praise than the king himself, with David's gain, he assumes, resulting in his own loss. Enviously Evil-Eyeing David, Saul wants both David and his praise destroyed. The following day, the narrative continues, Saul's

171. Casting an Evil Eye by looking menacingly at, or "overlooking," someone is a practice still known in modern time, as is indicated by the Scottish Highland expression for injuring with the Evil Eye—"to overlook"; see MacLagen 1902, *passim*.

172. For the idiom see also Num 32:13, Prov 24:16; Jer 52:2 etc.

173. Kittel, editor of the *Biblia Hebraica*, proposed reading *me 'ŏyén* here, in consonance with the same proposed reading at 1 Sam 2:29, 32.

174. Against Yamauchi (1983:189) who states that the verb employed here "simply means 'eyed' (so the RSV) or 'kept his eye upon' with no implication of envy or an Evil Eye.

malice remains. Overcome by an evil spirit, he tries to spear David to death (1 Sam 18:11).

The LXX follows the HT closely and renders the Hebrew particple *'ōyēn* with the Greek participial phrase *ēn hypoblepomenos*, literally, "was looking up from under [the eyebrows]," or, more colloquially, "was looking askance at." The expression is a synonym for "looking at with an Evil Eye" and indicates the *mode* of looking, i.e. askance.[175] The verb occurs again in Sir 37:10 ("one who looks askance at you with an Evil Eye," v. 10a) paralleling "those who envy (*zēlountôn*) you" (v. 10b). The association of looking askance with an Evil Eye and being envious in Sir 37:10 suggests the same association here, and this fits the context well. Saul's hostile looking askance involves an Evil Eye filled with envy directed against David. The Vulgate renders: "And Saul did not look on David with a good eye (lit., "good eyes") from that day and forward."[176] The formulation "not with a good eye" is identical in sense with the formulation "with an Evil Eye." KJV, JPS, RSV read: "And Saul *eyed* David," without indicating that the eyeing was envious and with malicious intent and hence the action of an Evil Eye. An Italian version (*La Sacra Bibbia*), on the other hand, makes the reference to Saul's Evil-Eyeing explicit: "*[Saul] guardò Davide di mal occhio*" ("Saul looked at David with an Evil Eye").

The dynamic here is complex. On the one hand, Saul's envies and resents David's receiving greater acclaim and counts this as his own loss of prestige (along the lines of limited good thinking). This sense of vulnerability to possible loss and the urge to preserve his rule is the emotion of jealousy. Here is a dramatic instance of a character torn by both emotions, though it is a case where envy and a hostile Evil Eye dominate the interaction.[177]

Two other passages of 1 Samuel/1 Kingdoms (2:29 and 2:32) *may* involve implicit references to the Evil Eye. The Hebrew wording of the texts, however, is not certain. The general context involves a divine condemnation of the priestly house of Eli (1 Sam 2:27–36). A man of God who had come to Eli recounts what the Lord had said concerning the house of Eli and how privileged it was: "And I chose him [Aaron, Eli's ancestor] out of all the tribes of Israel to be my priest, to go up to my altar, to burn incense, to wear an ephod before me; and I gave to the house of your father my offerings by fire from the people of Israel" (v. 28). A censuring question from the Lord

---

175. Compare the German *Scheelauge* ("squint-eye," "wandering eye") and *scheelen* ("to have/to look with a wandering eye," "look askance").

176. *Non rectis ergo oculis Saul adspiciebat David a die illa et deinceps.*

177. I am grateful to Prof. Gary Stansell for helping me see this complex dynamic.

then follows (v. 29), but there is disagreement in the Hebrew and Greek texts as to its wording and sense. One version of the Hebrew reads:

> Why do you kick at my sacrifice and at my offering, which I have commanded in my habitation, and honor your sons above me by fattening yourselves with the choicest parts of every offering of my people Israel?

The KJV follows this Hebrew text and translates: "Wherefore *kick ye* at my sacrifice and at mine offering . . ." (so also JPS). The sense of this action, however, is unclear and its wording is at variance with the LXX. The LXX reads:

> Why *have you looked with a shameless eye* (*ti epeblepsas. . . anaidei ophthalmôi*) on my incense offering and my meat offering, and have honored your sons above me, so that they bless themselves with the first fruits of every sacrifice of Israel before me?

Rudolf Kittel, editor of the *Biblia Hebraica*, proposed emending the Hebrew of the Leningrad Codex to accord with the Greek text of the LXX; in place of *tib'atu* ("kick") he proposed reading *tebbit* ("look"), and, in place of *ma'ôn* ("habitation"), reading *me'oyen* ("eyeing"). This would likewise be in accord with manuscripts of the Dead Sea Scrolls. The RSV and NRSV accept this emendation and translate v. 29:

> Why then *look with greedy eye at* my sacrifices and my offerings which I commanded. . . ?

In regard to the Hebrew of 1 Sam/1Kgdms 2:32, KJV (and JPS) accept the unaltered Hebrew text and translate:

> And *thou shalt see an enemy in my habitation*, in all the wealth which God shall give Israel.[178]

RSV and NRSV, on the other hand, accept Kittel's proposal for reading not *ma'ôn* ("habitation") but rather *me'oyen* ("eyeing") (in accord with some LXX and Dead Sea Scroll mss) and translate:

> Then in distress *you will look with envious eye* (NRSV: "*with greedy eye*") *on* all the prosperity which shall be bestowed upon Israel.[179]

178. JPS: "And *thou shalt behold a rival* in my habitation in all the good which shall be done to Israel."
179. Translating the Hebrew *tser* not "enemy" (KJV, JPS) but "in distress."

The LXX, along with emended Hebrew readings, may well imply looking with an Evil Eye. Looking with a "shameless eye" may imply an Evil Eye, but this would be a singular instance where "shameless eye" is equivalent to "Evil Eye."[180] The RSV translations (*look with greedy eye on*, v. 29 [so also NRSV at v. 32]; *look with envious eye on*, v. 32 [so also ESV]) draw closer to features of the Evil Eye complex. The sense of either "envious" or "greedy" eye would fit the context and be synonymous with looking with an Evil Eye, since envy and greed are both associated with an Evil Eye. Looking with an Evil Eye filled with *envy* would entail wishing the sacrifices and the prosperity destroyed. Looking with an Evil Eye filled with *greed* would involve Eli's desiring the sacrifices and prosperity for his own family alone.[181]

Other Old Testament passages likewise speaking of envy, though with no explicit mention of the eye or looking, may also imply reference to Evil Eye malice. This would include instances where words for "envy" and its family of terms appears.[182] This is the case because of the regular close association of the Evil Eye and envy, as indicated not only in the Greco-Roman sources but in the Old Testament as well. Envy is not only often paired with the Evil Eye; it also shares features in common with the Evil Eye. Envy, like the Evil Eye, is thought to arise in the heart: "Let not your heart envy sinners . . ." (Prov 23:17). Envy, also like the Evil Eye, is said to make the bones rot (Prov 14:30). Solomon, describing "what wisdom is" (Wis 6:22) states, "neither will I travel in the company of sickly envy (*phthonôi tetêkoti*), for it [envy] does not associate with wisdom." Inasmuch as the Evil Eye also is dissociated from wisdom (Sir 18:18), the reference to "sickly wisdom" could also evoke thought of an Evil Eye. As part of the *phthonos* family of words, the adjective *aphthonos* ("without envy," "generous," 3 Macc 5:2; 4 Macc 3:10) and the adverb *aphthonôs* ("without grudging," Wis 7:13) designate objects or actions *opposite* to the Evil Eye, inasmuch as the Evil Eye is linked with ungenerosity, stinginess, and giving begrudgingly.[183]

The phrase *phthonos kai zêlos* in 1 Macc 8:16 could also involve an implied reference to the Evil Eye. A flattering description of the Roman people states that "they all heed one man, and there is no *phthonos* and *zêlos* among

180. Sir 26:11 speaks of a headstrong daughter having a "shameless eye."

181. The passage also mentions the familiar association of eyes and heart (1 Sam 2:33); for the association of "haughty eyes/look" and "arrogant heart," see Ps 101:5; Prov 21:4.

182. Heb: *qanah*; Greek LXX: *zêlos: antizêlos, zêloô, zêlos, zêlotypeô zêlotypia, zêlôsis, zêlôtês, zêlôtos, homozêlia, parazêloô, parazêlôsis; phthoneô, phthoneros, phthonos*; see also *aphthonos* (3 Macc 5:2; 4 Macc 3:10); *aphthonôs* (Wis 7:13).

183. On *aphthonos*, see also Vol. 2.

them." *Zêlos* often was paired with *phthonos*[184] or was used interchangeably with *phthonos* in the same context.[185] *The Testament of Simeon* is an especially good example.[186] The combination of terms could identify two related but different emotions ("envy" and "jealousy"), as the RSV translates.[187] Or the combination could constitute a hendiadys in which two terms denote one phenomenon—in this case the disposition of envy.[188] Finally, *phthonos* could be a *substitution* for *baskania*, as occasionally occurs,[189] and the phrase is then best translated as "Evil Eye or envy."[190] The Old Testament contains numerous references to envious persons or episodes of envy, some of which were understood to involve the Evil Eye. A Christian writing of the first century CE, the first letter of Clement of Rome lists seven examples of envy (and Evil Eye) (*zêlos kai phthonos*) in *1 Clem.* 4:1–13: Cain envious of his younger brother Abel (*1 Clem.* 4:1–7; Gen 4:3–8); Esau envious of his younger brother Jacob (*1 Clem.* 4:8; Gen 38:22); the sons of Jacob envious of their younger favored brother Joseph (*1 Clem.* 4:9; Gen 37:11, *ezêlôsan*);[191] Moses fleeing from Pharoah and from what Clement takes to be the envy of his kinsmen (*1 Clem.* 4:10; Exod 2:11–15); Aaron and Miriam, understood by Clement as feeling envy (*zêlos*) toward Moses (*1 Clem.* 4:11; Num 12:1–14); Dathan and Abiram regarded by Clement as rebelling against Moses out of envy and consequently punished with death (*1 Clem.* 4:12; Num 16:1–35; Ps 106:16–18; Sir 45:18); and David envied not only by strangers but even by King Saul for David's greater popular acclaim (*1 Clem.* 4:13; cf. 1 Sam 18:6–8).

184. See, e.g., Democritus, Frag. B191 (ed. Diels and Kranz, FVS, 68 B 191); Lysias, *Funeral Oration* 48; Plato *Philebus* 47e, 50c; *Laws* 3.679C (*zêloi te kai phthonoi*); 1 Macc 8:16; *T. Sim.* 4:5; *1 Clem.* 3:2; 4:7, 13; 5:2.

185. Plato, *Symposium.* 213d; *Laws* 3.679c; Epictetus, *Disc.* 3.22.61; Plutarch, *De frat., Mor.* 485D, E; *De cap., Mor.* 86C; 91B; *De tranq. Mor.* 470C; 471A.

186. For *zêl*- terms see: 2:6, 7; 4:5, 9; for *phthon*- terms see 2:13, 14; 3:1, 2, 3, 4, 6; 4:5, 7; 6:2. See also *T. Dan* 1:6 and 2:5; *T. Gad* 4:5; 5:3; 7:4; *T. Benj.* 4:4; and *1 Clem.* 3:1–6:4.

187. A *distinction* of terms would be more likely if they were joined by "or" rather than "and."

188. See Democritus, fragment B191; Lysias, *Funeral Oration* 48; Plato, *Philebus* 47e, 50c; *Laws* 3.679c; *T. Sim.* 4:5; *1 Clem.* 3:2; 4:7; 5:2; cf. 4:14

189. See above, pp. 31, 33, 38, 40-41, 59 and Rakoczy 1996:41, 61–62, 83 n. 204; Matantseva 1994 (as illustrated on amulets).

190. For examples of the combination of terms of the *phthonos* and *baskania* word families, see also Dio Chrysostom, *Orat.* 45.53 (*phthonos kai baskania*); *Orat.* 77/78.15.6 (*phthonos kai to baskainein*); also *phthonos kai zêlotypia* (*Orat.* 44.8.6; 61.13.1; 61.15.6; 77/78.2.9;77/78.14.4); *zêlotypeô kai phthoneô* (*Orat.* 74.8.6); *zêloô* and *baskainô* (*Orat.* 77/78.37.7).

191. For the rabbinic tradition on Joseph enviously Evil-Eyed by his brothers, see Midrash *Genesis Rabbah* 84.10 and further texts in Vol. 4, chap. 1.

Other notorious cases of envy in the Old Testament include Sarah's envy and "browbeating" of Hagar (Gen 16:1–6).[192] According to the Jewish sages, Sarah cast on Hagar an envious Evil Eye (*Genesis Rabbah* 45.5). The matriarch Rachel likewise envied her co-wife Leah for her ability to bear children (Gen 30:1). The Philistines envied Isaac for his great possessions (Gen 26:14). Joshua envied Moses for selecting prophets (Num 11:29). Hannah envied her rival, Peninah, the other wife of Elkanah, father of Samuel (1 Sam 1:1–8), though envy is not explicitly mentioned. The *Wisdom of Solomon* traces the appearance of envy back to the Garden of Eden and the devil's envy of Adam and Eve: "God created the human for incorruption and made the human in the image of God's own eternity. But through the envy of the devil death entered the world, and those who belong to his party experience it" (Wis 2:23–24), probably referring to the deaths of Adam and Eve (Gen 3:19).

At least two of these cases connected envy with the Evil Eye. The discussion above of Saul's envy of David indicated how Saul's envious "eyeing" of David was a reference to the envious Evil Eye. As Saul's "eyeing" of David illustrates the connection of ocular activity, *looking* (with an Evil Eye), and *envy*, so other biblical episodes involving envy might also might imply the operation of an envious Evil Eye, though the term Evil Eye itself is not mentioned. In the case of the patriarch Joseph who was envied by his brothers, Jewish tradition has regarded Joseph as a hero who survived the envious Evil Eye and homicidal efforts of his brothers, favored as he was, not just by his father Jacob, but also by God. The *Testaments of the Twelve Patriarchs,* discussed in further detail below, recall Joseph's survival of sibling envy. The *Testament of Joseph* imagines Joseph's point of view concerning the envy and murderous intent of his brothers ("In my life I have seen envy (*ton phthonon*) and death . . . my brothers wanted to kill me, but the God of my fathers preserved me" (*T. Jos.* 1:3–4). The *Testament of Simeon* treats the malice of envy extensively. "I envied (*ezēlōsa*) Joseph," Simeon confesses, "because my father loved him more than all the rest of us" (*T. Sim.* 2:6). "The spirit of envy (*zēlou*) blinded my mind (*T. Sim.* 2:13).[193] Both *T. Jos.* and *T. Sim.* were assigned the title *Peri phthonou* ("Concerning Envy") in some textual manuscripts. The related *Testament of Issachar,* concerning another of Jacob's sons, expressly links envy and the Evil Eye. Regarding a person of integrity it is stated, "No envy (*zēlos*) will penetrate his thinking; no Evil Eye

---

192. A rabbinic reading of Gen 16:6 interprets this action as envy; see Ginsberg 1961 1:239.

193. For envy in *T. Sim.*, see also 2:14 3:1, 3, 4, 6; 4:5, 6, 7, 9; 6:2.

(*baskanos* or *baskania*) will dissipate his soul" (*T. Iss.* 4:5), with *T. Iss.* 4:6 also speaking of his making no room for "Evil Eyes" (*ophthalmous ponêrous*).

Before leaving this Israelite tradition concerning Joseph and his brothers and the envious Evil Eye, we might recall the continued prominence attributed Joseph as a successful survivor of the Evil Eye in post-biblical Jewish tradition and lore.[194] The rabbis taught, the Babylonian Talmud records, that Joseph survived the envious Evil Eye of his brothers and that this protection extended to all his descendents.[195] The apotropaic power of certain manual gestures against the Evil Eye is also traced to Joseph's survival of the envious Evil Eye of his brothers.[196] Both Joseph traditions are discussed in detail in Vol. 4, chap. 1.

King Solomon, whose extraordinary wisdom and special knowledge is celebrated in the Bible and legend, is not associated directly with the Evil Eye in the Bible. Proverbs mentioning the Evil Eye (Prov 23:6, 28:22) were attributed to Solomon (Prov 25:1). This attribution, as well as the *Wisdom of Solomon*, which also mentions the Evil Eye (Wis 4:12), transmit conventional wisdom rather than tradition peculiar to Solomon. In Josephus's time (first century CE) Solomon's great knowledge (1 Kgs 4:29–34; Wis 7:7–22) was thought to include astrological and occult lore, power over demons, and the art of healing.

> God granted him knowledge of the art used against demons for the benefit and healing of humans. He also composed incantations by which illnesses are relieved, and left behind forms of exorcisms with which those possessed by demons drive them out, never to return. (Josephus, *Ant.* 8.45, LCL)[197]

Accordingly, he was attributed a major role in the combating of evil forces and dangerous demons, including the Evil Eye and Evil Eye demon; he appears frequently on anti-Evil Eye amulets.[198] The *Testament of Solomon*, one of the several writings ascribed to Solomon, contains an important reference

194. See Billerbeck 1926 1:834; Shrire 1982:114; Ulmer 1991:351–52. On Joseph as the object of his brothers' envy in Christian memory see Acts 7:9–15. On the figure of Joseph in post-biblical Jewish history see Niehoff 1992.

195. See *b. B.M.* 84a; cf. *b. Ber.* 20a; *b. B.B.* 118; cf. also *Gen. Rab.* 97.

196. See *b. B.M.* 84a; cf. *b. Ber.* 20a, 55b; *b. B.B.* 118; cf. also *Gen. Rab.* 97. See also Blau 1907 5:280; Ulmer 1991:352; 1994:155. See also Blau 1907 5:280; Ulmer 1991:352; 1994:155.

197. See Josephus, *Ant.* 8.42–49 and Duling 1975. On Josephus's portrait of Solomon, see Feldmann 1976. On the occult in Josephus see M. Smith 1987.

198. On this aspect of Solomon and the powerful "Seal of Solomon" against the Evil Eye, see Vol. 4, chap. 1.

to the Evil Eye and is discussed below under the Old Testament Parabiblical Literature.

The creature named "basilisk" (LXX: *basiliskos*, LXX Ps 90:13 [MT 91:13]; Isa 59:5 [Heb: *tsiphoni*]),[199] while not directly associated with an Evil Eye, perhaps deserves mention because of the noxious power it was thought to have in common with an Evil Eye. It is mentioned in several OT verses (Ps 90/91:13; Prov 23:32; Isa 11:8, 14:29; 59:5). Modern translations prefer "serpent," "adder," "viper" etc.; but JPS renders "basilisk" at Isa 11:8, 14:29; 59:5). As noted in Vol. 2 (with illustration), this serpent-like creature was thought to emit noxious emanations that were lethal. Its gaze, breath, smell and touch could wither and destroy whatever it strikes, according to Pliny (*NH* 8.33.78; 29.19.66). It thus was held to inflict damage in a fashion simi-

Illus. 5

Sketch of a mythological basilisk, African style (from Seligmann 1910, 1:113, fig.)

lar to the noxious emanations of an Evil Eye. Centuries later Shakespeare still knew of the basilisk. In the play *Richard III*, the widow Lady Anne is complimented on her eyes by Richard, her husband's brother and muderer. She replies that she wishes her eyes were those of a basilisk so that she might kill him: "Would they were basilisk's, to strike thee dead!" (*Richard III*, Act 1, Scene 2).[200]

ADDITIONAL IMPLICIT OLD TESTAMENT REFERENCES TO THE EVIL EYE?

Old Testament texts making implicit rather than explicit mention of the Evil Eye include 1 Sam 18:9; 2:29; and 2:32; and Sir 31:14 and 23–24. Additional *implicit allusions to* Evil Eye belief and practice may be suspected in texts referring to dispositions associated with an Evil Eye such as envy. The Jewish rabbis regarded some instances of envy as cases of Evil Eye affliction. Envious Sarah, according to the rabbinic sages, cast the Evil Eye on Hagar and caused her to miscarry (*Gen. Rab.* 45.5). With her Evil Eye, they also said, she struck Hagar's child Ishmael in the desert with thirst, fever, and stomach cramps (*Gen. Rab.* 53.13). Joseph's envious brothers cast an Evil Eye on Joseph (*Gen. Rab.* 84.10), as Og the giant did on Jacob (*b. Ber.* 54b).

199. The Hebrew *tsephe'* derives from the obsolete root *tsapha'*, "to hiss."

200. See also *Cymbeline* Act 2, scene 4; *Henry VI*, Part 3, Act 3, Scene 2.

Manifestations of other dispositions such as miserliness, the lack of generosity and the begrudging of hospitality, or ocular actions of looking intently, looking askance at, or looking menacingly at someone also were linked by the rabbis to an Evil Eye. This is discussed in Vol. 4, chap. 1 on post-biblical Israel. Those who possess "a good eye, a humble spirit, and a lowly soul" are said to be the disciples of Abraham, in contrast to the followers of Balaam who are marked by "an Evil Eye, a proud spirit, and a haughty soul" (*m. Avot* 5:19). Rabbinic tradition also held that an Evil Eye caused the breaking of the first tablets of the Law (*Num. Rab.* 12.4) and the death of Daniel's three companions (*b. Sanh.* 93a).[201] The apotropaic amulets mentioned in Judg 8:21, 26 and Isa 3:20 (lunar crescents) and the eyes spoken of in Ezek 1:18 (cf. Rev 4:8) concern images which customarily were used to thwart the Evil Eye.[202] Whether or not an Evil Eye was originally implied in such cases cannot be determined, so that this remains only a possibility.

The mention of the Evil Eye (*baskania*) in conjunction with "roving desire" (*rhembasmos epithymias*) in Wis 4:12 relates an Evil Eye with an intense desire for what belongs to another, i.e. covetousness. Could this suggest that the proscription of covetousness (*epithymia*) in the Decalogue (Exod 20:17; Deut 5:21) may have been regarded by the popular mind as a proscription of an Evil Eye as well? Commenting on the tenth commandment in his 1946 book, *The Ten Commandments*, Joseph Lewis claims, with no supporting evidence, that "[i]n many languages, as well as in Biblical use, the words 'coveting,' 'enviousness,' 'sickness,' 'death' and the 'evil eye' are synonymous."[203] The proscription of covetousness in commandments nine and ten, he suggests, therefore included condemnation of an Evil Eye as well. Despite Lewis's extensive comment on the Evil Eye, his generalization remains unsupported and unconvincing speculation. The difference in the social dynamics of coveting (*epithymia*, *epithymeô*) and Evil Eyeing make this equation unlikely, as well as the fact that the Bible and ancient Evil Eye lore make no clear explicit association of Evil Eye and covetousness. *Epithymia* ("coveting," "covetousness") is the intense desire or craving to acquire something for oneself. In contrast to envy (and the Evil Eye), *epithymia*/coveting does not entail distress at the good fortune and possessions of others with the wish for their destruction, but rather the desire to *have these possessions for oneself*. Coveting aims at *gain for oneself*. Envy and an Evil Eye, by contrast, seek *loss for others*. The focus of *epithymia*, like

---

201. On the rabbinic tradition see Vol. 4, chap. 1.

202. Blau 1898:86–93; 1907:546–50; Koetting 1954:474–76.

203. Lewis 1946, E-text conversion and critical editing copyrighted by Cliff Walker 1998.

jealousy, is advantage to the *self*, rather than the dispossessing of *another*. *Epithymia* appears only rarely with "Evil Eye" (Philo, *Cher.* 33 is one singular instance) but is not paired with Evil Eye and never serves as a synonym for *bask-* terms or *ophthalmos ponêros*. It is likely that the ninth and tenth commandments neither implied a proscription of an Evil Eye nor were understood to do so.

Ecclesiastes 4:4–8 may contain "allusions to the evil eye," as Nili Wazana (2007) has proposed, but this is less than certain. The text reads:

> Then I saw that all toil and all skill in work come from a man's envy (Hebrew: *qanah*; LXX: *zêlos*) of his neighbor. This also is vanity and a striving after wind. A fool folds his hands and eats his own flesh . . . (A person who toils) . . . his eye/eyes is/are never satisfied with riches so that he never asks, "For whom am I toiling and depriving myself of pleasure?" This also is vanity and a striving after wind. (4:4–5, 8)

A literary inclusion demarcates Eccl 4:4–8 ("this also is vanity and a striving after wind," vv. 4, 8). In this unit, a tracing of toil and skill in work to a person's *envy* (*qanah/zêlos*) of his neighbor (v. 4) is joined by a reference to a fool who "eats his own flesh" (which could imply self-fascination, v. 5) and to one whose toil never ends while "his eye[204] is never satisfied with riches." This combination of *envy, wealth, self-destruction* (=self-fascination) and an *insatiable eye*[205] makes a reference to a greedy and self-destructive Evil Eyed person conceivable but not certain. The thought that "all toil and all skill in work" are driven by envy (4:4) makes an inclusive statement about human labor that extends far beyond the possession and exercise of an Evil Eye by some.[206]

Several articles by Zak Kotzé (2006, 2007a, 2007b, 2007c, 2007d, 2008, 2010) also are more speculative than cogent. In Gen 31:35 Kotzé claims to find a reference to an Evil Eye of Laban, Jacob's uncle (Kotzé 2006), though the conventional terminology for "Evil Eye" does not appear. The words on which Kotze concentrates (*'el yiher b'ene 'adoni*) are customarily translated, "Let not my lord be angry." A second article notes the ubiquity of Evil Eye belief and practice in the Ancient Near East and its frequent mention in

204. "Eye" (singular, LXX and many other mss) is preferable to plural "eyes" (HT).

205. Wazana (2007:700) adds solitude to his list of motifs; but this is not a regular feature of the Evil Eye belief complex.

206. Wazana (ibid.:697–89) mistakenly claims that "[t]his belief [in the Evil Eye] has left very few palpable traces in biblical literature" (ibid.:686). He proceeds, nevertheless, to cite as relevant several biblical texts (Deut 15:9; 28:54, 56; Prov 23:6–8; 28:22; and passages from Sirach). There seems to be confusion here as to what constitutes a reference to the Evil Eye or a "palpable trace" thereof.

the Hebrew Bible (Kotzé 2007). However, here Kotzé does not discuss the explicit conventional references to "Evil Eye" and fails to engage with the several articles treating the biblical references. He regards the Evil Eye as an instance of witchcraft and magic and then considers Prov 6:13; 10:10 (squinting of the eye/*qarats 'ayin*); in Pss 35:19; 141:4; Job 15:12; and 16:9 as references to the Evil Eye. He concludes that

> The evil eye seems to be a common theme in the wisdom litera-
> ture of the Hebrew Bible. Figurative expressions for the act of
> glaring present the eye as a magical organ with the power to do
> harm. In the Hebrew Bible the evil eye is most commonly en-
> countered as a witchcraft technique that was used in combina-
> tion with other magical gestures. The act is usually condemned
> and the corrupt nature of the possessor accentuated.[207]

The texts he cites, however, make no explicit mention of the Evil Eye and the biblical texts that do mention the Evil Eye explicitly are not brought into relation with these passages proposed by Kotzé. His view of the Evil Eye as something "magical" introduces a category not associated with the Evil Eye in the biblical texts. Kotzé also unconvincingly proposes that the Hebrew Bible speaks of YHWH having and exercising an Evil Eye (Kotzé 2008). Expressions of "setting the face against," or references to YHWH's eye in punitive or destructive contexts are posited as references to YHWH's Evil Eye. This, however, is inconsistent with the fact that there is no instance in the Bible where the conventional expressions for Evil Eye (*'ayin harah* or *r'' 'ayin*) are ever used of YHWH. Also undermining his theory is the fact that envy, so closely linked with the Evil Eye in the Bible and profane Greek sources, is never ascribed to YHWH; see Elliott 2007b, 2008.

Since iron, because of its magnetic properties, was regarded as a mys-
terious as well as powerful metal, iron amulets were worn as anti-Evil Eye protection.[208] The Kenites, a nomadic tribe of metalworkers in the land of Canaan, had a close relation to the Hebrews as early as in the thirteenth century BCE. They made their livelihood as metal craftsmen, inhabiting the country south of Tell Arad on the western slopes of the mineral-rich Wadi 'Arabah above Tamar (Num 24:21; Judg 1:16). If they are precursors of the modern Arab tribe, the Sleib, who also are nomadic smiths and who have a strong belief in the Evil Eye, the Kenites too may have been ancient transmitters of Evil Eye belief and practice.[209] There is, however, nothing in the biblical record to confirm this possibility.

207. Kotzé 2007:147

208. On iron warding off the Evil Eye see Vol. 2.

209. On the Kenites, their history, culture and possible relation to the Sleib, see

Might the account of Job's being struck blind for his miserliness (Job 22:5–11) imply that he had turned an Evil Eye against the needy? Job is accused of having behaved in a fashion described in Deut 15:7–11 as looking at the needy with an Evil Eye and withholding aid; cf. also Sir 14:8. Job is charged by the renown teacher Eliphaz:

> You have exacted pledges of your brothers for nothing,
>   and stripped the naked of their clothing.
> You have given no water to the weary to drink,
>   and you have withheld bread from the hungry . . .
> You have sent widows away empty,
>   and the arms of the fatherless were crushed. (Job 22:6–7, 9)

As a consequence, Eliphaz continues, "your light is darkened, so that you cannot see" (Job 22:11). Both Job's withholding of aid and his being struck blind are motifs associated with wielding an Evil Eye. Although a malevolent eye is not mentioned here, it may well have been implied in the narrative. When Job subsequently asserts the innocence of his behavior (31:1–40), he appears to respond directly to the charge of neglect of the needy (31:16–22):

> If I have withheld anything that the poor desired,
>   or have caused the eyes of the widow to fail,
> or have eaten my morsel alone,
>   and the fatherless has not eaten of it, . . .
> then let my shoulder blade fall from my shoulder,
>   and let my arm be broken from its socket. (vv. 16, 17, 22)

Again, no Evil Eye is explicitly mentioned, but could have been implied or assumed by listeners, given the thinking reflected in such texts as Deut 15:7–11; Sir 14:8; and Tobit 4:7, 16. The implication of Job 31:16b would be: I did not disdain and Evil-Eye the poor; no Evil Eye of mine caused the eyes of the widow to fail (as an Evil Eye is capable of doing; cf. Sir 18:18).[210]

Two further articles on the topic are similarly speculative but less than cogent. In the idiom contained in Ps 35:19, *qarats 'ayin*, usually rendered "sharpen the eye" (against someone), "wink the eye," Kotzé suspects reference to a malicious Evil Eye.[211] Noting that glaring/scowling causes a wound (Prov 10:10) and that squinting marks an evil person (Eccl 14:8), he proposes that in Ps 35:19 the idiom should be rendered, "those who hate me without

---

Mondriaan, 2011, esp. p. 417.

210. I am grateful to the perceptive eye of Prof. Gary Stansell for the suggestion of this possibility.

211. Kotzé 2010.

reason *cast their evil eye on* me."[212] In the phrase *kesuth 'enayim* "covering of the eyes," in Gen 20:16, Kotzé finds another implicit reference to the Evil Eye. His study finds it "reasonable to conclude that Abimelech's donation of a thousand pieces of silver to Abraham [upon his discovery that Sarah was Abraham's wife] was intended to have an apotropaic function against an Evil Eye, as suggested by his explanation that it will be a 'cover of eyes.'"[213] Kotzé is uncertain as to whether this donation was intended "as a protective gift for, or against, Sarah."[214] Once again the result is less than convincing. The Hebrew expression "covering of eyes" is not elsewhere associated with action of an Evil Eye or protection against an Evil Eye. Abimelek's gift, rather than having an "apotropaic function," is more likely to have served as an expiatory offering meant to exonerate Sarah from any whiff of sexual misconduct, as most commentators have long concluded and as acknowledged by Kotzé.[215] This previous interpretation is not shaken by Kotzé's conjectural and inconclusive study. Not every mention of eyes in the Bible is a reference to Evil Eyes. In his several studies on this topic Kotzé seems intent on discovering references to the Evil Eye in idiomatic expressions and texts that do not explicitly speak of an Evil Eye. This effort is admirable and welcome. However, sometimes a cigar, Herr Freud, is only a cigar.

A Good Eye

A "good eye" (*tov 'ayin / agathos ophthalmos*) is mentioned three times in the Old Testament: Prov 22:9 and Sir 35:8, 10. The passages refer not to a divine eye but to the eye of a generous human being. None mentions "good eye" in tandem with, or in contrast to, an Evil Eye. It is likely, however, that the Israelites thought of a good eye as an antithesis to an Evil Eye. This is suggested by Jesus's explicit combination and contrast of good eye and Evil Eye (Matt 6:22–23/Luke 11:34–35) and the similar contrast of good and Evil Eye in Israel's rabbinic tradition (*m. Avot* 2:9 and 5:19).

Proverb 22:9 (Heb) reads:

> He who has a *good eye* (*tov 'ayin*) will be blessed,
> for he shares his bread with the poor.

---

212. Kotzé 2010:145.
213. Kotzé 2011, esp. 494.
214. Ibid.
215. Ibid., 489–90.

"Good eye" in this context clearly denotes a generous eye and a person who gives liberally to the needy. The Septuagint interprets "good eye" (Heb) as *showing mercy* and *giving liberally*:

> He who shows mercy (*ho eleôn*) shall himself be maintained [by God],
>   for he has given from his own bread to the poor.
> He who gives liberally (*ho dôra dous*) secures victory and honor.
> (Prov 22:9 LXX)

A good eye is associated with an honorable person who is generous and merciful, especially to the poor.

LXX Sir 35:7–9 (RSV 35:8–10) also urges generosity in one's giving to God and twice speaks of acting with a "good eye" (*agathos ophthalmos*):

> 7 Glorify the Lord with a *good eye* (*en agathôi ophthalmôi*)
>   (RSV: "generously")
>   and do not stint the first fruits of your hands.
> 8 With every gift show a cheerful face,
>   and dedicate your tithe with gladness.
> 9 Give to the Most High as he has given [to you],
>   and [give] with a *good eye* (*en agathôi ophthalmôi*) as your
>   hand has found (RSV: "and as *generously* as your hand
>   has found"). (35:7–9)

The parallelisms involved in vv. 7 and 9 make it clear that "with a good eye" in each case has the sense of acting or giving *generously*, as rendered in the RSV.

Both Prov 22:9 and Sir 35:7, 9 regard having and acting with "a good eye" as being generous and liberal with one's possessions and gifts, both toward other humans and God. Thus the passages are consonant with the encouragement of generosity urged by such Evil Eye passages such as Deut 15:7–11; 28:53–57; and Tob 4:5–19, where the Evil Eye is generosity's opposite; see also Matt 20:1–15 and *m. Avot* 2:9; 5:13, 19. They are also consonant with the urging of generosity expressed in Sir 7:32–33:

> Stretch forth your hand to the poor,
>   so that your blessing may be complete.
> Give graciously to all the living,
>   and do not withhold kindness from the dead.

Thus both passages concerning the good eye should be seen as within the orbit of thinking concerning the Evil Eye, as underlying moral action consistent with God's will and as a contrast to the illiberal quality of an Evil Eye. Of course, the Evil Eye occasionally is weighted in the Greco-Roman world with negative moral connotation, especially when linked with, or connoting, envy and other forms of malice. In the Bible, however, this shameful and anti-social moral aspect of the human Evil Eye is especially underscored, often in connection with an appeal for generosity and liberality of heart, mind, spirit, and action.

References to the Evil Eye in Israel's parabiblical writings are consistent with the features and accents of Evil Eye belief and practice found in the biblical texts.

ISRAEL'S PARABIBLICAL LITERATURE

Pseudepigrapha of the Old Testament

Among the so-called Pseudepigrapha of the Old Testament, Israelite writings outside the canon and composed c. 200 BCE—200 C E, the *Testaments of the Twelve Patriarchs* and the *Testament of Solomon* contain explicit references to the Evil Eye. Possible allusions to the Evil Eye are contained in *Joseph and Asenath* and *2 Enoch*.

The Testaments of the Twelve Patriarchs

The *Testaments of the Twelve Patriarchs* make several references to the Evil Eye, both explicitly and implicitly. The composition is a pseudepigraphical work whose present form dates to the second or third century CE, but which includes earlier material datable to the beginning of the second century BCE. The individual testaments, each attributed to one of Jacob's twelve sons, are all inspired in their form (final words of instruction of the patriarch to his progeny before dying) by the account of Jacob's final blessing of his twelve sons in Genesis 49. As to content, the full Joseph saga from Genesis 37–50 lies in the background of these confessional and exhortatory speeches. Joseph was especially favored by his father Jacob and so targeted for slavery and death by his brothers. Their attempt to kill him, however, was trumped by God's rescue and elevation of Joseph and reconciliation of the patriarchal family. In the testaments, Joseph is remembered, with regret and repentance, as both innocent victim and successful survivor of the envious and hateful Evil Eye of his brothers (*T. Sim.* 1–2; *T. Dan* 1:6, 2:5; *T. Gad* 1–3; *T. Jos.* 1:3, 7; *T. Benj.* 3–6). The *Testaments* abound with over fifty references to envy and/or the Evil Eye.[216] Mention of envy, as is conventionally

216. For envy [*zêlos*] see *T. Reub.* 3:5, 6:4; *T. Sim.* 2:7, 4:5, 9; *T. Jud* 13:3; *T. Iss* 4:5; *T. Dan* 1:6; *T. Gad* 5:3; *T. Ash* 4:5; *zêloô: T. Reub.* 6:5; *T. Sim.* 2:6; *T. Levi* 6:3; *T. Iss.* 4:5;

the case, often implies the Evil Eye as well.²¹⁷ The most important text in this regard is the *Testament of Issachar*, which was given the title *Peri haplotêtos*, "Concerning Integrity." All the explicit references to the Evil Eye in the *T.12 Patr.* are found in this testament.²¹⁸

Toward the outset of his testament, Issachar provides an overview of his life (*T. Iss.* 3:1–8) in which he claims living with an integrity of heart that excludes envy and an Evil Eye. *Testament of Issachar* 3:1, 2, 3, 4, 6, 8 read in part:

1 I lived with rectitude of heart (*en euthytêti kardias*) . . .²¹⁹

2 I was living with integrity (*haplotêti*) . . .

3 I was no meddler in my dealings [with others]; I was *not envious and Evil-Eyed* (*phthoneros kai baskanos*) toward my neighbor

4 I lived my life with integrity of eyes (*en haplotêti ophthalmôn*)²²⁰

6 And my father rejoiced continuously at my integrity (*haplotêti*) . . .

7 God collaborated with my integrity (*haplotêti*) . . .

8 With integrity of heart (*en haplotêti kardias*) I supplied to the poor and oppressed everything from the good things of the earth.²²¹

The hendiadys, *envious and Evil-Eyed,* reflects the conventional proximity of these terms. Here both identify traits antithetical to living with integrity

---

T. Gad 7:4; *T. Benj.* 4:4; *phthoneros*: *T. Iss.* 3:3; *phthoneô*: *T. Sim* 2:14; 3:3, 6; *T. Gad* 3:3; 7:2; *T. Benj.* 4:4; *phthonos*: *T. Sim.* 2:13; 3:1, 2, 4, 6; 4:5, 7; 6:2; *T. Dan* 2:5; *T. Gad* 4:5; *T. Jos.* 1:3, 7; 10:3; *T. Benj.* 7:2, 5; 8:1. For Evil Eye, *baskania*: *T. Iss.* 4:5; *baskanos*: *T Iss.* 3:3, 4:5; *ophthalmos ponêros (in plural)*: *T. Iss.* 4:6; cf. *T. Dan* 2:5; see also *T. Benj.* 4:2 (*skoteinos ophthalmos*).

217. See Elliott 1994, esp. 68–73. The translation of the *T. 12 Patr.* by H. C. Kee in Charlesworth *OTP* 1993 1:775–828 is unreliable for our purposes. It often confuses envy with jealousy and mistranslates *zêlos* and its family of terms as "jealousy" rather than "envy." For example *T. Sim.* 2:6 ("was jealous" for *ezêlôsa*, despite 2:13–14, where Simeon speaks of his *envy* [*phthonou, phthonêsas*]of Joseph); *T. Gad* 7:4 (*mê zêlôsate* means "do not be envious," rather than "be jealous"; cf. *mê phthoneite*, 7:2 and *aphthonôs*, 7:6); *T. Sim.* 2:13 (means not "grudge," but "envy").

218. See *baskanos* (*T. Iss.* 3:3); *baskania* or *baskanos* (*T. Iss.* 4:5); *ophthalmos ponêros* in its plural form (*T. Iss.* 4:6).

219. Synonymous with "with integrity of heart" (*en haplotêti kardias*, 3:8; see also *haplotês* in 3:2, 6, 7)

220. Variant reading of the Codex Sinaiticus, omitted by Codex Alexandrinus.

221. In *T. Issachar*, *haplotês* appears in 3:2, 4, 6, 8; 4:1, 6; 5:1, 8; 6:1; 7:7; *haplous*, in 4:2. Elsewhere in the *T. 12 Patr.*: *haplotês* appears in *T. Reub.* 4:1; *T. Sim.* 4:5; *T. Levi* 13:1; *T. Benj.* 6:7. The phrases *en haplotêti kardias* (*T. Iss.* 3:8; 4:1) or *en haplotêti psychês* (*T. Iss.* 4:6a) and *en euthytêti kardias* (*T. Iss.* 4:6b) are used synonymously.

of heart or having integrity of eyes. The phrase "integrity of eyes," unique in the ancient literature, parallels "integrity of heart" and shows the conventionally assumed connection of eyes and heart. The final sentence describes the generous giving that is opposite to the Evil Eye behavior as described in several Old Testament texts previously discussed. The stress here on *haplotês* ("integrity," "singleness," "wholeness," "simplicity," "uprightness")[222] and its contrast to "Evil Eye" anticipate the similar contrast in Jesus's word concerning the Evil Eye (Matt 6:22–23/Luke 11:34).[223] *T. Iss.* 3:8 considers integrity as demonstrated by generosity to the poor and oppressed, and this appears to be the point of Jesus's Evil Eye saying as well.

As part of a following encouragement (*T. Iss.* 4:1–5:4) that his children likewise should "live with integrity of heart" (*en haplotêti kardias*, 4:1) Issachar states of a person of integrity (*ho haplous*, 4:2) that

> he is not greedy for gold, does not long for fancy foods, does not desire fine clothes (4:2) . . . but awaits only the will of God (4:3) . . . No envy (*zêlos*) pollutes his thinking, no Evil Eye malice dissipates his soul" (*ou baskania ektêkei tên psychên autou*, 4:5).[224] For he lives with integrity of soul (*en haplotêti psychês*) and views all things with rectitude of heart (*en euthytêti kardias*), making no room for Evil Eyes (*ophthalmous ponêrous*) (arising) from the world's error (4:6).

Two expressions for Evil Eye occur here: *baskania* and the plural form *ophthalmoi ponêroi*. Evil Eye and envy again are paralleled and contrasted to living with integrity of heart. Rectitude of heart (*en euthytêti kardias*) is parallel to and synonymous with integrity of soul (*en haplotêti psychês*) and integrity of heart (*en haplotêti kardias*). Envy and an Evil Eye are assumed to harm the envier and Evil-Eyed fascinator himself. Envy corrupts one's thinking and one's Evil Eye causes the dissipation and withering of one's own body, a notion we encountered previously in the Greco-Roman and Old Testament Evil Eye texts.[225] A person of integrity (*ho haplous*) is free of envy and an Evil Eye, and offers no welcome to others with Evil Eyes.

That this composition extolling integrity (*haplotês*) makes explicit mention of the Evil Eye is doubly significant. First, it shows how the Evil Eye and envy are considered antithetical to integrity and its implication of

222. See BDAG 104, sub *haplotês*; Spicq 1933.

223. On this saying of Jesus see below, chap. 2

224. Preferring *zêlos* to the verb *zêloi* (other Greek mss) and *baskania* to *baskanos* (other Greek mss) as constituting the most likely parallelism.

225. See above, pp. 40, 42–47 on Sir 14:5-7, and p. 81 regarding withering and self-injury.

generosity. Secondly, this opposition is important for our later understanding of Jesus's comment on the Evil Eye in Matt 6:22–23/Luke 11:34, where *haplous* (the adjective related to *haplotēs*) qualifies an eye (*ophthalmos haplous*) that Jesus contrasts to an Evil Eye (*ophthalmos ponēros*) and where an "integral eye" also implies a disposition of generosity.

Implicit references to the Evil Eye also are likely in the *Testaments of the Twelve Patriarchs*. Given the close association, combined mention, or synonymity of the Evil Eye and envy, and given their combined contrast to living with integrity, it is possible, if not likely. that where envy is mentioned, there the Evil Eye also is in mind, and where integrity (*haplotēs*, *haplous*) is urged, there envy and an Evil Eye are implicitly condemned.

The *topic of envy* is a major theme of the Testaments, is mentioned frequently,[226] and relates particularly to Jacob's sons's envy of their brother Joseph, their remorse, and his divine deliverance (Genesis 37; 39–52). The testaments emphasize that the vice provoking all the brothers to get rid of Joseph was their envy of him, "because father loved him more than the rest of us" (*T. Dan* 1:5). This envy lies in the background of all twelve testaments and is explict in many.

The *Testament of Simeon* was titled *Peri phthonou*, "Concerning Envy," and speaks often of the vice.[227] Simeon recounts his and his brothers' envy of Joseph and Joseph's divine deliverance.

> I envied (*ezēlōsa*) Joseph because my father loved him more than all the rest of us. I determined inwardly to destroy him, because the Prince of error and the spirit of envy (*zēlou*) blinded my mind so that I did not consider him as a brother. Nor did I spare Jacob, my father. But his God and the God of our fathers

---

226. For *phthonos* see *T. Sim.* 2:13; 3:1, 2, 4, 6; 4:5, 7; 6:2; *T. Dan* 2:5; *T. Gad* 4:5; *T. Jos.* 1:3, 7; 10:3; *T. Benj.* 7:2, 5; 8:1. For *phthoneō* see *T. Sim.* 2:14; 3:3, 6; *T. Gad* 3:3; 7:2; *T. Benj.* 4:4. For *phthoneros* see *T. Iss.* 3:3 (*phthoneros kai baskanos*); for *aphthonos* or *aphthonōs* see *T. Gad* 7:6.

For *zēlos* see *T. Reub.* 3:5; 6:4; *T. Sim.* 2:7 (*to pneuma tou zēlou*); 4:5, 9; *T. Jud.* 13:3 (*to pneuma tou zēlou*); *T. Iss.* 4:5 (some Greek mss); *T. Dan* 1:6; *T. Gad* 5:3; *T. Ash.* 4:5. For *zēloō* see *T. Reub.* 6:5 ("envy" or "vie with"); *T. Sim.* 2:6; *T. Iss.* 4:5 (some Greek mss, *ou zēloi . . . ou baskanos*); *T. Gad* 7:4 ("do not be envious"); *T. Benj.* 4:4 (*ou phthonei. . . ou zēloi*) . For *parazēlōsis* see *T Zeb.* 9:8. Both *phthonos* and *zēlos* word families mean "envy, to envy, to be envious," except for *T. Levi* 6:3 where *ezēlōsa* is best rendered "I was filled with zeal," concurring with Kee, *OTP* 1:790). *Pneuma tēs phthonou* (*T. Sim.* 4:7) and *pneuma tou zēlou* (*T. Sim.* 2:5; *T. Jud.* 13:3; *T. Dan* 1:6) both mean "spirit of envy."

227. See *T. Sim.* 2:6, 7, 13, 14; 3:1, 2, 3, 4, 6; 4:7 (*to pneuma tou phthonou* = *to pneuma tou zēlou* 2:7); 6:2; for *zēlos* see 2:7; 4:5, 9; for *zēloō* see 2:6. For the hendiadys *zēlos kai phthonos* see 4:5. *Phthonos* etc. and *zēlos* etc. are used synonymously.

sent his messenger and delivered him from my hands. (*T. Sim.* 2:6–8).[228]

Repenting of his envy that caused a withering of his hand, Simeon states,

> I prayed to the Lord God that my hand might be restored and that I might refrain from every defilement and (every act of) envy (*phthonou*) and from all folly, for I knew that I had contemplated an evil deed in the sight of the Lord and of Jacob, my father, on account of Joseph, my brother, in my envying (*phthonêsas*) him. (*T. Sim.* 2:13–14)

From this sibling envy he urges his descendents to take a lesson:

> Guard yourselves, therefore, my children, from all envy[229] and live with integrity of heart (*en haplotêti kardias*), so that God might shower your heads with grace, glory and blessing, as you have seen in Joseph . . . Each of you love his brothers with a good heart, and the spirit of envy (*to pneuma tou phthonou*) will depart from you. For this [spirit of envy] makes the soul savage and corrupts the body; it foments anger and war in the mind, excites the shedding of blood, drives the mind to distraction, arouses tumult in the soul, and trembling in the body. (*T. Sim.* 4:5, 7–8)

Dan likewise acknowledges that the "spirit of envy" (*pneuma tou zêlou*) drove him to envy his brother Joseph "because father loved him more than the rest of us" (*T. Dan* 1:5, 6). His hating heart aroused envy (*phthonon*) of his brother (*T. Dan* 2:5; cf. also *T. Gad* 3:3). Benjamin, with the brothers's envy of Joseph in mind, urges his progeny to "flee from envy (*phthonon*) and hatred of brothers" (*T. Benj.* 8:1). Joseph himself declares at the outset of his testament, "In my life I have seen envy (*ton phthonon*) and death . . . These, my brothers, hated me, but the Lord loved me" (*T. Jos.* 1:3, 4).[230]

Where one might be moved to envy, Gad advises an alternative course of action (*T. Gad* 7:1–7):

> If anyone prospers more than you, do not grieve, but rather pray for him that he may be completely prosperous. And if he

228. If "Prince of Error" (*ho archôn tês planes*) is an allusion to Satan, this is another example of the association of Satan and envy; see also Wis 2:24.

229. Taking *zêlou kai phthonou* as an hendiadys.

230. This *Testament of Joseph* was titled, like the *Testament of Simeon, Peri Phthonou*, "Concerning Envy," in some mss (Armenian), (Charles, *Patriarchs* 1908/1960:182, n. 1.). Other mss (Greek, Slavic) have the title *Peri sôphrosynês*, "Concerining Good Judgment."

is exalted still further, do not envy him (*mê phthoneite autôi*), but remember that all humanity dies. Offer praise to the Lord who provides good and beneficial things for all humanity . . . Even if someone becomes rich by evil scheming, as did Esau, your father's brother, do not be envious (*mê zêlôsate*), but wait for the Lord to set limits . . . One who is poor but who, free of envy (*aphthonôs*), praises the Lord for all things is richer than all . . . (7:1–3, 6)

In the *Testaments of the Twelve Patriarchs*, both *phthonos* and *zêlos* word families mean "envy, to envy, to be envious."[231] Envy is linked closely with the Evil Eye (*T. Iss.* 3:3; 4:5). Envy is also linked with anger and collaborates with hatred (*T. Dan* 2:2–5; *T. Gad* 4:5; *T. Jos.* 1:3–4). Joseph, Jacob's favored son, was a cardinal example of a victim of Evil-Eyed envy who was delivered by God.[232] Envy dominates one's mind, not permitting eating or drinking or doing anything good (*T. Sim.* 3:2). Envy "makes the soul savage and corrupts the body; it foments wrath and conflict in one's thinking; it arouses the shedding of blood, drives the mind to distraction, arouses tumult in the soul and trembling in the body" (*T. Sim.* 4:8). Envy targets those who are more highly favored over others, the successful, the acclaimed, and the rich (*T. Dan* 1:5; *T. Gad* 7:1–2, 4; *T. Benj.* 4:4). "Whenever the one who is envied flourishes, the envious one languishes" (*T. Sim.* 3:3)—an illustration of "limited good" reckoning. This is the notion associated with the Evil Eye complex of beliefs: in this "zero-sum game of life" all the good things of life are in limited and scarce supply so that whatever anyone gains comes at another's loss.[233] Envy also prods the envier to destroy what he envies (*T. Sim.* 3:3). Envy even brings harm to the envier. It blinds the envier's mind (*T. Sim.* 2:7). Simeon's envy of Joseph resulted in the Lord's binding of Simeon's hands and feet and in a withering of his hand (*T. Sim.* 2:13). Zebulon's nephews became sick and died because of Joseph, because they produced no mercy from within (*T. Zeb.* 5:4). Gratefulness to the Lord, on the other hand, is the opposite of envy (*T. Gad* 7:6). Humility kills envy (*T. Gad* 5:3); compassion and love cause the spirit of envy to vanish (*T. Sim.* 4:7).

231. The terms appear as parallels in *T. Sim.* 2:7; 4:7; *T. Gad* 7:2, 4. They also occur together in forming a hendiadys (*T. Sim.* 4:5) or are juxtaposed in the same context (*T. Sim.* 4:1—5:4).

232. See *T. Sim.* 2:6, 13–14; 4:2–5; 5:1; *T. Zeb.* 1:5–7; 2:1–9; 3:1–8; 4:10–13; 5:4; 8:4; *T. Dan* 1:4–9; *T. Naph.* 7:2–4; *T. Gad* 1:4–9; 2:1–5; 3:3; 5:6, 11; 6:2; *T. Jos.* 1:2–7; *T. Benj.* 2:1–6. "The good and pious man Joseph" was the model after whom all Israelites were encouraged to pattern their lives (*T. Sim.* 4:5; *T. Benj.* 3:1—4:5).

233. On the notion of "limited good," see Foster 1965, 1972; Malina 1979, 2001f; Graves 2014.

Given the association of envy and the Evil Eye, these features of envy are likely to have been associated with the Evil Eye as well. A further point of contact is the association of envy and the Evil Eye with having "a darkened eye," which is a likely metaphor for having for an Evil Eye. "A good person does not have a darkened eye (*skoteinon ophthalmon*) but is merciful to all," the *Testament of Benjamin* observes (4:2). "He does not envy (*phthonei*) anyone who glorifies himself. He is not envious (*zêloi*) of anyone who becomes rich" (*T. Benj.* 4:4). A "darkened eye" is equated with envying and is antithetical to showing mercy. It can also designate an eye made blind (Ps 69:23), and blindness, we recall, was viewed as a divine punishment for having and casting an Evil Eye. "Your light is darkened," Eliphaz chides Job, so that you cannot see" (Job 22:11).[234] Behind the comment is the assumption that a healthy body is full of light, which can be extinguished through blinding. In Job's case, this was blindness (darkness) brought about as divine punishment, so Eliphaz claimed, for Job's "great wickedness" and miserliness in stripping the naked of their clothing, refusing of water to the weary, withholding bread from the hungry, and despising the widows and orphans (Job 22:5–11). Was Job thought by his contemporaries, we might ask, to have been blinded for his miserly and ungenerous Evil Eye?

In the *Testament of Benjamin* 4:2, the expression appears to be metaphorical rather than denoting physically blinded eyes (as may also be the case with Job). Elsewhere anger, hatred, and envy are said to blind the eye and darken understanding (*T. Dan* 2:2–5). To have a darkened eye in a metaphorical sense is to be unmerciful toward others, similar to withholding aid to those in need—the trait typical of persons with an Evil Eye, as we have seen above. Envy and the Evil Eye, moreover, are both antithetical to *haplotês* and *haplous*, living with integrity. (*T. Sim.* 4:5; *T. Iss.* 4:1–5:4). These are features important for the interpretation of Matt 6:22–23/Luke 11:34 where an Evil Eye (*ophthalmos ponêros*) is contrasted to an *ophthalmos haplous* ("integral eye"), and having an Evil Eye is said to result in a body full of darkness.[235]

Before we leave this tradition concerning Joseph and his brothers and the envious Evil Eye, we might mention Joseph's prominence in later Israelite tradition and and lore.[236] Among the followers of Jesus, the story of Joseph as the object of his brothers' envy and of his divine rescue remained a

234. For eye(s) darkened, see Gen 27:1; 48:10; Deut 34:7; 1 Sam 3:2; Job 17:7; Ps 69:23; Lam 5:17; Zech 11:17.

235. For the bearing of the *T. 12 Patr.* on the Evil Eye passages of Matt 6:22–23/Luke 11:34 see Elliott 1994 and below, chap. 2.

236. See Billerbeck 1926 1:834; Shrire 1982:114; Ulmer 1991:351–52; and Vol. 4, chap. 1.

powerful and evocative memory. The speech of Stephen prior to his stoning, for example, refers explicitly to Joseph as victim and survivor of sibling envy (Acts 7:9–15). Joseph's story and his survival of sibling envy is also remembered in Israel's later rabbinic tradition, which tells of appeal to Joseph for protection against the Evil Eye.[237] The *Testaments of the Twelve Patriarchs* thus stand in a long line of Jewish Evil Eye lore extending down through late antiquity.

The Testament of Solomon 18:39

The *Testament of Solomon* (first to third century CE, possibly composed in Egypt), is a twenty-six chapter pseudepigraphic folktale concerning King Solomon and his control over spirit-demons.[238] It recounts Solomon's encounter with a spirit-demon that cast the Evil Eye and describes how it is thwarted.[239]

Solomon is portrayed as interrogating the spirits of thirty-six heavenly bodies that are divisions of the Zodiac (*T. Sol.* 18:1–42). These are the "world rulers of the darkness of this age" (*T. Sol.* 18:1–2) who cause various kinds of illnesses and conflicts. Solomon has been given "authority over all the spirits of the air" and asks each of the thirty-six spirits to identify itself. The thirty-fifth spirit-demon responds:

> I am called *Rhyx Phthêneoth.* I cast the Evil Eye (*baskainô*) on everyone. But the much-suffering eye (*ho polypathês ophthalmos*), when inscribed, thwarts me." (*T. Sol.* 18:39)[240]

Rhyx is likely a loan word from, or variation on, the Latin *rex,* "ruler, king, prince"; *Phtheneoth* is likely a variation on *phthonos*, Greek for *envy*, so that the statement is "*I am the ruler Envy.*" Here, as so often, envy and casting an Evil Eye (*baskainô*) again are linked. The second half of the sentence declares that the power of the Evil Eye is thwarted, annulled (*katargei*), by a graven image of the "much-suffering (Evil) Eye," or Evil Eye under attack. The image of the "much-suffering eye," as Campbell Bonner labeled it, appears frequently on amulets inscribed with an eye encircled by various

---

237. See *b. B.M.* 84a; *b. Ber.* 20a, 55b; *Gen. Rab.* 78:10.

238. On Solomon's power over demons see Josephus, *Ant.* 8.45; Billerbeck 1928 4:1.501–35, esp. 533–34; Winkler 1931; Verheyden, ed., 2012.

239. For the text in English translation with commentary see Duling 1993 1:935–87. For the standard text and earlier translation see McCown 1922b; cf. Fleck 1837; DiTomasso 2012:317–20. On the *Testament of Solomon*, see also Conybeare 1898; Duling 1988, 1992; Jackson 1988; Klutz 2003, 2005; Klutz, ed., 2003; Busch 2006.

240. Following the translation of Duling 1993 *OTP* 1:981.

creatures attacking it. There are numerous extant amulet examples.[241] "This representation of an Evil Eye attacked by powerful hostile forces was used as a potent anti-Evil eye amulet according to the principle of "like influences like" (*similia similibus*) or "fighting fire with fire." An instance of this Evil Eye under attack also may be present in the third-century CE synagogue at Dura Europos, Syria.[242] The appeal to and portrayal of Solomon (as rider on a horse and lancing an [evil] eye) and the expression "seal of Solomon" (*Sphragis Solomonis*) on several of these "much-suffering Evil Eye" or "Evil

Illus. 6

Byzantine silver Seal of Solomon medallion amulet portraying on the obverse (left) King Solomon as a cavalier spearing a prostrate demoness and on the reverse (right) an Evil Eye (alias *phthonos*/Envy) attacked (from Seligmann 1910 2:443, fig. 230; description in vol 2:313–14)

Illus. 7

King Solomon as cavalier spearing the prostrate demon Asmodeus (from Perdrizet 1922:12, fig. 5; cf. Gollancz, *The Book of Protection* 1912, Codex A, p. 55)

Eye under attack" amulets attest their use, if not likely origin, in Jewish circles, though these amulets were also employed by Christians and others as well.[243] Several such amulets depict Solomon on horseback spearing a prostrate demoness symbolizing the Evil Eye, who is once explicitly named *Baskosynê*, "Evil Eye."[244] Solomon likewise appears as an anti-Evil Eye figure

241. Bonner 1950:96–100. See Goodenough 1953 2:238–41 for depictions and discussion. On these amulets see Vols. 2 and 4. For illustrations see the items listed in Bonner 1950, Plates 14–15, nos. 292–303, 306.

242. So Bonner 1950; see Goodenough, 1953 2:238, and figs. 1065, 1066; and Duling *OTP* 1:981, n. q3; see Vol. 2 and Vol. 4, chap. 1.

243. Regarding the "seal of Solomon" on amulets see Schlumberger 1892a, 1892b, 1895; Perdrizet 1903, 1922; Goodenough, 1:168; 2:226–38; 7:198–200; 9:1044–67; Delatte and Derchain 1964, no. 371; Engemann 1981:290, illus. 7; 291, illus. 8.

244. For Solomon appearing on amulets as a cavalier lancing an Evil Eye demon

in the Syriac *Book of Protection* where he is depicted also as a cavalier spearing a prostrate demoness.[245]

The responses of the thirty-fourth and thirty-sixth demonic spirits in *T. Sol.* 18:38, 40 are likely related to 18:39. The thirty-fourth demon-spirit states:

> I am called Rhyx Autoth. I cause *envyings* (*phthonous*) and squabblings between those who love each other. But the letters Alpha and Beta (or "the alphabet") written down, thwart me. (v. 38)

The thirty-sixth demon spirit announces:

> And I am called Rhyx Mianeth. I am *envious against* (*epiphthonos*) the body; I demolish houses; I cause the flesh to rot. If anyone writes on the entrance of his house as follows, 'Melto Ardad Annath,' I flee from that place. (v. 40)

Illus. 8

Sketch of Perseus decapitating Medusa/Gorgo, Metope of Temple C, Selinus (modern Selinunte), Sicily, sixth century BCE (from Seligmann 1910, 1:76. fig. 2)

The features of these spirits are closely associated with those of the Evil Eye: envy and its hostility, destroying homes, causing human bodies to rot or wither, and the protection of homes afforded by anti-Evil Eye amulets (like *fascina* and mezuzahs).

Reference also is made in the *Testament of Solomon* to a female demon named *Obyzouth*, whose disheveled hair makes her resemble the snake-haired Medusa/Gorgo, caster of the Evil Eye (*T. Sol.* 13:1–7). She travels around the world by night, similar to the demonesses Lamashtu and Lilith, attacking pregnant women and strangling their newborn babies (13:3), also "injuring eyes, condemning mouths, destroying minds, and making bodies feel pain" (13:4).[246] She was thwarted by

see Schlumberger 1895 1:120, 134, 293; Seligmann 1910 2:313–15 and figs. 230–33; Perdrizet 1922; Bonner 1950:302, nos. 294–97 and Plate XIV; Delatte and Derchain 1964:261–64, nos. 369–77 (and 9 specimens in the Cabinet des Médailles. Bibliothèque Nationale, Paris); Bagatti 1971; Engemann 1975:25, fig. 1; Spier 1993:61–62; Michaelides 1994; Bohak 2008:213; See also Vols. 2 and 4.

245. Gollancz 1912. The illustration is reproduced in Budge 1978/1930:2/6.

246. The Mesopotamian demoness *Lamashtu*, the Hebrew demoness and "night hag" *Lilith* (Isa 34:14), and the demoness *Gyllou* also were feared for attacking birthing mothers and infant children and thereby were brought into the demonic Evil Eye orbit. For *Lilith* in the Dead Sea Scrolls see 4QSongs of the Sage (4Q510 frag. 11.4–6a). On Lilith in Israel's lore see M. Gaster 1900; Gordon 1957; Shrire, *Amulets* 1982:114–17.

pregnant women writing her name on a piece of papyrus which caused her to "flee from them to the other world." (13:6). Her being bound by her hair and hung up in front of the Jerusalem Temple (*T. Sol.* 13:7) recalls the Greek myth of Perseus's decapitation of the Evil-Eyed Medusa/Gorgo and his holding her decapitated head by her snake-like locks of hair. Her similarity to both the appearance of Medusa and the foul deeds of the Evil Eye demon/ demoness suggest a connection with the Evil Eye, though the Evil Eye is not specifically mentioned.

A further passage, *T. Sol.* 16:7, speaks of a bowl into which the demon *Kunopegos* was cast and contained. Such a bowl seems to resemble in function the so-called Aramaic Incantation Bowls, receptacles the size of soup bowls that were used for trapping or dispersing demons, including the Evil Eye demon. Inscribed with incantations spiraling on the inside bottoms, they were used to capture demons and thereby protect houses, families, and possessions. One such bowl inscription included the Evil Eye among the powers to be overcome:

> Sealed, countersealed and fortified against the male demon and female lilith and spell and curse and incantation and knock- ing and Evil Eye and evil black-arts, against the black-arts of mother and daughter, and against those of daughter-in-law and mother-in-law, and against those of the presumptuous woman, who darkens the eyes and blows away the soul, and against the evil black-arts that are wrought by men and against everything bad.[247]

Solomon, the seal of Solomon, and Solomon as slayer of the Evil Eye de- moness also figure prominently in further post-biblical Jewish amulets, as discussed in Vol. 4, chap. 1.

Shrire (1982:117) sees her as "the classical example of the succubus in Jewish mythol- ogy. She undoubtedly derives from very ancient sources appearing as Liatu 'a female demon' in Assyrian literature and earlier still as Lillaku in Sumerian tablets of the story of Gilgamesh in which she was supposed to have lived in a willow-tree."

247. C. H. Gordon 1934:324–26 (Text B, lines 5–8), in Duling *OTP* 1:948. The "seal- ring of El Shaddai" and the "seal-ring of King Solomon, the son of David, who worked spells on male demons and female liliths" are also enlisted in this inscription for protec- tion. See also Naved and Shaked 1987:173–75 on a Mesopotamian "Magic Bowl" (Bowl 8, fourth–seventh centuries CE, with the inscription: "Bound are the demons, sealed are the devs, bound are the idol spirits, sealed are the liliths, male and female; bound is the evil eye." On Aramaic incantation bowls and their texts see also Montgomery 1913; Isbell 1975; Naved and Shaked 1993; Schiffman and Schwartz 1992.

Possible allusions to the Evil Eye: Joseph and Asenath and 2 Enoch

JOSEPH AND ASENATH 4:11

The narrative of *Joseph and Asenath* (first century BCE–first century CE) is an expansion on the biblical account of the marriage in Egypt of the patriarch Joseph, son of Jacob, and the Egyptian Asenath, daughter of Pontiphera (LXX: Pentephres) (Gen 41:45). Early in the story, Joseph plans a visit to the home of Pentephres/Pontiphera, priest of Hierapolis in Egypt (*Jos. Asen.* 3:1–6). Pentephres tells his beloved daughter of the imminent arrival of Joseph, the mighty man of God and savior of Egypt from famine (4: 5–9). He announces his intent to give Asenath to Joseph in marriage (4:10) and receives a most negative response from his daughter:

> And when Aseneth heard what her father said, a great red sweat came over her, and she was furious and *looked askance/sideways with her eyes at her father.*[248] (*Jos. Asen.* 4:11)

She berated her father for wanting to marry her off to someone she took to be a foreigner, a fugitive, sold as a slave, immoral, and imprisoned (4:12–14). She flatly refused to be married to Joseph (4:15). Pentephres said nothing more, "for she had answered him arrogantly and in anger" (4:16). Later Asenath regretted having "spoken evil" of Joseph in ignorance (6:2, 4, 6, 7), and they eventually were married.

Asenath's "looking (*eneblepse*) askance/sideways (*plagiôs*)" at her father could imply her subjecting him to an Evil Eye, since "looking askance" (and an "oblique eye") are typical Evil Eye actions.[249] Asenath's look was accompanied by words described as "arrogant and angry." However, the looking is with "eyes" in the plural, not a singular eye that might suggest an Evil Eye. Moreover, her looking was with fury and anger, but not to harm her father. The remaining narrative makes nothing more of this "looking askance." So its being a gesture of an Evil Eye remains no more than a distant and unlikely possibility.

---

248. *eneblepse tois ophthalmois autês plagiôs tô patri autês.*

249. See Vol. 2.

2 ENOCH 52:7–8

Second Enoch is a late first century CE amplification of Gen 5:21–32 and covers events from Enoch's lifetime to the onset of the Flood. It is possible that 2 *Enoch* 52:7–8 alludes to looking with an Evil Eye. The text reads:

> Happy [is he] who looks carefully to the raising up of the works of his own hand. Cursed [is he] who looks [and is envious] to destroy another.[250]

The association of looking and envy could suggest the action of an Evil Eye, as could the notion of destroying by looking. The text, however, is too fragmentary to allow a conclusive decision.

From two uncertain allusions to the Evil Eye, we return to texts containing explicit references.

The Dead Sea Scrolls

The Dead Sea Scrolls include two explicit references to the Evil Eye. A reference to an Evil-Eyed fascinator occurs in 4QWisdom (4Q424), a collection of proverbs belonging to the "Wisdom Literature" of the Dead Sea Scrolls. Amidst advice on untrustworthy persons to be avoided (frag. 1, lines 6–13)[251] occurs a warning against a person with an Evil Eye, who is therefore unreliable as an estate manager:

> 10. A man with an Evil Eye (*'ish r' 'ayin*)—do not appoint him over [your wealth, for he will not] 11. mete out what remains to you to your satisfaction [. . .] 12 and in the time of accounting [harvest] he will be found a hypocrite." (4Q424, Frag. 1, lines 10–12)[252]

The translations generally render only according to sense ("miserly," "stingy" man).[253] The implication is that an Evil-Eyed person is unreliable and perhaps stingy or greedy so that he is not to be trusted with valued resources.

---

250. This is the modified translation of Andersen (*OTP* 1:178), the longer Slavic recension (J). His translation includes an addition from ms P, which he renders "and is jealous." It is, however, more likely that the looking is not with jealousy but with *envy*. It is envy, not jealousy, that wishes ill and destruction on another.

251. A slothful person, a collector of taxes, one with "twisted lips," and an impatient person.

252. Translation of Harrington 1996:61, modified by JHE.

253. García Martínez, *Dead Sea Scrolls*, 1996:393: "avaricious man."

The thought is consonant with biblical Evil Eye texts like Prov 28:22; Sir 14:3, 8–10; 18:8; 37:10–11; and Tob 4:7, 16.

A further Qumranic reference to the Evil Eye occurs in 4QDecrees (4Q477). 4Q477, frag. 1, col. 2.2–10, is a fragmentary text treating rules of behavior and those who were reproached for transgressing them.[254] Two individuals are reported as being reproached by the community for having the Evil Eye: Johanan, son of Matathias and someone (name lacking) identified as "son of Joseph."

> And they reproached] Johanan, son of Mata[thias because he [. . .] and was quick for anger, [and . . .] with him, and has the (Evil) Eye (*ha'ayin*), and also a boastful spirit . . . [. . .] And they reproached [. . .] son of Joseph, because he has the (Evil) Eye (*ha['ayin]*), and also because no-one . . ." (4Q477, frag. 1, col. 2.3, 4, 7)[255]

In the first case, an Evil Eye is associated with the negative vices of anger and boasting. In the second case, it is interesting that reproach falls on a "son of Joseph," who clearly did not embody the power of patriarch Joseph against the Evil Eye and envy.

Beyond these texts, further reference to the Evil Eye in the Dead Sea Scrolls is possible but uncertain. 4QBeatitudes (4Q525), involving a series of beatitudes or makarisms, contains the words "in the *evils of the eye* . . . to shed blood" (4Q525, frag. 13.2–3).[256] While "evils of the eye" associate the concepts of evil and eye, the phrase is not a conventional one for "Evil Eye" and the context is too fragmentary to allow any definitive judgment. A reference to the Evil Eye does not seem likely here.

The Manual of Discipline speaks of *spitting* in the midst of the Assembly of the Many (1QS 7:13). The act brings thirty days of punishment. The spitting may have been viewed either as an insulting gesture against a fellow member that causes strife within community, or as a gesture of protection against one suspected of casting an Evil Eye. Spitting for protection against an Evil Eye was customary among Greeks and Romans as we have seen in Vol. 2 and was likely practiced in Israel and Qumran, as Paul's mention of protective spitting indicates in his letter to the Galatians.[257] This Qumran text, however, is more likely referring not to spitting as a protective tactic but to spitting as a gesture of insult that would be judged and punished as

---

254. See García Martínez 1996:90–91.

255. Translation from ibid.:90–91.

256. Ibid.:397.

257. See Gal 4:14 and the discussion in chap. 2 below.

a socially disruptive act. Thus this text is not a likely allusion to an Evil Eye and its aversion.

This brings us to a consideration of the clear and explicit references to the Evil Eye in the writings of Philo and Josephus.

Philo of Alexandria

The voluminous writings of Philo, the Israelite philosopher of Alexandria, Egypt (first century CE), offer allegorical commentary on the Mosaic Law and Israelite tradition and contain numerous references to the Evil Eye. Philo uses terms of the *bask-* root some twenty-four times in his writings.[258]

The verb *baskainô* appears twice: *Agriculture* 112 and *Flaccus* 143. Commenting on behavior in competitions and contests, Philo encourages the honest acknowledgment that one's opponent

> has proved himself so vastly superior that even we, his antagonists, who might have been expected to begrudge [the victory] with an Evil Eye (*baskainein*), feel no envy (*mê phthoneisthai*)"(*Agriculture* 112)

The LCL translates *baskainein* with "grudge him his victory." This accurately renders the sense of the statement though it obscures the explicit reference to the Evil Eye in the original Greek. The combination of terms and the gist of the statement show that *baskainein* and *phthonein* are used as near synonyms.

In his account concerning the Roman prefect of Egypt, Flaccus, Philo tells of a certain citizen of Alexandria, Egypt, Isidorus, known to be a popularity hound and rabble-rouser. He was charged with instigating actions and insults against Flaccus and employing persons to supply money and wine to the people. Isidorus, it was declared, was always "Evil-Eyeing (*baskainôn*) the prosperous, and being a foe of law-abiding tranquility" (*Flaccus* 143). Isidorus here is the object of an Evil Eye accusation leveled against him in public. The accusation worked and Isidorus was forced to flee for his life. Since the prosperous conventionally are the objects of envy, the Evil-Eyeing here can involve envy, as the LCL translation proposes: "ever envious of the prosperous."

---

258. Philo: *baskainô* (2x): *Agriculture* 112; *Flaccus* 143b; *baskania* (10x): *Cherubim* 33; *Names* 95, 112; *Dreams* 1.107; *Abraham* 184; *Moses* 1.4, 246; *Spec. Laws* 1:241; *Virtues* 170; *QG* 4:191b; *baskanos* (11x): *Sacrifices* 32; *Agriculture* 64; *Prelim. St.* 71; *Abraham* 21, 199; *Joseph* 144; *Spec* 1:241; *Rewards* 83; *Flaccus* 29; *QG* 4:191c, 227; *abaskanos* (1x): *Posterity* 138.

The noun *baskania* appears ten times, all but *Abraham* 184 in combination with terms of the *phthon-* root.[259] The adjective/substantive *baskanos* appears eleven times.[260] Being Evil-Eyed (*baskanos*) is one of one hundred and forty-seven vices Philo names as typical of the "pleasure-lover" (*philê-donos*) (*Sacrifices* 32).[261] Describing the worthless human being (*phaulos*), Philo states that, among other things, he is always eager to learn of his neighbor's affairs, whether good or bad, and ready to envy (*phthonein*) the former and rejoice at the latter; for the worthless person is a creature that by nature is Evil-Eyed (*baskanos*) (*Abraham* 21).

Here being envious, Evil-Eyed, and given to Schadenfreude are treated as kindred malevolent dispositions. The idea that having an Evil Eye or being Evil-Eyed is determined by nature is typical of Greco-Roman thought, as we have seen in Vol. 2, and occurs elsewhere in Philo as well.[262] "The Egyptian disposition is, by nature Evil-Eyed (*baskanon*)." Philo declares in a fit of ethnic stereotyping, when describing the arrival of King Herod Agrippa in Alexandria and the reaction of the Alexandrian populace:

> But the citizens [of Alexandria in Egypt], bursting with envy (*phthonou*)—for the Egyptian disposition is by nature Evil-Eyed (*baskanon*)—considered that any good fortune to others was misfortune to themselves; and in their ancient, and we might say innate, hostility to the Judeans, they resented a Judean [Herod Agrippa] having been made a king, just as much as if each of them had thereby been deprived of an ancestral home. (*Flaccus* 29)

In this pregnant stereotyping statement, Philo indicates four important and typical features of the Evil Eye belief complex. (1) The Evil Eye is linked with envy;[263] (2) both the Evil Eye and envy are traits conferred by nature; (3) the Evil Eye is malevolent and seeks the deprivation of others; and (4) the Evil-Eyed envying of others is linked with the notion of limited good"—the gain of others comes only at a loss to oneself. This is a parade example of limited good, Evil Eye thinking. We will encounter this thinking again in chapter 2

259. *Cherubim* 33; *Names* 95, 112; *Dreams* 1:107; *Abraham* 184; *Moses* 1:4, 246; *Spec. Laws* 2:141; *Virtues* 170; *QG* 4:191b.

260. *Sacrifices* 32; *Agriculture* 64; *Prelim. St.* 71; *Abraham* 21, 199; *Joseph* 144; *Spec. Laws* 1:241; *Rewards* 83; *Flaccus* 29; *QG* 4:191c, 227.

261. *Baskania* ("Evil Eye malice") appears in the vice lists of 4 Macc 1:25–26 and 2:15–16. In the New Testament, Jesus lists an Evil Eye (*ophthalmos ponêros*) among twelve other vices.

262. See Philo, *Abraham* 199; *Prelim. St.* 71; *Rewards* 83.

263. An association typical of Philo's Hellenistic and Israelite culture; Milobenski 1964; Walcot 1978; Elliott 1992.

below in our examination of Jesus's parable of the generous vineyard owner and the envious workers (Matt 20:1–15). God, on the other hand, cannot be conceived as feeling envy or doubt (*QG* 1:55).

The adjective *abaskanos* ("free of an Evil Eye") occurs once (*Post.* 138). In this treatise, *The Posterity and Exile of Cain*, Philo describes the matriarch Rebecca offering water (of wisdom) to Eliezer, the servant of Abraham, and displaying the characteristics of a true and wise teacher (*Posterity* 136–138). "She has been taught the chief of all lessons, namely generosity (*philodôron*) free of an Evil Eye (*abaskanon*)." The Loeb Classical Library translation of *to abaskanon philodôron as "ungrudging generosity"* aptly conveys the sense of the Greek phrase, though again omitting explicit mention of the Evil Eye. *Ungrudging* for *abaskanon* is consistent with *bask-* terms elsewhere having the sense of *grudge, begrudge*; e.g. Sir 14:10; 18:18; 37:11. *Ungrudging* for *abaskanon* also is consistent with the antithesis of Evil Eye and generosity, as found in Deut 15:7–11; 28:54–57; Sir 14:3–10; Matt 6:22–23/Luke 11:34; and Matt 20:15.

The expression *ophthalmos ponêros* ("Evil Eye") does not occur in Philo.

To conclude concerning Philo, it is noteworthy how regularly Philo, in accord with conventional usage, combines terms of the *baskania* and *phthonos* word families, thereby illustrating the continued linkage of Evil Eye and envy.[264] In some of these combinations, the terms were used synonymously.[265] In others, they form a hendiadys.[266] As for occurrences of envy, the *phthon-* family of terms appears 238 times.[267] The *zel-* family of terms, also often designating *envy*, appears 150 times.[268]

From these Evil Eye passages we learn that Philo regards the Evil Eye as a natural phenomenon that Evil-Eyed persons have by nature (*Abraham* 21, 199; *Prelim. St.* 71; *Rewards* 83; *Flaccus* 29). Envy and an Evil Eye are directed against the victorious (*Agriculture* 112), the rich and prosperous (*Joseph* 144; *Virtues* 170; *Flaccus* 143; *QG* 4:19b) and strangers (*Agriculture* 64; *Moses* 1:246) and are attributed to strangers (*Agriculture* 64; *Prelim. St.* 71; *Abraham* 184; *Moses* 1:246). They are included among the vices (*Sacrifices*

---

264. For *phthonos* and *baskania* see *Cherubim* 33; *Names* 95, 112; *Dreams* 1:107; *Moses* 1:4, 246; *Spec. Laws* 2:141; *Virtues* 170; *QG* 4:191b; for *baskainein* and *phthonein*, *Agriculture* 112; for *phthoneo* and *baskanos*, *Joseph* 144.

265. See *Agriculture* 112; *Abraham* 21; *Joseph* 144; *Moses* 1.3–4, *Spec. Laws* 2:141; *Flaccus.* 29.

266. See *Cherubim* 33; *Names.* 95; *Dreams* 1.107; *Moses* 1:246; *QG* 4:191c.

267. *Phthoneô* (17x); *phthonos* (45x); *aphthonia* (51x); *aphthonos* (112x).

268. *Zêlos* (44x); *zêlotypeô* (2x); *zêlotypia* (8x); *zêlotypos* (2x); *zêloô* (55x); *zêlôsis* (7x). Further terms of the *zêl-* root include *zêlôtês* (27x); *zêlôtikos* (1x); and *zêlôtos* (4x).

32; *Prelim. St.* 71; *Names* 95; *Spec. Laws* 1:241; *Virtues* 170) and considered synonymous with "loving evil" (*Abraham* 21, 199). One text, *Flaccus* 29, illustrates how the notion of "limited good" fuels envy and Evil-Eyeing. Two other passages, *Posterity* 138 and *QG* 4:191c, indicate that envy and an Evil Eye are the antithesis of liberality and hospitality. Yet another, *QG* 4:227, expresses how an Evil Eye, like envy, grieves at the good fortune of others and wants it destroyed. Still another text, *Flaccus* 143, is an example of an Evil eye accusation which resulted in the disgrace and flight of the person charged.

Flavius Josephus

Flavius Josephus, Israelite soldier, statesman, and chronicler, writing in the latter half of the first century CE, employs, like Philo, terms of the *bask-* word group (thirteen occurrences) to denote the Evil Eye, casting the Evil Eye, envy, or begrudging (someone something).[269] Like Philo, Josephus makes no use of the phrase *ophthalmos ponêros.* Terms of the *bask-* family and of the *phthon-* (and *zel-*) families occur in tandem, showing that Josephus likewise assumed a connection of the Evil Eye with envy.[270]

According to Josephus, Israel's enemies and accusers Evil-Eye and envy them (*Ant.* 1.259; 3.268; 11.114; *Ag. Ap.* 1.72; 2.286). Israelites themselves, on the other hand, are not envious of the laws and institutions of other peoples (*Ag. Ap.* 2.271, 273). Nevertheless, Israel is hardly innocent of envy and the Evil Eye. King Saul, for instance, when recounting recent events to his kinsman Abner (*Ant.* 6.58–59), refrains from telling him about the affairs of the kingdom, fearing that this would arouse envy (*phthonon*) and distrust. So he said nothing, explaining that no one, not even a kinsman, shows unwavering loyalty, and when glorious honors are bestowed by God, "all are Evil-Eyed (*baskanoi*) toward these excellencies." Envy and an Evil Eye are equivalent and are aroused by the good fortune of others—standard notions associated with the Evil Eye. When Daniel and his relatives were made governors of Babylon by King Nebuchadnezzar, these

269. For the verb *baskainô* see *Ant.* 10.250, 257; *Life* 425; *Ag. Ap.* 1.72; 2.286; for the noun *baskania* see *Ant.* 10.250, 257; *Life* 425; *Ag. Ap.* 1.72; for the adjective/substantive *baskanos* see *War* 1.208; *Ant.* 1.260, 6.59; for the adverb *baskanôs* see *Ant.* 11.114; 14.266; for the adjective *abaskanos* see *War* 1.192.

270. See *Ant.* 10.212 (*phthonou kai baskanias*), 250 (*ephthonêthê, baskainousi,* and *blepontes* ["looking"]); 10.257 (*tou phthonou . . .baskainontes*);and *Ag. Ap.* 2.286 (*zeloun, baskainontes, epipthonou*); *War* 1.208 (*phthonon, tôn baskanôn*) . Terms of the *phthon-* word family appear a total of 155 times; terms of the *zêl-* word family (*zêlos, zêlotypos, zêlotypia, zêloô, zêlotês*) appear 120 times.

relatives "fell into dangerous exposure to envy and an Evil Eye" (*phthonou kai baskanias, Ant.* 10.212).[271] When Daniel is favored generously by King Darius, he "becomes prey to envy" (*ephthonêthê*). Linking the Evil Eye and envy. Josephus explains the social dynamic involved: "For people cast an Evil Eye (*baskainousi*) when they see (*blepontes*) other persons held by kings in greater honor than themselves" (*Ant.* 10.250).[272] Beholding and comparing, along with regarding honor as a limited good, arouses the Evil Eye of envy.[273] In this same context, Joseph again links envy and Evil Eye. The Persian satraps acted against Daniel "out of envy (*hypo tou phthonou*)," "imagining that King Darius might treat him with greater favor than they had expected," and might pardon Daniel even after he had shown contempt for the king's orders. "For this reason they Evil-Eyed (*baskainontes*) Daniel . . . and demanded that he be cast into the lion's den in accordance with the law" (*Ant.* 10.257).

The adverbial phrase *ou baskanôs* ("not with an Evil Eye") can have the more general sense of "without malice," as in *Ant.* 14.266. The related adjective *abaskanos* ("free of an Evil Eye") in the phrase "bore witness free of an Evil Eye" (*War* 1.192) can have the sense of "bore *ungrudging* witness" (LCL trans.).

Josephus states that he himself was a target of envy and an Evil Eye accusation. His privileged position with the Roman emperors Titus and Vespasian following the revolt in Judea, he notes, "exposed me to danger because of envy (*dia ton phthonon*)" (*Life* 423). "Persons who regarded my good fortune with an Evil Eye (*tôn baskainontôn*) brought numerous accusations against me; but by God's providence I escaped them all" (*Life* 425).[274] Envy and Evil-Eyeing again are treated as synonyms.

Josephus's references to the Evil Eye, in sum, manifest a continued association of the Evil Eye with envy or the use of the terms as synonyms. Good fortune and honors are the targets of envy and the Evil Eye, which is also associated with acting begrudgingly. An envious Evil Eye can prompt public accusation and result in life-threatening consequences.

---

271. The LCL rendition, "envy *and jealousy*" for *phthonou kai baskanias* is simply inaccurate; jealousy plays no role here. The paired terms represent a hendiadys (two terms for one entity and joined by "and"). The phenomenon is envious Evil-Eyed malice.

272. The LCL rendition, "for men are *jealous*," again is inaccurate; the verb *baskainousi* is "cast an Evil Eye," or "are Evil-Eyed" and the emotion is envy, not jealousy; for envy, see also *zêlotypousin* in the following paragraph (*Ant.* 10. 251).

273. A similar dynamic occurs in Jesus's parable of the envious vineyard laborers (Matt 20:1–15).

274. For envy and an Evil Eye aroused by success and renown see also *War* 1.208.

ANTI-EVIL EYE APOTROPAICS IN ISRAEL:
THE MATERIAL EVIDENCE

The amulets, so extensively employed in Israel (see above pp. 21, 75, 86–87), are a poignant illustration of the pervasive fear of hostile forces, including the Evil Eye, and attempts at self-defense. Hebrews, it has been noted, "like the nations round about them, made use of uninscribed amulets to protect them from the Evil Eye, and from hostile influences of every kind."[275] While the Epistle of Jeremiah contains the only *explicit* mention of an anti-Evil Eye apotropaic in the Bible, it is quite likely that the variety of apotropaics employed by Israelites that are mentioned in the Bible[276] included many that protected against the Evil Eye along with other forces of evil. Isaiah mentions crescents, pendants, bracelets, rings, and perfume boxes (3:19–21) that were likely worn as apotropaics as well as for ornamentation. Jewelry, as previously noted, generally served this double function.[277] Apotropaic lunar crescents were worn by both humans (Judg 8:26; Isa 3:18) and animals (Judg 8:21, 26 [camels]); see above, Illus. 1, p. 21.

The *phylacteries* (Hebrew: *tefillin*) worn by every observant male Israelite for daily prayer (Exod 13: 9, 16; Deut 6:4–8; 11:18; Matt 23:5) also were thought to protect against evil forces and the Evil Eye, as the name "phylactery" (from the Greek, *phylassô*, "to guard, protect") indicates.[278] See above Illus. 2, p. 22. *Mezuzahs*, small capsules containing biblical verses (Deut 6:9; 11:20), that were attached to the doorposts of homes as well as sanctuaries, likewise protected domiciles and their inhabitants.[279] See above, Illus. 4, p. 23. *Mezuzah* literally means "door post," "gate post." Originally *mezuzah* designated a Mesopotamian apotropaic with a cuneiform inscription affixed to the door post of a residence to drive away demons and evil spirits.[280] Their protective function was similar to that of the anti-Evil Eye *fascina* protect-

275. Budge 1978/1930:212.

276. On the use of apotropaics and amulets in Israel see above, p. 22 n. 55.

277. On the apotropaic function of jewelry, see Vol. 2, pp. 217–64.

278. On phylacteries/*tefillin* see Rodkinson 1893; Billerbeck 1928 4.1:250–76; Ben-Dor 1962:122; G. H. Davies 1962b; Yadin 1969. On their apotropaic function see Tigay 1979:51: "There is no lack of evidence that *tefillin* were ascribed apotropaic properties and used as such." Cf., e.g., Jerome (PL 26.128) and numerous rabbinic texts (e.g., R. Yohanan protected in the privy by his *tefillin*, *b. Ber.* 23a–b); also Tigay 1982.

279. See Casanowicz 1906; Seligmann 1910 2:338–39; Elworthy 1912; Koetting 1954:474–75; G. H. Davies 1962a; Trachtenberg 1970/1939:146–52. Five sheets of phylactery and mezuzah texts were found at Qumran: 4QPhyl G, 4QPhyl J, 4QMes A, 8QPhyl, XQPhyl 3. Josephus (*Ant.* 4.8.13) also attests the use of phylacteries and mezuzahs.

280. Oppenheim 1977:235.

ing the portals, thresholds, and vestibules of Greco-Roman residences.[281] Portals and thresholds were sacred spaces requiring protection from hostile forces including the Evil Eye. An analogous protective practice is performed daily in Tamil Nadu, South India, where women sweep and rearrange the thresholds of homes (= "making the Kôlam") "to guard against persons bearing an Evil Eye."[282]

Given the apotropaic power ascribed to the *colors red and blue* in the ancient Near East and Circum-Mediterranean against the Evil Eye,[283] it is likely that red and blue had a similar apotropaic function in Israelite cult and culture.

Blue, the color of the heavenly throne of God (Exod 24:10, sapphire pavement stone), was combined with red among the paraments of the tabernacle/temple and the priestly vestments. The *tabernacle* was adorned with ten curtains of "fine twined linen and blue and purple and scarlet stuff and fine twined linen (Exod 25:4; 26:1–6; 36:8; Num 4:6–7, 9 etc.). A veil or curtain in the tabernacle separating the Holy of Holies from the Holy Place was "of blue and purple and scarlet stuff and fine twined linen" (Exod 26:31, 31–35; 36:35; 2 Chr 2:7, 14; 3:14). A screen for the door of the tabernacle was "of blue and purple and scarlet stuff and fine twined linen" (Exod 26:36, 36–37; 36:37; 38:18). The gate of the court of the tabernacle had a screen "of blue and purple and scarlet stuff and fine twined linen" (Exod 27:16). The cover of the ark of covenant was blue, as was the table of the bread of the Presence (Num 4:6), the lamp stand for the night (Num 4:9), and the golden altar (Num 4:11). The vessels of the sanctuary were also put into a "cloth of blue" (Num 4:12). The Solomonic Temple likewise was adorned and protected by "purple, crimson, and blue fabrics" (2 Chr 2:7, 14; 3:14).

The *garments of Aaron and the priests* serving in the tabernacle were of "gold, blue and purple and scarlet stuff and fine twined linen" (Exod 28:5; 39:1). This included the ephod (28:5, 8; 39:2, 3, 5), the breast-piece of judgment (28:15; 39:8, 21). The priest's girdle was also "of fine twined linen and of blue and purple and scarlet stuff" (Exod 39:29). The plate of pure gold engraved with the words "holy to the LORD" was fastened to the priest's turban by "a lace of blue" (Exod 28:37). The robe of the ephod donned under the ephod was all of blue (Exod 28:31; 39:22) and on its skirts were "pomegranates of blue and purple and scarlet stuff, around its skirts, with bells of gold between them" (Exod 28:33; 39:24–26). The protective

281. On protection in thresholds and vestibules, see Vol. 2.

282. See the work of my USF colleague, Prof. Vijaya Najarajan 1993, esp. 200–201.

283. Seligmann 1910 2:242–59 on blue (246–47) and red (247–59); above Vol. 1:110, 112; Vol. 2:254-57.

function of the color blue and of the bells is made immediately clear: "And it [blue robe with bells] shall be upon Aaron when he ministers, and its sound shall be heard when he goes into the holy place before the Lord, and when he comes out, *so that he may not die*" (Exod 28:35). According to Josephus (*War* 5.5.5) "the bells signified thunder and the pomegranates, lightning." Qumran priests wore garments of blue, scarlet, and purple on the occasion of battle (1QM 7:10; cf. Exod 39:28–29),[284] as had Assyrian warriors before them (Ezek 23:6).

Lay Israelites were instructed to "make tassels on the corners of their garments . . . and to put upon the tassel of each corner a cord of blue" (Num 15:38–39).[285] These are the four blue tassels (*tzitzit*) on the prayer shawl (*tallit*) worn also by the observant Israelite Jesus of Nazareth (Matt 9:20; 14:36; Mark 6:56; Luke 8:44). See above, Illus. 3, p. 22. It is likely that for Israel the color blue was no mere decoration or marker of high social status or of piety, but, as in Mesopotamia, symbolic of heavenly and cultic power that also averted the Evil Eye and other forces of evil.[286]

Israelites applied the color *red/scarlet/crimson* (*tola*) to fabrics or yarns used in: (1) the equipment of the tabernacle (Exod 25–28 [scarlet and blue]; Num 4:8); (2) rites in cleansing lepers (Lev 14); (3) the ceremony of purification (Num 19:6); as well as (4) in royal apparel (2 Sam 1:24; Prov 31:21 etc.); (5) for marking thread (Gen 38:28, 30; Josh 2:18, 21); (6) for symbolizing sin (Isa 1:18); and (7) for adorning and protecting warriors' tunics and shields (Nah 2:4; 1 Macc 4:23).[287] This military practice was likely apotropaic, as it was for Greeks and Romans.[288] "Red is a color regarded everywhere as anti-demonic and anti-evil eye."[289] Red is ascribed protective power in Prov 31:21. Red thread amulets were employed by Israelites in the Hellenistic period (*t. Shabb.* 7:1) A custom continuing today consists of at-

---

284. Hermann 1969:379.

285. Later tradition regarded this as a constant reminder to follow God and not individual inclinations (Num 15:39–41).

286. On blue (*t'khelet*) as an apotropaic color in Israel, see also Schrire 1982:58 and Patai 1983:86–95. For blue in the Hebrew Scriptures, see also Est 8:15; Jer 10:9; Ezek 23:6; 27:7, 24. On *tekhelet* as "sky-blue" and produced from the secretions of a sea snail, the *Murex trunculus,* see Herzog and Spanier 1987; Sterman and Sterman 2012, 2013. The dark purple dye first produced from these secretions in the dye-making process, when exposed to light, "is transformed into pure indigo, thus leaving the dye an unadulterated sky-blue" (Sterman and Sterman 2013:28). On the debate concerning the color designated by *tekhelet,* see Sterman and Sterman 2012, 2013. On the *tzitzit* see Billerbeck 1928 4.1:277–92.

287. Hermann 1969:381.

288. So Hermann and Cagiano di Azevedo 1969:381, 393–408.

289. Trachtenberg 1970/1939:133.

taching a thread or ribbon of scarlet or blue to the wrist of infants or on the crib for protection against an Evil Eye.[290] It is analogous to the ancient Roman practice of suspending a protective anti-Evil Eye neck pouch (*bulla* containing a *fascinum*) from the necks of Roman children.[291] The Israelite practice may have some connection to the red thread attached to the newborn mentioned in Gen 38:27–30. Tamar, Judah's daughter-in-law, had become pregnant by Judah (Gen 38:13–18) and gave birth to twin boys. When she was in labor, one put out his hand "and the midwife took and bound on his hand a scarlet thread, saying, 'This one came out first.'" As he drew back his hand, "behold, his brother came out" and was named Perez. Afterward out came the brother "with the scarlet thread upon his hand" and he was named Zarah. In any case, the red and blue bracelets worn by infants have served as anti-Evil Eye protection for centuries. The Talmud reports that a

Illus. 9
Two Bronze composite amulets of winged phalluses with bells, Herculaneum (line drawing from Carcani, ed. 1771 2:399, no. 97)

Illus. 10
Bronze amulet of phallus with bells, Herculaneum (line drawing from Carcani, ed. 1771 2:403, Plate 98)

crimson thread also was placed between the eyes of a horse to avert the Evil Eye (*b. Shabb.* 53a; cf. *t. Shabb.* 4:5). The Christian church father and theologian John Chrysostom (fourth century CE) inveighed against the practice by Christians as well as pagans of attaching woven red bracelets to infants to

290. Moss and Cappannari 1976:8

291. On this Roman practice see Vol. 2, and for an illustration, Vol. 1:36, Illus. 1.10.

safeguard them from the Evil Eye.[292] On the whole, in both public cult and private life, the colors red and blue, while providing adornment, also played an important role in affording protection from the Evil Eye.[293]

The *bells* attached to the high priest's robe likely functioned similar to the *tintinnabula* used by Greeks and Romans; namely to produce a noise that would drive away the Evil Eye and other evil forces.[294] Just as *amulets with eyes* were used by Egyptians, Greeks, and Romans to ward off the Evil Eye, so the eyes mentioned in Ezek 1:18 and Rev 4:8 may have had a similar function.[295]

The apotropaic use of an *open hand* as protection against the Evil Eye has long been common in the Middle East and North Africa. In its Jewish adaptation it is identified as the *hamesh* or "Hand of Miriam" (sister of Moses and Aaron). Muslims know it as the *hamsa* or "Hand of Fatima" (Mohammed's daughter Fatima Zahra). *Hamesh* (Hebrew) and *Hamsa* (Arabic, also spelled *khamsa*) both mean "five," referring to the fingers of the hand. Hand-shaped amulets have been found in Egypt; hands also were inscribed on scarabs and depicted in magical texts.[296] The symbol of an open hand that was discovered in Judah, incised on the wall of a burial cave in Khirbet el-Qom, 12 km west of Hebron, is quite ancient (c. 7000 BCE) and may be a very early example of this anti-Evil Eye apotropaic.[297] Such open-hand images are still worn as jewelry today or placed on facades of modern buildings There is no certain reference to the Hand of Miriam amulet, however, in the Bible.

In general, it is in the design and use of amulets against the Evil Eye that we see the closest proximity of Israelite and Jewish practice to that of

---

292. John Chrysostom, *Hom. 1 Cor. 12:13* (PG 61.105); *Hom. Gal.* (PG 61.623); cf. Clement of Alexandria, *Strom.* 7.4.26. See also Hermann and Cagiano di Azevedo 1969:429–30.

293. On the color blue in general, see Ball 2001; Pastoureau 2001; Deutscher 2010, chs. 1 and 9. On red, see Greenfield 2006. On "the language of color" in the Mediterranean region see Borg 1999; see also Lamb and Bouriau 1995.

294. For the golden bells on the robe of the high priest and the sound they produce, see Exod 28:34–35; 39:25–26; Sir 45:7–9. See Gaster 1969:263–78 on the apotropaic function of these bells. On Roman apotropaic usage, see Jahn 1855, illustrations on pp. 77, 78, 81; Seligmann 1910 2:200 and figs. 189–91; Herzog-Hauser 1937. For phallic tintinnabula at Pompeii and illustrations, see Knight and Wright 1865, plates XXV, XXVI, XVII; also M. Grant 1975, 1982; Johns 1982; Gravel 1995, figs. 8.1, 8.2, 8.4, 8.5, 8; Moser 2006; and Vol. 2.

295. On apotropaic eye amulets see Vol. 1, chap. 2, and Vol. 2.

296. See Andrews 1994:70, illus. 67–70, 74d.

297. See Shroer 1984 who surveys the iconographic evidence from Egypt and Mesopotamia since the Old Babylonian period; see also the discussion by Wazana 2007:696–97.

their Greco-Roman, Egyptian, and ancient Near Eastern neighbors. Several slain soldiers of Judas Maccabees, when being prepared for burial, were found wearing under their coats "consecrated objects (*hierômata*) of the idols of Jamnia" (2 Macc 12:39–40), though forbidden by Judaean law (12:40). It is likely that these objects were worn as amulets, a practice that was common in the military. Pliny records that in his time (first century CE) persons were beginning to wear amulets decorated with images of Egyptian gods (*NH* 33.41). In the case of the slain Maccabean troops, the wearing of Egyptian amulets (possibly Eyes of Horus) was deemed idolatrous and the cause of their deaths (2 Macc 12:40).

A Jewish amulet discovered in a third-century CE child's grave near the Roman frontier city Carnuntum (close to modern Halbturn, Austria) consists of a silver capsule and a small gold leaf, inscribed with a Hebrew *Shemaʿ Yisrael* written in Greek letters. This practice of equipping the dead with amuletic protection mirrors that of Egyptian, Greek, and Roman customs.

Illus. 11

Jewish silver Hand of Miriam amulet (*Hamesh*) with the word *Shaddai* in palm (from Seligmann 1910 2:193, fig. 162)

A nine-line amuletic text in Hebrew on bronze foil (rabbinic period) implores that its bearer be safeguarded from the Evil Eyes of "his father, his mother, eye of women, eye of men, eye of virgins."[298] While the text is solely Jewish, an accompanying cross and other signs could identify this as a Christian amulet or point to a common Jewish-Christian provenance. Anti-Evil Eye amulets employed in post-biblical time by Jews and Christians show continuity with many of the biblical apotropaic devices as well as with parallel Mesopotamian, Egyptian, Greek, and Roman apotropaics.[299]

Illus. 12

Images of the Islamic Hand of Fatima (*Hamsa*) on a modern building, Andalucia, Spain (photo by John H. Elliott)

298. See Montgomery 1910–11.

299. On this point see also Vol. 4, chaps. 1 and 2.

CONCLUSION

The Evil Eye is mentioned frequently in the Old Testament in both the Hebrew and Greek Bibles. Explicit references to the Evil Eye are those employing the conventional language for "Evil Eye," "do evil with the eye," or "look with an Evil Eye," "look with malice," "look with envy," or "look with reluctance to give" (Deut 15:9; 28:54, 56; Prov 23:6; 28:22; Sir 14:3, 6, 8, 10; 18:8; 31:13; 37:10, 11; Wis 4:12; Tob 4:7, 16; 4 Macc 1:26; 2:15), or the expression for "Evil Eye amulet" (Ep Jer 69/70). The texts belong to literary contexts of legal prescription for dealing with poverty (Deut 15:7–11), an account of consequences and curses befalling Israel for infidelity to the commands of God (Deut 28:47–57), wisdom instructions on proper conduct (Proverbs, Sirach, Wisdom, Tobit), philosophical discussions of moral and immoral qualities (4 Maccabees), and a letter condemning alien idolatry (Epistle of Jeremiah). The references to the Evil Eye, like their Greco-Roman counterparts, reveal a range of characteristics associated with possessing an Evil Eye and looking with an Evil Eye. The content and context of these explicit texts provide a basis for considering further *implicit* references to the Evil Eye, as, for instance, where envy and envious looking are the subject (e.g., 1 Sam 2:29, 32; 18:9; Sir 31:23–24).

Israel's Evil Eye belief and practice is similar in several respects to that of its Mesopotamian, Egyptian, Greek, and Roman neighbors. The eye continues to be regarded as a preeminent organ of the body and projector of energy and light. Israelite authors continue to hold an extramission theory of vision. The eye continues to be viewed as a conveyor of emotions arising in the heart.

A wide range of dispositions and actions are associated in the Old Testament with having, and looking with, an Evil Eye, several of which are in common with their Greco-Roman counterparts. Emotions and thinking associated with the Evil Eye include fear, dread, feeling vulnerable to, and under attack by, hostile human forces, thinking of oneself as in competition with a rival (*antizêlos*) to whom one feels inferior; resenting the success and wellbeing of others and enviously wishing it destroyed because their gain is thought to involve one's own personal loss (Sir 37:10). Envy is significant among these emotions (1 Sam 2:32; 18:9; Sir 37:10; cf. also possibly 1 Sam 2:29; 4 Macc 1:25–26; 2:15–16). Miserliness and the withholding of generosity are dispositions that also receive notable emphasis (Deut 15:7–11; 28:54–57; Prov 23:6; Sir 14:3, 8, 10; Tob 4:7, 16). Envy, like the Evil Eye, is strongly condemned in the Old Testament and related sources, and has other features in common with the Evil Eye as well. "Wrath is cruel, anger is overwhelming; but who can stand before envy?" observes an Israelite sage

(Prov 27:4). "Envy makes the bones rot" (Prov 14:30). "Envy and wrath shorten (one's) days" (Sir 30:24). "Through the devil's envy, death entered the world" (Wis 2:24). Like the Evil Eye, envy is regarded as "the deadliest of evils." Philo complains of his own life being "plagued by the deadliest of evils, namely envy, the hater of the good (*ho misokalos phthonos*)" (*Spec. Laws* 3.1.2). Notorious examples of envy include Cain's envying Abel (Gen 4:6), Rachel's envying Leah (Gen 30:1); Joseph's brothers' envying Joseph (Gen 37:2–11; and Saul's envious "eyeing" of David (1 Sam 18:8–9). An Evil Eye is not explicitly mentioned in these latter texts, but its implication is likely. This linking of Evil Eye and envy continues in the New Testament, rabbinical commentary on the Evil Eye, and postbiblical Christian texts.[300] While the Evil Eye is closely associated with envy in the Old Testament, it is not identical with envy itself. When the adjective "envious" (*phthoneros*) is used to qualify the expression "evil eye" (*baskanos* or *ophthalmos ponêros*). As in Sir 14:10, "an Evil Eye is envious," (*ophthalmos ponêros phthoneros*), it is evident that the speaker did not regard *ophthalmos ponêros* as meaning "envy" or "envious" in and of itself. The adjective "envious" was added to make this association clear. An Evil Eye was viewed as the ocular mechanism that conveys envy.

Old Testament references to the Evil Eye also make it clear that, while Evil Eye and envy are closely and frequently linked, as in Greco-Roman texts, an "Evil Eye" could also convey emotions and dispositions other than envy. This is the case when an Evil Eye directed toward a neighbor in need involves turning away from and withholding food and aid from those in desperate straits (Deut 15:7–11; 28:53–57; see also Sir 14:8). Elsewhere an Evil Eye entails begrudging food at table (Prov 23:6) or giving a gift begrudgingly (Sir 18:18; Tob 4:7, 16). The verb "envy" likewise can assume the sense of "begrudge," "withhold," "refuse," as in Tob 4:7, 16, further illustrating the frequent synonymity or overlapping of Evil Eye and envy. The Evil Eye and envy, thus, are complementary rather than identical.

In the Old Testament, the Evil Eye also can involve feeling hostility and malice toward others, especially the poor and needy who seek help and material aid (Deut 15:7–11; 28:54–57; Prov 23:6–8; Sir 14:5–8, 10; 18:18; 37:11; Tob 4:7, 16). In these cases, it constitutes a reluctance to be generous, a disposition of *miserliness and stinginess*.

The Evil Eye can involve not only reluctance to give but also, occasionally, eagerness to get. It can connote being avaricious (Prov 28:22; Sir 14:9) or greedy (Sir 31:12–13) or ungrateful (Sir 37:11). As greed is a preoccupation with getting, being stingy or miserly is reluctance at giving. Both are

---

300. See below, chap. 2 and Vol. 4, chaps. 1 and 2.

dispositions linked with the Evil Eye, with the latter more frequently associated than the former. Several of these Evil Eye qualities overlap. The Evil Eye can be viewed as a fundamental manifestation of personal evil (Sir 14:6–7; 4 Macc 1:25–26; 2:15–16); the opposite of gratitude (Sir 37:11) and generosity (Deut 15:7–11; Tob 4:7, 16); and action obscuring what is good (Wis 4:12). It is thought to cause physical illness, vomiting, a dimming of eyesight or even blindness, a physical withering or diminution of life, dispossession of property, ruin, failure of one's rivals, or even death (Prov 23:6; 28:22; Sir 14:5; 18:18; 31:13). It likewise entails the notion that one can inadvertently injure, and bring loss to, oneself with one's own Evil-Eye (Prov 28:22; Sir 14:5–6, 9; 18:18).

Behavior and social interactions involving looking maliciously with an Evil Eye include looking enviously at, and wishing harm to others (1 Sam 2:29, 32; 18:9; Sir 14:10; 37:10, 11); the miserly and stingy withholding of aid or food to persons in need (Deut 15:7–11; 28:54–57; Prov 23:6–8; Sir 14:5–8, 10; 18:18; Tob 4:7, 16); the reluctant and begrudging providing of hospitality and food at one's table (Prov 23:6; Sir 14:10); being greedy and "hurrying after wealth" (Prov 28:22; Sir 14:9; cf. "roving desire," Wis 4:12); and gluttonous behavior at the table of others (Sir 14:9; 31:12–13; cf. 4 Macc 1:25–26). This association of the Evil Eye with stinginess, miserliness, niggardliness, parsimony, begrudging hospitality, a closed hand, averting one's eyes from the needy, or in modern terms, the "Scrooge Factor," appears repeatedly in the Old Testament, but only infrequently in Mesopotamian, Egyptian, and Greco-Roman sources. It is a major distinguishing feature of how the Evil Eye was viewed in the biblical communities and presented in the Bible. Among the biblical communities, the Evil Eye is viewed as the antithesis of generosity, liberality, altruism, unselfishness, and openhandedness toward others. Having and wielding an Evil Eye is deemed a grave moral failing incompatible with the will of God. It is listed among the vices as a malady of the soul (4 Macc 1:25–26) and a violent passion (4 Macc 2:15–16). It is described as a malice that obscures the good (Wis 4:12), and is lamented as the worst of all evils (Sir 14:6, 31:13).

Evil-Eyed persons, fascinators, embrace men and women, kings and newcomers (1 Sam 18:9), oneself (Sir 14:6, 9), persons of one's own family (Deut 28:53–57), patriarchs and matriarchs, hosts or guests at table (Prov 23:6, Sir 14:10; 31:12–13), those who envy (1 Sam 18:9; cf. 1 Sam 2:29, 32; Sir 14:10; 37:10, 11), those who are greedy (Sir 14:9) or miserly (Sir 14:3), who refuse aid or food to others (Deut 15:7–11; 28:54–57; Sir 14:8, 10) or who fail to show gratitude (Sir 37:11). Specifically identified are Joseph's envious brothers (Gen 37:11); envious King Saul (1 Sam 18:9); envious priests (1 Sam 2:32); envious co-wives (Sir 37:11); greedy priests (1 Sam

2:29); greedy pursuers of wealth (Sir 14:3, 9); hosts of banquets (Prov 23:6; Sir 14:10) and guests at banquets (Sirach 14:9; 31:12–13); famished parents (Deut 28:53–57); potential counselors (Sir 37:10, 11); and intemperate persons (4 Macc 1:25–26; 2:15–16). In later rabbinic and Christian traditions, fascinators include barren women envious of those who could bear children (e.g., Sarah, Rachel) as well as brothers envious of a favored sibling (Cain of Abel, Esau of Jacob, Joseph's brothers of Joseph), and a king (Saul) enviously Evil-Eyeing a more acclaimed subordinate (David).

Potential victims of the Evil Eye, the fascinated, include family members (Deut 28:53–57), co-wives (Sir 37:11), newborns and children, political rivals (1 Sam 18:9), the poor and needy (Deut 15:7–11; Tob 4:5–21), the starving (Deut 28:53–57), guests at table (Prov 23:6), the envied, persons who Evil-Eye themselves (Prov 28:22; Sir 14:5–6, 9; cf. 18:18; 31:13), and crops in the field (Ep Jer 69/70).

As elsewhere in the ancient world, mothers and children in Israel were particularly vulnerable to illness and death. Pregnancy and birth were precarious moments. Births could be premature (Eccl 6:4–5); miscarriages occurred (Exod 21:22–25); delivery was accompanied by pain (Isa 13:8; Jer 13:21; 22:23; 30:6; 49:24) and often by the mother's death (Gen 35:16–20; 1 Sam 4:19–21; 2 Kgs 19:3). Birthing mothers and newborns thus were considered especially vulnerable to an Evil Eye, as was also the case in Mesopotamian, Egyptian, Greek, and Roman cultures.

The *harm* wrought by an Evil Eye could involve desperate need and starvation left unrelieved (Deut 15:7–11; 28:53–57; Tob 4:1–21), vomiting of food while dining (Prov 23:6), failure to enjoy one's own good fortune (Sir 14:5), a dimming of one's own eyes, blindness (Sir 18:18) and injury to self (Sir 14:6), socially divisive envy (1 Sam 18:9), and the obscuring of what is good (Wis 4:12). The Evil Eye is the worst of evils and causes tears to fall from every face (Sir 31:13).

Measures for avoiding the Evil Eye of others include refusal to dine with Evil-Eyed persons (Prov 23:6); not taking their advice (Sir 37:10–11); wearing anti-Evil Eye amulets and protectives on one's person, and erecting anti-Evil Eye apotropaics in one's garden to protect crops from the Evil Eye of passersby (Ep Jer 69/70).

The Old Testament, in sum, shows that Israel shared with its neighbors a dread of the Evil Eye, a horror of being publicly labeled an Evil Eye possessor/fascinator, and similar stratagems for avoiding or warding off its injurious power. Biblical Greek (LXX) and Latin (Vulgate) *terminology* for the Evil Eye is that of the surrounding Greek and Roman cultures. Biblical comments on the Evil Eye reflect standard features of the ancient Evil Eye belief complex. The single explicit mention of an anti-Evil Eye apotropaic, the *probaskanion* of Ep Jer 69/70, involves a conventional Greek term for an anti-Evil eye apotropaic and an understanding of its function that mirrors Greek and Roman practice.

Belief in the Evil Eye in the biblical communities and ancient world generally formed part of a larger belief system involving concepts of demons, witchcraft, sorcery, and related extraordinary forces and agents affecting the natural and social environment and threatening human health as well as social well-being.[301] In a precarious natural environment, where economic survival for the greater portion of the population was uncertain, where a mixed economy and both economic and social disparity led to persistent competition and conflict over resources perceived as scarce and limited, where the eye was regarded as linked with the heart and the channel of its attitudes and dispositions, there ocular aggression and fear of the Evil Eye played a dominant role in human behavior and social interaction.

For the biblical communities, as for their neighbors, Evil Eye belief and practice was no more incompatible with belief in the high gods or in a sole deity, Yahweh, than was a fear of witches, sorcerers, or magicians. On the other hand, in contrast to their Mesopotamian, Egyptian, Greek, and Roman neighbors, the biblical communities never attributed the Evil Eye to their deity, who could be thought of as "jealous" of that which He possessed but never envious of, or malicious toward, his creatures. Nor did the biblical authors speak of an Evil Eye demon attacking them from without, or of a personified *Baskania* (Evil Eye) or *Phthonos* (Envy).

The Evil Eye constituted for them a predominantly *human* trait and moral quality, the very worst of the evils created by God, and a constant source of tears. It gave expression to the malicious emotion of envy and the mean-spirited disposition of miserliness and illiberality that refused or begrudged aid to the needy. It could cause vomiting at the table, tears to fall from every face, and injury to the fascinator and the community. Looking at another community member with an Evil Eye, hardening one's heart, and closing one's hand to neighbors in need violated the obligation of mutual aid and constituted a sin bringing divine judgment. In ambiguous occasions unregulated by formal laws or arrangements, the danger of an Evil Eye was invoked to promote traditional values such as generosity and the sharing of goods, especially with those in need. For the community defined and bound by the covenant established by YHWH, the Evil Eye symbolized unacceptable social and moral deviance. Avoidance of casting an Evil Eye and

---

301. On witches, witchcraft, and witchcraft accusation in the biblical communities see Bar-Ilan 1993; Schmitt 2012; and below, chap. 2.

practicing generosity, on the other hand, contributed to communal well-being and cohesion and fostered the values and ideals of covenantal justice.

References to the Evil Eye in Israel's parabiblical literature are consistent with what we find in the Old Testament. On the whole, the Evil Eye continues to be regarded as a human phenomenon and an expression of hostility toward other fellow humans. The *Testament of Solomon*, a noteworthy exception, conceives of the Evil Eye as a spirit-demon that can be thwarted by a powerful apotropaic eye. The biblical figure of King Solomon was renown in the period following the conclusion of the Hebrew and Greek Bibles as knowing an effective apotropaic against the Evil Eye (*T. Sol.* 18:39) and as a defender against the Evil Eye; see also Vol. 4, chap. 1). The patriarch Joseph likewise featured especially in this tradition as having survived the Evil Eye of his envious brothers (*T. 12. Patr.*). Appeal to this powerful figure, it was believed in the post-biblical period, afforded protection from envious Evil Eye attack (*b. Ber.* 55b; *b. B.M.* 84a; *Gen. Rab.* 78:10 on Gen 33:7). The rabbinic period saw an increase in the number of fascinators and enviers found in the Old Testament and in the strategies for warding off the Evil Eye's harmful power; see also Vol. 4, chap. 1).

In the pseudepigraphical writings of the Old Testament as well as the Dead Sea Scrolls, Philo, and Josephus, the Evil Eye is spoken of in terms and senses similar to those of the Hebrew and Greek Old Testaments, as well as Greek and Roman sources. It is particularly notable, however, that in this range of Israelite writings, possession and use of the Evil Eye is viewed so consistently in moral terms as a vehicle of malevolent emotions and dispositions unbefitting God's holy people. Persons with an Evil Eye lack integrity and generosity (*T. Iss.* 3:1–8, 4:1–5:4; *T. Sim.* 4:5). An Evil Eye is a "darkened eye" (*T. Benj.* 4:2). It conveys envy (*T. Iss.* 3:3, 4:5; *T. Sol.*18:39; cf. *T. Sim.* passim, Philo, Josephus). Those possessing an Evil Eye are untrustworthy (4Q424, frag. 1). Looking with an envious Evil Eye or casting an Evil Eye is an act of malevolence, hostility, and enmity against fellow humans, including one's own family, friends, and community. It manifests dispositions and a heart unattuned to the will of God and Israel's moral norms. It can cause injury to self as well as damage and loss to others. It can undermine the solidarity of families and the social body of Israel. Those beyond Israel's borders, specifically the Egyptians, were stereotyped as Evil-Eyed by nature and bursting with envy at the good fortune of others (Philo, *Flaccus* 29). The Evil Eye was attributed to strangers (Philo, *Agriculture* 64 etc.) and Evil Eye accusations could cause disgrace and flight (Philo, *Flaccus* 143). Targets of the Evil Eye included the prosperous and the victorious (Philo, *Joseph* 144 etc.; *Agriculture* 112), those singled out for favor (Josephus, *Ant.* 10.250, 257; *Life* 423, 425), and strangers (Philo, *Moses* 1:246 etc.). The material and iconographic evidence of Israel's apotropaic amulets, gestures, and actions express these same features of Israel's Evil Eye belief. This evidence in great part mirrors that of its neighbors while also showing adaptation to Israel's particular cultural and religious traditions.

What is striking about Israel's biblical and parabiblical tradition concerning the Evil Eye against the backdrop of Mesopotamian, Egyptian, Greek, and Roman tradition, is the absence of any mention of an Evil Eyed demon and of Israel's god as envious—in contrast to the Greek *baskanos daimon* and the envy and Evil Eye attributed to the Greek gods. The *Testament of Solomon* represents a singular exception in its association of the Evil Eye with a spirit-demon rather than a hostile human. Israel's sages spoke of the Evil Eye and the Evil-Eyed person as a *human* and *moral* phenomenon and as involving the volition of the agent. An Evil Eye, like envy with which it was so closely associated, betrays deviants acting out of synch with the values of the community and its distinctive emphasis on mutual communal support. An Evil Eye, miserliness, and envy place an individual at odds with the will and nature of a generous Creator who was zealous and jealous for His own people but never envious.

A "good eye" in a human represents the opposite of an Evil Eye, the alternative to a tight-fisted illiberality. A good eye is animated by a generous spirit and good will, particularly toward the poor and needy.

This broad sense of an Evil Eye, as we shall see in chap. 2 below, also typifies the teaching of Jesus and his early followers. Israel's distinctive stress on the immoral quality and intentional malevolence of the human Evil Eye sets the stage for our examination of references to the Evil Eye in the New Testament. There the Evil Eye is given a similar moral accentuation in the teaching of Jesus and the back-and-forth accusations of Paul and his opponents in Galatia.

2

THE NEW TESTAMENT CONCERNING THE EVIL EYE

INTRODUCTION

EVIL EYE BELIEF AND practice in Israel, as attested in the Old Testament, Israel's intertestamental writings, the Dead Sea Scrolls, and the writings of Philo and Josephus, continued in the early Jesus movement and, thereafter, in the rabbinic/Talmudic period and early Christianity down through Late Antiquity. Given the widespread and persistent dread of the Evil Eye over these centuries in Israel and the Greco-Roman world, it is hardly surprising to encounter it in the teaching of Jesus of Nazareth and a letter of the apostle Paul. Jesus mentions the Evil Eye on more than one occasion. Paul makes explicit mention of the Evil Eye in his letter to the Galatians and alludes to an exchange of Evil Eye accusations between himself and his rivals.

Like their fellow Israelites and their Greek and Roman contemporaries, Jesus and his earliest followers were persuaded that heavenly and earthly realms were populated by potent entities, spirits (both clean and unclean), angels, and demons. They too were convinced of the efficacious power of incantations, blessings and curses, spells, amulets, and powerful words and gestures.[1] They too knew of, and played a role in, many events of

1. They were familiar with, and ascribed to, the principle of "like influences like" (*similia similibus*), so fundamental to the presumed efficacy of apotropaics against the Evil

extraordinary healings, mass feedings, acts of human control over natural forces, altered states of consciousness, ascensions to the heavens, and revelations and auditions of heavenly voices. They too reckoned with ghosts, reappearing ancestors, witches, sorcerers, agents of the magical arts, necromancers, soothsayers, diviners, and Evil-Eyed fascinators. These were all deemed part of the natural order and thought to work mysteriously but effectively to influence human lives and destinies for good or evil. All are mentioned explicitly in the sacred writings. Jesus and one of his followers, Paul of Tarsus, we are told in the New Testament writings, also resorted to accusations of Evil Eye possession to denounce others of envy and deviation from the will of God.[2] Evil Eye belief and its accompanying practices were part of the Weltanschunung and "mental furniture" of this world of Jesus, Paul, and the communities described in the New Testament. Studies of Jesus's cultural world discuss Evil Eye belief as a telling feature of that

Eye. This notion, although not mentioned in the New Testament in connection with the Evil Eye, does feature, for example, in the presumed protection from poisonous serpents afforded to God's people in the wilderness by the bronze serpent crafted and lifted up by Moses and displayed for the people to look at (Num 21:4–9, esp. 21:9). The incident is mentioned by Jesus in his conversation with the Judean ruler, Nicodemus. John 3:1–21, esp. 3:14). Here it was a case of serpent protecting against serpents. On the principle of "like influences like" (*similia similibus*) see Vol. 2.

2. Among the numerous studies on the cultural and social scene of Jesus and his contemporaries relevant to our topic see especially Derrett 1973:31–174; Brox 1974; Neyrey 1990 (Paul); 1991 (Lk-Acts), 1998; Malina 1993, 2001; Esler 1994; Pilch 1995, 1996, 1999, 2004; Rohrbaugh 1996c, 2007; Malina and Rohrbaugh 2003; Malina and Pilch 2006; Neyrey and Stewart 2008. On demonology in Israel (biblical and postbiblical) see Conybeare 1895; Billerbeck (Str-B) 4/1 (1928/1961):501–35; Noack 1948; Langton 1949; Böcher 1970, 1981; Colpe et al., ed. 1976:546–797; Smith 1978; Ferguson 1984 and above, chap. 1, p. 5 n. 9.

culture.[3] This world, of course, shared the ecological, economic, and social conditions in which Evil Eye belief and practice have typically flourished.[4]

One major difference concerning Evil Eye belief in Israel and the Jesus movement, as opposed to that of their neighbors, however, stands out. Greeks and Romans, as the Mesopotamians before them, attributed an Evil Eye not only to humans but to a *baskanos daimôn*, an Evil-Eye demon. This demon belonged to the cast of hostile potencies thought to threaten humans, animals, and their welfare. There is no explicit reference to this demon in the biblical writings, which consistently speak of the Evil Eye only as a *human* phenomenon involving an active eye and internal human malevolent dispositions. It is not until the post-biblical period that Christians explicitly link the Evil Eye with an *external demonic force*, namely the chief of demons, the devil or Satan. On this development, see Vol. 4, chap. 2, on post-biblical Christian tradition. The Evil Eye spoken of in the New Testament writings is a strictly human phenomenon and is regarded as part and parcel of everyday human experience and conduct.

There are five explicit references to the Evil Eye in the New Testament. Four occur in the Synoptic Gospels as sayings of Jesus: Matt 6:22–23; 20:15; Mark 7:22; and Luke 11:34–35. In addition, preceeding Matt 6 and Luke 11 is the Q saying, Q11:34–35. All these sayings of Jesus are regarded by most scholars as authentic Jesus tradition. Paul also explicitly mentions the Evil Eye in his letter to the Galatians (Gal 3:1, *ebaskanen*), while also making further allusions to Evil Eye belief and behavior later in the letter (4:12–20).

3. For studies on, and brief references to, the Evil Eye in the New Testament and early Christianity, see Story 1877:152; Lightfoot 1866:133–34; Elworthy 1895/1958:5–6 and note 7a, 10; Elworthy 1958/1895:5, 6 and notes 7a, 10; Seligmann 1910 1:12–14; Leclerq 1924 1.2:1843–47 (citing Mark 7:22, Gal 3:1, Basil and Chrysostom); Cadoux 1941–42; Ryder Smith 1941–42, 1942–43; Duncan 1942–43; Percy 1942–43; Amiot 1946:59; Koetting 1954; Fensham 1967; Roberts Jr. 1963; Breech 1983:150–55; Yamauchi 1983:187–92 (describing it as a form of "black magic"); Chouraqui 1985:277; Allison 1987; Elliott 1988, 1990, 1991, 1992, 1993:67–69; 1994, 2004; 2005a, 2005b:159–64; 2007a, 2011, 2014, 2015; 2016a, 2016b, 2016c; Neyrey 1988a, 1998:224–24; Nanos 1999; 2000, 2002:181–91 and *passim*; Dunn 1993:151–52; Esler 1994:21, 1998:219, 228, 230; Derrett 1995; Bissoli 1996; Duff 1996, 2001; Rohrbaugh 1996:3–4, 2006:3–4; Rakoczy 1996:217, 276; Witherington 1997:202–04; Longnecker 1998:26, 153–57; Pilch 1996a, 1999:19, 119–21, 143–44; 2000a:19, 80, 85–86, 126, 133–34, 152; 2000b; 2002:51–52, 2004b, 2012:176–81; Hagedorn and Neyrey 1998:223–24; Pilch and Malina 1998:59–63,68–72, 122–27, 209–12; Fiensy 1999, 2007; Guijarro 2000; Aquaro 2001, 2004; Bridges and Wheeler 2001; Eastman 2001; Malina 2001:108–33; Perkins 2001:1–3; Snyder 2002:27; Malina and Rohrbaugh 2003b:50, 101–2, 176, 357–59; Aquaro 2004:20–70; Asano 2005:6, 238; Greenfield 2006:284–85; Malina and Pilch 2006:202–3, 209–10, 359–62; Apostolides 2008; Apostolides and Dreyer 2008; Hartsock 2008:143–46; Koivisto 2011.

4. See Roberts 1976; Garrison and Arensberg 1976; and previously, Vols. 1 and 2.

The letter to the Galatians is one of the authentic Pauline writings and these verses of Galatians likewise represent authentic words of Paul, with no suggestion of secondary addition. These New Testament references to the Evil Eye, while not as numerous as those found in the Old Testament, nevertheless provide further information on the Evil Eye and the social dynamics of Evil Eye accusation and counter-accusation. These passages indicate that nascent Christianity continued to take the Evil Eye with utmost seriousness. For Jesus and his followers, all of whom emerged within the cultural matrix of Second Temple Israel, the Evil Eye continued to bear serious moral and social overtones. The disdain, disapproval, and dread of the Evil Eye in both Israel and the emerging Church continued through Late Antiquity, as we shall see in Vol. 4. In the relevant New Testament texts discussed in this chapter, we encounter familiar elements of the Evil Eye belief complex: the eye taken as an active rather than a passive organ, emitting rather than receiving light and hence comparable to a lamp broadcasting light; an Evil Eye conveying malicious emotions arising in the heart; its close association with envy and ungenerosity; and the wielding of damaging Evil Eye accusations.

Full studies of these New Testament Evil Eye passages are few in number, which comes as a surprise given the ubiquity and intensity of the belief in this period. Since 1988, I have published a series of articles on the Evil Eye in the biblical writings.[5] Prompted by this research, Jerome Neyrey, Philip Esler, John Pilch, Richard Rohrbaugh, and others have noted references to the Evil Eye in the Bible and the need for their study in context.[6] Bruce Malina has discussed the link of the Evil Eye and envy in the biblical world,[7] and scholarly attention to this widespread and influential, yet exegetically neglected, belief appears to be growing.[8] Commentators on the relevant biblical passages, on the other hand, tend to discuss mainly philological points and appear unfamiliar with this widespread ancient belief.[9]

5. Elliott 1988, 1990, 1991, 1992, 1994, 2005a, 2005b, 2007a, 2011, 2014, 2015, 2016a, 2016b, 2016c.

6. Neyrey 1998, 1990; also 1998:223–224 on Matt 6:22–23; Esler 1994:19–24; Pilch 1996a; 1999:19; 2002:51–52; 2004; 2012:51–52; Rohrbaugh 2006:3–4; see also Bissoli 1996; Bridges and Wheeler 2001; Fiensy 2007:11–22.

7. Malina 2001:108–33

8. See Pilch and Malina 1998:59–63; Perkins 2001:1–3; Snyder 2002:27.

9. Welcome exceptions include Malina and Rohrbaugh on the Synoptic Gospels (2003:50, 101–2, 176, 357–59); Esler on Galatians (1998:219, 228, 230); Longenecker 1998:153–57 (on Galatians); Nanos 2002:181–82; 186–91, 279–80 (on Galatians); Malina and Pilch on Galatians (2006:202–3, 359–62); and the new annotations of Duling on Matt 6:23 and 20:15 in the SBL *HarperCollins Study Bible*, 2nd ed. 2006.

Thomas Rakoczy's excellent study on the Evil Eye in the Greco-Roman world looks only briefly at Evil Eye texts from Jesus to John Chrysostom (1996:216–26, "Christliche

THE EVIL EYE SAYINGS OF JESUS

The Evil Eye Saying in the Q Sayings Source (Q11:34–35)

Perhaps the earliest attestation of a word of Jesus concerning the Evil Eye is a saying contained in the so-called "Q" or "Sayings Source" (composed c. 50–60 CE): Q11:34–35. The Q Sayings Source, according to current exegetical theory, consisted of a collection of various sayings of Jesus (c. 242 verses) that circulated in oral form about 50–60 CE. The authors of the Gospels of Matthew and Luke each incorporated these sayings in their respective Gospels, producing a Matthean (Q^Matt) and a Lukan (Q^Luke) version of this material. The Q saying of Jesus on the Evil Eye, Q11:34–35, has been judged "undoubtedly an authentic word of Jesus."[10] Differing versions of the saying are given by Matthew (6:22–23) and Luke (11:34–35), both of whom were writing c. 80–90 CE. Matthew and Luke located the saying in different places of their narratives, with Luke expanding the saying by two verses (Luke 11:33, 36). Matthew situated the saying within a major unit popularly known as "the Sermon on the Mount" (5:1—7:28) in a sub-section (6:1–34)

Autoren: Der erste Paradigmwechsel"). In respect to the New Testament, he mentions only two texts (Matt 6:23 and Gal 3:1) in passing (Rakoczy 1996:217), with no analysis. In regard to the post-biblical Christian texts that he does examine, he describes the association of the Evil Eye with the Devil as a "paradigm shift." This association, however, occurs only in texts subsequent to the New Testament, so that the New Testament texts are not part of this "paradigm shift." The "shift" concerns regard of the Evil Eye as something *external* rather than (or in addition to) a personal human quality, thus representing a "dramatic difference" from previous ancient understanding (Rakoczy 1996:217). In a footnote (ibid.:217 n. 800), Rakoczy lists several references to the Evil Eye in the Greek Old Testament (LXX: Wis 4:12; Deut 28:54, 56; Sir 14:3, 6, 8; 18:18; 37:11; Prov 23:6; 28:22; 4 Macc 1:26; 2:15) but provides no discussion. He also opines that an absence of the Latin equivalent in the Christian writings, *malus oculus*, is probably no more than a coincidence of the tradition (ibid.).

In respect to this notion of a "paradigm shift," two points are crucial. (1) There is no evidence in the New Testament references to the Evil Eye of the "paradigm shift" that Rakoczy claims for Christianity as a whole. (2) The association of the Evil Eye with the Devil, an external force, is found *first* in the post-New Testament literature (*Mart. Polyc.* 17:1), and signals a *departure* from earlier Christian and Israelite thinking as found in the biblical writings. The association of the Evil Eye with a demonic force is by no means a novelty of Christian belief, but rather an adoption of the *baskanos daimôn* notion long a part of Mesopotamian and Greco-Roman belief. It is thus hard to find any evidence for the claim that in the Christian era a Christian doctrine emerged "that dramatically differentiated itself from the ancient (pagan) conception" (Rakoczy 1996:217). Rakoczy, however, is correct in noting that in Christian, as in pagan circles, Evil Eye belief and practice prevailed across the social strata and that Christians employed the same protective strategies against Evil Eye as their pagan neighbors (Rakoczy 1996:217 n. 799; see also Engemann 1975:22–23 for the parallels).

10. Davies and Allison 1988:641; cf also Allison 1987:81.

contrasting the attitudes and actions of his followers to those of the Phari-sees (6:1–18) and the Gentiles (6:32). Luke, on the other hand, located the saying not in his parallel to Matthew's Sermon on the Mount, namely Jesus's "Sermon on the Plain" (Luke 6:20–49), but in a latter narrative of Jesus' journey from Galilee to Jerusalem (9:51—19:27) containing much mate-rial unique to Luke. More specifically, the saying appears within a Lukan subsection concerning accusations against Jesus and his critical responses, along with critiques of the Pharisees and lawyers (Luke 11:14–54).[11]

Although the text of Luke's gospel generally is thought to provide the more likely original wording and sequence of the sayings in the Q source, in the case of the good and Evil Eye saying (Matt 6:22–23/Luke 11:34–35), Matthew's briefer version appears closer to the original wording and shape of Q than that of Luke (11:33–36). Luke's concluding verse (11:36) has no parallel in either Q or Matthew and the opening verse (Luke 11:33) is a saying (Q11:33) located elsewhere in Matthew (5:15).[12] The Markan gospel, of course, has no parallel to Matt 6:22–23/Luke 11:34–35 (= Q11:34–35).[13] However, certain terms and ideas similar to those of our Q saying, other than the contrast of eyes, are found in both Mark and the later *Gospel of Thomas*.[14] Nevertheless, since these similarities do not include mention of a good or Evil Eye, they can be excluded from our analysis.

In what follows, the wording of Q11:34–35 and Q11:33 are presented. In place of a separate analysis of the Q saying (11:34–35), our examinations of Matt 6:22–23 and Luke 11:33–36 will include attention to the Q saying as it was adopted and adapted by each evangelist. As to terminology, the term "integral" translates the Greek adjective *haplous*, which appears in Matt 6:22b; Luke 11:34, and hence in Q11:34b in the phrase *ophthalmos haplous* as a contrast to *ophthalmos ponêros* ("Evil Eye"). As the following discus-sion will indicate, this "integral eye" in all three texts connotes an eye and a person that is unreservedly *generous*, especially to those in need. It marks a

11. Matt 6:22–23 and Luke 11:34–35 are close in content and, because they repre-sent versions of the Q source, have no parallel in Mark. However, Mark 7:1–23 (refer-ring to the Evil Eye in 7:22) presents some interesting similarities to the larger literary context of Luke 11, particularly Luke 11:37–41, which, in turn, parallels material in Matthew 6 and Matthew 23.

12. The formulation of Q11:34–35 in *The Sayings Gospel Q* (Robinson, Hoffmann, Kloppenborg, eds. 2002:110–12) reflects this proximity; compare Allison 1987:71–73.

13. By definition, the hypothetical Q source consists of material common to Mat-thew and Luke but absent in Mark.

14. Concerning the use of a lamp for lighting compare Q11:33 (Matt:5:15/Luke 11:33) with Mark 4:21b-c and *Gos.Thom.* 33.2–3. Concerning light or darkness in a person (Q11:35) compare *Gos. Thom.* 24.3.

moral integrity manifested in openness, frankness, and unstinting liberality in contrast to a miserly Evil Eye.

A reconstruction of Q11:34–35 in this Q Sayings Source[15] reads as follows:

Q11:34–35
(Eye as Body's Lamp,
Contrast of Integral versus Evil Eye and of Light versus Darkness)

> 11:34a The lamp of the body is the eye.
> 11:34b If your eye is integral,
> 11:34c   your entire body is full of light;
> 11:34d if, however, your Eye is Evil,
> 11:34e   your entire body <<is>> full of darkness.
> 11:35a If, then, the light within you is darkness,
> 11:35b   how great the darkness![16]

> 11:34a *ho lychnos tou sômatos estin ho ophthalmos.*
> 11:34b *an ho ophthalmos sou haplous ê,*
> 11:34c   *holon to sôma phôteinon est[[in]]*
> 11:34d *an de ho ophthalmos sou ponêros ê,*
> 11:34e   *holon to soma sou skoteinon.*
> 11:35a *ei oun to phôs to en soi skotos estin,*
> 11:35b   *to skotos poson.*[17]

The structure of this saying involves an opening statement expressing the premise concerning the eye as the lamp of the body (11:34a) on which a

---

15. Robinson, Hoffmann, Kloppenborg, eds. 2002:110–13

16. Compare the translation of ibid.:111 and its heading, "The Jaundiced Eye Darkens the Body's Radiance" (Matt 6:22–23/Luke 11:34–35):

11:34a The lamp of the body is the eye.
11:34b If your eye is generous,
11:34c   your whole body [[is]] radiant;
11:34d but if your eye is jaundiced,
11:34e   your whole body <<is>> dark.
11:35a So if the light within you is dark,
11:35b   how great <<must>> the darkness <<be>>!"

My modifications in the text above involve a clearer paralleling in English of the three conditional statements, the rendition of *ponêros* with "Evil" rather than "jaundiced," of *haplous* as "integral" rather than "generous," and a briefer translation of 11:35b in place of "how great <<must>> the darkness <<be>>!"

17. The reconstructed Greek text is from ibid.:110–11), where double angle brackets << >> identify words added in the English translation according to sense and for a smooth flow of thought. Double square brackets [[ ]] mark an uncertain term. Single angle brackets <> indicate an emendation. On the reconstruction of this Q passage, compare Allison 1987:71–73.

contrast of two types of eyes is based (11:34b–34e). The conclusion (11:35ab) consists of the last of three parallel conditional "if" clauses (11:34b, 34d, 35a) and with its negative focus on darkness within a person brings the saying to a close.[18]

In the Sayings Source, Q11:34–35 follows Q11:33 (lamp providing light) and is connected through the linkword "lamp" (*lychnos*, 11:33, 34). Q11:33 reads:

> 11:33a No one light<s> a lamp and puts it [[in a hidden place]],
> 11:33b   but on the lampstand,
> 11:33c [[and it gives light for everyone in the house]].[19]

> 11:33a *Oudeis kai <ei>lychnon kai tithêsin auton [[eis kruptên]]*
> 11:33b   *all' epi tên lychnian,*
> 11:33c *[[kai lampei pasin tois en tê oikia]].*

The connection of these two Q sayings (11:33, 34–35) was retained by Luke (11:33–35). Matthew, on the other hand, separated Q11:33 from Q11:34–35 and used Q11:33 as part of Jesus's exhortation to his disciples early in the Sermon on the Mount (Matt 5:15). The disciples are urged to act like a lamp that sheds light and to let their light shine in the world through their good deeds (Matt 5:14–16). Other versions of the lamp saying appear in Mark 4:21b–c; Luke 8:16; and *Gos. Thom.* 33.2–3.[20] These parallels show

---

18. The Greek text as reconstructed in Robinson, Hoffmann, and Kloppenborg, eds. 2002:110–11. Q11:34a = Matt 6:22a; Luke 11:34a adds "your" (*sou*) (body)."

Luke 11:34b reads *hotan*; cf. Matt 6:22b *ean*;

Luke 11:34d reads *epan*; cf. Matt 6:23a *ean*

Q11:34b = Matt 6:22b/Luke 11:34b. Luke 11:34b has "whenever" in place of "if (therefore)" of Matthew.

Q11:34c = Matt 6:22c/Luke 11:34c; cp. Matt "will be" (*estai*) with Luke 11:34c "is" (*estin*).

Q11:34d = Matt 6:23a/Luke 11:34d. Luke omits "your eye" (*ho ophthalmos sou*) but this subject is clearly implied in the verb "it is" (*ê*) and its foregoing antithesis, "your eye (is good)," Luke 11:34b.

Q11:34e = Matt 6:23b/Luke 11:34e. Matt again has "will be" (*estai*), whereas Luke has an implied "is."

Q11:35 = the wording of Matt 6:23cd. This contrasts to the hortatory tone of Luke 11:35: "Therefore be careful lest the light in you be darkness."

19. As reconstructed in ibid.:110–11).

20. Mark 4:21b–c reads: "Is a lamp brought in to be put under the bushel basket, or under the bed, and not on the lampstand?" This is echoed and expanded on in Luke 8:16: "No one after lighting a lamp covers it with a vessel, or puts it under a bed, but puts it on a stand, that those who enter may see the light." See also *Gos. Thom.* 33.2–3 (Nag Hammadi II 2): (2) "For no one, kindling a lamp, puts it under a bushel, nor does one put it in a hidden place. (3) Rather, one puts it on a lampstand, so that everyone who comes in and goes out will see its light." See Robinson, Hoffmann, and Kloppenborg,

that the saying Q11:33 once circulated independently of the integral versus Evil Eye saying (Q11:34–35) so that a redactor of Q is likely responsible for the combination.[21] None of these parallel sayings, however, mentions an Evil Eye or a good eye. Therefore we can exclude them from our analysis, along with the content of Q11:33. In place of a separate analysis of Q11:34–35, we will examine the texts of Matt 6:22–23 and Luke 11:33–36 in their entireties, including their modifications of the Q saying.

The relation of Q11:33–35 to its immediate context in the Sayings Source is uncertain. According to the division of Q proposed by John Kloppenborg,[22] the two sayings belong to a major unit of the Q source treating "Controversies with Israel" (Q11:14–52). Their role in this unit, however, is not stated.

The Sayings Gospel Q in Greek and English translates the terms *haplous* and *ponêros* not literally but according to sense, rendering *haplous* ("integral") with "generous," and *ponêros* ("evil") with "jaundiced."[23] This creates an attractive assonance and gives a fitting sense for *haplous*. Moreover, there is some evidence that in antiquity jaundice was associated with the Evil Eye.[24] But for the modern reader, "jaundiced" does not communicate any such association with the Evil Eye. Nor is "jaundiced" a conventional or logical antithesis to "generous." "Miserly" is the more fitting contrast to "generous" and the likely implied quality of "Evil Eye" here and in Matt 6:23a and Luke 11:34d.[25]

The tradition represented in Q, as well as in Matthew, Luke, and as we shall see, Mark and the *Gospel of Thomas,* consists of varying sayings and combinations of sayings concerning lamps projecting light, light in the human body, and eyes (good or evil) as indications of human moral character

eds. 2002:110–12.

21. The formation, content, and attested existence of Q11:33–35 is a complex issue. Luke 11:33 (= Q11:33), the light on the lampstand saying, appears to be a doublet of Luke 8:16. Luke 8:16 parallels Mark 4:21 within the Mark-Luke double tradition, with Luke following Mark's sequence of material (Mark 4:1–25/Luke 8:4–18). Matt 5:15 is a further parallel to Mark 4:21/Luke 8:16/11:33. It does not follow Mark's sequence but rather parallels Luke 11:33 as part of the Matt-Luke double tradition (= Q). Luke 11:33 thus has affinity to both the Mark-Luke double tradition and the Matt-Luke Q source.

22. Kloppenborg 1987:92. Kloppenborg regards this as a secondarily redacted section he calls "Q2."

23. Robinson, Hoffmann, and Kloppenborg, eds. 2002:110–11.

24. Plutarch, in his account of a discussion on the Evil Eye (*Quest. Conv.* 5.7.1, Mor. 680C–683B), mentions the ability of the yellow-colored plover to heal a victim of jaundice (Mor. 681CD). On this text see Vol. 2.

25. On *integral* with the implication of *generous* as the appropriate translation of *haplous* in Q11:34b, Matt 6:22b, and Luke 11:34b, see below, on Matt 6:22b.

and conduct. Jesus's saying concerning a good/integral/generous eye versus an envious/miserly Evil Eye is one element of this tradition and appears in Q, Matthew, and Luke. Let us now examine the Matthean and then the Lukan versions of the saying.

The Evil Eye Saying in Matthew 6:22–23 and Luke 11:33–36

Matthew 6:22–23

22a The eye (*ophthalmos*) is the lamp of the body.
22b If, then, your eye (*ophthalmos*) is integral (*haplous*)
22c   your entire body will be full of light.
23a If, however, your eye (*ophthalmos*) is evil (*ponêros*),
23b   your entire body will be full of darkness.
23c If, then, the light in you is darkness,
23d   how great the darkness!

22a *Ho lychnos tou sômatos estin ho ophthlamos.*
22b *ean oun ê ho ophthlamos sou haplous*
22c   *holon to soma sou phôteinon estai.*
23a *ean de ho ophthlamos sou ponêros ê,*
23b   *holon to soma sou skoteineon estai.*
23c *ei oun to phôs to en soi skotos estin,*
23d   *to skotos poson!*

Matthew 6:22–23 is Matthew's rendering of Q11:34–35 and is closer to the wording of Q11:34–35 than is the Lukan version (11:34–35). Variants in the textual transmission are few and minor.[26] Matthew's version of the Q saying, in contrast to both Q and Luke, is not connected with a foregoing lamp saying and focuses not on the lamp but on the eye. The translation, which inverts the order of "eye" and "lamp," reflects this difference in focus.

THE LITERARY CONTEXT OF MATTHEW 6:22–23

Prior to the composition of Matthew, our Q saying concerning the Evil Eye (Matt 6:22–23/Luke 11:34–35) circulated as an independent logion, as the differing contexts of Matt 6:22–23 and Luke 11:34–35 suggest. It was then combined in the Q Sayings source with Q11:33. Matthew situated Jesus's saying on the integral and Evil Eye in the unit now known as the "Sermon on the Mount" (5:1—7:29).[27] This is the first of five major discourses of Jesus

26. For the variants, see below, p. 122 n. 33 at the discussion of Matt 6:22–23.

27. Elliott 1994 is an earlier and briefer analysis of Matt 6:22–23. On the Sermon on

as presented by Matthew, composed of numerous words of Jesus on different topics of his teaching and proclamation concerning life under the rule
of God.[28] More immediately, the saying is located in a section dealing with
contrasting priorities (6:19–21), divided loyalties (6:24), and a choice between (a) anxiety over material means of subsistence as typical of Gentiles
versus (b) trust in God and the pursuit of righteousness (6:25–34).[29] Flanking the contrast of an integral and an Evil Eye (6:22–23) are two sayings
contrasting earthly and heavenly wealth (6:19–21)[30] and loyalty to either
God or wealth/*mammôn* (6:24).[31] This series of contrasts gives a structural
and thematic coherence to 6:19–34 involving issues of contrasting priorities, opposing loyalties, and antithetical modes of belief and behavior. More
about this Matthean context in relation to heaven/earth and serving God/
mammon is discussed below. The thematic and structural consistency of
Jesus's integral and Evil Eye saying (6:22–23) with its immediate context
(6:19–34)[32] indicates that it was deliberately located here by Matthew.

Luke 11:33–36 is an expanded version of the saying and is located not
in Luke 6:27–45, Luke's "Sermon on the Plain," the parallel to Matthew's
"Sermon on the Mount," but elsewhere in the Lukan Gospel. Since the Lukan
writer is considered to have better preserved the order of Q, the Matthean
context suggests certain implications about the saying's meaning, at least in
the mind of the Matthean composer/redactor.

---

the Mount, see the magisterial study of H. D. Betz 1995. To account for both the similarities and differences between Matt 5:3–7:27 and Luke 6:20–49, Betz proposed that
Matt 5:3—7:27 was Matthew's adoption and adaptation of an earlier Sermon ("SM")
that he found in a recension of the Q Sayings Source (Q^Matt). Correspondingly, Luke
6:20–49 was Luke's adoption and adaptation of an earlier Sermon ("SP") that he found
in a different recension of the Q Sayings Source (Q^Luke) (Betz 1995:44). "Matthew as
well as Luke found the SM [Sermon on the Mount] and the SP [Sermon on the Plain],
respectively, in their recensions of Q (Q^Matt and Q^Luke)" (1995:44). "[T]he SM and the
SP represent, according to Betz, two substantially different elaborations of the same
materials" (1995:43) and in turn were used and reinterpreted differently by the evangelists Matthew and Luke. However the sources and redaction of the Matthean and
Lukan versions of this Evil Eye saying are to be judged, it is sufficient for our analysis to
concentrate on the Gospel stage of this development; namely, the saying as presented
by Matthew and Luke.

28. On theories concerning the pre-Matthean and pre-Synoptic sources of Matthew's Sermon see Betz 1995:32–44.

29. This section consists of a collocation of various Q sayings: Matt 6:19–21 =
Q12:33–34); 6:22–23 = Q11:34–35; 6:24 = Q16:13; 6:25–34 = Q12:22–32

30. The unit is framed by "treasure" (*thêsaurizete*, v. 19; *thesaurus*, v. 21)

31. The verse is framed by *dynatai* and *douleuein* (v. 24a, d) and two contrasting
masters (*kyrioi*, v. 24a; *theos* versus *mammôn*, v. 24d).

32. Betz (1995:54–57) identifies the larger literary context (6:19—7:12) as treating
"the conduct of daily life."

The Greek text of Matt 6:22–23 involves no variant readings that affect the meaning of these verses. Variations in the manuscript tradition are minor in number and significance.[33]

The Antithetical Structure and Grammar of Matthew 6:22–23

The saying consists of a stated premise concerning the human eye (v. 22a)[34] followed by a contrast of two antithetical types of eyes (vv 22b–23b), and a conclusion (v. 23cd). The premise is that the eye is an active rather than passive organ and therefore is comparable in function to that of a lamp, which casts light. Based on this premise (and with "eye" linking vv. 22b–23b to v. 22a), vv. 22b–23 contrast a *haplous* eye (v. 22bc) and an Evil Eye (v. 23ab) in two parallel couplets. A conclusion (v. 23cd) regarding the darkness in the body brought on by an Evil Eye completes the saying. The flanking verses, 6:19–21 and 6:24, also present general truisms (6:21, 6:24a, 24d) illustrated by positive-negative contrasts (6:19–20; 6:24bc). The actions encouraged and discouraged in 6:19–21 and contrasted in 6:24 suggest that 6:22–23 concerns not just a *state* of the body (light or dark), but also a positive versus a negative *form of action*, specifically regarding the handling of possessions, the subject common to 6:19–21 and 6:24 ("treasure," vv. 19–21, and material possessions ["mammon"], v. 24).

In terms of grammar and syntax, the causal condition is contained not in the protasis but in the apodosis,[35] as in other conditional sentences of this

---

33. In v. 22a, in contrast to the majority of witnesses, Codex Vaticanus and several Old Latin mss add *sou* ("your") or *tua* ("your"). In v. 22b, in contrast to the majority of witnesses, some mss omit *oun* ("then") (Codex Sinaiticus [ℵ], a few other mss, and lat syr^c mae bo^ms). Some mss locate the verb "is" (ê) after, rather than before, the noun "your eye." In v. 23a, in contrast to the majority of witnesses, some mss locate the verb "is" (ê) before the noun "your eye" (ℵ W 33 a few others). Matt 6:22c and 23b read *estai* ("will be"), in contrast to *estin* ("is") as found in the Lukan parallel (11:34c, 35a). The latter is the likely original reading. Matthew has added *estai* to parallel material seventeen times in his Gospel (Allison 1987:71) and the *estin* of Matt 6:23c confirms a present sense of the preceding *estai*.)

34. Matthew's version of the eye saying, in contrast to the Q Sayings Source and Luke, is not preceded by a statement about a lamp. Accordingly, its focus is not on a lamp but on the eye. For this reason the present translation begins with "the eye" as subject rather than "the lamp." This rendition is allowed by the Greek text which has "the eye" in the emphatic final position of the sentence and is consistent with the sequence of "eye" and "lamp" in v. 22bc and 23ab.

35. So Allison 1987:74–76.

type.[36] That is, the protasis provides evidence of the apodosis. "If your eye is *haplous*" (the protasis) shows the apodosis to be true: "your entire body is full of light." Similarly, "if your eye is evil" shows that "your entire body is full of darkness." Verse 23, finally, constitutes an ominous paradoxical or oxymoronic conclusion: "If then the light in you is darkness," that is, if your eye which should be a beacon of light is dark, "how great is the darkness!"

THE CONTRAST OF *HAPLOUS* AND *PONÊROS*

The quality that generally is contrasted to *ponêros* ("evil") is *agathos* ("good").[37] The second reference to the Evil Eye in Matthew (20:15) contrasts the good (*agathos*) vineyard owner to the Evil Eye (*ophthalmos ponêros*) of the grumbling, envious laborer(s). The Evil Eye saying of Sir 14:5 likewise contrasts *ponêros* and *agathos*. Matthew 6:22–23 and its Lukan parallel (Luke 11:34), however, contrast an Evil (*ponêros*) Eye to an eye that is *haplous*. The formation *ophthalmos haplous* occurs only in Matt 6:22–23 and its Lukan parallel. The adjective *haplous* in general has a positive sense and so here designates some type of "good" eye. This fits the positive-negative contrasts of Matt 6:19–21 and 6:24, as well as similar Evil Eye sayings. Since, however, the specific nature of the Evil Eye in Matt 6:22–23/Luke 11:33–36 conditions, and is conditioned by, *ophthalmos haplous*, it is necessary to consider more closely the implied sense(s) of *haplous* and its noun *haplotês*. On this point the *Testaments of the Twelve Patriarchs* are directly relevant, in particular the *Testament of Issachar*, which was given the title *Peri haplotêtos* (*Concerning Integrity*).[38] We will examine this text in due course.

Bible versions diverge considerably in their translations of the phrases *ophthalmos haplous* and *ophthalmos ponêros* in Matt 6:22–23/Luke 11:34 and show no consensus on their meaning or sense.

---

36. See Matt 12:28/Luke 11:20; Num 16:29; 1 Kgs 22:28; Prov 24:10 MT; Matt 12:26; John 9:41; Rom 7:20 8:9b; 14:15.

37. For this contrast in Matthew alone see 5:45; 7:11, 17–18; 12:35; 20:15; 22:10; 25:21, 23, 26.

38. On the *Testaments of the Twelve Patriarchs*, see above in this volume, chap. 1, pp. 79–86.

- *oculus simplex* vs. *oculus nequam* (Vulgate)
- *Auge einfältig* vs. *Auge ein Schalk* (Luther 1534); cf. Mark 7:22, "Schalksauge"
- *Auge lauter* vs. *Auge böses* (Luther, 1956 ed.; Zürcher Bibel)
- single eye vs. evil eye (KJV)
- good eye vs. bad eye (NKJV)
- sound eye vs. bad eye (NAB); sound eye vs. not sound eye (RSV; see also JB, NEB, Phillips)
- clear eye vs. bad eye (NAS); clear eye vs. diseased eye (NJB); clear eye vs. clouded eye (Scholars Bible)
- healthy eye vs. unhealthy eye (NRSV)
- *sain oeil* vs. *malade oeil* (BJ); *sano ojo* vs. *enfermo ojo* (La Biblia); *sano occhio* vs. *viziato occhio* (La Sacra Bibbia)

Some Versions even substitute a plural ("eyes") for the Greek singular: sound eyes vs. bad eyes (NAB); good eyes vs. bad eyes (NIV); sound eyes vs. no good eyes (TEV). Whereas older Versions assume a contrast of a morally integral eye and Evil Eye, recent translations assume a contrast of a physically healthy eye and physically unhealthy eye (or eyes).[39]

Modern exegetical studies of Matt 6:22–23/Luke 11:33–36 tend to refer to the phenomenon of the Evil Eye only briefly, if at all, with little attention to the history and details of Evil Eye belief and practice. There was, however, a brief exchange of views in 1942–1943, initated by a brief article by C. Ryder Smith writing on *ophthalmos ponêros* in Mark 7:22 and other biblical references to the concept. He described it as "one of the oldest and widest-spread ideas in the world."[40] The exchange surfaced varying proposals concerning the meaning of "Evil Eye" in the Bible ("evil motive," "malevolence," "stinginess," "envy") but arrived at no consensus.[41] Kari Syreeni's recent study on

---

39. Zilver (2002), a physical anthropologist, claims, unconvincingly, that *ophthalmos ponêros* here is a reference to astigmatism. Representing a quite different perspective on Matt 6:22–23, Gregory Thaumaturgus (c. 213–c. 270 CE) of Pontus and disciple of Origen in Palestine, takes the saying metaphorically as a contrast not of eyes but of opposing forms of love. The integral eye stands for an unfeigned love that enlightens the body; an Evil Eye represents a "pretended love, which is also called hypocrisy." Hypocrisy turns the light of genuine love into consuming darkness. See Gregory Thaumaturgus. "On the Gospel according to Matthew (6:22–23)," *ANF* 6:74.

40. Ryder Smith 1941/42:181–82, esp. 181.

41. See Ryder Smith 1941–42, 1942–43; Cadoux 1941–42; Duncan Percy 1942–43. For further older discussion on Matt 6:22–23, see, e.g., Fiebig 1916; Schwenke 1913. More recently see Sjöberg 1951; an exchange between Edlund 1952 and Cadbury 1954;

"A Single Eye: Aspects of the Symbolic World of Matt. 6.22–23,"[42] makes no mention of Evil Eye belief, although Syreeni is laudably desirous of "getting into Mathew's symbolic world" (1999:106). He appears unaware of the Evil Eye as a significant element of Matthew's symbolic and cultural world.

Lacking in these discussions was any consideration of ancient under-standing of the eye and how it operated. A turning point in the interpreta-tion of these texts, and of Matt 6:22–23 in particular, arrived with the studies of Hans Dieter Betz (1979),[43] Dale Allison (1987),[44] and the present author (1988).[45] All three authors stress the ancient extramission theory of vision underlying this saying and all biblical references to the Evil Eye. The saying of Jesus/Matthew comparing the eye to a lamp presumed a theory of vision that held that the eye was an active agent that projected light, rather than a passive organ receiving light.[46] Allison lists four ancient ocular theories, the ancient sources, and the scholarly literature.[47] Betz discusses "Ancient Greek Theories of Vision," without, however, mentioning by name "extramission" and "intromission" theories and without adequately commenting on their differences.[48] All three authors concur, nevertheless, that any interpretation or translation that ignores the actual theory of vision presumed in this text is doomed to confuse and mislead.[49]

Fensham 1967; Amstutz 1968; and Luz 1989. Billerbeck (1926 1:432) found no refer-ence to the Evil Eye in Matt 6:22–23, which, he claimed, is a concept that is "too narrow and not fitting the context."

42. Syreeni 1999.

43. See also Betz 1995:437–53.

44. See also Davies and Allison 1988:635–41 on Matt 6:22–23.

45. See also the subsequent Elliott articles on the Evil Eye (1990, 1991, 1992, 1994, 2005a, 2005b, 2007a 2011, 2013, 2014, 2015), followed then by Malina and Rohrbaugh 2003:50, 100–102; Apostolides and Dreyer 2008; Viljoen 2009; cf. also Marcus on Mark 8:22–26 (see below under Mark 7).

46. So Allison (1987) concurring with Betz (1979). Elliott (1988 and subsequent articles) arrives at the same position independently.

47. Allison 1987:61–66. For an earlier brief summary of the contrasting theories of vision see Wilpert and Zenker 1950, esp. 958.

48. Betz 1979.

49. Betz 1995:442–49. Betz (1979) is correct in noting the difference between an-cient and modern theories of vision and that Matt 6:22–23 represents the former con-cept of the eye as active agent (see also Betz 1995:445). He has not, however, justified his claim that in this text "the entire approach of Greek philosophical tradition is called into question" from a supposedly different "Jewish ethical point of view" (1979:55). Rather, as Allison (1987:66–71) correctly indicates, Israel shared with the Greeks an extramission theory of vision and moral censure of an Evil Eye, though for Israel this censure is much more pronounced. Betz and Allison justifiably reject any need for reconstructing an Aramaic version of the saying to ascertain the point of the saying;

An adequate understanding of our passage thus requires attention not only to its content and contextual setting in Matthew, but also to conventional thought about the eye's operation and, in particular, Evil Eye belief and practice. Several related issues require consideration:

1. The importance of the eye to the body (the most valued of the sense organs) and the eye as representative of the body (synecdoche, *pars pro toto*) and the person

2. The logic by which the eye is thought comparable to a lamp, and the presumed understanding of how the eye functioned, including the relation of eye and heart

3. The meaning of *haplous ophthalmos* and *ophthalmos ponêros* and the nature of the contrast, along with the best English rendering of each phrase

4. The consequences of having an integral or an Evil Eye

5. The affinity of this Evil Eye saying with other biblical Evil Eye texts and with Evil Eye belief and practice generally

6. The point of the saying and its relation to its immediate and remote Matthean contexts.

Let us consider each point in turn.

1. The importance of the eye to the body

The eye is mentioned over one hundred times in the New Testament. It plays a leading role among body parts. It functions as chief among the five senses[50] and preeminent verifier of facts and the truth. Truth was established through *eyewitness* evidence. Seeing was believing. Suspicion and aggression were expressed by wary or glaring eyes. It was this high valorization of the eye and seeing that lent power to dread of an Evil Eye. The eye, additionally, was considered the "window of the soul" (Plato, *Phaedra* 420E), reflector of emotions (Philo, *Abraham* 151–153), and the channel through which desires and dispositions arising in the heart were projected

---

compare Sjöberg 1951. They correctly identify a call for generosity as its main point, but appear unclear as to how *ophthalmos ponêros* represents not just "the ethical vocabulary of Judaism" but the tradition of Evil Eye belief and practice (as first presented by Elliott 1988). We will deal with this issue shortly.

50. According to Philo (*Abraham* 150–157), the eye is "the queen of the senses and set above them all" (*Abraham* 150). On the high valorization of the eye and sight see also above, chap. 1, pp. 16–19.

(voluntarily or involuntarily) out into the external world.[51] The verb "I see" (*horaô*) occurs 449 times in the New Testament, more than any other of the verbs for the five senses.[52] A kindred verb, *theoreô*, appears fifty-eight times. The eye as major organ could also stand as *pars pro toto* for the human person as a whole, including one's thoughts and dispositions (e.g., Prov 30:17; Ezek 16:5). A good or an evil eye could represent a good or an evil person (e.g., Prov 23:6 HT; Sir 14:10).

The eye is especially important to Matthew, who refers to this organ (*ophthalmos*) twenty-four times, more than all other New Testament writings.[53] Beside his two references to an Evil Eye (6:23; 20:15), Matthew presents Jesus as mentioning an offending eye or look (5:28–29; 7:3–5; 18:9) and imperceptive seeing (13:13–17 [Isa 6:9–10]).

2. The logic of the comparison of an eye to a lamp and its connection with the heart

What was the logic according to which the eye was thought comparable to a lamp (*lychnos*)? How was the eye thought to function and to be related to the heart? According to the ocular theory that prevailed in the ancient world, as we have previously noted, the eye was considered not a passive but an active agent.[54] The eye was full of light and emitted particles of light or energy, and thus was regarded analogous to a lamp, which also projected light. This understanding and similarity made possible and plausible a comparison of the eye to a lamp. The logic of the association of eye and lamp, in other words, rested on the presumption of the eye as emitter of energy and light (extramission theory of vision).[55]

51. For the association of eye and heart see below pp. 205–07 in relation to Mark 7:22.

52. See Duling 2014:158–59.

53. Matt 5:28, 38 (2x); 6:22 (2x), 23; 7:3 (2x), 4 (2x), 5(2x); 9:29, 30; 13:15 (2x), 16; 17:8; 18:9 (2x); 20:15, 33; 26:43; also *monophthalmos* ("one-eyed," 18:9).

54. On the history of theories of vision see van Hoorn 1972; Hahm 1975; Lindberg 1976; Beare 1996; and D. Park 1998. On the eye and vision in antiquity see also Wilpert and Zenker 1950; Michaelis 1956, 1967, 1976b; Déonna 1965; Chidester 1992:1–24; M. Jay 1993; C. Classen 1993; Viljoen 2009.

55. As noted by Betz (1979; 1995:445) Matt 6:22–23/Luke 11:34–36 "rejects the atomistic and Epicurean theories of vision, while approving of the Empedoclean and Platonic traditions, at least to the extent that vision occurs through light passing from the inside out." On the extramission theory of vision presumed for the Evil Eye and other comments on the eye in the New Testament see Allison 1987; Elliott 1988 and subsequent Elliott articles on the Evil Eye; also Davies and Allison 1988:635; Duff 2001; Malina and Rohrbaugh 2003:357; Malina and Pilch 2006:360–61; see also Marcus 1999

Whereas modern scientific theory beginning in the 1500s has held that the eye is a passive receptor of external light intromitted into the eye (intromission theory), the dominant theory among the ancients was that the eye, like a lamp or the sun, actively emitted rays and particles of light (extramission theory).[56] The eye, it was popularly believed, rather than being a passive receptor of light, actively produced and emitted rays of energy that struck the objects seen and exerted on them an active force.[57] This extramission theory of vision was advanced first by Empedocles (490–430 BCE.),[58] author of the first comprehensive theory of light and vision. It was held by numerous others including Plato (*Timaeus* 45b–d), and Euclid (*Optica*), and was given expression in Plutarch's "Table Talk" on the Evil Eye[59] and Heliodorus's novel *Aethiopica*,[60] as described in Vol. 2. "As Plutarch (*Quaest. Conv.* 5.7, *Mor.* 680F) explains it," Malina and Pilch (2003:357) recall, "odor, voice, and breath are all caused by streams of particles emanating from the physical body. When these emanations encounter another physical body, they excite the sense organs and thus produce a real physical effect." Similarly, "an active (the most active) stream of emanations comes from the eye, and like other bodily emanations, they can produce actual physical effects in whatever they happen to strike."

This view of the eye as active organ projecting light prevailed not only among Greeks and Romans (so Betz); it was also evident in Israel and other cultures (so Allison).[61] Israelites too conceived of the eye as a sun in miniature (2 Sam 12:11; 3 *Bar.* 8). They too spoke of "terrible sparks from their eyes" (Wis 11:18). They too likened eyes to torches and flames of fire.[62] Of

---

in respect to Mark 8:25.

56. See Vol. 2, pp. 73–81.

57. See Aeschylus, *Prom.* 356 (light comes from Typhon's eyes); Theocritus, *Id.* 24.18–19 (an evil fire comes from the eyes of snakes); Sophocles, *Ajax* 70 and Euripides, *Andr.* 1180 (eyes emit, cast forth, rays); Theophrastus, *De sensu* 26 quoting Alcmaeon; Plato, *Timaeus* 45 (eyes were given by the gods "to give light" . . . the "pure fire in us . . . they made to flow through the eyes"]; Aristotle, *De sensu* 437a22–26 (the eye contained a fire according to popular belief); Pseudo-Aristotle, *Prob. phys.* 31, 959b ("vision is fire"); *Prob. phys.* 31, 960b ("sight [is made] from fire, and hearing from air"); Philostratus, *Imagines* 1.28.1 (eyes of a wild boar flashing fire); cf. Allison 1987:61–69.

58. Empedocles, *Frag.* 84 (Diels and Kranz, FVS 1964 1.342.4–9 [31 B 84]).

59. Plutarch, *Quaest. Conv.* 5.7, *Mor.* 680C–683B, esp. 681A, 681AB.

60. Heliodorus, *Aethiopica* 3.7; cf. also Lucian, *Philopseudes* 22; Apollonius of Rhodes, *Argonautica* 4.1669–1672; Alexander of Aphrodisias, *Prob phys.* 2.53.

61. Betz 1979; Allison 1987:64–69; see Dan 10:2–9; Zech 4:1–14; 2 *Enoch* 42:1 [A]; T. *Job* 18:4; b. *Shabb.* 151b.

62. See Dan 10:6 ("his eyes like flaming torches"; and Rev 1:14 ("eye like a flame of fire"); 2:18; and 19:12 (of the eyes of Michael the angel and Jesus).

Noah it was said that "his eyes are like the rays of the sun" (1 *Enoch* 106:5, 10) and "when he opened his eyes, he lightened up the entire house like the sun" (1 *Enoch* 106:2, 10). According to Israelite wisdom, "the LORD gives light to the eyes" (Prov 29:13). A king "winnowed" all evil with his eyes (Prov 20:8). Sages spoke of "the light of the eyes" rejoicing the heart (Prov 15:30 HT; cf. also Ps 38:10). Concerning three rabbis, Eliezar ben Hyrcanus and Shimeon ben Yohai and his son, it was said that they possessed Evil Eyes of such power that everything upon which their glances fell was consumed by fire (b. B.M. 59b; b. *Shabb.* 33b). The eye also could become "dimmed" or "darkened,"[63] also in connection with Evil Eye possession (Sir 18:18).[64] "If you have no eyes," warns the sage, "you will be without light" (Sir 3:25).

Given this presumption of how the eye operated, the conventional comparison of the eye with a lamp and its association with light was a logical one. The lamp produces light and casts it forth (Matt 5:15); the eye does likewise. "The eye appears to give light."[65] Zechariah compares "seven eyes of the LORD" (4:10) to "seven lamps" (4:1). In the book of Job, Bildad speaks of the eye as a "light," a "flame of fire," and a "lamp" (Job 18:5–6).[66] Associating the eye with a "light" and a "lamp," a proverb observes: "The light of the righteous rejoices, but the lamp of the wicked will be put out" (Prov 13:9); see also Prov 24:19–20. *Second Enoch* 42:1 speaks of "the guards of the gates of hell . . . with their faces like lamps that have been extinguished." The *Testament of Job* (18:2) makes explicit this equation of eye and lamp: "my eyes, actings as lamps, searched out" (*hoi ophthalmoi tous lychnous poiountes eblepon*).[67]

Understanding this Matthean text, and all other biblical texts mentioning the eye, therefore, requires an awareness of this concept of the eye as an *active* rather than passive agent. Failure to grasp this fact, as one frequently encounters in numerous scholarly commentaries, not to mention modern sermons on these texts, results in an erroneous ocular physiology and an ethnocentric distortion of the import of these biblical texts.

In its Matthean context, as discussed in further detail below, our eye saying follows directly upon a heart saying (6:19–21), illustrating the ancient association of heart and eye. For Greeks and Romans, the eye was the

63. Gen 27:1; 48:10; Deut 34:7; Lam 5:17; Prov 13:9; 24:20; *T. Benj.* 4:2; Josephus, *Ant.* 8.268; *T. Job* 18:4; b. *Ber.* 16b.

64. For Philo, see *Abraham* 150–157; *Cherubim* 97; *Drunkenness* 88.

65. Derrett 1988:272.

66. See also Job 22:11; Prov 20:20.

67. On the eye as a lamp and emitter of light see also Allison 1987:69–71; Davies and Allison 1988 1:635; Elliott 1994:54, 66, 74, 77; Via 1994:356; Marcus 1999, concerning Mark 8:25; Zöckler 2001; Malina and Rohrbaugh 2003:50.

organ of perception closest to the heart and soul as well as the window to, and mirror of, heart and soul.[68] Eye and heart were similarly linked in Isra-elite thought.[69] A proverb in fact associates eyes, heart and lamp: "Haughty eyes and a proud heart, the lamp of the wicked, are sin" (Prov 21:4 RSV). The eye, connected to the heart, the organ of thought, intention, and moral disposition, was considered the channel through which the dispositions of the heart were expressed. For the ancients, a sound or healthy eye was not only a symptom of a sound and healthy body, as held in modern medicine. Since the eye was deemed to signal the thoughts and moral disposition of the heart, it could also be considered an indicator of a person's moral integrity or lack thereof. Thus both eye and heart point here in Matt 6 to the internal state of a person and its moral condition, a focus consistent with Evil Eye belief.[70] This, in turn, fits the broader Matthean context and its concern about wealth accumulation (6:19–21), mammon (6:24), and anxiety over food and clothing (6:25–34), as Cadbury (1954) has argued.

In sum, Jesus and Matthew, along with all biblical authors, regarded the eye as an active projector of light (extramission theory of vision), in contrast to the modern understanding of the eye as a passive receptor of light (intromission theory of vision). For this reason, the eye was deemed comparable to a lamp which also projected light.

Translations and commentaries that ignore or obscure these facts fail to convey the sense of this saying, with erroneous and misleading results. *The Scholars Bible* translation renders Matt 6:22–23: "The eye is the body's lamp. It follows that if your eye is clear, your whole body will be flooded with light. If your eye is clouded, your whole body will be shrouded in darkness. If, then, the light within you is darkness, how dark that can be!"[71] The commentary accompanying this erroneous translation reveals the unfounded assumption behind it. Robert W. Funk et al. (1993:151) state: "It was a common view in the ancient world that the eye admits light into the body (a commonsense notion). A clear eye permits the light to enter the body and penetrate the darkness." In actual fact, the prevailing "common view" in antiquity was exactly the opposite: the eye was not penetrated by light but

68. See Aeschylus, *Prom.* 356; Euripides, *Suppl.* 322; Aristophanes, *Equites* 631; Cicero, *Verr.* 3.6; 5.161; *Orat. pro dom.* 101; *Cael.* 49; Pliny, *NH* 28.17; Aelien, *Var. hist.* 2.44. See also Vol. 2.

69. See Deut 28:65; 1 Kgdm 9:3 LXX; Job 30:26–27; 31:1, 7, 9, 26–27; Prov 15:30; 21:4; Ps 73 (72):7; Isa 6:10; Jer 22:17; Lam 5:17; Sir 22:19; 1 Cor 2:9; Eph 1:18 ("eyes of the heart"); see also *1 Clem.* 36:2.

70. For the explicit link of heart and Evil Eye see Mark 7:21–22 and further discussion of the connection of eye and heart.

71. Funk et al., 1993 ad loc.

projected light. The popular German translation/paraphrase of Jörg Zink[72] displays a similar misunderstanding:

> Wenn nun *dein Auge seinen Sinn erfüllt,* ist dein ganzer Leib dem Licht offen.
> Wenn *dein Auge seinen Dienst verweigert,* ist dein ganzer Leib in der Finsternis.
> Wenn nun das Licht, das Gott deiner Selle gab, erloschen ist, wie abgrundtief muss die Finsternis sein!

> When your eye fulfills its purpose, your entire body is open to light.
> When your eye refuses its duty, your entire body is in darkness.
> When the light that God gave your soul is extinguished, how vastly deep the darkness must be!

Here the errors multiply: (a) There no linguistic basis for the concept "fulfills its purpose." (b) An intromission theory rather than extramission theory of vision is mistakenly presupposed according to which light is sent to the soul from God. (c) The result is not a body in darkness, as Zink states, but darkness in the body, as the Greek states. Zink and the Scholars Version exemplify a distorting modernization of ancient thought and language. These misguided translations join the list of other mistaken Versions that reflect no awareness of the widespread and ancient tradition concerning the Evil Eye; some imagine that the contrast here concerns states of physical or psychic health rather moral versus immoral behavior.[73] That the contrast concerns *morality* rather than health becomes even clearer when we examine the contrast of *haplous* eye and Evil Eye.

72. Zink 1965 ad loc.

73. The comments of Nolland on the passage (2005:300–302) are similarly unconvincing. He curiously claims that ancients viewed the eyes as *both* projecting and receiving light in the single action of vision. "The light from the eyes was thought to merge with the light coming from the object . . . and then to flow or bounce back to the eye and to penetrate through the eye into the person, where sight was registered" (301). His reasoning about the eye, however, restricts attention to what he describes as its receptive or "absorbative" nature. "As the lamp is an image for the eye, so the eye in turn is an image for the human capacity to absorb from what is available externally . . . The imagery is of light coming into the body through the eyes and illuminating the whole interior of the person" (301). He translates *haplous* as "healthy" and *ponêros* with the rarely attested "diseased" (300). He is aware that an "Evil Eye" is associated with "those who are miserly, envious, or grasping" (302), but claims that common among its various senses "is a narrowed or distorted way of viewing things . . . and this allows a bridge to the idea of a diseased eye" (302). Merging extramission and intromission theories of vision, his interpretation of this saying focuses virtually exclusively on the imagery of "light coming into the body" (302) and the antithesis of healthy vs. diseased eye, producing a rather confused and confusing interpretation of the passage.

3. The meaning of *ophthalmos haplous* and *ophthalmos ponêros*, the nature of the contrast, and the preferable English rendition of each phrase

The formulation *ophthalmos ponêros* is one of multiple conventional designations for "Evil Eye." The adjective *ponêros* modifies *ophthalmos* ("eye")—as in Sir 14:10; 31:13; Mark 7:22; and Luke 11:34d—and forms with "eye" the expression "Evil Eye." In each case *ponêros* means "evil" in a moral sense, not "ill," "sick" or "unsound" in a physical sense. *Ponêros* in general concerns "being morally or socially worthless, *wicked, evil, bad, base, worthless, vicious, degenerate.*"[74] Only in rare instances was *ponêros* used to denote an unhealthy physical condition, a "sick" body.[75] The related noun, *ponêria*, likewise only rarely denotes a physical malady.[76] The formulation to which *ophthalmos ponêros* is contrasted here and in Luke 11:34 (and Q), *ophthalmos haplous,* is unconventional and rare, but clearly implies something positive overgainst the negative "Evil Eye."[77] The antithesis of *haplous* versus *ponêros* occurs only in Matt 6:22–23/Luke 11:34–35 in the biblical writings. The more recurrent lexical contrast of "good" and "evil" involves *agathos* vs. *ponêros*, as found elsewhere also in Matthew.[78] The contrast of "good (person)" versus "Evil Eye" appears in Matthew's other reference to the Evil Eye, Matt 20:15. The rabbis, like Jesus, also contrasted a good eye to an Evil Eye (*m. Avot* 2:9, 11; 5:13, 19).

Sirach 14 also is relevant here in three ways. First, Sir 14:5 constitutes a prior Israelite wisdom saying involving the Evil Eye and a contrast of good and evil.[79] Second, the passage speaks of an Evil-Eyed person afflicting himself with his Evil Eye (Sir 14:6), not enjoying his own riches (14:5) and having evil injustice wither his soul (14:9). Matthew 6:23 likewise envisions an Evil Eye bringing about harm to oneself ("your entire body will be full of darkness"). Third, Sir 14 relates an Evil Eye to possessing wealth but being reluctant to share it (14:3, 4, 5, 8, 10; cf. also Deut 15:7–11; 28:54–57; Tob

74. BDAG 851 *s.v.*

75. Plato, *Protagoras* 313a; cf. the adverb *ponêrôs*, "badly off (in health)," Thucydides, *Peloponnesian War* 7.83.3.

76. For "illness of the feet" (*podôn ponêria*) and "illness of the eyes" (*ponêria ophthalmôn*) see Plato, *Hippias Minor* 374d.

77. The adjective *haplous* is not attested elsewhere as combined with "eye" until the fifth–sixth century CE writing of Damascius (*Vita Isidori* 16), with reference to frank expression ("unjaundiced," "sincere," BDAG 2000:104); this is four hundred years after the Matthean and Lukan formulations.

78. See Matt 5:45; 7:11, 17, 18; 12:34–35; 20:15; 22:10.

79. See also Wis 4:12: "for the Evil Eye (*baskania*) of wickedness obscures the good (*ta kala*)."

4:7, 16). Our saying stands in this tradition and the unwillingness to be generous appears to be the issue here in Matt 6:22–23 as well.

In defining *haplous* and its related noun *haplotês,* the standard lexicon of biblical Greek, Bauer-Danker-Arndt-Gingrich (BDAG 2000:104), states that *haplous* pertains "to being motivated by singleness of purpose so as to be open and aboveboard, *single, without guile, sincere, straightforward.*" In respect to the eye, it means "single = unjaundiced, sincere" (BDAG 2000:104). *Haplotês,* BDAG indicates, appears "[i]n our lit.[erature] esp. of personal integrity expressed in word or action, *simplicity, sincerity, uprightness, frankness*" (ibid.). LSJ notes that *haplous* is a contraction of *haploos,* with the meanings "*I. single; II. Simple, plain, straightforward;* of persons, words, thoughts, acts, *simple, open, frank; III. Simple* [as opposed to *compound, mixed*]; *unalloyed. Haplotês,* used of persons, can mean *simplicity, frankness, sincerity; open-heartedness, liberality* (2 Cor 11:3; 8:2; 9:11, 13; cf. 11:3)." There are New Testament instances where the context clearly implies a sense of generosity and liberality in particular; see Rom 12:8; 2 Cor 8:2, 9:11, 13. The related verb *haploô* can mean "make single, unfold, spread out" (LSJ).

Haplous and its family of terms thus have a broad range of meanings in both non-biblical and the biblical sources, with both moral and non-moral senses, but in the biblical writings only with positive force.[80] No instance prior to Matthew has been found where *haplous* or *haplotês* refer to physical (or mental) health with the meanings "good health," "healthy" or "sound."[81] As already mentioned, *ponêria* on rare occasion could denote "illness" (of feet or of eyes) as is also true of *ponêros* denoting "unhealthy;" but there are no instances where *haplous* and *ponêros* were employed to contrast healthy and unhealthy eyes. This speaks against all biblical translations and exegetical studies rendering *haplous* and *ponêros* as "healthy/unhealthy," "sound/unsound," "clear/unclear" (see below).

In respect to its biblical occurrences, the adjective *haplous* appears only rarely in the Bible: once in Matt 6:22/Luke 11:34 and once in the LXX (Prov 11:25). Proverbs 11:25 is part of a couplet (11:24–25) whose members are parallel in form and meaning. The Hebrew reads:

> One person gives freely, yet grows richer;
> another withholds what he should give and only suffers want.

---

80. Bacht 1959:821–830; see also Spicq 1933; Sjöberg 1951; Edlund 1952; Schlatter 1963:222–223; Amstutz 1968; Baumbach 1963:77–79; Dibelius and Greeven 1976:77–79; Schramm 1990; Moss 2011:760–62; for the papyri see Moulton–Milligan 58–59.

81. Subsequent to Mathew and Luke centuries later see Damascius, *Vita Isidori* 16.

> A generous person (lit. "a blessed soul," *nephesh berakah*) shall
>> be made rich,
> and he that satisfies abundantly shall himself be satisfied.
> (JHE trans.)

The LXX reads:

> There are some that scatter their own and make more;
>> and there are some that gather but have less.
> Every integral person (*psychê haplê*) is praised;
>> an angry person, on the other hand, is not admired.
> (JHE trans.)

Thus LXX *psychê haplê* renders the Hebrew *nephesh berakah*, with both phrases identifying persons who are commendably *generous* and *liberal* in spirit.[82] The following verse (Prov 11:26) similarly contrasts miserliness and generosity:

> The people curse him who holds back grain,
>> but a blessing is on the head of him who sells it. (RSV)

The praise of generous giving and its contrast to miserliness is characteristic of Evil Eye texts, as already observed. Matthew's use of *haplous* to modify "eye" and to form a contrast to "Evil Eye" thus is consonant with the sense of *haplous* in Prov 11:25. The related noun *haplotês* occurs seven times in the LXX,[83] with "integrity (of heart)," "sincerity," and "innocence" as related meanings or connotations. The verb *haploun* appears only once in the LXX (Job 22:3b): "Is it gain to [the Lord] that you *make your ways blameless* (or 'whole,' translating the Hebrew *tamêm*, 'make blameless')?" The sense is *living with integrity* in accord with God's will; Job 22:3b is parallel to "living righteously" (Job 22:3a).

The noun *haplotês* appears in the New Testament seven times.[84] The contexts of Rom 12:8 and 2 Cor 8:2; 9:11, 13 favor the meaning "generosity, liberality."[85] In Eph 6:5–6 and Col 3:22, "singleness/integrity of heart" (Eph 6:5, Col 3:22) is contrasted to the rare term *ophthalmodoulia* (lit. "eye service"), which connotes the insincere service of slaves to owners meant only to impress. The adverb *haplôs* occurs once in the New Testament, of God

---

82. The LXX specifically contrasts a *psychê haplê* to an angry person, so that this context suggests "irenic person" for *psychê haplê*. However, *psychê haplê* (v. 25) parallels "some that scatter their own" (v. 24), suggesting generous giving which "makes more."

83. 2 Kgdm 15:11 [Heb: *tom*]; 1 Chr 29:17 [Heb.: *yoser levav*; LXX: *haplotêti kardias*]; Wis 1:1; Sus 63; 1 Macc 2:37; 2:60; 3 Macc 3:21.

84. Rom 12:8; 2 Cor 8:2; 9:11, 13; 11:3; Eph 6:5; Col 3:22.

85. Contrast 2 Cor 11:3 ("integrity," "singular devotion").

who gives "generously" (Jas 1:5). "Generous, generosity, generously" thus are recurrent meanings of this word family in the Bible.

None of the aforementioned occurrences, however, juxtapose *haplous* and its forms with terms for the Evil Eye. This juxtaposition, however, does occur in certain writings of the *Testaments of the Twelve Patriarchs*. This, in turn, provides essential semantic background for determining the meaning and implications of *haplous* and of the general sense of Matt 6:22–23/Luke 11:34–35.

The Testaments of the Twelve Patriarchs and Matthew 6:22–23

The *Testaments of the Twelve Patriarchs* and their references to the Evil Eye have been examined in chapter 1 above. The twelve individual testaments are expansions on the biblical saga of Joseph and his brothers (Gen 37–50) and are inspired in their form (the patriarch's final words of instruction to his progeny before dying) by the account of Jacob's final blessing of his twelve sons in Genesis 49. Looming as a shadow over these testaments of Jacob's twelve sons is the event of their collective envying and Evil-Eyeing of their brother Joseph.

Two of these testaments are particularly helpful for understanding our Matthean text. The *Testament of Issachar*, which is titled *Peri Haplotês*, ("Concerning Integrity"), contrasts integrity and the Evil Eye. The *Testament of Simeon*, which is titled, *Peri Phthonou*, "Concerning Envy," illustrates the association of envy and the Evil Eye as well as their contrast to integrity of heart.[86] In conjunction with material from the other Testaments, they illustrate four important points relative to our Matthean text.

1. The terms *haplous* and *haplotês* denote *moral integrity* in various specific manifestations depending on context: singleness of heart and of eyes; innocence; absence of duplicity, greed, and avarice; undivided commitment (equivalent to righteousness); love of God and neighbor; and compassion and generosity toward the poor and needy (*T. Sim.* 4:4–7; *T. Iss.* 3:8; 5:2).

2. This moral integrity, epitomized by Joseph (*T. Sim.* 4:4–5; *T. Benj.* 3:1—6:7), or occasionally by one of his brothers (*T. Iss.*), is contrasted to the Evil Eye and envy once manifested by Joseph's brothers against Joseph (*T. Sim.* 2:6–14; *T. Iss.* 3:2–8; 4:1—5:2; *T. Gad* 7:6–7).

86. The translations that follow are my own; those of Charles (1913) and Kee (1983) lack consistency in regard to translation of the terms for Evil Eye (*baskanos*) and envy (*phthonos, zêlos,* and paronyms).

3. The moral integrity denoted by *haplous* and *haplotês* is directly linked with eye and heart, just as the malice of an Evil Eye is linked with eye and heart.

4. An Evil Eye is equivalent to a "darkened eye" (*T. Benj.* 4:2); it stands in contrast to an integral eye that is full of light (*T. Benj.* 3:1—6:7).

These points can be considered in more detail.

In the *Testaments of the Twelve Patriarchs*, the adjective *haplous* (*T. Iss.* 4:2 in 4:1–6) and its noun *haplotês*[87] designate the same quality as they do in the LXX, the translations of Aquila and Symmachus, and early Christian literature;[88] namely, disposition and behavior that is integral, pure of motive, innocent, without duplicity or deception, and devoid of evil intent. *Testaments of Benjamin* 6:7 contrasts "twofold" to "singular:" "the works of Beliar are twofold (*dipla*), they lack singularity/integrity (*haplotêta*)." In some biblical texts, as in *Testaments of the Twelve Patriarchs*, *haplotês* is combined with heart (*kardia*) in the expression "singleness of heart" or "integrity of heart" (1 Chr 29:17; Wis 1:1; Eph 6:5).

The *Testament of Issachar* which bears the title, *Peri Haplotês*, "Concerning Integrity," has integrity of heart (and eye) as its chief topic. Issachar, fifth son of Jacob and Leah and elder brother of envied Joseph, speaks as a farmer who has lived with rectitude of heart (3:1), integrity of eyes (3:4) and integrity of heart (3:8; 4:1); scorning luxuries and wealth; free of envy, an Evil Eye and greed; shuning lust; offering freely to God and to the poor; and prospering by God's grace. He urges his children to likewise pursue integrity of heart and to avoid envy and the Evil Eye (4:1—6:4). The relevant verses from chaps. 3–5 read as follows:

> When, therefore, I grew up, my children, I lived with rectitude of heart (*en euthytêti kardias*) . . . and my father blessed me, for he saw that I lived with integrity (*haplotêti*) before him. And I

87. *T. Reub.* 4:1; *T. Sim.* 4:5; *T. Levi* 13:1; *T. Iss.* 3:2, 4, 6, 7, 8; 4:1, 6; 5:1, 8; 6:1; 7:7; *T. Benj.* 6:7; note the phrases *haplotês kardias* ("integrity of heart," *T. Reub.* 4:1; *T. Sim.* 4:5; *T. Iss.* 3:8; 4:1; 7:7); *haplotês ophthalmôn* ("integrity of eyes," *T. Iss.* 3:4 *v.l.*).

88. *haplous*: Prov 11:25; Aquila: Gen 25:27; Job 1:8; 9:20; Ps 15 [16]:1; 63 [64]:5; Prov 10:29. Symmachus: Gen 42:11; Job 33:3; Ps 24 [25]:8; 35[36]:11; Eccl. 7:30[29]. Cf. also *haplous*: Josephus, *Ag. Ap.* 2.190; *Ps-Phoc.* 50; Philo, *Migration* 153; *Barn.* 9:2; *1 Clem.* 23:1.

Haplotês: 2 Kgdm 15:11; 1 Chr 29:17; Wis 1:1; Dan LXX Sus 63; 1 Macc 2:37, 60; 3 Macc 3:21; Aquila: Job 4:6; 21:23; Ps 7:9; 25[26]:1, 11; 40[41]:13; 77[78]:72; Prov 10:9; 28:6. Symmachus: Gen 20:5; Job 2:9; 27:5; Ps 7:9; 36[37]:37; 40[41]:13; 77[78]:72; Prov 10:9; 28:6); Rom 12:8; 2 Cor 1:12 *v.l.*; 8:2; 9:11, 13; 11:3; Eph 6:5; Col 3:22; *1 Clem.* 60:2 *v.l.*; Hermas *Vis.* 1.2.4; 2.3.2; 3.1.9; 3 8.5, 7; *Mand.* 2.7; *Sim* 9.15.1 etc. For relevant discussions see also Amstutz 1968:16–41; Edlund,1952:53–61; Garrett 1991:96–105.

was not a busybody in my actions, nor envious (*phthoneros*),
nor an Evil-Eyed person (*baskanos*) toward my neighbor. I
spoke against no one nor did I disparage anyone's life. I lived
my life with integrity of eyes (*en haplotêti ophthalmôn, v.l.*) . . .
My father always rejoiced in my integrity (*haplotêti*) . . . and
knew that God aided my integrity (*tê haplotêti mou*). For to all
the poor and oppressed I supplied the good things of the earth
in the integrity of my heart (*en haplotêti kardias mou*). (3:1–4,
6–8).[89]

Issachar then proceeds to portray in detail an integral person (*ho haplous*), *implicitly himself,* whom his children are urged to emulate (4:1–6):

And now, heed me, children, and walk in the integrity of your
hearts (*en haplotêti kardias humôn*) . . . The integral person (*ho
haplous*) is not greedy for gold, he does not defraud his neighbor, he does not yearn for fancy foods or want fine clothes. He
does not make plans to live a long life, but awaits only the will of
God. And the spirits of error have no power over him, since he
does not include feminine beauty in the scope of his vision, lest
by allowing distraction he corrupt his mind. No envy (*zêlos; v.l.
zêloi*) enters his thinking; no Evil Eye (*baskania, v.l.; baskanos*)
dissipates his soul. For he lives by integrity of soul (*en haplotêti
psychês*) and sees all things by the rectitude of his heart (*en
euthutêti kardias*); he avoids Evil Eyes (*ophthalmous ponêrous*)
made evil by the world's error, so that he might not see any turning aside from the Lord's commands.

Issachar continues by urging his children to live with the integrity that he
has demonstrated (5:1–8):

Therefore, my children, keep the Law of God. Acquire integrity
(*tên haplotêta*) and live without malice . . . have compassion on
the poor and the weak . . . live with your father's integrity (*tê
haplotêti patros hymôn*). (5:1, 2, 8)

The signficance of these words from the *Testament of Issachar* for our
Matthean text lies, first, in their clarification of the meaning of *haplous* as
"integrity" and their illustration of the nature of the integrity of eye and
heart. The context gives a helpful specificity to the abstract concept of "integrity" or "singleness." Second, they entail explicit contrasts of *haplous*

89. Compare Col 3:22/Eph 6:5–6, which contrast integrity of heart to *ophthal-modoulia* (flattering "service of the eyes").

(and integrity) to an Evil Eye (3:3; 4:5, 6), as occur in Matt 6:22–23/Luke 11:34–35.

Haplous and *haplotês* identify qualities of a person who lives and acts with integrity, singleness of purpose and undivided allegiance. Integrity is associated with the organs of both eye and heart (vision and intention, *T. Iss.* 3:1, 4, 8; 4:1, 6) and, for Israelites, is equivalent to living righteously in accord with the will of God (4:3; 5:1) and receiving God's blessing (3:7). Living with integrity includes scorning luxury and wealth (4:2), loathing avarice and greed (4:2, 5), feeling malice toward no one (3:4; 5:1), and especially being compassionate and generous toward all in need (3:8; 5:2).[90] These features of an integral person are qualities, which in Evil Eye belief, as we have seen, are associated with persons free of an Evil Eye and envy so that the explicit contrast here between *haplous* and Evil Eye (3:3) is both logical and consistent with tradition. In our discussion of Matt 20:1–15 we will return to the *Testaments of the Twelve Patriarchs* and this link of Evil Eye and envy as illustrated by the *Testament of Simeon* and the Joseph tradition in general.

In the light of the foregoing, the phrase *ophthalmos haplous* in Q11:34b; Matt 6:22b; and Luke 11:34b is best rendered "integral eye," which in the context of Matt 6:22–23 in particular implies a *generous eye*, i.e. *a generous person*.[91] In all three cases. "integral eye" connotes a "generous eye," contrasted to an Evil Eye which conveys miserliness and stinginess. This is supported by several factors.

(i) This is the connotation of the term *haplous* in Prov 11:24–26 and in *T. Iss.* 4:2 in its context (4:1—5:4). Its related noun *haplotês* also has this sense in *T. Sim.* 4:4–7; *T. Iss.* 3:8; 5:2;[92] also Rom 12:8; 2 Cor 8:2; 9:11, 13.

---

90. It is not that the terms *haplous* and *haplotês* in and of themselves signify generosity, as proposed by Cadbury 1954 and opposed by Thienemann 1955 and Amstutz 1968. It is rather that they *assume* this sense in hortatory contexts and as they contrast to an Evil Eye. The Evil Eye, as we have seen, can involve miserliness that resists sharing with those in need. Cadbury, nevertheless, is correct in sensing that the intent of the saying of Matt 6:22–23/Luke 11:34–35 on the whole is a "condemnation of miserliness over against generosity" (1954:69, 72).

91. It is generally the case with *haplous* and *haplotês* that their contexts determine which aspect of integrity is intended, and, in the case of moral integrity, how this integrity is concretely manifested (so Edlund 1952:62–78). The more specific sense of integrity, as indicated above, is open to a range of possibilities. Eric Sjöberg (1951) proposed a retroversion of the Greek of Matthew into Aramaic, which rendered *haplous* as *shelim* (= "whole," "without defect"; = Hebrew *tam;* cf. Billerbeck 1926 1:431), a term used of unblemished animals for sacrifice. This would be one form of integrity, namely physical integrity as required by the cult. However, the force of *haplous* in our saying is not cultic but moral integrity.

92. Charles, "Testaments of the Twelve Patriarchs" in *APOT* 2:326 on *T. Iss.* 3:8: "disinterested generosity."

This is the case also of the adverb *haplôs* in Jas 1:5 ("God gives generously to all persons") and Hermas, *Mand.* 2.4 ("give generously to all in need"). *The Sayings Gospel Q* (2002:110–11) in respect to Q11:34 also translates *haplous* according to sense with "generous."[93]

(ii) "Generous eye" fits the contrast of *ophthalmous haplous* to *ophthamos ponêros*. Generosity is the antithesis to the stinginess and miserliness associated with an Evil Eye.[94] Two biblical Evil Eye texts make it especially clear that the contrast of an Evil Eye to generosity has a long pedigree: Deut 15:7–11 and Tob 4:7–11, 16. Deuteronomy 15:7–11, we recall, reads:

> 7 If there is among you in need, a member of your community in any of your towns within the land that the Lord your God is giving you, do not harden your heart or shut your hand against your needy neighbor. 8 You should rather open your hand, willingly lending enough to meet the need, whatever it may be. 9 Be careful lest there be an evil thought in your heart and you say: "The seventh year, the year of remission [of debts], is near," and *your eye be evil* against your neighbor (or *you cast an Evil Eye upon* your neighbor) and you give nothing, and your neighbor cry to the Lord against you, and you be guilty of sinning. 10 Give liberally and do not let your heart be evil when you do so, for because of this the Lord your God will bless you in all your work and in all that you undertake. 11 Since there will never cease to be some in need in the land, I therefore command you, Open your hand wide to the poor and needy neighbor in your land. (JHE trans.)

The Evil Eye saying of Tobit (4:7–11, 16) echoes Deut 15:7–11, and, beside thematic similarity, has additional specific affinities with Matt 6:22–23 and its context. Tobit's instruction concerning generous giving makes a direct connection between the topics of generous almsgiving (4:7–11, 16), laying up treasure in heaven (4:9), not acting with an Evil Eye (4:7, 16), and darkness (4:10), all features of which appear also in Matt 6:22–23:

> 7 Give alms (*poiei eleêmosynên*) from your possessions to all who live uprightly,
> and do not begrudge with an Evil Eye (*mê phonesatô sou ho ophthlamos*: cf. Matt 6:23a) the alms when you give them.

93. *The Sayings Gospel Q* translation of *ponêros* with "jaundiced" has mild support in Evil Eye tradition (Pliny, *NH* 30.94; Plutarch, *Quaest. Conv.* 5.7, *Mor.* 681CD) where an Evil Eye occasionally is associated with jaundice. But this connection would be unknown to modern readers of the Bible and perhaps unknown to Jesus, Matthew, and Luke as well.

94. Deut 15:7–11; 28:54–57; Prov 23:6–8; Sir 14:3–10; 37:11; Tob 4:7–11, 16.

Do not turn away your face from any poor man,
and the face of God will not be turned away from you [echoing
Deut 15:7, 10].
8 If you have many possessions,
give alms from them in proportion [to what you have];
if you have few possessions,
do not worry about giving according to the little you have.
9 In this way you will be laying up a good treasure (*thêsaurizeis*)
[cf. Matt 6:19, 20, 21] for yourself
against the day of necessity.
10 For the generous giving of alms delivers from death
and keeps you from entering the darkness (*skotos*) [compare
Matt 6:23bcd].
11 And for all who practice it,
giving alms is an excellent gift in the presence of the Most High
. . .
16 Give of your bread to the hungry,
and of your clothing to the naked [compare Matt 25:31–46].
Give all your surplus for alms,
and do not begrudge with an Evil Eye (*mê phonesatô sou ho ophthalmos*) [compare Matt 6:23a] the alms when you give them.
(Tob 4:7–11, 16)

The commonalities between Matt 6:22–23/Luke 11:34–35 and these two OT
texts are not specific or extensive enough to indicate oral or literary depen-
dence on Deut 15:7–11 or Tob 4:7–11, 16 on the part of Jesus or Q, Matthew
or Luke. They are sufficient, however, to demonstrate that an Evil Eye was
long regarded in Israel as the antithesis to generosity.

A similar contrast of generosity vs. illiberality (but without reference
to an Evil Eye) is made in Prov 11:24–26, the only LXX instance of *haplous*
(11:25, *psychê haplê* = "generous person"). In the more clearly formulated
Hebrew text it declares:

One person gives freely, yet grows all the richer;
    another withholds what he should give and only suffers want.
A generous person will be enriched,
    and one who waters will himself be watered.
The people curse one who holds back grain,
    but a blessing is on the head of one who sells it.

Here too a generous or liberal person is contrasted to one who holds back
in miserly fashion.

Thus the sense of "integral eye" as *generous eye* accords with the use and connotation of *haplous* and *haplotês*, just as the sense of "miserly eye" accords with the use and connotation of *ophthlamos ponêros*.

(iii) The expression "good eye" (Prov 22:9; Sir 35:8, 10) can imply "generous eye," i.e. the eye of one who is generous and the opposite of an Evil-Eyed person. The Hebrew of Prov 22:9 reads:

> One who has a good eye (*tov 'ayin*) will be blessed,
>   for he shares his bread with the needy.[95]

Sir 35:8–11 likewise equates a "good eye" with cheerful giving:

> Glorify the Lord with a good eye (*en agathôi ophthalmôi*)
>   (RSV: *generously*)
>   and do not stint the first fruits of your hands.
> With every gift show a cheerful face,
>   and dedicate your tithe with gladness.
> Give to the Most High as He has given,
>   and with a good eye (i.e. generous eye, *en agathôi opthalmôi*)
>   as your hand has received.[96]
> For the Lord is one who repays,
>   and He will repay you sevenfold.[97]

(iv) Concern with generous giving implied in "generous eye" is consistent with the frequent biblical encouragement of generosity as an honorable quality blessed by God.[98]

(v) "Generous eye" as contrasted to "miserly eye" (Evil Eye) fits the immediate and larger contexts of Matthew's gospel.

(a) In Matt 6:19–24, vv. 22–23 are part of a set of three sayings (6:19–21, 22–23, 24), focusing on the proper, God-pleasing handling of possessions and "the generous treatment of the fellow human being."[99] In this contrast of

95. The wording of the LXX differs in not rendering "good eye," but the sense remains the same: "He that shows mercy (*ho eleôn*) to a poor person shall himself be maintained; for he has given of his own bread to the poor." LXX recasts "good eye" as showing mercy and generosity to the poor. Cf. RSV: "He who has a bountiful eye; NRSV: "Those who are generous."

96. RSV: "as generously as your hand has found."

97. See also Prov 28:27: He who gives to the poor will not want; but he who hides his eyes will get many a curse." The linking of generosity, eye, and divine recompense recalls Deut 15:7–11.

98. See, e.g., Exod 35:5; Ps 37:21; Prov 14:31; 19:6, 17; 21:26, 28:27; Sir 4:4–6; Luke 3:11; Acts 2:44–46; 10:4; Rom 15:26; 2 Cor 8:2, 20; 9:5–15; 1 Tim 6:17–19; *Did.* 4:5–8; *Barn.* 3:3, 5; 19:11. For God as generous: see, e.g., Matt 6:30; Luke 11:13; Rom 5:20, 6:23, 8:32, 10:12; 1 Tim 1:14; Jas 1:17.

99. Derrett 1995:68.

eyes, notes Ulrich Luz, "the relationship to possessions remains central."[100] The "treasure in heaven," of which 6:19–21 speaks, is associated in 19:21 with generosity toward the poor.

(b) Matthew 6:1–4, commenting on the giving of alms, also pertains to generous giving to those in need. Focus on "treasure," almsgiving, and generosity was encouraged in Tob 4 also in conjunction with not having an Evil Eye (Tob 4:7–11, 16).

(c) The parable of Matt 20:1–15 contrasts an Evil Eye of disgruntled laborers to the generosity of a "good" vineyard owner (20:15).[101]

Numerous factors thus support the conclusion that in Matt 6:22–23 an "integral eye" has the sense of a "generous eye" contrasted to an "Evil Eye" connoting a "miserly eye" or "stingy eye."[102] A "generous eye" represents a generous person and a "miserly eye," a miserly person unwilling to share personal resources, especially with those in need.[103] The claim made over half a century ago by Henry Cadbury and predecessors is essentially correct: the saying of Jesus in both Matthean and Lukan versions "is a condemnation

100. Luz 1989:398.

101. Amstutz (1968:96–102) proposed that *haplous* could have the sense of "without envy." Envy, admittedly, is the emotion most frequently associated with an Evil Eye and in *T. Iss.* 3:3 and 4:5–6 envy (*phthoneros, zêlos*) is joined with Evil Eye (*baskanos, ophthalmous ponêrous*) as alien to a person of integrity (*ho haplous*, 4:2). *Testament of Simeon* 4:5 equates behaving with integrity of heart (*en haplotêtos kardias*) with guarding against all envy (*zêlou kai phthonou* as a hendiadys). The context of Matt 6:22–23, however, namely Matt 6:19–24, argues against "envious Evil Eye" and rather for "miserly Evil Eye (as a logical antithesis to "generous"). This is in contrast to Matt 20:15 where "Evil Eye" clearly implies envy, as the social dynamic of the parable indicates.

102. Scholars favoring *generous* for *haplous* or *generous* as a connotation of "integral" or "simple" include Cadbury 1954 (following earlier scholars: Lightfoot, Wettstein, Schlatter, Bornhäuser, Allen, Weinel, Fridrichsen, 105–7); Filson 1960:100; R. L. Roberts 1963; Schlatter 1963:222–224; Derrett 1988:272–73 (versus evil eye = "mean," 273); Malina and Rohrbaugh 2003:358. Luz translates "sincere eye" vs "evil eye" (1989:391), but observes that "the 'sincere' eye means a form of human behavior, primarily generosity, but, beyond it, honesty and uprightness in obedience to God as such" (1989:397); cf. Fensham 1967: "goodness of intention." Derrett (1995:68, also 1988:273) takes "Evil Eye" to imply "meanness," which he sees as refusing generosity. Allison (1987) and Davies and Allison (1988) also consider generosity to be the chief point, but fail to explore and explain the bearing of *ophthalmos ponêros* and Evil Eye tradition on this interpretation.

103. Senior (1998:87) renders "healthy eye" and "unhealthy eye," but regards the phrases as metaphorsl for "one who is generous" and" one who is possessive or stingy," respectively.

of miserliness over against generosity."[104] Other renderings of *haplous* fail to match this weight of support for "generous."[105]

Since, as indicated above, there are no cases prior to Matthew where *haplous* means "healthy," only rare cases where *ponêros* can mean "sick," and no cases where *haplous* and *ponêros* were employed together to compare healthy and unhealthy eyes, translations and commentaries proposing contrasts of "healthy/unhealthy" or "sound/unsound" or "clear/unclear" are to be rejected.[106] This sense, moreover, is incongruous with the context, which concerns not issues of physical health but of morality and making proper moral choices with one's possessions (Matt 6:19–21, 24).[107] It is likewise inconsistent with the fact that the standard meaning of *ophthalmos ponêros* is "Evil Eye," not "unhealthy eye," and consistently points to a moral condition rather than one of health.[108] John Chrysostom, in his homily on Matt 6:22–23, observes that *ophthalmos ponêros* here indicates not a sick eye that looks or sees (badly), but someone that looks "with Evil Eye malice (*meta baskanias*) originating in an evil soul."[109] Chrysostom explicitly identifies *ophthalmos ponêros* as *baskania* and expresses the conventional notion of an Evil Eye conveying the malice arising in the heart/soul. Chrysostom is surely correct and to be followed in seeing Jesus's saying as referring to moral behavior and not to a matter of physical health.

---

104. Cadbury 1954:72; he made this point over against Edlund (1952), who rejected "generous" and preferred "genuine," claiming that "generous" was too restricted to envy and did not fit the context of either Matthew or Luke (Edlund 1952:107, 113). In actuality, however, "generous" is not so bound to envy as its opposite and does indeed fit Matthew's context.

105. The entry on *haplous* in the *EDNT* (Schramm, 1 [1990]):124 recognizes that this saying [of Matt and Luke] "is based on the image from the Hebrew-Aramaic thought world of the 'good' and 'evil' [i.e. envious] eye," though *haplous* is rendered variously as "pure, gracious," or "without envy" (citing Amstutz 1968:101–2), and as referring to "the human will in its entirety." The *EDNT* entry on "eye" (*ophthalmos*) by M. Völkel (*EDNT* 2 [1991]), on the other hand, shows no recognition of Evil Eye tradition in Matt 6/Luke 11 and proposes the renditions "pure, sincere" (*haplous*) and "bad" (*ponêros*). Neither entry adequately captures the sense or implications of the contrast.

106. Against Betz, among others. Betz translates, "healthy/good eye" vs. "sick/evil eye" (1995:450, 451) as implying a "well-functioning" vs. a "malfunctioning" eye (1995:451). He mentions the Evil Eye only in passing (1995:451) and it plays no role in his interpretation of this saying.

107. So, correctly, Luz 1989:360–61. See also the similar moral contrasts of Matt 7:17–18 and 12:34–35.

108. The meaning of *ophthalmos ponêros*, which is the more conventional and recurrent expression, controls the meaning of its unusual counterpart *ophthalmos haplous* and not vice versa.

109. John Chrysostom, *Hom. Matt.* 20.3–6 [on Matt 6:22–23] (*PG* 57.290–92).

The contrast of an integral/good eye versus an Evil Eye is paralleled and continued in the contemporary rabbinic tradition. Rabban Johanan ben Zakkai (c. 80 CE) once said to his five disciples:

> Go forth and see which is the good way to which a man should cleave. R. Eliezer [ben Hyrcanus,c. 90 CE] said, A good eye. R. Joshua said, A good companion. R. Jose said, A good neighbor. R. Simeon said, One that sees what will be. R. Eliezar [ben Arak] said, A good heart . . . He [R. Johanan b. Zakkai] said to them to them: Go forth and see which is the evil way which a man should shun. R. Eliezar said, An Evil Eye. R. Joshua said, An evil companion. R. Jose said, An evil neighbor. R. Simeon said, He that borrows and does not repay . . . R. Eleazar said, An evil heart." (*m. Avot* 2:9)

In a further instance, a comparison of four types of almsgivers includes two whose intentions typify ungenerous begrudging Evil-Eye behavior. These are contrasted to a saintly man and an evil man:

> There are four types of almsgivers:[1] he that is minded to give, but not that others should give—he begrudges [with an Evil Eye] what belongs to others; [2] he that is minded that others should give, but not that he should give–he begrudges [with an Evil Eye] what belongs to himself; [3] he that is minded to give and also that others should give–he is a saintly man; [4] he that is minded not to give himself and that others should not give–he is an evil man. (*m. Avot* 5:13)[110]

Mention of the Evil Eye in connection with almsgiving recalls especially the exhortation of Tob 4:5–19.

Finallly, the rabbis contrasted a good eye to an evil eye in a comparison of the disciples of Abraham with those of Balaam: those who are disciples of Abrahan have "a good eye and a humble spirit and a lowly soul," but disciples of Balaam have "an Evil Eye, a haughty spirit, and a proud soul." The former "enjoy this world and inherit the world to come;" the latter "inherit Gehenna and go down to the pit of destruction" (*m. Avot* 5:19).

In these contrasts, an Evil-Eyed person is one who is ungenerous, miserly, reluctant to share one's resources, begrudging of hospitality to others, begrudging the generosity of others, and haughtiness. This portrait is

---

110. These rabbinical passages of *Pirke Avot* are far closer and more relevant than the "partial" parallel Turan (2008) finds in *b. Ta'an.* 24a where "eye," he proposes, is a microcosm and indicator of the broader physical health of a person (2008:81). Turan appears unfamiliar with Evil Eye tradition in antiquity. On the references to the Evil Eye in the *Pirke Avot* (2:9–11; 5:13–19), see Vol. 4 of the present study.

consistent with the qualities and actions of Evil-Eyed persons described in numerous Old Testament texts (Deut 5:7–11; 28:53–57; Sir 14:3, 8, 10; 18:18; 37:11). There is thus a long and consistent tradition in Israel in which having an Evil-Eye is considered the opposite of being generous and liberal with one's possession. This tradition further supports viewing the antithesis of "integral eye" vs. "Evil Eye" in Matt 6:22–23/Luke 11:34–35 as implying a contrast of a generous person to a miserly person reluctant to aid poor and needy neighbors.

The multivalence of the Greek term *haplous* (designating various types of singularity, sincerity, or integrity) is best captured by the similarly ambiguous English term "integral." To whatever realm of life and action *ophthalmos haplous* and *ophthalmos ponêros* might have alluded in the Q stage of this saying, it is evident that Matthew has used the logion to support a point about the proper management of one's wealth (6:19–21)[111] and putting allegiance to God before servitude to wealth (6:24).[112] In this context, the expression *ophthalmos haplous* implies a person whose integrity consists of the moral quality of generosity and liberality, and is best rendered "generous eye." Its counterpart, *ophthalmos ponêros*, best rendered with the conventional translation "Evil Eye" (as in Sir 14:10; 31:13; Q11:34d/Luke 11:34d; Mark 7:22), implies in this context a person who is stingy, miserly and unwilling to share possessions with those in need. A modern instance of this sense of the Evil Eye as the opposite of generosity is offered by an ethnographic study by D. K. Pocock of the Patidar, a caste of Central Gujerat, India. Pocock reports that the Evil Eye (*najar*) "was attracted not by mere envy but by meanness and a refusal to share good things."[113] "When some do accumulate wealth, the fear of *najar* defines the ways in which wealth may be enjoyed, that is with modesty; it requires all men to be generous according to their means."

4. The consequences of having an integral or an Evil Eye

The consequences of having an integral or an Evil Eye (Matt 6:22c, 23b/Luke 11:34c, 34e) are stated in terms of light or darkness in the body. In regard to the eye functioning like a lamp (Matt 6:22a/Luke 11:34a), an integral eye produces light throughout the entire body, but an Evil Eye shrouds the body

---

111. In Matt 20, Jesus's condemnation of an Evil Eye (20:15) is joined to the incident of the young man's unwillingness to be generous to the poor (Matt 20:16–22)

112. As reinforced by Peter's assertion, "We have left everything and followed you" (Matt 19:27).

113. Pocock 1992:208.

in darkness. In moral terms, a person with an integral/generous eye displays a generosity that benefits his neighbors and his community. A person with a miserly Evil Eye, by contrast, is one whose stinginess undermines the well-being of the entire community and ruins his own reputation, earning himself no reciprocal benefits, but only divine displeasure.

Matthew 6:22–23, like Q11:34d–35 and unlike Luke 11:33–36, ends on a negative note stressing darkness in the body brought on by an Evil Eye (6:23cd).[114] Matthew's version, also like Q11:34–35 and in contrast to Luke 11:33–36, devotes more words to having an Evil Eye than to having an integral eye, so that Matthew's redaction of the eye saying focuses chiefly on acting with an Evil Eye and its dark implications.

A saying of Jesus in the *Gospel of Thomas* (24c–f), also on light or darkness in a person, likewise concludes on the negative note of darkness; it reads:

> [Light] exists [inside a person of li]ght,
> [and this person (*or* light) shines on the whole] world.
> [If this person (*or* light) does not shine,
> then] there is [darkness] (*or* "this person" *or* "light" is dark).

> [*phôs es*]*tin* [*en anthrôpô ph*]*ôteino,*
> [*kai phôtizei tô k*]*osmô* [*holô*].
> [*ean mê phôtiz*]*ê,*
> [*tote skoteinos e*]*stin.*[115]

This saying makes no reference to an integral or Evil Eye and so is no exact parallel to Matt 6:22–23/Luke 11:34–35. It is, however, similar in theme and terminology to elements of Q11:34/Matt 6:22c, 23b/Luke 11:34c, e. The saying is part of a set of three sayings (24c–26), which, following 24c–f, continues:

> Jesus said,
> "Love your brother as your soul;
> keep him as the apple of your eye."

114. Luke adds a saying (11:36) that brings 11:33–36 to a positive conclusion stressing a body full of light and providing light like a shining lamp.

115. P.Oxy. 655. The more expanded Coptic parallel (Nag Hammadi II 2) reads: "Light exists inside a person of light, and he (*or* it) shines on the whole world. If he (*or* it) does not shine, there is darkness." See *The Saying Gospel Q* 2002:112–13. See, similarly, *Dialogue of the Savior* 125:18—126:1 ("The savior said, 'The lamp [of the] body is the mind; as long as you (sing.) are upright [of heart]—which is [. . .]—then your (pl.) bodies are [lights]. As long as your mind is [darkness], your light which you wait for [will not be]." Here "mind" replaces "eye."

Jesus said,
>"You see the speck in your brother's eye,
>but you do not see the log which is in your own eye.
>When you take the log out of your own eye,
>then you will see to take out the speck from your brother's eye."

Of these three sayings, the first (24c–f) concerns light or darkness in a person, which is similar, though not identical, to Q11:34c, 34e, 35/ Matt 6:22c, 23b/Luke 11:34c, 34e, 35, 36a–c, as well as Matt 5:15. The second and third are two "eye sayings" (§§25–26) that are linked by the motif "eye," along with action toward a brother. One (§25) urges loving a brother "as the apple of your eye." The other (§26) instructs about a speck in a brother's eye and a beam in one's own eye. This third saying parallels the Q eye saying concerning the speck and beam (Q6:41–42 contained in Matt 7:3–5/Luke 6:41–42). *Gospel of Thomas* 25 has no exact equivalent in the four canonical gospels; but variants of all of its three sayings occur.

Gospel of Thomas 24–26 thus appears to be an assemblage of three originally separate sayings subsequently joined in the *Gospel of Thomas* on the basis of their related terms and subjects of light or darkness in the body, and the eye (regarded as an organ of light or darkness).[116] This combination shows how eye sayings were gradually drawn together and how the motifs of darkness and light continued to be associated and combined with the subject of the eye. Here in *Gospel of Thomas* 24 it is the *person*, rather than the *eye* (as in Matt/Luke), that is said to shine or be dark. Since "eye" however can can serve as *pars pro toto* for the entire human being, the variation is insignificant. The association of eye, lamp, and light (as in Q11:34–35/Matt 6:22–23/Luke 11:33–36 and conventional thinking regarding the eye) suggests that this association implicitly lay behind the joining of Saying 24c–f to Sayings 25 and 26. The independence of these sayings in Matthew and Luke points to their combination by the composer of the *Gospel of Thomas*.

Similar to the negative ending of Q11:35 and Saying 24c–f of the *Gospel of Thomas*, Matt 6:23 closes on a negative note. This negative ending gives the saying and the contrast of integral and Evil Eye a tone not simply of exhortation but of warning: casting an Evil Eye extinguishes the light in the body and plunges the body in darkness—do not do it! An Evil Eye (and its exercise), according to Matt 6:23 (and Q11:34–35/Luke 11:34–35) fills the body with darkness, in contrast to an integral/generous eye that fills the body with light (v. 22). The adjectives *phôteinos* ("full of light [*phôs*]," "radiant") and *skoteinos* ("full of darkness [*skotos*]," "dark") constitute a

---

116. On *Gos. Thom.* 24 specifically, see Zöckler 2001.

contrast[117] paralleling and qualifying "integral eye" and "Evil Eye" respectively, and continuing the comparison of an eye to a lamp.

In regard to "full of light," "full of darkness," it is important to note that ancient Mediterraneans conceived of light and darkness as objective and opposed realities that could be unconnected with any source of light and darkness other than themselves.[118] "Darkness was an objectively present reality, the presence of dark and not the absence of light as it is for modern readers. Dark pushes out light just as light can push out dark."[119] "The sun did not 'cause' daylight, nor did the moon or stars 'cause' light at night. Genesis describes the creation of sun, moon, and stars *after* the creation of light and darkness (Gen 1:3–5, 14–19).[120] Plato (*Republic* 7. 516) imagines someone coming in from the sun and having his "eyes full of darkness." Speaking of one who stumbles around at night, Jesus declares that "the light is not in him" (John 11:10).

The contrast of light and darkness was conventional and recurrent in Israel's literature.[121] For Israel, light was essential to life and symbolized positive, life-giving qualities, and, accordingly, the divine realm. God is "clothed with light" (Ps 104:2). God the creator gives light to the eyes of poor and oppressor alike (Prov 29:13; cf. 20:12). Light symbolized salvation and union with God; darkness, alienation from God.[122] Darkness, physically, was a dangerous state and symbolized negative, death-dealing qualities, the forces of evil, the realm of death and the dead, or a form of punishment from God. Job lamented: "When I looked for good, evil came; and when I waited for light, darkness came" (Job 30:26). Light was associated with truth (Ps 43:3) and uprightness (Ps 97:11; Isa 2:5), and darkness, with ignorance (Job 12:24–25) and immorality (Job 24:13–17). The followers of Jesus, the "light of the world" (John 3:19; 8:12; 9:5), interpreted salvation as being called by God "from darkness to God's marvelous light" (1 Pet 2:9). They considered themselves "children of light" (Luke 16:8; John 12:36; 1 Thess 5:5; Eph 5:8) who through baptism were "delivered from the realm of darkness" and given an inheritance of the sons of light" (Col 1:12–13).

---

117. For the contrast, see also Xenophon, *Mem.* 3.10.1; 4.3.4; Plutarch, *Cons. ux.*, *Mor.* 610E; *Prim. frig.*, 953C; *1 Enoch* 22:2.

118. See, e.g., Gen 1:3–4 regarding the creation of light and darkness independent of and prior to the creation of celestial lights in the firmament ruling night and day (Gen 1:14–18).

119. Malina and Rohrbaugh 2003:42, 50; see also Malina and Pilch 2006:360

120. Malina and Pilch 2006:360.

121. For many Biblical, post-Biblical, apocryphal, and pseudepigrahical examples, see Aalen 1951.

122. See Ps 56:13; Isa 9:2; 42:16; 1 Pet 2:9; Job 10:21–22; Matt 8:12; 22:13.

Matthew (4:16, citing Isa 9:1) uses the contrast of darkness and light (as symbols of negative vs. positive life situations) to announce the coming of Messiah Jesus. Darkness is said to have engulfed the earth with Jesus's death on Golgotha (Matt 27:45). "What I tell you in the dark," instructed Jesus, "utter in the light." (Matt 10:27).

Used metaphorically to describe moral states and actions, light and darkness symbolized good and evil persons, righteous and unrighteous conduct. "The light of the righteous rejoices," observes the sage, "but the lamp of the wicked will be put out" (Prov 13:9; see also Ps 97:11). The Qumran community distinguished socially and morally between themselves, the righteous "Sons of Light," and the unrighteous "Sons of Darkness" (1QS 1.9–10; 3.17—4.1; 1QM). The Sons of Darkness have greedy minds and blind eyes (1QS 4.9–11). *Testament of Naphtali* 2:10 observes: "For if you request the eye to hear, it cannot; so neither while you are in darkness can you do the works of light." "Choose for yourselves light or darkness, the Law of God or the works of Beliar" (*T. Jud.* 19:1).

Accordingly, Jesus speaks of darkness displacing the light (*phôs*) in the body of an Evil-Eyed person and making the body "dark" (*skoteinon,* 6:23ab). Jesus states that an Evil Eye (and its exercise) makes one's body *full of darkness* (*skoteinon*) in contrast to an integral eye (and its exercise) that makes the body *full of light* (*phôteinon*) (Q11:34–35; Matt 6:22–23; Luke 11:34–35). The adjective *skoteinos* and the concept of darkness were already associated with envy (and an Evil Eye) in the *Testament of Benjamin,* another of the *Testaments of the Twelve Patriarchs,* discussed above.[123] The *Testament of Benjamin* also urges integrity (*haplotês,* 6:7), which it contrasts to the duplicity of the demon Beliar (6:7) and his evils, the first of which is envy (*phthonos,* 7:2).[124] Positively, the main concern of the *Testament of Benjamin* is to hold up Joseph as a model of the "good and holy man" (3:1), the one who with God's aid had successfully survived the envy and Evil Eye of his brothers and the spirits of Beliar (3:3–4). Benjamin's children are exhorted to "flee evil-doing, envy (*phthonon*), and hatred of brothers, and cleave to goodness and love (8:1). They are each to be a "good man" who has no "darkened eye": *T. Benj.* 4:2, 4, 5; and 5:3 read:

> The good man (*anêr agathos*) does not have a darkened eye
> (*skoteinon ophthalmon*), for he shows mercy to all, even though
> they be sinners" . . . he does not envy (*phthonei . . . zêloi*) . . . he

---

123. See above, chap. 1, pp. 79–86.

124. Charles (*APOT* 1913 2:357 n. 2) conjectures *phonos* ["murder"]; but see the *phthonos* of Cain also in 7:6. Envy and Evil Eye are combined in the *Testaments of the Twelve Patriarchs,* as elsewhere, and often form a hendiadys.

shows mercy to the impoverished; to the ill he shows compassion; he reveres God . . . for where one has reverence for good works and light for understanding, even darkness flees from him.

A "darkened eye" is spoken of in terms similar to those used of an Evil Eye and thus appears equivalent to "Evil Eye." Having a darkened eye, moreover, is the opposite of being a good person who shows not miserliness or envy but rather is merciful and generous to the poor.

A darkened eye, like an Evil Eye, can be a blind(ed) eye in either a physiological or a moral sense or both.

(a) It can designate a blind eye that cannot see physically (Ps 68:24 LXX; Zech 11:17). This darkening is comparable to a physical "dimming" of the eyes in advancing old age (Gen 27:1; 48:10; Deut 34:7; 1 Sam 3:2) or in sorrow (Job 17:7). It can also identity someone whose understanding and mental capacity is "darkened" in the sense of "crippled." Such a darkened mind can lead to the urge to kill (*T. Gad* 4:5; 5:1), but genuine repentance "drives away darkness and enlightens the eyes" (*T. Gad* 5:7).[125] Darkening and blinding are synonomous in these formulations. The spirit of envy (*zêlou*) and anger consumed Dan (*T. Dan* 1:6), another brother of Joseph, and *blinded* him (2:2); "for the spirit of anger ensnares a person in the nets of deceit, *blinds his eyes, darkens his understanding* by means of a lie and provides him with its own particular perspective (*horasin*)" (2:7).[126]

(b) A darkened eye (or mind or heart) can also designate an eye (and a person) that is morally evil, blinded by malevolent emotions, and unwilling to be compassionate and generous (*T. Gad* 4:1—5:4). A darkening of an eye in this case is comparable to a "melting" of an eye. "The gift of an Evil-Eyed person (*baskanou*), states Sirach, "melts the eyes" (Sir 18:18). An inscription from Arsameia, Anatolia, recording a declaration by Antiochus I of Commagene, c. 50 BCE,[127] mentions, *inter alia*, envy of another's good fortune resulting in the envier's "melting" of his own eye.[128] A earlier passage of Job is also relevant. Eliphaz, in his excoriation of Job's wickedness (22:1–30), states, "your light is darkened, so that you cannot see" (22:11). This darkening of Job's eye, Eliphaz claims, is divine punishment for Job's "great wickedness" and miserliness in "stripping the naked of their clothing, refusal of water to the weary, withholding bread from the hungry, and despising

125. See also *T. Gad* 6:2, "the spirit of hatred darkened my mind"; *T. Dan* 2:2, 4; Eph 4:18.

126. See also *T. Sim.* 2:7: "the spirit of envy (*to pneuma tou zêlou*) blinded my mind."

127. *I.Arsameia*, Antiochus I, lines 210–220.

128. Text in Danker 1982:251.

the widows and orphans (22:5–9).[129] Darkening of the eye here is divine punishment for the refusal of generosity toward those in need. Proverbs 20:9 LXX relates eyes to a lamp and the darkness brought upon the eyes (by God) for gross immorality:

> the lamp (*lamptêr*) of the one who speaks disparagingly of father
> or mother will be extinguished
> and the pupils of his eyes (*hai korai tôn ophthalmôn*) shall
> see [i.e. experience] darkness.

(c) Finally, a darkened Evil Eye can designate a human condition and behavior that are *both* physically and morally flawed. The psalmist curses his enemies, "Let their eyes be darkened so that they cannot see" (Ps 69:23, cited by Paul in Rom 11:10). This can refer to either physically blinded eyes or to eyes incapable of perception. Metaphorically, a darkened eye is equivalent to a "darkened mind" blinded by malevolent dispositions and a reluctance to show compassion. Gad observes that hatred and envy "darken the mind," which leads to the urge to kill (*T. Gad* 4:5; 5:11). Genuine repentance, on the other hand, "drives away darkness and enlightens the eyes (*T. Gad* 5:7). Since it is God who grants sight (Exod 4:11), a darkened eye and blindness could also be considered a divine punishment for having sinned[130] or for having cast an Evil Eye.[131] Tradition concerning the apostle Paul, as we shall see below, reports that he was both blinded by God for persecuting the Jesus movement (Acts 9:3–19; 22:4–16) and accused of having an Evil Eye (Gal 3:1; 4:12–20; cf. *Acts of Paul and Thecla* 3).

In these texts, then, a darkened eye is an eye (and a person represented by "eye") that is physically blinded or beclouded by malicious dispositions such as envy, avarice, greed, and malice toward others. It identifies a person lacking in generosity, compassion and mercy, i.e. by the features conventionally associated with an Evil Eye and its possessors. This all points to a "darkened eye" as equivalent to an "Evil Eye." This, in turn, gives sense to Jesus' connecting an Evil Eye with a body full of darkness.

"If then the light in you is darkness" (Matt 6:23c = Q11:35a) connects to the foregoing v. 22 through the terms "light" (*phôs*, related to "full of light" [*phôteinon*, v. 22a] and. by implication, "lamp" [*lychnos*, v. 22]), and

129. For darkening of the eye as punishment for wickedness see also Prov 13:9; 24:20; Lam 5:17.

130. See Gen 19:11; Deut 28:28; 2 Kgs 6:18; Prov 13:9; and 24:20 ("the lamp of the wicked will be put out"); John 9:1–2; Acts 9:8–9 (Saul/Paul); Acts 13:11. As punishment by the gods, see Hesiod, Frag. 52; Sophocles, *Oed. Col.* 868; Herodotus, *Hist.* 2.111; 9.93.

131. For an Egyptian curse text mentioning Horus blinding the eyes of those casting an Evil Eye see Bourghouts 1978:2, citing Schott 1931:106–10.

"darkness" (*skotos*, related to *skoteinon*, v. 23b); and it combines the motifs of light and darkness. This statement concerning light being darkness seems oxymoronic. The underling presumption of the formulation in terms of the functioning of the eye is clear: a good person projects light from a good/integral/generous eye; a malevolent person projects darkness from an Evil Eye. Inasmuch as good or evil eyes represent good or evil persons (as in Prov 23:6; Sir 14:10), an Evil-Eyed person is thought to be moved by evil intentions (in this saying an unwillingness to be generous) and to project from his Evil Eye malignant atoms of (dark) energy that engulf and harm those struck by the gaze. In this way light normally projected from the eye is extinguished or thwarted and replaced by darkness and its evil effect. Luke's transformation of this part of the saying (Q11:35a) into an exhortation ("See to it that the light in you not be darkness.") still retains this paradox of light possibly becoming darkness. The idea that "the light in you is darkness" recalls the word of Bildad, friend of Job:

> The light of the wicked is put out,
>   and the flame of his fire does not shine.
> The light is dark in his tent
>   and his lamp above him is put out. (Job 18:5–6)

Here too is an association of light and lamp, darkness and evil, as well as light identified as darkness.

The apparent sense of Jesus's statement is that the light projected from an integral eye can be extinguished and replaced by the darkness associated with an Evil Eye. If the light in you is darkness, i.e. if what should be the light in you is actually a darkness filling your entire body, how desolate your condition! Matthew's version of the saying thus concludes with an exclamation about the severity of darkness wrought by an Evil Eye: "how great the darkness!" (Matt 6:23d = Q11:35b). Luke, on the other hand, replaces this exclamation with an exhortation: "see to it, therefore that the light in you not be darkness" (Luke 11:35). Luke's modification, however, may just make explicit what is implicit in Matthew, namely that Matthew's exclamation also has hortatory force, like that of other Evil Eye texts.[132]

Jesus associates an Evil Eye with deep darkness, although the precise nature of this darkness is not stated. In Matthew's gospel, Jesus speaks of darkness as marking the eschatological state of the doomed (Matt 8:12; 22:13; 25:30). According to *T. Naph.* 2:10, "If you bid the eye to hear, it cannot; so neither while you are in darkness can you do the works of light." For Matthew, darkness within persons would prevent them from letting "their

---

132. See Deut 15:7–11; Prov 23:6–8; Sir 31:12–13; 37:10–11; Tob 4:1–21.

light shine" with good works and thereby glorifying God (Matt 5:14–16).[133] In general, the projecting of light benefits the eye's owner and all his/her family and neighbors; darkness benefits no one. Similarly, being "light in the world: (Matt 5:14) benefits humanity and leads to the glorification of the Creator (5:14–16), just as a bright-shining lamp benefits all in the household. Darkness causes people to stumble or lose their way, in the world as in the house. This darkness is injurious not only to others but to the Evil-Eyed person as well. This injury to self is suggested by the belief that, with their Evil Eye, fascinators can harm themselves.[134]

With integral eye and Evil Eye, light and darkness, signaling generous or miserly persons, a generous eye (and person) is viewed as a boon to all; gratitude and honor return to the generous donor along with favor from God. A miserly Evil Eye (and person) ignores those in need, disregards the common good, and alienates the self from both fellow humans and God. As Sirach advised long ago, "Whoever accumulates by depriving himself accumulates for others, and others will live in luxury on his goods. If a man is miserly to himself, to whom will he be generous? He will not enjoy his own riches" (Sir 14:4–5).

Implied in this Matthean conclusion is a warning against possessing and casting an Evil Eye. This warning has a purpose similar to accusations of possessing or casting an Evil Eye as found in Matt 20:15 and Gal 3:1:[135] Its aim is to uphold the virtue of generosity and condemn the miserly hoarding of goods in a culture rife with competition and conflict over scarce resources and to promote attitudes and actions contributing to the harmony and wellbeing of the comunity. In Jesus's teaching, these are virtues and actions typical of life under the reign of God and they distinguish the children of God from the mammon-focused, anxiety-ridden non-believing Gentiles (Matt 6:25–34).[136]

133. See also Acts 13 :47, citing Isa 49:6; Rom 2:19.

134. See Prov 28:22; Sir 14:6; Plutarch, *Quaest. Conv.* 5.7; *Mor.* 682B, 682EF.

135. On Evil Eye accusations, see below on Matt 20:1–15 and Paul's letter to the Galatians.

136. Betz, ignoring the implications of this explicit reference to the Evil Eye, proposes a different point to the saying. He concludes that "the eye does not itself contain the light but receives it from another source. . .'the light within you' [Matt 6:23c]" (1995:452) . . . If the 'inner light' shines, the eye will serve as the lamp that illuminates the body. The inner light enables the eye to be *haplous* ('sound') and thus function normally" (1995:453). According to Betz, the aim of the saying is "to stir up the conscience and prompt the question, 'What if my inner light is darkness? How can it be made to shine again?'" (1995:453).

5. The affinity of this Evil Eye saying with other biblical Evil Eye texts and with Evil Eye belief and practice generally

Our analysis has shown how this Evil Eye saying of Matthew (and of Q and Luke) is consistent with several features of Evil Eye belief.

- Because the eye is understood here, as generally in antiquity, to be an active organ projecting light (or darkness), it is compared to a lamp that projects light.

- The phrase *ophthalmos ponêros* is a conventional formulation for "Evil Eye"[137] and is best rendered "Evil Eye," not "unhealthy/unsound/unclear eye."

- Having and using an Evil Eye, looking with a hostile Evil Eye, is a *moral* defect, not an issue of health.

- An Evil Eye is the antithesis to a good, integral eye (and generous person, cf. Matt 20:15). The contrast accords with other "good versus evil" contrasts in Matthew (7:17–19; 12:34, 35; 20:15; 22:10).

- An Evil Eye is associated here with darkness (*skoteinos*) as it is in *T. Benj.* 4:1 and Tob 4:10. Elsewhere an Evil Eye also is said to darken/dim/melt the eyes (Sir 18:18).[138]

"Evil Eye" here connotes a miserliness/stinginess/ungenerosity conveyed through a hostile eye in contrast to a good eye communicating generosity and liberality. J. D. M. Derrett observes, correctly, "'Bad [i.e. Evil] eye' does not mean 'wickedness,' it means a disposition which is ungenerous, illiberal, unloving . . . 'Good eye' means a generous, favourable disposition."[139] "'Evil Eye,'" he comments, "expresses the idea of niggardliness or meanness, in contexts where society expects, and rewards, generosity."[140] "It is mistaken to translate *haplous* in Matthew 6.22 as 'pure,' 'simple' or the like. Disregarded, but correct, is the long tradition that it means, there and in associated passages, 'generous.'"[141] Centuries following the composition of the Gospel of Matthew, John Chrysostom (c. 347–407 CE) takes the phrase

137. See Sir 14:10; 31:13; Q11:34b; Matt 20:15; Mark 7:22; cf.also *ophthalmos* + verb *ponêreuô* in Deut 15:9; Tob 4:7, 16.

138. The darkness that Tobit envisions, however, seems closer to the "outer" eschatological darkness of Matt 8:12, 22:13, 25:30 than to the bodily darkness of Matt 6:23/ Luke 11:34–36.

139. Derrett 1988:272.

140. Derrett 1995:68.

141. Derrett 1988:272.

ophthalmos ponêros to imply envy,[142] which is conceivable given the close link of Evil Eye and envy. However, an Evil Eye often also is the weapon of miserly/stingy ungenerous persons and actions (Deut 15:7–11; 28:54–57; Prov 23:6; Sir 14:3, 5, 8, 10; 18:18; 37:11; Tob 4:5–19; *m. Avot* 5:13). This sense better fits the context of Matt 6 with its instruction on the giving of alms (6:2–4) and "laying up treasure in heaven" (6:19–21)—in contrast to Matt 20:15 where the context does imply envy. This sense thus accords closely with the advice of Tobit to his son Tobias (4:7–11, 16):

> *Give alms (poiei eleêmosynên)* from your possessions to all who live uprightly, and *do not begrudge with an Evil Eye* the alms when you give them. Do not turn your face away from any poor man, and the face of God will not be turned away from you. If you have many possessions, *give alms* from them in proportion [to what you have]; if you have few possessions, do not worry about giving according to the little you have. In this way you will be laying up a *good treasure (thêsaurizeis)* for yourself against the day of necessity. For the generous giving of alms delivers from death and keeps you from entering the *darkness (skotos)*. and for all who practice it, *giving alms* is an excellent gift in the presence of the Most High . . . Give of your bread to the hungry, and of your clothing to the naked. Give all your surplus as *alms*, and *do not begrudge with an Evil Eye* the *alms* when you give them.

Tobit's association of generous giving, not acting with an Evil Eye, laying up treasure,[143] and darkness attests to the logical relation of these elements in Matt 6:19–23 and may also explain Matthew's rationale for connecting vv. 22–23 to vv. 19–21.

An Evil Eye can bring harm not only to others but to the Evil-Eyed person him/herself.[144]

The opposition of an Evil Eye to integrity, as expressed in the *Testaments of the Twelve Patriarchs,*[145] reveals a further implication of Matthew's passage. The essence of integrity *(haplotês)* was not simply personal uprightness but also fidelity to God and commitment to communal cohesion in resistance to Hellenistic enculturation. Matthew's Gospel, with its stress on undivided loyalty to, and trust in, God, and differentiation of Christian be-

142. John Chrysostom, *Hom. Gal.* (PG 61.648).

143. See also Sir 29:8–13 where giving generously to the poor and almsgiving is described as "laying up treasure" (29:11, 12) rather than letting one's money rust (29:10).

144. See also Prov 28:22; Sir 14:5, 6, 9; 18:18; Plutarch, *Quaest. Conv.* 5.7, *Mor* 682B, 682EF.

145. *T. Sim.* 4:5; *T. Iss.* 3:1—5:8; cf. also *T. Benj.* 4:1–5.

havior from that of Pharisees and Gentiles, displays similar social concerns. For Matthew, an Evil Eye is not only a symptom of an ungenerous heart but also a signal of that heart's disloyalty toward God and community. Jesus's word concerning the Evil Eye, Matthew indicates, must be understood in relation to his call for singular devotion to God and a distinctive mode of social behavior that differentiates children of God and their confidence in God's providential care from outsiders and their anxiety over accumulation and survival. "If you are not involved in abundant and joyful giving, then your life is corrupt, your piety worthless, and your discipleship only a sham."[146]

6. The point of the saying and its relation to its immediate and remote Matthean contexts

The structure and thrust of the saying, as it encourages the generous sharing of resources, is consistent with emphases of the immediate and broader contexts of Matthew's Gospel. The immediate context (6:19–24) presents Jesus's instruction on the proper handling of wealth and setting of priorities (6:19, 24).[147] The connection of 6:22–23 with 6:19–21 reflects the conceptual link of eye (vv. 22–23) and heart (v. 21); see also Matt 5:8. The terms "treasure," "lay up treasure" (6:19, 20, 21) are a motif in the Evil Eye saying of Tobit (4:7–11),[148] to which Matt 6:22–23 is closely related; they show the logic behind Matthew's connection of vv. 22–23 with vv. 19–21. Laying up imperishable treasures in heaven refers to the sharing of material resources. The connection of an Evil Evil (vv. 22–23) with *mammon* (v. 24) is illustrated by a Jewish midrash on the book of Numbers: "The wealthy person whose Eye is Evil and his mammon go out of this world" (*Sifre Num.* 110). God vs. mammon mirrors integral vs. Evil Eye. All three sayings contrast positive and negative actions concerning the management of possessions. The antitheses of earth vs. heaven (vv. 19–21) and God vs. mammon (v. 24) suggest that the antithesis of integral vs Evil Eye (vv.22–23) also implies attitude and action consistent or inconsistent with commitment to God. Betz regards Matt 6:22–23 as a statement "on vision" and the proper shining of one's "inner light."[149] He says little of their relation to preceding and follow-

---

146. So Schlatter (1963:224). On generosity in Israel as expressed in private charity (biblical and post-biblical) and works of love see Billerbeck 4/1 (1928/1961):536–58, 559–610.

147. Luz 1989:393; Davies and Allison 1988:635.

148. See esp. Tob 4:9; cf. also Sir 29:8–13.

149. Betz 1995:437–39, 453.

ing verses.[150] Reading these words in the light of everyday Evil Eye belief, however, shows that they are an encouragement of generosity by both Jesus and Matthew. In Matthew they cohere closely with both their immediate and more remote contexts.[151]

Coherence of Matt 6:22–23 with the broader context of the Sermon on the Mount includes the relation of an integral eye with Jesus's insistence on integrity in 5:21–48;[152] not being anxious about the resources necessary for daily living (6:25–34); the association of heart, eye and intention (5:21–48; cf. Matt 9:4; 15:19); the relation of generous giving (6:22–23) to generous almsgiving (6:2–4, as in Tob 4:7, 16); Matthew's portrayal of management of possessions as a further sign of "righteousness" (5:20–48, 6:1–18); and identification of "treasure laid up in heaven" (6:19–21) as care for the poor (19:16–22; cf. 25:31–46 and Tob 4:9). "It [this Evil Eye saying] is part of a sermon in favour of the generous treatment of the fellow human being."[153]

Within the Gospel as a whole, Matthew's Jesus again praises generosity as an act typical of the reign of God in his parable of the generous vineyard owner and the Evil-Eyed workers (20:1–15). The owner's generosity contrasts to the ungenerosity of the young man reluctant to give his goods to the poor (19:16–22). Throughout the Gospel, moreover, generosity is extolled as a quality typical of God and those under God's rule,[154] and stress is given to one's obligation to fellow members under God's reign.[155]

150. On "inner light" see earlier, Brandt 1913; Betz 1979:56; Allison 1987; and Moss (2011:773–76). Moss contends that this riddle-like saying of Jesus aimed at arousing confusion in the hearers/readers and uncertainty concerning their salvation. She distinguishes (a) an "earliest form" of the saying denouncing the Evil Eye from (b) a pre-Matthean modification and (c) a Matthean use of the logion deliberately "to sow seeds of uncertainty in the minds of the listeners" concerning their own salvation" so as to prompt self-inspection and "monitoring of one's own thoughts and actions" (2010:776). This unconvincing theologizing and psychologizing of the Mathean pericope illustrates the consequence of ignoring the extensive Evil Eye tradition underlying and informing this saying of Jesus and its reformulations by Matthew and Luke.

151. Neyrey, taking "Evil Eye" to imply envy, comments that "Evil Eye aggression can be seen as another form of honor challenge" in the honor and shame culture of the time. "Jesus warns that such envy, i.e., the pursuit of honor that harms another, is simply wrong, or worse, shameful" (1998:223–24). This accurate observation about the connection of an Evil Eye accusation with the values of honor and shame actually is more relevant to Matt 20:15 and the Evil Eye accusation there than to Matt 6:22–23 where stinginess rather than envy is the likely disposition implied.

152. See also Matthew's stress on the integrity of word and deed: 7:24–27; 12:33–37; 23:1–36.

153. Derrett 1995:68.

154. See Matt 5:6, 7, 12, 44–45, 48; 6:7; 7:7–12; 9:13/12:7; 18:23–35; 19:29; 22:1–10; 23:23.

155. See Matt 5:21–48; 6:1—7:27; 10:40–42; 18:23–35; 19:16–22; 25:31–46.

Summary and Conclusion concerning Matthew 6:22–23

1. The logic and meaning of this saying (in Q11:34–35; Matt 6:22–23; and Luke 11:34–35) are governed by certain conventional notions about the eye in general and the Evil Eye in particular. The saying as a whole entails no theological novelties but rather expresses proverbial wisdom and popular abhorrence of the Evil Eye and its malice while encouraging its opposite, generosity.[156]

A. In this Matthean saying, the eye is conceived as an important organ of the body and one that emits light, in accord with the prevailing ancient extramission theory of vision.

B. It is therefore logical for Jesus, like others, to compare the eye to a lamp and for the eye to be described metaphorically as the lamp of the body, again in accord with ancient thought.

C. All theological interpretations incorrectly imagining the eye as a receptive organ and treating "lamp" and "light" as references to God's granting light to Jesus's followers, or providing them discernment of what is truly good, are misguided. Equally erroneous is the notion that lamp and light connote the good news about Jesus *entering* the hearts and minds of receptive persons, as opposed to "darkness" signifying persons resistant to Jesus and the good news. Such interpretations are illogical since they presume a modern intromission theory of vision alien to Jesus and his followers. These expressions of modern theological imagination are inconsistent with the ancient extramission theory of vision underlying these words and are oblivious to the Evil Eye belief that dominates this saying. An Evil Eye does not constitute "the impossibility of discerning what is truly good."[157] It rather conveys via a hostile glance something evil—in this case the refusal of aid to any fellow-believers in need

2. *Ophthalmos haplous* means "integral eye," which in this context has the sense of "generous eye." *Ophthalmos ponêros* means "Evil Eye," which in this context has the sense of "miserly/stingy eye." The common moral focus of the three related sayings of Matt 6:19–21, 22–23, and 24, and the traditional meaning of *ophthalmos ponêros* as "Evil Eye" representing a malicious person rule out *ophthalmos haplous* and *ophthalmos ponêros* as references to physically healthy or unhealthy eyes.

3. Inasmuch as "eye" stands for the entire person (*pars pro toto*), "integral/generous eye" represents a generous person living with integrity. "Evil

---

156. Schlatter 1963:222–23; Luz 1989:396–98.

157. Against Patte 1987:262.

Eye" represents a miserly/stingy person unwilling to share his/her material resources with others in need.

4. The gist of our saying is this: having an integral eye or an Evil Eye reflects the moral condition of the entire person and affects her/his fate. An integral person, an individual living with integrity and unequivocally devoted to God's will, is generous to all in need so that her/his body is full of light and radiates light similar to a properly functioning lamp. An Evil-Eyed person, who is miserly with her/his possessions and unwilling to aid those in need, has a darkened eye and a body flooded with darkness. This is an individual who cannot see (in either or both a physical and moral sense), who is alienated from God, and who is imperceptive of and unresponsive to to the predicament of the poor. This person causes harm to others rather than affording help.

5. This word of Jesus is an exhortation as well as an instruction: live with integrity and be generous toward those in need so that your light shines and provides light for all. This is equivalent to "laying up treasure in heaven" and "serving God." Be free of an Evil Eye, for an Evil Eye is equivalent to "laying up treasure on earth" and "serving mammon." Do not let your eye be dark or blind to the plight of others, for such ungenerosity brings harm to all concerned and alienates from a generous God. "Remember that an Evil Eye is a bad thing. What has been created more evil than an Evil Eye? It sheds tears from every face!" (Sir 31:13). A word of Isaiah also comes close in language and spirit to the point of our saying with its contrast of darkness-light and stress on generous giving:

> If you pour yourself out for the hungry and satisfy the desire of
>   the afflicted,
> then shall your light rise in darkness and your gloom be as
>   noonday. (Isa 58:10)

The saying is not an abstract reflection "on vision" and one's "inner life."[158] It is rather a concrete encouragement of generosity in one's everyday life, along with a dire warning against brandishing a miserly Evil Eye against those in need.

We have in this passage a call for generosity and a subtle warning against acting toward others with a miserly Evil Eye. The saying reflects and affirms notions and values typical of Evil Eye cultures in general and of the biblical communities in particular: compassion and benevolence toward those in need and disdain for those who close their heart to the poor and with a miserly Evil Eye begrudge their support. Its specifically Israelite

---

158. Against Betz 1995:437–53.

coloration lies in the association of the Evil Eye with a moral disposition and behavior that is inconsistent with the will and generosity of God. For both Jesus and Matthew such integrity and generosity are essential characteristics of the people called to imitate the compassion of the Creator and to be integral as God himself is integral and perfect (5:48). They are likewise qualities that are essential to the social cohesion and mutual support of the fledgling messianic community.

The biblical parallel to Matt 6:22–23 is Luke 11:34–35 (33–36). Before leaving this Matthean saying and turning to the other passage of Matthew referring to the Evil Eye (20:1–15/16), a discussion of the Lukan version of Q11:34–35 is in order.

Luke 11:33–36

33a   No one, after lighting a lamp (*lychnos*), puts it in a crevice or under a bushel
33b   but rather on a lampstand (*lychnian*),
33c   so that those who enter may see the light (*to phôs*).
34a   The lamp (*lychnos*) of the/your body is your eye (*ophthalmos*).
34b   When your eye (*ophthalmos*) is integral (*haplous*)
34c   your entire body is also full of light (*phôteinon*);
34d   when, however, it [your eye] is evil (*ponêros*)
34e   your body is also full of darkness (*skoteinon*).
35   See to it, therefore, that the light (*phôs*) in you not be darkness (*skotos*).
36a   If, therefore, your body [is] entirely full of light (*phôteinon*),
36b   having no dark part (*skoteinon*),
36c it will be entirely full of light (*phôteinon*),
36d   as when a lamp (*lychnos*), by its shining forth, provides you light (*phôtizêi*).

33a *Oudeis lychnon hapsas eis krypton tithêsin oude hypo ton modion*
33b *all' epi tên lychnian,*
33c   *hina hoi eisporeuomenoi to phôs blepôsin.*
34a *Ho lychnos tou sômatos estin ho ophthalmos sou.*
34b *hotan ho ophthalmos sou haplous ê*
34c   *kai holon to sôma sou phôteinon estin .*
34d *epan de ponêros ê,*
34e *kai to soma sou skoteinon*

35 *skopei oun mê to phôs to en soi skotos estin.*

36a *ei oun to soma sou holon phôteinon,*

36b *mê echon meros ti skoteinon,*

36c *estai phôteinon holon*

36d *hôs hotan ho lychnos tê astrapê phôtizei se.*

Luke 11:33–36 in its entirety is a combination of three sayings (vv. 33, 34–35, 36).[159] Verses 33 and 36, added to introduce and conclude vv. 34–35, emphasize the motifs of lamp and light, comparing a body full of light to a lamp providing illumination. In contrast to the negative ending of Matt 6:22–23 and Q11:35, the Lukan passage concludes on a positive note (v. 36).

The Lukan version of the Q11:34–35 integral versus Evil Eye saying is close in wording and sense to Matthew's formulation (6:22–23). It likewise contrasts an integral eye and an Evil Eye with much the same language. Luke's version of the saying *differs* from Matthew's in three chief ways: (1) Luke 11:35 transforms an exclamation (Q11:35 = Matt 6:23cd) into an exhortation. (2) Luke 11:34–35 is joined to, and framed by, two sayings (11:33 and 11:36) to create a new set of three sayings concluding on a positive note in contrast to the negative ending of Matt 6:23cd. (3) The location of the saying in Luke's narrative differs from its location in Matthew's narrative. Having examined the Q and Matthean versions of our saying, we can concentrate now on the expansions and unique features of Luke's version, and on the sense of the saying in its Lukan context.

The Greek formulation of the integral versus Evil Eye saying of Luke (11:34–35) is very similar, although not identical, to that of Matt 6:22–23, which is closer to the formulation of Q[160] than is Luke's version.

- Luke 11:34a = Q11:34a/Matt 6:22a, with Luke adding *sou* ("your") to modify "eye."

- Luke 11:34b = Q11:34b/Matt 6:22b, with minor differences.[161] In the New Testament, *haplous* occurs only here and Matt 6:22b.

- Luke 11:34c = Q11:34c/Matt 6:22c, with minor differences. Luke adds "also" (*kai*) to the beginning of this clause (and the clause of 11:34e). Luke reads "is" (*estin*) rather than Matthew's "will be" (*estai*).

159. Or it could be described as a combination of two sayings and a generalizing Lukan conclusion (v. 36).

160. Robinson, Hoffmann, and Kloppenborg, eds. 2002:110–12. On Luke 11:34–35//Matt 6:22–23, see Hartsock 2008:143–46.

161. Luke reads "when" (*hotan*) rather than "if" (*ean*) in Q and Matthew; Luke lacks the "therefore" (*oun*) of Q and Matt, and places the verb "is" before "eye" rather than at the end of the clause.

- Luke 11:34d = Matt 6:23a with minor differences. Luke reads "when" (*epan*) rather than "if" (*ean*) and lacks "your eye" (*ho ophthalmos sou*), which is, however, implied, as shown by the context and the Matthean parallel.[162]

- Luke 11:34e = Matt 6:23b with minor differences.[163]

- The difference of Luke 11:35 from Q11:35/Matt 6:23c is more substantial; it reads as an exhortation rather than as the exclamation of Q and Matthew. The conditional particle "if" (*ei*) is omitted, the imperative verb "see to it" (*skopei*) is added to open the clause along with the negative particle *mê* ("not"). The concluding exclamation "how great the darkness" is omitted, thereby creating the command, "see to it, therefore, that the light in you not be darkness."[164]

The biblical translations of Luke 11:34–35 are similar to those of Matt 6:23–24, but show much diversity and little agreement on the meanings of the qualifications of *ophthalmos*, namely *haplous* and *ponêros*. One finds in addition to *simplex* versus *nequam* (Vulgate), "einfältig" vs. "Schalk" (Luther), and "good" vs. "bad" (NKJV). Incongruous contrasts have also been put forward: "single" vs. "evil," (KJV); "sound" vs. "bad" (NAB, Phillips), "clear" vs. "bad" (NAS), "lauter" vs. "böser" (Zürcher). Erroneous renditions referring to health abound: "sound" vs. "not sound" (RSV); "healthy" vs. "not healthy" (NRSV); "sain" vs. "malade" (BJ); "clear" vs. "diseased" (NJB); "sano" vs. "enfermo" (La Biblia—La Casa de la Biblia); "sano" vs. "viziato" (*La Sacra Bibbia*); see also eyes good vs. bad (NIV); eyes "sound" vs. "no good" (TEV).

Behind Luke 11:34–35, as behind Matt 6:22–23, is the conventional ancient view that the eye of the human body is comparable in its nature and function to a lamp in a human household. Luke introduces vv. 34–35 with a saying (v. 33) that states the light-projecting function of a household lamp. Verse 34 then proceeds from the lamp in a house (v. 33) to the "lamp" in a human body, namely the eye as vessel and conveyer of light. Following the contrast of integral and Evil Eye, light or darkness in the body (v. 34),

162. For a similar Lukan omission see Luke 6:45 where 6:45ab reads *agathos anthrôpos . . . agathou thesaurou*, while its antithesis of 6:45c reads *ponêros . . . ponêrou* (omitting an implied *anthrôpos* and *thêsaurou*).

163. Luke adds "also" (*kai*) at the beginning of the clause, but lacks "entire" before "body" and also lacks a concluding verb (cp. "will be" [*estai*]), which, however, is implied by its parallel in v. 34c and by the presence of a verb in Matthew. The verb *estai* is supplied secondarily by P45 and a few other mss.

164. In respect to v. 35, Codex Claremontanus and several Old Latin mss have the same reading as Matt 6:23cd. Various Old Latin mss and the Vulgate support the reading *skopei . . . estai phôteinon holon kai hôs [ho] lychnos [tês] astrapês phôtisei se*.

hearers are warned to make sure that it is light that fills the body, not darkness. Verse 36 assures that a person's body that is full of light with no hint of darkness (cf. vv. 34–35) provides light, similar to a lamp which shines forth (cf. v. 33). The pairing of vv. 33 and 36 with the eye saying of vv. 34–35 provides strengthened illustration of the understanding of the eye as active rather than passive organ. Luke's term *astrapê* ("by its shining forth," v. 36d) expresses this as well.[165] While "integral eye" and "Evil Eye" still have the likely connotations of "generous eye/person" versus a miserly eye/person," as in Matthew,[166] the Lukan form and setting of the saying focus more on the projecting of light than on the Evil Eye and darkness.[167] This fact is obscured when the eye erroneously is assumed to receive rather than project light.[168]

In Luke 11:34, as in Matt 6:23, *ophthalmos ponêros* refers to the pernicious Evil Eye.[169] Luke joined this eye saying (vv. 34–35) to two other sayings about lamp and light, one to introduce (v. 33) the set of three sayings and the other (v. 36) to conclude it. The linkwords "lamp" (vv. 33, 36) and "light" (vv. 33, 36) frame the unit.[170] The result is a unit that highlights the positive light-projecting function of the eye and of the human being represented by

165. The term is used to designate lightning as well as the light of a lamp and also occurs in the expression "flashing of the eyes" (Sophocles, Frag. 474). Allison (1987:79) proposes that v. 36 was "an early interpretative addition to the saying about the lamp as eye" prior to Luke and that it illustrates the presumption of an extramission theory of vision.

166. For the contrast of good (*agathos*) versus evil (*ponêros*) persons see Luke 6:45 where "good" may also connote generous; see also 11:13.

167. For the contrast of darkness and light see also Luke 12:3.

168. See, e.g, Garrett (1991:105 n. 33), who thinks that "the Lucan version is concerned with the ability of the eye to "receive the light, i.e. perceive and accept Jesus or his Gospel." She notes the studies of Betz and Allison on the eye as active rather than passive (Garrett 1991:100 n. 22), but ignores this basic fact and its implications for the meaning of 11:33–36. Robert Tannehill (1996:196) also claims, "the eye either admits the light of God's word or does not." These theological interpretations fail, since they erroneously presume the eye to be a passive rather than active agent. Jesus/Luke, however, is not speaking of a body "truly receptive of light" or "accept[ing] illumination from the true light" (Fitzmyer 1985:939], but of an eye *projecting* light.

169. Plummer (1922:308) unconvincingly takes *haplous* to mean "free from distortion, sound" and *ponêros* to mean "diseased." Joseph Fitzmyer (1985:938–41) rightly opts for the moral sense of *haplous* ("clear-sighted") and *ponêros* ("bad"). He acknowledges that *ophthalmos ponêros* designates "Evil Eye" in Matt 20:15 and Mark 7:22, but claims that this meaning "is not suitable here," though with no explanation (1985:940–41). In this context, "clear-sightedness," he states, "becomes a dedication to the word of God preached ('the light'); and the badness results in a 'darkened' existence."

170. In Luke 11:33, *pheggos* ("radiance") as an alternative to *to phôs* ("light") has some good Mss support (including Codex Alexandrinus) and is preferred in editions of the Nestle-Aland edition of the Greek text prior to Nestle–Aland[27] Other variant readings concern scribal efforts to harmonize the Lukan and Matthean texts.

the eye.[171] The point of Luke 11:33–36 is that one's body should be full of light, and, like a lamp, should cast forth that light—action that is impeded by having and casting an Evil Eye. This new positive stress on lamp and light, however, is no logical grounds for concluding that *ophthalmos ponêros* has lost its meaning of "Evil Eye."[172] The meaning of the phrase "the light that is in you" (v. 35) also is obscured when the eye is erroneously assumed to be a passive rather than active agent. Even as astute a commentator as Joseph Fitzmyer is among those who miss this cultural point. He renders *to phôs to en soi* as "the light which *enters* you"[173] because he mistakenly assumes the point about light to be about its *entering* the body instead of being *projected from* the body. Light and darkness, he asserts, symbolize acceptance or rejection of the person and preaching of Jesus.[174] Fitzmyer also comments: "If the body is truly receptive of light . . . it will accept illumination from the true light when it shines—the word of God preached by Jesus."[175] His translation is inconsistent with the comparison of the eye to a lamp which *projects* light.[176]

In actuality, Luke, like Matthew (and Q), and his contemporaries in general, regards the eye as an active organ—as is made clear by the comparison of eye and lamp (v. 34a) and the addition of v. 33 on the light-casting function of a lamp. An active integral eye discloses a body full of light and projects light, as the eye is intended to function. An active Evil Eye discloses a body full of darkness and projects darkness, with no light provided. As in Matthew's version, and in keeping with qualities associated with the Evil Eye, an integral eye signals generous giving to those in need. An Evil Eye, by contrast, signals reluctance in giving and the begrudging of generosity.

The Structure, Context, and Point of Luke 11:33–36

Luke combines Jesus's integral versus Evil Eye saying (11:34–35) with two other sayings about "lamp" and "light" that introduce (v. 33) and conclude (v. 36) a newly formed unit, vv. 33–36. Verse 33 is a saying of Q that is

171. By contrast, the Q saying and Matt 6:22–23 end on the negative implications of having an Evil Eye.

172. Against Fitzmyer 1985:940–41.

173. Ibid.:938, 940.

174. Ibid.:940.

175. Ibid.:939.

176. Tannehill's interpretation (1996:196) is similarly problematic: "The eye that is single in this sense [completely focused on God] is open to God's illumination, enabling the self to be 'full of light.'" In actuality, the eye as active agent does not receive illumination from God but rather provides illumination.

located elsewhere in Matthew's narrative.[177] Verse 36 has no Matthean parallel; it expands on and combines elements of vv. 34–35, focuses on a body full of light,[178] and concludes with the motif of lamp and light introduced in v. 33. Terms pertaining to "lamp" and "light" link the verses and form an inclusion that frames the unit.[179] In contrast to Matt 6:22–23, Luke 11:33–36 ends with a positive stress on a body full of light and providing light. Verse 36 also illustrates the conventional notion of the eye as comparable to a lamp projecting light. The verses surrounding the eye saying of Luke differ in content from the sayings framing the eye saying of Matthew (6:19–21, 24) just as the location of the three sayings in Luke's narrative differs from the location of the eye saying in Matthew. In contrast to Matthew, who locates the saying within Jesus's first major discourse, the "Sermon on the Mount," Luke situates 11:33–36 not within Luke's equivalent "Sermon on the Plain" (Luke 6:17–49), but within a unique Lukan account of Jesus's final journey to Jerusalem (9:51—19:27). More immediately, the verses follow a series of warnings by Jesus (11:14–32) and precede a condemnation of Pharisees and lawyers (11:37–54).

The connection of Luke 11:33–36 to its immediate context and the rhetorical function of the unit are not immediately clear. Alfred Plummer (1922:308) sees 11:33–36 as continuing Jesus's reply to the demand for a sign and as a reference to "spiritual sight . . . not darkened by indifference and impenitence" and thus having no need of a sign from heaven. Fitzmyer sees a connection between a "bad" eye (v. 34) of Jesus's hearers and "this *evil* generation" (*autê genea ponêra*, v. 29) with its untrusting demand for signs.[180] Verse 34 "comments on the condition of those who listen to the preaching of Jesus."[181] Charles Talbert views 11:33–36 as the third of Jesus's threefold response (11:16–36) to the charge that Jesus casts out demons and healed in league with Beelzebul, the prince of demons (11:14–16).[182] "The unit [11:33–36] likens Jesus' ministry to a light that illuminates those who enter a house." "The failure to respond properly [to the light provided by Jesus] "is a spiritual analogue to the person whose body is full of darkness because of a diseased or blind eye (vv. 34–35). Hence the call for a sign

177. Luke 11:33 = Matt 5:15; cf. Mark 4:21 and the Lukan doublet, Luke 8:16, and *Gos. Thom.* 33b.

178. See also *Gos. Thom.* 24c: "There is light within a person of light, and this person (or light) illumines the entire world."

179. "Lamp" (*lychnos*): vv. 33a, 34a, 36d; cf. lampstand (*lychnia*, v. 33b); "light" (*phôs, phôteinos, phôtizei; astrapê*): vv. 33c, 34c, 36a, 36c, 36d).

180. Fitzmyer 1985:939.

181. Ibid.

182. Talbert 1989:138–39.

(11:29–32) is a symptom of spiritual blindness." Susan Garrett, ignoring any connection of 11:34–35/Matt 6:22–23 to Evil Eye belief, assumes a modern introspective theory of vision.[183] She proposes that the verses are connected to the testing of Jesus and the seeking of signs (11:16, 29). This she takes as manifesting the absence of a *haplous* eye or heart" (1991:101–102), as illustrated by the Pharisees (11:37–44).[184] For her, 11:33–36 issues a theological and eschatological warning. To those who are testing him and seeking signs Jesus declares that "only one whose eye is single, *haplous*, will 'see' a favourable outcome at the judgment" (1991:105). Tannehill (1996:196), following Garrett (1991:103), may be correct in seeing the Phariseees and lawyers "presented as examples of those who lack singleness of heart and eye."[185] The evil of the Evil Eye could relate to the "evil" of this generation (11:29) and of the Pharisees. As Luke 11:27–36 concerns reception or rejection of Jesus, the "Evil Eye" and "this evil generation" identify persons whose bodies are dark and unproductive of light, contrary to the function of lamps and the intended conduct of Jesus's followers.[186] Since 11:33–36 in its entirety, however, stresses the *positive* projecting of light rather than the darkness of an Evil Eye, it is likely that this unit affirms something *positive* in its context as well. These proposals of Garrett and Tannehill concentrate on a negative rather than positive thrust of 11:33–36, while at the same time overlooking the bearing of biblical Evil Eye tradition on the meaning vv. 34–35 and their function in context. Taking the latter into consideration, we note that the integral versus evil contrast of Luke 11:34 relates to the contrast of good and evil in 11:13. This verse, which concludes Jesus' statement about human and divine generosity (11:5–13), affirms that even evil persons can give good gifts, with God's goodness exceeding even this human generosity:

> If then you who are evil (*ponêroi*) know how to give good gifts (*domata agatha*) to your children, how much more will the heavenly Father give (*dôsei*) the Holy Spirit to those who ask him! (Luke 11:13)

This generous giving accords with the generosity associated with an integral eye as well as with the generosity of the "good eye" described in Prov 22:9

183. Garrett 1991.

184. Ibid.:103, 105.

185. It is interesting that Luke 11:37–41 parallels elements of Mark 7:1–23, where Jesus, also in criticism of the Pharisees' purity practice at meals and their attention to external ritual matters rather than internal moral concerns, contrasts outside and inside, assures that all is clean, and likewise mentions the Evil Eye (7:22). Mark 7:1–23 is discussed below.

186. See Matt 5:15; Mark 4:21; *Gos. Thom.* 24.3; 33.2–3.

and Sir 35:8, 10.[187] Generosity, moreover, also is involved in the giving of alms to which Jesus later refers in his critique of the Pharisees (Luke 11:41), and is a major theme that pervades this Gospel.[188] The broader context of Luke 11, where Jesus urges generosity and a willingness to aid persons in need, resembles the context of the Evil Eye saying of Matt 6, which speaks of almsgiving to the poor (Matt 6:2–4) and laying up treasure in heaven (= generosity to the poor, Tob 4:9). Thus, like the Evil Eye saying of Matt 6:22–23 and of Tob 4:7, 16 (cf. also Deut 15:7–11), the Evil Eye in this Lukan version also denotes a person who is miserly and stingy with his/her possessions and unwilling to be generous, especially toward the poor and needy.

This suggests that in this Lukan context, the words about lamp and light, integral and Evil Eye, were meant to encourage among Jesus's followers the practice of generosity and avoidance of miserliness, similar to their intent in Matthew. The warning of v. 35 that hearers should have light rather than darkness filling their bodies implies an admonition not to look at others with a miserly Evil Eye since this would fill the viewer's body with darkness. See to it that your eye is an integral, generous eye providing light, and never a stingy Evil Eye extinguishing the light. Always be a person disposed to being generous rather than miserly or stingy. Showing mercy and giving alms to the needy rather than hoarding your wealth is the practice that accords with God's will. The warning is thus similar in sense to the Evil Eye admonitions of Deut 15:7, 9, 10 and Tob 4:7–11, 16,[189] as well as Matt 6:22–23.

Luke's exhortation makes this warning even stronger than Matthew's exclamation (Matt 6:23cd). Luke's set of sayings ends on a positive rather than a negative note: integrity and generosity fill the body with light; this light shines brightly in this evil generation and distinguishes the children of God from those who, instead of being generous, load on people burdens too difficult to bear (Luke 11:45).

Our analyses of Matt 6:22–23 and Luke 11:33–36 have shown that many modern commentators and Bible translators are unaware of, or ignore, the the active nature of the eye presumed in this saying and throughout the Bible. Many also appear unacquainted with the concept of the Evil Eye, and consequently propose interpretations incompatible not only with ancient physiological understanding of the eye but also unappreciative of

187. Quoted above in relation to Matt 6:22–23.

188. See also Luke 1:53; 3:1; 6:29–31, 35, 36, 38, 45; 7:13; 8:3; 10:29–37; 11:5–13; 12:32–34; 14:12–14; 16:22–23, 31; 18:22; 19:8; 21:1–4. cf. Acts 2:45; 3:6; 4:32, 34–35; 10:23;11:29.

189. For these passages see above, chap. 1, pp. 24–31 (Deut 15) and pp. 57–61 (Tob 4).

cardinal moral values such as generosity. The result is theological interpretation oblivious to Israel's Evil Eye belief that flies in the face of the everyday reality and thought-world of Jesus and his earliest followers.

The Evil Eye Saying in Matthew 20:1–15/16

A Parable about a Generous Vineyard Owner and a Malocchio of Malcontents

Returning to the Gospel of Matthew, we now take up the second of Matthew's references to the Evil Eye. It appears as part of the conclusion to Jesus's parable concerning a generous vineyard owner and envious Evil-Eyed workers. This parable, unique to Matthew, tells of an interaction between the owner of a vineyard and his workers as an illustration of some quality of the kingdom of heaven (Matt 20:1). The parable climaxes and concludes with the owner posing a rhetorical question to a worker grumbling about the owner's generous payment of the last-hired laborers: "Is your Evil Eye envious," the owner asks—an implicit Evil Eye accusation—"because I am generous? (*ho ophthalmos sou ponêros estin hoti egô ê agathos eimi*, 20:15).

Bible Versions and exegetical studies show no consensus on the translation of v. 15, on the content and length of the parable, or on its meaning and point for Jesus or for Matthew. The inadequacies of discussions reflecting modern dogmatic biases[190] are frequently underscored by commentators on this text.[191] But the proposals of new approaches[192] or a new interpretive "key" to the parable[193] have yet to lead to a new consensus.[194] Most interpretations recognize a reference to the Evil or envious Eye in the

190. E.g., Billerbeck 1926/1961 1:833–34; 4/1:484–500. As an example, Herman Waetjen (2011:103 n. 28) points to the study of A. Hultgren (2000): "Hultgren concludes that Jesus's 'outlandish parable' reveals that 'we are accepted and loved by God, and saved by God, not because of our efforts but purely by God's won grace.' In his exposition, 42–43, his Lutheran application of the parable destroys its character and spitiualizes its objective."

191. See, e.g., Dupont 1965; Derrett 1977:50; Haubeck 1980:95–96; Schottroff 1984:137–38; esp. Herzog 1994:79–97.

192. E.g., Crossan 1973; Schottroff 1984; Dietzfelbinger 1983; Scott 1989:281–98; Herzog 1994:79–97.

193. Derrett 1977:50, 59–63.

194. For diverging interpretations of Matthew's treatment of the parable see, e.g., Jeremias 1963:33–38, 136–39; Schottroff 1984:129–47; 2006:209–17; Patte 1987:261–80; Tevel 1992; Herzog 1994:79–97; Verhoefen 2007; Vearncombe 2010 (rich economic detail on viticulture); Waetjen 2011; Van Eck and Kloppenborg 2015 (extensive economic detail on viticulture).

parable's conclusion and offer some brief comment.[195] Few, however, accord it significance for the meaning of the parable as a whole.[196] When analyzed, however, in the light of Evil Eye tradition, this parable can be seen to make a powerful statement about generosity and Evil-Eyed envy.

The following analysis expands on an earlier study of mine (Elliott 1992), which subsequently has informed a recent publication of Herman Waetjen (2011).[197] Waetjen sees the parable as a censure of envious Evil Eyed laborers and an affirmation of generosity meeting workers' needs. An examination of the parable with features of ancient Evil Eye belief in mind clarifies the cultural script latent in this story and shows how this reference to an Evil Eye constitutes a fitting punchline to the parable.

The Literary Context of the Parable

In the overall structure of Matthew's narrative, our parable is situated within an account of Jesus' teaching and ministry in Judaea following his departure from Galilee (19:1) and preceding his entry into Jerusalem (21:1–11). Matthew, who in general is here following his Markan source (Matt 19:1–20:34//Mark 10:1–52), adds this parable as a further illustration of preceding teaching concerning the nature of the kingdom of heaven, conditions for attaining salvation and eternal life, and the fact that with God all things are possible (19:13–30).[198] He has shaped the introduction (20:1) and has

195. See, e.g., Billerbeck 1926/1961 1:833–35 (listing additional references in the rabbinic tradition); Jeremias 1963:138; Schniewind 1964:207; Derrett 1977:54; Haubeck 1980:104; Dietzfelbinger 1983:127, 133; Schottroff 1984:137; Schenke 1988:263–64; Donahue 1988; Malina 2001:123; Vearncombe 2010; Waetjen 2011.

196. Exceptions include Breech (1983:150–56), who identifies the dynamic of envy at work in the parable's second half. See also Schenke (1988:264–65) who, however, speaks of the grumblers' egocentric "jealousy" [*Eifersucht*] rather than envy, and Patte (1987:261–80) who postulates a link of the "bad eye" saying to what he takes to be the dominant theme of 19:1—20:16, namely, hardness of heart and its contrast to the goodness of God.

197. Waetjen 2011:99 and nn. 16, 18, 100, 102.

198. A compositional pattern and linkage with earlier teaching of Matthew are evident here. The motif of "treasure in heaven" (19:21) echoes "treasures in heaven" (6:20), thereby linking chs. 19–20 with preceding teaching of the Sermon on the Mount. Repeated reference here to the related theme "kingdom of heaven" (19:12, 13, 21, 23, 24; 20:1) likewise links chs. 19–20 with the Sermon on the Mount (5:3, 10, 19, 20; 7:21). In chs 19–20, the saying concerning the refusal of the rich young man to be generous to the poor and his loss of treasure in heaven (19:16–22) is followed by a parable concerning a generous landowner and an Evil-Eyed reaction (20:15/16). Matthew 19:16—20:16 repeats an earlier structure of ch. 6 in which a saying on earthly and heavenly treasures (6:19–21) is followed by an Evil Eye saying (6:22–23) implicitly

added a generalizing conclusion concerning a reversal of priorities (v. 16) to fit the parable to its literary context. At the outset of the parable, Matthew added a conjunctive "for" (*gar*, 20:1) to indicate that the appended parable is logically connected to what precedes it (19:1–30). As a new conclusion to the parable, Matthew added v. 16,[199] which is introduced with a conjuctive "thus" (*houtôs*), suggesting that this saying summarizes the point of the parable. In actuality, however, v. 16 connects only to the terms "first" (vv. 8, 9, 16) and "last" (vv. 8, 12, 16) and one feature of the story; namely, that the last-hired are the first paid.[200] It is similar to the saying of Matt 19:30, which also speaks of a reversal of "first" and "last." The sequences of "last-first" or "first-last" are adapted to fit their specific contexts. The reversal of expectations is thus a theme that frames 20:1–15 in its Matthean setting.[201]

What of the meaning and point of the parable as originally told by Jesus and what of its Evil Eye accusation in particular? To answer these questions we turn to an examination of the parable's content, structure and conclusion.

The Parable in Detail

Jesus's parables generally reflect aspects of ancient Palestinian everyday life and outlook, while at the same time defying expectations and shocking into new states of awareness. Our parable fits this pattern. The behavior of the laborers is typical, including the resentment of some over any perceived preference given other workers. The behavior of the owner, on the other

---

condemning ungenerosity.

199. For Matt 20:16 as a Matthean addition see, e.g., Bultmann 1963:177; Dodd 1935:92, 94; Jeremias 1963:34–37; Hagner 1995:569; Davies and Allison 1988 3:67. Some scholars reduce the original parable to vv. 1–13 (e.g., Crossan [1973:112–13], followed by Patte [1987:280 n. 21] or to vv. 1–14a (Scott 1989:282).

200. This saying of Matt 20:16 occurs also in Luke (13:30; cf. also *Barn.* 6:13). Luke uses this Q saying as a conclusion to teaching of Jesus concerning the kingdom of God (Luke 13:18, 20, 29) but in a different context (Luke 13:22–30). Expressing a notable feature of God's extraordinary reign and unexpected action, this reversal saying appears frequently and in varying formulations; see Mark 10:31/Matt 19:30; Matt 23:12/ Luke 18:14; *Gos. Thom.* 4; *P. Oxy.* 654.3. For the reversal theme see also Mark 10:43–44/ Matt 20:26–27/Luke 22:26; Matt 5:3–12/Luke 6:20–23; Matt 21:31; 22:14; 25:31–46; Mark 9:35/Luke 9:48; Luke 14:11; Jas 1:9, 4:6 = 1 Pet 5:5c; *Barn.* 4:14.

201. Concluding v. 16 some witnesses (C D W 038, ff1,13 Textus Receptus, Latin, Syriac, Middle Egyptian, Coptic) add a further saying, "Many are called but few are chosen." This is lacking in other textual witnesses (ℵ B L Z 085 892 1424 sa bopt) and is likely a secondary addition taken from Matt 22:16; cf. Metzger 1994:41. Like Matt 22:14, it is "one of those common generalizing conclusions, in this case taken from Matt 22.14 and probably inserted before the end of the first century" (Jeremias 1963:34).

hand, is very untypical of human owners, but, as Israelites believe, quite characteristic of divine largess. "The story is quite plausible in all its details," Luise Schottroff observes, "only the employer's generosity is unusual. The dispute that this generosity occasions is the point to which the parable is meant to lead."[202]

Neither Jesus nor Matthew states explicitly to whom the parable is addressed. Matthew seems to suggest that it was addressed to followers of Jesus (19:23), disciples who appear unclear about the nature of the kingdom of heaven (19:10–15, 23–30).[203] Also present at the scene, however, were Pharisees challenging him on points of law (19:3–9) and a wealthy man reluctant to part with his wealth (19:16–22). Originally Jesus may have addressed it more broadly to the crowds (cf. 19:2, 16–22), since the conclusion (20:15) has wide applicability and not just significance for disciples or critics alone.

The parable (20:1–15) consists of two halves (vv. 1–7, 8–15) and four phases of action: (1) a hiring of laborers throughout the day (vv. 1–7), (2) their compensation at the day's close (vv. 8–10), (3) a complaint by the first-hired and longest working laborers criticising the owner (vv.11–12), and (4) the owner's response (vv. 13–15). Verse 8 is the hinge of the story and vv. 8–10 create the tension around which the ensuing confrontation turns.

Verses 1–7 introduce the story as a parable illustrating the nature of the kingdom of heaven (20:1). "The kingdom of heaven is like" has the sense of "the nature of life under God's reign is as follows." These opening seven verses relate a first series of events: the hiring of five groups of day laborers at different times of the day by a householder owning a vineyard and intent on harvesting his produce. The multiple hirings took place at "early" morning (sunrise), and at the third, sixth, ninth, and eleventh hours, the last being an hour before sunset, the end of the working day. Those hired first agreed to work for one denarius, the standard wage for a full day's work (twelve hours from sunrise to sunset) of an unskilled laborer (v. 9).[204] Those hired at the third, sixth, and ninth hours were promised as a wage "whatever

202. Schottroff 1984:132; cf. also Schottroff 2006:209–17, esp. 212–14 (although in this latter essay she seems to retract, or at least qualify, her earlier position [2006:211]); see also Herzog 1994:53–73. "The true message of the story concentrates on the generosity of the owner of the vineyard" (Hoppe 1984:16).

203. See also Matt 19:10, 13, 27, 28.

204. The denarius, a Roman coin made of silver (3.8 grams), was the basic unit of coinage throughout the Roman Empire and the most frequently mentioned coin in the New Testament. Douglas Oakman (1987:36) calculates that one denarius would buy three days worth of food for a peasant family of four. It has been estimated that a peasant family of four subsisted on 200 denarii per annum in ancient Italy; see Harl 1996:278–80.

is just" (*dikaion*, v. 4a); a specific amount is not mentioned. Lastly, some still unemployed toward the close of the day were hired at the eleventh hour, one hour before sunset (vv. 7–8).

The details fit the workaday agricultural situation of Palestine in Jesus's day.[205] The *oikodespotês* ("householder," RSV: "landowner," NRSV, 20:1, 11)[206] owned a vineyard and was intent on quickly gathering the grapes. His repeated hiring suggests that the timing of the harvest was an urgent matter. The hired workers (*ergatai*, vv. 1, 8) accord with the picture of Mediterranean peasants and day laborers. The latter were among society's poorest, apart from the totally destitute. With no land, little material means of support, and no regular income, they hired themselves out each day for whatever wages they could get, optimally one denarius for a full twelve hours of work frpm sunrise to sunset. Any work at all, however, for any length of time, was a stroke of good fortune, given the high rate of unemployment in Palestine at the time.[207] Pay at the end of the day also was the custom (see Lev 19:13; Deut 24:14–15). The verses that follow (vv. 8–15), on the other hand, tell of a very unconventional mode of payment, a surprising act of generosity on the part of the owner, and a response typical of workers feeling themselves shortchanged and openly shamed.

Verses 8–10 describe the payment of the laborers by the owner's field manager (*epitropos*, v. 8) at the end of the day and the action creating the tension of the story. By an unusual directive of the owner, the laborers are paid in the reverse order in which they were hired—"from the last to the first" (v. 8).[208] More surprisingly, the last-hired who had worked only one hour were paid the same amount (a full denarius, v. 9)[209] as that contracted by the first- hired for a full day's work (v. 2). As payment to persons working only one hour, this full denarius was more a gift than a wage. The owner was treating them less as workers being paid a contracted sum—no such sum is mentioned by the owner—and more like needy relatives to whom he was

---

205. See Schottroff 1984:129–35; Herzog 1994:53–73; Vearncombe 2010; Van Eck and Kloppenborg 2015 for further details.

206. Another harvest parable illustrating the kingdom of God and featuring an *oikodespotês* is Matt 21:33–46. Jesus's parable of the great banquet (Luke 14:16–24) describes an *oikodespotês* whose generosity and inclusive hospitality is like that of the owner here. In all three parables, the householder appears to be a metaphor for God.

207. Schottroff 1984:132–35; Herzog 1994:84–90.

208. No evidence exists in extant sources for such a procedure. For "first," see Matt 20:8, 10, 16; for "last," 20:8, 12, 14, 16.

209. Presumably together with all those hired since the third hour.

being generous.[210] Here it is an action that is crucial to the dynamic of the story.

The *reversed order of payment* and its occurrence in the sight of all the workers required that the first-hired wait for and witness the payment of the last-hired. With this *reversed order of payment*, the first- hired *saw with their own eyes* the denarius given to each of the last-hired (implied but not explicitly stated). These first-hired, upon seeing that the last-hired received a full denarius for only one hour's work, so the story implies, then *compared* themselves to the first-hired and concluded that "they would receive more" than the one denarius paid the last-hired—and thus more than the wage they initially had agreed upon (v. 10a). Their expectation was based on the assumption that the wage for all workers would be proportionate to the length and conditions of the work performed, as v. 12 makes clear. "If the wage being paid for one hour's work is one denarius, then we could possibly receive twelve denarii for our twelve hours of labor," they could have reckoned. However, they too received one denarius (v. 10b). This payment then leads to resentment and protest.

A confrontation erupts between the discontented first-hired and the owner (vv. 11–15). The payment of the same wage for different lengths and conditions of work moved the first-hired to grumble at the owner that he made the last-hired "equal to"[211] to themselves who had borne the heat and burden of the entire day (v. 12). Their explicit complaint is that the wage paid out made the last-hired and first-hired "equal" despite their unequal lengths and conditions of labor. An accompanying *implict* and unspoken complaint of the first-hired is that by comparison with the favored last-hired, they were made to look like chumps "stuck with the short end of the stick" in the eyes of all the workers (and perhaps other villagers as well—the word will hit the gossip grapevine). Based on the notion of limited good prevalent in their society, as in peasant societies generally,[212] they reckon that the gain and good fortune of the last-hired amounts to their loss and "comes out of their hide," so to speak.

---

210. In regard to types of exchange in antiquity, exchanges that occurred within the immediate family and kin groups were based on need, loyality and unlimited generosity ("generalized reciprocity"); exhanges among neighbors and friends, village buyers and sellers, were based on equal *quid pro quo* arrangements ("balanced reciprocity"); and exchanges with strangers and those beyond one's group involved maximizing one's own gain at whatever loss to the "other" ("negative reciprocity"); cf. Malina 1986:98–11.

211. The adjective *isous* means "equal to" or "the same as" and expresses some form of parity.

212. On the concept of limited good See Foster 1965; Pilch and Malina 1998: 122–27; Malina 2001:81–107; and Vol. 2, pp. 87, 92–94, 155, 156, 271.

The owner then responds (vv. 13–15). He replies to one of the grumblers by defending himself and the justness of his action, and by intimating that the malcontents were guilty on their part of having an Evil Eye. "Friend, I am doing you no wrong. Did you not agree with me for a denarius?" (v. 13; cf. v. 2). The first half of vv. 14–15 which follow is a chiastic formulation in which "what belongs to you" (*to son*, v. 14a) parallels and is contrasted to "what belongs to me" (*tois emois*, v. 15a) and frames "what I want to give" or "what I want to do" (*thelô . . . dounai*, v. 14b, *thelô poiesai*, v. 15a):

> A. You take <u>what belongs to you</u> and go;
>
> > B. <u>I want</u> *to give* to this last person as (I give) to you.
> >
> > B.' Do I not have the authority to *do what* <u>I want</u>
>
> A.' with <u>what belongs to me</u>?

A further parallel construction, an antithetical parallelism contrasting the owner and the grumbler(s), concludes the parable (v. 15b): "or is your Evil Eye envious (*ê ho ophthalmos sou ponêros estin*) because I am generous (*hoti egô agathos eimi*)?"[213]

This rhetorical and accusatory question brings the parable to a logical and dramatic close. It telescopes attention on two main character sets, (a) the owner and (b) a worker representing grumbling first-hired laborers; and it contrasts the goodness of the owner to grumblers's Evil Eye. By its position as the climax to the parable, this reference to the Evil Eye, a *malocchio* of the malcontents, is given special prominence. Together with its counterpart, the goodness of the owner, it forms a climax and summary of the parable's basic point.

In what precisely did the goodness of the owner and the Evil Eye of the grumbler(s) consist? He speaks of himself as *agathos* (lit., "good"). *Agathos* ("good") is the quality generally contrasted to *ponêros* ("evil").[214] The details of this parable point more specifically to the "goodness" of the owner as his being *generous*, especially to the last-hired and paying them far more than

---

213. The Greek formulation involves a complete parallelism of subjects–adjectives–verbs:

your eye	evil	is
I	good	am

As indicated below, the *sense* of this question is best rendered by the translation: "Is your Evil Eye envious because I am generous," with "evil" in this context implying *envious*, "eye"implying *Evil Eye*, and "good" implying *generous*.

214. See Aeschines, *Tim.* 69; Aristotle, *Eth.eud.* 1240b; Sir 14:5; Matt 5:45; 7:11, 17–18; 12:35; 22:10; 25:21, 23, 26; Luke 6:45; 11:13; *Barn.* 4:12.

their labor had earned.[215] The antithesis of an Evil Eye, moreover, often is generosity, as in Matt 6:22–23 and the Evil Eye texts cited there. The opposite of an Evil Eye, namely a "good eye" (*agathos ophthalmos*), as Sir 35:7, 9 (RSV 35:8, 10) illustrate, can imply a "generous eye;" i.e. a generous person who gives generously. The owner's generosity comprises not only his liberality with the last-hired[216] but also his giving work to those who could get no work (v. 7). It could also involve paying those hired since the third hour for a full day's work, although this is not stated. The owner, moreover, commits himself to a wage that is "just" (v. 4) (rather than miserly) and pays the standard (not minimal) wage for a full day's work. [This is] "the behaviour of a large-hearted man who is compassionate and full of sympathy for the poor."[217] "The householder is generous," giving "the twofold gift of work in the vineyard and of wages."[218] Generosity was ranked by Israel and the followers of Jesus among the highest of the virtues.[219]

This generosity, the owner's question implies, is opposed by the grumbler's Evil Eye. Matthew 20:15b reads, literally, "Is your eye (*ophthalmos*) evil (*ponêros*) because I am good (*agathos*)?" The formulation *ophthalmos*+ *ponêros* appears also in Matt 6:23,[220] Mark 7:22 and Sir 14:10; 31:13, and denotes "Evil Eye" in these passages. The contrast of *Evil Eye* and *good/generous person* also recalls Matt 6:22–23/Luke 11:34 and Sir 14:5, which are Evil Eye texts.[221] In Matt 6:22–23/Luke 11:34 and Sir 14:5, a generous eye or an Evil Eye are contrasting attributes of *one* person. Matthew 20:15 contrasts *two* persons, one who is generous and the other who has an envious Evil Eye. In these and several other Evil Eye texts, generosity is regularly the antithesis of an Evil Eye (Deut 15:7–11; 28:54–57; Prov 23:6–8; Sir 14:3–5, 8; 18:18; 37:11; Tob 4:7, 16). Generosity, moreover, also is antithetical to

215. For *agathos* with the sense of "generous" or "benevolent" see BDAG, *s.v.*, p. 4; Louw and Nida, *GEL* 1:§57.110; see Ps 134:3 LXX; Matt 25:21, 23; Luke 19:17; 23:50; 1 Pet 2:18.

216. The pay for only one hour's work would be insufficient for feeding a family for even just one day. "It is because of his pity for their poverty that the owner allows them to be paid a full day's wages." (Jeremias 1963:37).

217. Jeremias 1963:37; also Dodd 1935:122.

218. Patt 1987:275.

219. See Prov 11:24–26; 14:31; 19:17; 21:26; 28:27; Sir 4:4–6; Tob 4:7–11, 16; Matt 6:2–4, 22; 7:11/Luke 11:13; Acts 2:33; 10:4; Rom 10:12; 2 Cor 8:2; 9:5–15; Gal 5:22; Jas 1:5.

220. It is *implied* in the Lukan parallel, Luke 11:34 [*ponêros*, with *ophthalmos* implied].

221. For further contrasts of *ponêros* versus *agathos* in Matthew, see Matt 5:45; 6:22–23; 7:11; 7:17, 18; 12:34, 35; 20:15; 22:10 (good/evil persons); see also 22:18 (*ponêria* of the Pharisees; RSV: malice).

envy. Envy seeks to deprive; generosity seeks to bestow. Envy is destructive; generosity is constructive.

The sense of "good" (*agathos*) as "generous" in v. 15b is assumed in most translations and commentaries on this passage.[222] Among commentators, William Herzog represents a rare but important exception.[223] Concerning the translation and sense of *ophthalmos ponêros*, however, there is little agreement.[224]

Some Versions translate *ophthalmos ponêros* literally as "Evil Eye" (Vulgate [*oculus nequam*], KJV, NKJV, *La Sacra Bibblia* [*vedi tu di mal occhio*], *Nueva Biblia Espanola* [*ves tu con malos ojos*]). Luther was acquainted with the Evil Eye as an oblique glance and rendered *ophthalmos ponêros* as an ocular action: "*Siehest du darum scheel, dass ich so gütig bin?* ("*do you look askance* because I am so generous?"). The actual terms "eye" and "evil" are left unmentioned. Most Versions substitute an emotion such as envy for the combination of "eye" and "evil."[225] In some cases, the emotion chosen is patently wrong, as when *jealous* is chosen instead of *envious* (BJ, Phillips, TEV). As previously noted in Vol. 2, in antiquity envy and jealousy were associated but carefully distinguished, just as *Eifersucht* is related to but distinguished from *Neid* in German. The concepts involve different social

222. Luther, RSV, NRSV, NAB, NASV, TEV, JB, NJB, Zürcher Bibel, Goodspeed, Phillips, Nueva Biblia Espanola; compare NEB ("kind"). Senior 1998:223 is representative of most commentators.

223. He regards the householder as a greedy exploiter of an economically threatened labor force and by no means a stand-in for God. Herzog rather insists that "[f]ar from being generous, then, the householder is taking advantage of an unemployed labor force to meet his harvesting needs by offering theme work without a wage agreement" (Herzog 1994:86). Herzog's contention is convincingly critiqued by Waetjen 2011:97–101.

224. The *Greek-English Lexicon* of Louw and Nida vascillates on the meaning of *ophthalmos ponêros* in Matt 20:15. In section 57.108 (vol. 1:570) they list *ophthalmos ponêros* in the section on "Give" (57.71–124) within Domain 57 ("Possess, Transfer, Exchange"). They describe the phrase as an "idiom, literally 'evil eye'" meaning "to be stingy—'stingy, miserly.'" They render Matt 20:15, "are you stingy because I am good?" They also allow, however, that *ophthalmos ponêros* in Matt 20.15 possibly "is to be understood in the sense of 'jealous,' see 88.165 [*ophthalmos ponêros* as instance of "Envy, Jealousy," 88.160–166]; see also 23.149 [on *ponêros*])." In connection with the sub-domain "Envy, Jealousy" (88.160–166) under the main domain 88 ("Moral and Ethical Qualities") they list *ophthalmos ponêros* (88.165) as an instance of "jealousy and resentment," unfortunately failing to distinguish between jealousy and envy. They translate Matt 20:15, "or are you jealous because I am generous?" They also neglect to explain that *ophthlamos poneros* and *baskainô* (53.98; 88.159) are related as terminology for "Evil Eye."

225. For example, "are you envious" (NAB; cf. also JB, NIV, NJB, NRSV, *La Biblia* (La Casa de la Biblia) or "ist dein Auge neidisch" (Zürcher Bibel).

dynamics.[226] *Jealousy/Eifersucht* is the fear I have of your taking from me what is mine. *Envy/Neid* is the grief I feel at the sight of your good fortune and my wish that it be destroyed. Jealousy is defensive; envy is aggressive. *Envy* involves an array of features including a displeasure from viewing the assets and success of another, a resentful consciousness of inferiority to the person(s) envied, a sense of impotence to acquire what is desired, and a malevolent wish to harm the envied one and to see him/her deprived of his/her success or good fortune. The parable describes an act of envy, not jealousy. The first-hired were not fearful of losing something to the last-hired, as "jealous" would imply. Rather they were envious of the good fortune of the last-hired and wanted it destroyed because merely beholding it brought them to grief. Envy, moreover, and not jealousy, is the emotion most frequently associated with the Evil Eye. Translating *ophthalmos* and *ponêros* with only "envy," however, leaves the reader uninformed that Jesus expressly spoke of the Evil Eye.[227] The preferred rendition of Matt 20:15b in consonance with its context is: "Is your Evil Eye envious because I am generous."

Among the commentators, some recognize in Matt 20:15 a reference to the Evil Eye similar to 6:23.[228] Others take the expression as an idiom for envy, jealousy, stinginess or begrudging, with minimal consideration of the social dynamic involved and its bearing on the interpretation of the parable as a whole.[229] Still other scholars appear unaware of Evil Eye belief and do not find it here in the formulation of *ophthalmos* + *ponêros*.[230] Inasmuch, however, as this reference to the Evil Eye invokes a powerful concept of Jesus's and Matthew's culture and, in addition, occurs at the climactic point in the parable, a closer examination of its meaning and implications is called for.

Several questions need addressing. What relevance or connection does the concept of the Evil Eye have to the interaction and emotions portrayed

226. See also Elliott 2007a, 2007b, 2008, and Vol. 2, pp. 85–92.

227. RSV ("Or do you begrudge me my generosity?") gives a possible sense of *ophthalmos ponêros* but likewise leaves Evil Eye unmentioned.

228. For example, Jülicher 1910 2:465; Billerbeck 1924/1961 1:833–835; Schlatter 1963:590; Dietzfelbinger 1983:127; Jeremias 1963:138; Elliott 1988, 1992, 1994; Derrett 1995, 1997; Senior 1998:223; Malina 2001; Malina and Rohrbaugh 1992; Waetjen 2011.

229. For example, Jeremias 1963:138, 139; Haubeck 1980:104 n. 33 (preferring "begrudging," "Missgunst, Hartherzigkeit, Lieblosigkeit"); Gundry 1982; Schottroff 1984, 2006; Herzog 1994. For exceptions, see Breech 1983 and Schenke (1988:264–265), who, however, mistakenly sees here a reference to jealousy rather than envy as do Louw and Nida (*GEL* vol. 1, §88.165).

230. For example, Harrington 1983; Kingsbury 1986; Patte 1987. Crossan (1973: 112–13), Patte (1987:280 n. 21), and Scott (1989:287) unconvincingly eliminate v. 15 from the parable altogether.

in this story? What particular emotion associated with the Evil Eye fits the disposition of the grumblers and the dynamics of the interaction? If "Evil Eye" here implies the emotion of envy, as several translations and commentators propose, what do we know about the Evil Eye and envy that might support this equation? How might the unusual structure of the action of the story set the stage for an outbreak of envy? How is an envious Evil Eye prompted by a show of generosity? How does this attribution of an envious Evil Eye to the grumbler(s) and its contrast to the good/generous owner provide a fitting climax to the parable?

Taking up these questions, we can first establish that the conventional and frequent association of the Evil Eye and envy in all cultures of the ancient Circum-Mediterranean, including the biblical communities, makes it quite possible that *ophthalmos + ponêros* here implies the emotion of envy. The details of the story, as we shall see, make it likely. The situation portrayed here has all the basic ingredients of an occasion where envy typically is aroused. The story is specifically constructed to present a situation for envy to emerge.

To recall how the ancients regarded the phenomenon of envy—its features, circumstances, and dynamic—we can consider two ancient discussions of the topic which chronologically frame the early Christian period; namely, those of Aristotle (384–322 BCE) and the Christian church father Basil of Caesarea in Cappadocia (c. 330–379 CE).[231]

Aristotle, in his treatise on rhetoric, notes that envy (*phthonos*), like indignation, "is a disturbing pain aroused by the prosperity of others":

> We feel it towards our equals [in birth, relationship, age, disposition, distinction or wealth] not with the idea of getting something for ourselves, but because the other people have it . . . We feel envy also if we fall but a little short of having everything . . . Ambitious men are more envious than those who are not . . . and small-minded men are envious, for everything seems great to them . . . The deeds or possessions which arouse the love of reputation and honour and the desire for fame, and the various gifts of fortune, are almost all subject to envy; and particularly if we desire the thing ourselves, or think we are entitled to it, or if having it puts us a little above others, or not having it a little

231. For studies on envy from antiquity onward and its association with the Evil Eye see, *inter alia*, Stevens 1948; Odelstierna 1949; Milobenski 1964 [from the pre-Socratics to Plutarch]; Walcot 1978, esp. pp. 77–90 on "The Evil Eye [and envy]"; Dunbabin and Dickie 1983; Johnson 1983, esp. 334–46; Francis Bacon 1985 [1625]; Schoeck 1987; de la Mora 1987; Malina 2001:108–33; Elliott 1988, 1992, 1994, 2007a, 2007b, 2008, 2014, 2015; Nusser 2000. See further the extensive Excursus on Envy in Vol. 2, 83–113.

below them . . . We envy those who are near us in time, place, age or reputation . . . hence the saying, 'Potter against potter.' We also envy those whose possession or success in a thing is a reproach to us: these are our neighbors and equals . . . We also envy those who have what we ought to have, or have got what we did have once. Hence old men envy younger men, and those who have spent much envy those who have spent little on the same thing. And men who have not got a thing, or not got it yet, envy those who have got it quickly. (Aristotle, *Rhet.* 2.10, 1387b–1388a; cf. also 2.9)

Over six hundred years later, the Christian Church Father Basil the Great of Caesarea in Cappodocia calls attention to many of these same features of envy in his famous homily "Concerning Envy" (*Peri phthonou/De invidia*).[232] From the homily's outset he juxtaposes *phthonos* (envy) and its paronyms with *baskania* (Evil Eye) and its paronyms and uses the terms synonomously.

No feeling (*pathos*) more pernicious than envy (*phthonos*) is implanted in human souls (PG 31.372) . . . As rust wears away iron, so envy corrodes the soul it inhabits (373) . . . Envy (*phthonos*) is pain caused by our neighbor's prosperity. Hence an Evil-Eyed/ envious person (*ton baskanon*) is never without cause for grief and despondency. If his neighbor's land is fertile, if his house abounds with all the good of this life, if he, its master, enjoys continual gladness of heart—all these things aggravate the sickness and add to the pain of the Evil-Eyed/envious person (*tô baskanô*) . . . Is someone else rich and eager to lavish his wealth in alms to the poor and charitable constributions, and does he receive great praise from the beneficiaries of his charity? All these blessings are like so many blows and wounds piercing the envious person to the heart's core (373) . . . The sick man awaits only one alleviation of his distress—that he may see one of the persons whom he envies (*tôn phthonoumenôn*) fall into misfortune. This is the goal of his hatred—to behold the victim of his envy pass from happiness to misery, that he who is admired and emulated might become an object of pity (373) . . . What could be more fatal than this sickness (*nosou*)? It ruins our life, perverts our nature, arouses hatred of the goods bestowed on us by God, and places us in a hostile relation toward God (376).

232. Basil, *Peri phthonou/De invidia/ Concerning Envy* (Homily 11), PG 31.372–85; English translation by Wagner 1950:464–74 (modified by JHE).

Though not citing Matt 20:1–15, Basil, like Jesus (Matt 20:15), envisions an envious Evil Eye aroused by a display of generosity.

While citing biblical examples of envy (Cain of Abel, Joseph by his brothers, Saul of David) including envy of Jesus by those who handed him over to Pilate, his executioner (Mark 15:10/Matt 27:18), Basil asks in words also reminiscent of our parable:

> Why do you grieve, my friend, when you yourself have suffered no misfortune? Why are you hostile to someone who is enjoying prosperity, when he has in no way caused your own possessions to decrease? (376)

Again, in terms similar to the dynamic of our parable, he observes that the envious person "is more distressed by the resources of his benefactor than he is thankful for the benefits received" (376). Once again, like Aristotle and our parable, he notes that

> a person is exposed to envy (*zêlos*) from his neighbor . . . among acquaintances, neighbors and fellow workmen, or those who are otherwise brought into close contact, and among these again, those of the same age and kinsmen and brothers. In short, as the red blight is a common pest to corn, so envy is the plague of friendship. (380)

Broaching the traditional association of envy and the Evil Eye, he observes that

> persons who suffer from this malady of the Evil Eye/envy (*hoi nosountes tên baskanian*) are supposed to be even more dangerous than poisonous animals, since these [latter] inject their venom by piercing their victim; then, gradually, putrefaction spreads over the infected area. But some think that envious persons bring about damage merely by looking (lit. "by their eyes" [*di' ophthalmôn*]), so that the bodies of healthy persons in the full flower and vigor of their prime are made to pine away by their Evil-Eyed glance (*katabaskainomena*), suddenly losing all their plumpness, which dwindles and wastes away under the eyes of the envious (*tôn phthonerôn ophthalmôn*). (380)

At the conclusion of his homily (380), Basil declares that God is good (*agathos*) and devoid of envy (*aphthonos*), repeating a similar declaration at the homily's outset (372.1), with God's goodness contrasted to envy and the Evil Eye, as in Matt 20:15. Beside urging his hearers to "flee from this abominable wickeness (*kakon*), which is "a cause of losing the kingdom (of God)" (380), he calls for positive action (381.27–50; 384.1—385.36). This includes the practice of generosity. The man of wealth "will be generous (*aphthonos*, lit. "without envy") in giving of his possessions to the needy and he will offer physical assistance to the infirm and regard the surplus part of his wealth as belonging to any destitute person as much as it does to himself" (384).

In sum, these authors, Aristotle and Basil, writing half a millennium apart reflect the longstanding conventional wisdom that envy is displeasure caused by our neighbors' prosperity, those equal to us in role and rank. It is aroused by a comparison of our lot with that of those close to us and sees their sudden gain as a diminishment of our status and wellbeing. It is resentment at not having that to which we believe ourselves entitled. Our envy resents both the good fortune of beneficiaries and the generosity of benefactors although in actuality these in no way diminish our own condition. It gnaws away at our own health, perverts our nature, and endangers the harmony and well-being of the community.

Basil makes no specific reference in the homily to our Matthean parable, nor, for that matter, to Aristotle. But the continuity of ancient thought on the nature of envy and the Evil Eye is readily apparent and tallies at important points with the detail and dynamics of our Matthean parable.

This ancient understanding of envy including its inseparable connnection with the *Evil Eye*, is echoed centuries later in Francis Bacon's celebrated essay "Of Envy" (1625). These key features of envy similarly reappear in the definition of envy given by Immanuel Kant, which Helmut Schoeck in his comprehensive study of the the subject (1987), regards as "one of the most complete definitions" of envy ever offered:

> Envy (*livor*) is a tendency to perceive with displeasure the good of others, although it in no way detracts from one's own, and which, when it leads to action (in order to diminish that good) is called qualified envy, but otherwise only ill-will (*invidentia*); it is, however, only an indirect, malevolent frame of mind, namely a disinclination to see our own good overshadowed by the good of others, because we take its measure not from its intrinsic worth, but *by comparison with the good of others* and then go on to symbolize that evaluation.[233]

Sociologist Alvin Gouldner, commenting on the "Greek contest system" characteristic of the ancient Hellenic world,[234] has noted that envy, like competition and conflict, is endemic in this and similar societies where the cultural assumption prevailed that all goods were in limited supply and

---

233. Quoted in Schoeck 1987:201, emphasis added.
234. Gouldner 1969:41–77.

could never be increased but only redistributed.[235] Here in a competitive conflict situation, governed by the rules of honor and shame, life assumed the character of a "zero-sum game" in which one person's gain presupposed another's loss. Gouldner's observations concerning Mediterranean antiquity thus coincide with those of anthropologist George Foster concerning the image of limited good in peasant societies and its connection with envy. Like Foster, Gouldner directly associates envy with these prevailing cultural patterns. "Within the contest system," he observes,

> men can get ahead in either of two ways, and there are two ways in which they can lose out. They can rise relative to others by (1) raising themselves absolutely and leaving the other man behind or by (2) maintaining their own absolute position and cutting the other man down. Conversely, they can fall (1) by moving down while the man above has not changed his absolute position; or they can fall (2) *relative to him*, even when their own absolute position remains the same or improves if his happens to improve still more. Consequently in the contest system, men's satisfaction with their own position decreases to the extent that other's positions are improved. The good things that happen to others are therefore hurtful to them. This is precisely the nature of envy, which is the feeling of dissatisfaction that arises from the success of others. Envy is particularly apt to occur in a contest system because every success experienced by others-whether or not it means an absolute decline in one's own status—does mean a decline in status relative to theirs; it means a diminution of one's own relative superiority, and it is this relative advantage that is most prized.
>
> Envy is prone to occur in a social system where a man's own situation is appraised and experienced as satisfying or dissatisfying by comparing it with another's. In such a system one is more likely to find, as Aeschylus remarks, that a man 'winces again to the vision of a neighbor's bliss,' all the more so as competitive animus disposes him to deny that the superior reward is justified by superior merit. (Gouldner 1969:56)

Biblical authors ranked an envious Evil Eye among the worst of sins. "Remember that an Evil Eye is a wicked thing. What has been created more evil than an Evil Eye?" (Sir 31:13). "An Evil-Eyed person is envious of bread, and it is lacking from his table (Sir 14:10). Israel's history is replete with notorious examples of insidious envy: Cain envying Abel (Gen 4:1–16), Philistines envying Isaac (Gen 26:14), Rachel envying Leah (Gen 30:1), Joseph

---

235. Ibid.:53–58.

envied by his brothers (Gen 37:11), Moses envied by Dathan and Abiram (Ps 106:16), Peninah envied by Hannah (1 Sam 1:1–8), David envied by Saul (1 Sam 18:9).[236]

The *Testaments of the Twelve Patriarchs*, which, as we have seen, help to clarify the contrast of integral/generous eye and Evil Eye in Matt 6:22–23/ Luke 11:34, are relevant for determining the sense of *ophthalmos ponêros* in Matt 20:15 as well.[237] Behind the confessional and exhortatory speeches of the twelve sons of Jacob contained in these Testaments looms the saga of Joseph and his envious brothers recounted in Gen 37–50.

Joseph, eleventh son of Jacob and first-born of Rachel, Jacob's favorite wife, was the favored son of Jacob as the "son of his old age" (Gen 37:3). His brothers, driven by resentment and envy of his favored treatment by their father, sold Joseph him into slavery. But in Egypt where he was taken, Joseph, by the favor of God, was elevated by the pharaoh to command over all Egypt. In this capacity he met, forgave, and assisted his family in a time of dire famine. In Israel's history, Joseph is remembered as the quintessential example of fraternal envy overcome by God. He was innocent victim and successful survivor of the envious and hateful Evil Eye.

In the *Testaments of the Twelve Patriarchs* this theme of envy receives extensive elaboration.[238] The individual Testaments abound with over fifty references to envy and/or the Evil Eye.[239] The *Testament of Simeon*, subtitled *Peri Phthonou*, "Concerning Envy," recalls the Joseph story explicitly and illustrates the contrast of integrity of heart and envious Evil Eye. "In the time of my youth," Simeon confesses,

> I envied (*ezêlôsa*) Joseph, because my father loved him more than all the rest of us. I determined inwardly to destroy him because the Prince of error spirit of envy (*to pneuma tou zêlou*) blinded my mind so that I did not consider him as a brother. Nor did I spare Jacob my father . . . my right hand was half-withered for seven days. And I knew, my children, that this had happened to

236. *1 Clem.* 4:1–13 lists seven Old Testament cases.

237. On the *Testaments of the Twelve Patriarchs* see above in this volume, chap. 1, pp. 70, 79–86, and in this chap. 2, pp. 135–38.

238. See *T. Sim.* 1–2; *T. Dan* 1:6, 2:5; *T. Gad* 1–3; *T. Jos.* 1:3, 7; *T. Benj.* 3–6.

239. For envy see the noun *zêlos* (*T. Reub.* 3:5, 6:4; *T. Sim.* 2:7, 4:5, 9; *T. Jud.* 13:3; *T. Iss.* 4:5; *T. Dan* 1:6; *T. Gad* 5:3; *T. Ash.* 4:5) and its verb *zêloô* (*T. Reub.* 6:5; *T. Sim.* 2:6; *T. Levi* 6:3; *T. Iss.* 4:5; *T. Gad* 7:4; *T. Benj.* 4:4); also the noun *phthonos* (*T. Sim.* 2:13; 3:1, 2, 4, 6; 4:5, 7; 6:2; *T. Dan* 2:5; *T. Gad* 4:5; *T. Jos.* 1:3, 7; 10:3; *T. Benj.* 7:2, 5; 8:1); its adjective *phthoneros* (*T. Iss.* 3:3); and its verb *phthoneô* (*T. Sim.* 2:14; 3:3, 6; *T. Gad* 3:3, 7:2; *T. Benj.* 4:4). For Evil Eye see the noun *baskania* (*T. Iss.* 4:5); the adjective/substantive *baskanos* (*T. Iss.* 3:3, 4:5); and *ophthalmos(-oi) ponêros(-oi)* (*T. Iss.* 4:6; cf. *T. Dan* 2:5; *T. Benj.* 4:2 [*skoteinos ophthalmos*]).

me because of Joseph and I repented and wept. Then I prayed to
the Lord God that my hand might be restored and that I might
refrain from all pollution and envy (*phthonou*) and all folly, for
I knew that I had perpetrated an evil deed (*ponêron pragma*)
in the sight of the Lord and of Jacob, my father, on account of
Joseph my brother, because of my envying (*phthonêsas*) him. (*T.
Sim.* 2:6–7, 13–14)

After recounting how in his youth he had envied his brother Joseph,
suffered the punishment of a half-withered hand, and then had repented (*T.
Sim.* 2:6–14), Simeon urges his children and descendents (*T. Sim.* 3:1—4:8):

Listen to me, my children, and beware of the spirit of deceit
and envy (*phthonou*). For envy dominates the whole of man's
mind and does not permit him to eat or drink or do anything
good. Rather it keeps prodding him to destroy the one whom he
envies (*ton phthonoumenon*). Whenever the one who is envied
(*ho phthonoumenos*) flourishes, the envious one (*ho phthonôn*)
languishes. And I came to know that liberation from envy
(*phthonou*) occurs through fear of the Lord. If anyone flees to
the Lord for refuge, the evil spirit (*ponêron pneuma*) will quickly
depart from him, and his mind will be eased. From then on he
has compassion on the one whom he envied (*tou phthonoum-
enou*) and has sympathy with those who love him and thus his
envy (*phthonou*) ceases (3:1–6) . . . Guard yourselves, therefore,
my children, from all envy[240] and live with integrity of heart (*en
haplotêti kardias*), so that God might shower your heads with
grace, glory and blessing, just as you have seen in Joseph (4:5)
. . . And you, my children, each one of you love his brothers with
a good heart, and the spirit of envy (*phthonou*) will withdraw
from you (4:7). For this [spirit of envy] makes the soul savage
and corrupts the body; it foments anger and war in the mind,
excites the shedding of blood, drives the mind to distraction,
arouses tumult in the soul, and trembling in the body (4:8).

Simeon enumerates the pernicious qualities of envy, and, by implication, of the Evil Eye. He contrasts envy to integrity of heart and eye, and
stresses how envy can be overcome by fear of the Lord and brotherly love.

Later echoes of the association of Joseph and the envious Evil Eye are
found in the continued prominence attributed to Joseph as successful survivor of the Evil Eye in post-biblical Jewish tradition and lore.[241] The rabbis

240. Taking *zêlou kai phthonou* as an hendiadys.

241. Billerbeck 1926 1:834; Shrire 1982:114; Ulmer 1991:351–52. On Joseph as
the object of his brothers' envy in Christian memory see Acts 7:9–15. On the rabbinic

firmly believed that Joseph was protected against the Evil Eye and that this protection extended to all his descendents. This belief was based not only on the Genesis account of Joseph's successful survival of the envy of his brothers in general, but on a variant reading of Gen 49:22 in particular. This verse, recounting Jabob's final blessing of Joseph, reads: "Joseph is a fruitful bough, a fruitful bough by a spring . . ." The Hebrew word translated "spring" (*'ayin*), however, can also be rendered "eye" as was the case in a midrash on this text. A further variant of this midrash is recorded in the Talmud in an anecdote about Rabbi Yohanan, who invoked his descendency from Joseph as protection against the Evil Eye:

> Rabbi Yohanan used to go and sit at the gate of the ritual bath. "When the daughters of Israel ascend from the bath let them meet me first, that they may bear sons as beautiful and as learned as I." . . . The rabbis said to him: "Do you not fear an Evil Eye when you expose yourself to be seen?" He said to them: "I am of the seed of Joseph, against whom an Evil Eye is powerless." It is written: Joseph is a fruitful bough, even a fruitful bough by a well (*ayin*) . . . Rabbi Abahu said: "Do not read 'by a well' but 'above the power of the Eye.'" Rabbi Yose ben Rabbi Hanina said it from the following: "Multiply abundantly like fish in the midst of the earth'" (Gen 48:16). Just as fish in the sea are covered by water and the Eye has no power over them, so also the seed of Joseph—the (Evil) Eye has no power over them. (*b. B.M.* 84a; cf. *b. Ber.* 20a)

Another midrash recounts that for protection against the Evil Eye when entering a strange town, the stranger joins his hands, puts each thumb in the palm of the other hand, and recites the words: "I, so-and-so, am of the seed of Joseph over which the Evil Eye has no power, as it says" [citation of Gen 49:22 follows] (*b. Ber.* 55b). Yet another midrash on Genesis (*Gen. Rab.* 78:10 on Gen 33:7) declares that Joseph also protected others, notably Rachel, from the Evil Eye of Esau. The *Testaments of the Twelve Patriarchs*, with their focus on envy and the Evil Eye thus stand in a long line of Israelite Evil Eye lore extending down through Late Antiquity.[242]

With these contours of envy and the Evil Eye in mind, we can now return to our parable and piece together the diverse aspects of the picture: the reference to the Evil Eye in the parable's climax, the association of the

---

tradition see Vol. 4, chap. 1.

242. For further discussion of envy in Greek, Roman, Old Testament, and New Testament sources see Hagedorn and Neyrey 1998; Elliott 1992, 1994, 2007a, 2007b, 2008, and below regarding Mark 7:22, pp. 198–212.

Evil Eye with envy, ancient conceptions of envy and the Evil Eye, and the conditions and dynamics of the envying process.

In the light of foreging observations it becomes clear that our parable embodies typical features and stages of *an envy process* as conventionally conceived. These can be summarized as follows. A process of envy includes (1) an occurrence involving neighbors in close proximity (in our case an owner and hired workers in a village); (2) a triangular relationship between three parties (in our case an owner, first-hired workers and last-hired workers);[243] (3) an interaction among the parties that is witnessed by the persons involved and that allows a comparison of status or treatment to be made between persons considered of equal status (in our case a comparison among day laborers on the same social level); (4) a comparison that is actually made by one of the parties; and (5) as a result of this comparison, the emergence in the comparing party of a sense of unfairness or lack of balance in this interaction and a feeling of inferiority and indignation that this party has somehow been short-changed. This arouses (6) a feeling of envy directed at the person(s) perceived as favorably treated to the envious party's detriment (based on a notion of limited good),[244] coupled with the malevolent wish that the privileged parties be "dispriviledged" and their good fortune be destroyed and their status reduced.[245] This envious, malevolent emotion lingers on and is irremediable because it is a feeling that either is not culturally permissible to acknowledge (so that the occasioning event remains unresolved), or that is expressed obliquely in terms of anger against the putative "injustice" of the benefactor deemed responsible for the "unfairness" in the first place. This lingering quality of Evil-Eyed envy negatively affects both the envious individuals and the social relations of

243. This triangular relationship is typical of envy situations. Jealousy, by contrast, involves only two parties: one person or group anxious about holding on to what is owned and a second party feared to be intent on dispossessing party one of something it possesses.

244. We recall that the premise of the notion of limited good is that it is best when things stay on an even keel, with minimal changes to social arrangments. If gifts are made, they must be shared by all in order to avoid arousing envy. If sharing does not occur, those not receiving a benefaction will become resentful and envious of those who do, because they assume that the gain of their neighbors occurs at their own loss.

245. This is illustrated in Greek, Roman, and Israelite sources that tell of the competition of rivals for perceived limited resources and the action of an envious and begrudging Evil Eye (Neyrey and Rohrbaugh 2001; Elliott 2007a, 2007b, 2008). On envy associated with, and spurred on by, a notion of limited good see Foster 1965; 1972; 108–33; Malina 1979, 2001:81–107, 108–33; Pilch and Malina 1998:59–63, 122–27; Hagedorn and Neyrey 1998:20–22; Neyrey and Rohrbaugh 2001; on Evil Eye, envy, and limited good see Elliott 1988, 1990, 1991, 1992, 1994, 2005a, 2005b, 2007a, 2011, 2014, 2015.

the community to which they belong. In Evil Eye cultures, manifestations, or suspected occurrences, of envy are judged as evidence of the envier's possessing and exercising an Evil Eye. Accordingly, (7) envy situations can conclude with Evil Eye accusations meant to publicly stigmatize and denounce the suspected envious party, with the aim of ridding the community of smouldering resentment, hostility and discord.

The parable embodies most of these elements and in both its content and structure constitutes a carefully crafted story about generosity opposed by Evil- Eyed envy, with implied praise of the former and implied denunciation of the latter. The structure of the parable masterfully creates the occasion for envy to emerge, and the final words of the parable expose the Evil-Eyed envy obsessing the grumblers. This unconventional sequence of payment procedure of the last workers paid first, together with the equality of payment, creates precisely that situation where a feeling of envy might emerge and rear its ugly head. The story, in other words, deliberately constructs an occasion for an invidious comparison.[246] Beginning with the payment of the laborers (v. 8), a *triangular relationship* typical of envy situations, is set up between the householder, the first-hired, and the last-hired.[247] With this reversed payment sequence, the first-hired are required to wait for their pay until the last-hired were compensated. Because of this they saw the one denarius that the first-hired received. This set the stage for a comparison to be made which would not have taken place had the first been paid first and then left before witnessing the payment of the last-hired. The reversed order of payment is thus absolutely crucial to the dynamic and tension of the story. "Now when the first came, [on the basis of what they had just witnessed], they thought they would receive more; but each of them also received a denarius" (v. 10).[248] With this reckoning and ensuing grumbling (v. 11–12) *an invidious comparison* is given shape and momentum. Seeing

246. Against Jeremias (1963:35), who sees the stipulated sequence as an "unimportant detail" with "no great significance." Also against Crossan (1973:113) and Scott (1989:287–89), who eliminate vv. 14–15 altogether, and against Scott's eliminating the words "beginning with the first until the last" (v. 8c) from the parable's so-called "originating structure." In actuality, v. 8b (echoed in v. 14b) creates the tension of the story so that vv. 8b and 14b are essential to the unfolding of this case of envy.

247. Jealousy, by contrast, involves only two parties: one person or group anxious about holding on to what is owned and a second party feared by party one to be intent on dispossessing party one of what it possesses.

248. Kyle Snodgrass (2008:377) finds here the interpretive key to the parable: "those hired first thought they would receive more. The parable breaks any chain of logic connecting reward, work, and human perceptions of what is right. God's judging is not regulated by human perceptions of justice, and lurking behind that statement is a whole theology of mercy."

others leads to comparison, comparison leads to envy, and envy is projected by an Evil Eye.

The first-hired are moved to envy at the sight of the payment of the last-hired equaling their own pay, but on their part receiving only what was contracted. They "feel pain," as Aristotle describes envy (*Rhet.* 2.9, 1386b), "at the good fortune of others" and wish that this good fortune be removed.[249] In regard to the envy process and the perception of limited good, they could have reckoned as follows: In *absolute* terms we have received what the last have received, a *denarius*, the wage upon which we had originally agreed (v. 2). But in *relative* and comparative terms, we have been shortchanged, disfavored, shamed. For the last-hired worked only one hour for their *denarius*, whereas we have labored long and hard the entire day for the same wage. In comparsion to payment of the last hired, we then should have received more on the basis of "more pay for more work." By making these last-hired "equal" to us in pay, you, the owner, have demeaned, short-changed, and disfavored us. Given the limit to the overall payment being made, their gain from your generosity entails our loss.

In this connection, we recall Gouldner's comment that "in a contest system [and perceived zero-sum game], even when persons' *absolute* position remains constant [in the parable, reception of a denarius for work performed], they will perceive their *relative* position to have been diminished to the extent that the position of others has improved" [in the parable, laborers working less but being paid the same denarius].[250] Their comparing themselves and their pay with the last-hired, and their reckoning with a limit to the payment available for distribution (= the limited good), leads them to conclude that the gain of the last-hired has come at their expense. The last-hired have been favored whereas, by comparison, we have been disfavored. Our grueling labor has been devalued in comparison with their brief stint at work, and with this payment we have lost standing in the public eye. Their envy directed at the last-hired demands that these last-hired lose their good fortune or at minimum have it proportionately reduced.

The consequences of this feeling and reasoning are grave. In focusing only on their own supposed "loss" in dignity and status due to the elevation of the last-hired through their favored treatment (maximum pay for minimum work), the malcontents blinded themselves to the actual goodness of the owner and his relief of the desperate plight of all those hired, themselves included. Only envy toward the last-hired filled their eyes and

249. The activated emotion is envy, not jealousy. The grumblers do not fear losing what they have, but are grieved by the good fortune of the last-hired and wish it removed.

250. Gouldner 1969:56.

heart, an envy masked by a complaint against the owner. Rather than admitting to envy—envious perons never admit this most grievous vice—the first-hired complain to the owner about what *he* has done: he has made the one hour workers "equal to" the twelve hour workers despite the disparity in the length and condition of the work performed (v. 12). The malcontents mask their actual feeling—envy directed at the last-hired—with a complaint to the owner about the unfairness of equal pay for unequal work. Their complaint is directed at the owner for his having aroused their displeasure with his generosity to the last-hired, but their resentment and envy is aimed at the last-hired who were so favored by the owner.

A similar modern scenario involving Evil-Eyed envy has been described by anthropologist Joel Tietelbaum in his analysis of Tunisian Evil Eye behavior: "As often noted, Tunisian folk explanations [of the Evil Eye] maintain that the harmful effect of the eye results from feelings of jealousy, envy, greed, and frustration on the part of those who find themselves obliged to admire the good fortune or well-being of another."[251]

In Jesus's parable, the owner's response exposes the real problem. His reply to one of the grumblers (vv. 13–15) is fourfold. First, he assures the malcontent, "I do you no injustice" (v. 13b, *ouk adikô se*; the verb is related to the "just" [*dikaion*] wage promised earlier, v. 5). Second, he reminds the grumbler that they both agreed on a *denarius* for the labor (v. 13b; cf. v. 2)[252] and that is what the grumbler received, so "take what is yours (*to son*)" (namely the contracted denarius) and leave" (v. 14a). Third, the owner contrasts "what is yours" (*to son*, v. 14a) to "what is mine" (*tois emois*, v.15a). This contrast is clear in the chiastic arrangement of vv. 14–15a. Having told the grumbler "take what is yours and leave," he asserts that he himself has the authority (*exestin moi*) to do what he wants (*thelô*) with what is his (*en tois emois*) (v. 15a). What he wants (*thelô*) is to give to the last-hired what he gave to the first-hired (v. 14c). The malcontent received what belonged to him—the contracted denarius. The owner exercized what belonged to him—the freedom to be generous. His generosity to the last-hired was no skin off the nose of the first-hired, as the first-hired had erroneously assumed. No zero-sum game was in play here; "no Peter, so to speak, was robbed to pay Paul." Lastly, with a third (cf. v. 13b, 15a) and final rhetorical question the vineyard owner exposes that which he detects is gnawing at the malcontents. If the problem is not a case of injustice, then it must be an instance of Evil-Eyed envy: "is your Eye Evil envious because I am good?"

---

251. Teitelbaum 1976:64–65.

252. Waetjen 2011:100–101 argues for the better attested reading, "Did I not agree with you (*synephonêas soi*)" as "the better text for verse 13."

(v. 15b).[253] The actual contrasting words "Evil Eye" and "good" in this context imply an envy chanelled through an Evil Eye opposed to the moral goodness of a householder manifested in an act of generosity. With his final question, the owner implies that behind the complaint of the first-hired lies the green-eyed monster of envy that is so grieved by the generous goodness of the owner and the good fortune of the last-hired (v. 15b). The church father John Chrysostom long ago perceptively captured the point of the story and its stress on envy and the Evil Eye. The complaining workers, he observed, "were indignant, and very displeased at the good of others, which was proof of [their] envy and Evil-Eyed malice (*phthonou kai baskanias*)." The householder, "in justifying himself with respect to them, and in making his defense to him that had said these things, convicts him [the complaining malcontent] of evil (*ponêrias*) and Evil-Eyed malice (*baskanias*) when he says 'Is your eye evil, because I am good?'"[254]

Here in Matt 20:15, as in numerous other biblical cases, an Evil Eye is associated with the familiar disposition of envy.[255] In the parable, this envy and resentment of the good fortune of other laborers is coupled with a resentment as well of the generosity of the author of that good fortune. The envy is directed at the good fortune of the last-hired, but it is concealed by the malcontents's accusation of the owner. In reply, the owner exposes the actual cause and object of their displeasure—their Evil-Eyed envy of the generous wage received by the last-hired The noxious effect of this Evil-Eyed envy is not only poisoned relations among the workers and between owner and laborers, but also a ruined reputation, and possibly ruined health, of the enviers, as well as expected damage to the harvest—typical calamitous results of an Evil Eye at work.[256]

Verse 15 thus forms a dramatic and fitting conclusion to the parable. It concentrates attention on its two chief contrasted characters, the owner and

253. RSV includes this translation in a footnote as an alternative to "do you begrudge me my generosity?"

254. John Chrysostom, *Hom. Matt.* 64.3 [on Matt 20:1–16] (PG 58.612–13). Chrysostom adds that in heaven, by contrast, there is no such complaining and self-justification. "For that place is entirely free of envy (*phthonou*) and Evil-Eyed malice (*baskanias*)."

255. See 1 Sam 2:29, 32; 18:9; Wis 4:12; Sir 14:3, 5–7, 8, 9; 31:13; 37:11; cf. Gen 37:11; also *T. Iss.* 3:2–3. Some commentators appear unaware of the association of the Evil Eye and envy. Nolland (2005:811–12), for example, denies that *ophthalmos ponêros* refers to the Evil Eye and sees no connection between the Evil Eye and envy. Yet he regards the emotion of the grumblers as "resentment" manifested in their eyes, a condition virtually indentical with Evil-Eyed envy.

256. See Prov 28:22; Sir 14:5, 6; 18:18; 31:13; Matt 6:23; *T. Sim.* 4:8. The anti-Evil Eye scarecrow set up in the cucumber field (Ep Jer 69/70) was used for crop protection.

a worker representing grumbling first-hired laborers. It affirms the generous goodness of the former and the Evil Eyed envy of the latter, thereby expressing the twofold point of the parable. The traditional title of the parable, "The *Workers* in the Vineyard," captures only the latter in the vaguest of terms. Jeremias's alternative label, "the parable of the good employer" (Jeremias 1963:136) captures only the former. Both features, however, are equally important as opposite sides of the same coin. The parable is double-edged, highlighting both generosity and the envy such generosity can arouse. . To an owner, who is generous beyond anticipation and against expectation, it contrasts workers, who resist this generosity with an envious Evil Eye aimed at their co-workers, and who, according to Evil Eye belief, bring down disaster upon themselves and their community.

The rhetorical question contains an implied *Evil Eye accusation* whose effect is to denounce and publicly shame the envious malcontents. Such accusations are resorted to in Evil Eye cultures where there is an absence of formal or legal mechanisms for adjudicating disagreements and conflicts among groups living in close proximity. The intent of the accusation is to publicly label, tarnish, disgrace and discredit the accused by shaming them as envious Eye Evil possessors and thus as individuals who threaten the social welfare and well-being of the entire community. In Galatia, as we shall see, Paul's accusers as well as Paul himself engaged in a process of Evil Eye accusation and counter-accusation. In the environment of Jesus, Paul and Matthew, an Evil Eye accusation, like witchcraft accusations in general, would have been heard as a powerful condemnation of persons disrespecting sacred values like generosity and engaging in disruptive social behavior.[257] The accusation denounces the first-hired as malicious enviers while upholding the norm of generosity according to which the owner acted. The former behaved shamefully, while the vineyard owner behaved honorably.[258]

The parable told by Jesus to the crowds makes a moral point about human behavior: people are to be generous, especially to the needy, and when faced with exhibitions of generosity by others, they should never enviously

257. See Elliott 1988, 1990; Malina and Neyrey 1988a; Neyrey 1986, 1988. On the shape and substance of witchcraft accusations see Douglas 1963, 1970a, 1987. On the comparison of witchcraft and Evil Eye accusations see Garrison and Arensberg 1976:321, chart 15.1

258. Neyrey (1998:223–24), taking "Evil Eye" to imply envy at 6:23, aptly notes that "Evil Eye aggression can be seen as another form of honor challenge" in the honor and shame culture of the time. "Jesus warns that such envy, i.e., the pursuit of honor that harms another, is simply wrong, or worse, shameful" (Neyrey 1998:223–24). This accurate observation about the connection of an Evil Eye accusation with the values of honor and shame actually is more relevant here in 20:15, where envy is in fact the disposition under censure.

Evil-Eye the beneficiaries, but honor the liberality of the benefactor.[259] The high value assigned by Israel to generosity has already been recalled in connection with our examination of Matt 6:22–23. The generosity of God, especially toward the destitute, is a repeated theme in Israelite tradition.[260] Jesus, too, according to Matthew, proclaimed and practiced the generosity and indiscriminate liberality of God[261] and urged his audiences to do likewise.[262] Generosity, Jesus asserts, is precisely the mode of benevolence that prevails or should prevail in a society animated by God's generous compassionate rule. As also noted in connection with Matt 6:22–23, generosity frequently was contrasted, as here, to an Evil Eye (Deut 15:7–11; 28:54–57; Sir 14:8; Tob 4:8–10, 16–17; *T. Sim.* 2:6–7; 3:1–6). In Matt 20:15, however, "Evil Eye" connotes envy, while in 6:23 it connotes miserliness.[263] Thus Matt 20:15 is in accord with other biblical comments about an envious Evil Eye such as "an Evil-Eyed person is envious of bread" (Sir 14:10); the envious Evil Eye that is denounced in 1 Sam 2:29, 32; 18:9; Sir 37:10–11; and the envious Evil Eye referred to in the *Testaments of the Twelve Patriarchs*. This envy associated traditionally with an Evil Eye fits exactly the social dynamic sketched by the parable. Grumbling first-hired workers resent the good fortune enjoyed by the last-hired and enviously wish it voided. The Evil Eye accusation by the owner exposes their real feeling—disgraceful envy, not displeasure about

259. Interpretations of the parable, which find here critique by Jesus of theological beliefs miss its actual point, as Schottroff (1984:137–38) points out. Notions that the parable attacks an Israelite concept of recompense (so Paul Billerbeck (1928 4/1:484–500) on "work righteousness," i.e. attaining the kingdom of God through human effort or legalistic Pharisees and legalism (Via 1967:154), or a faulty Israelite conception of God, are far from the parable's moral point. On opposing opinions concerning the parable's point see also Davies and Allison 1988 3:61.

260. See, e.g., Pss 12:5; 140:12; Isa 41:17; Luke 1:52, 72, 78; Rom 5:20; 6:23; 8:32; 10:12; Jas 1:5, 17; 2:5; 5:11.

261. Matt 6:25–33; 10:8; 11:28–30; 14:14–21; 15:32; 18:23–35; 20:34; 21:22; 22:1–10; 25:31–46.

262. Matt 5:42, 43–47; 7:7–11; 10:8; 19:21; 25:31–46; for generosity as a quality blessed by God see Exod 35:5; Deut 15:7–11; Ps 37:21; Prov 14:31; 19:6, 17; 21:26, 28:27; Sir 4:4–6; Luke 3:11; Acts 2:44–46; 10:4; Rom 15:26; 2 Cor 8:2, 20; 9:5–15; 1 Tim 6:18.

263. Matt 20:15 is both similar to and different from 6:23. Both verses speak of the *ophthalmos ponêros*, the Evil Eye, and in both verses the Evil Eye is contrasted to the quality of generosity. Matthew sets both 6:22–23 and 20:1–15 into sections dealing with wealth and the handling of possessions, and for both the kingdom of heaven is an issue. In terms of our Evil Eye topic, they differ in two respects. In Matt 6:22–23, an integral or an Evil Eye are alternate characteristics of the same person; in Matt 20:15 "good" and "Evil Eye" are attributes of opposing persons. Secondly, whereas in Matt 6 Evil Eye has the sense of stingy/miserly eye, the content of the parable indicates that *ophthalmos ponêros* in 20:15 has the sense of an envious Evil Eye.

equality—and brings the parable to a dramatic close. The Evil Eye charge concludes the parable just as the negative comment on an Evil Eye concludes the saying of Matt 6:22–23.

Joachim Jeremias held that "[t]he parable is clearly addressed to those who resembled the murmurers, those who criticized and opposed the good news, the Pharisees, for example. Jesus was minded to show them how unjustified, hateful, loveless, and unmerciful was their criticism."[264] Jesus justifies his association with outcastes and the despised and shows "[t]his is what God is like, so good, so full of compassion for the poor, how dare you revile him?"[265] Jeremias's acute analysis captured one aspect of the parable's point but missed a second. His interpretation, and all the subsequent readings it has influenced, focuses one-sidedly on the notion of the generosity of God, shortchanging the equal importance of the Evil Eye accusation. It also finds in the parable connections to Jesus's ministry and opponents (Pharisees) not mentioned in the story itself. The parable itself is rather a commentary on how persons are to conduct themselves under the rule of God. They are to be generous, especially to the needy, and never to envy with an Evil Eye the good fortune of beneficiaries of generosity. The parable is thus similar in its dynamic to the parable of the generous father, the prodigal son, and the envious elder brother (Luke 15:25–32). To his father's generosity toward the younger brother, the elder brother responds with resentment and envy of his brother, although this envy is not explicitly named.

The Parable in its Matthean Context

Matthew, as already noted, is the only evangelist to include this parable and he has modified it to fit the emphases of his narrative. The conjunctive "for" (*gar*) added to the parable's opening words (20:1a) asserts a logical connection of the parable to what precedes it (19:16–30). The addition of the saying of v. 16 (introduced by an added "thus" [*houtôs*]) provides a new Matthean generalizing conclusion to the parable. In actuality, however, this statement, "thus the last shall be first and the first, last," does not summarize the point of Jesus's parable (as Jeremias 1963:37 also noted), but connects to only the substantives "first" (vv. 8, 9, 16) and "last" (vv. 8, 12, 16) and the feature of the story stating that the last-hired are the first paid.[266] The

---

264. Jeremias 1972:38.

265. Ibid.

266. This saying (Matt 20:16) occurs also in Luke (13:30; cf. also *Barn.* 6:13) and appears to be a Q saying that circulated independently. Luke also uses this Q saying as a conclusion to teaching of Jesus concerning the kingdom of God (13:18, 20, 29) but in a

reversal saying is similar to that of Matt 19:30 ("first/last, last/first") which concludes 19:23–29, instruction on the nature of discipleship and God's reign (19:23, 24). The sequences of these two sayings ("last/first" or "first/last") are adapted by Matthew to fit their specific contexts. Matthew 19:30 appears to summarize the contrast between the rich young man (19:16–22) and the disciples who have abandoned everything (19:23–29).[267] Matthew 20:16 repeats the reversed sequence of 20:8–9.

The parable is now framed in Matthew by two sayings that emphasize a reversal of first and last and that connect the parable to its preceding and following contexts.[268] Matthew interpolates the parable (20:1–15), to which he has added v. 16, into the structure of his Markan source, between Mark 10:31 and Mark 10:32–34. The surrounding material in Matthew involves debate with the Pharisees concering divorce (19:3–9), engagement with a rich young man over generosity as the way to eternal life (20:16–22), and instruction of the disciples (19:10–12, 13–15, 23–30; 20:17–19, 20–30) with repeated reference to the kingdom of heaven, as in 20:1.

Explaining the nature of the kingdom of heaven (20:1a), the parable connects with preceding and following instruction on this eschatological theme.[269] The adjective "good" (20:15), which modifies an implied "God" in 19:17 ("There is One who is good"), strengthens the identification of the good owner of the parable with God who is good.[270] The parable presents a pendent to the encounter of Jesus with the rich young man seeking to enter eternal life (19:16–22). Treasure in heaven, Jesus tells him, results from generosity to the poor, in line with the exhortation of the Evil Eye texts of Deut 15:7–11 and Tob 4:5–21.[271] The rich young man asks about doing "good"

---

different context (Luke 13:22–30). Expressing a notable feature of God's extraordinary reign and unexpected action, this reversal saying appears frequently and in varying formulations; see Matt 19:30/Mark 10:31; cf. *P. Oxy.* 654. 3. For the reversal theme see also Mark 9:35; 10:43–44/Matt 20:26–27/Luke 22:26; Matt 5:3–12/Luke 6:20–23; 21:31; 22:14; 23:12/Luke 18:14; 25:31–46; Mark 9:35/Luke 9:48; Luke 14:11; *Barn.* 4:14; *Gos. Thom.* 4.2; *P. Oxy.* 654.3.

267. Schlatter 1963:586, 592.

268. Matt 19:1–30 and 20:17–34, which precede and follow 20:1–16, reproduce the content and sequence of Mark 10:1–52.

269. See "kingdom of heaven" (19:12, 14, 23), "kingdom of God" (19:24), "your kingdom" (20:21), "eternal life" (19:16, 29), "treasure in heaven" (19:21), and "new world/rebirth" (19:27).

270. *Oikodespotês* ("householder/land owner," 20:1; also *kyrios*, "owner," v. 8) as a metaphor for God occurs in another harvest parable illustrating the kingdom of God, namely Matt 21:33–46 (v. 33). In Jesus's parable of the great banquet (Luke 14:16–24, v. 21), the *oikodespotês*, whose generosity and inclusive hospitality resembles that of the owner here, is also a likely stand-in for God.

271. With "you will have treasure in heaven" (Matt 19:21) compare Matt 6:20,

(*agathos*, 19:16, 17a); Jesus replies that God is "good" (*agathos*, 19:17b); and the vineyard owner, now a stand-in for God, claims to be "good" (*agathos*, 20:15). To the refusal of the rich young man to be generous and to follow Jesus (19:22) Matthew contrasts the generosity of the good landowner illustrating the generosity of God (20:15) and constituting a model for faithful followers of Jesus and inhabitants of the kingdom. The concerns of the disciples regarding wealth (19:16–30) and status (19:13–15, 23–30; 20:20–28) may suggest that the issue of envy lurks in the background throughout this section of the narrative, but this is not stated explicitly by Matthew.

These contextual links are not accentuated by Matthew. His overriding concern, as 19:30 and 20:16 (and 20:26–28) show, is with the reversal of first and last persons in the kingdom of heaven. In Matthew's design, the parable now illustrates theologically how in the new age (19:27) the inheriting of eternal life (19:16, 30; cf. 19:23, 24) and entering the kingdom of heaven (19:12, 14, 23; cf. 20:1) will reverse conventional expectation. The last and lowest on the social ladder—propertyless disciples (19:27–29; 20:20–28) and infants (19:13–15)—will enter first, while the first on the social ladder—the wealthy (19:16–22, 23–24)—will enter last. Laborers finding only one hour of work a day will be compensated equally to those paid a full day's wage.[272]

In terms of the larger context of Matthew's gospel, this kingdom-of-heaven parable with its contrast of good and evil (20:15) resembles other vineyard and harvest parables that likewise contrast good and evil, with a focus on eschatological judgment (e.g. Matt 21:28–32; 21:33–46; see also

---

"treasures in heaven"), a saying joined to the other Evil Eye passage of Matt 6:22–23.

272. Other interpretations viewing the "first" as Israelites or those who were with Jesus from the beginning, and the "last" as Gentiles or recent converts to the Matthean community are less convincing.

Daniel Patte (1987:261–80) takes a different tack. He sees "hardness of heart" (19:8) as "the main theme of 19:1—20:16" (1987:263). This is illustrated by the Pharisees (19:8), questioning disciples (19:10), their rejection of children (19:13), and is further addressed in 19:16–22 and 19:23–30). 20:1–16, is "the key for understanding 19:1–19" (1987:263). The "bad eye" of the parable (20:15), Patte claims, is equivalent to a "hard heart;" both prevent people from doing God's will (1987:263, 277). "[H]aving a hard heart or a bad eye is being unable to perceive what is truly good according to God's revelation and thus being unable to make God's will one's own will. The source of such hardness of heart (or bad eye) is ultimately the inability to accept or envision the goodness of God" (1987:263; also 278). Patte, however, exaggerates the function of hardness of heart as the theme uniting 19:1—20:16; he unduly minimizes Matthew's intentional stress on the reversal of first and last; and with the rendition "bad eye" (also in Matt 6:23) shows no awareness of *ophthalmos ponêros* as designating an Evil Eye associated with the dispositions of envy and miserliness. For other interpretations of Matthew's treatment of the parable see Jeremias 1963:33–38; Herzog 1994:79–81; Schottroff 1984:139–46, and 2006:214–17.

Luke 13:6–9). Matthew 20:1–15 has features in common with the parable of Matt 18:23–35 (forgiveness of much versus refusal of forgiveness of little). Both are kingdom-of-heaven parables and both compare the generosity of a social superior (king or vineyard owner) to the begrudging of forgiveness or of generosity on the part of underlings. Throughout his Gospel, morever, Matthew extols the generosity and compassion of God and Jesus and presents them as models for all God's creatures to emulate.[273] In its other appearance in Matthew (6:22–23), an Evil Eye is likewise contrasted to generosity (a generous eye) and condemned as hindering the storing of treasure in heaven and impeding undivided commitment to God (6:19–24).[274]

Matthew links this parable encouraging generosity and deploring Evil-Eyed envy with other themes of his Gospel such as the conditions for entering the kingdom of heaven, qualities of discipleship and leadership, resistance to the teaching and ministry of Jesus, the terms of eschatological judgement, and its illustration of the radical reversal of values prevailing in the kingdom of heaven.

In a fledgling community of Christ-followers where the have-nots were dependent on the generosity of the haves, to regard one's neighbor or co-worker with an envious Evil Eye and begrudge generosity was not only to belie the generosity of one's God, but to turn a blind eye to the plight of one's fellow workers. Jesus tells the parable to praise generosity (of humans and conceivably also of God), to urge liberality on the part of all people, including his disciples, in the spirit of Deut 15:7–11 and Tob 4:1–21, and to condemm Evil-Eyed envy of fortunate beneficiaries. Matthew uses the parable to imply that goodness and generosity were traits not only of humans but of God, who is "good" in both his fidelity to his commitments and his generosity to all creatures. There is no limit to God's favor and mercy and no predicting its sudden appearance. Under God's rule, one person's gain does not entail another's loss. "Generosity in the last analysis trumps justice."[275] Evil Eyed envy, on the other hand, manifests a failure to comprehend or trust that the Creator's benefactions are unlimited and fall on "the evil and the good, the just and the unjust" (Matt 5:45). Evil-Eyed envy wallows in

273. See Matt 5:6, 7, 12, 44–45, 48; 9:13/12:7; 18:23–35; 19:29; 20:1–16; 22:1–10; 23:23.

274. Vearncombe (2010:221) claims that the grumblers "were not 'envious,' but were operating from their understanding of the prevailing economic system, an understanding radically shaken by the landowner's uncharacteristic display of reciprocal solidarity." This ignores the fact, however, that the climax of the parable itself and the condemning words of the vineyard owner in v. 15 explicitly reproach the malcontents's envious Evil Eye and their anger at his generosity.

275. A spot-on succinct summary of the parable by my friend and weekly Lectionary discussion partner, Rev. Dr. Robert McKenzie.

unwillingness to renounce "business as usual" and defy prevailing economic structures—in opposition to God's reversal of values (Matt 19:30, 20:16). It refuses to rejoice in the blessings unexpectedly enjoyed by others. To those who questioned or opposed Jesus' good news of a God who was generous and compassionate even toward supposedly "undeserving" sinners, this story served both as an illustration of human and divine generosity and as a condemnation of those who resented and condemned his ministry to the poor, the outcast, and the sinners.[276] In Matthew's narrative context, v. 15 becomes a warning directed to the disciples and critics alike about how the generosity of God can be met by humans who enviously Evil-Eye blessed recipients of God's limitless benefaction. This word of Jesus regarding the Evil Eye serves in Matthew as an admonition to the community against competition for favor and status and as an appeal for undivided loyalty and commitment, trust in God's surprising generosity, and solidarity with the poor and "undeserving." The parable as a whole in its Matthean setting serves as an affirmation of God's unlimited compassion[277], a vindication of Jesus' own ministry to the needy and marginalized, and as a potent condemnation of Evil-Eyed envy and its socially divisive power.

Matthew 20:1–16: Conclusion

Envy and the Evil Eye, the biblical communities believed, injure and destroy human beings, their health and possessions, human relationships, and the social fabric of the community in general. Therefore dread of the Evil Eye was a constant, everyday reality. Informal moral and social constraints were employed to identify, expose, and discredit Evil-Eyed persons as social deviants threatening the well-being of the entire group.

Examining this parable in the light of ancient Evil Eye belief and behavior situates it in its ancient context and exposes its likely contextual meaning. Five results might be mentioned. (1) Investigating the link between the parable's reference to the Evil Eye and the pervasive dread of the Evil Eye in ancient culture has directed closer attention to an ignored feature of the parable's dramatic conclusion and its cultural overtones. (2) Evil Eye belief and behavior manifests a regular association of the Evil Eye and the vice of envy, an association that appears here as well. (3) Consideration of this link and of

276. On the contrast between Jesus' use of the Evil Eye motif and rabbinical usage see Hezser 1990:244–45.

277. According to Hultgren 2000:33–45, this parable, like that of the Unforgiving Slave (Matt 18:23–35), underlines the quality of "God's extraordinary forgiveness and grace."

the dynamic of the envy process, in turn, has revealed the manner in which the parable is logically and dramatically structured as a story about envy and invidious comparison, thereby confirming the present integrity of the text and arguing against the necessity of any textual exclusions or additions. (4) The parable on the whole is a story about the showing of generosity in accord with God's will and a censure of invidious comparison and Evil-Eyed envy as incompatible with life in the kingdom of God. The malignant Evil Eye and the socially destructive force of its envy serve here as a negative foil for Jesus's solidarity with the marinalized and his encouragement of generosity to the poor and "undeserving." With this Evil Eye parable Mtthew affirms the unlimited nature of divine compassion, the importance of communal sharing and social cohesion, and a calculus according to which the last shall be first and the first last. (5) Reading the parable in the light of Evil Eye belief and practice provides a fresh understanding of the significance and function of this parable in both the teaching of Jesus and that of Matthew, while also illustrating the extent to which Jesus and the early Church shared with their surrounding cultures one of its most widespread beliefs; namely, belief in the envious Evil Eye and its malignant and divisive power.

The Evil Eye in Mark 7:22[278]

The Context: Mark 7:1–23

According to the Gospel of Mark, the earliest of the written Gospels (c. 70 CE), Jesus included the Evil Eye in an enumeration of evil dispositions and vices that originate in the human heart and defile a person (Mark 7:21–22 within 7:1–23). The occasion of this statement by Jesus, according to Mark,[279] was a dispute in Galilee initiated by certain Pharisees and scribes (lawyers) from Jersualem. They objected to Jesus's disciples' not washing and ritually purifying their hands prior to eating (7:1–5). Mark's explicit mention in this episode of the "Evil Eye" (*ophthalmos ponêros,* v. 22) is obscured by the numerous translations that render the Greek with such terms as "envy" or "jealousy" (see below).

Mark 7:1–23, framed by the term and topic of defilement (*koinais,* v. 1; *koinoi,* v. 23), consists of several sub-units: 7:1–13 (7:1–8, 9–13) and

278. The following draws on material in Elliott 1988:60, 2005a, and 2007a.

279. As Rudolf Bultmann observed (1963:324), the unit as a whole (7:1–23) has been constructed by Mark: "The sayings about outward observance of the law (7:9–13) and inward defilement (7:14–16 [–23]) are added [by Mark] to the controversy about purity (7:1–8)." This compositional activity is typical of all the evangelists (Bultmann ibid.:322–28).

7:14–23 (14–16, 17–23). As designed by Mark, vv. 1–13 are focused on the Pharisees, vv. 14–16 on the crowd, and vv. 17–23 on the disciples and their non-understanding (v. 18) of Jesus's parabolic words (vv. 14–16).[280] Rudolf Bultmann (1963:17–18) saw the material of this "conflict story" deriving from early Palestinian tradition, except for vv. 20–23, a catalogue of vices that he assigned to a "hellenistic author," or "Mark himself" (1963:17–18).[281] The expression *ophthalmos ponêros* (v. 22), however, as we have seen, is found on Jesus' lips elsewhere in the Gospels (Matt 6:23, 20:15; Luke 11:34); it has an equivalent in the rabbinic tradition (*m. Avot* 2:9; 5:19; cf. also 5:13); and it points to a belief long held in Israel. It is therefore likely to reflect the language and thought of Jesus, whatever the origin of the full list of vices in vv. 20–22.[282]

The issues of purity and defilement, diet and dining (when, where, how, what to eat and with whom) were critical for the rabbis of Mark's time (late 60s-early 70s CE) as for the Pharisees of Jesus's time (early 30s). The rules relevant to these issues were instrumental in maintaining Israel's fidelity to the Mosaic law and affirming the distinctive identity, conduct and boundaries of Israel versus non-Israelite outsiders. The identifying features of Israel became a vital issue in Mark's day marked by the collapse of the Jerusalem temple, priesthood and cult. There was, in their place, a turn to Torah and a fresh rabbinic interrogation of its instruction for a new day. Food and the circumstances of its consumption, including related matters of pure and impure modes of consumption, were vital issues of concern. For Mark's community, Jesus's position on the origin of impurity and defilement was determinative for its, and all Israel's, understanding and practice as well.[283] The occasion of dining raises the question of appropriate preparation for eating in a state of purification and avoiding defilement. Where have Jesus and his followers stood on this issue? The question concerns not just dining habits and the origin of defilement, but guidelines for appropriate behavior, matters of group identity, and the relation of the Jesus movement to other representatives of Israel.

280. The disciples' non-understanding or misunderstanding of Jesus's remarks and teachings is a major theme of the Markan gospel; see 4:10–13; 6:52; 7:18; 8:17–18, 21, 32–33; 9:6; 14:40.

281. See also Lohmeyer (1963:142) concerning vv. 20–22: "hier die spätere Gemeinde spricht" ("the later community is speaking here").

282. For perceptive comments on this passage in general, see Pesch 1976:367–84; Malina 1988; Pilch 1988; Dunn 1990; Bartchy 1992; and on its reference to the Evil Eye, Malina and Rohrbaugh 2003:174–76, 357–59.

283. See also Matt 23 with its excoriation of what is deemed the hypocrisy of the Pharisees concerning internal and external defilement, as well as Galatians 2 on the controverted issue of table fellowship and who could eat what with whom.

Mark presents Jesus as addressing the issue of defilement and where it originates, and, by implication, how to avoid it. Mark's narrative (7:1–23) expands on a confrontation between Jesus and his disciples and the Pharisees, as the several clarifying comments indicate (7:3–5, 11, 19b). Jesus's saying or "mashal" about purity and defilement (v. 15, cf. 18c, 20) is reckoned by critics as authentic tradition (see also Luke 11:40–41).[284] The list of vices (vv. 21–22) illustrating the point of Jesus's saying about defilement in v. 15, derives from Hellenistic and Second Temple Israelite tradition.[285] On the whole, Mark presents us with an interpretation by the early Jesus movement of Jesus's instruction of his disciples on this matter of purity and defilement (vv. 17–23) as the movement, in the generation after Jesus's death, confronts problems emerging within Jesus groups composed of both Israelites and non-Israelites.[286] The Evil Eye sayings on the lips of Jesus in Matt 6:22–23/ Luke 11:34–35 and Matt 20:15 show that the early Jesus movement easily recalled or imagined Jesus speaking of the Evil Eye. Mention of the Evil Eye in Mark 7:22 is consistent with, and further confirms, that conviction.

The Pharisees, as presented by Mark, advocated a rigorous observance of purity laws as a means for asserting the separate holy identity of Israel and its exclusive fidelity to the God of the covenant over against the allure and encroachments of Greco-Roman culture and the danger of Israelite cultural accommodation. Impurity and unholiness, they claimed, characterized all "others" beyond the pale of Israel, the ungodly gentiles. Israel, by contrast, was to be "holy as I the LORD your God am holy" (Lev 19:2).[287] Pharisees, along with all Judeans, Mark explains, did not eat without first washing their hands and ritually purifying themselves, in accord with their interpretation and application of the tradition of the elders (vv. 3–4). In this purification requirement, Pharisees were applying requirements for the priests to themselves and other lay Israelites. Yair Furstenberg argues that this hand washing requirement stands in contrast to the biblical priestly purity system and was introduced by the Pharisees influenced by Greco-Roman hand washing practice. "Jesus confronted it with the conception of ritual purity found in Leviticus."[288] "The biblical law (which Jesus favours) posits the person as a source of contamination of foods and vessels, whereas the Pharisees are

284. So Pesch 1976 1:383.

285. Vögtle 1936; Pesch 1976 1:382.

286. Pesch 1976 1:384

287. On purity and defilement see Booth 1986; Kazen 2002. On purity and Israel's purity system in general, see Douglas 1966; Neusner 1973, 1976a, 1976b; Elliott 1991b; Neyrey 1996; Malina 2001:161–97. On purity and defilement in Mark, see Neyrey 1986, 1988.

288. Furstenberg 2008:200.

concerned with the effects of contamination on the person."[289] Spotting Jesus's disciples eating with unwashed, unpurified hands, the Pharisees and scribes/lawyers asked Jesus their leader why his disciples ate with defiled hands contrary to the tradition of the elders (v. 5).[290] In directing their question to Jesus, they were putting him on the spot in public and maneuvering to shame and thereby discredit him.

In response, Jesus accused his interrogators of hypocrisy for honoring God with their lips but not their heart (v. 6),[291] and for their disrespecting and neglecting the commandment of God in favor of human precepts and tradition (vv. 7–8), even to the point of neglecting and dishonoring their own parents contrary to the requirement of the Decalogue (vv. 9–13; see Exod 20:12; 21:17; Lev 20:9; Deut 5:16).

Jesus, turning to the gathered crowd (vv. 14–15) and thereafter to the disciples privately (vv. 17–23), repeatedly insisted that defilement originates not *outside* the human body, as some Pharisees and scribes insisted, but rather from *within*, namely the human heart (vv. 14–15, vv. 18–23).[292] This applies to supposedly unclean hands (vv. 2–5) as well as unclean food (vv. 15–19). He thus implies that a washing of the hands does not eliminate defilement since it does not reach the source of defilement. His first statement (v. 15) is general in formulation; neither hands, food or eating is expressly mentioned but all are implied by the meal context (vv. 2–5):

> 7:15a There is nothing outside a person (*exothen tou anthrôpou*), which, by going into (*eisporeuomenon*) him/her, can defile (*koinôsai*) him/her;[293]
>
> 7:15b it is rather the things that go out of a person (*ek tou anthrôpou ekporeuomena*) that defile (*koinounta*) a person.

The repetition of this principle to the disciples (vv. 17–20) is connected by Mark explicitly to the issue of defiled food at meals by Jesus's reference to

289. Ibid.

290. That the question concerned the conduct of Jesus's *disciples* (rather than Jesus's own practice) shows that this issue remained relevant for Jesus's followers years after his death.

291. That is, honoring God *externally* with lip service but disrespecting God *internally* in their hearts, a distinction addressed in Mark 7:14–23. Matt 23:25–26 and Luke 11:37–40 report Jesus's criticizing their focus on cleansing the *outside* of the cup and dish while *inside* they are full of corruption and evil. Like white-washed tombs, clean on the outside but polluted within, they appear righteous externally but within are "full of hypocrisy and iniquity" (Matt 23:27–28).

292. Neusner 1976 argues that Jesus was opposing a position of the Pharisees of the House of Shammai and that he is close to the position of the House of Hillel.

293. Compare Lev 11–15; Deut 14:3–21; Dan 1:8; 4 Macc 7:6.

the stomach and his declaration that all foods are clean (vv. 18–19b). The point Jesus made with the crowd (vv. 14–15) is thus repeated for the benefit of his dense and uncomprehending disciples: "Do you not see that whatever goes into a person from outside cannot defile (*koinôsei*) him?" (v. 18b; cf. v. 15a) and "it is rather what goes out of a person [from inside] that defiles a person" (v. 20).[294] The reason given is that whatever *enters the body from without*—including food—enters not the heart (*kardia*) but the stomach (*koilia*) and then exits into the latrine/shitsack.[295] Excrement and where it is stored in the body may be ugly and repulsive, but excrement is not unclean according to the Mosaic law and Pharisaic standards.[296] Excrement is the result of food that entered the body from without; it was ingested, digested, and excreted, but it did not defile. On the other hand, it is that which is *internal*, Jesus asserts, and then *comes out of a person from within* that defiles that person (v. 20).

> 7:18a [Jesus to the disciples] "Are you too without understanding?
>
> 18b Do you not see that whatever goes into (*eisporeuomenon*) a person from outside (*to exôthen*) cannot defile (*koinôsei*) a person,
>
> 19a since it does not go into (*eisporeuetai*) one's heart but into one's stomach
>
> 19b and then goes out (*ekporeuetai*) into the latrine/shitsack?"
>
> 19c [This, Jesus said], declaring all foods clean (*katharizôn panta ta brômata*).
>
> 20 And he [Jesus] said, "It is rather what goes out (*ekporeuomenon*) of a person that defiles (*koinoi*) a person."

Jesus's contrast of what enters and what exists the body is accompanied by a contrast of heart (vv. 19a, 21; cf. v. 6) to stomach (v. 19a). According to his understanding and that of his contemporaries, the stomach is the organ that processes food entering the body, whereas the heart is the organ where thoughts, dispositions and feelings arise. The stomach receives food coming in and passing through. The heart gives birth to thoughts, dispositions, and feelings going out (through eye and mouth, as it was believed). Verse 19b, as indicated by the translation, is taken to be Mark's own interpretation of

294. Compare the saying of Jesus preserved in *Gos. Thom.* 14: "For what will go into your mouth will not defile you, but what comes out of your mouth; that is what will defile you."

295. The Greek term *aphedrôn* rendered "latrine" is a very vulgar word that could also be translated "shitsack"; so Malina 1988:23, following Mayer 1983:38–39.

296. Neyrey 1988b:86; Malina and Rohrbaugh 2003:176.

Jesus's words.[297] "Jesus' concern . . . lies not with bodily surfaces and orifices, but with bodily interior and heart. Hence, lips and mouth do not need to be guarded, but the heart should be constantly examined."[298] It is a person's heart, the organ of thought, feeling, and intention, that produces what is pure or polluted; see, similarly, Luke 6:45. To illustrate defiling things that arise in the heart, Jesus lists thirteen vices, one of which is the Evil Eye (7:21–22).

> 7:21 For from within (*esôthen*), out of the heart of persons, come out (*ekporeuontai*) wicked thoughts; acts of immorality, of theft, of murder, of adultery,
>
> 22 of greed, of maliciousness (*ponêriai*); (along with) deceit, immoderate conduct, an Evil Eye (*ophthalmos ponêros*),[299] blasphemy, arrogance, lack of good sense.
>
> 23 All these evil things (*ta ponêra*) come out from within (*esôthen ekporeuetai*) and defile (*koinoi*) a person.

With the final remark of v. 23, in which he classifies all thirteen vices as "evil things" (*ta ponêra*), Jesus concludes his teaching on defilement, and Mark brings the entire episode (7:1–23) to a close. The stress on defilement in this final verse (*koinoô*, v. 23; cf. vv. 15, 18, 20) repeats that of verse 2 (*koinos*, cf. also v. 5) and forms a literary *inclusio* bracketing the entire unit of vv. 1–23.

"Evil Eye" in Mark 7:22

Bible translations of *ophthalmos ponêros* in Mark 7:22 vary, with the majority opting for "envy." The Vulgate, KJV (1611), and NKJV render *ophthalmos*

---

297. But see also Luke 11:41b. For a divine declaration that all foods are clean see Acts 10:14–15, 28; 11:8–9. The Matthean parallel (15:1–20, esp. vv.17–20) lacks this statement; Jesus's own words only imply food and the act of eating, referring explicitly only to the internal origin of defilement.

298. Neyrey 1988b:86.

299. Inexact or partial parallels to Mark 7:1–23 in the Gospels of Matthew (15:1–20 = Mark 7:1–23) and Luke (Luke 11:37–41 = Mark 7:1–6a; cf. *Gos. Thom.* 14) contain no mention of *ophthalmos ponêros*. Luke has no parallel to Mark 7:6b–23. Matthew's shorter list of only seven vices (15:19), using the Decalogue as a model and omitting vices unrelated to commandments five through eight, contains no mention of the Evil Eye. Since Matthew includes in his Gospel two other references to the Evil Eye, its absence in 15:19 cannot be attributed to reluctance on Matthew's part to speak of an Evil Eye or to record Jesus speaking of the phenomenon. It rather appears that Matt 15:19 has reduced Mark's longer list to a group of seven (omitting, beside *ophthalmos ponêros*, also *ponêriai, dolos, aselgeia, hyperêphania,* and *aphrosynê*). This would be consistent with Mathew's practice of using the content of Mark but reducing its formulation.

ponêros as "Evil Eye." Luther employs an older Germanic variant for Evil Eye, namely *Schalksauge.*[300] The Italian *La Sacra Bibbia* conveys the sense of Evil Eye with *squardo maligno* ("malicious glance"), which captures the ocular action involved in an Evil Eye. The *Zürcher Bibel* (*neidischer Blick* = "envious glance") conveys the connection of malevolent ocular glance with the emotion of envy.[301] Remaining versions read just "envy" (BJ, *La Biblia*, NJB, NAB, NAS, NIV, RSV, NRSV, Philipps, Zink) or "jealousy" (TEV). This is unsatisfactory for at least three reasons. (1) While envy indeed is associated with the Evil Eye, the terms and concepts are not synonymous, as already noted. Envy is a disposition and an emotion, whereas an Evil Eye is the physical mechanism of eye and glance which is thought to convey envy and work its destructive effect. (2) Translations reading "envy" or "jealousy" fail to inform the reader that it is "Evil Eye" that stands in the original Greek text and, as Matt 6:22–23 and Matt 20:15 also indicate, that Jesus held this belief and warned against it repeatedly. (3) While envy is in fact related to the Evil Eye, jealousy is not and therefore an inappropriate rendition here in any case. A preferable, more comprehensive and culturally accurate translation of *ophthalmos ponêros* here would be "Evil-Eyed envy" or "envious Evil Eye."

In this Markan narrative concerning defilement related to eating, predining purification, and the issue of where defilement and evil have their origin, what is to be said about Jesus's reference to the Evil Eye here? Several observations can be made.

(1) The formulation itself, *ophthalmos ponêros*, is the one consistently used by, or attributed to, Jesus in the Gospels when he speaks of the Evil Eye.[302]

(2) This same formulation, *ophthalmos ponêros*, appears in the LXX,[303] the other prominent and related semantic field being *baskainô* and

---

300. Compare Luther's related rendition of Matt 6:22: *Ist dein Auge ein Schalk.*

301. The *Zürcher Bibel* rendition of Matt 20:15 likewise conveys the association of eye and envy: "ist dein Auge neidisch?."

302. See also Matt 6:23; 20:15. The Lukan parallel to Matt 6:23, Luke 11:34, reads only *ponêros*, but *ophthalmos* is clearly implied by context. Jesus himself would have used the Aramaic formulation '*eyna' bisha.*'

303. Sir 14:8, 10; 31:13; cf. also the verbal formulation of Deut 15:9 (*kai ponêreusetai ho ophthlamos sou*), Deut 28:54, 57 (*baskainô + tôi ophthalmôi*), and Tob 4:7, 16. See also *T. Iss.* 4:6; cf. *T. Dan* 2:5; *T. Benj.* 4:2.

paronyms.[304] Outside of Israel and Christianity, by contrast, *ophthalmos ponêros* is, with one exception, not attested.[305]

(3) Since the Evil Eye was considered one of the worst human vices according to Sir 31:13, it is hardly surprising that Jesus possibly includes it and Mark definitely lists it with twelve other vices marking immoral or morally "defiled" individuals. This inclusion is consistent with the mention of the Evil Eye in other lists of vices (4 Macc 1:25–26; 2:15–16; Philo, *Sacrifices* 32). Such catalogues of vices were a typical component of Israelite moral exhortation.[306] They were adopted and used by the Jesus movement as well.[307] Lists of virtues and vices were used to identify and illustrate actions and dispositions considered morally appropriate or inappropriate for one's group or people. They were tools of instruction and exhortation that clarified the moral norms and values that distinguished one group from other groups or that signalled values held in common by different groups.

(4) Jesus's association of the Evil Eye and other vices with the *heart* (Mark 7:21; cf. vv. 6, 19) is consistent with the ancient understanding of the heart as the seat of thought, disposition, feeling, and imagination.[308]

304. See Deut 28:54, 57; Prov 23:6; 28:22; Wis 4:12; Sir 14:3, 6, 8; 18:18; 37:11; Ep Jer 69/70; 4 Macc 1:26; 2:15. For the New Testament see Gal 3:1.

305. For the few Christian texts of the post-biblical period employing *ophthalmos ponêros* see Vol. 4, chap. 2. The exception and single instance of the plural, *ophthalmoi ponêroi*, appears in Artemidorus (second century CE), *Onirocriticon* 1.26, line.68. Billerbeck notes (1924 2:14) that in the rabbinic literature "Evil Eye" and "good eye" are recurrent ("gang und gäbe"); see e.g., *m. Avot* 2:9, 11; 5:19 and, for further texts, Billerbeck 1926 1:833–35. On these texts, see Vol. 4, chap. 1.

306. See Wis 14:25–27; Sir 7:1–21; 4 Macc 1:26, 2:15; *1 Enoch* 8:1–4; *2 Enoch* 10:4–6; 34:1–2; *2 Bar.* 73:4; 1QS 4:9–11; 10:21–23; *T. Reub.* 3:3–6; *T. Dan* 1:6; 2:4; *T. Sim.* 3:1; *T. Jud.* 16:1; Philo, *Sacrifices* 32 [147 vices!]; Josephus, *Ag. Ap.* 2.19–28; *T. Mos.* 7:3–10.

307. See Matt 15:19/Mark 7:21–22; Rom 1:29–31; 13:13; 1 Cor 5:10–11; 6:9–10; 2 Cor 12:20–21; Gal 5:19–21; Eph 4:25–31; 5:3–13; Col 3:5–9; 1 Tim 1:9–10; 6:4–5; 2 Tim 3:2–5; Tit 3:3, 9; 1 Pet 2:1; 4:3; Rev 21:8; 22:15; *Did.* 2–5; 5:1–2 [the "way of death" and 22/23 examples of *ponêra*]; Hermas *Mand.* 8.3; *Sim.* 6.5.5; 9.15.3; Polycarp, *Phil.* 4:3; 5:2, 3; 6:1. On New Testament vice and virtues lists see Easton 1932; Vögtle 1936; Wibbing 1959.

308. For example, Gen 6:5; 8:21; 27:41; Exod 4:14; 35:35–36; Deut 29:19; 2 Sam 6:16; 1 Kgs 3:9; Esth 6:6; Prov 6:14, 18 (perverted heart devising evil); Prov 8:5; 15:30; 21:4; 23:17 (the heart envies); Pss 4:7; 10:6; 14:1; 33:11; 34:7; Ps 58:2 (working wickedness in heart); Jer 11:8, 13:10, 18:12; ; Dan 2:30; Matt 5:28; 9:4; 12:24; 13:15; 15:19; 18:35; Mark 2:6; 3:5; 11:23; Luke 1:51; 2:35; 3:15; 5:22; 9:47; 24:38; John 12:40; Acts 28:27; Rom 1:24 (lusts of the heart); Jas 3:14; cf. Str-B I (1926):721–22 on the heart as agent of thought and feeling. For the heart in Mark see also 2:6, 8; 6:52; 8:17; 11:23; 12:30, 33. For a "base heart" as the locus of envy and evil dispositions see also the inscription, *I. Arsameia, Antiochus I* (Danker 1982 §42, pp. 247–55). Lines 215–216 state that: an envious person "melts his own eye over someone else's good fortune;" line 229 continues the thought and links envy and a melting eye with a base heart: "Pierced

It is also consistent with the assumed connection of eye and heart, as we noted above (pp. 126–30) regarding the joining of Matt 6:19–21 (heart) with 6:22–23 (eye).[309] Three assumed zones of the human body were associated with aspects of thought, communication and action:[310] the *zone of eyes-heart* enabling emotion-fused thought; the *zone of ears-mouth* enabling self-expressive speech; and the *zone of hands/feet* enabling purposeful action. The harmonious functioning and coordination of all three zones signaled a person of integrity. Humans cannot see into the heart so as to detect disposition and intention, but must rely on external appearance, such as the condition of the eye and the look of the face. Cicero explains that feelings "are mirrored by the face and expressed by the eyes . . . Nature has given us eyes . . . to indicate the feelings of the heart" (*De or.* 3.221–223; cf. also Quintillian, *Inst. Orat.* 11.75–76). God, by contrast, "sees in secret" (Matt 6:4, 6, 18) and "knows the heart" (Luke 16:15; Acts 1:24; 15:8). "Man looks on the outward appearance, but the Lord looks on the heart" (1 Sam 16:7). The notion of the "singleness of heart" (Eph 6:5; Col 3:20) replicates the "singleness/integrity of eye," which is the opposite of an Evil Eye (Matt 6:22–23). Similarly, a "darkening of heart" (Rom 1:21) matches a "darkening of eye" (= the Evil Eye).[311] According to this assumed connection of eye and heart, dispositions associated with the Evil Eye were thought to arise in the heart and then exit the body through the eye as charged particles of energy, the theory described in the *Table Talk* of Plutarch and resting on Democritus's theory of the eye as an active agent and projector of particles.[312] Joel Marcus (1999) has shown in connection with Mark 8:22–26 (recounting the healing of a blind man) how Mark, like his contemporaries, also presumed this extramission theory of vision.[313]

(5) The vices of the Markan list include both *actions* (theft, murder, adultery, immoderate conduct, and blaspheming/maligning others) and *dispositions* (deceit, arrogance, and lack of good sense) that prompt action. Both these aspects are associated with the Evil Eye as well. As has become clear in the present study, the expression *ophthalmos ponêros* always means

---

in his base heart, the root of his wicked life."

309. For this connection in Israel see Deut 15:9; 28:65; 1 Kgs 9:3 LXX; Job 30:26–27; 31:7, 26–27; Prov 15:30; 21:4; 23:26; Ps 73 (72):7; Isa 6:10; Jer 22:17; Lam 5:17; Sir 22:19; Tob 4:7. 16, 19; *T. Iss.* 4:1–6; 1 Cor 2:9; Eph 1:18 "eyes of your heart; cp. "blindness of their heart," Eph 4:18; Col 3:22); *1 Clem.* 36:2; *Gos. Thom.* 28.

310. Malina 2001:58–80, based on de Géradon 1958.

311. For examples of both concepts see above on Matt 6:22–23 and Elliott 1994.

312. For Plutarch on the Evil Eye see Vol. 2:48–56 and passim.

313. On Mark 10:46–52, blindness and the Evil Eye, see also Guijarro 2000. On the prevailing extramission theory of vision see above, pp. 126–30; see also Vol. 2:73–81.

"Evil Eye," whose specific meanings can vary according to context. *Ophthalmos ponêros* could denote the *malevolent eye* itself or *physically injuring* or bringing illness or death upon another person or object through the noxious glance. Or the expression could denote a *malevolent disposition or emotion* prompting the noxious glance in the first place (such as miserliness and disregarding the needy, begrudging of generosity to others, greed, avarice, or envy.[314] We have already seen that an Evil Eye can entail dispositions and actions other than envy. In the scenarios of Deut 15:7–11 and 28:53–57, directing an Evil Eye against a needy neighbor or family member is motivated not primarily by envy but by miserliness. In these texts it involves a malevolent withholding of aid and food. This is similar to an Evil-Eyed person disregarding the needy (Sir 14:8) or withholding food at table (Prov 23:6) or giving a gift begrudgingly (Sir 18:18; Tob 4:7, 16). It can also denote being avaricious (Prov 28:22; Sir 14:9) or greedy (Sir 31:12–13), or ungrateful (Sir 37:11). In general, an Evil Eye obscures what is good (Wis 4:14).

(6) In this particular Markan context, *ophthalmos ponêros* most likely connotes Evil-Eyed *envy*. This is the emotion most frequently associated with the Evil Eye as our foregoing review of the evidence attests. In fact, *phthonos* ("envy") and its semantic field often were used as synonyms of *ophthalmos ponêros* and its semantic field and vice versa. Jerome's Vulgate translation of *ophthalmos ponêros* here is *oculus malus*. But he also was aware of the association of Evil Eye and envy since he used terms of the *invid-* family to translate "Evil Eye" of the Hebrew or Greek; see Deut 28:54, 56 (*invidebit*); Prov 23:6 (*homine invido*); and Prov 28:22 (*invidet*). In the ancient world, the dread and condemnation of *phthonos* and *invidia* ("envy") was matched only by that of *ophthalmos ponêros* and *baskania* ("Evil Eye"). In catalogues of vices like that of Mark, envy is among the vices

---

314. An exchange of opinion occurring in the early 1940s in Great Britain had C. Ryder Smith taking *ophthalmos ponêros* in Mark 7:22 and elsewhere in the Bible to mean "evil motive" which could include envy (Ryder Smith 1941–1942) or as "malevolence" (1942–1943). In response, C. J. Cadoux (1941–1942) insisted on "stinginess" in all instances. J. Duncan Percy (1942–1943), responding to both, favored "envy—the dark and evil passion that grudges and grieves at another's good." Exegetical commentator Ernst Lohmeyer (1963:142, 143) translates "neidisch Auge" ("envious eye"), but curiously insists that "Mit dem 'bösen Auge' ist im NT niemals das aus dem Volksglauben und Magie bekannte 'böse Blick' gemeint; es ist dem 'Neid' des Armen auf besser Gestellte nahe verwandt (s[iehe] Mt 20, 15)" ("In the New Testament 'bad eye' never means "Evil Eye" as known in popular piety and magic; it is closely related to the 'envy' of the poor of the more well-to-do (see Matt 20:15)." By contrast, the classicist Peter Walcot in his study on envy in the Greek world underlines the association of envy with the Evil Eye and regards *ophthalmos ponêros* in Mark 7:22 as indeed meaning Evil Eye (Walcot 1978:87).

most frequently mentioned.[315] Envy also figures prominently in Mark's passion narrative, which states that "it was out of envy (*phthonos*) that the chief priests handed over" Jesus to Roman authority (Mark 15:10; cf. Matt 27:18). Mark attributes Jesus's death to the envy of his opponents just as Plato presents Socrates attributing his condemnation and death to the envy, slander, and malice of his enemies (Plato, *Apology* 2.54). Acts 5:17 records a further instance where the high priest and his Sadducean cohorts are said to have arrested apostles of the risen Jesus out of envy (*zêlos*).[316] A dynamic of envy on the part of those seeking Jesus's death, in fact, has been shown by Hagedorn and Neyrey to pervade Mark's story of Jesus.[317] Mark's mention of the Evil Eye here in 7:22 is an essential feature of Mark's "anatomy of envy."[318] Thus while *ophthalmos ponêros* here could imply any number of motivating malevolent dispositions, the overall Markan context favors taking the phrase to imply an *envious Evil Eye* or *Evil-Eyed envy*.[319]

The term "envy" alone is an inadequate rendition. Although the Evil Eye and envy were intimately linked in the ancient world, they nevertheless were distinguishable; envy was the disposition, an Evil Eye was the conveying mechanism. Consequently, while *ophthalmos ponêros* may *imply* envy, it ought not be translated as "envy" alone here in Mark 7:22. Use of the adjective "envious" (*phthoneros*) to qualify the expression "Evil Eye" (*baskanos*. or *ophthalmos ponêros*), as in Sir 14:10 (*ophthalmos ponêros phthoneros*) makes it evident that the speaker/author did not regard *ophthalmos ponêros* as meaning "envy" in and of itself. Instead the adjective "envious" was added to make this association explicit. *Envy is a disposition* conveyed through the *medium of an Evil Eye and noxious glance.* Inasmuch as Jesus includes *ophthalmos ponêros* with other vices aborning in the heart, it is likely that *ophthalmos ponêros* here referred to both (a) the malice of envy arising in the heart and (b) the Evil Eye through which this envy was externalized and directed toward its victim. The preferable translation capturing both these aspects is "an envious Evil Eye" or "Evil-Eyed envy."

(7) By associating the Evil Eye with other immoral actions and with the heart as organ of thought, feeling, and intention, Jesus (and Mark) indicate

315. See *phthonos*: Rom 1:29; Gal 5:21; Phil 1:15; 1 Tim 6:4; Tit 3:3; 1 Pet 2:1; *zêlos*: Sir 40:5; Rom 13:13; 2 Cor 12:20; Jas 3:16, cf. Jas 4:2.

316. For hostile envy against the followers of Jesus see also Acts 13:45; 17:5.

317. See Hagedorn and Neyrey 1998, who list nine aspects of envy, in addition to the crucial charge of envy in 15:10, constituting Mark's "anatomy of envy."

318. See Elliott 2007a expanding on Hagedorn and Neyrey 1998.

319. Pesch 1976:382: "Das 'böse Auge' (vgl. Dt 15, 9; 28, 54) bezeichnet die Missgunst, den Neid (*phthonos*)" ("The 'evil eye' [cf. Deut 15:9; 28:54] denotes ill will, envy (*phthonos*)."

that they *do not view the Evil Eye as something that operates inadvertently* and thus free of moral culpability. It rather involves personal intention and the will to harm—malicious designs that must be guarded against and over which control can and must be exercised. This seems to be the case in all biblical references to the Evil Eye. In contrast to Greco-Roman notions of the Evil Eye, which imagine that it can be inherited and passed on from one generation to another (Pliny, *NH* 7.16–18), the Evil Eye of which Jesus and the biblical authors speak involves a disposition and act for which each individual has personal responsibility.

(8) Jesus's including the Evil Eye with other actual dispositions and recurrent acts indicates that he did *not regard the Evil Eye as something magical* or belonging to the realm of the occult or dismissable as ignorant superstition. Like Paul and the sages preceding him, Jesus deemed the Evil Eye an everyday reality of the human condition—powerful and dangerous but as human as miserliness, theft, and murder.

(9) The *focus* of Jesus' attention here is *not on the Evil Eye of others* at the meal, but rather on the possibility of *oneself* having and exercizing an envious Evil Eye. His concern is not with the threatening Evil Eye of one's neighbor or enemy or host or fellow diners, but with the Evil Eye and defiling dispositions of *one's own heart*. This concern is consistent with his concentration on the internal human condition rather than the external state, that is, on the heart (internal) in contrast to the external hands (7:3, 5) and lips (7:6).

(10) In his linking the Evil Eye with the human heart, Jesus does *not connect the Evil Eye with some hostile demon attacking humans from without.* This contrasts to Mesopotamian and Greco-Roman notions of an *Evil Eye demon* (*baskanos daimôn*) roaming about ready to invade homes and strike vulnerable victims.[320] The Bible consistently portrays the Evil Eye as a negative *human* phenomenon. It was a malignancy brewing in the human heart and transmitted through the projections of the human eye. Just as Greeks and Romans in the Hellenistic period focused ever more attention on envy and its mastery as a personal and moral issue,[321] so the biblical writers and Jesus likewise concentrated on the Evil Eye (and envy) as human vices needing to be mastered. Along with the other vices Jesus mentioned, when put into action, it brought about a person's defilement and pollution, thereby setting that person at odds with his family, his community, and his God.

Nowhere in the biblical writings is the Evil Eye associated with, or attributed to, the devil/Satan. This connection is made only later in the

320. For illustrative texts see Vols. 1 and 2.

321. Walcot 1964:116–34.

post-biblical period by Christians, who view both envy and the Evil Eye as originating with the prince of demons, the devil/Satan.[322] An Israelite sage had observed centuries earlier that "through the devil's envy, death entered the world" (Wis 2:24). Given the connection between envy and the Evil Eye, and between the devil and envy (as well as all forms of evil), it is not surprising that eventually the Evil Eye would be traced to the devil/Satan as well.

(11) The mention of an Evil Eye on an occasion of *dining* is also noteworthy. This accords with the prevailing notion that meals were situations where an Evil Eye is likely to be experienced. As we recall from Vol. 2, Aristotelian tradition prescribed that the herb rue should be ingested prior to meals in order to ward off the Evil Eye of other diners and avoid vomiting (Pseudo-Aristotle, *Prob. phys.* 20.34). Israel shared this dread of the Evil Eye at the table, where it could ruin the food, bring discomfort or illness to the diners, and manifest a begrudging spirit on the part of the host. Israelite sages warn against eating the bread of one with an Evil Eye, for "you will vomit up the little you have eaten and you will waste your pleasant words" (Prov 23:6–8). An Evil-Eyed person is envious of [or begrudges] bread and it is lacking from his table" (Sir 14:10). "If you sit at a bountiful table, do not be gluttonous at it and do not say, 'there is lots of food on it.' Remember that an Evil Eye is a wicked thing. What has been created more evil than an (Evil) Eye?" (Sir 31:13).[323]

Conclusion to Mark 7 and the Evil Eye

Jesus's mention of the Evil Eye in Mark's narrative concerns more than its inclusion in a list of immoral and anti-social acts or dispositions. As Mark tells the story, it is part of Jesus's instruction concerning Israel's purity system, ritual defilement at mealtime, and, more broadly, the place where defilement and evil arise. Jesus distinguishes himself from Pharisees and scribes/ lawyers who view defilement and evil as external in origin, as though defilement could be avoided and purity assured by an external washing of hands or an ingesting of kosher food. Here, as on other occasions, Jesus insists that observance of purity rules and adherence to ancient tradition focused on externals does not and can not eliminate defilement and evil.[324] This is the

322. See, e.g., *Mart. Polyc.* 17:1 and thereafter, and especially the writings of Basil, Jerome, and John Chrysostom—all discussed in Vol. 4, chap. 2.

323. Deut 28:54–57 describes a gruesome occasion of the Evil Eye and desparate eating to stay alive.

324. See Luke 11:37–41 (cf. Matt 23:25–28) for a similar critique as well as Matt 5:21–48, where Jesus ranks disposition and intention as important as act, and Matt 6:1–18 contrasting the external orientation of the Pharisees and the internal focus of

case because defilement and evil are *internal matters of the heart*, the heart from which also the dispositions of the Evil Eye emanate.

An Evil Eye and its malevolent glance convey envy and other malicious emotions stirring in the human heart. From the heart this envy and malevolence proceeds to the eye and then via the ocular glance outward toward its victims. The Evil Eye, for Jesus and Mark and all the biblical authors, is not an instance of ignorant superstition. Nor is it something operating unintentionally. Instead, like the other vices listed in Mark 7:21–22, it involves a malevolent moral disposition and action that can and must be controlled. If given expression, it can injure or destroy a victim's health and personal well-being and also ruin healthy social relations of the community, whether the family, village or larger group. In the total context of the Markan Gospel and its whole gestalt of envy (Hagedorn and Neyrey 1998), the fatal consequences of envy and casting an envious Evil Eye become clear. An envious Evil Eye not only defiles. As can be seen in the case of Jesus as its victim, envy and the Evil Eye can lead to violence and even murder. "The Evil Eye," Derrett (1996:69) aptly observes, is an antisocial disposition, capable of being detected and reprehended in any individual within his society. Its cure, if any, lies in a religious conversion, perhaps a 'rebirth.'"

This confrontation between Jesus and his critics brings to expression conflicting views on the nature and source of evil and defilement and, on Jesus's part, an implicit call for an inner transformation and purification that is fundamental to external action consistent with God's will. In the last analysis, defilement for Jesus is not only a ritual issue, but a moral one. The social meaning and ethnic implications of the point made in Mark 7:1–23 is illustrated by the narrative of Mark 7:24–30. Jesus, a "clean" Israelite, in "unclean" territory (Tyre and Sidon), interacts with an "unclean" Greek woman, Syrophoenician by birth, and heals (= "makes clean," cf. 1:40–45) her unclean, demon-posssessed daughter. Persons are no more automatically unclean than are formerly classified unclean foods or acts. A similar scenario concerning clean and unclean persons, places, and foods is described in Acts 10–11.

Since defilement is a moral issue, what is required for purity is not (merely) the washing of hands and feet or ostentatious giving of alms or public display of prayer (Matt 6:1–18), but a repentance and purity that is *internal* in nature, a complete change of mind and heart (*metanoia*), a transformation of attitude, will, and conduct—an inner purification of heart.[325] In such a transformed heart, an Evil Eye and envy have no place.

Jesus (and God).

325. Mark's Jesus does not state this in so many words in this particular episode

PAUL, GALATIANS, AND EVIL EYE ACCUSATIONS

"O uncomprehending Galatians, who has injured you with
an envious Evil Eye?" (Gal 3:1)

Paul's celebrated letter to the Galatians has remained through the centuries an inexhaustible source of inspiration and fascination. For historians it provides information that is basic for a reconstruction of Paul's early career and the early course of Christian history. It also provides a graphic insight into the practical struggles of Israel's messianic movement as it sought to gain not only Israelite but also Gentile adherents to its gospel of salvation in Christ and the Holy Spirit. For theologians it has represented a revolutionary "magna charta of Christian freedom" in which Paul contrasts a trust in the grace of God available to all who are one with Jesus Christ and the Holy Spirit, on the one hand, to an observance of a Mosaic law that demarcates Israel from the Gentiles and excludes these *goyim* from the company of the saved. The Augustinian monk, Martin Luther, ridden with guilt and *Angst*, embraced this epistolary celebration of freedom as his beloved wife, his other Katherine von Bora.

This letter is valuable for a further reason as well. It provides rich evidence of the social and cultural world which Paul and his contemporaries inhabited. This was an environment marked by constant competition and conflict, a world viewed as inhabited by spirits and humans with extraordinary powers who played a regular and threatening role in human affairs, a world in which the mysterious forces of demons, witchcraft, and the Evil Eye were thought to be everywhere at work.[326]

Witchcraft, Witchcraft Societies, and the Evil Eye

Writing on Paul's letter to the Galatians and the cultural environment in which and for which it assumed shape, Jerome Neyrey analyzed a significant feature of this world, described by anthropologists as that of a "witchcraft society."[327] "Witchcraft," since the milestone research of E. E. Evans Pritchard among the Azande (1929, 1931, 1937), is viewed as the use of an *innate, inherited* mystical power on the part of certain individuals to harm

---

where it is more tacit than explicit, but he does so elsewhere; see Mark 1:15 (summarizing Jesus's entire message); 6:12; 12:29–30; cf. also Matt 4:17; 5:8, 21–48; 6:1–18; 11:20–21; 22:37; Luke 6:45; 8:15; 10:27; 21:34.

326. For earlier versions of the following, see Elliott 1988:62–67, 1990, 2005b:159–64, 2011:118–22.

327. Neyrey 1988a, 1990a.

(or, in fewer cases, help) others. Witchcraft is generally now distinguished from sorcery, which entails an *acquired* ability and *deliberate intention* to *manipulate certain substances* in order only to *harm* others.[328] In witchcraft societies, humans see themselves subject to the powers of demons, spirits, and malicious forces lurking everywhere and often operating through human agents.[329] The Circum-Mediterranean region, since Mesopotamian civilization, George Murdock has pointed out (1980:57–63), has long been the home of these witchcraft and Evil Eye societies.[330] In such witchcraft societies, the Evil Eye is regarded as a physiological phenomenon of nature that must be carefully reckoned with because of its noxious power. Here belief in witches and the Evil Eye play a significant role in identifying causes of failure, misfortune, illness, loss, and death.[331] Evil Eye belief, like witchcraft belief, also is instrumental in the regulation of behavior and social interaction. In these "witchcraft societies," certain persons were deemed to be witches or Evil Eye possessors or both.[332] Medea, for example, was both

328. See Willis 2002:562–64; Marwick, ed. 1982 passim.

329. On witchcraft, witchcraft societies, and the rationale and operation of witchcraft accusations see Evans-Pritchard 1937; Kluckhohn 1944; M. Wilson 1951; Lea 1939; Middleton and Winter 1963; Douglas 1963, 1967, 1970a:99–124, 1970b:xiii–xxxviii, 1999a:77–94; Baroja 1965; Hughes 1965; Marwick 1965; Weidman 1968; Mair 1969; Nash 1973; Rush 1974; Dionisopoulos-Mass 1976; Murdock 1980:21, 37–40, 49, 50–51, 58, 61–62, 66 (witchcraft causing illness); Herzfeld 1981; Marwick, ed. 1982; Buonanno 1984; Warwick 1987 (containing numerous examples of witchcraft accusations); Abush 1989; Apostolides and Dreyer 1989; Ben-Yehuda 1989; Russell 1989; Levack, ed., 1992 vols. 1, 2, 4, 9, 10, 12; ibid., 2004; Stevens 1996; Greenwood 2000; Lehmann and Meyers 2006; Greenwood 2000; Willis 2002; Levack, ed. 2004; Devish 2005; Bowie 2006; Moro, Myers, and Lehmann 2008.

On witchcraft in antiquity see Jastrow 1905 1:285; Frachtenberg 1918; Baroja 1965:17–40; Mair 1969; Ward 1980; Luck 1985:195–204, 213–16; Abush 1987, 1989; Malina and Neyrey 1988:1–32 (Jesus as witch); Russell 1989; Neyrey 1990:181–217; Levack, ed. 1992b vol. 2; Duff 1996; Ankarloo and Clark 1999; Collins 2000; Ogden 2002:78–145; Levack, ed. 2004:5–29; Kotzé 2007; Stratton 2007; Apostolides 2008; Apostolides and Dreyer 2008; Schmitt 2012.

330. Other features of Circum-Mediterranean cultures correlated with witchcraft and the Evil Eye include writing (invented in Sumer), belief in concerned high gods, patrilineal descent, payment of a bride price in marriage, and money as medium of exchange, see Murdock 1980:57–71.

331. See Maloney, ed. 1976:v–xvi, 135–38; Dionisiopoulos-Mass 1976; Garrison and Arensberg 1976; J. M. Roberts 1976; and Murdock 1980:57–63.

332. On the relation of witchcraft and the Evil Eye in various societies, including the biblical communities, see Jastrow 1905 1:285 (Evil Eye of a witch); Baroja 1965:38, 132, 234–35. Rush 1974:33–34, 57–77, Appendix I on "Evil Eye Ritual" with photographs of the ritual procedure (137–44); Dionisopoulos-Mass 1976; Spooner 1976; Murdock 1980:58; Evans-Pritchard 1937:26 n. 1; Neyrey 1986b, 1988a, 1990a, 1990b; 1990c; Malina and Neyrey 1988:1–32; Gravel 1995:6–7; Lehman and Meyers 2006; Devish

an archtypical witch and wielder of an Evil Eye.[333] The poet Ovid tells of a witch, Dipsas, casting an Evil Eye, and mentions the same means (garlic) employed for averting witches and defending against fascinators (Ovid, *Amores* 1.8.15–16). These dangers to society were thought to possess the power to harm humans and livestock, cause illness and death, destroy valuable property, and upset the tranquility and harmony of villages and communities.[334] Consequently, witches and Evil Eye possessors were feared or at least, like porcupines, "treated with great care." The public was constantly on the lookout for their presence, so that telltale physical signs of a witch or a fascinator were important to know and verify.

In such societies, labeling someone a "witch" or an "Evil Eye possessor" (*baskanos, fascinator*) and making the labels stick in the mind of the public, was an effective way of denigrating, neutralizing and defeating rivals, especially in competitions for leadership and control. Apuleius, a Platonist philosopher and traveling lecturer (second century CE), presents in his *Apology* (25–43) examples of witchcraft accusations. He himself fends off accusations that he had won the affection of his wealthy wife through witchcraft, and that he had he bewitched a boy by an incantation.[335] In his *Metamorphoses/The Golden Ass* (2.21–30), Apuleius tells of a woman accused of bewitching and murdering her new husband in order to cover up a love affair and get possession of his money.[336] Pliny the Elder recounts an incident concerning a certain Caius Furius Cresimus, who was more successful at farming than were his envious neighbors. He was accused by them of having used spells (*veneficiis*) to entice away their crops to his own property. He was indicted but acquitted because of his eloquent defense of his innocence (Pliny, *NH* 18.41–43).

The cultural breeding grounds for these beliefs have been extensively studied. Witch beliefs, like Evil Eye beliefs, flourish "in small-scale societies with inadequate control of their environment and dominated by personal relationships, societies in which people think in personal terms and seek personal causes for their misfortunes." This hypothesis of anthropologist

---

2005:389–90, 402–3; Bowie 2006; Kotzé 2007; Apostolides and Dreyer 2008. Garrison and Arensberg in Maloney, ed. 1976:321, adapting Douglas1970:xxvi–xxvii, present a chart (fig. 15.1, p. 321) comparing and demonstrating the similarity of witchcraft and the Evil Eye as threats to the community and the functions of the accusations.

333. See, e.g., the *Argonautica of* Apollonius of Rhodes.

334. One significant difference is that witches, in contrast to Evil Eyed persons, could also be engaged for *positive* purposes such as healing, attracting the affection of another, or attaining some desired goal, whereas the Evil Eye brought about only loss.

335. See the text in Luck 1985:109–13; Levack, ed. 2004:10–13.

336. See the text in Luck 1985:212–17.

Monica Hunter Wilson writing in 1951[337] has been amply supported by decades of subsequent research. Anthropologist Mary Douglas has identified six distinctive features of the social circumstances typical of such witchcraft societies: (1) external social boundaries (distinguishing "us" from "them") are clearly marked; (2) internal social relations are confused and characterized by competing positions of rivals; (3) close and unavoidable social interaction prevails; (4) tension-relieving mechanisms are weak or lacking; (5) control by a central authority also is lacking; and (5) there is intense, disorderly ongoing competition for leadership.[338] Similar conditions prevail in Evil Eye cultures.[339]

Under these general conditions, Evil Eye accusations, like witchcraft accusations, are employed to criticize conduct of which one's group does not approve. The accusations are leveled at specific individuals or groups to blame them for having caused misfortune, illness, or social disruption. This tactic aims at publically discrediting rivals, having them viewed as dangerous deviants, and defeating them. The accusations occur generally, but not exclusively, within face-to-face groups, villages, or local communities.

If the public finds the accusation credible, the accused stands denounced, discredited, and dishonored. Whatever the judgment of the public, however, the accusation alone has the effect of bringing the accused into suspicion and disrepute. Since the truth of such accusations is virtually impossible to ascertain on the basis of concrete evidence, the reputations of accusers and accused, and whatever influence they have with the public, ultimately determines the success or failure of the accusation. These accusations served to clarify contested group values, encourage conformity with social and moral norms, to identify and condemn allegedly deviant or malevolent conduct, neutralize rivals and opponents, disable internal enemies, mark social boundaries and thereby maintain the solidarity and vitality of the group.[340] What Mary Douglas observes concerning witchcraft accusations applies to Eye Eye accusations as well. "The accusation is itself a weapon for clarifying and strengthening the [social] structure. It enables

---

337. Monica Hunter Wilson, "Witch-beliefs and Social Structure" (1951), reprinted in Marwick, ed. 1982:276–85, esp. 284.

338. Douglas 1970b:xxvi–xxvii; see also Malina and Neyrey 1988:20–30.

339. See Maloney, ed., 1976:passim. Garrison and Arensburg in Maloney, ed. 1976:321, adapting Douglas 1970b:xxvi–xxvii, present a chart (fig. 15.1, p. 321) comparing and demonstrating the similarity of witchcraft and the Evil Eye as perceived threats to the community, with the functions of the accusations also compared.

340. See Douglas 1970b; Teitelbaum 1976; Garrison and Arensberg 1976; Herzfeld 1981; Esler 1994:131–46.

guilt to be pinned on the source of confusion and ambiguity" (Douglas 1990a:107).

Among these closely-knit communities, defined primarily by geographical proximity, ethnic affiliation, group loyalty, and face-to-face contact, *the stranger or outsider* in particular, is generally perceived as a threat to the common weal, and thus a likely Evil Eye fascinator with malicious or envious designs. *Within* such communities that are subject more to custom than a centralized and effective system of law, accusations of Evil Eye possession and injury are effective frequent means employed by rival factions for discrediting and disabling their opponents. Accusing an opponent of being a fascinator or Evil Eye possessor, like an accusation of witchcraft, serves as an informal but effective social mechanism for marshalling public opinion against that person, classifying him or her as a social deviant, censuring his behavior, discrediting his honor and credibility, and isolating him as a danger to the community.[341]

Attention to these details of Paul's cultural world has advanced a more accurate reading of the Galatian letter by situating it in its actual cultural context and by considering beliefs and aspects of the prevailing cultural script generally unconsidered by modern interpreters.

Paul's Letter to the Galatians

A close reading of Galatians indicates that a strategy of Evil Eye accusation and counter-accusation played a prominant role in Paul's confrontation with his opponents in Galatia. Rival Israelite and Gentile factions of the messianic movement had clashed over the social and moral implications of a gospel and a household of faith founded not on fidelity to the Mosaic law but on solidarity with a crucified Messiah. In his initial visit to Galatia (c. 53 CE), Paul had preached a gospel proclaiming good news of a salvation available to Israel and Gentiles alike. It is offered as a divine gift of the Spirit and accepted by trust in a divine promise rather than by submission to the Mosaic law. Soon after his departure from Galatia, this teaching was challenged by rival Israelite followers of Jesus Christ demanding continued observance of the Mosaic law, kosher food laws, circumcision, and Israel's traditional calendar, in addition to faith in Jesus as the Christ. They also challenged Paul's apostolic authority and tried to discredit him with

341. On witchcraft accusations in the Jesus movement, see Malina and Neyrey 1988, esp. 27–30; Neyrey 1986:160–70; 1990a:181–206, 207–17; Malina and Neyrey in Neyrey, ed. 1991:97–122. On Evil Eye accusations see Elliott 1988:63–67, 1990, 1992, 2005b, 2013a.

a variety of *ad hominem* arguments. Their attack had produced debilitating cleavages within the Galatian churches and had seriously undermined Paul's credibility and authority.

Receiving disturbing news of this situation, Paul fires off a highly emotional letter to the Galatian churches expressing his surpise and dismay at their turning away so quickly from his proclamation (1:6–9). Paul attempts to repair the damage to the community, restore order, and regain the upper hand and the moral high ground. This response includes a historical retrospective of his own career, his apostolic credentials and defense of his own person, actions, and motives (1:1, 10—2:14; 6:17); a reiteration and elaboration of his gospel (2:15–21; 3:6—4:11; 4:21–31; 5:14–15); a deploring of the Galatians' abandonment of his gospel (1:6) and their falling victim to injury caused by an Evil Eye of Paul's opponents (3:1, 2–5); a recalling of his earlier relations with the Galatians (4:12–20); a counter-attack upon his opponents (1:7–9; 3:1; 4:17; 5:7–12; 6:12–13, 17); and a concluding appeal for standing fast in freedom, and maintaining faith active in love, communal solidarity, and cooperation within the "household of faith" and "Israel of God" (5:1–6, 13—6:10, 11–16, 18).

After first clarifying his gospel and defending his own activiites since being called by God (1:6–2:21), Paul turns to the Galatians and regrets how they have been diverted from the gospel he proclaimed when he first visited them and how they have returned to observance of the Mosaic Law as necessary for salvation (3:1—4:20). At the outset of this section he asks rhetorically, "O uncomprehending Galatians, who has injured you with an envious Evil Eye? (3:1). At the section's close he mentions actions that also point to Evil Eye accusation and counter-accusation (4:12–20).

With the rhetorical question of 3:1 Paul implicitly accuses his opponents of having gravely injured the Galatians with an envious Evil Eye, thereby weakening the commitment of the Galatians to God, Jesus Christ, and one another. This damaging role of an envious Evil Eye is strikingly similar to the Evil Eye injury done to the illustrious figures of history, Dion and Brutus, as Plutarch describes it in his *Parallel Lives.* Comparing the lives of the Greek Dion and the Roman Brutus, Plutarch remarks that it was what happened to them rather than what they chose to do that made their lives similar. They both died prematurely without accomplishing their goals and both were warned about this by an ill-boding spectre from heaven. (*Dion* 2.1–2). From this spectre, which these educated men took quite seriously, Plutarch continues, they learned that they would be targets of evil spirits, the Evil Eye, and envy, which would attack their virtue and honor:

But if Dion and Brutus, men of solid understanding and philo-sophic training and not easily cast down or overpowered by anything that happened to them, were so affected by a spectre that they actually told others about it, I do not know but we shall be compelled to accept that most extraordinary doctrine of the oldest times: that mean and Evil-Eyed spirits (*ta phaula daimonia kai baskana*), in envy of (*prosphthonounta*) good men and in opposition to their noble deeds, try to confound and ter-rify them, causing their virtue to rock and totter, in order that they may not continue erect and inviolate in the path of honour and so attain a better portion after death than the spirits them-selves. (Plutarch, *Dion* 2.5–6)[342]

Paul, however, is speaking not about Evil-Eyed *spirits* harming the Galatians, but rather Evil-Eyed *humans*—those competing with Paul for the hearts and minds of the Galatians.

References and Allusions in Galatians to the Evil Eye

The first of multiple references or allusions to the Evil Eye is the explicit mention of the Evil Eye in Gal 3:1. Paul initially has criticized and cursed perverters of the gospel at Galatia (1:6–9) and has accounted for himself, the divine origin of his gospel, and its practical implications (1:10—2:21). He then addresses the Galatians directly. He chides them for turning away from the Holy Spirit they had earlier received and instead relying once again on obedience to the Mosaic Law as necessary for salvation (3:1—4:20). His opening statement (3:1) is part of a rhetorical question (3:1–5) with accusa-tory overtone:

O uncomprehending Galatians, who has injured you with an envious Evil Eye (*ebaskanen*), you before whose very eyes Jesus Christ was publicly portrayed as crucified?

O anoêtoi Galatai, tis hymas ebaskanen, hois kat' ophthalmous Iêsous Christos proegraphê estaurômenos. (3:1)[343]

---

342. LCL translation by Bernadotte Perrin (Plutarch, *The Parallel Lives*, Vol. 6: *Dion and Brutus. Timoleon and Aemilius Paulus*, 1918), modified by JHE.

343. The verb *baskainô* occurs only here in the New Testament according to the most reliable manuscript evidence. Ms 075 includes it a second time at 5:7, *tis hymas ebaskane*, where *ebaskane* replaces the better supported verb *enekopsen* ("hindered"). This is a secondary and weakly supported reading clearly influenced by the similar formulation of 3:1, *tis hymas ebaskanen*; cf. Nanos 2002:188 n. 183.

At the section's close (4:12–20), Paul again mentions actions and affections conventionally associated with the Evil Eye (4:12–20) and again refers to an event of the past when he and the Galatians first met (4:12c–15). Thus 3:1 and 4:12–20 are related in terms of both retrospective temporal focus and subject matter.[344]

Bible versions and commentators vary in their translations of *ebaskanen*, with most of them obscuring the fact that Paul here is referring explicitly to the action of an Evil Eye, which is regularly associated with the malice of envy. The verb of this rhetorical question,[345] *ebaskanen*, is, as we have seen in this study, the conventional term used throughout the Hellenic and Hellenistic world for "injure with an Evil Eye," often with the implicaton of envy.[346] F. T. Elworthy, in his classic 1895 study, *The Evil Eye*, observed over one hundred years ago that with *ebaskanen* Paul is saying "that some evil eye had 'overlooked' [Elworthy's term] them and worked in them a blighting influence. It was an apt allusion to the then, and still, universally prevalent belief in that power of 'dread fascination' which the writer of the Epistle so well knew they [the Galatians] would comprehend."[347]

Jerome's Vulgate translation had rendered the Greek *ebaskanen* with *fascinavit*, the standard Latin equivalent also meaning "injure with an Evil Eye." In his commentary on this Pauline text Jerome observed that the poet Virgil had used this same Latin verb in referring to the Evil Eye: "I do not know which Evil Eye has injured (*fascinavit*) my tender lambs" (Virgil, *Ecl.* 3.103).[348] The related noun *fascinatio*, Jerome further notes in this connection, renders "Evil Eye malice" (*baskania*) in Wis 4:12 (Vulgate). Jerome regards *baskania*, *fascinatio* and *invidia* as synonyms. He explains that in everyday speech *fascinavit* signifies "envy" (*invidia*): "Among us [speakers

---

344. Martin Luther, following John Chrysostom, saw in this relation of 3:1–5 and 4:12–20 a balance of the censure of the Galatians in 3:1–5 with their praise in 4:12–20.

345. This is one of several accusatory rhetorical questions posed throughout the letter; see also 3:2, 3, 4, 5; 4:9, 15, 16, 21; 5:7, 11.

346. The term *baskainô* appears only here in the New Testament. It is useful to keep in mind that simply uttering the word *baskainô* and its family of terms was deemed a dangerous matter, hence its occasional replacement with *phthoneô* (envy); see Rakockzy 1996:41, 61–62; Matantseva 1994 (as illustrated on amulets). Among Italians of Napoli, speaking the dangerous word *malucch* or *jettatura*, "Evil Eye," in public still is avoided and compared to shouting "fire!" in a packed theater because of the fear it aroused; see Rakockzy 1996:83 n. 204.

347. Elworthy 1895/1958:5. See also Story, *Castle St. Angelo* 1877:152; Budge 1978/1930:387: Paul "most certainly" referred to the Evil Eye in Gal 3:1." Earlier, see Burder 1822 2:397, noting the reference to fascination in Gal 3:1.

348. This line from Virgil is cited by Jerome in his commentary on Galatians (*Comm. Gal.* [PL 26.347 §417]).

of Latin] *invidus* ["envious person"] is more meaningfully recorded in Greek as *fascinator* [= *baskanos* = "Evil-Eyed person"] (*Comm. Gal.* [PL 26.347 §417; similarly, PL 30.847]).

This conventional meaning of the Greek verb in antiquity is generally obscured by modern translations. Among modern versions, *La Biblia* correctly reads: *ha fascinado*. Most versions, however, render not literally but according to what they take to be the sense of the verb *ebaskanen: bezaubert; verzaubert; bewitched; cast a spell over* (Luther,[349] Zürcher Bibel, KJV, NKJV, NAB, NAS, NEB, NIV); *behext* (Zink); *a ensorceles* (BJ); *ha ammaliati* (La Sacra Bibbia); *embrujó* (La Biblia Versión Popular); *put a spell on* (NJB, TEV); *cast a spell over* (Phillips). These renditions according to assumed sense obscure the verb's explicit reference to the Evil Eye or fail to convey to modern readers the ancient association of spells and bewitchment with the Evil Eye.

The standard Greek–English lexicon of Danker-Bauer-Arndt-Gingrich gives two meanings for *baskainô*: (1) "to exert an evil influence through the eye, *bewitch*, as with an 'evil eye'" and (2) "to be resentful of someth[ing] enjoyed by another, *envy*."[350] The entry indicates that even "bewitch" must be understood as occurring through the operation of an evil *eye* and that such ocular Evil-Eyeing often is prompted by, or a channel of, feeling envious. Ample illustration of this comment has been provided in the pages of our present study. A translation of 3:1 that combines both aspects would read: "who has harmed you with an envious Evil Eye?"

Gerhard Delling's entry on *baskainô* in the *Theological Dictionary of the New Testament* is somewhat misleading.[351] Delling states that *baskainô* can mean "to bewitch," (involving 'harm through hostile looks") or "to revile," or "to envy." In regard to Gal 3:1, however, he says that the verb means "to bewitch (by words),[352]" claiming that this involved "real harm to the *nous* ["thinking"] of the Galatians (*anoêtoi*)."[353] "The dangerous feature is that the Galatians have willingly yielded to these magicians and their influence without realizing to what powers of falsehood they were surrendering."[354] Thomas Rakoczy, who translates, "who has hexed you with the Evil Eye?" ("Wer hat euch mit dem bösen Blick verhext?") appropriately rejects Del-

349. Although Luther translates "bezaubert" ("bewitched"), he explains that "to bewitch means to do harm with an evil look . . . the Greek word [*ebaskanen*], as Jerome attests, means not only to bewitch but also to envy [with an evil look/eye]" (*LW* 27:244).

350. BDAG *s.v.*, 171; citing, *inter alios*, Elliott 1988, 1994.

351. Delling 1964 1:594–95.

352. Ibid., 595.

353. Ibid.

354. Ibid.

ling's reduction of the meaning of *baskainô* to "bewitching *by words*" as too narrow since all exegetes in antiquity saw here a clear reference to the working of an ocular Evil Eye, i.e. a malevolent *gaze*, as illustrated by the comments of Jerome and John Chrysostom (discussed below).[355]

In their *Greek–English Lexicon*, J. P. Louw and E. A. Nida list and define *baskainô* twice, with differing translations and unsatisfactory commentary. Once they list *baskainô* (53.98)[356] under the Subdomain J ("Magic," 53.96–101) of Main Domain 53 ("Religious Activities," 53.1–105). They define *baskainô*, "to bewitch a person, frequently by use of the evil eye and with evil intent—'to bewitch, to practice magic on'" (53.98). They cite Gal 3:1 and translate, "who has bewitched you." They claim (53.98) that "*baskainô* differs from *mageuô* 'to practice magic' (53.96) in that the former involves the use of so-called 'black magic,' but for a different interpretation of *baskainô* in Ga.3.1, see 88.159." *Baskainô* is listed again (88.159)[357] under semantic Subdomain U ("Mislead, Lead Astray, Deceive" (88.152–159) of Main Domain 88 ("Moral and Ethical Qualities," 88.1–318). This definition contains no mention of "Evil Eye" but expresses the aspect of deception: "to deceive a person by devious and crafty means, with the possibility of a religious connotation in view of the literal meaning 'to bewitch' (see 53.98)—'to deceive, to bewitch, to beguile.'" Citing Gal 3:1, Louw and Nida translate: "you foolish Galatians, who has deceived you." They add, "It is also possible that *baskainô* in Ga. 3.1 is to be understood literally in the sense of bewitching by means of black magic (see 53.98)."[358]

These comments are erroneous and misleading. The verb, as we have seen, does not mean "deceive" but "harm with an Evil Eye." Nor does the act involve "black magic." No mention is made here in 3:1 of black magic or black magic's usual media (potions, elaborate utterances, formulae, objects). Nor do the ancients link the Evil Eye with black magic. Louw and Nida also fail to mention that *baskainô* is related to *ophthalmos ponêros* in that both are expressions for "Evil Eye," and that *baskainô* can also imply the involvement of the emotion of envy.

Commentators also diverge in their translations and explanations of the verb. Some judge the verb to be used metaphorically. Burton, for example, translates "bewitched," allowing for the meaning "envy," but making no reference to an Evil Eye or ocular activity and viewing "bewitched" to mean

355. Rakoczy 1996:217 n. 801.
356. Louw and Nida, *GEL* 1:545.
357. Ibid.:1:760.
358. Ibid.

"to pervert, to confuse the mind."[359] Other commentators are aware that the verb refers to the Evil Eye. Of these, some nevertheless inconsistently translate figuratively. Heinrich Schlier, for example, translates *ebaskanen* with "verzaubert" ["bewitched"], although he speaks of "bewitchment *by means of the ocular glance*," similar to Luther.[360] The implication is that "the Galatians are fascinated by a [demonic] power and are about to fall victim to it."[361] In the light of our previous discussion, however, it is more likely that Paul has in mind not an an Evil-Eyed *demon* but Evil-Eyed *humans* who are harming the Galatians, as 4:17–18 indicate. Hans Dieter Betz knows that originally the verb referred to the Evil Eye,[362] but translates "bewitched," reckoning that *ebaskanen* is "used figuratively."[363] However, the support he gives for this opinion is a statement of Socrates (Plato, *Phaedo* 95b), which he translates "My friend, . . . do not be boastful lest some *evil eye* put to rout that argument that is to come." Betz's correct translation of Plato with "evil eye" unfortunately does not influence his translation of Paul ("bewitched").[364] Others assuming a metaphorical sense also are inconsistent in their choices.[365]

359. Burton 1921:142–44. See also Bligh 1969:227; Lührmann (1978 ad loc.): "verzaubert." Paul Althaus (1962:23) takes the verb to refer go "dämonische Zauber" ["demonic magic"]; likewise Arnold 2005:446, although he correctly sees that "the implied subject [of the verb] is Paul's Jewish-Christian opponents" [2005:446 n. 65]). Derrett (1995:71 n. 9) appears to favor "bewitch" and does not include Gal 3:1 in his list of Evil Eye texts in the New Testament (1995:68–69).

360. Schlier 1962:118.

361. Ibid.:119.

362. Betz 1979:121, 131 n. 31.

363. See also Longnecker 1990:100; contrast, however, Longnecker 1999:94 for a more reasonable conclusion.

364. Betz also faults Schlier for emphasizing "the magical element" over what Betz considers its strictly rhetorical force (1979:131). Betz regards both *ebaskanen* and the reference to the Galatians' "eyes" (3:1b) as "from the rhetorical tradition" (1979:131), and apparently not from folk belief and practice concerning the Evil Eye. He claims that the verb was generally employed "to characterize opponents and their sophistic strategies." The verb, he opines, suggests "something 'irrational'" happening to the Galatians to cause their abandonment of Paul's original proclamation (1979:132). This notion, however, focuses too narrowly on use of the verb in intellectual debates, overlooking the more frequent employment of this and other terms of the *bask-* word family to denote an actual Evil Eye and its malignant power.

365. See. e.g., Ridderbos 1957 ad loc. Bruce (1982:148) gives as possible meanings "fascinate" or "bewitch (originally by means of the evil eye)," but implausibly prefers the translation "who has hypnotized you?" S. Williams (1997:83) renders "has cast a spell on you," even though stating that "Paul uses a verb (*baska[i]nein*) that, in the classical Mediterranean world, means to harm someone through the 'evil eye'" (1997:83). He regards the verb not as an Evil Eye accusation but as "a suggestive metaphor underscoring

There are, however, commentators that do translate with expressions referring to the Evil Eye, sometimes also discussing its implications. J. B. Lightfoot translated *ebaskanen* with "fascinated" as well as "bewitchment."[366] He saw the verb deriving "from the popular belief in the power of the evil eye." This implied both the "baleful influence on the recipient [the Galatians]" and the "envious spirit of the agent [the "Judaizers"]." Jerome Neyrey points out that the Evil Eye belief manifest in Gal 3:1 is a typical feature of Paul's witchcraft society and opines that the verb implies an act of bewitchment. "Paul is using it [*ebaskanen*] in its formal sense as an accusation that someone has bewitched the Galatians."[367] The classicist Thomas Rakoczy includes Gal 3:1 in his recent discussion of Evil Eye texts in the ancient world and, as we have noted, translates "who has hexed you with an Evil Eye?" ("wer hat euch mit dem bösen Blick verhext?")[368] My proposal, "who has injured you with an (envious) Evil Eye," presented in a series of articles,[369] is a literal rendition of the verb and has been accepted by a number of scholars.[370] Explicit mention of "Evil Eye" is also preferred by others,[371] although occasionally with some unconvincing accompanying comments.[372]

---

how inexplicable, unreasonable, and deleterious is their yielding to the preachments of the agitators" (ibid.). Martyn also translates "cast a spell" (1997:5, 282) although he similarly explains that *baskainô* means "'to bewitch,' 'to put the evil eye upon.'" (1997:282 n. 5). The verb, he mistakenly claims, belongs to "the language of magic:" "the Teachers must indeed have been virtual magicians to have made the Galatians long to come under the Law . . . When Gentiles take up observance of the Law as though that were salvific, they gives themselves over to—or they return to (4:9)—a belief in magic" (1997:282–283). How observance of the Law is tantamount to a belief in magic or "falling under magic" (1997:283) Martyn does not say. The erroneous premise of this flawed "magic theory" is that the Evil Eye was deemed to be something magical, which of course it was not. As noted from the outset of this study, the ancients, when speaking of humans casting an Evil Eye, regarded the Evil Eye as a dangerous yet *natural* phenomenon and as a physical conveyer of negative emotions arising in the human heart; see Vol. 2:119–21; and in this volume, chap. 1 above. On the ambivalence of G. H. R . Horsley (1987:31) see p. 234 n. 414 below.

366. Lightfoot 1866:132.

367. Neyrey 1988a:72–73.

368. Rakoczy 1996:217.

369. Elliott 1988, 1990/2010, 2005, 2011a, 2011b, 2013.

370. See Esler 1994:20–21; 1998:219; Malina 2001:123; Nanos 2000:175, 187 ("who has cast the evil eye upon you?"); see also pp. 13, 22, 49–56, 184–91, 278, 279–83, 339); Snyder 2002:27 ("You foolish Celts! Who has given you the evil eye?"); Malina and Pilch 2006:202–3, 209–10, 359–62; Oakes 2015:100–103.

371. See Dunn 1993:151–52; Witherington 1998:200–204; Longnecker 1999:94; Cosby 2009; Oakes 2015:100.

372. Longnecker (1999:94) renders, "injure with the evil eye," but mistakenly sees this as a "charge of "sorcery" (1999:96) and an implication of "demonic spirits"

The problem with all renderings of *ebaskanen* according to a figurative or metaphorical sense rather than literally is that Bible readers are left uninformed of yet another Biblical reference to the Evil Eye. Consequently they, like many commentators, will not be aware of the explicit mention in this letter of contention over an Evil Eye, and will not be on the lookout for further references or allusions to features of Evil Eye belief and practice in the letter.

Closer to Paul's time and reflecting the thought world of antiquity, Jerome (c. 342–420 CE) and John Chrysostom (c. 347–407 CE) and, following them centuries later, Martin Luther (1483–1546), were all convinced that it was indeed the Evil Eye to which Paul was referring in Gal 3:1 and that this fascination posed a danger to children in particular. Jerome, as previously noted, rendered *ebaskanen* with *fascinavit*, the standard Latin verb for "injure with an Evil Eye." In his commentary on Galatians, he observes that the verb *baskainein* is a familiar everyday word (*verbum quotidianae sermocinationis*) and that the envier (*invidus*) is more aptly known as a *fascinator*, i.e. *baskanos*, an Evil-Eyed person.[373] Equating Evil-Eyeing and envying he recalls that

---

(1999:99). Alternately, Susan Elliott (2003 and no relation to J. H. Elliott) proposes that *ebaskanen* should be interpreted literally, but as a reference to *the Evil Eye of the Mother of the Gods*, a locally worshiped Anatolian deity. Disagreeing with John Elliott, Susan Eastman inconsistently renders *ebaskanen* "put under the curse" (2001:72) and "cast the evil eye" (2001:87). She argues, unconvincingly, that with these words Paul is invoking a supposedly Deuteronomic "curse" referring to parents casting the Evil Eye (*baskanei tôi ophthalmôi,* Deut 28:53–57, esp. vv. 54, 56) to introduce both the theme of blessing and curse (Gal 3:8–14) and the parent-child imagery of Gal 4:19–31.

Peter Oakes (2015:101–3), rejecting a figurative sense of *baskainô* (against Betz 19789:131; Witherington 1998:203; and de Boer 2011:170) takes the verb as referring to the pervasive belief in the evil eye and translates: "O foolish Galatians! Who has cast the evil eye on you—you to whom Jesus Christ was presented before your very eyes as having been crucified?!" He suspects (2015:101, 102) that 3:1 constitutes "the kind of question that is based on counterfactual irony. In that case Paul would be saying to the Galatians that, in view of their awareness of Christ's crucifixion, their behavior is so irrational that it surely cannot be explained (he says sarcastically) without [reference to] the malign effect of the evil eye. In favor of this explanation, Paul's stress here is not the nature of his opponents (as possessors of the evil eye; contra J. Elliott 2011) but on the stupidity of the Galatians." This, however, is a false alternative. The foolish behavior of the Galatians (3:1, 2–4), Paul's rhetorical question implies, was occasioned by the opponents' injuring them and their sound judgment with an Evil Eye. As an illustration of evil eye belief in biblical times, Oakes (2015:102, figure 6), presents a photograph of a block of stone from a wall of the Greek city of Thasos. It portrays a huge pair of eyes serving as an apotropaic "to ward off any evil eye that might emanate from the next town."

373. Jerome, *Comm. Gal.* (PL 26.347 §417).

> We are taught . . . that, on the one hand, the envier (*invidus*) is
> pained by the prosperity of others; on the other hand, that any-
> one possessing something precious suffers injury from another
> who casts the Evil Eye (*fascinante*), that is, who looks with envy
> (*invidente*).[374]

Jerome further recalls the traditional opinion that the Evil Eye is especially
injurious to children and causes them to suddenly grow lean, waste away,
twist about as if in pain, and sometimes to scream and cry out.[375] He finds
this relevant to the Galatians, noting that they were a young community and
so, as *children* in the faith, were especially vulnerable to the Evil Eye.[376] Paul's
calling the Galatians "my children" (4:17) also hints at their vulnerability to
the Evil Eye and his paternal concern for their well-being.

Recalling also the conventional notion that the Evil Eye causes diners
at a meal to vomit up their food,[377] Jerome describes these Galatian "children" as having been struck by an Evil Eye that caused them to "vomit up
the food of the Holy Spirit" (with which Paul had earlier fed them).[378]

Another early Christian commentator on Galatians, Marius Victorinus (fourth century CE), also sees in *ebaskanen* a reference to the Evil Eye
(*fascinum*), which he too links with envy.[379] He himself also appears to have
held the belief.[380]

As to the possible collaboration of demons in Evil Eye actions, Jerome
expresses uncertainty:

> Whether or not this is true God alone must decide. For it is
> possible that demons (*daemones*) assist with this sin. And
> whomever they spot initially busy in God's work or already well
> advanced, this one they divert from doing what is right.[381]

374. *Docemur. . . quod vel invidus aliena fecunditate crucietur, vel is in quo bona
sint aliqua,, alio fascinante, id est invidente noceatur"* (*Comm. Gal.* PL 26.347) In his
Explicatio in epistolam ad Galatas (PL 30.847) on Gal 3:1, Jerome again explains that
in the common tongue *fascinavit* signifies "envy" and quotes Wis 4:12 for illustration.

375. Jerome, *Comm. Gal.* (PL 26.347).

376. Ibid.

377. See Pseudo-Aristotle, *Prob. phys.* 20.34, 926 b21–31; Alexander of Aphrodisias, *Prob. phys.* 2.53; Prov 23:6–8; Sir 14:10; 31:12–13; cf. Rakoczy 1996:142–44.

378. Jerome, *Comm. Gal.* (PL 26.347): *et stomacho fide nauseante Spiritus Sancti
cibum evomuerint.*

379. Marius Victorinus, *In epistulam Pauli ad Galatas liber 1* (PL 8.1166–67) on Gal
3:1: *"non patiuntur fascinum, nisi qui in bono aliquo pollent, et patiuntur a malignis et
invidis"*); cf. also Ambrosiaster, *Comm. Gal.* [on 3:1] (PL 17.372).

380. So Dickie 1995:26.

381. Jerome, *Comm. Gal.* (PL 26.347).

The ancient Greek association of the Evil Eye with a demon or demons (*baskanos daimôn*)[382] was adopted by Christians in the post-biblical period, as we shall see in detail in Vol. 4, chap. 2. But it is not present here in Paul or in the Bible generally where the Evil Eye is always viewed as a *human* vice.[383] Basil the Great of Caesarea, in his homily on envy and the Evil Eye, explicitly named the Devil/Satan as the power behind human envying and Evil-Eying.[384] John Chrysostom, whose homilies are the earliest complete commentary on the letter of Galatians, sees *ebaskanen* in 3:1 implying "the malignity of a demon, whose breath had blasted their prosperous well-being."[385] However, he specifically treats the Evil Eye that injured the Galatians as a *human* malignity—the Evil-Eyed *envy* of those opposing Paul's gospel.[386] It is not the eye itself that causes injury, he explains, but the envy arising internally, flowing from the eye, and "beholding in an evil manner." His comment illustrates how he associates and equates the Evil Eye (*baskainein, baskania, ophthalmos ponêros*) and envy (*phthonos, zêlos*):

> And when you hear of envy (*phthonos*) here [*ebaskanen* in Gal 3:1] and in the Gospel [Matt 6:22–23] of an Evil Eye [*ophthalmos ponêros*], *which means the same (to auto dêlounta)*, do not suppose that the glance of the eye has any capacity to injure those who look upon it. For the eye, that is, the organ itself, cannot be evil; but Christ in that place [Matt 6:22–23] means envy [*phthonos*] by the expression [*ophthalmos ponêros*]. The function of the eye is simply to behold (*to horan*). To behold, however, in an evil manner (*to de ponêrôs horan*) belongs to a mind internally depraved . . . Because through this sense the knowledge of visible objects enters the soul, and because envy [*phthonos*], for the most part, is generated by wealth, and because wealth, political powers and their guardians are beheld by the eye, therefore he [Jesus Christ] calls the eye evil (*ponêron ophthalmon*)—not as merely beholding, but as beholding with Evil-Eyed malice (*baskanias*) spawned by some moral evil (*kata psychên ponêrias*). Therefore by the words, "who has injured you with the Evil Eye?" (*tis hymas ebaskanen*) he [Paul] implies that

382. See Vol. 2, pp. 15, 27–28, 118, 141–42; Rakoczy 1996:104–20.

383. On the Christian demonization of the Evil Eye see Rakokzy 1996:216–26. See also Vol. 4, chap. 2.

384. Basil, "Concerning Envy," *Homily* 11.4 (PG 31.379–80); cf. also earlier, Tertullian, *Virg.* 15 (PL 2.959).

385. John Chrysostom, *Hom. Gal.* (PG 61.648).

386. Chrysostom speaks often of the Evil Eye and always as an actual, known reality: see *Hom. Gen.* 14.1 (PG 53. 111); *Hom. Gen.* 1.4 (PG 54.586); *Hom. Matt.* 12.4 (PG 57.207); *Paralyt.* (PG 51.49); *Delic.* (PG 51.348); cf. Rakoczy 1996:219 n. 809.

the persons in question acted not from positive concern, not to supply defects, but to mutilate what existed [among the Galatians]. For envy (*phthonos*), far from supplying what is wanting, subtracts from what is complete, and ruins the whole. And he [Paul] speaks thusly, not as if envy (*phthonos*) had any power of itself, but meaning that those teaching these things [cf. 1:7, 9] did so from Evil-Eyed malice (*baskania*).[387]

Paul's opponents, according to Chrysostom, have cast an Evil Eye "out of envious motives," intent on ruining the Galatians. Chrysostom, like Basil, envisioned humans exercizing an Evil Eye under the influence of the Devil/Satan so that the action involved both demonic and human malignity.[388]

Jerome and John Chrysostom, however, vascillated in their personal opinions regarding the Evil Eye.[389] On the one hand, *baskania/fascinatio* denoted for them, as for all the church fathers who commented on the phenomenon, a "supernatural force, envious of good fortune, prosperity, beauty, and virtue," which they attributed to the devil.[390] When commenting on Gal 3:1, however, Jerome, like John Chrysostom, speaks of *humans* casting an Evil Eye (citing Sir 18:18; Wis 4:12; Virgil, *Ecl.* 3) as relevant to the situation in Galatia.[391] Jerome states concerning the verb *fascinavit* of Gal 3:1 that it designates not an eye that can injure but an envy that can harm:

It is not that he [Paul] knows this to be *fascinum,* which is thought to do harm. But he is using a word of everyday speech (*verbum quotidianae sermocinationis*), as we read in Proverbs [i.e. Sirach] 'the gift of an envious man (*invidi*) torments the eye (*Donum invidi cruciat oculos*)' [Sir 18:18]. The word *invidus* ("envious") among us [Latin speakers] is stated more meaningfully in Greek as *fascinator* [i.e. *baskanos,* "one who fascinates," "one who casts an Evil Eye"]. And in the Wisdom ascribed to Solomon it says, 'fascination/the Evil Eye of malice obscures what is good' (*fascinatio malignitatis obscurat bona*) [Wis 4:12].[392]

387. John Chrysostom, *Hom. Gal.* [on 3:1] (PG 61.647–48). My translation is a modification of that by G. Alexander, NPNF, vol. 13, series one, 1956:74–75.

388. Rakoczy (1996:219) sees Gal 3:1 reflecting a new development in thinking about the Evil Eye, namely, relating it to false theological teaching, as 3:2–5 and following indicate. In actuality, Paul connects the Evil Eye to the envy of the *teachers* as well as to their errant teaching.

389. On this point see Vol. 4, chap. 2.

390. Dickie 1995:30; see 1995:18–34

391. Jerome, *Comm. Gal.* [on 3:1] (PL 26.347–48 §§416–17).

392. Ibid. (PL 26.347 §417). See also Jerome's brief comment on 3:1 in *Explicatio in epistulam ad Galatas* (PL 30.847). There he also states that *fascinavit* means envy

Jerome takes these passages and terms to be referring to *envy*, which he then describes in detail:

> By these examples we have shown either that the envious person (*invidus*) is tormented by the happiness of another, or he in whom there are some good things suffers harm by one who fascinates/casts an Evil Eye (*fascinante*), that is, by one who envies (*invidiante*). It is said that the Evil-Eyer (*fascinus*) is particularly harmful to infants and the young of age and to those who do not yet leave behind a firm footprint. Accordingly, one of the pagans [Virgil] has said, 'I do not know what (Evil) Eye (*oculus*) is harming with an Evil-Eye (*fascinat*) my tender lambs.'[393]

Jerome, however, also appears to accept the notion that an Evil Eye can operate physically and cause vomiting, as Prov 23:6 and Aristotlean tradition[394] assert. For he adds concerning the Galatians that

> [i]t is as though someone has injured them with an Evil Eye (*fascinante*) and they have vomited out the food of the Holy Spirit" (*Comm. Gal.* [PL 26.348 §417–18]).

Jerome's underlining the association of the harmful Evil Eye with children, moreover, is significant for the sense of the later passage of 4:12–10, where Paul explicitly declares the Galatians to be "my little children" (4:20).[395]

Ultimately Jerome leaves the issue of the actuality of an Evil Eye unresolved, while also connecting it with demons:

> God will see whether or not it be true, since it is possible that even demons (*daemones*) are in service to this sin, turning away from good works those who they recognize have begun or have made progress in the work of God. We think that the reason he

---

(*invidia*) in the popular tongue (*per vulgi*) and also cites Wis 4:12, again treating *fascinatio* as implying envy.

393. Jerome, *Comm. Gal.* [on 3:1] (PL 26.347 §417, citing Virgil, *Ecl.* 3.103: *Nescio quis teneros oculus mihi fascinat agnos*).

394. Pseudo-Aristotle, *Prob. phys.* 20.34, 926b 20–31, discussed in Vol. 2.

395. Thomas Scheck's recent translation of Jerome's commentary on Galatians (2010) is to be welcomed. But his rendering of Jerome's references to the Evil Eye (*fascinare, fascinus, fascinatio*) in 3:1 with "bewitch," "bewitching," "witchcraft" (ibid.:112) obscures Jerome's explicit references to the Evil Eye, his equating it with envy, and associating it directly with infants and with the Galatians as vulnerable children—all in line with conventional notions of the Evil Eye. Scheck appears to be among those scholars unfamiliar with ancient Evil Eye tradition. Scheck (ibid.) also misconstrues and mistranslates Jerome's term *fascinator*, which means "one who fascinates/harms with an Evil Eye" and not "bewitched." Jerome is speaking of the *agent*, not the victim, of envy and an Evil Eye.

[Paul] has taken this example from popular thinking is that, just as the tender age is said to be harmed by the Evil Eye (*fascino*), so also the Galatians, recently born in the faith of Christ and nourished with milk, not solid food, have been injured.[396]

This ancient pagan association of the Evil Eye with a demon or demons was a notion also shared by John Chrysostom, Basil of Caesarea and the Christian church fathers in general.[397]

Jerome remained undecided on the Evil Eye as an actual phenomenon capable of causing injury. On the one hand, he denies that Paul is referring to a force that can do harm and regards *baskania* and *fascinatio* as references to envy. On the other hand, he knows and mentions instances of an Evil Eye causing harm, particularly to children, and ultimately leaves the truth of the matter to God.

John Chrysostom, on his part, denied that the eye itself is evil and instead maintained that it is envy conveyed by the eye that is damaging. Paul, Chrysostom observes,

calls the Eye Evil—not as beholding merely, but as looking enviously from some moral depravity. Therefore by the words, "Who has injured you with an Evil Eye?" he implies that the persons in question acted not from concern, not to supply defects, but to mutilate what existed. For envy, far from supplying what is wanting, subtracts from what is complete and vitiates the whole. He speaks in this manner, not as if envy had any power of itself, but to point out that those advancing these [false] teachings did so from envious motives.[398]

Even on this view, the agents are human persons not demons. Jerome and John Chrysostom treated *ebaskanen* in Gal 3:1 as a reference to envy rather than to an actual physical Evil Eye. But their stance on the physical actuality of a harmful Evil Eye remained ambiguous.[399] Ambrosiaster (later half of the fourth century CE),[400] underlines in his commentary on Galatians how

396. Jerome, *Comm. Gal.* (PL 26.347–48 §417); trans. Scheck, with modification by JHE.

397. See Rakokzy 1996:104–20, 216–26. On Greece and Rome, see Vol. 2; on post-biblical Christian texts see Vol. 4, chap. 2.

398. John Chrysostom, *Hom. Gal.* (PG 61.648), trans. G. Alexander, NPNF vol. 13, series one, 1956:74–75.

399. On Jerome, John Chrysostom, and the Church Fathers concerning the Evil Eye, see Vol. 4, chap. 2.

400. Ambrosiaster, a.k.a. Pseudo-Ambrosius, is the name given to the anonymous author of the earliest complete Latin commentary on the thirteen epistles of Paul.

the condition of the fascinated victim is caused to shift from good to evil, as from liberty to servitude:

> For everyone who is struck by an Evil Eye (*fascinatur*) crosses over from good to evil, like those who cross over from liberty and security to servitude and distress.[401]

A millennium later, the great German reformer and biblical scholar Martin Luther (1483–1546), in his Wittenberg lectures on Galatians (1519/1523 and again in 1535), devoted extensive attention to the Evil Eye and these same associations. Writing in both Latin and German, he translated *ebaskanen* (Gal 3:1) with *fascinavit* (Jerome's Vulgate rendition which he cites) and then with *bezaubert*.[402] "To bewitch [*bezaubern*], states Luther, "means to do harm with an evil look . . . the Greek word [*ebaskanen*], means not only to bewitch (*bezaubern*) but also to envy, as Jerome states" (*LW* 27:244). Like Jerome, Luther also mentioned the line from Virgil, "I do not know what (Evil) Eye (*oculus*) is Evil-Eyeing (*fascinat*) my tender lambs" (*Ecl.* 3.103), to indicate the connection of *ebaskanen*, *fascinavit* and envy. He also noted the threat that the Evil Eye poses to children, including the Galatians "who were like new-born infants in Christ." Whereas Jerome questioned whether Paul actually believed in such "witchcraft," Luther affirmed its reality for both the apostle and himself:

> Paul does not deny that witchcraft exists and is possible; for later on, in the fifth chapter (5:20) he also lists 'sorcery,' which is the same as witchcraft [*sic*], among the works of the flesh. Thereby he proves that witchcraft and sorcery exist and are possible. (*LW* 26:190)

Luther considered witchcraft and the Evil Eye as realities in his own day.

> As I have said, I believe that with God's permission those witches, with the aid of devils, are really able to harm little infants for the punishment of unbelievers and the testing of believers, since, as is evident from experience, they also work many other kinds of harm in the bodies of men as well as of cattle and everything. And I believe that the apostle was not unaware of this. (*LW* 27:245)

---

401. Ambrosiaster, *Comm. Gal.* [on 3:1] (PL 17.372a). *Omnis enim qui fascinatur, de bono transit in malum, sicut et hi de libertate et securitate ad servitium et sollicitudinem transierunt.*

402. Luther, *Lectures on Galatians*, LW 27:243–45; WA 8:1945–1951; also the lectures of 1519/1523: LW 26:189–98; WA 40:309ff.

Citing experiences from his own time, Luther comments on the illness of children caused by the Evil Eye:

> This, I believe, is the ailment of little infants that our women-folk commonly call *die elbe* or *das hertzgespan*, in which we see infants wasting away, growing thin, and being miserably tormented, sometimes wailing and crying incessantly. The women, in turn, try to counter this ailment with I know not what charms and superstition; for it is believed that such things are caused by those jealous [JHE: actually "envious"] and spiteful old hags if they envy some mother her beautiful baby." (*LW* 27:244)[403]

The Galatians, according to Luther echoing Jerome, also are injured children, vulnerable infants that have fallen victim to the advocates of the Mosaic Law. Paul accuses these advocates of being Evil-Eyed bewitchers in league with Satan (*LW* 26:194, 197). In contrast to these false apostles, according to Luther, Paul implies that "we are laboring both by exhortation and by writing to break the spell with which the false apostles have bound you, so that those among you who have been taken captive by this bewitchment many be set free by us." Luther perceives in Gal 3:1 an implied contrast between the false teachers and Paul's own mission, a contrast that will reappear in 4:12–20.

Writing on the Evil Eye within decades of Luther's death, Leonardus Vairus (1540–1603), bishop of Pozzuoli, Italy, in his essay, *De fascino* (Paris, 1583), also reckons with the reality of the Evil Eye. He comments on Gal 3:1:

> Let no man laugh at these stories [about the Evil Eye/fascination] as old wives' tales (*aniles nugas*); nor, because the reason passes our knowledge, let us turn them into ridicule. For infinite are the things which we cannot understand (*infinita enim prope sunt, quorum rationem adipisci nequimus*). Rather than turn all miracles out of Nature because we cannot understand them, let us make that fact the beginning and reason of investigation. For does not Solomon in his Book of Wisdom say, '*Fascinatio malignitatis obscurant bona* [For the Evil Eye of wickedness obscures the good]' [Wis 4:12] and does not Dominus Paulus cry out to the Galatians, '*O insensate Galatae, quis vos fascinavit?* [O uncomprehending Galatians, who has injured you with an envious Evil Eye?]' [Gal 3:1] which the best interpreters admit to refer

---

403. As a further example of satanic bewitchment, Luther mentions the tragic suicide of his contemporary, Dr. Krause of Halle (*LW* 26:195–96).

to those whose burning eyes (*oculos urentes*) with a single look blast all persons, and especially boys?"[404]

Vairus regards the Evil Eye as a phenomenon of nature whose malignity is attested repeatedly in the biblical tradition. Similarly in accord with ancient lore, he understands the Evil-Eyeing of which Paul speaks to involve burning eyes injuring victims, particularly children.

In more recent time J. B. Lighfoot has pointed out that *baskainein*, fascinating with an Evil Eye, involves both "the baleful influence on the recipient and the envious spirit of the agent" (1866:132), with noxious effect especially on children, as Jerome stressed centuries ago. The link of Evil Eye and envy, as we have seen, is conventional and in the case of Gal 3:1 has long been suspected.[405]

In sum, conventional ancient usage of the verb *baskainô* and the understanding of its meaning and connotations in the ancient church and for centuries thereafter constitute a solid basis for rendering *ebaskanen* in Gal 3:1 with "injured with an envious Evil Eye."[406]

The immediate literary context of *ebaskanen* also supports the verb as a reference to the Evil Eye, when we keep in mind elements of the Evil Eye complex as indicated by Jerome and John Chrysosom.

(1) Paul follows up this reference to Evil Eye (3:1a) with a striking reference to the "eyes" of the Galatians: "(you) before whose very eyes (*ophthalmois*) Jesus Christ was portrayed as crucified" (3:1b). Even though Paul in his previous proclamation had painted before their eyes a vivid picture of the crucified Christ, the Galatians fell easy victim to the envious Evil Eye of the false teachers and their deceptive "gospel." It is true that this formulation of 3:1b underlines the "vividness with which Paul had initially presented the Crucified One."[407] It is also true that the ancients held the eyes to be the chief organ for confirming the truth of something—"seeing is believing." It is, however, also the case that in Paul's day various objects were employed as

---

404. Translation by Story 1877:152.

405. For *ebaskanen* implying envy see also Bligh 1969:227; Nanos 2002:186, 187, 191, 279–80, pointing out the relative social parity of Paul and his opponents, a condition typical of incidents of envy (Aristotle, *Rhet.* 2.10.1–2; Cicero, *De or.* 2.52.209; Hagedorn and Neyrey 1998:27–28).

406. Opperwall (1982:210) is representative of those scholars who interpret *ebaskanen* only "firguatively to denote the Galatians' captivation by the falsehood into which the Judaizers had led them."

407. Williams 1997:83. Martyn 1997:281 aptly translates: "in spite of the fact that in my sermons a picture of Jesus Christ marked by crucifixion was painted before your eyes."

amulets to ward off the power of the Evil Eye.[408] Paul could be alluding here to that practice. In late antiquity a Christian adaptation of the Greco-Roman apotropaic practice involved holding up a crucifix and fixing one's eyes on it as defense against an Evil Eye. One inscription, for example, asserts that the *ophthalmos baskanos* loses its power in the presence of the cross's power.[409] It has been suggested that Paul may be implying something similar here:[410] the fixing of your eyes on the cross should have defended you against the Evil Eye—so how could you have fallen victim to its harmful power?[411] Independently, Bruce Malina and John Pilch (2006:202) make a similar point:

> Paul continues the evil eye allusion by noting that it was before the Galatians' *eyes* 'that Jesus Christ was publicly exhibited as crucified.' This sight should have forearmed them against the evil eye of others. These others are those who would have the Galatians follow Mosaic Torah. They are envious of the gospel that the Galatians have accepted and the behavior entailed by that proclamation . . . [S]omehow they have been made oblivious to what faith in God who raised Jesus effected, something that an evil eye hexing can obviously do![412]

There also was a notion that harm from an Evil Eye could be avoided by not looking into the eye of the fascinator (an aspect of the Medusa/Gorgo myth).[413] It is possible that Paul, with this stress on the Galatians' *eyes,* was intimating that if they had steadfastly kept their eye fastened on the Crucified One, they would not have fallen victim to an Evil Eye. In any event, this emphasis on *eyes* makes sense with the *Evil Eye* notion lurking in the background.[414] Mention of an Evil *Eye* sparks a mention of *eyes,* just as it

---

408. On anti-Evil Eye amulets in the Greco-Roman world see Vol. 2, pp. 217–64, and for studies Vol. 2, pp. 158 n. 525.

409. See Bartelink 1983:394.

410. See Racokzy 1996:217 n. 801.

411. See also Lightfoot 1866:133; Bligh 1969:227. On the cross as apotropaic in later time see John Chrysostom, *Catech. illum.* (PG 49.246); *De adoratione pretiosae crucis* (PG 58.838); *Hom. Eph.* (PG 62.357–59); ses also Dölger, *Antike und Christentum* 1932 3:81–116.

412. Malina and Pilch 2006:202–3. On the connection of Evil Eye and envy, see also ibid.:361–62; also Malina 2001:108–33.

413. On this myth, see the comments on Medusa/Gorgo in Vol. 2.

414. G. H. R . Horsley (1987:31), although claiming that at Gal 3:1 "Paul uses the verb [*baskanen*] there figuratively," nevethess aptly observes that "it cannot be doubted that he is entirely alert to its association with the evil eye, in view of his inclusion of the words *kat' ophthalmous* in the following vivid clause."

does later where Paul speaks of the Galatians' tearing out their *eyes* on Paul's behalf as proof of their not treating him as an Evil-Eyed stranger (4:15).

(2) Paul's address of his readers here as *anoêtoi Galata* (3:1a) also relates to his concern about an Evil Eye. This is a second rebuke of the Galatians and of those confusing them, expanding on that of 1:6–9. His vivid portrayal of the crucified Christ before their very eyes (3:1b) should have inured them to damage from the Evil Eye of the false teachers. But they were *anoêtoi* (3:1a), says Paul—uncomprehending and immature and hence especially vulnerable to the power of the Evil Eye. This is a point underscored by Jerome and Luther. The adjective *anoêtoi* can mean "unintelligent, foolish, or dull-witted."[415] In this context, it means not so much "foolish" or "stupid," as "lacking in experience, knowledge, wisdom, and good sense"[416]—as is the case with infants—and uncomprehending as to who posed a danger to them. Gerhard Delling perceptively asks, "does *anoêtoi* mean that, like children, those addressed have proved incapable of resisting the *baskanos*?"[417] Indeed, the adjective likely gives the reason that his readers succumbed to an Evil Eye: as recent converts to the gospel, they were *inexperienced and unsuspecting* and so fell victim to certain Evil-Eyed persons as infants are wont to do. Their immaturity and naivete in the faith allowed their easy deception by the false teachers, along with their credulous acceptance of the teachers' charge that Paul was their enemy and with his gospel was trying to dazzle them with flattery (1:10) and untruths (5:11–12). These are among the accusations that Paul's letter aims to refute. This infantile naiveté and vulnerability is consistent with Paul's later addresseeing them explicitly as "my children" in 4:19. Jerome explains that it was their being *children* in the faith that made them so vulnerable, for children were considered most in danger of Evil Eye attack.[418] "If they had been grown-ups, walking steadily along the path of the true faith, they would not have succumbed to this fascination."[419] *Anoêtoi* "does not mean that they do not 'know,' but that they do not understand the implications of what they 'should' know."[420] In this connection, Jerome also describes the *effect* of their having been Evil-Eyed: "they vomited up the food of the Holy Spirit," so to speak. Behind his com-

415. BDAG, 84. In Rom 1:14 the adjective is paired with *aphrôn* ("lacking good sense") and opposed to "wise" (*sophos*); cf. also Prov 17:28 and *ô anoête* (Philo, *Dreams* 2.181).

416. See Lightfoot 1866:132: "senseless."

417. Delling 1964:595 n. 12.

418. Jerome, *Comm. Gal.* on 3:1 (PL 26.347–48 §417). On children as chief victims of the Evil Eye see Vol. 2, and in this volume, pp. 107, 225

419. Bligh 1969:227.

420. Nanos 2002:46 n. 51.

ment is the notion, discussed earlier in this study, that an Evil Eyed person can cause diners to vomit up their food.[421]

The second relevant aspect of the direct address of 3:1 is the identification of the addressees as "Galatians."[422] *Galatai* is a variant form of *Keltai* or *Keltoi*, "Celts" (in Latin, *Galli* = "Gauls"); see the cognates Gallia, Galicia, and Wales, for example, as regions settled by the Celts. Those who had settled in this central-northern Anatolian region (of modern-day Turkey) to which they gave their name ("Galatia") were Celtic tribes (primarily the Trocmi, the Tectosages, and the Tolistobogii) who had migrated eastward from Gaul (modern France) to Anatolia in the late third century BCE.[423] Paul, perhaps with Silvanus (according to Acts), first visited Galatia on an extended journey from Antioch through Asia Minor and Greece, returning eventually to Antioch.[424] Along with those with him, he sent this letter "to the churches of Galatia" (1:2) soon after having evangelized there.[425] In later time, a westward migration took the Celts to Spain (Galicia) and the British isles.

It is interesting that Paul's one explicit reference to the Evil Eye in all his extant correspondence is in a letter addressed to Celts who have had a long history of interest in the Evil Eye down to the modern period.[426] Graydon Snyder, writing on the formation of early Irish Christianity, has traced migrations of the Celts from Gaul (modern France) eastward to Anatolia, the Christianization of some there by Paul, and then their movement westward to Spain (cf. Galicia) and northward to Ireland and Scotland, with Gaelic as their modern tongue.[427] This Celtic *Völkerwanderung* provided one of the durable transmission routes of Evil Eye belief and practice in the

421. See Pseudo-Aristotle, *Prob. phys.* 20.34; Prov 23:6–8; see Vol. 2 and above, pp. 35–37.

422. See also Gal 1:2: "to the churches of Galatia." The "you" of 3:1a is a 2nd person plural pronoun with "Galatians" as its antecedent.

423. On the Celts in Anatolia see Mitchell 1993.

424. For Luke's account of the journey see Acts 15:36—18:22, esp. 16:6. Paul refers to the initial visit in Gal 4:13.

425. See Gal 1:6. The letter thus was written either on the so-called "second" (Acts 15:36—18:22, c. 53 CE) or "third" missionary journey (Acts 18:23—21:16, c. 55 CE) shortly after the visit reported in Acts 16:6 or 18:23. The churches are not associated with specific cities, contrary to other letters of Paul. This is consistent with the predominantly rural nature of this area of Galatia and its minimal urbanization. On Galatia, see Mitchell, *Anatolia*, vol. 1 and 2:3–51; Elliott 2000:87–88.

426. See Mackenzie 1895; Carmichael 1900; MacLagan 1902; Henderson 1910; MacCorkill 1925; Krappe 1927; Davidson 1949; Dillon and Chadwick 1967; Borsje 2012; and Manco 2015.

427. Snyder 2002.

western part of the ancient Circum-Mediterranean world. Snyder is one of the few scholars to recognize Paul's reference to the Evil Eye and connect it with the Celtic identity of the addressees.[428] He translates 3:1a: "You foolish Celts! Who has given you the evil eye?"[429] Down to the modern period, Evil Eye belief and practice has remained strong in Ireland and Scotland, especially in its rural areas.[430]

(3) Various scholars have read *ebaskanen* as implying envy. Given what we know of the close association of envy with the Evil Eye, this is likely in the context of this letter. An appropriate translation would then be, "who has injured you with an envious Evil Eye?" This, in turn, would constitute a further connection of 3:1 with 4:12–20, where in 4:17–18 Paul denounces the envy (envious Evil Eye) of his opponents.[431]

(4) The rhetorical nature of Paul's question in 3:1 implies that Paul has an answer in mind as to who was Evil-Eyeing the Galatians. In 4:17 he provides that answer: it is those teaching a gospel different from Paul's who are harming the Galatians with their Evil-Eyed envy.

These connections of 3:1 to 4:12–20, which we consider in detail below, point to a larger context which supports the conclusion that in 3:1 Paul is making clear that part of the social dynamic involving himself and his opponents concerns the accusation that someone has injured the Galatians with an Evil Eye. In the light of 4:12–20, it becomes clear that his question in 3:1 is in fact an implied Evil Eye accusation directed against his opponents.[432] The singular subject of the verb *ebaskanen* refers most likely not to a single individual (acting as representative) but to Paul's rivals as one group all collectively casting an Evil Eye.[433]

Paul does not state explicitly what injury by the Evil Eye he envisions, but it can be surmised from details of the context: It would have included

428. Ibid.:2002:23–45.

429. Snyder 2002:27; see also ibid.:44 n. 10, referring to, *inter alios*, Elliott 1990; Perkins 2001:1–3. See earlier Lightfoot 1866:132: "O ye senseless Gauls . . ."

430. On the Celts see also the informative study of Brigitte Kahl 2010.

431. The translation of Lightfoot (1866:132), while rendering *ebaskanen* with "bewitchment" rather than "Evil Eye," nevertheless includes expressions ("withering eye," "fascination," "envious gaze") indicating that Lightfoot is certain that Evil Eye malice is implied here: "O ye senseless Gauls, what bewitchment is this? I placarded Christ crucified before your eyes. You suffered them to wander from this gracious proclamation of your King. They rested on the withering eye of the sorcerer. They yielded to the fascination and were rivetted there. And the life of your souls has been drained out of you by that envious gaze."

432. Elliott 1990, 2005:159–64; so also Neyrey 1988a; Longnecker 1999:93–97; Nanos 2002:187–88.

433. Nanos (2002:187–188) raises and comments aptly on this point.

a misleading of the Galatians to reject Paul's gospel (1:6–9) resulting in a loss of the surety of salvation they had been promised because of their trust in Jesus Christ as God's Messiah.[434] Losing their freedom in Christ entailed a (re)submission to requirements of the Mosaic law (3:2–5; 4:21) including circumcision (5:1–5, 11; 6:12–15), dietary restrictions (2:11–14), and particular calendaric observation (4:8–10). Their loss also would have included a reassertion of barriers between Judeans and Greeks, males and females, slaves and free persons (3:28), the fomenting of rival factions (1:6–9; 2:11–14; 5:20–21), debilitating envying (4:17–18; 5:21, 26), and a vicious "devouring one another" within the churches (5:15, 26). The object of the envy transmitted by the Evil Eye of Paul's opponents, as the context indicates, would have included the Galatians' reception of the Spirit, the working of powerful deeds among them (3:3, 5; 5:5, 16–19, 22–26), and the freedom in Christ they enjoyed (5:1, 13).

When Paul turns from accounting for himself and his understanding of the gospel and its practical implications (1:10—2:21) to the troubling condition of the Galatians, his first move, we have seen, is to ask who has injured them with an envious Evil Eye (3:1). He then immediately directs attention to the moment when he first visited the Galatians and their initial reception of the Spirit of God (3:2–5). He returns to a review of that initial meeting of his with the Galatians in 4:12–16. Thus 3:1–5 and 4:12–16 are related to each other as recollections of what occurred at the initial meeting of Paul and Galatians. A closer look at the more inclusive unit of 4:12–20 reveals that 3:1 and 4:12–20 are related by refererences to the Evil Eye as well.

Beyond Galatians 3:1—The Evil Eye as Subtext in 4:12–20

Paul's agitated response to the confusion and vascillation on the part of the Galatians from 3:1 onward includes a section in which he returns to the issue of the Evil Eye, namely 4:12–20. Here, for the purpose of self-vindication,[435] he recalls his intimate and positive relation to the Galatians from the outset and criticizes those whom he holds responsible for enviously Evil-Eyeing

---

434. In 3:1, the additional words in some manuscripts (C D^c K L P Psi most minuscules vg^cl syr^h goth eth, others, Textus Receptus), "to not obey the truth" (*têi alêtheiai mê peithesthai*), are a secondary addition influenced by 5:7 (cf. Metzger et al. 1994:524) and state a sense of the damage. The words *tis hymas* occurring in 5:7 as well as in 3:1 perhaps prompted certain scribes to see a connection between the two verses and so to add these words of 5:7 at 3:1.

435. "Apologia," as John Chrysostom calls it (*Hom. Gal.*, PG 61.659).

238 Beware the Evil Eye

the Galatians.[436] The explicit mention of the Evil Eye in 3:1 is the exposed tip of a submerged iceberg.

4:12–20: CONTEXT AND CONTENT

In 4:12–20 Paul turns from the major theological issue of the freedom of the Galatian believers from the law and slavery (4:1–7, resumed in 4:21–30, 5:1) and their deplorable resubmission to the law (4:8–11) to a reflection on the kinship in Christ shared by the Galatians and Paul since they first met. The section 4:12–20 forms a unit of thought whose content is distinct from what precedes (4:8–11) and follows (4:21–31). The section opens with a direct address of the addressees, "brothers (and sisters in the faith)," which affirms the intimate kin-like degree of their relationship (4:12), as it does repeatedly in the letter (1:11, 3:15; 4:28, 31; 5:11, 13; 6:1, 18). The section closes with Paul addressing the Galatians with another intimate term of kinship, "my children" (v. 19).[437]

Paul recalls here the affectionate reception the Galatians initially lavished on Paul when he first visited them (vv. 14c–15). He expresses puzzlement over their present relationship (v. 16). He levels an accusation against persons troubling and envying the Galatians (vv. 17–18) and follows this with a declaration of his own intense devotion to the Galatians (v. 19) and his wish to be present with them (v. 20). The difficult matters that Paul addresses here—his defense against false charges (4:13–15), his new prickly relationship with the Galatians (4:15a, 16) and his condemnation of his opponents (4:17)—are set within a positive frame (vv. 12, 19–20) that affirms the bond still uniting Paul and his addressees.

> 12b [When I first visited you] you did me no wrong. 13 You know that it was because of a bodily ailment that I first preached the gospel to you; 14 and although my condition was a trial to you, you did not scorn or spit (*exeptusate*), but welcomed me as an angel of God, as [you did] Christ Jesus. 15 What has become of the good will you felt? For I testify that, had it been possible, you would even have ripped out your own eyes (*tous*

436. Nanos's outline of the letter (2002:71–72) captures well the connection between 1:6–9 (initial "ironic rebuke and theme applied to exigence"), its restatement in 3:1–5 (second ironic rebuke and restatement of theme), and 4:12–20 ("ironic appeal to previous experience of theme")—each of the passages constituting situational rather than narrative or transition material.

437. On Paul's customary fictive kinship language see Bossman 1996:163–71; Bartchy 1999.

ophthalmous hymôn) and given them to me. 16 Have I now become your enemy in telling you the truth?

17 They [my opponents and detractors] envy (*zêlousin*)
you—but not for a good reason (*ou kalôs*) (v. 17a); they want
to exclude you (v. 17b) in order that you [are forced to] envy
(*zêlousin*) them (v. 17c). 18 It is always good (*kalon*), however,
to be envied (*zêlousthai*) for a good reason (*en kalôi*)" (v. 18a),
and not only when I am present with you (v. 18b).

19 My children (*tekna mou*), with whom I am again in
birth pangs until Christ be formed in you, 20 I wish I could be
present with you now and change my tone, for I am perplexed
about you. (JHE trans.)

Addressing the Galatians as "brothers (and sisters)" (v. 12), Paul recalls that when he first brought to them the good news, he was suffering
some kind of illness or physical imparement or disfigurement (*astheneian
tês sarkos*, v. 13). Along with his being a stranger, this malady tested (*peirasmon*) the Galatians as to their welcoming him or turning him away (v. 14).
In actuality, Paul stresses, their reception was most positive. They did him
no wrong (v. 12b); they did not disdainfully reject him or spit (v. 14a). To
the contrary, "you received me as a messenger/angel from God, as [you did]
Christ Jesus" (v. 14b). "You would even have ripped out your eyes and given
them to me" (v. 15). Wondering "what has become of your good will toward
me" (v. 15a), he then asks rhetorically if the Galatians now regard him as
their enemy for having told them the truth (v. 16). At this point he turns
the spotlight on his opponents as the real enemies of the Galatians. He accuses them of envying the Galatians for their new freedom in Christ and of
mistreating them for their [the opponents'] own selfish ends (vv. 17–18). In
contrast to these envious false teachers, Paul assures his readers, he, Paul,
cares for them as "my children" in whom, or among whom, Christ is still
being given shape in their lives by God (v. 19). Perplexed at recent developments in Galatia, Paul yearns to rejoin them and assume a more positive
tone (v. 20).

In this section, most commentators note, Paul's language is elusive,
leaving much that is implied but unstated. This has created much room for
divergent translations and differing opinion concerning the intended sense
and even the intended grammer of this text segment. Some commentators
present interpretive options rather than asserting one interpretation as final.
What I offer here is, in my estimation, a plausible scenario involving an Evil
Eye charge that underlies these verses and that harks back to Paul's earlier
reference to the Evil Eye in 3:1 The plausibility of this proposal rests on a
complex of five items present here, each of which is associated with Evil Eye

belief and practice. Responding to an accusation of his opponents that he has Evil-Eyed the Galatians, Paul defends himself and accuses them of injuring the Galatians with their Evil-Eyed envy. In appealing to the behavior of the Galatians when they first met Paul (4:12c–14, 15b), the apostle refers to the same point in time mentioned earlier in 3:1b ("before whose eyes Jesus Christ was publicly portrayed as crucified") and in the further rhetorical questions of 3:2–4. In 4:12–20 he picks up the issue of the Evil Eye introduced in 3:1. Some scholars, including Luther, have noticed the connection of 4:12–20 with 3:1.[438] To my knowledge, however, my publications on the Evil Eye and this present monograph are the first to argue that 4:12–20 contains several allusions to the Evil Eye which relate this unit to 3:1 and point to a social dynamic of Evil Eye accusation and counter-accusation.[439]

These verses raise several tantalizing questions. Why is Paul's tone so defensive in vv. 12c–16? Is he responding to some accusation brought against him? Why does he make such an odd mention of the Galatians' "not spitting" when they first met (v. 14)? Why his hyperbolic comment about their "ripping out their eyes" (v. 15c). To what behavior is v. 17 referring? Why does Paul call the Galatians his "children" (v. 19)? To what form of social interaction might these phenomena be pointing? Can all these individual "dots" be connected? The answer, we shall see, is that it is Evil Eye belief and practice that helps connect these dots.

In 4:12b–15 Paul reminds his Galatian readers of their behavior toward him when they met for the first time. He mentions two unusual actions: they did not *spit* (but received him as a messenger from God), and (2) they would have *ripped out their eyes* and given them to Paul.

As to the first, "You did not spit" is the literal meaning of *oude exeptusate*, although this is not evident in most modern biblical translations and commentaries.[440] Some translations and commentators add "me" as object of the verbs *exouthenêsate* ("despise") and *exeptusate,* but "me" is not present in the original Greek. If it had been present, it would be impossible for *exeptusate* to mean "spit" because "you did not spit me" would make no sense. Addition of "me" in the translation, on the other hand, makes it easier

438. Luther (*Lectures on Galatians*, 1519, 1535) proposes that Paul's praise of the Galatians in 4:12–20 was meant to balance the censure of them expressed in 3:1–5. Nanos (2002:71–72) sees a structural connection, as noted above. Longnecker (1999:97–99, 105) also recognizes the connection of 4:12–20 to 3:1, but misses the allusions to the Evil Eye linking this unit (4:12–20) to the explicit mention of the Evil Eye in 3:1.

439. Those accepting and following my proposal (1988, 1990) include Nanos 2002:186, 190–91, and Malina and Pilch 2006:209–10, 362.

440. This is the sole occurrence of this compound verb in the LXX and NT. The words are lacking in Papyrus 46.

to imagine and accept the sense of *ouk exeptusate* as "you did not *reject* me. "Spit" requires no addition of "me" and makes good sense once the Evil Eye implications of this verb are understood.

The Vulgate *neque respuistis,* "nor did you spit," literally reproduces the Greek, as do a few later translations.[441] The majority of modern Bible Versions, however, render an assumed sense of the verb: *reject, despise, loathe, treat with scorn; show contempt, revulsion* etc.[442]

The Greek verb *ptuô* and its compound forms (*apoptuô, ekptuô, emptuô, epiptuô, proptuô*), denote various forms of spitting (spitting, spitting out, spitting on or into the face of, spitting on the ground etc.). The action noun *emptusma* ("spitting"), *ptuelos* ("spit," "spittle"), and *ptusma* ("spittle") are also part of this large word family that appears in both the LXX and the New Testament.[443] Spitting entails not only a physical expulsion of saliva but also a dramatic gesture. One *gesture* of spitting expresses in biblical cultures a *feeling* such as defiance, scorn, contempt, repulsion and the like.[444] The verbs meaning "to spit" could also asume a figurative sense: *disapprove, dislike, despise, disdain, scorn, reject, condemn, show contempt, put to shame* etc. Spit and spittle also were thought to have curative power[445] so that spit and spitting were employed to heal by Greeks, Romans and Israelites alike.[446] Spitting also was practiced to ward off demons and evil spirits as part of the healing process or to prevent their damage of others. It was employed as protection against those having fits and epileptic seizures in particular.[447]

441. See Luther 1984 edition: "nicht . . . vor mir ausgespuckt"; Zink: "nicht vor mir ausgespien").

442. Luther (1545 ed.) : *noch verschmähet.* In his *Lectures on Galatians,* paraphrasing 4:14, he translates, "(not) spat on me" (*LW* 26:421).

443. For Hebrew see *yaraq* (verb, "spit"); *roq* (noun, "spittle"). The equivalent word family in Latin includes *spuo, adspuo, conspuo, despuo, inspuo, respuo, sputo, insputo.* Latin *saliva* = saliva; *sputum* ("spittle"); cf. also English *spew;* German, *speien.*

444. See Num 12:14; Deut 25:9; Job 17:6; 30:10; Isa 50:6; Mark 10:34; Mark 14:65/ Matt 26:67; Mark 15:19/Matt 27:30; Luke 18:32.

445. Pliny, *NH* 28.35–39.

446. See Pliny, *NH* 26.69 and in the New Testament, Mark 7:33; 8:23; and John 9:6. Vespasian is reported to have cured a blind man with his spittle (Tacitus, *Hist.* 4.81; Suetonius, *Vesp.* 7; Dio Cassius, *Hist.* 65.8). The third century CE text of Christian rites and practices at Rome, the *Apostolic Tradition,* records how spitting was employed by Christians to purify the body, with saliva compared to the sanctifying water of baptism: "For when it [saliva] is offered with a believing heart, just as from the font, the gift of the Spirit and the sprinkling of washing sanctifies him who believes" (*Apost. Trad.* 41.17). On the actual and metaphorical aspects of saliva see Nicholson 1897; Elbogen 1916; on saliva charms see Bergen 1890, also Vol. 2: 174–78.

447. See Theophrastus, *Char.* 16.14; Pliny, *NH* 10.23, 33.

Finally, spitting, as we have seen in Vol. 2, was practiced frequently to ward off a specific form of evil, namely an Evil Eye.[448] "We Romans," noted Pliny,

> spit (*despuimus*) on epileptics (*comitiales morbos*), in this way repelling the contagion. Similarly, [by spitting] we ward off Evil Eyeing (*fascinationes*) and the evil that follows from meeting a person who is lame in the right leg. (Pliny, *NH* 28.35)

The Greeks likewise spat for protection against the Evil Eye (Theocritus, *Idylls* 6.39). Since strangers were deemed potential bearers of an Evil Eye, spitting was customary in their presence. Spitting was used to protect children in particular from the Evil Eye. Pliny observes:

> Upon the entrance of a stranger, or when a person looks at an infant while asleep, it is usual for the nurse to spit three times upon the ground (*adspui*) [or in the baby's face, *despui* as a variant], even though infants already are under the divine protection of the god *Fascinus*. (Pliny, *NH* 28.39)

Persius, the Roman satirist and another contemporary of Paul and Nero, tells of a grandmother protecting her infant grandson against the Evil Eye (*urentis oculis*)[449] by spitting, applying saliva to his forehead and displaying a *digitus infamus*.[450] Even male adult pigeons were thought to spit on the newborn chicks to protect them against the Evil Eye.[451] Centuries after Paul, John Chrysostom deplored the fact that in the public baths Christian midwives and nurses were still applying a mixture of spittle and mud with their middle finger to the foreheads of their infants "to ward off the Evil Eye and envy" (*ophthalmon apostrephei kai baskanian kai phthonon*).[452] The practice, in fact, continues still in modern time in Greece[453] and with mothers in Tunisia.[454] Spitting, we can thus conclude, in Galatia and Paul's day was an act of protection against harm from an Evil Eye. But, Paul insists, the Galatians did not make this gesture when first meeting him, a key point in his self-defense.

---

448. On the Greco-Roman custom see Vol. 2, pp. 174–78. Theocritus, *Idylls* 6.39 (the herder Democtas spits three times on his chest to ward off the Evil Eye); 7.126–127; Pliny, *NH* 28.35, 39; Strato, *Anthologia Palatina* 12.229. On spitting among the Essenes and Qumran community see Atkinson and Magness 2010, esp. 326–29.

449. An expression indicating the scorching and withering effect of the Evil Eye.

450. Persius, *Sat.* 2.31–34; cf. also Petronius, *Sat.* 131.4.

451. Pseudo-Aristotle, Frag. 347; Athenaeus, *Deipn.* 9.394B; Aelian, *Varia hist.* 1.15.

452. John Chrysostom, *Hom. 1 Cor.* 12.7 (PG 61.106).

453. Jahn 1855:82 n. 223.

454. Teitelbaum 1976:64.

Modern scholarly opinion on the translation of *exeptusate* in Gal 4:14 and the significance of the act diverges widely. Many commentators render only the *assumed sense* of the Greek verb with no mention of its literal meaning: "you did not depise, reject, show contempt" etc.[455] Others (e.g., Betz, Bruce, Martyn) acknowledge that the verb means "spit (out)" with possible apotropaic overtones, but still translate it according to an assumed sense: "reject," "despise."[456]

Still others translate the verb literally, "spit (out)" and explain that spitting was an apotropaic maneuver to protect oneself against evil spirits and demons thought to cause illness. Heinrich Schlier, for example, insists emphatically that *exeptusate*

> is not used here in the metaphorical sense of 'to expose,' 'to despise,' 'to reject' etc., but quite literally in the sense of the ancient gesture of spitting out as a defense against sickness and other demonic threats. The Galatians resisted the temptation to see in Paul someone demoniacally possessed because of his sickness, but received him as an angelic manifestation, indeed, as Christ Jesus himself."[457]

Schlier, Lührmann, Williams, and others mention spitting to repel evil forces thought to cause illness, but without connecting it to Evil Eye practice. More specifically and more frequently attested, however, is the act of spitting to

455. Burton (1921:242), for some undisclosed reason, considered a literal meaning of the verb an "impossibility" and prefered a "tropical meaning, 'to reject.'"

456. Betz (1979:200, 225); Longnecker (1990:192). Bruce (1982:209) allows that the verb could mean, literally, "to spit out" (as a gesture for averting the Evil Eye) or could express "a feeling or reaction of disgust or disdain" (1982:209). He too cites scholars who associate spitting with aversion of the Evil Eye and the exorcising of demons, but translates the verb "reject." See also BDAG 309, *s.v.*, but translating the verb "disdain." s.v. Although Martyn is aware that the verb means "to spit out" (1997:421), he translates the phrase *oude ekptusate* "nor regarded me with contempt." (1997:7, 418, 421) His comments, however, dwell more on spitting than on contempt. He imagines that the Galatians could have been "[t]empted to view the sick apostle as an evil magician momentarily overcome by the malignant powers he normally used to control others" and "could have reacted by spitting, hoping to cleanse their mouths of the unclean oders they inhaled at his presence" (1997:421). This leaves unexplained what might have prompted the Galatians to view Paul as "a sick and evil magician" in the first place. As for the spitting, Martyn, like many others, appears to be unfamiliar with Evil Eye belief and practice, which, with other detail of this section, offers a simpler and more elegant explanation.

457. Schlier 1962:448; see also ibid.:207, 210; Althaus 1962:36; Lührmann 1978:70, 74; Williams 1997:120. Moulton and Milligan (1930:198) note authors who think *exeptusate* is to be understood literally and that it denotes a prophylactic step taken at the sight of invalids and especially of epileptics.

repel an Evil Eye (which could be viewed as the cause of maladies, especially those concerning the eyes).[458] These scholars, however, do not connect spitting here with Evil Eye belief and practice.

Keeping in mind the fact that spitting was practiced not only to drive off evil demons in general but to repel the Evil Eye in particular, I have proposed rendering the verb literally ("you did not spit") and connecting this comment (and all of 4:12–20) with Paul's earlier reference to the Evil Eye in 3:1.[459] Malina and Pilch, accepting this proposal, note that *exeptusate* means "spit" and that "[s]pitting was a "way to protect oneself from the evil eye and its deleterious effect."[460] Paul points out, they note, that the Galatians did not fear Paul's gaze but showed him hospitality.[461]

Paul's earlier mention of the Evil Eye in 3:1 and the custom of spitting to ward off the Evil Eye, along with other allusions to the Evil Eye in 4:12–20, give a cogent basis for translating *exeptusate* literally rather than figuratively and for regarding this spitting as an apotropaic gesture for warding off the dreaded Evil Eye. Paul's point is that, when they first met, the Galatians did not spit as they customarily would have, had they suspected him of having an Evil Eye.

There are two facts about Paul that might have fed this suspicion and provoked an act of spitting. For one thing, Paul was a *stranger* when they first met, and strangers were deemed potential wielders of an Evil Eye. Second, Paul's *ailment and physical appearance* could have suggested that he had an Evil Eye.

In Evil Eye cultures, even to this day, *strangers* are suspected of having a harmful Evil Eye, so it is imperative to spit to protect oneself, one's family members, and valued possessions. Pliny the Elder, as we have seen above, comments on the custom in his own day (*NH* 28.39).[462]

---

458. Pheme Perkins (2001:1–3, 83) correctly senses that "the eye problem may have been an 'evil eye,'" but incorrectly explains the point of spitting. Spitting was not thought to "cure" the Evil Eye, as she proposes, but to ward it off.

459. Elliott 1988, 1990, 2005, 2011a, 2011b, 2013.

460. Malina and Pilch 2006:209–10, esp. 209; also Oakes (2015:146, 147) observing that "Paul's assertion that the Galatians would have given him their eyes suggests that his physical problem probably involved his eyes. A disfigurement relating to one or both eyes would incline a Mediterranean audience to view the sufferer as possessing an evil eye (J. Elliott 2011)."

461. Ibid. Goddard and Cummins 1993 *ad loc.*, on the other hand, regard the reference to spitting as a metaphor with no connection to Evil Eye practice.

462. See also Pseudo-Aristotle, Frag. 347 (ed. Rose); Athenaeus, *Deipn.* 9.394B; Aelian, *Varia hist.* 1.15. Theocritus, *Idylls* 20.11; Tibull., *Elegies* 1.2.98; . Persius, *Sat.* 2.31–34. Petronius, *Sat.* 131.4 (a nurse taking mud made from spittle and applied with middle finger (= *medio digito = digitus infamis*) to forehead of infants to avert the Evil

There also was the belief that even the mere *uttering* of the Greek word *ptuô* thrice—*ptuô, ptuô, ptuô* ("I spit, I spit, I spit")—effectively wards off the Evil Eye. The Roman satirist Juvenal tells of Roman women of lower rank who inquire as to their futures "with much smacking of lips [*poppusma*] against evil influences" (*Sat.* 6.584).[463] This smacking of the lips was made "to avert the evil eye or similar maleficent influences."[464] *Poppusma* (the same term in both Greek and Latin) is an explosive term representing or resembling the sound of *ptui-ptui-ptui*, another explosive.[465] The later German expression *toi-toi toi,* (which is equivalent in sense and function to the English saying "knock on wood" [(to ward off evil forces or wish good luck]) most likely derives from this threefold Greek term and custom.

Second, protective spitting could have been prompted against Paul by his physical ailment (*astheneian tês sarkos,* v. 13) or for his having a physical appearance associated with the Evil Eye. In Evil Eye cultures, as documented profusely in the anthropological and historical evidence, physical ailments such as epilepsy or lameness, or physical disfiguration such as having a humped back, or ocular impairment (such as blindness, ophthalmia, strabismus, weak eyesight, having only one eye, and even having joined eyebrows), have signalled their bearers as potential possessors of the Evil Eye.[466] To protect themselves against such suspected fascinators, as previously noted, persons spit in their presence. This combination of Evil Eye elements occurs in Gal 4:14–15 where Paul states that "although my physical condition was a trial to you, you did not show contempt or spit." Many maladies have been proposed, but none has been proved beyond doubt.[467]

Eye. This practice was known to and condemned by the Christian church father John Chrysostom centuries latter (John Chrysostom, *Hom. 1 Cor. 12:7* [PG 61.105–6]).

463. *Juvenal, the Sixteen Satires* 1974:149, trans. Peter Green.

464. Peter Green in *Juvenal,* 1974:160 n. 41.

465. For the Greek paronym *poppusmos* see Xenophon, *Eq.* 9.10; Plutarch, *Quaes. Conv., Mor.* 713B. For the Latin *poppusmus* (the sound made when seeing lightning) see Pliny, *NH* 25.25 (plural).

466. On one-eyedness see Seligmann 1910 1:78; 1922:232–233. On the one-eyed monster Polyphemus the Cyclops, see Vol. 2:121, 136–37.

467. For example, malaria, epilepsy, blindness, ophthalmia, debilitation caused by imprisonment and flogging, or an indeterminate illness have all been proposed. This ailment, whatever its specific nature, was likely referred to by Paul in his Corinthian correspondence as a "physical weakness" (1 Cor 2:3; 2 Cor 10:10; 11:29–30; 12:5, 9, 10) and in 2 Cor 12:7 as a "thorn in the flesh." It may also be connected with an unexpected warning Paul issues at the very close of the Galatian letter: "henceforth let no one trouble me, for I bear on my body the marks of Jesus" (*ta stigmata tou Iêsou,* 6:17). As in 4:12–20, Paul appears in 6:17 to be defending himself against some accusation, this one concerning physical marks on his body (wounds? scars?) that may be claimed to undermine his authority and credibility. In response he calls them "the marks of

In any case, it was some sort of physical infirmity or impairment or disfiguration that was so offensive that it posed a serious test (*peirasmon*) of the Galatians' acceptance or rejection of the apostle (v. 14). It also provided ammunition to Paul's rivals for use against him. Paul's following comment about the Galatian's willingness to tear out their *eyes* and give them to him, however, points to the possibiltilty that the ailment or appearance may have involved some kind of *ocular* impairment or disfigurement.[468]

Edwin Yamauchi lists several points favoring the likelihood that the ailment, described by Paul here as a physical ailment (4:13) and in 2 Cor 12:7 as a "thorn in the flesh," was an "acute ophthalmia, brought on in part by the blinding vision on the road to Damascus."[469] "This widely prevalent disease," Yamauchi points out, "was both excruciatingly painful and disfiguring."[470] This severe ocular impairment would then help explain certain details of the text. (1) "It would explain why Paul wrote with such 'large letters' (Gal 6:12) his greeting to the Galatians." (2) An eye inflammation would further explain (a) why the Galatians would have been "tempted to regard Paul as one with an evil eye (Gal. 4:14)," and (b) "why they were willing to pluck out their own eyes to give them to Paul (Gal 4:15) and c) why Paul now rebukes them for falling under the evil eye of the Judaizers (Gal 3:1)."[471] Such an ocular ailment could indeed have prompted among the Galatians the suspicion that it marked Paul as fascinator and wielder of an Evil Eye.

Before pursuing this point further, let us recall two traditions about Paul and his eyes that are relevant here. One is recorded three times in Acts (9:3–19; 22:4–16; 26:9–18). It recounts Paul's being struck blind (presumably by God for persecuting Jesus' followers, Acts 9:4) and having his sight restored in the course of his being called by God for a mission to bring the good news of salvation to the Gentiles. Could it be that the ailment of which Paul speaks in Galatians is an ocular after-effect of this blindness? Its relevance to our Evil Eye topic is that blind persons were thought to wield an Evil Eye, or that their blindness is divine punishment for having cast an

---

Jesus," i.e. acquired because of his association with the wounded and crucified Jesus of Nazareth. The unusual appearance of this defiant remark at the letter's conclusion indicates that the accusation weighs heavily on Paul's mind.

468. Elliott 1988, 1990, 2005, 2011a, 2011b; Perkins 2001:1–3, 83.

469. Yamauchi 1983:190, following the proposal of Farrar 1903:265.

470. Yamauchi, 1983:190 cites Farrar 1903:265, who imagines Paul going on to say, "at that time weak, agonized with pain, liable to fits of delirium, with my eyes red and ulcerated by that disease by which it pleases God to let Satan buffet me, you might well have been tempted to regard me as a deplorable object."

471. Yamauchi 1983:190.

Evil Eye. In the Sophoclean tragedies, "the blind are seen not only as having transgressed mortal boundaries and as a source of pollution, but also as capable of inflicting the evil eye," as in the case of the blind king and the blind beggar in *Oedipus Tyrannus* (1306) and *Oedipus at Colonus* (149–156).[472] An Egyptian curse text mentions Horus blinding the eyes of those casting an Evil Eye.[473]

The other tradition is a striking detail about *Paul's eyebrows* that appears in the earliest extant description of the apostle's physical appearance—the *Acts of Paul and Thecla* (c. 185-195 CE), compiled in Lykaonia of Asia Minor adjacent to Galatia. The account describes various features of Paul's anatomy, including, of all things, his *knitted eyebrows*. After Paul had arrived in Iconium, a town in Southern Galatia, the narrative recounts, a resident named Onesiphorus, went out to meet him, paying attention to details provided him by a certain Titus.

> And he saw Paul coming, a man of small stature, with a bald head and crooked legs, in a good state of body, with *eyebrows meeting (synophryn)* and nose somewhat hooked, full of friendliness. (*Acts of Paul and Thecla* 3)[474]

Why this strange detail about eyebrows joined together?[475] It is possible that the detail reflects a memory of Paul having been connected with an Evil Eye, perhaps in conjuction with the memory of his earlier blindness? For knit eyebrows, one of several unusual ocular features, were considered a telltale indicator of an envier and an Evil Eye possessor.[476] Aesop, we recall,[477] was described as hunchbacked (*kyphos*) and *squint-eyed* or with *knit eyebrows*

472. Bernidaki-Aldous 1987:1.

473. Bourghouts 1978:2, citing Schott 1931:106–10.

474. *Acta Apostolorum Apocrypha*, ed. R. A. Lipsius, Part 1, 1959:237; English translation by R. McL. Wilson, in Hennecke-Schneemelcher 1965 2:354.

475. The noun *hê ophrys* can denote either "eyebrow" or "brow" [of forehead]. Aristotle refers to "right eyebrow and left" (*PA* 671b 32; cf. *Pr.* 878b 28), speaking of *eyebrows* rather than brow of the forehead; cf. LSJ 1279 *s.v.*). See also Homer, *Iliad* 14.493. The plural likewise would denote *eyebrows* (e.g., Homer, *Iliad* 13.88). The related adjective *synophrys* similarly can denote either "meeting eyebrows" (Aristotle, *Phgn.* 812b 25; P.Petr. 2nd ed., docs. 3, 16, 17, 18, 24; Theocritus, *Idylls* 8.72) or "knitted brow" [of forehead], LSJ 1724, *s. v.*).

476. See Pliny, *NH* 11.114, 274–75; Seligmann 1910:1:66–78, esp. p. 75; see also Vol. 2, pp. 122–24. For knit eyebrows as indicator of an Evil Eye possession see also Basil, *Homily 11 on envy* (PG 31.380.57). On Paul's knit eyebrows and other examples and associations of eyebrows, see Malina and Neyrey 1996:127–30, 141–42 (a symbol of Paul's "manliness"). Grant 1982 claims that knit eyebrows was a stereotypical feature of a military general.

477. See Vol. 2, pp. 121, 126, 142.

(*streblos*); he was considered so ugly that his fellow slaves quipped that he was bought only to serve as an anti-Evil Eye protective (*prosbaskanion*) for the owner's shop.[478]

Whatever Paul's physical malady may have been, Pauline tradition associated him with two telltale markers of Evil Eye possessors—blindness and knit eyebrows. Blindness, the loss of one's eyesight and possibly of one's eyes, was regarded in antiquity, as we have seen, both as a punishment for having an Evil Eye and as a condition prompting the exercise of an envious Evil Eye.

We might recall that epilepsy, another illness proposed as Paul's malady, also is related to the Evil Eye. This so-called "sacred illness" (Hippocrates, *De morbo sacro* 1, fifth century BCE) sent by the gods was thought to be divine punishment for having and wielding an Evil Eye.[479] Epileptics, like Pope Pius IX of modern time, were held to be Evil Eye possessors. Epilepsy, like the Evil Eye, was thwarted by spitting, perhaps because of the connection of epilepsy and Evil Eye. Theophrastus (*Char.* 16.14) observes that the superstitious man "shudders when he sees someone who is mad or has epileptic fits, and he spits on his chest."[480] Pliny the Elder writes:

> We [Romans] spit (*despuimus*) on epileptics (*comitiales morbos*), in this way repelling the contagion. Similarly, [by spitting] we ward off Evil Eyeing (*fascinationes*) and the evil that follows from encountering a person who is lame in the right leg. (Pliny, *NH* 28.35)

Various factors thus point to the possibility, if not the likelihood, that Paul could have been viewed as possessor and wielder of an Evil Eye.[481]

Paul's arrival at Galatia as both a *stranger* and one *suffering an ailment or disfiguration* likely associated with his *eyes*, along with his *knit eyebrows*, could have exposed him to the charge that he was a dangerous Evil-Eye possessor or fascinator. At this point in his letter Paul addresses this issue

478. *Vita Aesopi,* recension G 16, ed. Perry 1952; cf. also *Vita Aesopi,* recension W 16. See Trentin 2009:134–39.

479. On epilepsy, a.k.a "the falling sickness," see Temkin 1971 and Lesky and Waszink 1965. Since "chronic sufferers, like those afflicted by epilepsy or those living in regions infested with malaria, would probably wear their talismans throughout the course of their lifetime" (Kotansky 1991:120), it is possible that if Paul's malady ("thorn in the flesh") was epilepsy, he too wore such an anti-epilepsy amulet. PGM 114 (= GMPT 1986:313) concerns a phylactery for epileptic seizures caused by demonic attacks.

480. Theophrastus, *Char.* 16.14: *mainomenon de idôn ê epilêpton phrixas eis kolpon ptusai,* See also Apuleius, *Apology* 43–44 (Thalles suffering from epilepsy, with fellow servants spitting on him).

481. So Elliott 1988, 1990, 2005, 2011a, 2011b; Perkins 2001:1–3, 83.

and insists that the Galatians did not treat him as such. The fact that they did not scorn him or spit in his presence, Paul reminds them, is a powerful indication of their not regarding him as an Evil-Eyed fascinator.

Indeed, rather than treat him as a maimed and Evil-Eyed stranger, they did the opposite: "you received me as an angel/messenger of God, as [you did] Christ Jesus" (v. 14c). Then in a flourish of hyperbole illustrating their hearty welcome, Paul adds, "you would have *ripped out your eyes* and given them to me" (v. 15). The image is a curious piece of exaggerated rhetoric and is as rare as it is gruesome. The eyes were considered the "most precious members of the body."[482] Why any thought of tearing them out? Betz considers this another "literary motif" demonstrating the intensity of the friendship binding Paul and the Galatians.[483] More than a mere literary motif, however, seems in play here. Since Paul has just referred to the physical ailment he suffered when he first visited the Galatians (vv. 13–14), it is likely that his mention of "eyes" is prompted by the nature of that ailment; namely, some kind of ocular impairment or disfiguration as just described.[484] Not only did the Galatians not regard his ailment as indication of his having an Evil Eye. They were so enthusiastic about Paul that they would have responded to his ocular ailment by giving him their own eyes—their good eyes for his poor ones. "Instead of treating him as a person with the evil eye, Paul attests they would have given their eyes if Paul needed them."[485]

Now Paul's startling statement concerning the Galatians' willingness to rip out their eyes and give them to Paul makes good sense. A reference to eyes is on Paul's lips because the Evil Eye is on Paul's mind, as was also the case in 3:1.

In regard to 4:12–15 we can conclude that Paul's mention of the Galatians's not spitting, the reference to "eyes," and the possible ocular nature of Paul's physical condition and appearance all point to the Evil Eye as an issue on Paul's mind here and as an important factor in his choice of language. Paul is making the point that although the Galatians might have had reason to suspect him of having an Evil Eye, they did not treat him as such. (1) They did not show scorn or spit, but (2) did the opposite—they embraced him as a messenger from God. (3) They would even have torn out their own eyes and given them to Paul. The defensive cast of these words, along with their

482. So Burton 1921:244; so also Schlier 1962:211; Betz 1979:227.

483. Betz 1979:227–28. He refers to Lucian's *Toxaris* whose story of friendship includes two friends sacrificing their eyes. So also Martyn 1997:421.

484. This is allowed as a possibility by Burton (1921:244) but judged "precarious." It is favored by others: Schlier (1962:211); Lührmann (1978:74: poor eyesight, poor vision); Elliott 1988, 1990, 2011a, 2011b.

485. Malina and Pilch 2006:210; see also Perkins 2001:1–3, 83.

content, suggest that Paul saw himself accused by his opponents of harming the Galatians with an Evil Eye. Harm from an Evil Eye already was broached in 3:1. His recollection here of details of their first encounter (vv. 12c–15), along with his assurance of his continual concern for them (vv. 19–20), are meant to disprove and refute this accusation of Paul's wielding an Evil Eye as malicious and unfounded.

The following unit, 4:16–20, contains two further steps of Paul to address the Evil Eye accusation: a counter-accusation directed against his opponents, the false teachers, who are aroused by self-centered envy (v. 17), and a depiction of his Galatian addressees as "children" (v. 19).

Turning from a recounting of the past (4:12–14, 15c) to the present, Paul first asks his readers sarcastically, "Have I now become your enemy in telling you the truth?" (v. 16).[486] The rhetorical question indicates his awareness that some in Galatia are denouncing him as a dangerous stranger, and it helps explain the defensive thrust of vv. 12–15. How could his truth-telling possibly make him an enemy, as his opponents claim him to be? He then shifts abruptly from self-defense to censure and presents his readers with the unvarnished truth. Meeting accusation with counter-accusation, he declares, in effect, that "it is not I but others who are harming you." The specific identity of the "they" and "them"[487] to whom Paul is referring is not stated, but is clear from the larger context of the letter. They are the ones who, in Paul's words, are troubling the Galatians (1:7; 5:10, 12) and Paul (6:17). They are, from Paul's perspective, hindering the Galatians from obeying the truth (5:7), proclaiming a different gospel, and prodding the Galatians to desert Paul (1:6). They are perverting Paul's gospel of Christ (1:7). They are allied with the "false brothers" in Jerusalem (alias the "circumcision party," 2:12) who are spying out our freedom (2:4) and who are intent to "put us under bondage" (2:4). They insist on the necessity of circumcision and observance of the Mosaic law for salvation (4:10, 21; 5:2, 12–13; cf. 3:2–5). They have misrepresented Paul's position regarding circumcision (5:11–12; 6:12–15) and accused him of inconsistency (2:18). They are "the people who have come into your churches with their false gospel,"[488] who have also been criticizing and denegrating Paul and his gospel. They claim that he is no genuine apostle (1:1), that he seeks to win over the Galatians through flattery (1:10–11), that his gospel is a human concoction (1:11—2:10), that his tenuous ties with the mother church in Jerusalem expose him as a maverick

486. This is the truth conveyed by the gospel (the "truth of the gospel," 2:5, 14; cf. 5:7), which he initially proclaimed.

487. "They" is the subject of the third person plural verbs *zêlousin* (v. 17a) and *thelousin* (v. 17b). "Them" (*autous*) is the direct object of the verb *zêloute* in v. 17c.

488. Martyn 1997:422.,

figure and loose cannon (2:1–10), that he hides the truth from the Galatians and so is a false teacher (5:11; 1:10), that he is inconsistent about circumcision—"preaching" it (5:11) while not practicing it—and that the physical marks on his body (6:17) and his bodily ailment (4:13) cast grave doubt on his apostolic identity and authority. These are the persons to whom Paul refers by implication with his rhetorical question of 3:1a: "who has injured you with the Evil Eye?" and the "they" and "them" of 4:17. This is indicated by the further rhetorical questions of 3:2–5 concerning preoccupation with (circumcised) flesh and the law.

What Paul accuses them of doing in 4:17–18 is much debated. There is no consensus among the Bible Versions and commentators concerning the rendition of the verbs *zêlousin* (v. 17a), *zêloute* (v. 17c) and *zêlousthai* (v. 18a) or the point being made by Paul.[489] The Bible Versions present a broad variety of translations: "emulate" (*aemulare*, Vulgate); "be eager," "eagerly court" (*eifern; eifrig umwerben, werben,* Luther; Zürcher Bibel); "zealously affect" (KJV); "zealously court," "be zealous" (NKJV); "be zealous to win over, "be zealous" (NIV); "show interest in" (NAB); "be devoted to" (NJB; cf. BJ: *attachement, attacher, s'attacher*); "show deep interest in" (TEV, La Biblia; Dios habla hoy-La BibliaVersión Popular); "make much of" (RSV, NRSV); "envy" (NEB, La Sacra Bibbia: *zelare, zelo*).[490] Each translation captures an aspect of this polysemous verb except the RSV and NRSV for whose translation there is no apparent textual support in ancient Greek usage.

The verb *zêloô*, meaning, at base, "feel intensely, burn with ardor," can take either a positive or negative direction. It can mean "to have intense positive or negative feeling toward a person or cause," "be zealous," or "be jealous." Taken negatively, it also can mean "be envious." The context and social dynamic of the action are determinative.[491] BDAG and LSJ, *sub voce*, propose "zealously court" for Gal 4:17; the majority of Bible Versions and commentaries concur.[492]

John Chrysostom, commenting on Gal 4:17 (*Hom. Gal.* [PG 61.660]), takes the verbs to refer to some aspect of "being zealous." He distinguishes, however, between a "good zeal" (*zêlos agathos*) that emulates (*mimêsasthai*)

489. The secondary addition at the end of v. 17 of *zêloute de ta kreittô charismata* in some MSS (D* G Ambrose), "but you *zealously seek* the superior spiritual gifts," presumably occurred under the influence of 1 Cor 12:31 containing the same words.

490. NEB footnote gives "court" as an alternative but less preferable possibility.

491. BDAG 427. See Elliott 2007b, 2008 on this term, its word family, biblical usage, and criteria for translation

492. See, e.g., Luther, Schlier 1962:208 (*sich bemühen, umwerben*); Lührmann 1978:74 (*eifern*); Betz (1979:220, 229); Bruce (1982:207), Martyn (1997:418): "court [favor]"); Longenecker 1990:193 ("earnestly court"), 1999:104 ("seek").

virtue, and an "evil zeal" (*zêlos ponêros*) that seduces [lit. "casts out," *ekbal-lein*] from virtue the one who is on the right path, and "seduces from perfect knowledge." The self-serving aim of their *zêlos,* notes Chrysostom, is to attain the elevated rank of teachers, and to degrade the Galatians, who now stand higher than they, to the reduced position of disciples. The struggle is over social status and lines of dependency. The wide range of translations illustrate the polysemous nature of terms of the *zêl*-family.

The preference of the NEB and *La Sacra Bibbia* for *envy,* however, has much to commend it. The NEB reads:

> The persons I have referred to are envious of you, but not with an honest envy. What they really want is to bar the door to you so that you may come to envy them. It is always a fine thing to deserve an honest envy—always, and not only when I am present with you, dear children.[493]

"To envy" is one of the prominent meanings of the verb *zêloô* in both the LXX and the New Testament, with the noun *zêlos* also meaning "envy."[494] *Zêlos,* moreover, occurs twenty-two times in *1 Clement,* another Christian letter from the first century CE. In all twenty-two cases it has the meaning "envy," as indicated by context and social dynamic, often referring to instances of envy in Israel's past history.[495] In Galatians, as in *1 Clement*[496] and elsewhere,[497] *zêloô* (Gal 4:17, 18) and *zêlos* (Gal 5:20) are used as

---

493. In a recent study of Gal 4:12–20, Lappenga (2012) is aware that *zêl-* and paronyms can mean "envy" (2012:787–88). He chooses, however, to render *zêlousin hymas* (v. 17a) "are zealous for you," *autous zêloute* (v. 17c) "emulate them," and *zêlousthai* (v. 18a) "to be zealously pursued." In addition to this translational inconsistency and not sufficiently weighing the sense of envy in Paul's argument, Lappenga appears unaware of allusions in 4:12–20 to Evil Eye tradition.

494. *Zeloun* meaning "to envy" in the LXX: Gen 26:14; 30:1; 37:11; Num 11:29; Ps 36:1 (HT 37:1); Ps 72:3 (HT 73:3); Prov 3:31; 23:17; 24:1, 19; Isa 11:13b; Ezek 31:9. In the New Testament: Acts 7:9, 17:5; 1 Cor 13:4; Jas 4:2. For *zêlos* in the LXX meaning envy: Job 5:2; Prov 27:4; Qoh 4:4; 9:6; Isa 11:13a; for *zêlos* meaning envy in the the New Testament: Acts 5:17, 13:45; Rom 13:13; 1 Cor 1:3; 2 Cor 12:20; Jas 3:14, 16. In five cases, the noun could mean either envy or jealousy (Rom 13:13; 1 Cor 3:3; 2 Cor 11:2; Jas 3:14, 16) since neither context nor social dynamic is determinative.

495. *1 Clem.* 3:2, 4 ("unrighteous envy"; cf. 45:4); 4:7, 8, 9, 10, 11, 12 (cf. 43:2; 63:2), 13; 5:2, 4, 5; 6:1, 2, 3, 4; 9:1; 14:1; 39:7 (citing Job 5:2); 43:2 (cf. 4:12; 63:2); 45:4 (cf. 3:4); 63:2 (cf. 4:12; 44:1).

496. In *1 Clement,* *zêlos* and *phthonos* also appear as a hendiadys: *1 Clem* 3:2; 4:7; 5:2; cf. 4:13.

497. See *T. Sim. zêl-* terms: 2:6, 7; 4:5, 9; *phthon-* terms 2:13, 14; 3:1, 2, 3, 4, 6; 4:5, 7; 6:2; cf. also *T. Dan* 1:6 and 2:5; *T. Gad* 4:5; 5:3; 7:4; *T. Benj.* 4:4.

synonyms of *phthoneô* and *phthonos*.[498] *Zêlos* often is used interchangeably with *phthonos* ("envy") in the same contexts.[499] It also often appears with *phthonos* as a hendiadys.[500]

The rendition of *zêloo* with "envy" in 4:17–18 is favored by several factors: the polysemic quality of the verb and its paronyms; its meaning "envy" in numerous biblical and related texts; its regular place in the Evil Eye complex with the meaning "envy" (as noted frequently in this study); and its present literary context in Galatians;[501] words about the rivalry between Paul and his opponents that breeds envy.[502] Envy, moreover, is censured elsewhere in the letter (Gal 5:20, 21, 26) and Evil-Eyed envy is implied by *ebaskanen* in 3:1. Jerome (*Comm. Gal.* [PL 26.383–384]) commenting on 4:17–18, notes that the verb *zêlô* can have either positive or negative senses. He translates *zêlousin* with *aemulantur* ("they are improperly zealous"), a Latin verb also with possible positive ("emulate") and negative ("envy") senses. He takes Paul to be referring negatively to his opponents' envy (*zelo et aemulatione perversa*), which resembles that of Joseph's brothers (Gen 37:11; Acts 7:9), as well as the envy of Miriam and Aaron of their brother Moses (Num 12:1–15), and Cain's envy of brother Abel (Gen 4:1–16). In reference to v. 17, Lightfoot rightly concludes: "The false teachers envy the Galatians this liberty in Christ" (1866:133) and have an interest in subjecting them.[503] Commenting on *zêlos* (Gal 5:20) and *phthonos* (5:21) in the

---

498. For instance, in *1 Clem.* 3:4 the statement, "impious envy (*zêlon adikon*) by which also death came into the world" alludes to Wis 2:24, "through the envy of the devil (*phthonou diabolou*) death came into the world." The statement of *1 Clem.* 4:13 ("Because of envy [*zêlos*], David incurred envy [*phthonon*] not only from strangers but also suffered persecution from Saul, king of Israel"), refers to 1 Sam 18:6–8 and Saul's enviously Evil-Eyeing David.

499. See, e.g., *T. Sim.* (*zêl*- terms: 2:6, 7; 4:5, 9; *phthon*- terms 2:13, 14; 3:1, 2, 3, 4, 6; 4:5, 7; 6:2); cf. also *T. Dan* 1:6 and 2:5; *T. Gad* 4:5; 5:3; 7:4; *T. Benj.* 4:4.

500. See Democritus, Frag. B191; Lysias, *Funeral Oration,* 48; Plato, *Philebus* 47e; *Laws.* 3.679c; 1 Macc 8:16; *T. Sim.* 4:5; *1 Clem* 3:2; 4:7; 5:2; cf. 4:13.

501. Other instances of the formation *zêloun* + personal object (*hymas*), "they envy you," e.g., Prov 23:17, 24:1, speak of *envying* evil persons, rather than of "courting their favor."

502. On competitiveness and rivalry as typical of ancient Mediterranean society and as the breeding ground for envy see Gouldner 1969; Esler 1998:65–66, 228, 230; Hagedorn and Neyrey 1998:20–25; Malina 2001:108–33.

503. Nanos (2002:186, 187, 191, 279–80) also sees envy implied in the verb *ebaskanen* (3:1) and in 4:17–18, and correctly distinguishes between envy and jealousy (2002:251 n. 76). His translation, however, of 4:17 is odd: "They are jealous for you . . . in order that you would be jealous for them" (2002:251). He immediately states, "There is nothing wrong in principle with being jealously sought or seen when it is for good . . . But it is to be feared when that jealousy is envious, thereby begrudging one the good that one has gained, it is of this of which the influencers are accused." His mistaken

list of vices in 5:20–21, Jerome stresses the difference between their two Latin equivalents, *aemulatio* (for which he gives *zelus* as a synonym), and *invidia*, respectively. *Zelus* [like its Greek equivalent *zêlos*], he explains, can have either positive or negative force, and in the latter case can mean "envy." *Invidia* [like its Greek equivalent *phthonos*] always means "envy," which is always weighted negatively and involves being "tormented by the prosperity of another."[504] Jerome then gives biblical examples of *zelus*-as-envy (Joseph envied by his brothers, Miriam and Aaron envious of Moses).[505]

When the verb *zeloô* is taken to mean "envy" in Gal 4:17–18, Paul is thus saying:

> They [my opponents and detractors] envy you—but not for a good reason (*ou kalôs*) (v. 17a); they want to exclude you (v. 17b) in order that you [are forced to] envy them" (v. 17c).[506]

Censure (v. 17a) is then supported by explanation (v. 17bc). Envy emerges between rivals over some valued good possessed by the one and admired and envied by the other, according to Aristotle.[507] In Galatia, Paul and his opponents were rivals, each seeking to win over the hearts and minds of the Galatians. According to Paul, his rivals, as the proponents of an alternate gospel, envy the Galatians and not for a good reason.[508] They do not envy in admiration of the treasured good the Galatians possess, namely freedom in Christ, union with God, and solidarity with Paul. To the contrary, his rivals want to exclude (*ekkleisai*) and cut off the Galatians from their newly gained bond with Christ, God, and Paul so that these Galatians are forced to admire and envy the false teachers of what they claim to possess, namely surety of salvation and the favor of God because of their obedience of the Mosaic law. They envy you not for the good you possess, but in order to exclude you, so that you envy them for the good they possess. John Chrysostom, commenting on Gal 3:1,[509] observes that Paul equates the Evil Eye with envy, and in his rhetorical question intimates that the false teachers

---

equation of jealousy and envy confuses his accurate point about envy being the focus of Paul's accusation.

504. Jerome, *Comm. Gal.* (PL 26.347 §§416, 417).

505. Scheck, *Galatians* 2010:237, mistakenly renders *aemulatio/zelus* as "jealousy" and erroneously regards the biblical examples as instances of jealousy rather than envy.

506. Verse 17 is constructed chiastically, like 4:12 ("you, I—I, you"): they envy you (v. 17a) so that you envy them (v. 17c).

507. Aristotle, *Rhet.* 1.11,1370b–1371a; 2.6,1384a; 2.9–11,1387–1388.

508. This is the likely sense of the general negative modifier *ou kalôs*, which means, lit., "not in a laudable way"; cf. BDAG 505.

509. John Chrysostom, *Hom. Gal.* (PG 61.647–48).

acted "from an envious Evil-Eyed motive." This is precisely the point that Paul is making here in 4:17.[510] This self-serving motive of the false teachers and their malicious envy stand in stark contrast to the affection that binds Paul and the Galatians (vv. 12–15, 18b–20).

Paul follows this negative censure of the envy of his rivals in Gal 4:17 with a generalizing statement concerning a *positive* aspect of envy: "it is always good (*kalon*), however, to be envied (*zêlousthai*) for a good reason (*en kalôi*)" (v. 18a).[511] Being envied is a dilemma, a win-and-lose moment. On the one hand, to be envied can potentially involve the loss of something valuable caused by an envious or malevolent look. On the other hand, being an object of envy shows to the public that one has something of value, which in turn increases one's social prestige and ranking in the group. "Who would not wish to become envied, friends?" asked Epicharmus. "It is obvious that a man who is not envied is of no account."[512] Themistocles, Plutarch noted, while still a youth said, "he was doing nothing remarkable, as he was not yet envied."[513]

The second half of v. 18 relates the general axiom to the specific situation of Paul and the Galatians. For the Galatians to be envied[514] for a *good* reason would *always* (*pantote*) speak well of them, whether Paul was present (as he was at the beginning) or absent (as he is now). From this point of view, there is something positive about the Galatians being envied, but nothing positive about the false teachers doing the envying. Their Evil-Eyed envy of the Galatians is focused not on some good possessed by the Galatians. Their envious intent is to alienate the Galatians from Paul and to become the object of the Galatians' attention and admiration. Translating *zêloô* as "envy" in this context makes perfect sense, since envy emerges where rivalry is present. Commentators preferring to translate *zêloô* as "court" or "woo," fail to explain how, in what manner and with what means, the false teachers were supposedly wooing the Galatians; and secondly, how their courting of the Galatians could cause the latter to ultimately court the false teachers.

510. Philip Esler (1998:227–30) is one of the few recent commentators aware of this association here of envy and the Evil Eye.

511. *kalon de zêlousthai en kalôi pantote*, contrasting (a) envying and being envied for a good reason (*en kalô*, v.18a) to (b) envying and being envied for a dishonorable reason (*ou kalôs*, v. 17a), with *de* functioning as an adversative particle. *Zêlousthai* (A, C, several other Greek mss; cf. *to zêlousthai* [D G byz]) is preferable to *zêlousthe* (א, B, a few Greek mss, Vulgate, Origen) and must be taken as a passive since there is no instance of its use as a middle (so Burton 1921:247).

512. Epicharmus in Stobaeus 3.38.21; cf. Gouldner 1969:43, 55–58.

513. Plutarch, *De invidia et odio, Mor.* 537.

514. The Galatians are the *objects* of envying in v. 17 and therefore the more likely implied subjects of the passive "to be envied" of v. 18.

Taking the verb to refer to "envying" and "being envied," on the other hand, makes the social dynamic understandable and makes clear the relation of envying here to the Evil-Eyed envying of 3:1. As John Chrysostom observed in commenting on Gal 3:1,

> By the words, "who has injured you with the Evil Eye?" (*tis hymas ebaskanen*) he [Paul] implies that the persons in question acted not from positive concern, not to supply defects, but to mutilate what existed [among the Galatians]. For envy (*phthonos*), far from supplying what is wanting, subtracts from what is complete, and ruins the whole. (John Chrysostom, *Hom. Gal.*, [PG 61.647–48])

Galatians 4:19–20 concludes 4:12–20 and contains one final allusion to the Evil Eye as Paul affirms his earnest concern for the Galatians.

> My children, with whom I am again in birth pangs until Christ be formed in you (v. 19). I wish I could be present with you now[515] and change my tone, for I am perplexed about you. (v. 20).[516]

In contrast to his opponents' envious abuse of the Galatians (v. 17), and far from being an "enemy" (v. 16), Paul is intent on protecting and nourishing them in their new faith as "my children" (*tekna mou*).[517] This portrayal of the addressees as "children" does double duty here. First, "my children" describes their condition as recent converts won by Paul to faith in Jesus Christ, and as persons and communities[518] in whom Christ is still taking shape, with the aid of Paul and the Holy Spirit.[519] "My children" expresses as well the intimate bond of affection uniting Paul and the Galatians.

---

515. Paul yearns to be present with them now (*pareinai pros hymas arti,* v. 20a) as he was earlier (*pareinai me pros hymas,* v. 18b). His absence from Galatia and the roiling situation there puts him at a distinct disadvantage. His positive desire for the Galatians (*êthelon,* v. 20a) contrasts to that of the self-serving enviers (*thelousin,* v. 17b)

516. The unit 4:12–20 is thus framed by an opening and close stressing the intimate bond of fictive kinship uniting Paul to the Galatians. "Brothers [and sisters]" at the opening (v. 12a) is matched by "children" at the close (v. 19). For "brothers [and sisters]" elsewhere in Galatians see 1:11; 3:15; 4:28, 31; 5:11, 13; 6:1, 18.

517. This is the reading of ℵ* B D* F G, many others, Tert Did Ambst. Other manuscripts read "my little children" (*teknia mou*): ℵ² A C D² M ψ lat Clem Alex. The difference does not effect the meaning.

518. So Martyn 1997:424.

519. "Again in birth pangs" implies that his initial "birthing" of the Galatians into the family of God on his first visit (4:13) is being repeated following their defection from Paul's gospel "until Christ be (fully) formed in you;" see Martyn 1997:424. For Paul as metaphorical parent of his converts see 1 Cor 4:15 and Phlm 10.

Secondly, "children" also depicts them as objects especially vulnerable to the Evil Eye. For, as we have seen, it was children whom the ancients saw as the most vulnerable victims of Evil Eye attack.[520] Jerome and Martin Luther both comment on this connection of "children" and Evil Eye. Jerome, in respect to Gal 3:1, connects the belief that the Evil Eye is injurious to children to the Galatians' being a young community and therefore especially endangered by the Evil Eye.[521] Martin Luther, commenting on Gal 3:1, follows Jerome in citing Virgil, "I do not know what eye is Evil-Eyeing my tender lambs" (*Nescio quis teneros oculus mihi fascinate agnos. Ecl.* 3.103). He notes the threat that the Evil Eye poses to children as "tender lambs," including the Galatians "who were like new-born infants in Christ."[522]

As "children," the Galatians have fallen victim to the Evil Eyed envy of the false teachers (v. 17; 3:1). As the figurative parent who has given them birth in Christ, Paul assures them of his unwavering concern for their protection and well-being (v. 19). Perplexed at recent developments, he yearns to be with them and assume a more positive tone in speaking with them (v. 20). Paul's implication is that, in contrast to the false teachers who enviously Evil-Eye the Galatians and harm them socially and spiritually, he regards the Galatians as his dear children whose wellbeing and growth in Christ are his ardent concern.

Our examination of 4:12–20 has shown, in conclusion, that familiarity with the complex of beliefs and practice associated with the Evil Eye has enabled us to discern in Paul's remarks allusions to five items conventionally associated with the Evil Eye. The first (1) is the Galatians' *not spitting* when they first met Paul. They did not employ, that is, the gesture frequently used to ward off an Evil Eye (v. 14b) . The second (2) is their willingness to tear out their *eyes* and give them to Paul (v. 15c). This supports the possibility or likelihood, third, that the *physical ailment* mentioned by Paul (v. 13) concerned an ocular impairment or disfigurement of some kind. References in the Pauline tradition to Paul's blindness (Acts 9:9, 18; 22:11, 13) and his knit-together eyebrows (*Acts of Paul and Thecla* 3) further illustrate attention to ocular impairments or features of the apostle that qualified him for

520. On children as victims of the Evil Eye see Plutarch, *Quaest. Conv.* 5.7, *Mor.* 680C, 682A; 682F; Plutarch, *Is. et Os.* 17 (357D–E); Pliny, *NH* 7.16; Alexander of Aphrodisias, *Prob. phys.* 2.53; Lactantius, *Div. Inst.* 1.20.36; *b. Bava Batra* 141a; cf. Brav in Dundes, 1992:48 and previously, Vol. 1, chap. 2, and Vol. 2. The vulnerability of children is attested especially in numerous ancient personal letters that include the conventional wish that the recipient's children "be kept safe from the Evil Eye;" see Vol. 2:1–4 and Vol. 4, chap. 2.

521. Jerome, *Comm. Gal.* (PL 26.347).

522. For Luther's reference to children of his own day who had fallen victim to the Evil Eye see above, above, p. 231.

suspicion or accusation of being an Evil Eye possessor. (4) Paul's addressing the Galatians as "my *children*" (v. 19) relates them to those persons thought most vulnerable to the Evil Eye, namely babies and infants. (5) Conventional association of the Evil Eye with envy argues for rendering the *zêloô* verbs of vv. 17–18 as "envy. Paul accuses his opponents of *envying* the Galatians (v. 17), a vice condemned elsewhere in the letter (5:21, 26) and the malicious action most frequently associated with casting an Evil Eye.

Evil Eye belief and practice is the phenomenon with which all five factors are connected. Our heuristic model of this belief and associated practices has enabled us to identify and then connect some literary and social "dots"—seemingly unrelated at first—to form a coherent picture of Paul's aim and argument here and its function within the strategy of the letter as a whole.

This unit of Gal 4:12–20 thus is not an "interlude" or an excursus on the topic of friendship as some commentators have suggested.[523] It rather addresses a graver and more sinister issue that Paul raised earlier in his rhetorical question of 3:1. Taken together, these associated features of the Evil Eye phenomenon make it clear that accusations of Evil Eye possession and injury loomed large on the horizon of the Galatian conflict. Luther also noted that in 4:12–20 Paul was refuting accusations made against him by his rivals:

> [T]herefore with his honeyed and soothing words he [Paul] wants to prevent the false apostles from having an opportunity to slander him and twist his words in a captious way, as follows: "Paul is treating you in an inhuman manner, calling you insane, bewitched, and disobedient to the truth. This is a definite sign that he is not interested in your salvation but regards you as damned and rejected by Christ."(*LW* 26:422 on Gal 4:15)

Luther aptly senses the dynamic here of accusation and defense. It is the substance of the accusation and counter-accusation, however, that needs amplification. For it concerns not just false teaching and insult, but injuring with an Evil Eye. In 4:12–20 Paul defends himself against the charge of his rivals that he has injured the Galatians with an Evil Eye,[524] and he lauches a counter-accusation: it is not I but they, my rivals, who have done you harm

---

523. Betz (1979:221) opines that "[w]hat Paul offers in the section is a string of topoi belonging to the theme of 'friendship,'" which constitutes "a lighter section" than the preceding material.

524. Elliott 1988;63–66, followed by Longnecker 1999:96; see also Elliott 1990, 2005b, 2011, 2014.

with their envious Evil Eye.[525] Thus Gal 4:12–20 is Paul's response to his accusatory rivals concerning the person(s) actually injuring the Galatians with an Evil Eye, a topic the apostle introduced earlier in Gal 3:1.

The Evil Eye in Galatia—Conclusion

In his letter to the Galatians, a people long familiar with Evil Eye belief and practice, Paul poses a question, "O uncomprehending Galatians, who has injured you with an envious Evil Eye?" (3:1). It is a rhetorical question to which Paul already knows he will soon provide the answer. Once this explicit mention of the Evil Eye in 3:1 is recognized, a look out for further Evil Eye references or allusions becomes appropriate. (Of course, translations which do *not* render *ebaskanen* literally obscure this reference to the Evil Eye and leave readers with no clue that the Evil Eye is under discussion anywhere in the letter.) Familiarity with the complex of beliefs and practices associated with the Evil Eye has enabled us to see in 4:12–20 five additional allusions to the Evil Eye and to understand the relation of the content of 4:12–20 to Paul's question concerning the Evil Eye in 3:1 This ensemble of data throws a spotlight on a powerful *ad hominem* accusation made against Paul by his rivals and a counter-argument launched by Paul. Although it could be inferred from 3:1 that Paul himself first introduced the issue of the Evil Eye, a close examination of the letter suggests a different scenario.

The picture that emerges is a struggle between Paul and his rivals for the hearts and minds of the Galatians waged on two levels. One is on the conceptual, theological level, which is the usual focus of commentaries and studies on this letter. The other is the battle waged on the personal and social level, with pernicious charges hurled back and forth concerning harm done with an Evil Eye. Paul parrys an Evil Eye accusation directed against him prior to his letter with a counter-accusation levelled against his opponents. This scenario may be reconstructed as follows.

After Paul's departure from Galatians, rivals of Paul proclaimed a gospel different from his (1:6), just as his was different from that of the mother church in Jerusalem. "Galatians fairly bristles with a sense of rivalry and competition."[526] For Paul's rivals, the situation in the Galatian churches

525. It has been suggested that notice of this exchange of Evil Eye accusation and counter-accusation, while possible, "make[s] the argument more convoluted than is necessary" (Murphy-O'Connor 2000:45 n. 18). Despite the degree of complexity, it is, however, necessary for a compete exegesis of the letter and its social dynamic to expose the *ad hominem* dimension of this battle between Paul and his rivals for the hearts and minds of the Galatians.

526. Neyrey 1988a:97.

was rife with confusion, ambiguity, and deviation from orthodox Israelite behavior. Paul, they charged, was the one responsible for this confusion. Paul was a defective apostle delivering a defective and deluding message. This was not a mere matter of name-calling but of character assassination. These rivals challenged Paul's authority as an apostle from God, opposed his gospel and its novel social implications, and leveled numerous accusations against him including the *ad hominem* charge that he, the stranger and interloper, was harming the Galatians with his Evil Eye.

From Paul's response to this accusation in 4:12–20 it is possible to glean further detail on the substance and basis of this accusation. In addition to Paul's being a stranger, it is likely that Paul's "physical ailment," which, he conceded, was a "trial" to the Galatians when Paul and they first met (4:13–14), was some form of ocular impairment or appearance to which the opponents pointed as telltale evidence supporting their Evil Eye accusation. This fits the ancient view that being a stranger and/or presenting infirmity or deformity, blindness or epilepsy—all suspected at one time or another as the nature of Paul's ailment—were deemed grounds for being suspected of having an Evil Eye. An external deformity or peculiarity was taken as a signal of an inner defect, hostility, envy and the wish to do harm. Paul's claim that the Galatians were ready to tear out their own eyes and give them to Paul (4:15) points to the ailment as some kind of ocular impairment or peculiarity. Two Pauline traditions strengthen this probability. First, three accounts in the book of Acts describe Paul being struck with *blindness* in the course of his being called by God as an apostle to the Gentiles. A second tradition regarding Paul's eyes is part of the first physical description of the apostle (*Acts of Paul and Thecla* 3), which mentions a further remarkable and curious ocular feature of Paul—the fact that *his eyebrows were knit together*. In Paul's world, both the loss of eyesight and joined eyebrows were considered telltale indicators of a person with an Evil Eye.

This Evil Eye accusation by Paul's rivals, along with their other charges, had been an attempt to make the dispute public and galvanize public opinion against Paul. The charge was ruinous and could not go unanswered. If the accusation was made to stick, the consequences would be disastrous for Paul. The Galatian community as a whole would be moved to perceive Paul as bearing malice against them and intending to harm them with his Evil Eye. He would be seen as a lethal threat to their well-being. No matter how eloquent and powerful his message might have been, it would stand no chance of acceptance if he were successfully stigmatized as an Evil Eye possessor intent on harming the Galatians. Paul had to turn back this accusation as groundless and ludicrous so as to regain the confidence of his audience and regain a fair hearing of his message. If he did not counter and disprove it, Paul (and those with him, 1:1) would be publicly disgraced, degraded and dreaded as a danger to the health and well-being of the Galatian community. His apostolic credibility would be undermined and his proclamation dismissed as fraudulent and self-serving. So if Paul's entire mission and message in Galatia were not to be discredited and derailed, he had to respond to this damaging charge and prove it false.

Paul met accusatory fire with fire; to the accusation of his opponents he responded in kind. He answered not only with a brilliant theological argument making the case for a gospel of divine promise and grace rooted in the promise to Abraham, prior to the Mosaic law, and conveyed by the Spirit. He also parried their Evil Eye accusation with one of his own, implying in Gal 3:1 that it was *not he but they, his opponents,* who with their Evil-Eyed envy were afflicting the Galatians and destroying their community. John Chrysostom perceived this implied accusation also in another rhetorical question in 5:7. Commenting on Paul's censure of the Galatian agitators in Gal 5:7, "You were running a good race; who hindered you from obeying the truth?" Chrysostom links the "hinderers" with the persons implied earlier in his rhetorical question of 3:1: "These are the words of one who is exclaiming and lamenting, as he said before, 'Who injured you with an envious Evil Eye?'"[527]

After posing a rhetorical question identifying harm from an Evil Eye as an issue of grave concern (3:1), Paul answers his own question in 4:12-20. His response involves a self-defense, on the one hand (4:12c-15, 18-20), and a counter-accusation,on the other (4:17). Recalling the details of the Galatians' first encounter with Paul (4:12c-15), Paul insists that their own treatment of him at that time shows that they never had considered him an Evil Eye possessor, despite factors that his accusers might have suggested as pointing in that direction. The Galatians' unguarded and cordial reception of him (though a stranger with a manifest physical malady and striking markings on his body; cf.6:17), their not spitting in his presence, their not averting their eyes from him (cf. 3:1), their willingness, in fact, to give him their own eyes, their embracing him as a messenger of God—all these details of 4:12-15 disprove the allegation of his rivals that he was intent on injuring the Galatians with an Evil Eye.

This defensive maneuver is then followed by an offensive attack. Paul counters the Evil Eye allegation of his opponents with an Evil Eye accusation of his own: It is *my rivals*, my accusers, who are those actually harming you with their Evil-Eyed envy (4:17). It is *they* who are taking advantage of you as vulnerable children in faith (cf. 4:19). It is *they* who are envious of

---

527. John Chrysostom, *Hom. Gal.* (PG 61.666).

your liberty and exploit you for their own self-seeking purposes and wish exclude you from union with God, the believing community, and me, your very parent in Christ (4:17, 19). Beyond this segment of the letter, further accusation continues in a similar vein:It is *they* whose envy engenders envy and dissension within the community (cf. 5:19–21, 26) in contrast to my gospel of liberty and love in the Spirit (cf. 5:1–6:16). It is *they*—preoccupied with physical appearance, circumcision, and bodily stigmata and ailment—who reveal themselves as slaves of the flesh rather than children of the Spirit (5:2–26; 6:11–15, 17). It is *they* and their alien would-be gospel that are accursed (1:6–9; 3:10).

The accusation by Paul's opponents that he was intent on harming the Galatians with an Evil Eye is parried by Paul with a self-defense (4:12–16, 18–20; 6:17), counter-accusations (3:1; 4:17; cf. 1:6–7; 5:7–12; 6:12–14) and a general denunciation of envy (5:21, 26). Paul and his rivals confronted each other with equal claims to authority: apostolic credentials and the word of God. In this competitive situation where a central legal authority for adjudicating conflicts is absent and where "ambiguous social relations"[528] prevail, theological argumentation is combined with *ad hominum* Evil Eye accusation intended to disable the competition, discredit their positions, and reduce their status in the court of public opinion. If the Galatians were persuaded by Paul's counter-accusation, then Paul's reputation and credibility were saved, and it was his opponents who would suffer shame, loss of credibility, and perhaps dismissal as persons inimical to the well-being of the Galatians.

The implied Evil Eye accusation of Gal 3:1 (and 4:17) is similar in form, content, and aim to another in the New Testament, namely that of the vineyard owner in Matt 20:15 (1) In both Galatians and Matthew the Evil Eye charge is formulated in terms of an accusatory rhetorical question: "Who has injured you with an envious Evil Eye?" (Gal 3:1); "Is your Evil Eye envious because I am generous?" (Matt 20:15). (2) In both, the question is an insinuation: "It is not *I* but *you* who cast the Evil Eye" (Gal 3:1); "It is not *I* who am unjust, but *you* with your Evil-Eyed envy" (Matt 20:15b). (3) Both accusations concern Evil-Eyed envy. (4) In both, the Evil Eye accusation is employed in a situation involving persons in close geographical and social proximity where formal means of adjudicating competing complaint and conflict are absent. (5) In such situations, the Evil Eye accusation operates as an informal, but still potent, maneuver to target, label, discredit, dishonor,

528. Douglas 1970a:103.

and incapacitate persons purported to violate moral norms and values and to thereby threaten the wellbeing of the community.[529]

Galatians and the Evil Eye—Conclusion

Our investigation of Galatians has proceded along the "intercultural" lines of which Philip Esler has spoken.[530] We have sought to enter the world of Paul, his Galatian churches, and his rivals by reading his words in the light of ancient Evil Eye belief and practice. In terms of method, we have seen how a model of a particular belief complex and its associated practices and social implications can be used to as a heuristic means for probing and illuminating the social contours of a literary text. As a consequence, we have learned that the conflict in which Paul and his opponents were engaged involved not only theological debate about divine grace, Jesus as Messiah, Torah observance, freedom, and life animated by the Spirit of God. It also entailed a battle over the more mundane issue of Evil Eye possession—who menaced the Galatians and who really had the Galatians' interests and wellbeing at heart. By tracing the manifest and latent references to Evil Eye belief and practice in this letter we have discovered textual connections (3:1 and 4:12–20) and allusions to the Evil Eye that often elude conventional studies. Our identifying and connecting the dots, so to speak, brings to light *the social dynamic* to which these Evil Eye references point and we can grasp *the coherence* of this dynamic with broader features of this writing, its situation and socio-rhetorical strategy.

This Galatian letter in which the Evil Eye figures prominently is also a letter where baptism plays a veiled but presumed and central role. The divine grace and freedom which believers enjoy, and the new unity with God and Jesus Christ that is theirs, have been conferred at the moment of their rebirth as children of God (3:23—4:7; 4:28–31), namely at their baptism. As newborn children of God, they were particularly vulnerable to a hostile and lethal Evil Eye. The liturgical tradition of the Greek Orthodox Church has preserved this ancient connection of baptism and Evil Eye. "In the early Orthodox Church, prayers were offered in the sacrament of baptism to forestall the evil eye and to exorcize satanic powers in the case of *vaskania*."[531] In

---

529. Two centuries later, according to the apocryphal *Acts of Thomas*, another apostle, Thomas, was accused of wielding an Evil Eye. On his mission to India, he was denounced by the husband of a wife, whom the apostle was attracting to the faith. Thomas was accused of having and casting an Evil Eye or being an agent of the Evil Eye demon (*Acts of Thomas* 44, 100). The text is discussed in Vol. 4, chap. 2.

530. Esler 1998:1–28; also 235–39.

531. Soderlund and Soderlund 2010:17.

modern time, Greek Orthodox prayers for the deliverance of the newborn from injury by the Evil Eye are still in practice.[532]

Scholarly comment on the Galatian letter, as on the biblical writings generally, tends to restrict attention to theological issues and religious ideas. Social interaction, personal rivalries and conflicts, put-downs and accusations generally get short shrift, especially when high-flying theological ideas are at stake. The social dynamics accompanying conceptual debates, however—often left implicit in the texts—are always important to uncover and examine. For they give us fuller, more balanced scenarios, and hence a more complete picture of human life and engagement at the practical, everyday level of reality. Attention to the role played by Evil Eye accusations in Galatia enables us to grasp more concretely the *social* as well as theological strategies at work in the Galatian conflict and to appreciate more fully the persuasive and nuanced nature of Paul's letter and his engagement with the Galatians.

IMPLICIT REFERENCES TO THE EVIL EYE IN THE NEW TESTAMENT?

Our discussion of explicit references to Evil Eye belief and practices in the New Testament is now complete. Are there additional, *implicit* references as well, or instances where allusion to an Evil Eye would have been suspected by the hearers and readers? A few cases might be mentioned; none is absolutely certain.

First, there are references to *eyes* or to the act of *looking intently* that invite consideration. Jesus, for example, warned of an eye (Matthew: "right eye" that "causes you to offend" (Mark 9:47–48/Matt 5:29/Matt 18:9).[533] Such an eye should be removed, for "it is better for you to enter the kingdom of God (Matthew: "life") with one eye than with two eyes to be thrown into Gehenna." This eye saying completes a triad of sayings concerning an offending hand, foot, and eye (Mark 9:43–48/Matt 18:8–9), which follows and expands on a warning against offending (*skandalisê*) little ones who trust in Jesus (Mark 9:42). A Matthean doublet of this saying appears in Matt 5:29 where Jesus instructs: "if your right eye causes you to offend (*skandalizei se*), pull it out and remove it from you; for it is better that you lose one of your members than that your whole body be thrown into Gehenna." This is paralleled by a similar instruction concerning an offending right hand (v. 30). Both are attached to a saying in which Jesus explains the prohibition of adultery (v. 27; cf. Exod 20:14; Deut 5:17) to include *looking desirously at*

532. For the prayers see Vol. 4, chap. 2.
533. Mark 9:47: *skandalizê se*; Matt 5:29/18:9: *skandalizei se*.

(*blepôn gynaika pros to epithymêsai autên*) *the wife* of another man.[534] Here an offending eye is one that looks intently at the wife of another man with the aim of alienating the affection of that wife (= commiting adultery). In neither of these offending eye sayings is the eye or the looking said to harm or envy the object on which the ocular glance falls. Nor are children said to be the objects of an offending eye. Thus a reference here to looking with an Evil Eye seems most unlikely.

The eye saying of Jesus reported in Luke 6:41–42/Matt 7:3–5 (= Q) is intriguing. It reads,

> Why do you see the speck that is in your brother's eye,
>   but do not notice the log that is in your own eye?
> (Luke 6:41/Matt 7:3).[535]

The rhetorical question makes no mention of an Evil Eye, but is strikingly similar to a fragment of a Greek comic poet that does. A questioner asks accusingly,

> why do you look sharply at the evil of another, you foulest of Evil-Eyed enviers (*baskanôtate*), but look past your own evil?"
> (*Comica adespota* 359).[536]

Jesus's saying, included in a statement about not judging fellow believers (Luke 6:37–42/Matt 7:1–5), contrasts noticing a tiny speck in a fellow believer's eye to ignoring a huge plank in one's own eye. The point of this metaphorical statement is that one must first "clean up one's own messy act" before finding any tiny peccadillo in others. The conditions of the eyes represent the differently flawed moral conditions of their possessors. Each of the eyes is faulty but neither is said to be an Evil Eye that injures or envies others. The problem is not an Evil Eye as such, but elements in the eyes representing character flaws of differing seriousness. The explicit mention of Evil Eye in the comic fragment makes it possible that an Evil Eye is also implied of the brother and fellow believer who searches for specks in the eyes of others while ignoring his own more substantial shortcomings. Jesus's is making a point similar to that of the comic poet, but his language is sufficiently different as to question any allusion on his part to an Evil Eye.[537]

---

534. See also the same connection of eye and adultery in Justin Martyr, *First Apology* 15:1–3.

535. See also P. Oxy. 1.1; *Gos. Thom.* 26.

536. *ti tallotrion, anthrôpe baskanôtate/ kakon oxuderkeis; to d' idion parablepeis? Comica adespota* 359 (Kock, ed., 1888 3:476).

537. Derrett (1988) likewise disallows any reference here to an Evil Eye.

The expression "lust of the eyes" (*epithymia tôn ophthalmôn*) in 1 John 2:16), like its parallel phrases, "lust of the flesh" and "pride of life," illustrate features of this fallen human world that are "not from (God) the Father" and that will pass away (1 John 2:16–17). The eyes here are envisioned to be the site and channel of lust (*epithymia*), i.e. intense desire. This emotion, while problematic, is not conventionally associated with an Evil Eye.

The terms *epithymia, epithymeô* occurring in the last two of the Ten Commandments (Exod 20:17/Deut 5:21; Rom 7:7; 13:9) with the sense of "covet," "desire to possess," have been suspected as an allusion to coveting with an envious or Evil Eye. But this too is unlikely. Desiring to acquire someone or something possessed by another person is not the same as envying. The one who desires intensely or covets wishes not to destroy but to gain and possess. One who envies is not so much interested in acquiring for oneself as in destroying something of worth possessed by another simply because the sight of another's pleasure gives him grief.

Nor does Rev 2:18–23 attribute an Evil Eye to the Son of God as has been claimed.[538] The fourth of seven letters to seven churches of Asia Minor (Rev 2:1—3:22) opens with words identifying the ultimate speaker dictating the letter:

> And to the angel of the church in Thyatira write: "The words
> of the Son of God, who has eyes like a flame of fire, and whose
> feet are like burnished bronze" (2:18; cf. 1:14, "his eyes were like
> a flame of fire and his feet were like burnished bronze;"; also
> 19:12, "his eyes are like a flame of fire.")

This Son of God condemns the Thyratiran prophetess Jezebel who leads his disciples astray in the practice of idolatry and refuses to repent (vv. 20–21). He therefore will strike her ill (v. 22) and strike her children dead (v. 23). The Evil Eye was thought capable of causing illness and death, but the reference here is not to a single Evil Eye but to a *pair of eyes*. As discussed earlier, eyes, considered as active agents, were often compared to the sun projecting rays or were spoken of as projecting flames of fire. This analogy illustrates the conceptualization of the eyes in general being active agents casting forth particles of energy, whether of gods or humans. This conceptualization underlies the understanding of how an Evil Eye in particular operates, but not every flashing eye constituted an Evil Eye. In the present case, it is the flashing eyes (plural) of the Son of God that, like the burning rays of the sun, that did the punitive damage, but not a single Evil Eye. Nor is it likely that

538. Against the contention of Duff (1997). His desire to contextualize this passage of Revelation is welcome, but his argument reveals a limited familiarity with the Evil Eye complex and Evil Eye tradition.

a follower of Jesus Christ, the Son of God, would attribute to him a malignant Evil Eye.[539] Duff acknowledges that "the label 'evil eye' is misleading."[540]
Claiming that in this text "the phenomenon revolves around power rather
than any moral distinction, he declares that "the eye of the 'evil-eyed' individual is not actually evil."[541] This self-contradictory notion runs counter to
all that is said in antiquity about the Evil Eye as a constantly immoral entity.
Duff's discussion of "the Son of God's evil eye" and his equation of the Son
of God with Hekate lacks convincing support.[542]

It has been suspected that Paul's "looking intently" (*atenisas*) as mentioned in Acts 13:9 involved an Evil Eye glance,[543] but this is far from certain.[544] Acts, recounting a visit of Paul and Barnabbas to the city of Paphos
on the island of Cyprus (Acts 13:4–12), tells of their encounter with a certain
magician, a Judean "false prophet" by the name of Elymas Bar-Jesus. The latter was with the Roman proconsul in control of the island, Sergius Paulus,
who had invited Paul and his colleague Barnabas to inform him concerning
the word of God they were proclaiming (13:7). Elymus, however, opposed
them, "seeking to turn away the proconsul from the faith" (13:8). So Paul,
alias Saul,

> filled with the Holy Spirit, *looked intently at him* (*atenisas eis
> auton*) [Elymas], and said, "You son of the devil, you enemy of
> all righteousness, full of deceit and villany, will you not cease
> making crooked the straight ways of the Lord? And now behold,
> the hand of the Lord is upon you and you shall be blind and
> unable to see the sun for a time." (vv. 9–11b RSV)

539. Nowhere in either Testament of the Bible is God or a divine representative, or
Jesus, said to possess an Evil Eye. Nor is God ever said to be envious. On this latter point
see Elliott 2007a, 2008.

540. Duff 1997:119.

541. Ibid.

542. Ibid., 121–26. Also in regard to the book of Revelation, Boll (1914:68) has observed in connection with the locust mentioned in Rev 9:3, 7, that a locust was thought
to have and convey an Evil Eye, and so also could ward it off, citing the 1912 study of
E. Fehrle on locust. On locust warding off the Evil Eye see also Seligmann 1910 1:135;
2:120, 155, 311 and, vice versa, on a *jettatore* hired to ward off locust, see Seligmann
1910 1:220.

543. Billerbeck 1924 2:713–14.

544. Seligmann, in connection with his comment on the ocular glance (1910
2:436), mentions Paul's intense staring at and cursing of Elymas resulting in the latter's
blindness as an example of the combination of ocular glance and verbal suggestion. But
he does not identify this text as an instance of Evil-Eyed staring.

The magician was immediately enshrouded by mist and darkness and could not see (v. 11). The pronconsul, seeing what had happened, was astonished at the teaching of the Lord and believed (v. 12).

Evil Eye lore holds that an oblique glance, a gaze, a glaring or staring, or looking intently can be actions of an Evil Eye. (Note the German accent on "Blick" [= "glance, look"] in the conventional German equivalent of "Evil Eye," namely *böser Blick*). The Evil Eye, moreover, as noted frequently in this study, also was considered a major cause of illness and death,[545] while blindness was deemed more a punishment for having and using an Evil Eye. The verb *atenizô*, however, is not conventionally used in connection with "Evil Eye." Furthermore, none of the other numerous instances of *atenizô* in Luke-Acts means "look with an Evil Eye."[546] The context in fact points to "the hand of the Lord" (v. 11) as the blinding agent. Luke, author of both the Gospel and Acts, knew and used the conventional expression for Evil Eye (Luke 11:34d), but did not employ it here. If he meant *atenisas* to imply "looking intently with an Evil Eye," this would be the only instance in the entire New Testament where a follower of Jesus was said to possess and intentionally use an Evil Eye—apart, that is, from the Evil Eye accusation of Paul's rivals against Paul. An implication of a staring Evil Eye cannot be totally ruled out, but is extremely unlikely.

Instances of *envy* might imply an Evil Eye lurking in the background, given the close association of the two in ancient thinking. This is the case with the reference to the brothers of Joseph who envied him (*zêlôsantes*) as stated in Acts 7:9 (cf. Gen 37:11). As the Joseph tradition, *The Testaments of the Twelve Patriarchs*, and the *Testament of Solomon* have shown,[547] envy and the Evil Eye were not only closely linked but in many instances virtually equivalent. The envy of the high priests against Jesus (Mark 15:10/ Matt 27:18), which led to their delivering him to Pilate (Mark 15:1–15/ Matt 27:1–23), would certainly have been associated in the popular mind with an Evil Eye.[548] The elder son (Luke 15:25–32) in Jesus's parable of the prodigal son, generous father, and resentful elder brother (Luke 15:11–32) is not said explicitly to have envied his younger brother because of the lavish

---

545. See Murdock 1980 concerning the Circum-Mediterranean generally, and Vols. 1 and 2 passim. For rabbinic texts on the Evil Eye as a cause of death and destruction and on the *Strafblick* [punishing glance] of the rabbis see Billerbeck, *Str-B* 2 1924:713–14 and Vol. 4, chap. 1.

546. See Luke 4:20 ("look at intently:"); 22:40 ("look at suspiciously"); Acts 1:10; 3:4; 6:15; 7:55; 14:9; 23:1—all "look at intently"; 3:12 ("stare at"); 10:4 ("look at in terror"); 11:6 ("look at carefully").

547. See above, pp. 69–72, 79–86, 105–109, 135–38, 149–50, 183–85.

548. See Hagedorn and Neyrey 1998; and Elliott 2007a.

love bestowed on him by a forgiving father. Nevetheless, it was clearly envy that he felt, and in the popular mind this was associated with a malevolent Evil Eye.[549] The expression "to be in the gall of bitterness" (*eis cholên pikrias einai,* Acts 8:23) is an idiom for "to be envious or resentful of someone." Accordingly, Simon of Samaria, who offered the apostles money to acquire their power to confer the Holy Spirit, is urged by Peter to repent of his envy of Peter and John and their bequest of the Holy Spirit (Acts 8:9–24). No reference, however, to Simon's casting an Evil Eye is apparent.

Since the Evil Eye is linked with, and is a subset of, the forces of evil in general, *references to evil* may at points imply an Evil Eye. The final petition of the Lord's Prayer (Matt 6:9–13/Luke 11:2–4) according to Matthew (6:13), for example, reads: "deliver us from evil" (*rhusai hêmas apo tou ponêrou*). The term *tou ponêrou* can be read (a) as the genitive of a neuter substantive (*to ponêros*) denoting evil generically. Or *ponêrou* could be read (b) as the genitive of a masculine substantive (*ho ponêros*) denoting "the evil one" alias the devil/Satan.[550] This same masculine substantive *ho ponêros* also could denote (c) "the Evil (Eye)" (*ophthalmos ponêros*): "deliver us from the Evil Eye."[551] Other occurrences of *ponêros* allow this as a grammatical possibility (1 Cor 5:13; Eph 6:16; 2 Thess 3:3; 1 John 2:13; 5:18, 19). The question is whether this interpretation of *ponêros* is semantically plausible. The text and context allow no definitive answer. The petition, moreover, could be taken in either of two ways: (a) deliver us from evil/the evil one/the Evil Eye that could harm us as victims; or (b) deliver *us* from casting an Evil Eye/perpetrating evil on *others*. Traditionally, of course, "Evil Eye" was not assumed here and option b, to my knowledge, has never been proposed. It is worth recalling, however, that the traditional rite of baptism in the Greek Orthodox church did in fact include a specific prayer that the baptizand be kept safe from falling victim to an Evil Eye; for this prayer see Vol. 4, chap. 2.

In addition to references to envy and evil, there are still other subjects mentioned in the New Testament that could involve allusions to the Evil Eye. Since in antiquity and down to the present the Evil Eye has been

---

549. The emotion felt was not jealousy but envy, not fear of loss but resentment of a brother's gain. For envy in the New Testament see Acts 7:9; Rom 1:29; 13:13; 1 Cor 3:3; 13:4; 2 Cor 12:20; Gal 5:20–21, 26; Phil 1:15; 1 Tim 6:4; Jas 3:14, 16; 4:2; 1 Pet 2:1.

550. Matt 13:19 ("the evil one")/Mark 4:15 ("Satan")/Luke 8:11 ("the devil"); cf. also Matt 13:19; John 17:15.

551. Luke 11:34 refers to the Evil Eye with simply *ponêros*, with *ophthalmos* implied (as the parallel Matt 6:23 indicates) but not written. Lochman (1988:130–34) lists studies on *ponêros* favoring either the neuter or masculine/personal option. For *ponêros* as either masculine or neuter see also Matt 5:37, 39; John 17:15; 1 Cor 5:13; Eph 6:16; 2 Thess 3:3; 1 John 2:13, 14; 3:12; 5:18, 19. For the combination see Luke 6:45.

thought to be a major cause of illness,[552] attack from an Evil Eye may have been suspected where illnesses were reported, even though the Evil Eye is not mentioned explicitly.[553] John Pilch, in his astute analysis of illness and healing in the New Testament, for example, suspects that the ill boy healed by Jesus as reported in the Gospel of John (4:46–54) "was suffering from the effects of the evil eye . . . Given the high rate [of disease and death] in the culture at this time, a healthy son would certainly be the object of envy, and thus an opportunity to exercize the evil eye."[554] On the same cultural reasoning, the twelve year old girl who was ill and died (Mark 5:21–24, 35–43/Matt 9:18–18, 23–26) may also have been regarded as a victim of an Evil Eye.[555] The blind man described in John 9:1–41 also could have had his blindness regarded as punishment for having an Evil Eye, since, as we noted in Vol. 2 and as Pilch reminds his readers, "blind people were invariably suspected of possessing and giving the Evil Eye."[556] This may also have been the public perception of Saul/Paul as well, who, as we noted above, was struck blind as divine punishment for persecuting the followers of Jesus (Acts 9:8–9; 22:11–13)—perhaps out of envy of their success?[557] Jesus's spitting and use of saliva to heal the blind person (John 9:1–41, esp. 9:6), Pilch opines, would also have been seen by those present as means to heal someone with an Evil Eye. "He [Jesus] uses saliva (see also Mark 7:33; 8:23) because it was widely believed that saliva gave protection particularly against the evil eye, which perhaps the majority of people there would have assumed the blind man possessed."[558] Both the malady and the means of its cure suggest that the public could have deemed the blind man to be an Evil-Eye possessor. Might the public who witnessed Jesus's healing of another blind person (Mark 8:22–26) have held a similar view, considering the similar combination of blindness and spitting? Spitting and spittle were generally used to *avert* an Evil Eye, not *cure* the effect of one. However, we might recall the incident in the *Satires* of Petronius, where an old woman with spittle and her middle

552. See Maloney, ed. 1976:14, 138–39, 166, 171, 184, 315–19; Murdock 1980; Simons and Hughes 1985:487; Herzfeld 1986; Pilch 2000a:19, 85–86, 126, 133–34, 152.

553. Derrett (1995:69–70) concluded his review of New Testament references to the Evil Eye with the judgment that nowhere in the New Testament is the Evil Eye explicitly said to be the cause of illness. Silence on the matter, however, may be no more than circumstantial.

554. Pilch 2000a:126; see also Pilch 1999:145–46.

555. Pilch 1999:145.

556. Pilch 2002a:133.

557. For Oedipus struck blind for having an Evil Eye see Sophocles, *Oedipus Tyrannus* 1306 and *Oedipus at Colonus* 149–156; Bernidaki-Aldous 1988; and Vol. 2:121–22.

558. Pilch 2000a:134.

finger (otherwise employed to *avert* an Evil Eye) *healed* Encolpius who was struck impotent by an Evil Eye.[559] In the popular mind, however, as Pilch has emphasized, illnesses could well have been considered caused by a malevolent Evil Eye as well as by demons and unclean spirits.[560] Pilch describes this perception as a "culture-bound syndrome" and as typical of the biblical communities and their neighbors.

> A syndrome is a group of signs and symptoms that occur together and characterize a particular health abnormality. A culture-bound syndrome is an abnormality that is distinctive in a culture because that cluster of signs and symptions is given an interpretation that is usually not biomedical but rather social or cultural. Culture-bound syndromes are those folk-conceptualized disorders, that is, illnesses that include alterations of behavior and of experiences among their symptomology. The effects of being the object against whom someone has cast an evil eye form a culture-bound syndrome in circum-Mediterranean cultures.[561]

Finally, a practice that likely involved concern about the Evil Eye— without its explicit mention—is the custom of observant Israelite males at daily prayer donning leather phylacteries (Aramaic: *tefillin*; Greek: *ta phylaktêria*), Matt 23:5) and prayer shawls (*tallit*) with blue tassels (Hebrew: *tzitzit*; Greek: *kraspeda*) attached at the four corners. As noted above in chap. 1, the phylacteries, prescribed by Torah (Exod 13:9, 16; Deut 6:8), were leather capsules containing words of Torah bound on the forehead and left arm of the worshipper. They were worn by Pharisees (Matt 23:5) and other strict observers of Torah (*Letter of Aristeas* 159), not only as a reminder of Israel's deliverance from Egypt,[562] but also as protection (*phylactery* from the Greek, *phylassein*, "to guard, protect") against the forces of evil, including the Evil Eye.[563] The attachment of blue tassels (Hebrew: *tzitzit*; Greek:

---

559. Petronius, *Satyricon* 131.4–5; see Vol. 2:148–49.

560. See Pilch 2000a:19, 126, on John 4:46–54; and Pilch 2000b:132 concerning John 9:1–41 on blindness and the Evil Eye; also Pilch 1999:145–46.

561. Pilch 2000a:152.

562. Exod 13:1–16; Deut 6:4–9; 11:13–21.

563. On phylacteries/*tefillin* see Rodkinson 1893; Billerbeck 1928 4.1:250–76; Trachtenberg 1939:145–46; Bonner 1950; Eckstein and Waszink 1950; Ben-Dor 1962:122; G. H. Davies 1962b; Yadin 1969; Schürer 1979 2:480; Tigay 1979; BDAG 1068. On their apotropaic function see Tigay 1979:51: "There is no lack of evidence that *tefillin* were ascribed apotropaic properties and used as such;" cf. e.g., Jerome (*PL* 26.128) and numerous rabbinic texts (e.g., R. Yohanan protected in the privy by his *tefillin*, *b. Ber.* 23a-b. See also above, chap. 1, pp. 21–23, 98–99.

kraspeda) to the four corners of the garment worn for prayer is commanded in the Torah (Num 15:37–41; Deut 22:12) and reinterpreted as a reminder to "remember and keep all of my [God's] commandments." Jesus. well aware of the Evil Eye (Matt 6:22–23/Luke 11:34–36; Mark 7:22), wore such tassels on his garment (Matt 9:20/Luke 8:44), combining a signal of orthodox piety and a means of protection against the Evil Eye.[564] A mere touching of these powerful tassels was said to provide healing to the infirm (Matt 14:36; Mark 6:56; cf. Mark 5:24–34). It is also interesting to note that the horses of the destroying angels mentioned in Rev 9:13–21 had breastplates colored red and blue (Rev 9:17), which were the main colors employed then, as they are today, to defend against an Evil Eye. This image reflects the widespread practice of protecting domestic animals, including horses, camels and live-stock, with cloths, colors, and bells intended to ward off the Evil Eye.[565]

A similar dual purpose was served by the *mezuzah* ("doorpost"), a small recepticle affixed by Israelites to the right door-posts of their houses and rooms. The receptacle contained small fragments of parchment on which was written (according to Deut 6:4–9 [the *Shema*] and 11:20) verses of Deut 6:4–9 and 11:13–21. Their use displayed orthodox piety while also protecting homes and residents from the Evil Eye and other hostile forces.[566] Mezuzahs are not mentioned in the New Testament but their presence in the Israel of Jesus's day can be assumed from their requirement in the Old Testament and continued evidence of the practice in postbiblical time.[567] (For illustrations of phylacteries, fringes, and mezuzahs, see above, chap. 1.) Similar strategies were employed in the Greco-Roman world where *fascina* attached to the doorposts of homes or depicted in the mosaics of thresholds were meant to protect house and inhabitants from the Evil Eye and hostile demons.[568] The custom continues in modern time. A similar pratice of pro-tecting homes against the Evil Eye occurs in present-day India. Each morn-ing the wife (re-) arranges the ground area at the house's threshold to keep the house and its residents safe from the Evil Eye. In Tamil Nadu, South In-dia, Vijaya Nagarajan reports, a daily threshold design, *the Kôlam*, is made

564. So also Pilch 1999:19. On the blue (and white) tassels see Billerbeck 1928 4.1:277–92; Schürer 1979 2:479. On blue as an apotropaic color against the Evil Eye see Blau 1898; Seligmann 1910 1:248; 2:20, 101 etc.; Schrire 1982:58; and above, chap. 1, pp. 99–100, 102. See also Vol. 2, pp. 254–57.

565. On this practice, see Vol. 2:147, 150.

566. On mezuzahs see Blau 1898:61, 86–87; Trachtenberg 1939:146–52; Schürer 1979 2:479–80; Eckstein and Waszink 1950:406–7 (for pagan amulets protecting homes see col. 406).

567. See, however, the *Letter of Aristeas* 158; see also Vol. 4, chap. 1.

568. On the practice, see, Vol. 2, pp. 171–74; 199–200.

by the woman of the residence to invite the goddess Lakshmi and also "to prevent the effect of the evil eye" and protect against covetousness and envy . . ." "The kôlam acts as a net, as a catcher of emotion-laden feelings, and as a protective screen for the emotions cast out by those who pass by the doorway, and for those who cross the threshold" . . . "Making the kôlam protects not only the home but also the self against both the Evil Eye of others and one's own Evil Eye of envy and evil intentions toward others."[569]

As scholars familiarize themselves with the full extent of the Evil Eye belief complex, it is possible that in the future other allusions to the Evil Eye in the New Testament will be uncovered.

EVIL EYE BELIEF AND PRACTICE IN THE NEW TESTAMENT—CONCLUSION

The dread of the malignant Evil Eye that pervaded the ancient world of the Circum-Mediterranean and Near East overshadowed the biblical communities as well. The New Testament, like the Old Testament, contains several explicit references to the Evil Eye. The general character of the Evil Eye as it appears in the biblical writings, however, arouses less dread than disapproval, deprecation, denunciation, and condemnation. The Evil Eye is spoken of as an immoral human quality, dishonorable and damnable—"the worst of evils" (Sir 31:13). Generosity is a fundamental obligation of observant Israelites and a prominent feature of Israel's distinctive morality. Possessing and casting an Evil Eye is a grievous refusal of this obligation.

Jesus and Paul and their circles shared the pervasive belief in the Evil Eye and its malice. They spoke of it in terms similar to those of their Israelite forebears. On one occasion, Jesus contrasted an Evil Eye to an "integral"eye, as reported variously by the evangelists Matthew (6:22–23) and Luke (11:33–36). The contexts of these passages, together with features of Evil Eye lore, indicate that an "integral eye" (*ophthalmos haplous*) connoted an eye and a person who was generous (especially *Testaments of the Twelve Patriarchs*). An "Evil Eye" (*ophthalmos ponêros*), by contrast, connoted a person who was *miserly* or *stingy*, as illustrated by several Old Testament Evil Eye texts (Deut 15:7–11; 28:54–57; Sir 14:3, 8, 10; Tob 4:7, 16). The *antithesis of generosity and Evil Eye* is pronounced in the accusation that concludes Jesus's parable of the generous vineyard owner and the hired workers (Matt 20:1–15). The association of the Evil Eye with *envy* is a related feature of this parable. The detail and structure of the parable were designed to show how human envy can arise when generosity is shown and invidious comparison

569. Nagarajan 1993:200–201.

is at play. Jesus teaches that both miserliness and envy are inconsistent with life under the rule of God and antithetical to God's own generosity and freedom from envy. Jesus's mention of the Evil Eye in connection with a controversy concerning purification prior to dining and the actual origin of defilement (Mark 7:1–23, esp. v. 22) is another condemnation of Evil-Eyed envy. Envy, like other malicious dispositions and emotions, Jesus admonishes, arises in the heart and is transmitted outward through an Evil Eye and its malevolent glance. The controversy's setting (meals and dining) is similar to that of other Old Testament Evil Eye texts, as is the linking of Evil Eye and the heart.

The fact that we encounter references of Jesus to the Evil Eye in the Gospels of Matthew, Mark, and Luke indicates no reluctance on the part of the evangelists to deny or suppress the fact that Jesus and his contemporaries shared this widespread belief. Moreover, the values affirmed by Jesus' words about the Evil Eye in all cases are consonant with Jesus's general stress upon integrity (Matt 5:21–48; 19:21), the antithesis and mutual exclusion of good and evil states and actions (Matt 5:45; 7:17–18; 12:35/Luke 6:45; Matt 22:10), and the necessary coherence of inward states and moral action (Matt 7:15–20/Luke 6:43–45; Matt 12:33–37). His comments on the Evil Eye likewise are consistent with his demonstration of (Matt 11:5/Luke 7:22; Matt 11:28) and call for generosity, mercy (Matt 12:7; Luke 6:36) and the sharing of possessions in emulation of a generous God and in obligation to fellow creatures under the reign of God.[570]

Paul's letter to the Galatians contains both a direct reference to exercise of an Evil Eye (*ebaskanen*, 3:1) and several allusions, including Paul's physical condition and appearance, the practice of spitting to avert the Evil Eye, a hyperbolic statement about ripping out eyes, an accusation of envy, and the vulnerability of the Galatians as "children" to the menace of the Evil Eye (4:12–20). Galatians, it becomes evident, alludes to an exchange of accusations concerning injury with an Evil Eye that is a subtext of a clash over alternative versions of the good news announcing salavation and new life. Paul, accused by his rivals of harming the Galatians with an Evil Eye, insists that it was *not he but they* who were Evil-Eyeing the Galatians, preaching a faux gospel, curtailing the Galatians' freedom in Christ, and undermining the wellbeing of the community. All features of the Evil Eye in these New Testament texts are consistent with characteristics of Evil Eye belief and practice found in Old Testament texts, the parabiblical evidence, and Greek and Roman sources.

---

570. See Matt 6:2–4, 25–34; 7:7–12; 10:42/ Mark 9:41; Matt 18:5–6/Mark 9:37/Luke 9:48; Matt 18:23–35; Matt 19:16–22/Mark 10:17–22/Luke 18:18–23; Matt 22:1–10.

Ancient witchcraft societies holding Evil Eye beliefs, including the biblical communities, may strike the modern Bible reader as distressingly strange and uncomfortably alien in their "primitive" beliefs and "superstitious" practices. Modern biblical translators and commentators with a worthy concern for the Bible's contemporary relevance may even resort to minimizing or domesticating its alien features for modern consumption. Ironically this effort at "sanitizing" the text keeps current Bible readers from noticing or considering any connection between modern Evil Eye belief and practice and that of the biblical forebears. For those, however, who are committed to understanding the word of God in all its historical and cultural particularity, the only course possible is to study and comprehend these texts as products of and witnesses to their own historical, social, and cultural contexts, including their characteristic perceptions of the world, constellations of beliefs, and patterns of behavior.

EVIL EYE BELIEF AND PRACTICE IN THE BIBLE—CONCLUSION

The Bible as a whole views with furrowed brow all manifestations of an Evil Eye and what it represents. The biblical communities feared and abhorred the Evil Eye similar to their neighbors, and regarded its menace as omnipresent. They shared with their neighbors not only the belief itself but also, of course, the ecological conditions in which Evil Eye belief and practice typically flourish. Here too we find small-scale societies marked by fragile ecologies, unrationalized economies, ineffective laws and intense social competition. These societies held a firm belief in witches, witchcraft, and the Evil Eye. It is in so-called "witchcraft societies" like those of the Old and New Testament and surrounding societies, that Evil Eye belief and practice most typically flourish. The reality of an Evil Eye, like that of witches and sorcerers, diviners, soothsayers and necromancers, demons and evil spirits, was part of the "mental furniture" of the age and of this region of the world.[571] The Evil Eye was regarded as one of the many mysterious forces of nature, akin to, but not equateable with, the mysterious power of witches and wizards. In the Bible, witchcraft and wizards are repeatedly proscribed.[572] The Evil Eye, on

571. See Derrett 1973:31–165, 205–15, as representative of the general view concerning the social, economic, political, and "mental and intellectual" terrains of the biblical writings.

572. See Exod 22:18; Lev 19:26, 31; 20:6, 27; Deut 18:10–12, 20. For witchcraft and sorcery as practiced by Israel or its neighbors, see also Exod 7:11; 1 Sam 15:23; 2 Kgs 9:22; 21:6; 23:24; Isa 8:19; 47:9, 12; Jer 27:9; Mic 5:12; Nah 3:4; Dan 2:2; Mal 3:5; Gal 5:20; Rev 9:21; 18:23; 21:8; 22:15.

the other hand, is abhorred but never legally forbidden. Never is it classified or prohibited in the Bible as a form of witchcraft, sorcery or magic. The Evil Eye is seen rather as a physiological condition conferred by nature (Philo, *Abraham* 21; *Flaccus* 29, etc.), or, more frequently, a moral failure that can be controlled and rectified.

The biblical communities shared the notion that having and looking with an Evil Eye was (a) a negative quality of the Evil Eye possessor and (b) as involving malevolent hostility toward other human beings, creatures, and objects. The eye was understood as an active organ that projects light or particles of energy. It did not receive light from outside, but projected energy outward, similar to the light of a lamp. There is a close relation, these communities believed, between an Evil Eye and feeling envious, which entailed displeasure and resentment at the good fortune of others and the wish for its destruction. Envy, in turn, was fueled by the presumption that all the resources and goods of life were in scarce and limited supply. These communities, of which both Jesus and Paul were a part, considered an Evil Eye a conveyor of malicious dispositions that arise in the heart: envy (1 Sam 18:9; Sir 37:10, 11; *Testaments of the Twelve Patriarchs*; Philo; Josephus; Matt 20:15; Mark 7:22), greed (1 Sam 2:29, Prov 28:22; Sir 14:3, 9; 31:12–13 [gluttony]; Wis 4:12) and ungenerosity, illiberality, miserliness or stinginess with one's possessions, especially toward the poor and needy (Deut 15:7–11; 28:54–57; Sir 14:3; 18:18; Tob 4:1–21; *Test. 12 Patr.*, Matt 6:22–23/ Luke 11:34–35). These dispositions were regarded as incompatible with the will of God and injurious to communal wellbeing as well as personal health. An Evil Eye projected the negative energy of envy or stinginess or greed that arose in the heart and then flowed outward through the eye. The noxious glance of the eye and the dispositions it conveyed brought injury, illness, or loss on whomever or whatever this poisonous glance fell (Prov 23:6–8; 28:22; Sir 14:3,5, 6, 9; 18:18; Wis 4:12; Matt 6:22–23/Luke 11:34). A person looking with an Evil Eye, it was thought, could not only injure others, but also harm him/herself (Sir 14:5, 6, 9; 31:13; 18:18?). The Evil Eye was linked with a "darkened eye," darkness, and blindness.

Like their neighbors, the biblical communities were on constant lookout for possessors of the Evil Eye, and were especially wary of strangers, the physically deformed, those struck blind, and those with ocular impairment or unusual ocular features. Fear of strangers was typical along with the stereotyping of aliens and "outliers" as agents of harm and wielders of an Evil Eye (Philo, *Agriculture* 64; Josephus, *Ant.* 1.259; 3.268). They anticipated an Evil Eye at occasions of eating and dining (Deut 28:54–57; 1 Sam 2:29; Prov 23:6; Sir 14:9, 10; 31:12–13; Mark 7:1–23; cf. 4 Macc 1:25–26?) and when persons who were poor or destitute or famished requested aid (Deut

15:7–11; Deut 28:54–57; Tob 4:1–21; cf. 4 Macc 1:25–26), when the issue of generosity or its opposite, stinginess or illiberality, arose (Matt 6:22–23/ Luke 11:33–36), when praise or admiration were expressed, whenever one person or group was viewed as having been favored to the detriment of another person or group (Matt 20:1–15), or when rival persons (as with rival wives, Sir 37:11) or rival groups (as with Paul and his opponents in Galatia) sought to demean or degrade the other and promote themselves and their cause.

All persons, creatures, and objects, they believed, were vulnerable to an Evil Eye, but especially birthing mothers, infants and children (Gal 4:19), and those who enjoyed unusual or unanticipated good fortune (Matt 20:1–15). Evil Eye accusations also continued to be made against persons targeted for disapproval, denunciation, and disgrace (Matt 20:1–15; Gal 3:1, 4:12–20). Methods for protecting against and warding off an Evil Eye likewise were the same as, or similar to, those of their contemporaries such as the wearing or deploying of anti-Evil Eye amulets (Ep Jer 69/70) and apotropaic phylacteries; bells; mezuzas; items marked with the protective colors of blue and red (Exod 13:9, 16; 28:33–34; 39:25–26; Num 15:37–41; Deut 6:4–9; 22:12; Isa 3:18–23; Sir 45:9; Matt 9:20; 14:36; 23:5; Mark 6:56; Luke 8:44; Rev 9:17); spitting (Mark 8:23; John 9:6; Gal 4:14); inscribed images of an Evil Eye under attack (*T. Sol.* 18:39; cf. 18:38, 40), and resort to envious Evil Eye accusations to discredit and defeat rivals (Matt 20:15; Gal 3:1; 4:.17–18). *Allusions* to the Evil Eye in the Bible, beyond explicit references, may be suspected in texts commenting on the *eye* (Mark 9:47–48/Matt 5:29/ Matt 18:9; Luke 6:41–42/Matt 7:3–5), or on *envy* (Mark 15:10/Matt 27:18; Luke 15:25–32; Acts 7:9; *T. Sol.* 18:38, 40) or *miserliness* since both vices are closely associated with an Evil Eye. Allusions may also include references to evil (Matt 6:13) or to *means* conventionally employed for warding off the Evil Eye and other noxious forces (phylacteries, fringes on prayer shawls).

The numerous warnings against having and wielding an Evil Eye or being an Evil-Eyed person were meant to encourage generosity, hospitality, charity, and liberality of spirit and to discourage miserliness, tight-fistedness, greed, and envy. The parable of the vineyard owner and his workers (Matt 20:1–15) provides an instructive example of the process of Evil-Eye envying and its exposure. The action proceeds from ocular observance of the good fortune of another perceived as a rival, to comparing one's situation and status with that of the rival, to reckoning with a notion of limited good and feeling inferior or deprived in relation to the fortunate rival. This in turn leads to feeling pain and displeasure over the other's good fortune and the wish that this good fortune be destroyed. This feeling of envious malice is conveyed with a malevolent ocular glance directed at the fortunate rival.

Jesus's condemnation of an ungenerous Evil Eye and praise of a generous eye (Matt 6:22–23/Luke 11:33–36) is consistent with his urging of generosity as recorded in Luke 6:30, 35 and is consonant with such Old Testament Evil Eye texts as Deut 15:7–11; 28:54–57; Tob 4:5–21; and Sir 14:3–10, as well as later rabbinic tradition regarding the generosity of one with a "good eye": "He that has a good eye shall be blessed, for he gives of his bread to the poor" (b. Ned. 38a, in connection with Moses as an example of the "good eye" of Prov 22:9). Possessors of the Good Eye were given the honor of reciting blessings: "We give the cup of blessing for the grace after meals to the one who has a Good Eye" (b. Sota 38b). Whoever gives the most for the heave offering for priests (terumah) has a Good Eye; whoever provides the least has an Evil Eye (Sifre Num. 110). The association of a "good eye" with generosity and "Evil Eye" with its opposite, illiberality and stinginess, is explicit in this tradition.

Paul's agitated letter to the Galatians shows us how personal *ad hominem* attacks and Evil Eye accusations accompanied intense theological disputation. Though these Evil Eye accusations are more covert than overt in Paul's letter to the Galatians, they are a graphic example of how in Paul's culture rivalries and struggles for influence and control included the hurling of Evil Eye labels to discredit and neutralize one's opponents. Such accusations served as a means to "put down" and socially neutralize one's rivals, denounce unapproved behavior, mobilize public censure, and marginalize social deviants.

Israel and the followers of Jesus put particular stress on the moral implications of having and casting an Evil Eye. They continued to consider the phenomenon, however, a *physiological* reality and not only a moral metaphor. This is made clear by the occasionally explicit references to the act of malicious *looking* accompanying references to the Evil Eye, the continued regard of the *eye as an active organ* emitting particles of energy, and the belief that *visible amulets and demonstrative apotropaic actions* were effective in thwarting the noxious glance of an Evil Eye. The darkness, moreover, involved with an Evil Eye was not only moral depravity but physical blindness.

Differences and Distinctive Biblical Emphases

In general, the notion of the malignant and socially injurious Evil Eye is symptomatic of a prevailing perception of the human condition and its vulnerability to hostile forces both human and demonic. Comments, advice or warnings concerning the Evil Eye reveal the assumed properties of human physiology and affections, the assumed moral and immoral propensities of human behavior, and the social behavior presumed necessary for communal stability.

Biblical conceptions of the Evil Eye, while generally similar to those attested in Mesopotamian, Egyptian, Greek and Roman cultures, also display some noteworthy differences and distinctive accents.

(1) In contrast to Mesopotamian, Egyptian, and Greco-Roman sources, the biblical authors make *no mention of an Evil Eye demon*, a *baskanos daimôn*,[573] alias the "demon of envy" (*phthoneros daimôn*).[574] This Evil Eye demon was associated with Hades and, often in funerary inscriptions and tomb epitaphs, said to be responsible for the deaths of those remembered in the epitaphs.[575] In the Bible, the Evil Eye is never presented as a demon attacking humans from without. It is rather always depicted, lamented, and warned against as a *human* defect arising within the human heart and communicated by an ocular glance. Only in the post-biblical period was the Evil Eye associated by the Christian communities with Satan/the Devil. This view of the Evil Eye as instrument of the chief of demons, Satan, as found in the Christian church fathers, represents a noteworthy divergence from how the Evil Eye is presented in the biblical wrirtings as a human, not demonic, malady, as an *internal* matter of evil and malevolent disposition arising in the human heart. This linking of the Evil Eye with the Devil/Satan is, in effect, a turn to, and agreement with, a pagan view of the Evil Eye and an attribution of evil to *external* demonic agency alongside human agency.

(2) The Evil Eye, furthermore, is *never attributed to God*, but only to humans. Israelites and Christians never attributed an Evil Eye or envy to Yahweh, in contrast to the Greeks who ascribed both to the gods.[576] The God of Israel rather is portrayed as rescuing his favorites from the baneful effect of the Evil Eye in typically unexpected or unpredictable ways, as the stories of Joseph and David make evident. The Evil Eye, along with the associated qualities of envy, miserliness or ungenerosity, are presented in the Bible solely as human malignancies

---

573. See CIG 2.3715, *baskanos hêrpase daimôn*; Kaibel 1878: no. 345, line 1.

574. See CIG 4.6858, *tôi phtonerôi daimoni*.

575. See Kaibel 1898: no. 496, line 6: *[b]askainei tois agathoi[s Aidês]*; cf. also no. 381, line 3, a metrical epitaph concerning a four year old girl caused to die by the Evil Eye/malevolence of Hades (*Aideô baskaniois*); see Bernand 1991:99 for the complete text. See also Kaibel, 1898: no. 734, line 2: *baskanôi pikrôi*, "by bitter *baskanos* [causing death] (cematery of Priscilla in Rome).

576. See Rakoczy 1996:7–11, 63–72, 247–70; Elliott 2007a, 2007b, 2008, and Vol. 2 passim.

(3) The Bible, in contrast to the neighboring cultures,[577] *never attributes the Evil Eye to animals, alive or dead, as fascinators.* Animals, however, were thought vulnerable to an Evil Eye and therefore protected by amulets (Judg 8:21, 26; Zech 14:20).

(4) The Bible says nothing about an *Evil Eye being inherited,* or characteristic of particular families of peoples that pass it on from generation to generation.

(5) An Evil Eye, the biblical texts indicate, is *activated primarily by intention, by allowing envy, miserliness, or malevolence to arise and take effect in unimpeded fashion.* Evil-Eyeing can result in self-injury (Sir 14:5, 6, 9; 18:18), but this is a consequence and by-product of deliberate, not inadvertent, Evil-Eyeing of others.

(6) *No mention* is made in the biblical writings of *Medusa/Gorgo or any other mythological figure* or force conventionally associated with the Evil Eye (and envy) in Mesopotamian, Egyptian, Greek, and Roman traditions.[578] There is likewise *no mention of Horus or an amuletic Eye of Horus.* There is *no mention of an Evil Eye demon.*

(7) There is *no explanation* in the Bible of *how the Evil Eye was thought to operate.* This, however, can be surmised from evidence that is available both in the Bible and comparable parabibblical and extra-biblical sources.

(8) It has been claimed that nowhere in the Bible is the Evil Eye explicitly named a *cause of illness,* in contrast to other cultures. Derrett's assertion to this effect (1995), however, exceeds the evidence. Proverbs 23:6–8 speaks of the Evil Eye causing the vomiting of food, and the loss mentioned in Prov 28:22 could include health as well as wealth. Other Evil Eye passages (Sir 14:6, 9; 18:18; 31:13; Matt 6:22–23/Luke 11:33–36) speak of the grief, injury and "darkness" (blindness) wrought by an Evil Eye. Biblical cases of blindness, in particular, could have been perceived as punishment for exercising an Evil Eye. This is despite the fact that Israelite and early Christian authors were more prone to attribute illness to the work of demons and unclean spirits than were their Greco-Roman contemporaries.[579] Latter rabbinic texts speak of the Evil Eye causing illness, shortness of life, and death, and this surely reflected the thought of earlier biblical authors and characters as well, even where not stated explicitly.[580]

577. On animals as fascinators in Greek and Roman texts see Vol. 2.

578. On the sole possible exception of the basilisk (also rendered "serpent," "viper" and mentioned in LXX Ps 90:13 [MT 91:13]; Prov 23:32; Isa 11:8, 14:29; 59:5 [*tsiphoni*]), see above, p. 72.

579. Nutton 2004:283–91.

580. See *m. Avot* 2:16; *b. Arak.* 16a; *b. B.M.* 107b; *b. Ned.* 7b; *y. Shabb.* 14, 14c; *Gen. Rab.* 53:13. On these texts see Vol. 4, chap. 1. On the conventional notion of the Evil

(9) The Bible contains *no texts describing remedies* for healing injuries specifically caused by an Evil Eye. Mark 8:22–26 could represent an exception if the blindness cured by Jesus' spittle was imagined to have been due to an Evil Eye—blindness either as caused by an Evil Eye or as punishment for having an Evil Eye. The same holds true for Paul's blindness and cure as recounted in Acts (9:8–9, 17–18; 22:11–13)—if the blindness is regarded as punishment for Paul's Evil Eyeing (and envying) those whom he persecuted (Acts 8:1a; 9:1–2, 4–5; 22:4–5, 7–8, 11–13, 20).

(10) A significant *distinctive* feature of biblical commentary on the Evil Eye is *association of an Evil Eye with reluctance to be generous toward those in need*. Repeatedly the biblical authors, and also Jesus, warn against and condemn displays of stinginess, miserliness, looking with a hostile eye and closing ones's hand to the poor and destitute (Deut 15:7–11; 28:54–57; Prov 23:6; Sir 14:3, 8, 10; 18:18; Tob 4:7, 16). This reluctance to share one's resources and the withholding of food and support comes under frequent censure and appears implied in Jesus' teaching as well where he contrasts a good eye and an Evil Eye (Matt 6:22–23/Luke 11:34–35). Here an "integral eye" represents a generous person, and an Evil Eye, an ungenerous, illiberal, and miserly individual. This association of an Evil Eye with reluctant giving and resentful sharing of resources is a distinctive emphasis of the biblical Evil Eye references. It points to a moral code that envisions the sharing of material resources, especially with the poor and needy, as essential to the well-being and stability of the community and as consonant with the will of God.

The biblical references thus focus on the Evil Eye as a human moral problem, its noxious effects, and, by implication, how it can be contained and controlled through the avoidance of envy, miserliness, greed, gluttony and the cultivation of moderation in affect and especially generosity and liberality toward all in need.

(11) There are various references in the Bible to *strategies and means of protection* for warding off an Evil Eye. These include the anti-Evil Eye figure (*prosbaskanion*) for protecting a cucumber field mentioned in Ep Jer 69/70, and Paul's mention of *spitting* in Gal 4:14. Additional means for warding off the Evil Eye in biblical times in all likelihood also included the affixing of *mezuzahs* to the doorposts of domestic residences (Deut 6:9; 11:20), the donning of phylacteries (*phylaktêria*) at prayer (Exod 13:9, 16; Deut 6:8; 11:8; Matt 23:5), the blue fringes (*tzitzit, kraspeda*) attached to prayer shawls (Num 15:37–41; Deut 22:12; Matt 9:20; 14:36; 23:5; Mark 6:56; Luke 8:44).

Eye as cause of illness see Murdock's world survey on theories of illness, including the Evil Eye (1980 and esp. 57–71). See also Maloney, ed. 1976:14, 166, 315–19 and passim; Herzfeld 1986; Plich 2000:19.

the tabernacle and temple materials and vestments also of the apotropaic color blue (Exod 25:4; 26:1, 4; 28:5–6, 8, 15; Num 4:6–7 etc.; 2 Chr 2:7, 14; 3:14, and the bells attached to the garment of the high priest (Exod 28:33–35; 39:25–26; Sir 45:7–9; Josephus, *War* 5.5.5). The color red similarly was attributed apotropaic power and adorned fabrics in the tabernacle (Exod 25–28; Num 4:8), warriors' tunics and shields (Nah 2:4; 1 Macc 4:23), and threads attached to the wrists of infants (Gen 38:27–30).

The references to apotropaics and the host of amulets found among the biblical communities also before and after the composition of the biblical writings indicate not only that in Israel and early Christianity Evil Eye belief and practice continued unabated over millennia, but also that these amulets and protective practices were shaped by distinctive Israelite and Christian traditions. In the post-biblical period, notable biblical figures such as Joseph and Solomon, key biblical verses or excerpts of prayers, sacred names of God, Jesus, and angels, and references to the cross of Christ and popular saints all figured in the Jewish and Christian adaptation of Circum-Mediterranean and Near Eastern Evil Eye practices.[581] The Evil Eye belief and practice of Israel and the nascent Jesus movement are marked by distinctive features of their religious traditions. On the whole, however, the cultural similarities shared by the various Circum-Mediterranean peoples in respect to Evil Eye belief and practice outweigh the differences.

It is futile to attempt a distinction between physiological and metaphorical senses of "Evil Eye" in the biblical texts. Here, as in the relevant evidence from Mesopotamian, Egyptian, Greek and Roman tradition, the frequent mention of "seeing," "looking," and acts of vision that accompany references to the Evil Eye down through Late Antiquity indicates that "Evil Eye" explicitly and implicitly presumes physical ocular activity conveying malevolent dispositions and energy arising in the heart.

The Various Capacities of Evil Eye Belief

In the biblical communities, as in other Evil Eye cultures, the concept of the malignant and menacing Eye operated on multiple levels (biological/physiological, psychological, economic, social, and moral) and served a variety of purposes.

Belief in the Evil Eye was instrumental in (1) accounting for sudden and otherwise inexplicable causes of misfortune, injury, loss, or death; (2) identifying and explaining manifestations of personal and social evil, (3) identifying, expressing and promoting particular values of the community

581. See Vol. 4, chaps. 1 and 2.

such as generosity, a liberal spirit, and the sharing of possessions, and, on the other hand, discouraging envy, stinginess, greed, and unrestrained ambition, which threatened group concord and cohesion; (4) reinforcing with extraordinary sanction attitudes and actions fostering the common weal and group harmony and unity; and (5) encouraging patterns of behavior and social interaction consistent with the will of God. (6) Evil Eye interactions and accusations played a role in the adjudication of conflict in groups and villages where central authority was absent or ineffective. They helped to define, mark and enforce the social identity and boundaries of groups. Evil Eye accusations provided a modicum of social control in situations lacking formal enforcement of law. These accusations, if made to stick, discredited and degraded the accused in the court of public opinion. The accused were branded as persons seriously out of line with moral expectations and community standards, and dangerous to the harmony of the community and its well being.

Explicit biblical references to the Evil Eye in the original languages have been obscured by modern translations that render the Hebrew and Greek according to suspected sense rather than literally. As a result, modern readers relying on biblical translations are left uniformed of the frequent mention of this phenomenon in the Bible, the role that the Evil Eye played in ancient biblical life, and the relation of biblical Evil Eye belief and practice to the beliefs and practices of their own modern cultures.

Approaching the Biblical World

Familiarity with this fascinating feature of ancient belief and practice brings us modern readers one step closer to that foreign world of the Biblical communities, their conceptual horizons, and the cultural scripts according to which they thought and felt and acted. In the case of Paul's letter to the Galatians, to take but one example from our list of biblical Evil Eye texts, anxiety about the present evil age (Gal 1:4), enslavement to the elemental spirits of the universe (Gal 4:3), use of harmful magic (*pharmakeia*, Gal 5:20), and resort to curses (Gal 1:8–9; 3:10), to solemn warning (6:17), and to charges of Evil Eye possession (3:1) and counter-accusations of Evil –Eyed envy (4:17), are all vivid features of the witchcraft society in which Jesus, Paul, and the early churches were at home. The role of Evil Eye belief and practice in Galatians and other biblical documents should serve as an important reminder to exegetes and theologians often preoccupied exclusively with lofty theological concepts and arguments always to keep at least one good eye also on the popular culture which informed the biblical authors and provided the cultural scripts according to which they thought, acted, and communicated.

Dread of the Evil Eye and resort to manifold measures of defense continued in the communities of Israel and Christianity long beyond the first century of the Common Era. Evil Eye belief and practice in these communities down through Late Antiquity are the subjects of the final volume of this study, Vol. 4, chaps. 1 and 2.

BIBLIOGRAPHY

PRIMARY SOURCES

Old Testament (Hebrew, Greek)

Elliger, K., and W. Rudolph, eds. 1977. *Biblia Hebraica Stuttgartensia*. Stuttgart: Deutsche Bibelstiftung.

Kittel, Rudolf, and Paul Kahle, eds. 1951. *Biblia Hebraica*. 9th ed. Stuttgart: Privilegierte Württembergische Bibelanstalt.

Rahlfs, A., ed. 1935, 1952. *Septuaginta, id est Vetus Testamentum graece iuxta LXX interpretes*. 2 vols. Stuttgart: Privilegierte Württembergische Bibelanstalt.

Septuaginta Vetus Testamentum Graecum. 1967–. Auctoritate Academiae Scientiarum Gotting-ensis editum. Göttingen: Vandenhoeck & Ruprecht.

Bible (Latin Vulgate)

Biblia Sacra. Vulgatae Editionis Sixti V Pontificis Maximi iussu recognita et Clementis VIII Auctoritate edita. Albani (Rome): Paulinae, 1957 (1907).

Biblia Sacra iuxta Latinam Vulgatam versionem. 18 vols. Rome: Typis Polyglottis Vaticanis, 1926–1995.

Weber, R., ed. 1969. *Biblia Sacra: Iuxta Vulgatam versionem*. 2 vols. Stuttgart: Württembergische Bibelanstalt.

Apocrypha and Pseudepigrapha

Black, Matthew. 1970. *Apocalypsis Henochi Graece*. In *Pseudepigrapha Veteris Testamenti graece*. Vol. 3. Edited by A. M. Denis and M. de Jonge. Leiden: Brill.

Busch, Peter. 2006. *Das Testament Salomos: Die älteste christliche Dämonologie, kommentiert und in deutscher Erstübersetzung*. TUGAL 153. Berlin. de Gruyter.

Charles, R. H., ed. 1913. *The Apocrypha and Pseudepigrapha of the Old Testament in English*. 2 vols. Oxford: Clarendon.

————. 1908. *The Greek Versions of the Testaments of the Twelve Patriarchs*. Reprinted, Ancient Texts and Translations. Eugene, OR: Wipf & Stock, 2008.

————. 1913. "The Testaments of the Twelve Patriarchs." In *APOT*, 2:282–367.

Charlesworth, James H., ed. 1983, 1985. *The Old Testament Pseudepigrapha*. 2 vols. Garden City, NY: Doubleday.

Denis, A.-M., ed. 1970. *Fragmenta Pseudepigraphorum quae supersunt graeca*. PsVTG 3. Leiden: Brill.

Duling, Dennis C. 1983. "Testament of Solomon." In *The Old Testament Pseudepigrapha*. Vol. 1, *Apocalyptic Literature and Testaments,* edited by James H. Charlesworth, 935–87. Garden City: Doubleday.

Fleck, Ferdinand Florenz. ed. 1837. "*Testamentum Salomonis.*" In *Wissenschaftliche Reise durch das südliche Deutschland, Italien, Sicilien, und Frankreich* 2/3. Anecdota maximam partem sacra, 111–40. Leipzig: Barth. [Ms. P , now in Bibliotheque Nationale, Paris.]

Jonge, Marinus de, ed. 1978. *The Testaments of the Twelve Patriarchs: A Critical Edition of the Greek Text.* PVTG 1.2. Leiden: Brill.

Levi, I., ed. 1969. *The Hebrew Text of the Book of Ecclesiasticus, with Introduction, Notes and Selected Glossary.* Semitic Study Series, 3. Leiden, Brill.

Marböck, Johannes. 2010. *Jesus Sirach 1–23.* HTKAT. Freiburg: Herder.

Milik, J. T., ed. 1976. *The Books of Enoch. Aramaic Fragments from Qumrân Cave 4.* Oxford: Oxford University Press.

Miller, David M., and Ken M. Penner, eds. 2006. "Testament of Solomon." Edited by David M. Miller, and Ken M. Penner. Edition 1.0. In *The Online Critical Pseudepigrapha.* Edited by Ian W. Scott, Ken M. Penner, and David M. Miller. Atlanta: Society of Biblical Literature. Online: http://www.purl.org/net/ocp/testament-of-solomon.

Oesterley, W. O. E., and G. H. Box. 1913. "The Book of Sirach." In *APOT* 1:268–517.

Sauer, Georg. 2000. *Jesus Sirach/Ben Sira.* ATD Apokryphen 1. Göttingen: Vandenhoeck & Ruprecht.

Schreiner, Josef. 2002. *Jesus Sirach: 1–24.* Die neue Echter Bibel. Altes Testament 38. Würzburg: Echter.

Simpson, D. C. 1913. "The Book of Tobit." In *APOT* 1:174–241.

Skehan, Patrick W., and Alexander A. Di Lella. 1987. *The Wisdom of Ben Sira: A New Translation with Notes.* AB 39. New York: Doubleday.

Testamentum Salomonis. PG 111.1316–1358 (BHG 2390).

Winston, David. 1979. *The Wisdom of Solomon. A New Translation with Introduction and Commentary.* Anchor Bible 43. Garden City, NY: Doubleday.

Zapff, Burkard M. 2010. *Jesus Sirach: 25–51.* Die neue Echter Bibel. Altes Testament 39. Würzburg: Echter.

Ziegler, Joseph, ed. 1980. *Wisdom of Jesus Ben Sirach. Sapientia Iesu Filii Sirach.* Edited by Joseph Ziegler. Vetus Testamentum Graecum. Auctoritate Academiae Scientiarum Gottingensis editum. Vol. 12.2. 2nd ed. Göttingen: Vandenhoeck & Ruprecht (1962).

New Testament

Aland, Kurt, ed. 1976. *Synopsis Quattuor Evangeliorum*. Stuttgart: Württembergische Bibelanstalt.

Aland, Kurt et al., eds. 1994. *Greek New Testament*. New York: United Bible Society.

Nestle, Eberhard et al., eds. 1993. *Novum Testamentum Graece*. 27th ed. Stuttgart: Deutsche Bibelgesellschaft.

Dead Sea Scrolls

García Martínez, Florentino. 1996. *The Dead Sea Scrolls Translated. The Qumran Texts in English*. Translation by Wilford G. E. Watson. 2nd ed. Leiden: Brill, 1996.

Garciá Martínez, Florentino, and Eibert J. C. Tigchelaar, eds. 1997, 1998. *The Dead Sea Scrolls. Study edition*. 2 vols. Leiden: Brill.

Harrington, Daniel J. 1996. *Wisdom Texts from Qumran*. New York: Routledge.

Lohse, Eduard, ed. 1971. *Die Texte aus Qumran: Hebräisch und Deutsch*. 2nd ed. Darmstadt: Wissenschaftliche Buchgesellschaft.

Tov, Emmanuel, with Noel B. Reynolds and Kristian Heal, eds. 2006. *The Dead Sea Scrolls Electronic Library*. Leiden: Brill.

Wise, Michael et al., eds. 1996. *The Dead Sea Scrolls: A New Translation*. New York: HarperCollins.

Philo of Alexandria

Colson, F. H. et al., trans. 1929–1962. *Philo*. 12 vols. LCL. Cambridge: Harvard University Press.

Cohn, L., and P. Wendland, eds. 1896–1930. *Philo. Opera quae supersunt*. 7 vols. Berlin: de Gruyter.

Flavius Josephus

Thackeray, H. St. J. et al., trans. 1926–1965. *Josephus*. 10 vols. LCL. Cambridge: Harvard University Press.

Rabbinic Writings and Jewish Sources

Mishnah

Danby, Herbert, ed. and trans. 1933. *Mishnah*. Oxford: Oxford University Press.

Neusner, Jacob, ed. and trans. 1988. *The Mishnah*. New Haven: Yale University Press.

Midrashim

Eisenstein, D. ed. 1915. *Otsar Midrashim: A Library of Two Hundred Minor Midrashim.* 2 vols. Reprinted, 1969.

Friedmann, H., and M. Simon, trans. 1939. *Midrash Rabbah.* 10 vols. London: Soncino.

Talmudim

Daiches, S., and H. Freedman, eds. 1962. *Hebrew-English Edition of the Babylonian Talmud, Baba Mezi'a.* London: Traditional Press.

Epstein, I., ed. 1935–1960. *The Babylonian Talmud.* 34 vols. in 6 parts. London: Soncino.

Guggenheimer, Heinrich Walter. 2000. *The Jerusalem Talmud.* Translated by Heinrich Walter Guggenheimer. *First Order: Zeraim, Tractates Peah and Demay.* Berlin: de Gruyter.

Talmud Yerushalmi. 1866. Krotoschin; Zitomir, 1860–1867; Vilnius, 1922.

Targumim

Diez Macho, Alejandro. 1968. *Neophyti 1: Targum Palestinense MS de la Biblioteca Vaticana,* Vol. 1, *Genesis.* Madrid: Consejo Superior de Investigaciones Científicas.

Etheridge, J. W., ed. 1862–1865. *The Targums of Onkelos and Jonathan Ben Uzziel on the Pentateuch, with the fragments of the Jerusalem Targum from the Chaldee.* London: Longman, Green, Longman, and Roberts.

McNamara, Martin, ed. 1992. *Targum Neofiti 1: Genesis.* The Aramaic Bible 1A. Collegeville, MN: Glazier.

Sperber, Alexander, ed. 2012. *The Bible in Aramaic based on old manuscripts and printed texts,* Second Impression. Volume I: *The Pentateuch according to Targum Onkelos* with a foreword by Robert P. Gordon. Volume II: *The Former Prophets according to Targum Jonathan.* Volume III: *The Latter Prophets according to Targum Jonathan,* Volume IV A: *The Hagiographa. Transition from translation to Midrash.* Volume IV B: *The Targum and the Hebrew Bible.* Leiden: Brill.

Tosefta

Lieberman, Saul, ed. 1955. *Tosefta.* New York: Jewish Theological Seminary.

Other Jewish Sources

Levene. Dan. 2003. *A Corpus of Magic Bowls: Incantation Texts in Jewish Aramaic from Late Antiquity.* Kegan Paul Library of Jewish Studies. London: Kegan Paul.

Naveh, Joseph, and Shaul Shaked, eds. 1987. *Amulets and Magic Bowls: Aramaic Incantations of Late Antiquity.* 2nd ed.; 3rd ed., 1998.

———, eds. 1993. *Magic Spells and Formulae: Aramaic Incantations of Late Antiquity.* Jerusalem: Magnes.

Noy, David, ed. 1993. *Jewish Inscriptions of Western Europe*. Vol. 1. Cambridge: Cambridge University Press.

Noy, David, and Hanswulf Bloedhorn, eds. 2004. *Inscriptiones Judaicae Orientis*. III. *Syria and Cyprus*. Texts and Studies in Ancient Judaism 102. Tübingen: Mohr/ Siebeck.

Margalioth, Mordecai, ed. 1966. *Sepher Ha-Razim*. Jerusalem: Yediot Achronot.

Morgan, Michael A., trans. 1983. *Sepher Ha-Razim. The Book of Mysteries*. SBL Texts and Translations 25. Pseudepigrapha Series 11. Chico, CA: Scholars.

Early Christian Writings

Acta Apostolorum Apocrypha. Edited by R. A. Lipsius and M. Bonnet. 2 vols. in 3 parts. Vol. 1 (1891); vol. 2.1 (1898); vol. 2.2 (1903). 1891–1903; reprinted, Darmstadt: Wissenschaftliche Buchgesellschaft, 1959.
> *Acts of Paul and Thecla*. Vol. 1:235–272.
> *Acts of John*. Vol. 2.1:151–216.
> *Acts of Thomas*. Vol. 2.2:99–291.

Basil of Caesarea. 1895. *Basil: Letters and Select Works*. In *Nicene and Post-Nicene Fathers of the Christian Church*. 2nd series. Vol. 8. Edited by Philip Schaff. Reprinted, Grand Rapids: Eerdmans, 1968.

———. 1950. "Homily 11, Concerning Envy/*Peri phthonou*." (PG 31. 372–386). In *Saint Basil. Ascetical Works*, 463–474. Translated by M. Monica Wagner. *The Fathers of the Church: A New Translation*. New York: Fathers of the Church.

Elliott, J. K., ed. 2005. *The Apocryphal New Testament: A Collection of Apocryphal Christian Literature in an English Translation*. Oxford: Oxford University Press.

Gregory Thaumaturgus. 1886. "On the Gospel according to Matthew (6:22–23)." In *Ante-Nicene Fathers*, Vol. 6.2. Translated by S. D. F. Salmond. Edited by Alexander Roberts, James Donaldson, and A. Cleveland Coxe Buffalo, NY: Christian Literature Publishing.

Hennecke, Edgar, and Wilhelm Schneemelcher, eds. 1963, 1965. *New Testament Apocrypha*. 2 vols. Philadelphia: Westminster

Jerome. *Commentarius in epistulam ad Galatas*. PL 26. 307–438.

———. 1969. *Commentarius in Matthaeum*. Edited by D. Hurst and M. Adriaen. CCSL 77. Turnholti: Brepols.

———. *Explicatio in epistulam ad Galatas*. PL 30.811 [abbreviated version of 26.346–48].

———. 1977, 1979. *Commentaire sur S. Matthieu*. 2 vols. Edited by Emile Bonnard. SC 242, 259. Paris: Cerf.

John Chrysostom. *Catecheses ad illuminandos*. PG 49. 223–40.

———. *De adoratione pretiosae crucis*. PG 58.838

———. *De futurae vitae deliciis*. PG 51.347–54.

———. *Homiliae in epistulam ad Galatas commentarius*. PG 61:611–82.

———. *Homiliae in Genesim 1–67*. PG 53.21–385; 54.385–580.

———. *Homiliae in Iohannem 1–88*. PG 59.23–482.

———. *Homiliae in Matthaeum 1–90*. PG 57.13–58.794.

———. *Homiliae in Matthaeum XV–XXIV*. PG 57.223–328.

———. *Homiliae in primam epistulam ad Corinthios 1–44*. PG 61.9–382.

————. *In paralyticum demissum per tectum.* PG 51.47–54.

————. 1886–1890. *Saint Chrysostom: Homilies on the Epistles of Paul to the Corinthians.* Translated by Talbot W. Chambers. Nicene and Post-Nicene Fathers of the Christian Church 12. Edited by Philip Schaff. Reprinted, Grand Rapids: Eerdmans, 1956.

————. 1886–1890. *Saint Chrysostom: Homilies on Galatians, Ephesians, Philippians, Colossians, Thessalonians, Timothy, Titus, and Philemon.* Vol. 13. Nicene and Post-Nicene Fathers of the Christian Church. Translated by Gross Alexander. Edited by Philip Schaff. Reprinted, Grand Rapids: Eerdmans, 1956.

————. 1839. *Sancti Patris Johannis Chrysostomi archepiscopi Constantinopolitani Homiliae in Matthaeum, XV–XXIV.* Edited by F. Field. Vol. 1:186–356. Cambridge: Officina academica.

John Chrysostom (Pseudo-). 1988. *Opus imperfectum in Mattheaeum.* Edited by J. van Banning. CCSL 87B. Turnholt: Brepols.

Marius Victorinus. 1986. *In epistulam Pauli ad Ephesios, In epistulam Pauli ad Galatas, In epistulam Pauli ad Philippenses.* Edited by F. Gori. CSEL 83.2. Vienna: Universität Salzburg.

————. *In epistulam Pauli ad Galatas liber 1.* PL 8. 1145–98.

Migne, Jacques-Paul, ed. 1857–1889. *Patrologiae cursus completus: Series Graeca.* 176 vols. Paris: Garnier.

————, ed. 1844–1864. *Patrologiae cursus completus: Series Latina.* 221 vols. Paris: Garnier.

Robinson, James M., ed. 1996. *The Nag Hammadi Library in English.* 4th ed. Leiden: Brill.

Greek and Roman Writings

Aeschylus. 1952. "The Plays of Aeschylus." Translated by G. M. Cookson., *Great Books of the Western World,* 5:1–91. Chicago: Encyclopaedia Britannica.

Alexander (Pseudo-) of Aphrodisias. 1841. *Problemata Physica.* In *Physici et Medici Graeci minores,* 1:3-80. Edited by I. L. Ideler. 2 vols. Berlin: Reimer. Reprinted, Amsterdam 1963.

Apollonius of Rhodes. 1912. *Argonautica.* Translated by R. C. Seaton. LCL. Cambridge: Harvard University Press.

Aristotle. 1934. *Aristotle in 23 Volumes.* Translated by H. Rackham et al. Cambridge: Harvard University Press.

————. 1927–1952. *The Works of Aristotle.* 12 vols. Edited by W. D. Ross and J. A. Smith; translated by W. D. Ross et al. Oxford: Clarendon

————. 1854–1874. *Aristotelis opera omnia. Graece et latine.* Edited by Ulco Cats Bussemaker, Friedrich Dübner, and Emil Heitz. 5 vols. Paris: Didot. Vol. 4 edited by U. C. Bussemaker (1857) includes an Appendix containing Aristotle (Pseudo-), *Problemata inedita* (3 books).

————. *On Rhetoric: A Theory of Civic Discourse.* Newly translated, with Introduction, Notes, and Appendices, by George A. Kennedy. New York: Oxford University Press, 1991.

————. *Rhetoric.* Translated by John H. Freese. LCL. New York: Putnam, 1926.

Aristotle (Pseudo-). 1913. *Physiognomonica*, edited and translated by E. S. Forster. In Aristotle. *Opuscula: De coloribus, De audibilibus, Physiognomonica*, by T. Loveday and E. S. Forster. *De Plantis*, by E. S. Forster. *De mirabilibus auscultationibus*, by L. D. Dowdall. *Mechanica*, by E. S. Forster. *De lineis insecabilibus*, by H. H. Joachim. *Ventorum situs et cognomina*, by E. S. Forster. *De Melisso, Xenophane, Gorgia*, by T. Loveday and E. S. Forster. Oxford: Clarendon.

Problemata (physica). In *The Works of Aristotle*. 12 vols. Edited by W. D. Ross and J. A. Smith. Translated by W. D. Ross et al. Vol. 7, translated by E. S. Forster. Oxford: Oxford University Press, 1927.

Problemata inedita. 1857. In *Aristotelis opera omnia. Graece et latine*. Vol. 4, edited by U. C. Bussemaker. 5 vols. Paris: Didot.

Diels, Hermann, and Walter Kranz, eds. 1951–1952. *Die Fragmente der Vorsokratiker*. 3 vols. 6th ed. Berlin: Weidmann. *Testimonia* 1–170 (siglum A); *Fragmenta* 1–298a (siglum B).

Euripides. 1995. *Children of Heracles. Hippolytus. Andromache. Hecuba*. Translated by David Kovacs. LCL. Cambridge: Harvard University Press.

Heliodorus. 1957. *An Ethiopian Romance*. Translated with an introduction by Moses Hadas. Ann Arbor: Ann Arbor University of Michigan Press.

———. 1961. *Ethiopian Story*. Translated by W. R. M. Lamb. Everyman's Library 276. London: Dent.

Heliodorus. 1935–43. *Héliodore: Les Éthiopiques. Téagène et Chariclé*. Edited by R. M. Rattenbury and T. W. Lumb. Translated by J. Maillon. 3 vols. Paris: "Les Belles Lettres."

Kaibel, Georg, ed. 1878. *Epigrammata Graeca ex lapidibus conlecta*. Berlin: Reimer. Reprinted 1965.

Kock, Theodor. 1888. *Comicorum Atticorum fragmenta*. Vol. 3. Leipzig: Teubner.

Lysias. 1930. *Lysias. Orations*. Translated by W. R. M. Lamb. LCL. Cambridge: Harvard University Press.

Philostratus the Elder of Lemnos, Philostratus the Younger. 1931. *Elder Philostratus, Younger Philostratus, Callistratus*. Translated by Arthur Fairbanks. LCL. Cambridge:, Harvard University Press. (*Imagines* vol. 1 by Philostratus the Elder; *Imagines* vol. 2 by Philostratus the Younger).

Plato. 1900. *Platonis Opera*. 5 vols. Edited by J. Burnett. Scriptorum Classicorum Bibliotheca Oxoniensis. Oxford: Clarendon.

———. 1969. *Plato*. 12 vols. Edited by P. Shorey. Translated by H. N. Fowler et al. LCL. Cambridge: Harvard University Press.

Plutarch. 1914–1926. *The Parallel Lives*. 11 vols. Translated by Bernadotte Perrin. LCL. New York: Macmillan.

———. 1918. *The Parallel Lives*. Vol. 6. *Dion and Brutus. Timoleon and Aemilius Paulus*. Translated by Bernadotte Perrin. LCL. New York: Macmillan.

———. 1976. *Moralia*. 16 vols. Translated by F. C. Babbitt et al. LCL. Cambridge: Harvard University Press.

Sophocles. 1994. *Sophocles. Ajax. Electra. Oedipus Tyrannus*. Edited and translated by Hugh Lloyd-Jones. Vol. 1. LCL. Cambridge: Harvard University Press.

Stobaeus, Johannes. 1894–1923. *Ioannis Stobaei Anthologium* [Eclogues, Books 1–2; Florilegium, Books 3–4]. 3 vols. and appendix. Edited by Curtius Wachsmuth and Otto Hense. Berlin: Weidmann.

Theocritus. 1901. *The Idylls of Theocritus*. Translated by R. J. Cholmeley. London: Bell & Sons.

Theophrastus. 1915. *Theophrastus. Characters. Herodas, Cercidas and the Greek Choliambic Poets*. Edited and translated by J. M. Edmonds and A. D. Knox. LCL. Cambridge: Harvard University Press.

———. 1917. *De Sensu et sensilibus. Theophrastus and the Greek Physiological Psychology* before Aristotle. Translated by George M. Stratton. London: Allen & Unwin.

Thucydides. 1919. *History of the Peloponnesian War*. 4 vols. Translated by C. F. Smith., LCL. Cambridge: Harvard University Press.

Tibullus, Albius. 1878. *Albii Tibulli Elegiarum libri duo. Accedunt Pseudotibulliana*. Edited by Emil Baehrens. Leipzig: Teubner.

Virgil. 1916. *Eclogues, Georgics, Aeneid*. Translated by H. R. Fairclough. LCL. Cambridge: Harvard University Press.

Xenophon. 1914–1940. *Xenophon*. Translated by C. L. Brownson et al. 7 vols. LCL. Cambridge: Harvard University Press

PAPYRI

Mahaffy, J., and J. Smyly. 1891–1905. *The Flinders Petrie Papyri*. 3 vols. Dublin: Academy House.

Grenfell, B. P., and A. S. Hunt et al., eds. 1898–1972. *The Oxyrhynchus Papyri*. 72 vols. London: Egypt Exploration Society.

SECONDARY STUDIES AND REFERENCE WORKS

Aalen, Sverre. 1951. *Die Begriffe "Licht" und "Finsternis" im Alten Testament, im Spätjudentum und im Rabbinismus*. Skrifter utgitt av det Norske Vedenskaps-Academi I Oslo. Historisk-filosofisk Klasse 1951:1. Oslo: Dybwaad.

Abusch, I. Tzvi. 1987. *Babylonian Witchcraft Literature: Case Studies*. Brown Judaic Studies 132. Atlanta: Scholars.

———. 1989. "The Demonic Image of the Witch in Standard Babylonian Literature: The Reworking of Popular Conceptions by Learned Exorcists." In *Religion, Science, and Magic in Concert and in Conflict*, edited by Jacob Neusner et al., 27–58. New York: Oxford University Press.

Alexander, P. S. 1986. "Incantations and Books of Magic." In Emil Schürer, *The History of the Jewish People in the Age of Jesus Christ (175 BC—AD 135)*, edited and revised by Geza Vermes et al., Vol. 3/1:342–79. Edinburgh: T. & T. Clark.

Allison, Dale C. 1987 "The Eye is the Lamp of the Body (Matthew 6.22–23 = Luke 11.34–36)." *NTS* 33 (1987) 61–83.

———. 1997. "The Eye as a Lamp: Finding the Sense." In *The Jesus Tradition in Q*, 133–67. Harrisburg, PA: Trinity.

Alonso-Schökel, Luis, and Juan Mateos. 1976. *Nueva biblia espanola: Edicion Latino-americana*. Edited by Luis Alonso-Schökel and Juan Mateos. Madrid: Cristianidad.

Amiot, François. 1946. *Saint Paul; Epitre aux Galates. Epitre aux Thessaloniciens*. Paris: Beauchese.

Amstutz, J. 1968. *HAPLOTES: Eine begriffsgeschichtliche Studie zum jüdisch-christlichen Griechisch.* Theophania 19. Bonn: Hanstein.

Ankarloo, Bengt, and Stuart Clark. 1999. *Witchcraft and Magic in Europe: Ancient Greece and Rome.* Philadelphia: University of Pennsylvania Press.

Anonymous. 1974. "Evil Eye." In *Encyclopedic Dictionary of Judaica.* Edited by Geoffrey Wigoder, 181. New York: Amiel.

Apostolides, Anastasia. 2008. "Western Ethnocentrism: A Comparison between African Witchcraft and the Greek Evil Eye from a Sociology of Religion Perspective." Masters thesis, University of Pretoria, South Africa.

Apostolides, Anastasia, and Yolanda Dreyer. 2008. "The Greek Evil Eye, African Witchcraft, and Western Ethnocentrism." *HTS Teologiese Studies* 64/2:1021–42.

Aquaro, Robert A. 2001. "*Vaskania*: Envy and the Evil Eye in the Bible." MA thesis, St. Vladimir's Seminary.

———. 2004. *Death by Envy: The Evil Eye and Envy in the Christian Tradition.* New York: iUniverse.

Arnold, Clinton E. 2005. "'I Am Astonished That You are So Quickly Turning Away!' (Gal 1:6): Paul and Anatolian Folk Belief." *NTS* 51:429–49.

Atkinson, Kenneth, and Jodi Magness. 2010. "Josephus's Essenes and the Qumran Community." *JBL* 129:317–42.

Avemarie, Friedrich. 2002. "Das Gleichnis von den Arbeitern im Weinberg (Mt 20, 1–15)—eine soziale Utopie?" *Evangelische Theologie* 62:272–87.

Avrahami, Yael. 2011. *The Senses of Scripture: Sensory Perception in the Hebrew Bible.* Library Hebrew Bible/Old Testament Studies 545. London: Bloomsbury T & T Clark.

Bacht, Heinrich. 1959. "Einfalt." In *RAC* 4:821–40.

Bacon, Francis. 1985. "Essay IX. Of Envy." In *The Essayes or Counsels, Civill and Morall* [1625], edited by Michael Kiernan, 27–31. Cambridge: Harvard University Press.

Bagatti, B. 1971. "Altre medaglie di Salomone cavaliere e loro origine." *Revista di archeologia cristiana* 47:331–42.

Ball, Philip. 2001 "The Problem of Blue." In *Bright Earth: Art and the Invention of Color,* 231–49. Chicago: University of Chicago Press.

Balz, Horst, and Gerhard Schneider, eds. 1993. *Exegetical Dictionary of the New Testament.* 3 vols. Translated by James W. Thompson and John W. Medendorp. Grand Rapids: Eerdmans.

Bar-Ilan, Meir. 1993. "Witches in the Bible and in the Talmud." In *Approaches to Ancient Judaism,* edited by Herbert W. Basser and Simcha Fishbane, 7–32. Atlanta: Scholars.

Barkay, Gabriel. 1992. "The Priestly Benediction on Silver Plaques from Ketef Hinnom in Jerusalem." *Tel Aviv* 19:139–92.

———. 2009. "The Riches of Ketef Hinnom." *BAR* 35/4–5:22–35, 122–26.

Barkay, Gabriel et al., eds. 2004. "The Amulets from Ketef Hinnom: A New Edition and Evaluation." *BASOR* 334:41–71.

Baroja, Julio Caro. 1965. *The World of Witches.* Translated by O. N. V. Glendinning. Chicago: University of Chicago Press.

Bartchy, S. Scott. 1992. "Table Fellowship." In *Dictionary of Jesus and the Gospels,* 796–800. Downers Grove, IL: InterVarsity.

———. 1999. "Undermining Ancient Patriarchy: The Apostle Paul's Vision of a Society of Siblings." *BTB* 29:68–78.

Bartelink. G. 1983. "*Baskanos*: Désignation de Satan et des démons chez les auteurs chrétiens." *Orientalia Christiana Periodica* 49:390–406.

Baumbach, Günther. 1963. *Das Verständnis des Bösen in den Synoptischen Evangelien.* Theologische Arbeiten 19. Berlin: Evangelische Verlagsanstalt.

Baumgärtel, Friedrich and Johannes Behm. 1965. "*kardia* etc." In *TDNT* 3:605–14.

Bayardi, Ottavio Antonio and Pasquale Carcani, eds. 1757–79. *Le pitture antiche d'Ercolano e contorni incise con qualche spiegazione.* 5 vols. Edited by Accademia ercolanese di archeologia. Naples: Regia Stamperia.

Bell, Richard H. 1994. *Provoked to Jealousy. The Origin and Purpose of the Jealousy Motif in Romans 9–11.* WUNT 2/63. Tübingen: Mohr/Siebeck.

Ben-Dor, I. 1962. "Amulets." In *IDB* 1:122.

Benoit, P. 1953. "L'Oeil, lampe du corps." *Revue Biblique* 60:603–5.

Ben-Yehuda, Nachman. 1989. "Witchcraft and the Occult as Boundary Maintenance Devices." In *Religion, Science, and Magic: In Concert and in Conflict*, edited by Jacob Neusner et al., 229–60. Oxford: Oxford University Press.

Bergen, Fanny D. 1890. "Some Saliva Charms." *Journal of American Folklore* 79:51–59.

Bernidaki-Aldous, Eleftheria. 1988. "The Power of the Evil Eye in the Blind: *Oedipus Tyrannus* 1306 and *Oedipus at Colonus* 149–56." In *Text and Presentation. The University of Florida Department of Classics. Comparative Drama Conference Papers*, Vol. 8. Edited by Karelisa Hartigan, 39–48. New York: University Press of America.

Betz, Hans Dieter. 1979a. *Galatians: A Commentary on Paul's Letter to the Churches in Galatia.* Hermeneia. Philadelphia: Fortress.

———. 1979b. "Matthew vi.22f. and Ancient Greek Theories of Vision." In *Text and Interpretation. Studies in the New Testament Presented to Mattthew Black*, edited by E. Best and R. McL. Wilson, 43–56. Cambridge: Cambridge University Press. Reprinted in Betz 1985:71–87; and Betz 1992:140–54.

———. 1985. *Essays on the Sermon on the Mount.* Philadelphia: Fortress.

———. 1992. *Synoptische Studien.* Tübingen: Mohr/Siebeck.

———. 1995. *The Sermon on the Mount: A Commentary on the Sermon on the Mount, Including the Sermon on the Plain (Matthew 5:3—7:27 and Luke 6:20–49).* Hermeneia. Minneapolis: Fortress.

———. 1997. "Jewish Magic in the Greek Magical Papyri (PGM VII. 260–71)." In *Envisioning Magic: A Princeton Seminar and Symposium*, edited by Peter Schäfer and Hans G. Kippenberg, 45–63. Studies in the History of Religions 75. Leiden: Brill.

Billerbeck, Paul. 1922–1961. [and Hermann L. Strack]. *Kommentar zum Neuen Testament aus Talmud und Midrasch.* 6 vols. 3rd ed. Munich: Beck, 1922–1961.

———. 1926a. *Das Evangelium nach Matthäus.* Vol. 1 in *Kommentar zum Neuen Testament aus Talmud und Midrasch.* 3rd ed. Munich: Beck.

———. 1926b. *Das Evangelium nach Markus, Lukas und Johannes und die Apostelgeschichte.* Vol. 2 in *Kommentar zum Neuen Testament aus Talmud und Midrasch.* 3rd ed. Munich: Beck.

———. 1928. *Exkurse zu einzelnen Stellen des Neuen Testaments.* In *Kommentar zum Neuen Testament aus Talmud und Midrasch* 4.1. 3rd ed. Munich: Beck.

Exkurs 21. "Zur altjüdischen Dämonologie." 4.1:501–35.

Exkurs 22. "Die altjüdische Privatwohltätigkeit." 4.1:536–58.

Exkurs 23. Die altjüdische Liebeswerke." 4.1:559–610.

Birnbaum, Philip. 1975. "Evil Eye." In *A Book of Jewish Concepts*, 462–63. Rev. ed. New York: Hebrew Publishing.

Bissoli, Giovanni. 1996. "Occhio semplice e occhio cattivo in Lc 11,34 alla luce del Targum." *SBFLA* 46:45–51.

Black, Stephen K., ed. 2014. *To Set at Liberty: Essays on Early Christianity and Its Social World in Honor of John H. Elliott*. Social World of Biblical Antiquity 2/11. Sheffield: Sheffield Phoenix.

Blau, Ludwig. 1898. *Das altjüdische Zauberwesen*. Jahresbericht der Landes-Rabbinerschule in Budapest für das Schuljahr 1897–98. 1914. Reprinted. Westmead, UK: Gregg International, 1970.

———. 1907a. "Amulet." *JE* 1:546–550.

———. [and Kaufmann Kohler]. 1907b. "Evil Eye." *JE* 5:280–81.

Bligh, John. 1969. *Galatians. A Discussion of St. Paul's Epistle*. London: St. Paul Publications,

Böcher, Otto. 1970. *Dämonenfurcht und Dämonenabwehr: Ein Beitrag zur Vorgeschichte der christlichen Taufe*. BWANT 90. Stuttgart: Kohlhammer.

———. 1981. "Dämonen." *Theologische Realenzyklopädie* 8:270–74.

Boer, Martinus C. 2011. *Galatians: A Commentary*. New Testament Library. Louisville: Westminster John Knox.

Bohak, Gideon. 2008. *Ancient Jewish Magic. A History*. Cambridge: Cambridge University Press.

Boll, Franz. 1914. *Aus der Offenbarung Johannis: Hellenistische Studien zum Weltbild der Apokalypse*. Berlin: Teubner.

Bonneau, Danielle. 1982. "L'apotropaïque 'Abáskantos' en Égypte." *Revue de l'historie des religions* 99/1:23–36.

Bonner, Campbell. 1950. *Studies in Magical Amulets Chiefly Graeco-Egyptian*. Ann Arbor: University of Michigan Press. Online: http://classics.mfab.hu/talismans/pandecta/1537

Booth, Roger P. 1986. *Jesus and the Laws of Purity*. JSNTSup 13. Sheffield: JSOT.

Borg, Alexander, ed. 1999. *The Language of Color in the Mediterranean: An Anthropology of Linguistic and Ethnographic Color Terms*. Stockholm: Almqvist and Wiksell.

Borghouts, Joris F. 1978. *Ancient Egyptian Magical Texts*. Nisaba 9. Leiden: Brill.

Borsje, Jacqueline. 2012. *The Celtic Evil Eye and Related Mythological Motifs in Medieval Ireland*. Studies in the History and Anthropology of Religion 2. Leuven: Peeters.

Bossman, David M. 1996. "Paul's Fictive Kinship Movement." *BTB* 26:163–71.

Botterweck, G. Johannes, and Helmer Ringgren, eds. 1974–2015. *Theological Dictionary of the Old Testament*. 15 vols. Translated by David Green et al. Grand Rapids: Eerdmans.

———. 1975–1976. *Theologisches Wörterbuch zum Alten Testament*. 2 vols. 2nd ed. Munich: Kaiser.

Böttrich, Christfried. 2004. "Verkündigung aus 'Neid und Rivalität'? Beobachtungen zu Phil 1,12–18." *ZNW* 95 (2004) 84–101.

———. 2008. "Die 'Anatomie des Neides' im Spannungsfeld zwischen jüdischer und christlicher Paränese." *BThZ* 25:52–74.

Bourghouts, J. F. 1978. *Ancient Egyptian Magical Texts*. Nisaba 9. Leiden: Brill.

Bowie, Fiona. 2006. "Witchcraft and the Evil Eye." In *The Anthropology of Religion*, 200–236. 2nd ed. Oxford: Wiley-Blackwell.

Brandt, W. 1913. "Der Spruch vom *lumen internum*." *ZNW* 14:97–116, 177–201.

Brav, Aaron. 1908/1992. "The Evil Eye among the Hebrews." *Ophthalmology* 5:427–35.

Breech, James. 1983. *The Silence of Jesus*. Philadelphia: Fortress.

Brenk, Frederick E. 1986. "In the Light of the Moon: Demonology in the Early Imperial Period." In *ANRW* 16.3:2068–145.

Bridges, Carl B., and Ronald E. Wheeler. 2001. "The Evil Eye in the Sermon on the Mount." *Stone–Campbell Journal* 4:69–79.

Brox, Norbert. 1974. "Magie und Aberglaube an den Anfängen des Christentums." *Trierer Theologische Zeitschrift* 83:157–80.

Bruce, F. F. 1982. *The Epistle of Paul to the Galatians: A Commentary on the Greek Text*. NIGTC. Grand Rapids: Eerdmans.

Budge, E. A. Wallis. 1978/1930. *Amulets and Superstitions*. 1939. Reprinted, New York: Dover, 1978.

Bultmann, Rudolf. 1963. *The History of the Synoptic Tradition*. Translated by John Marsh. New York: Harper & Row.

Burder, Samuel. 1822. *Oriental Customs, or an Illustration of the Sacred Scriptures*. Vol. 2. 6th exp. ed. London: Longman et al.

Burkert, Walter. 1977. "Air-Imprints or Eidola: Democritus' Aetiology of Vision." *Illinois Classical Studies* 2:97–109.

Burton, Ernest de Witt. 1921. *A Critical and Exegetical Commentary on the Epistle to the Galatians*. ICC. Edinburgh: T. & T. Clark.

Buttrick, George Arthur. 1962. *The Interpreter's Dictionary of the Bible*. 4 vols. New York: Abingdon.

Cadbury, Henry J. 1954. "The Single Eye." *HTR* 47:69–74.

Cadoux, C. J. 1941–42. "The Evil Eye." *Expository Times* 53:354–55.

Canaan, T. 1929. *Dämonenglaube im Lande der Bibel*. Leipzig: Hinrichs.

Carter, Timothy Leonard. 2002. *Paul and the Power of Sin: Redefining beyond the Pale*. SNTSMS 115. Cambridge: Cambridge University Press.

Casanowicz, I. M. 1906. "Mezuzah." In *JE* 8:531–32.

———. 1917. "Two Jewish Amulets in the United States National Museum." *JAOS* 37:43–56.

Cheyne, T. K. 1899. "Eye." *Encyclopedia Biblica* 2:1453–56.

Cheyne, T. K., and John S. Black, eds. *Encyclopedia Biblica*. 4 vols. London: Adam & Charles Black, 1899–1903.

Chidester, David. 1992. *Word and Light: Seeing, Hearing, and Religious Discourse*. Urbana: University of Illinois Press.

Chouraqui, A. 1985. *L'univers de la Bible*. Paris: Lidis.

Coenen, Lothar, and Klaus Haacker, eds. 1983. *Theologisches Begriffslexikon zum Neuen Testament*. 3 vols. 3rd ed. Wuppertal: Brockhaus, 1967–1972. 6th ed., 1983. (New ed. 1997–).

Colpe, Carsten et al. 1976. "Geister (Dämonen)." In *RAC* 9:546–797.

Conybeare, F. C. 1895–96. "The Demonology of the New Testament." *JQR* 8:576–608.

———. 1898. "The Testament of Solomon." *JQR* 11:1–45.

Corbo, Virgilio. 1978. "Piazza e villa urbana a Magdala." *Liber Annuus* 28:232–40 + figs. 71–76.

Cosby, Michael. 2009. *Apostle on the Edge: An Inductive Approach to Paul*. Louisville: Westminster John Knox, 2009.

Crim, K., ed. 1976. *The Interpreter's Dictionary of the Bible. Supplementary Volume*. Nashville: Abingdon.

Crossan, John Dominic. 1973. *In Parables: The Challenge of the Historical Jesus*. Reprinted, Sonoma, CA: Polebridge, 1992.

Danker, Frederick W. 1982. *Benefactor: Epigraphic Study of a Graeco-Roman and New Testament Semantic Field*. St. Louis: Clayton.

———, rev. and ed. 2000. *A Greek-English Lexicon of the New Testament and Other Early Christian Literature*. 3rd ed. Based on Walter Bauer's *Griechisch-deutsches Wörterbuch zu den Schriften des Neuen Testaments und der frühchristlichen Literatur*. 6th ed., edited by Kurt Aland und Barbara Aland, with Viktor Reichmann, and on previous English editions by W. F. Arndt, F. W. Gingrich, and F. W. Danker. Chicago: University of Chicago Press.

Davidson, William L. 1923. "Envy and Emulation." In *HERE* 5:322–23.

Davies, G. Henton. 1962a. "Mezuzah." In *IDB* 3:363.

———. 1962b. "Phylacteries." In *IDB* 3:898–899.

Davies, T. W. 1979. "Charm, charmer." In *ISBE* 1:636–37.

Davies, W. D., and Dale C Allison. 1988. *The Gospel according to Saint Matthew*. 3 vols. Vol. 1, *Matthew 1–7*. ICC. Edinburgh: T. & T. Clark.

Davis, Basil S. 1999. "The Meaning of *proegraphe* in the Context of Galatians 3.1." *NTS* 45:194–212.

Deichgraeber, K. 1957. "Blick." In *RGG*³ 1:1321

de la Mora, Gonzalo Fernàndez. 1987. *Egalitarian Envy. The Political Foundations of Social Justice*. Translated by Antonia T. de Nicholàs. New York: Paragon.

Delatte, A. and P. Derchain. 1964. *Les intailles magiques gréco-égyptiennes*. Cabinet de médailles, Bibliothèque nationale. Paris: Bibliothèque nationale.

Delling, Gerhard. 1964. "*Baskainô*." In *TDNT* 1:594–95.

Déonna, Waldemar. 1965. *Le Symbolisme de l'Oeil*. Travaux et Mémoires des anciens Membres étrangers de l'Ecole et de divers Savants, Fasc. 15, Ecole française d'Athènes. Paris: de Boccard.

Derrett, J. Duncan M. 1973. *Jesus's Audience: The Social and Psychological Environment in which He Worked*. New York: Crossroad.

———. 1977. "Workers in the Vineyard: A Parable of Jesus." In *Studies in the New Testament*. Vol. 1:48–75. Leiden: Brill. Reprint of: "Workers in the Vineyard: A Parable of Jesus." *JJS* 25 (1974) 64–91.

———. 1988. "Christ and Reproof (Matthew 7:1–5/Luke 6:37–42)." *NTS* 34: 271–81.

———. 1995. "The Evil Eye in the New Testament." In *Modelling Early Christianity: Social-Scientific Studies of the New Testament in Its Context*, edited by Philip F. Esler, 65–72. London: Routledge.

Deutscher, Guy. 2010. *Through the Language Glass: Why the World Looks Different in Different Languages*. New York: Metropolitan Books.

Devish, René. 2005. "Witchcraft and Sorcery." In *A Companion to Psychological Anthropology: Modernity and Psychocultural Change,* edited by Conerly Casey and Robert B. Edgerton, 389–416. Oxford: Blackwell.

De Wet, Chris Len. 2007. "The Homilies of John Chrysostom on 1 Corinthians 12:a Model of Antiochene Exegesis on the Charismata." MA Thesis, University of Pretoria, South Africa.

Dietzfelbinger, Christian. 1983. "Das Gleichnis von den Arbeitern im Weinberg als Jesuswort." *Evangelische Theologie* 43:126–37.

Dillon, Myles and Nora K. Chadwick. 1967. *The Celtic Realms*. London: Weidenfeld & Nicolson.

DiTomasso, Lorenzo. 2012. "Pseudepigrapha Notes IV: 5. The Testament of Job. 6. The Testament of Solomon." *Journal for the Study of the Pseudepigrapha* 21:313–20.

Dobschütz, Ernst von. 1910. "Charms and Amulets (Christian)." In *HERE* 3:413–30.

Dodd, C. H. 1935. *The Parables of the Kingdom.* 3rd ed. Reprinted, New York: Scribner 1958.

Dickie, Matthew W. 1992. "Envy." In *ABD* 2:528–32.

Domeris, William Robert. 2007. *Touching the Heart of God. The Social Construction of Poverty among Biblical Peasants.* Library of Hebrew Bible/Old Testament Studies 466. New York: T. & T. Clark.

Douglas, Mary Tew. 1963. "Techniques of Sorcery Control." In *Witchcraft and Sorcery in East Africa,* edited by John Middleton and E. H. Winter, 123–41. London: Routledge & Kegan Paul.

———. 1966. *Purity and Danger: An Analysis of Concepts of Pollution and Taboo.* New York: Praeger.

———. 1967. "Witch Beliefs in Central Africa." *Africa* 37:72–80.

———. 1970a. *Natural Symbols: Explorations in Cosmology.* London: Routledge & Kegan Paul.

———, ed. 1970b. *Witchcraft Confessions & Accusations.* New York: Tavistock.

———. 1999a. "Sorcery Accusations Unleashed: The Lele Revisited." In *Implicit Meanings: Essays in Anthropology,* 77–94. New ed. London: Routledge & Kegan Paul.

———. 1999b. *Implicit Meanings: Essays in Anthropology.* New ed. London: Routledge & Kegan Paul.

Downing, F. Gerald. 2003. "Magic and Scepticism in and around the First Christian Century." In *Magic in the Biblical World: From the Rod of Aaron to the Ring of Solomon,* edited by Todd Klutz, 86–99. JSNTSup 245. Sheffield: Sheffield Academic.

Duff, Paul B. 1996. "'I Will Give to Each of You as Your Works Deserve': Witchcraft Accusations and the Fiery-Eyed Son of God in Rev 2.18–23." *NTS* 43:116–33.

———. 2001. "Vision and Violence: Theories of Visions and Matthew 5:27–30." In *Antiquity and Humanity: Essays on Ancient Religion and Philosophy. Presented to Hans Dieter Betz on His 70th Birthday,* edited by Adela Yarbro Collins and Margaret M. Mitchell, 63–75. Tübingen: Mohr/Siebeck.

Duling, Dennis C. 1975. "Solomon, Exorcism, and the Son of David." *HTR* 68:235–52.

———. 1984. "The Legend of Solomon the Magician in Antiquity: Problems and Perspectives [Presidential Address, EGLBS]." *Proceedings: Eastern Great Lakes Biblical Society* 4:1–22.

———. 1985. "The Eleazar Miracle and Solomon's Magical Wisdom in Flavius Josephus's *Antiquitates Judaicae* 8.42–49." *HTR* 78:1–25.

———. 1988. "The Testament of Solomon: Retrospect and Prospect." *JSP* 2:93–95.

———. 1992. "Solomon, Testament of." In *ABD* 6:117–19.

———. 2014. "Following Your Nose: Social-Historical and Socio-Scientific Directions in New Testament Osmology." In *To Set at Liberty: Essays on Early Christianity and Its Social World in Honor of John H. Elliott.* Edited by Stephen K. Black, 145–69. Social World of Biblical Antiquity 2nd ser., 11. Sheffield: Sheffield Phoenix.

Dunbabin, Katherine M. D., and M. W. Dickie. 1983. "*Invidia Rumpantur Pectora*: The Iconography of *Phthonos/Invidia* in Graeco-Roman Art." *JAC* 26:7–37 + plates 1–8.

Duncan Percy, J. 1942–43. "An Evil Eye." *Expository Times* 54:26–27.

Dundes, Alan. 1992a. "Proverbs (23:1–8) and the Evil Eye in 'The Wisdom of Sirach.'" In *The Evil Eye: A Casebook*, edited by Alan Dundes, 41–43. 2nd exp. ed. Madison: University of Wisconsin Press.

———. 1992b. "Wet and Dry, the Evil Eye: An Essay in Indo-European and Semitic Worldview." In *The Evil Eye: A Casebook,* edited by A. Dundes, 257–312. 2nd exp. ed. Madison: University of Wisconsin Press.

Dundes, Alan, ed. 1992. *The Evil Eye: A Casebook.* 2nd exp. ed. Madison: University of Wisconsin Press, 1992. (1st ed.: *The Evil Eye: A Folklore Casebook*, New York: Garland, 1981).

Dunn, James D. G. 1990. "Jesus and Ritual Purity: A Study of the Tradition-History of Mark 7,15." In *Jesus, Paul and the Law: Studies in Mark and Galatians*, 37–60. Louisville: Westminster John Knox.

———. 1993. *A Commentary on the Epistle to the Galatians.* BNTC. London: Black.

Dupont, Jacques. 1965. "Les ouvriers de la vigne." *Assemblées du Seigneur* 22:28–51.

Eastman, Susan. 2001. "The Evil Eye and the Curse of the Law: Galatians 3.1 Revisited." *JSNT* 83:69–87.

Edlund, Conny. 1952. *Das Auge der Einfalt: Eine Untersuchung zu Matth. 6,22–23 und Luk. 11,34–35.* Acta Seminarii Neotestamentici Upsaliensis 19. Lund: Gleerup.

Egger-Wenzel, Renate, and Jeremy Corley, eds. 2012. *Emotions from Ben Sira to Paul.* Deuterocanonical and Cognate Literature Yearbook 2011. Berlin: de Gruyter.

Eitrem, S. 1950. *Some Notes on the Demonology in the New Testament.* Symbolae Osloensis Suppl. 12. Oslo: Brogger.

Elbogen, I. "Saliva." 1916. In *HERE* 11:100–104.

Elliott, John H. 1988. "The Fear of the Leer: The Evil Eye from the Bible to Li'l Abner." *Forum* 4/4:42–71.

———. 1990. "Paul, Galatians, and the Evil Eye." *Currents in Theology and Mission* 17:262–273. Reprinted in Jerome Neyrey and Eric C. Stewart, eds., *The Social World of the New Testament. Insights and Models.* 223–34. Peabody, MA: Hendrickson, 2008.

———. 1991a. "The Evil Eye in the First Testament: The Ecology and Culture of a Pervasive Belief." In *The Bible and the Politics of Exegesis: Essays in Honor of Norman K. Gottwald on His Sixty-Fifth Birthday*, edited by David Jobling et al., 147–59 + 332–36. Cleveland: Pilgrim.

———. 1991b. "Household and Meals vs. Temple Purity. Replication Patterns in Luke-Acts." *BTB* 21:102–8.

———. 1992. "Matthew 20:1–15:A Parable of Invidious Comparison and Evil Eye Accusation." *BTB* 22:52–65.

———. 1993. *What Is Social-Scientific Criticism?* Guides to Biblical Scholarship New Testament Series. Minneapolis: Fortress.

———. 1994. "The Evil Eye and the Sermon on the Mount. Contours of a Pervasive Belief in Social Scientific Perspective." *Biblical Interpretation* 2:51–84.

———. 2004. "Look It Up: It's in BDAG." In *Biblical Greek Language and Lexicography. Essays in Honor of Frederick W. Danker*, edited by Bernard A. Taylor et al., 48–52. Grand Rapids: Eerdmans.

———. 2005a. "Jesus, Mark, and the Evil Eye." *Lutheran Theological Journal* (Festschrift in honor of Victor C. Pfitzner) 39:157–68.

———. 2005b. "Lecture socioscientifique: Illustration par l'accusation du Mauvais Oeil en Galatie." In *Guide des nouvelles lectures de la Bible,* edited by André Lacocque, 141–67. Traduction de Jean-Pierre Prévost. Paris: Bayard.

———. 2007a. "Envy and the Evil Eye: More on Mark 7:22 and Mark's 'Anatomy of Envy.'" In *In Other Words: Essays in Honor of Jerome H. Neyrey*, edited by Anselm Hagedorn et al., 87–105. Social World of Biblical Antiquity 2nd ser., 1. Sheffield: Sheffield Phoenix.

———. 2007b. "Envy, Jealousy and Zeal in the Bible: Sorting Out the Social Differences and Theological Implications—No Envy for YHWH." In *To Break Every Yoke: Essays in Honor of Marvin L. Chaney,* edited by Robert Coote and Norman K. Gottwald, 344–63. Social World of Biblical Antiquity 2/3. Sheffield: Sheffield Phoenix.

———. 2008. "God—Zealous or Jealous but Never Envious: The Theological Consequences of Linguistic and Social Distinctions." In *The Social Sciences and Biblical Translation*, edited by Dietmar Neufeld, 79–96. SBL Symposium Series 41. Atlanta: Society of Biblical Literature.

———. 2011 "Social-Scientific Criticism: Perspective, Process, Payoff: Evil Eye Accusation at Galatia as Illustration of the Method." *Hervormde teologies studies* 67:114–23.

———. 2015a. *Beware the Evil Eye: The Evil Eye in the Bible and the Ancient World.* Vol. 1, *Introduction, Mesopotamia, and Egypt.* Eugene, OR: Cascade Books.

———. 2015b. "Jesus, Paulus und der Böse Blick: Was die modernen Bibelversionen und Kommentare uns nicht sagen." In *Alte Texte in neuen Kontexten: Wo steht die sozialwissenschaftliche Bibelexegese?*, edited by Wolfgang Stegemann and Richard E. DeMaris, 85–104. Stuttgart: Kohlhammer.

———. 2016a. *Beware the Evil Eye: The Evil Eye in the Bible and the Ancient World.* Vol. 2. *Greece and Rome.* Eugene, OR: Cascade Books.

———. 2016b. "Evil Eye." In *The Ancient Mediterranean Social World: A Sourcebook.* Edited by Zeba Crook. Grand Rapids: Eerdmans, forthcoming.

Elliott, John H. et al. 2016. "Envy." In *The Ancient Mediterranean Social World: A Sourcebook.* Edited by Zeba Crook. Grand Rapids: Eerdmans, forthcoming.

Elliott, Susan. 2003. *Cutting Too Close for Comfort: Paul's Letter to the Galatians in Its Anatolian Cultic Context.* JSNTSup 248. London: T. & T. Clark.

Elworthy, Frederick Thomas. 1895/1958. *The Evil Eye: An Account of This Ancient and Widespread Superstition.* Reprinted with an Introduction by Louis S. Barron. New York: Julian, 1958.

———. 1912. "The Evil Eye." In *HERE* 5:608–15.

Encyclopaedia Britannica. Chicago: Encyclopaedia Britannica Inc. 11th ed., 1911; 14th ed, 1973; 15th ed., 1974.

Engemann, Josef. 1975. "Zur Verbreitung magischer Übelabwehr in der nichtchristlichen und Christlichen Spätantike." *JAC* 18:22–48.

———. 1980. "Der 'Corna' Gestus—Ein antiker und frühchristlicher Abwehr- und Spottgestus?" *Pietas: Bernhard Kötting Festschrift,* edited by Ernst Dassmann and K. Suso Frank, 483–98. JAC Ergänzungsband 8. Münster: Aschendorff.

———. 1981. "Glyptik." In *RAC* 11:270–313.

Engemann, Josef, and S. H. Fuglesang, G. Vikan, and M. Bernardini. 1991. "Amuleto." *Enciclopedia dell' Arte Medievale* (1991). Online: www.trecanni

Esler, Philip F. 1994. *The First Christians in Their Social Worlds: Socio-Scientific Approaches to New Testament Interpretation.* London: Routledge.

———, ed. 1995. *Modelling Early Christianity. Social-scientific Studies of the New Testament in Its Context.* London: Routledge, 1995.

———. 1998. *Galatians.* New Testament Readings. London: Routledge

Evans-Pritchard, E. E. 1937. *Witchcraft, Oracles and Magic among the Azande.* Oxford: Clarendon. 2nd ed. 1950.

Farrar, F. W. 1903. *The Life and World of St. Paul.* London: Cassell.

Fensham, F. C. 1967. "The Good and Evil Eye in the Sermon on the Mount." *Neotestamentica* 1:51–58

Fehrle, Egen. 1912. "Die Heuschrecke im Aberglauben." *Hessische Blätter für Volkskunde* 11/2:207–18.

Feldman, Louis H. 1976. "Josephus as an Apologist to the Greco-Roman World: His Portrait of Solomon." In *Aspects of Religious Propaganda in Judaism and Early Christianity,* edited by Elisabeth Schüssler Fiorenza, 69–98. Notre Dame: University of Notre Dame Press.

Ferguson, Everett. 1984. *Demonology of the Early Christian World.* Symposium Series 12. New York: Mellen.

Ficker, Johannes. 1896. "Amulett." In *Realencyklopädie für Protestantische Theologie und Kirche,* edited by J. J. Herzog and Albert Hauck, Vol. 1:467–76. Leipzig: Hinrichs.

Fiebig, Paul. 1916. "Das Wort Jesu vom Auge." *ThStK* 89:499–507.

Fiensy, David A. 1999. "The Importance of New Testament Background Studies in Biblical Research: The 'Evil Eye' in Luke 11:34 as a Case Study." *Stone-Campbell Journal* 2:75–88.

———. 2007. *Jesus the Galilean: Soundings in a First Century Life.* Piscataway, NJ: Gorgias, 2007.

Fitzmyer, Joseph A. 1985. *The Gospel According to Luke X–XXIV.* AB 28A. Garden City, NY: Doubleday.

Foerster, Werner. 1964. "*Daimon* etc.; *deisdaimonia.*" In *TDNT* 2:1–20.

Foster, George M. 1965. "Peasant Society and the Image of Limited Good." *American Anthropologist* 67:293–315.

———. 1972. "The Anatomy of Envy: A Study in Symbolic Behavior." *Current Anthropology* 13:165–202.

Fox, Michael V. 2009. *Proverbs 10–31: A New Translation with Introduction and Commentary.* AYB 18B. New Haven: Yale University Press.

Frachtenberg, Leo. 1918. "Allusions to Witchcraft and Other Primitive Beliefs in Zoroastrian Literature." In *The Dastur Hoshang Memorial Volume.* Bombay: Fort Printing Press.

Frankel, Ellen, and Betsy Platkin Teutsh. 1992. *The Encyclopedia of Jewish Symbols.* Northvale, NJ: Aronson.

Freedman, David Noel, ed. *The Anchor Bible Dictionary.* 6 vols. New York: Doubleday, 1992.

Fridrichsen, Anton. 1946. "*Propter invidiam*: Note sur I Clém.V. i." *Eranos* 44:161–74.

Friedenwald, Harry. 1939. "The Evil Eye (*Ayin Hara-ah*)." *Medical Leaves,* 44–48.

Frisk, Hjalmar. 1960–1973. *Griechisches etymologisches Wörterbuch.* 3 vols. Heidelberg: Winter.

Fritz, Kurt. 1953. "Democritus; Theory of Vision." In *Science, Medicine, and History: Essays on the Evolution of Scientific Thought and Medical Practice Written in*

Honour of Charles Joseph Singer, edited by E. Ashworth Underwood, 1:83–99. 2 vols. Oxford: Oxford University Press.

Funk, Robert W. et al. 1993. *The Five Gospels: The Search for the Authentic Words of Jesus.* New York: Macmillan.

Furstenberg, Yair. 2008. "Defilement Penetrating the Body: A New Understanding of Contamination in Mark 7.15." *NTS* 54:176–200.

Galling, Kurt et al., eds. 1957–65. *Die Religion in Geschichte und Gegenwart.* 3rd ed. 6 vols. and index. Tübingen: Mohr/Siebeck

Garrett, Susan, R. 1991. "'Lest the Light in You Be Darkness': Luke 11:33–36 and the Question of Commitment." *JBL* 110:93–105.

Garrison, Vivian, and Conrad M. Arensberg. 1976. "The Evil Eye: Envy or Risk of Seizure? Paranoia or Patronal Dependency?" In *The Evil Eye,* edited by Clarence Maloney, 286–328. New York: Columbia University Press.

Gaster, Moses. 1900. "Two Thousand Years of a Charm against the Child-stealing Witch." *Folklore* 11:129–62.

———. 1910. "Charms and Amulets (Jewish)." In *HERE* 3:451–55.

Gaster, Theodor H. 1962. "Demon, Demonology." In *IDB* 1:817–24.

———. 1969. *Myth, Legend and Custom in the Old Testament.* New York: Harper.

———. 1987. "Amulets and Talismans." In *Encyclopedia of Religion,* edited by Mircea Eliade, 1:243–46. New York: Macmillan, 1987. Reprinted in *Hidden Truths: Magic, Alchemy, and the Occult. Religion, History, and Culture,* edited by Lawrence E. Sullivan, 145–50. New York: Macmillan, 1989.

Géradon, Bernard de. 1958. "L'homme a l'image de Dieu." *Nouvelle Révue Théologique* 80:683–95.

Gifford, Edward S. 1958. *The Evil Eye: Studies in the Folklore of Vision.* New York: Macmillan.

Gilmore, David. 1982. "Anthropology of the Mediterranean Area." *Annual Review of Anthropology* 11:175–205.

Ginsberg, Louis. 1961. *The Legends of the Jews.* 7 vols. Philadelphia: Jewish Publication Society of America.

Goddard, A. J., and S. A. Cummins. 1993. "Ill or Ill-Treated? Conflict and Persecution as the Context of Paul's Original Ministry in Galatia [Galatians 4.12–20]." *JSNT* 52:93–126.

Goodenough, E. R. 1953–1968. *Jewish Symbols in the Greco-Roman Period.* 13 vols. Bollingen Series 37. New York: Pantheon.

———. 1953. "Charms in Judaism;" "Amulets." In E. R. Goodenough, *Jewish Symbols in the Greco-Roman Period,* 2:153–295; 3:379–81, 999–1209. New York: Pantheon.

Gordon, Benjamin Lee. 1937. "*Oculus fascinus* (Fascination, Evil Eye)." *Archives of Ophthalmology* 17:290–319. Reprinted as "The Evil Eye." *The Hebrew Medical Journal* 2 (1961):261–92 [in Hebrew].

Gordon, C. H. 1934. "Aramaic Magical Bowls in the Istanbul and Baghdad Museums." *ArOr* 6:324–26.

———. 1937. "Aramaic and Mandaic Magic Bowls." *ArOr* 9:84–106.

———. 1957. "A World of Demons and Liliths." In *Adventures in the Ancient Near East,* 160–84. London: Phoenix.

Gottwald, Norman K. 1993. "Social Class as an Analytic and Hermeneutical Category in Biblical Studies." *JBL* 112:3–22. Reprinted, in Gottwald, *Social Justice and the*

Hebrew Bible, vol. 1, 21–43. Center and Library for the Bible and Social Justice Series. Eugene, OR: Cascade Books, 2016.

Gouldner, Alvin W. 1969. *The Hellenic World: A Sociological Analysis.* [Part I of *Enter Plato: Classical Greece and the Origins of Social Theory.* New York: Basic Books, 1965]. New York: Harper & Row, 1969.

Grant, Robert M. 1982. "The Description of Paul in the Acts of Paul and Thecla." *Vigiliae christianae* 36:1–4.

Graves, Christina. "Limited Good, Envy, the Evil Eye, and Bible Translation." Graduate Institute of Applied Linguistics. *GIALens* 8/1. http://www.gial.edu/documents/gialens/vo18–1/graves_limitedgood.pdf.

Greenfield, Amy Butler. 2006. *A Perfect Red. Empire, Espionage and the Quest for the Color of Desire.* New York: Harper Perennial, 2006.

Greenfield, Richard P. 2006. "Evil Eye." *Encyclopedia of Ancient Greece.* Edited by Nigel Guy Wilson, 284–85. New York: Routledge.

Grünbaum, M. 1877. "Beiträge zur vergleichenden Mythologie aus der Hagada." *Zeitschrift der Morgenlandischen Gesellschaft* 31:183–359. Online: http://menadoc.bibliothek.uni-halle.de/dmg/periodical/pageview/26627.

Grunwald, M. 1901. [On the Evil Eye] *Mitteilungen der Gesellschaft für Jüdische Volkskunde* 5, part 7, 40–41, 47–48.

Gryglewitz, F. 1957. "The Gospel of the Overworked Workers." *CBQ* 19:190–98.

Guijarro, Santiago. 1999. "The Politics of Exorcism: Jesus' Reaction to Negative Labels in the Beelzebul Controversy." *BTB* 29:118–29.

———. 2000. "Healing Stories and Medical Anthropology: A Reading of Mark 10:46–52." *BTB* 30:102–112.

Gundry, Robert. 1982. *Matthew: A Commentary on His Literary and Theological Art.* Grand Rapids: Eerdmans.

Hagedorn, Anselm C., and Jerome H. Neyrey. 1998. "'It Was Out of Envy That They Handed Jesus Over' Mark (15:10): The Anatomy of Envy and the Gospel of Mark." *JSNT* 69:15–56.

Hagner, Donald A. 1993, 1995. *Matthew.* 2 vols. WBC 33A, 33B. Dallas: Word.

Hahn, Ferdinand. 1973. "Die Worte vom Licht. Lk. 11, 33–36." In *Orientierung an Jesus: Zur Theologie der Synoptiker,* edited by Paul Hoffmann et al., 107–38. Freiburg: Herder.

Hanauer, J. E. 1935. *Folk-Lore of the Holy Land.* London: Sheldon.

Hanson, G. W. 1994. *Galatians.* NTCS 9. Downers Grove, IL: InterVarsity, 1994.

Harder, G. 1968. "*Ponêros, ponêria.*" In *TDNT* 6:546–66.

Harl, Kenneth. 1996. *Coinage in the Roman Empire, 300 B.C. to A.D. 700.* Baltimore: Johns Hopkins University Press.

Harrington, Daniel J. 1983. *The Gospel according to Matthew.* Collegeville Bible Commentaries 1. Collegeville, MN: Liturgical.

Harrison, Roland K. 1979. "Amulet." In *ISBE* 1:119.

Hartsock, Chad. 2008. *Sight and Blindness in Luke-Acts: The Use of Physical Features in Characterization.* Biblical Interpretation Series 94. Leiden: Brill.

Hasting, James et al., eds. 1908–1926. *Encyclopaedia of Religion and Ethics.* 13 vols. Edinburgh: T. & T. Clark. 4th edition (reprint), 1958.

Haubeck, Wilfrid. 1980. "Zum Verständnis der Parabel von den Arbeitern im Weinberg (MT 20, 1–15)." In *Wort in der Zeit: Neuetestamentliche Studien: Festgabe für Karl*

Heinrich Rengstorf, edited by Wilfred Haubeck and Michael Bachmann, 95–107. Leiden: Brill.

Hauck, Robert J. 2006. "'Like a Gleaming Flash': Matthew 6:22–23, Luke 11:34–36 and the Divine Sense in Origen." *Anglican Theological Review* 88:557–73.

Hays, Richard B. 2000. "Galatians." In *New Interpreter's Bible*, edited by Leander E. Keck, 11:181–348. Nashville: Abingdon.

Heller, Bernard. 1928. "Amulett." In *Encyclopedia Judaica* (German, Berlin), 2:735–46.

Herrmann, Christian. 1994. *Ägyptische Amulette aus Palästina/Israel*. Orbis Biblicus et Orientalis 138. Göttingen: Vandenhoeck & Ruprecht.

Herrmann, Christian. 2002. *Ägyptische Amulette aus Palästina/Israel II*. Orbis Biblicus et Orientalis 184. Göttingen: Vandenhoeck & Ruprecht.

Herzfeld, Michael. 1981. "Meaning and Morality: A Semiotic Approach to Evil Eye Accusations in a Greek Village." *American Ethnologist* 8:560–74.

Herzog, Isaac, and Ehud Spanier. 1987. *The Royal Purple and the Biblical Blue—Argaman and Tekhelet: The Study of Chief Rabbi Dr. Isaac Herzog on the Dye Industries in Ancient Israel and Recent Scientific Contributions*. Jerusalem: Keter.

Herzog, William R., II. 1994. *Parables as Subversive Speech: Jesus as Pedagogue of the Oppressed*. Louisville: Westminster John Knox.

Herzog-Hauser, Gertrud. 1937. "Tintinnabulum." In *PW* 6A:1406–10.

Hezser, Catherine. 1990. *Lohnmetaphorik und Arbeitswelt in Mt 20, 1–16: Das Gleichnis von den Arbeitern im Weinberg im Rahmen rabbinischer Lohngleichnisse*. Novum Testamentum et Orbis Antiquus 15. Göttingen: Vandenhoeck & Ruprecht.

Hirsch, Emil G. 1892. "The Evil Eye." *The Folk-Lorist* 1:69–74.

Hoppe, Rudolf. 1984. "Gleichnis und Situation: Zu den Gleichnissen vom guten Vater (Lk 15, 11–32) und gütigen Hausherrn (Mt 20. 1–15)." *Biblische Zeitschrift* 28:1–21.

Horsley, G.H.R. 1987. "Roman Job." In *New Documents Illustrating Early Christianity: A Review of the Greek Inscriptions and Papyri Published in 1979*. Vol. 4. Edited by G. H. R. Horsley, 30–31. North Ryde, Australia: Macquarie University, Ancient History Documentary Research Centre.

Hultgren, Arland J. 2000. *The Parables of Jesus: A Commentary*. Grand Rapids: Eerdmans.

Isbell, Charles D. 1975. *Corpus of Aramaic Incantation Bowls*. SBLDS 17. Missoula, MT: Scholars Press, 1975.

Jackson, Howard M. 1988. "Notes on the Testament of Solomon." *JSJ* 19:19–60.

Jahn, Otto. 1855. *Über den Aberglauben des bösen Blickes bei den Alten*, 28–110 + 5 plates. Berichte der Sächsischen Gesellschaft der Wissenschaften zu Leipzig. Philologisch-Historische Classe. Leipzig: Hirzel.

James, M. R. 1922. "The Testament of Solomon." *JTS* 24 (1922) 468.

Jacques, Xavier. 1972. *List of Septuagint Words Sharing Common Elements*. Subsidia Biblica 1. Rome: Biblical Institute Press, 1972.

Jastrow, Marcus, ed. 1950. *Dictionary of the Targumim, the Talmud Babli and Yerushalmi, and the Midrashic Literature*. 2 vols. New York: Pardes. Reprinted, Peabody, MA: Hendrickson, 2005.

Jeffers, Ann. 1996. *Magic and Divination in Ancient Palestine and Syria*. Studies in the History and Culture of the Ancient Near East 8. Leiden: Brill.

Jenni, E., and D. Vetter. 1976. "עין 'ajin Auge." In *THAT* 2:259–68.

Jenni, Ernst, and Claus Westermann, eds. 1971–1976. *Theologisches Handwörterbuch zum Alten Testament*. 2 vols. Munich: Kaiser.

———. 1997. *Theological Lexicon of the Old Testament*. 3 vols. Translated by Mark E. Biddle. Peabody, MA: Hendrickson.

Jeremias, Joachim. 1972. *The Parables of Jesus*. 2nd rev. ed. New York: Scribner.

Jirku, A. 1912. *Die Dämonen und ihre Abwehr im Alten Testament*. Leipzig: Deichert, 1912.

Johnson, Luke T. 1983. "James 3:13–4:10 and the Topos *peri phthonou*." *Novum Testamentum* 25:327–347.

Jülicher, Adolf. 1910. *Die Gleichnisreden Jesu*. 2 vols. Tübingen: Mohr/Siebeck.

Kahl, Brigitte. 2010. *Galatians Re-imagined: Reading with the Eyes of the Vanquished*. Paul in Critical Contexts. Minneapolis: Fortress, 2010.

Kaufman, R. 1939. "Amulets." *Universal Jewish Encyclopedia* 1:288–291.

Kazen, T. 2002. *Jesus and Purity Halakhah: Was Jesus Indifferent to Impurity?* Stockholm: Almqvist & Wiksell.

Keel, Othmar. 1996. *Corpus der Stempelsiegel-Amulette aus Palästina/Israel: Von den Anfängen bis zur PerserZeit. Katalog Band I: Von Tell Abu Farag bis 'Atlit*. Göttingen: Vandenhoeck & Ruprecht, 1996.

Keener, C. S. 1999. *A Commentary on the Gospel of Matthew*. Sacra Pagina 1. Grand Rapids: Eerdmans.

Kennedy, A. R. S. 1910. "Charms and Amulets (Hebrew)." In *HERE* 3:439–41.

Kim, Angela Y. 2001. "Cain and Abel in the Light of Envy: A Study in the History of the Interpretation of Envy in Genesis 4.1–16." *JSP* 12:65–84.

Kingsbury, Jack Dean. 1986. *Matthew*. Proclamation Commentaries. 2nd ed. Philadelphia: Fortress.

Kirschenblatt-Gimblett, Barabra, and Harris Lenowitz. 1973. "The Evil Eye (The Good Eye) Einehore." *Alcheringa* 5:71–77.

Kittel, Gerhard, and Gerhard Friedrich, eds. *Theological Dictionary of the New Testament*. 10 vols. Edited and translated by Geoffrey W. Bromiley. Grand Rapids: Eerdmans, 1964–76.

Klatzkin, Jacob et al., eds. 1928–34. *Encyclopaedia Judaica*. 10 vols. Berlin: Eshkol.

Klausner, Theodore et al., eds. 1950–. *Reallexikon für Antike und Christentum*. 25+ vols. Stuttgart: Hiersemann.

Kloppenborg, John S. 1987. *The Formation of Q: Trajectories in Ancient Wisdom Collections*. Studies in Antiquity & Christianity. Philadelphia: Fortress.

Kluckhohn, C. 1944. *Navaho Witchcraft*. Boston: Beacon.

Klutz, Todd. 2003. "The Archer and the Cross: Chorographic Astrology and Literary Design in the *Testament of Solomon*." In *Magic in the Biblical World: From the Rod of Aaron to the Ring of Solomon*, edited by Todd Klutz, 219–44. JSNTSup 245. Sheffield: Sheffield Academic.

———, ed. 2003. *Magic in the Biblical World: From the Rod of Aaron to the Ring of Solomon*. JSNTSup 245. Sheffield: Sheffield Academic.

———. 2005. *Rewriting the Testament of Solomon*. Library of Second Temple Studies 53. London: T. & T. Clark.

Koehler, Ludwig et al. *The Hebrew and Aramaic Lexicon of the Old Testament*. 2 vols. Translated and edited under the supervision of M. E. J. Richardson. Leiden: Brill, 1994.

Kötting, Bernhard. 1954. "Böser Blick." In *RAC* 2:474–82.

Koivisto, Jussi Kalervo. 2011. "Martin Luther's Conception of *Fascinare* (Gal 3:1)." *Biblical Interpretation* 19:471–95.

Kosior, Wojciech. 2014. "'It Will not Let the Destroying [One] Enter.' The Mezuzah as an Apotropaic Device according to Biblical and Rabbinic Sources." *Polish Journal of the Arts and Culture* 9/1:127–44.

Kotansky, Roy. 1991. "Two Inscribed Aramaic Amulets from Syria." *Israel Exploration Journal* 41:267–81.

Kotzé, Zak. 2006. "Laban's Evil Eye: A Cognitive Linguistic Interpretation of אל יחר בעיני אדני (*ʾel yiḥar bʾene ʾadoni*) in Gn 31:35." *OTE* 19:1215–24.

———. 2007a. "Magic and Metaphor: An Interpretation of Eliphaz' Accusation in Job 15:12." *OTE* 20/1:152–57.

———. 2007b. "The Evil Eye as Witchcraft Technique in the Hebrew Bible." *Journal for Semitics* 16:141–49.

———. 2007c. Linguistic Relativity and the Interpretation of Metaphor in the Hebrew Bible: The Case of לטש עינים in Job 16:9." *OTE* 20:387–394.

———. 2007d. "A Cognitive Interpretation of the Combination עצה עינים in Proverbs 16:30." *Journal for Semitics* 16/2:1–11.

———. 2008. "The Evil Eye of YHWH." *Journal for Semitics* 17:207–18.

———. 2010. "An interpretation of the idiom קרץ עין in Psalm 35:19." *Journal for Semitics* 19:141–48. First published in Van Hecke, P and A.Labahn, eds., *Metaphor in the Hebrew Bible*. BETL 231. Leuven: Peeters, 2009

———. 2011. "An Interpretation of כסות עינים in Genesis 20:16." *Journal for Semitics* 20/2:487–96.

Kuhnert, Ernst. 1909. "Fascinum." In *PW* 6.2:2009–14.

Lafaye, G. 1926. "Fascinum, fascinus." In *Dictionnaire des antiquités grecques et romaines*, edited by Charles Daremberg and Edmund Saglio, 2:983–87. Paris: Hachette.

Lamb, Trevor, and Janine Bourriau, eds. 1995. *Colour: Art & Science*. Darwin College Lectures. Cambridge: Cambridge University Press, 1995.

Landman, Isaac, ed. 1939–1943. *The Universal Jewish Encyclopedia*. 10 vols. + Index. New York: Universal Jewish Encyclopedia.

Langton, Edward. 1949. *Essentials of Demonology: A Study of Jewish and Christian Doctrine, Its Origin and Development*. London: Epworth.

Lappenga, Benjamin J. 2012. "Misdirected Emulation and Paradoxical Zeal: Paul's Redefinition of 'The Good' as Object of Emulation of *zēlos* in Galatians 4:12–20." *JBL* 131:775–96.

Lea, Henry Charles. 1939. *Materials toward a History of Witchcraft*. 3 vols. New York: AMS, 1986.

Leclercq, Henri. 1924. "Amulettes." In *Dictionnaire d'archéologie chrétienne et de liturgie*, edited by Fernand Cabrol, 1.2:1784–1860. Paris: Letouzey & Ane. ["Le mauvais oeil," cols. 1843–47].

———. 1936. "Oeil." In *Dictionnaire d'archéologie chrétienne et de liturgie*, edited by Fernand Cabrol, 12.2:1936–43. Paris: Letouzey & Ane. ["I. Le mauvais oeil," cols. 1936–41.]

Lehmann, Arthur C., and James E. Meyers, eds. 2006. *Magic, Witchcraft and Religion. An Anthropological Study of the Supernatural World*. 4th ed. Mountain View, CA: Mayfield.

Lesky, E., and J. H. Waszink. 1965. "Epilepsie." In *RAC* 5:819–31.

Levack, Brian P., ed. 1992, vol. 1. *Anthropological Studies of Witchcraft, Magic, and Religion*. Vol. 1 of *Articles on Witchcraft, Magic & Demonology: A 12-Volume Anthology of Scholarly Articles*. New York: Garland.

———. 1992, vol. 2. *Witchcraft in the Ancient World and the Middle Ages*. Vol. 2 of *Articles on Witchcraft, Magic & Demonology: A 12-Volume Anthology of Scholarly Articles*. New York: Garland.

———. 1992. *The Literature of Witchcraft*. Vol. 4 of *Articles on Witchcraft, Magic & Demonology: A 12-Volume Anthology of Scholarly Articles*. New York: Garland.

———. 1992, vol. 9. *Possession and Exorcism*. Vol. 9 of *Articles on Witchcraft, Magic & Demonology: A 12-Volume Anthology of Scholarly Articles*. New York: Garland.

———. 1992, vol. 10. *Witchcraft, Women and Society*. Vol. 10 of *Articles on Witchcraft, Magic & Demonology: A 12-Volume Anthology of Scholarly Articles*. New York: Garland.

———. 1992, vol. 12. *Witchcraft and Demonology in Art and Literature*. Vol. 12 of *Articles on Witchcraft, Magic & Demonology: A 12-Volume Anthology of Scholarly Articles*. New York: Garland.

———, ed. 2004. *The Witchcraft Sourcebook*. New York: Routledge.

Leeb, Carolyn. 2008. "Translating the Hebrew Body into English Metaphor." In *The Social Sciences and Biblical Interpretation*, edited by Dietmar Neufeld, 109–25. SBL Symposium Series 41. Atlanta: Society of Biblical Literature.

Levi, Doro. 1941. "The Evil Eye and the Lucky Hunchback." In *Antioch-on-the-Orontes. Publications of the Committee for the Excavation of Antioch and Its Vicinity*, 3:220–32. 5 vols. Princeton: Princeton University Press, 1934–72.

Lévy, Isaac Jack, and Rosemary Lévy Zumwalt. 1987. "The Evil Eye and the Power of Speech among the Sephardim." *International Folklore Review* 5:52–59.

———. 2002. *Ritual Medical Lore of Sephardic Women. Sweetening the Spirits, Healing the Sick*. Urbana: University of Illinois Press, 2002.

Levy, Israel. 1969. *The Hebrew Text of the Book of Ecclesiasticus*. Semitic Studies Series 3. Leiden: Brill, 1969.

Levy, Jacob, ed. 1924. *Wörterbuch über die Talmudim und Midraschim*, nebst Beiträgen von H. L. Fleischer. Zweite Auflage mit Nachträgen und Berichtigungen von Lazarus Goldschmidt. 4 vols. Reprinted, Darmstadt: Wissenschaftliche Buchgesellschaft, 1963.

Lewis, Charlton T., and Charles Short. 1975. *A Latin Dictionary*. Oxford: Clarendon (orig. ed., 1879).

Lewis, Joseph. 1946. *The Ten Commandments: An Investigation into the Origin and Meaning of The Decalogue and an Analysis of Its Ethical and Moral Value as a Code of Conduct in Modern Society*. New York: Free Thought Press. E-text conversion and critical editing copyrighted by Cliff Walker 1998. Online: http://www.positiveatheism.org/hist/lewis/lewten101.htm

Liddell, H. G., R. Scott, and H. S. Jones. 1968. *A Greek–English Lexicon*. Oxford: Clarendon.

Lietzmann, Hans. 1932. *An die Galater*. 3rd ed. HNT 10. Tübingen: Mohr/Siebeck.

Lightfoot, Joseph Barber. 1866. *Saint Paul's Epistle to the Galatians: A Revised Text with Introduction, Notes and Dissertations*. 2nd rev. ed. London: Macmillan.

Lilienthal, Regina. 1924. "Ayin hara (Eyin hore)." *Yiddische Filologye* 1:245–71.

Lincicum, David. 2008. "Scripture and Apotropaism in the Second Temple Period." *Biblische Notizen* 138:63–87.

Löwinger, Adolf. 1926. "Der Böse Blick nach jüdischen Quellen." *Menorah* 4:551–69.

Longenecker, Bruce W. 1990. *Galatians*. WBC 41. Dallas: Word.

———. 1998. *The Triumph of Abraham's God: The Transformation of Identity in Galatians*. Nashville: Abingdon.

———. 1999. "'Until Christ Is Formed in You': Suprahuman Forces and Moral Character in Galatians." *CBQ* 61:92–108.

Louw, Johanes P., and Eugene A. Nida. 1988. *Greek-English Lexicon of the New Testament Based on Semantic Domains*. 2 vols. New York: United Bible Societies.

Lührmann, Dieter. 1978. *Der Brief an die Galater*. Zürcher Bibelkommentare. Zürich: TVZ.

Lust, J. et al., eds. 1992–. *A Greek-English Lexicon of the Septuagint*. Stuttgart: Deutsche Bibelgesellschaft.

Luther, Martin. 1883–2009. *D. Martin Luthers Werke: Kritische Gesammtausgabe*. 121 vols. Weimar: Hermann Böhhau. [=*Weimarer Ausgabe* (WA)].

———. *In epistolam Pauli ad Galatas, M. Lutheri commentarius*. [Second Lecture on Galatians 1518/1519, 15232]. Weimarer Ausgabe [WA] 2:438–618.

———. *In epistolam S. Pauli ad Galatas. Commentarius ex praelectione D. Martini Lutheri collectus*. [Third Lecture of 1531, collected 1535]. Weimarer Ausgabe [WA] 40/1–2.

———. 1963. *Lectures on Galatians 1535. Chapters 1–4*. Luther's Works 26, edited by Jaroslav Pelikan and Walter A. Hansen. St. Louis: Concordia.

———. 1964. *Lectures on Galatians, Chapters 5–6, 1535; Lectures on Galatians, Chapters 1–6, 1519*. Luther's Works 27. edited by Jaroslav Pelikan. St. Louis: Concordia.

Luz, Ulrich. 1989. *Matthew 1–7: A Commentary*. Translated by Wilhelm C. Linss. Continental Commentaries. Minneapolis: Augsburg.

———. 2001. *Matthew 8–20: A Commentary*. Translated by James E. Crouch. Hermeneia. Minneapolis: Fortress.

Lykiaropoulos, Amica. 1981. "The Evil Eye: Towards an Exhaustive Study." *Folklore* 92:221–30.

Maclagan, Robert Craig. 1902. *Evil Eye in the Western Highlands*. London: Nutt.

Mair, Lucy. 1969. *Witchcraft*. New York: McGraw-Hill, 1969.

Malina, Bruce J. 1979. "Limited Good and the Social World of Early Christianity." *BTB* 8:162–76.

———. 1986. *Christian Origins and Cultural Anthropology: Practical Models for Biblical Interpretation*. Reprinted, Eugene, OR: Wipf & Stock, 2010.

———. 1988. "A Conflict Approach to Mark 7." *Forum* 4/3:3–30.

———. 1989. "Dealing With Biblical (Mediterranean) Characters: A Guide for U.S. Consumers." *BTB* 19:127–41.

———. 1990. "Mary—Woman of the Mediterranean: Mother and Son." *BTB* 20:54–64.

———. 1992. "Is There a Circum-Mediterranean Person? Looking for Stereotypes." *BTB* 22:66–87.

———. 2001a. "Clean and Unclean: Understanding Rules of Purity." In *The New Testament World: Insights from Cultural Anthropology*, 161–97. 3rd rev. ed. Louisville: Westminster John Knox.

———. 2001b. "Envy—The Most Grievous of All Evils." In *The New Testament World: Insights from Cultural Anthropology*. 3rd rev. ed., 108–33. Louisville: Westminster John Knox.

———. 2001c. "The First-Century Personality: The Individual and the Group." In *The New Testament World: Insights from Cultural Anthropology*, 58–80. 3rd rev. ed. Louisville: Westminster John Knox.

———. 2001d. "Honor and Shame: Pivotal Values of the First-Century Mediterranean World." In *The New Testament World: Insights from Cultural Anthropology*, 27–57. 3rd rev. ed. Louisville: Westminster John Knox.

———. 2001e. *The New Testament World: Insights from Cultural Anthropology*. 3rd rev. ed. Louisville: Westminster John Knox, 2001

———. 2001f. "The Perception of Limited Good: Maintaining One's Social Status." In *The New Testament World: Insights from Cultural Anthropology*, 81–107. 3rd rev. ed. Louisville: Westminster John Knox.

Malina, Bruce J., and Jerome H. Neyrey. 1988. *Calling Jesus Names: The Social Value of Labels in Matthew*. Sonoma: Polebridge Press.

———. 1996. *Portraits of Paul: An Archaeology of Ancient Personality*. Louisville: Westminster John Knox.

Malina, Bruce J., and John J. Pilch. 2006. *Social-Science Commentary on the Letters of Paul*. Minneapolis: Fortress.

Malina, Bruce J., and Richard L. Rohrbaugh. 2003a. *Social-Science Commentary on the Gospel of John*. 2nd ed. Fortress: Minneapolis.

———. 2003b. *Social-Science Commentary on the Synoptic Gospels*. 2nd ed. Minneapolis: Fortress.

Maloney, Clarence. 1976a. "Don't Say 'Pretty Baby' Lest You Zap It with Your Evil Eye—The Evil Eye in South Asia." In *The Evil Eye*, edited by Clarence Maloney, 102–48. New York: Columbia University Press.

Maloney, Clarence, ed. 1976. *The Evil Eye*. New York: Columbia University Press.

Malul, Meir. 2002. *Knowledge, Control, and Sex: Studies in Biblical Thought, Culture, and Worldview*. Tel Aviv: Archaeological Center Publication.

———. 2009. "The Ceremonial and Juridical Background of Some Expressions in Biblical Hebrew." In *Studies in Bible and Exegesis*, vol. 9, presented to Moshe Garsiel. Edited by S. Vargon et al., 299–327. Ramat Gan; Bar-Ilan University. [Hebrew]

Manco, Jean. 2015. *Blood of the Celts: The New Ancestral Story*. London: Thames & Hudson.

Marcus, Joel. 1999. "A Note on Markan Optics." *NTS* 45:250–56.

Martyn, J. Louis. 1997. *Galatians. A New Translation with Introduction and Commentary*. AB 33A. New York: Doubleday.

Marwick, Max. 1965. *Sorcery in Its Social Setting*. Manchester: Manchester University Press.

———, ed. 1982. *Witchcraft and Sorcery: Selected Readings*. 2nd ed. Baltimore: Penguin.

Matera, Frank J. 1992. *Galatians*. Sacra Pagina 9. Collegeville, MN: Liturgical.

Mayer, Anton. 1983. *Der zenzierte Jesus: Soziologie des Neuen Testaments*. Olten: Walter.

McCown, Chester C. 1922a. "The Christian Tradition as to the Magical Wisdom of Solomon." *JPOS* 2:1–24.

———. 1922b. *The Testament of Solomon*. Untersuchungen zum Neuen Testament 9. Leipzig: Hinrichs.

McKim, D. K. 1982. "Envy; envious." In *ISBE* 2:108.

McNutt, Paula M. 1994. "The Kenites, the Midianites, and the Rechabites as Marginal Mediators in Ancient Israelite Tradition." *Semeia* 67:109–32.

Meisen, Karl. 1950. "Der böse Blick und anderer Schadenzauber in Glaube und Brauch der alten Völker und in frühchristlicher Zeit." *Rheinisches Jahrbuch für Volkskunde* 1:144–77.

Meiser, Martin. 2007. *Galater*. Novum Testamentum Patristicum 9. Göttingen: Vandenhoeck & Ruprecht, 2007.

Metzger, Bruce M. et al., eds. 1994. *A Textual Commentary on the Greek New Testament*. 2nd ed. New York: United Bible Societies.

Michaelides, D. 1994. "A Solomonic Pendant and Other Amulets from Cyprus." In *Tranquillitas: Melanges en l'honneur de V. Tran Tam Tinh*, edited by M. O. Jentel et al., 403–12. Collection "Hier pour aujourd'hui." 7 Quebec: University of Laval.

Michaelis, W. 1967a. "*Horaô* etc." In *TDNT* 5:315–382.

———. 1967b. "*Ophthalmos*." In *TDNT* 5:375–378.

Milobenski, Ernst. 1964. *Der Neid in der Griechischen Philosophie*. Klassisch-Philologische Studien 29. Wiesbaden: Harrassowitz.

Mitchell, Steven. 1993. *Anatolia: Land, Men, and Gods in Asia Minor*. Vol. 1, *The Celts in Anatolia and the Impact of Roman Rule*. 2 vols. Oxford: Clarendon.

Mondriaan, Marlene E. 2011. "Who Were the Kenites? *OTE* 24:414–30.

Montgomery, James A. 1910–11. "Some Early Amulets from Palestine." *JAOS* 31:272–81.

———. 1913. *Aramaic Incantation Texts from Nippur*. University of Pennsylvania, The Museum, Publications of the Babylonian Section 3. Philadelphia: University Museum.

Moore, Carey A. 1996. *Tobit. A New Translation with Introduction and Commentary*. AB 40A.New York: Doubleday.

Moro, Pamela A. et al., eds. 2008. *Magic, Witchcraft, and Religion: An Anthropological Study of the Supernatural*. 7th ed. New York: McGraw-Hill.

Moss, Candida R. 2011. "Blurred Vision and Ethical Confusion: the Rhetorical Function of Matt 6:22–23." *CBQ* 73:757–76.

Moulton, James Hope, and George Milligan. 1930. *The Vocabulary of the Greek Testament Illustrated from the Papyri and Other Non-Literary Sources*. London: Hodder & Stoughton.

Moulton, W. F. et al., eds. 1996. *A Concordance to the Greek Testament: According to the Texts of Westcott and Hort, Tischendorf and the English Revisers*. 5th ed. Edinburgh: T. & T. Clark.

Mowinkel, Sigmund. 1962. *The Psalms in Israel's Worship*. 2 vols in 1. Translated by D. R. Ap-Thomas. Nashville: Abingdon. Reprinted with a new foreword by James L. Crenshaw. Grand Rapids: Eerdmans, 2004.

Murdock, George Peter. 1980. *Theories of Illness: A World Survey*. Pittsburgh: University of Pittsburgh Press.

Murphy-O'Connor, Jerome. 2000. "'Even Death on a Cross': Crucifixion in the Pauline Letters." In *The Cross in Christian Tradition: From Paul to Bonaventure*, edited by Elizabeth A. Dreyer, 21–50. Mahwah, NJ: Paulist.

Nador, George, ed. 1975. *An Incantation against the Evil Eye*. Academia Maimonideana. Documenta inedita 2. Middlesex, UK: Bina.

Nanos, Mark. D. 1999. "O Foolish Galatians, Who Has Cast the Evil Eye [of Envy] upon You? (Gal 3:1a–b): The Belief System and Interpretive Implications of Paul's Accusation." A Paper presented at the Annual Meeting of the Society of Biblical Literature, Boston, 1999.

———. 2000. "The Inter- and Intra-Jewish Political Contexts of Paul and the Galatians." In *Paul and Poliitcs: Ekklesia, Israel, Imperium, Interpretation. Essays in Honor of Krister Stendahl,* edited by Richard A. Horsley, 146–59. Harrisburg, PA: Trinity.

———. 2002. *The Irony of Galatians: Paul's Letter in First-Century Context.* Minneapolis: Fortress, 2002.

Nash, Dennison. 1973. "A Convergence of Psychological and Sociological Explanations of Witchcraft." *Current Anthropology* 14:545–46.

Naveh, Joseph, and Saul Shaked. 1987. *Amulets and Magic Bowls: Aramaic Incantations of Late Antiquity.* 2nd ed. Jerusalem: Magnes. 3rd ed. 1998.

———. 1993. *Magic Spells and Formulae: Aramaic Incantations of Late Antiquity.* Jerusalem: Magnes.

Neusner, Jacob. 1973. *The Idea of Purity in Ancient Judaism.* Studies in Judaism in Late Antiquity 1. Leiden: Brill.

———. 1976a. "'First Cleanse the Inside.' Halakhic Background of a Controversy Saying." *NTS* 22:485–95.

———. 1976b. *History of the Mishnaic Law of Purities.* 22 parts. Studies in Judaism in Late Antiquity 6. Leiden: Brill.

Neyrey, Jerome H. 1986a. "The Idea of Purity in Mark." In *Social-Scientific Criticism of the New Testament and Its Social World,* edited by John H. Elliott, 91–128. Semeia 35. Decatur, GA: Scholars.

———. 1986b "Witchcraft Accusations in 2 Cor 10–13: Paul in Social Science Perspective." *Listening* 21:160–70.

———. 1988a. "Bewitched in Galatia: Paul and Cultural Anthropology." *CBQ* 50:72–100.

———. 1988b "A Symbolic Approach to Mark 7." *Forum* 4/3:63–92.

———. 1990a "Bewitched in Galatia: Paul's Accusations of Witchcraft." In *Paul, In Other Words: A Cultural Reading of His Letters,* 181–206. Louisville: Westminster John Knox. [A revised version of Neyrey 1988a].

———. 1990b. *Paul, In Other Words: A Cultural Reading of His Letters.* Louisville: Westminster John Knox, 1990.

———. 1990c "Seduced in Corinth: More Witchcraft Accusations." In *Paul, In Other Words. A Cultural Reading of His Letters,* 207–17. Louisville: Westminster/John Knox. [A revised version of Neyrey 1986b].

———, ed. 1991. *The Social World of Luke-Acts: Models for Interpretation.* Peabody, MA: Hendrickson Publishers.

———. 1996. "Clean/Unclean, Pure/Polluted, and Holy/Profane: The Idea and the System of Purity." In *The Social Sciences and New Testament Interpretation,* edited by Richard L. Rohrbaugh, 80–104. Peabody, MA: Hendrickson.

———. 1998. *Honor and Shame in the Gospel of Matthew.* Louisville: Westminster John Knox.

Neyrey, Jerome H., and Anselm C. Hagedorn. 1998. "'It Was Out of Envy That They Handed Jesus Over' (Mark 15.10): The Anatomy of Envy and the Gospel of Mark." *JSNT* 69:15–56.

Neyrey, Jerome H., and Richard L. Rohrbaugh. 2001. "'He Must Increase, I Must Decrease' (John 3:30): A Cultural and Social Interpretation." *CBQ* 63:464–83.

Neyrey, Jerome H., and Eric C. Stewart, eds. 2008. *The Social World of the New Testament: Insights and Models.* Peabody: Hendrickson.

Nicholson, Frank W. 1897. "The Saliva Superstition in Classical Literature." *Harvard Studies in Classical Philology* 8:23–40.

Niehoff, M. R. 1992. *The Figure of Joseph in Post-Biblical Jewish History*. Arbeiten zur Geschichte des antiken Judentums und des Urchristentums 16. Leiden: Brill.

Nigosian, Solomon. 2008. *Magic and Divination in the Old Testament*. Portland, OR: Sussex Academic.

Noack, Bengt. 1948. *Satana und Soteria: Untersuchungen zur neutestamentlichen Dämonologie*. Copenhagen: Gads.

Nolland, John. 2005. *The Gospel of Matthew: A Commentary on the Greek Text*. New International Greek Testament. Grand Rapids: Eerdmans.

Nordheim-Diehl, Miriam, von. 2012. "Der Neid Gottes, des Teufels und der Menschen: eine motivgeschichtliche Skizze." In *Deuterocanonical and Cognate Literature Yearbook 2011: Emotions from Ben Sira to Paul*, edited by Renate Egger-Wenzel and Jeremy Corley, 431–50. Berlin: de Gruyter.

Noy, David. 1971. "Evil Eye." In *Encyclopedia Judaica* 6:997–1000.

Nusser, Karl-Heinz. 2000. "Neid." In *TRE* Part 2, 24:246–54. Berlin: de Gruyter.

Oakes, Peter. 2015. *Galatians*. Paideia Commentaries on the New Testament. Grand Rapids: Baker.

Oakman, Douglas E. 1986. *Jesus and the Economic Questions of His Day*. Studies in the Bible and Early Christianity 8. Lewiston, NY: Mellen.

———. 1987. "The Buying Power of Two Denarii. A Comment on Luke 10:35." *Forum* 3/4:33–38.

———. 1991. "The Ancient Economy in the Bible. BTB Readers Guide." *BTB* 21:34–39.

Odelstierna, Ingrid. 1949. "*Invidia, Invidiosus*, and *Invidiam Facere*: A Semantic Investigation." *Uppsla Universitets Arsskrift* 10. Uppsala: A.-B. Lundequistska Bokhandeln.

Ogden, Daniel. 2002. *Magic, Witchcraft, and Ghosts in the Greek and Roman Worlds: A Sourcebook*. New York: Oxford University Press. 2nd ed., 2009

Olyan, Saul M., ed. 2012. *Social Theory and the Study of Israelite Religion: Essays in Retrospect and Prospect*. SBLRBS 71. Atlanta: Society of Biblical Literature.

Opperwall, Nola J. 1982a. "Eye." In *ISBE* 2:249.

———. 1982b. "Evil Eye." In *ISBE* 2:210.

Orr, James et al., ed. 1929. *The International Standard Bible Encyclopaedia*. 4 vols. Chicago: Howard-Severance, 1929. Revised edition by Melvin G. Kyle, Grand Rapids: Eerdmans, 1939. Revised and edited by Geoffrey W. Bromiley. Grand Rapids: Eerdmans, 1979–88.

Park, Roswell. 1912. *The Evil Eye, Thanatology, and Other Essays*. Boston: Badger.

Patai, Raphael. 1983b. "T'khelet-Blue." In *On Jewish Folklore*, 86–95. Detroit: Wayne State University Press.

Patte, Daniel. 1987. *The Gospel according to Matthew: A Structural Commentary on Mathew's Faith*. Philadelphia: Fortress.

Paul, Shalom M. 1994. "Euphemistically 'Speaking' and a Covetous Eye." In *Hebrew Annual Review* 14, edited by T. J. Lewis, 193–204. Columbia, OH. Reprinted in *Divrei Shalom: Collected Studies of Shalom M. Paul on the Bible and the Ancient Near East 1967–2005*, 213–22. Culture and History of the Ancient Near East 23. Leiden: Brill, 2005.

Paulys Real-encyclopädie der classischen Altertumswissenschaft. Edited by A. F. Pauly. Vols. 1–6 (1839–1852). New Edition begun by G. Wissowa et al. 70+ vols. Stuttgart: Metzler, 1892–1980.

Percy, J. Duncan. 1942–43. "An Evil Eye." *Expository Times* 54:26–27.

Perdrizet, Paul. 1900. "Melanges Epigraphiques." *Bulletin de Correspondance Hellénique* 24:285–323.

————. 1903. "Sphragis Solomonis." *Revue des études grecques* 16:42–61.

————. 1922. *Negotium perambulans in tenebris,* 5–38. Publications de la Faculté des Lettres de l'Université de Strasbourg, 6. New York: Columbia University Press.

Perdrizet, Paul. 1922. *Negotium perambulans in tenebris.* Publications de la Faculté des Lettres de l'Université de Strasbourg, 6, 5–38. New York: Columbia University Press.

Peringer von Lillieblad, Gustaf. 1685. *De amuletis Hebraeorum dissertatio.* Uppsala University. Holmiæ: Johann Georg Eberdt.

Perkins, Pheme. 2001. *Abraham's Divided Children.* Harrisburg, PA: Trinity Press.

Pesch, Rudolf. 1976. *Das Markusevangleium. I. Teil. Einleitung und Kommentar zu Kap. 1,1–8,26.* Freiburg: Herder.

Peterson, Erik. 1926. *Eis Theos: Epigraphische, formgeschichte und religionsgeschichtliche Untersuchungen.* Forschungen zur Religion und Literatur des Alten und Neuen Testaments n.F. 24. Göttingen: Vandenhoeck & Ruprecht.

————. 1982. "Das Amulett von Acre." In *Frühkirche, Judentum, und Gnosis: Studien und Untersuchungen,* 346–54. Darmstadt: Wissenschaftliche Buchgesellschaft,

Philonenko, M. 1988. "La parabole sur la lampe (Luc 11:33–36) et les horscopes qoumraniens." *ZNW* 79:145–51.

Pilch, John J. 1988. "A Structural Functional Approach to Mark 7." *Forum* 4/3:31–62.

————. 1993. "Insights and Models for Understanding the Healing Activity of the Historical Jesus." In *SBLSP 1993,* edited by Eugene H. Lovering, Jr., 154–77. Atlanta: Scholars.

————. 1995. *The Cultural World of Jesus: Sunday by Sunday, Cycle A.* Collegeville, MN: Liturgical.

————. 1996. "Actions Speak Louder Than Words." *The Bible Today* 34/3:172–76.

————. 1999. *The Cultural Dictionary of the Bible.* Collegeville: Liturgical Press.

————. 2000a. *Healing in the New Testament: Insights from Medical and Mediterranean Anthropology.* Minneapolis: Fortress.

————. 2000b. "Improving Bible Translations: The Examples of Sickness and Healing." *BTB* 30:129–34.

————. 2002. *Cultural Tools for Interpreting the Good News.* Collegeville, MN: Liturgical.

————. 2004a. *Visions and Healing in the Acts of the Apostles: How the Early Believers Experienced God.* Collegeville, MN: Liturgical, 2004.

————. 2004b "A Window into the Biblical World: The Evil Eye." *The Bible Today* 42/1:49–53

————. 2012. *A Cultural Handbook to the Bible.* Grand Rapids: Eerdmans.

Pilch, John J. and Bruce J. Malina, eds. 1998. *Handbook of Biblical Social Values.* 2nd expanded edition. Peabody, MA: Hendrickson, 1998. "Envy (and Evil Eye) (59–63)"; "Eyes-Heart" (68–72); "Limited Good" (122–27); "Zeal/Jealousy (209–12).

Pilhofer, Peter, and Ulrike Koenen, 1998. "Joseph I (Patriarch)." In *RAC* 18:715–48.

Pirke Avoth. http://www.chabad.org/library/article_cdo/aid/680274/jewish/Ethics-of-the-Fathers-Pirkei-Avot.htm.

Pocock, D. F. 1992. "The Evil Eye—Envy and Greed among the Patidar of Central Gujerat." In *The Evil Eye: A Casebook*, edited by A. Dundes, 201–10. 2nd exp. ed. Madison: University of Wisconsin Press. Reprinted from D. F. Pocock, *Mind, Body and Wealth: A Study of Belief and Practice in an Indian Village*, 25–33, 39–40. Totowa, NJ: Rowman & Littlefield, 1973.

Plummer, A. 1922. *The Gospel according to S. Luke*. 5th ed. ICC. Edinburgh: T. & T. Clark.

Preisendanz, K. 1956. "Salomon." In *PW* Suppl. 8 (1956) 660–704.

Qimron, Elisha, and John Strugnell. 1994. *Qumran Cave 4: V Miqsat Maʻase HaTorah*. Discoveries in the Judaean Desert 10. Oxford: Oxford University Press, 1994.

Rad, Gerhard von. 1966. *Deuteronomy*. Translated by Dorothea Barton. Old Testament Library. Philadelphia: Westminster.

Rakoczy, Thomas. 1996. *Böser Blick, Macht des Auges und Neid der Götter: Eine Untersuchung zur Kraft des Blickes in der griechischen Literatur*. Classica Monacensia 13. Tübingen: Narr.

Rapport, Angelo S. 1937. *The Folklore of the Jews*. London: Soncino.

Ridderbos, H. N. 1957. *The Epistle of Paul to the Churches of Galatia*. NICNT. Grand Rapids: Edermans.

Ringe, Sharon H. 1985. *Jesus, Liberation, and the Biblical Jubilee: Images for Ethics and Christology*. Overtures to Biblical Theology. Philadelphia: Fortress.

Roberts, John M. 1976. "Belief in the Evil Eye in World Perspective." In *The Evil Eye*, edited by Clarence Maloney, 287–328. New York: Columbia University Press.

Roberts, R. L., Jr. 1963. "An Evil Eye (Matthew 6:23)." *Restoration Quarterly* 7:143–47.

Robinson, James M., Paul Hoffmann and John S. Kloppenborg, eds. 2002. *The Sayings Gospel Q in Greek and English, with Parallels from the Gospels of Mark and Thomas*. Hermeneia Supplements. Minneapolis: Fortress.

Rodkinson, Michael Levi. 1893. *History of Amulets, Charms, and Talismans: A Historical Investigation into their Nature and Origin*. New York: New Talmud Publishing.

Rohrbaugh, Richard L. 1978. *The Biblical Interpreter: An Agrarian Bible in an Industrial Age*. Philadelphia: Fortress.

———. 1991 "The Pre-Industrial City in Luke-Acts: Urban Social Relations." In *The Social World of Luke-Acts: Models for Interpretation*, edited by Jerome H. Neyrey, 125–49. Peabody, MA: Hendrickson. [Reprinted in Rohrbaugh 2006]

———. 1993. "A Peasant Reading of the Talents/Pounds: A Text of Terror?" *BTB* 23:32–39. [Reprinted in Rohrbaugh 2006]

———. 1996a. "Introduction." In *The Social Sciences and New Testament Interpretation*, edited by Richard L. Rohrbaugh, 1–15. Peabody, MA: Hendrickson.

———. 1996b. "The Preindustrial City." In *The Social Sciences and New Testament Interpretation*, edited by Richard L. Rohrbaugh, 107–25. Peabody, MA: Hendrickson. [Reprinted in Rohrbaugh 2006]

———, ed. 1996c. *The Social Sciences and New Testament Intepretation*. Peabody, MA: Hendrickson.

———. 2006. *The New Testament in Cross Cultural Perspective*. Matrix. Eugene, OR: Cascade Books.

Rosenzweig, A. 1892. *Das Auge in Bibel und Talmud*. Berlin: Mayer & Müller.

———. 1905. *Kleidung und Schmuck im biblischen und talmudischen Schrifttum*. Berlin: Poppelauer.

Ross, Barry. 1991. "Notes on Some Jewish Amulets: *'ayin ha-ra'* and the Priestly Blessing." *Journal of the Association of Graduates in Near Eastern Studies* 2:34–40.

Roth, Cecil, and Geoffrey Wigoder, eds. 1972. *Encyclopedia Judaica*. 14 vols. Jerusalem: Keter. 2nd ed., Fred Skolnik, editor in chief. 22 vols. New York: Thomson Gale, 2006.

Rowe, A. 1938. *A Catalogue of Egyptian Scarabs, Scaraboids, Seals, and Amulets in the Palestine Archaeological Museum*. Government of Palestine, Department of Antiquities. Cairo.

Rush, John A. 1974. *Witchcraft and Sorcery: An Anthropological Perspective on the Occult*. Springfield, IL: Thomas.

Russell, Jeffrey Burton. 1977. *The Devil: Perceptions of Evil from Antiquity to Primitive Christianity*. Ithaca, NY: Cornell University Press.

———. 1982. "The Evil Eye in Early Byzantine Society: Archaeological Evidence from Anemurium in Isauria." *Jahrbuch der Oesterreichischen Byzantin-istik* 32/3. XVI. Internationaler Byzantinistenkongress 1981. Akten II/3:539–48. Vienna: Oesterreichische Akademie der Wissenschaften.

———. 1989. "Witchcraft." Selected from *Encylcopedia of Religion* (1987). In *Hidden Truths: Magic, Alchemy, and the Occult. Religion, History, and Culture,* edited by L. E. Sullivan, 69–81. New York: Macmillan.

Ryder Smith, C. 1941–42. "An Evil Eye (Mark vii, 22)." *Expository Times* 53:181–82.

———. 1942–43. "The Evil Eye." *Expository Times* 54:26.

Sauer, G. 1976. "קנא *qin'ā* Eifer." In *THAT* 2:647–50.

Schenke, Ludger. 1988. "Die Interpretation der Parabel von den 'Arbeitern im Weinberg' (Mat 20, 1–15) durch Matthäus." In *Studien zum Matthäusevangleium,* edited by L. Schenke, 245–68. Stuttgarter Bibelstudien. Stuttgart: Katholisches Bibelwerk.

Schiffman, Lawrence H., and Michael D. Swartz. 1992. *Hebrew and Aramaic Incantation Texts from the Cairo Geniza*. Semitic Texts and Studies 1. Sheffield: JSOT Press.

Schlatter, Adolf. 1963. *Der Glaube im Neuen Testament*. Stuttgart: Calwer.

Schlier, Heinrich. 1962. *Brief an die Galater, übersetzt und erklärt*. KEK 7. 12th ed. Göttingen: Vandenhoeck & Ruprecht.

———. 1964. *"ektuô."* In *TDNT* 2:448–49.

Schlumberger, Gustave Leon. 1892a. "Amulettes byzantins anciennes destinés à combattre les maléfices et maladies." *Revue des études grecques* 5:73–93.

———. 1892b. *Amulettes byzantins anciens*. Paris: Leroux.

———. 1895. *Mélanges d'archéologie Byzantine: Monnaies, médailles, méreaux, jetons, amulettes, bulles d'or et de plomb, poids de verre et de bronze, ivoires, objets d'orfèvrerie, bagues, reliquaires, etc.* 8th ed. Paris: Leroux.

Schmidt, Brian B. 2002. "Canaanite Magic vs. Israelite Religion: Deuteronomy 18 and the Taxonomy of Taboo." In *Magic and Ritual in the Ancient World,* edited by Paul Mirecki and Marvin Meyer, 242–59. Religions in the Graeco-Roman World 141. Leiden: Brill.

Schmitt, Rüdiger. 2004. *Magie im Alten Testament*. AOAT 313. Münster: Ugarit-Verlag.

———. 2012. "Theories Regarding Witchcraft Accusations and the Hebrew Bible." In *Social Theory and the Study of Israelite Religion: Essays in Retrospect and Prospect,* edited by Saul M. Olyan, 181–94. SBLRBS 71. Atlanta: Society of Biblical Literature.

Schniewind, Julius. 1964. *Das Evangelium nach Matthäus*. NTD 2. Göttingen: Vandenhoeck & Ruprech.

Schoeck, Helmut. 1987. *Envy: A Theory of Social Behaviour*. 1970. Reprinted, Indianapolis: Liberty Press. [German orig. 2nd ed., 1968].

Schott, S. 1931. "Ein Amulett gegen den bösen Blick." *Zeitschrift für Ägyptischen Studien* 67:106–10.

Schottroff, Luise. 1984. "Human Solidarity and the Goodness of God: The Parable of the Workers in the Vineyard." In *God of the Lowly: Socio-Historical Interpretations of the Bible*, edited by Willy Schottroff and Wolfgang Stegemann, 129–47. Translated by Matthew J. O'Connell. Maryknoll, NY: Orbis.

———. 2006. *The Parables of Jesus*. Translated by Linda M. Maloney. Minneapolis: Fortress.

Schreiner, S. 1996. "Review of *The Evil Eye in the Bible and Rabbinic Literature*, by Rivka Ulmer." *Zeitschrift für die alttestamentliche Wissenschaft* 108:324.

Schrire, Theodore. 1973. "Amulet." In *Encyclopedia Judaica* 11:906–15.

———. 1982. *Hebrew Magic Amulets: Their Decipherment and Interpretation*. 1966. Reprinted, New York: Behrman.

Schroer, Silvia, and Thomas Staubli. 2001. *Body Symbolism in the Bible*. Translated by Linda M. Maloney. Collegeville, MN: Liturgical.

Schulze, W. A. 1957. "Das Auge Gottes." *Zeitschrift für Kirchengeschichte* 68:149–52.

Schüssler Fiorenza, Elisabeth, ed. 1976. *Aspects of Religious Propaganda in Judaism and Early Christianity*. University of Notre Dame Center for the Study of Judaism and Christianity in Antiquity, 2. Notre Dame, IN: University of Notre Dame Press.

Schwencke, Friedrich. 1913. "Das Auge ist Leibes Licht (Mt 6, 22f., Lk 11, 33–36)." *ZWTh* 55:251–60.

Scott, Bernard Brandon. 1989. *Hear Then the Parable: A Commentary on the Parables of Jesus*. Minneapolis: Fortress.

Seawright, Helen L. 1988. *The Symbolism of the Eye in Mesopotamia and Israel*. MA Thesis. Wilfried Laurier University 1988. Theses and Dissertations (Comprehensive): http://scholars.wlu.ca/etd/94.

Seligmann, Siegfried. 1910. *Der Böse Blick und Verwandtes: Ein Beitrag zur Geschichte des Aberglaubens aller Zeiten und Völker*. 2 vols. Berlin: Barsdorf. Reprinted, Hildesheim: Olms, 1985.

———. 1922. *Die Zauberkraft des Auges und das Berufen*. Hamburg: Barsdorf.

———. 1927. *Die magischen Heil-und Schutzmittel aus der unbelebten Natur, mit besonderer Berücksichtigung der Mittel gegen den Bösen Blick: Eine Geschichte des Amulett-wesens*. Stuttgart: Strecker & Schroeder.

Senior, Donald. 1998. *Matthew*. Abingdon New Testament Commentaries. Nashville: Abingdon.

Shachar, I. 1981. *Jewish Tradition in Art: The Feuchtwanger Collection of Judaica*. Translated by R. Grafman. Jerusalem: Israel Museum.

Shanks, Hershel. 2007. "Magic Incantation Bowls: Charms to Curse, to Cure, to Celebrate." *BAR* 33/1:62–63, 65.

Siebers, Tobin. 1983. *The Mirror of Medusa*. Berkeley: University of California Press.

Sinai, Turan (Tamas). 2008. "'Wherever the Sages Set Their Eyes, There Is Either Death or Poverty': On the History, Terminology, and Imagery of the Talmudic Tradition about the Devastating Gaze of the Sages." *Sidra* 23:137–205. [Hebrew, with English summary, viii–ix].

Singer, Isidor, ed. 1927. *The Jewish Encyclopedia*. 12 vols. 3rd ed. New York: Funk & Wagnalls.

Sjöberg, Eric. 1951. "Das Licht in dir: Zur Deutung von Matth. 6,22 f. par." *Studia Theologica* 5:89–105.

Smith, Jonathan Z. 1978. "Towards Interpreting Demonic Powers in Hellenistic and Roman Antiquity." In *ANRW* II.16.1:425–39.

Smith, Morton. 1987. "The Occult in Josephus." In *Josephus, Judaism and Christianity*, edited by Louis Feldman and Gohei Hata, 236–56. Detroit: Wayne State University Press.

Snodgrass, Klyne, 2008. *Stories with Intent: A Comprehensive Guide to the Parables of Jesus*. Grand Rapids: Eerdmans.

Snyder, Graydon. 2002. *Irish Jesus, Roman Jesus: The Formation of Early Irish Christianity*. Harrisburg, PA: Trinity.

Soderlund, O. and H. 2013. "The Evil Eye in Cultural and Church History." http://aslansplace.com/wp-content/uploads/2013/07/The_Evil_Eye_In_Cultural_and_Church_History-Soderlund.pdf.

Sophocles, E. A., ed. 1914. *Greek Lexicon of the Roman and Byzantine Periods (From B.C. 146 to A.D. 1100)*. 2 vols. Cambridge: Harvard University Press (1887).

Spicq, Ceslas. 1933. "La vertus de simplicité dans l'Ancien et le Nouveau Testament." *Revue des sciences philosophiques et théologiques* 22:1–26.

———, ed. 1994. *Theological Lexicon of the New Testament*. 3 vols. Translated by James Ernest. Peabody, MA: Hendrickson.

Spier, Jeffrey. 1993. "Medieval Byzantine Magical Amulets and Their Tradition." *Journal of the Warburg and Courtauld Institutes* 56:25–62 + 6 plates.

Stendebach, F. J. 1989. " '*ajin*." In *TWAT* 6:31–48.

———. 1999. " '*ajin*." In *TDOT* 11:28–44.

Sterman, Baruch, with Judy Taubes Sterman. 2012. *The Rarest Blue: The Remarkable Story of an Ancient Color Lost to History and Rediscovered*. Guilford, CT: Lyons.

Sterman, Baruch and Judy Taubes Sterman. 2013. "The Great Tekhelet Debate—Blue or Purple?" *BAR* 39/5:28, 73.

Stevens, E. B. 1948. "Envy and Pity in Greek Philosophy." *American Journal of Philology* 69:171–89.

Stevens, Phillips, Jr. 1996. "Sorcery and Witchcraft." In *The Encyclopedia of Cultural Anthropology*, edited by David Levinson and Melvin Ember, 1225–32. New York: Holt.

Stolz, F. 1971. "*Léb, Herz*." *THAT* 1:862–67.

Stratton, Kimberly B. 2007. *Naming the Witch: Magic, Ideology, and Stereotype in the Ancient World*. Gender, Theory, and Religion. New York: Columbia University Press.

Stumpf, Albrecht. 1964. "*zêlos* etc." In *TDNT* 2:877–88.

Sullivan, Lawrence E., ed. 1989. *Hidden Truths. Magic, Alchemy, and the Occult. Religion, History, and Culture*. Selections from the *Encyclopedia of Religion*, edited by Mircea Eliade. New York: Macmillan.

Swartz, Michael D. 2010. "ReViews: Repelling the Evil Eye." (Review of *Angels and Demons: Jewish Magic through the Ages*, edited by Filip Vukosavovic. Jerusalem: Bible Lands Museum, 2010). *BAR* 36/5:70–71 (and two photos).

Syreeni, Kari. 1999. "A Single Eye: Aspects of the Symbolic World of Matt. 6.22–23." *StTh* 53:97–118.

Talbert, Charles H. 1989. *Reading Luke: A Literary and Theological Commentary on the Third Gospel.* New York: Crossroad.

Tamborino, Julius. 1909. *De antiquorum daemonismo.* Religionsgeschichtliche Versuche und Vorarbeiten 7.3. Giessen: Töpelmann.

Tannehill, Robert C. 1996. *Luke.* Abingdon NT Commentaries. Nashville: Abingdon.

Teitelbaum, Joel M. 1976. "The Leer and the Loom—Social Controls on Handloom Weavers." In *The Evil Eye*, edited by Clarence Maloney, 63–75. New York: Columbia University Press.

Temkin, Owsei. 1971. *The Falling Sickness. A History of Epilepsy from the Greeks to the Beginnings of Modern Neurology.* 2nd ed. Baltimore: Johns Hopkins University Press.

Tevel, J.M. 1992. 'The Labourers in the Vineyard: The Exegesis of Matthew 20,1–7 in the Early Church." *Vigiliae Christianae* 46:356–80.

Thienemann, T. 1955. "A Comment on an Interpretation by Prof. Cadbury." *Gordon Review* 1:9–22.

Thompson, R. Campbell. 1908. *Semitic Magic: Its Origins and Development.* London: Luzac, 1908. Reprinted, New York: KTAV, 1971. New York: AMS Press, 1976; York Beach: Red Wheel/Weiser Books, 2000.

———. 1910. "Charms and Amulets (Assyro-Babylonian)." In *HERE* 3:409–11.

Thompson, Stith. 1955–1958. *Motif-Index of Folk-literature: A Classification of Narrative Elements in Folktales, Ballads, Myths, Fables, Medieval Romances, Exempla, Fabliaux, Jest-books, and Local Legends.* 6 vols. Revised and enlarged edition. Bloomington: Indiana University Press.

Thomsen, Marie-Louise. 1992. "The Evil Eye in Mesopotamia." *Journal of Near Eastern Studies* 51:19–32.

Thomson, William McClure. 1880. *The Land and the Book: Or, Biblical Illustrations Drawn from the Manners and Customs, the Scenes and Scenery of the Holy Land.* 2 vols. New York: Harper & Bros.

Tigay, Jeffrey H. 1979." On the Term Phylacteries (Matt 23:5)." *HTR* 72:45–53.

———. 1982. "On the Meaning of *T(W)TPT* (totafot)." *JBL* 101:321–31.

Tilford, Nicole. 2015a. "Evil Eye." In *Oxford Bibliographies*, edited by Christopher Matthews. Last modified: 25 November 2014. http://www.oxfordbibliographies.com/view/document/obo-9780195393361/obo-9780195393361–0112.xml.

Tilford, Nicole. 2015b. "The Affective Eye: Re-examining a Biblical Idiom." *Biblical Interpretation* 23:207–21.

Tolmie, D. François. 2005. *Persuading the Galatians: a text-centered rhetorical analysis of a Pauline letter.* WUNT, 2nd series, 190. Tübingen: Mohr/Siebeck.

Trachtenberg, Joshua. 1970/1939. *Jewish Magic and Superstition. A Study in Folk Religion.* New York: Behrman, 1939; reprinted, New York: Atheneum, 1970.

Turan, Sinai (Tamas). 2008. "A Neglected Rabbinic Parallel to the Sermon on the Mount (Matthew 6:22–23; Luke 11:34–36)." *JBL* 127/1:81–93.

Ulmer, Rivka Brigitte Kern. [aka Kern-Ulmer] 1991."The Power of the Evil Eye and the Good Eye in Midrashic Literature." *Judaism* 40:344–53.

———. 1992/93 "Zwischen ägyptischer Vorlage und talmudischer Rezeption: Josef und die Ägypterin." *Kairos* 24/25:75–90.

———. 1994. *The Evil Eye in the Bible and in Rabbinic Literature.* Hoboken, NJ: Ktav.

———. 1998. "Die Macht des Auges (der böse Blick) in der rabbinischen Literatur." In *Approaches to Ancient Judaism* New Series 13, edited by Jacob Neusner, 121–38. South Florida Studies in the History of Judaism 164. Atlanta: Scholars.

———. 2003. "The Divine Eye in Ancient Egypt and in the Midrashic Interpretation of Formative Judaism." *Journal of Religion and Society* 5:1–17.

Van Eck, Ernest, and John S. Kloppenborg. 2015. "An Unexpected Patron: A Social-Scientific and Realistic Reading of the Parable of the Vineyard Labourers (Mt 20:1–15)." *HTS Teologiese Studies/ Theological Studies* 71:1–11. http://dx.DOI.org/10.4102/hts.v71i1.2883.

Vearncombe, Erin. 2010. "Redistribution and Reciprocity: A Socio-economic Interpretation of the Parable of the Labourers in the Vineyard (Matthew 20.1–15)." *Journal for the Study of the Historical Jesus* 8:199–236.

Verhey, A. D. 1982. "Evil." In *ISBE* 2:206–10.

Verheyden, Joseph, ed. 2012. *The Figure of Solomon in Jewish, Christian and Islamic Tradition. King, Sage and Architect.* Themes in Biblical Narrative: Jewish and Christian Traditions 16. Leiden: Brill.

Verhoefen, P. 2007. "The First Will Be First: The Labourers in the Vineyard." In *Listening to the Parables of Jesus*, edited by Edward F. Beutner, 41–50. Jesus Seminar Guides 2. Santa Rosa, CA: Polebridge.

Vermes, Geza. 2004. *The Complete Dead Sea Scrolls in English.* New York: Penguin.

Via, Dan. 1967. *The Parables: Their Literary and Existential Dimension.* Philadelphia: Fortress. Reprinted, Eugene, OR: Wipf & Stock, 2007.

———. 1994. "Matthew's Dark Light and the Human Condition." In *The New Literary Criticism and the New Testament*, edited by Elizabeth Struthers Malbon and Edgar V. McKnight, 348–66. JSNTSup 109. Sheffield.

Viljoen, Francois P. 2009. "A Contextualised Reading of Matthew 6:22–23: 'Your Eye Is the Lamp of Your Body.'" *Hervormde theologies studies* 65:166–70.

Vögtle, Anton. 1936. *Die Tugend- und Lasterkataloge im Neuen Testament exegetisch, religions- und formgeschichtlich untersucht.* Neutestamentliche Abhandlungen 16,4/5. Münster: Aschendorff.

Vukosavovic, Filip, ed. 2010. *Angels and Demons: Jewish Magic Through the Ages* [Catalogue of a Bible Lands Museum exhibit in 2010]. Jerusalem: Bible Lands Museum.

Waetjen, Herman C. 2011. "Intimation of the Year of Jubilee in the Parable of the Workers in the Vineyard." In *Liberating Bible Study: Scholarship, Art, and Action in Honor of the Center and Library for Bible and Justice*, edited by Laurel Dykstra and Ched Myers, 93–104. The Center and Library for the Bible and Social Justice Series 1. Eugene, OR: Cascade Books.

Wagner, M. Monica, trans. 1950. *Saint Basil, Ascetical Works.* In *The Fathers of the Church. A New Translation.* Vol. 9:463–74. New York: Fathers of the Church. ET of Basil, "Homily 11. Concerning Envy/*Peri phthonou*." PG 31. 372–86.

Walcot, Peter. 1978. *Envy and the Greeks: A Study of Human Behaviour.* Warminster, UK: Aris & Phillips.

Ward, J. O. 1980. "Witchcraft and Sorcery in the Later Roman Empire and the Early Middle Ages." *Prudentia* 12/2:93–108.

Warwick, Max, ed. 1987. *Witchcraft and Sorcery: Selected Readings.* 2nd ed. New York: Viking/Penguin.

Wazana, Nili. 2007. "A Case of the Evil Eye: Qohelet 4:4–8." *JBL* 126:685–702.

Weidman, Hazel Hitson. 1968. "Anthropological Theory and the Psychological Function of Belief in Witchcraft." In *Essays on Medical Anthropology,* edited by Thomas Weaver, 23–35. Athens: University of Georgia Press.

Wigoder, Geoffrey. 1974. *Encyclopedic Dictionary of Judaica.* New York: Amiel.

Williams, Sam K. 1997. *Galatians.* ANTC. Nashville: Abingdon.

Willis, Roy. 2002. "Witchcraft and Sorcery." In *Encyclopedia of Social and Cultural Anthropology,* edited by Alan Barnard and Jonathan Spence, 562–64. New York: Routledge.

Wilpert, Paul, and Sibylla Zenker. 1950. "Auge." In *RAC* 1:957–69.

Witherington, Ben III. 1998. *Grappling with Grace in Galatia: A Socio-Rhetorical Commentary on Galatians.* Grand Rapids: Erdmans.

Yamauchi, E. M. 1983. "Magic in the Biblical World." *Tyndale Bulletin* 34:169–200.

Yadin, Yigael. 1969. *Tefillin From Qumran (XQPhyl 1–4).* Jerusalem: Israel Exploration Society and Shrine of the Book.

Yardeni, Ada. 1991. "Remarks on the Priestly Blessing on Two Ancient Amulets from Jerusalem." *Vetus Testamentum* 41:176–85.

Yitshaqi, Y. 1976. *Lahash We-Qami'a [Amulet and Charm].* Tel Aviv: Shaqed.

Zilver, Robert. 2002. *The New Evil Eye Theory.* Electronic Book/CD published by the Polyopie Stichting, Netherlands, March 2002. Online: http://www.polyopiestichting.nl/

Zink, Jörg, trans. 1965. *Das Neue Testament.* 3rd ed. Stuttgart: Kreuz.

Zöckler, Thomas. 2001. "Light Within the Human Person: A Comparison of Matthew 6:22–23 and Gospel of Thomas 24." *JBL* 120:487–99.

Zumwalt, Rosemary Lévy. 1996. "Let it go to the garlic:" Evil Eye and the Fertility of Women among the Sephardim." *Western Folklore* 55:261–80.

INDEX

APOCRYPHA

GREEK OLD TESTAMENT TRANSLATIONS

PHILO OF ALEXANDRIA

MODERN